An Introduction to Special Education

An Introduction to Special Education

Second Edition

William H. Berdine and A. Edward Blackhurst, Editors
University of Kentucky, Lexington

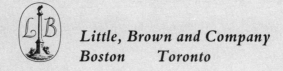

Little, Brown and Company
Boston   Toronto

This text is dedicated to our students, who have taught us much about teaching.

Library of Congress Cataloging in Publication Data
Main entry under title:

An Introduction to special education.

  1. Handicapped children — Education.   I. Berdine,
William H. II. Blackhurst, A. Edward.
LC4019.I57 1985   371.9   84-20101
ISBN 0-316-09891-4

Library of Congress Catalog Card No. 84-20101

ISBN 0-316-09891-4

9 8 7 6 5 4 3 2 1

HAL

Published simultaneously in Canada by Little, Brown & Company (Canada) Limited

Printed in the United States of America

Cover illustration: Marjorie Minkin. *Fire and Ice*. Acrylic on cotton duck canvas. 50 x 60. © Marjorie Minkin, 1980. Courtesy Stavaridis Gallery, Boston, MA.

Picture Researcher: Susan Van Etten

PHOTOGRAPH CREDITS
Title page: Alan Carey/The Image Works, Inc.
Part 1 opening photo: Bob Daemmrich/Texastock, Inc.
Chapter 1: p. 8, Paul Conklin; p. 26, Sybil Shelton/Peter Arnold, Inc.; p. 38, Claudia Lewis.
Chapter 2: p. 46, 51, Paul Conklin; p. 56, Alan Carey/The Image Works, Inc.; p. 79, Claudia Lewis.

Continued on page 660

Preface

This text is an introduction to, and a comprehensive survey of, the field of special education. Special education is that branch of education responsible for meeting the needs of exceptional children — those who are gifted or who have impairments that affect intellectual, physical, emotional, or sensory abilities. We will examine the body of contemporary literature for each of the traditional areas of special education and strive to develop an understanding of the developmental and learning characteristics of exceptional persons. Also, for each of the areas of exceptionality we will describe the types of educational services that have been found to be effective in helping persons with special needs to reach their potential. Although this book is not a methods of teaching or a curriculum text, we will describe some specific teaching techniques and curricular approaches that are becoming common to special education.

Whether you are a student entering a special education teacher training program, or planning to pursue a career in any of the number of professional areas that have an impact on exceptional persons, or simply interested in broadening your knowledge of exceptional individuals, you will find the information in this text to be current and useful. After completing the reading of the text, you should be able to accomplish the following:

- define the terms that are commonly used in special education
- understand the major issues and trends in special education and explain how these relate to general education and other related fields
- define the various traditional categories of exceptionality and explain reasons for de-emphasizing categorical labels
- describe the developmental and learning characteristics of exceptional children
- describe the various educational services available to exceptional children
- describe the various types of supportive services needed by exceptional persons and their families

ORGANIZATION

The fourteen chapters making up this book are divided into four parts. Part I, the first three chapters, contains information critical to an understanding of all areas of special education. We define major terms and basic concepts and we trace the growth of the field. The role of modern systems and media technology, including the growing use of microcomputer technology in learning settings for exceptional individuals, is also examined. In the second chapter we analyze the critical issues confronting both teachers and special education students in today's society. The chapter focuses on student identification, normalization, individualized instruction, and cultural diversity. Lastly, we explore the basic principles of child development within the context of early childhood special education. It is our contention that knowledge of normal child development is a prerequisite to the understanding of disabilities.

Upon the broad foundation created in Part I, we go on to examine communication and sensorimotor disabilities. Because communication skills lie at the base of much of what we do in special education, we begin Part II with a chapter on communication disorders. We go on to discuss the significant impact that hearing disorders have on learning and development, and we study visual impairments and the ways teachers can assist visually impaired learners to attain maximum benefit from school and society. This section closes with a chapter on the broad array of physical and health-related disabilities.

In Part III we examine individual differences in learning and behavior. Chapters on mental retardation, learning disabilities, behavior disorders, severe developmental disabilities, and the gifted and talented are included. Although we believe that the kind of educational services created should not be determined solely by the type of exceptionality being addressed, we have examined the various categories of exceptionality in separate chapters. This approach not only helps facilitate your understanding of the different developmental characteristics and varying needs of exceptional children, but it also enables us to present information in an organized manner.

The text concludes with Part IV, Complementing Special Education Services. We discuss the development of career and vocational education programs for exceptional learners. Lastly, we consider the rather significant role the families of exceptional persons play in assisting them to achieve their fullest potentials.

FORMAT

This book has a number of distinctive features that will help you master the content.

Competency statements. In each chapter we identify key principles that we believe you should learn in an introductory course in special education. These competency statements, set off in the text by horizontal lines, are followed by discussion of related content. The competency statements will help focus your attention as you read through each chapter.

Page margin questions. Throughout the text's page margins you will find questions pertaining to key content. The questions help call attention to important facts, concepts, and principles and will facilitate your mastery of the content.

Probes. Lists of questions, called probes, appear at various points within the chapters. There is one probe or set of questions for each competency statement. The probes will enable you to check whether you have learned the material that has been presented. We encourage you to answer each probe as you come to it. This will enhance your learning and retention of the material and will become an invaluable tool along with the competency statements and marginal questions for reviewing chapters. Answers to the probes are provided at the end of the book.

Task sheets. Each chapter concludes with a task sheet. The task sheet contains activities that are designed to supplement the information presented in the text. Generally, the activities involve some sort of field experience, such as observing actual special education programs or interacting with people who work with exceptional children. The variety of possible field experiences will depend on your access to children and the time you will be able to allocate to them. For those of you who are unable to schedule field experiences, an alternative such as a library research project is included. We also urge you to design your own field experiences that can best suit your special circumstances.

Technology in action vignettes. Each chapter features a brief vignette describing how modern technology is playing an active role in the respective areas of special education. The vignettes are intended to provide interesting and educationally relevant information.

Human interest features. Examples, anecdotes, and excerpts from popular literature have been incorporated into the text. They will give you insight into some of the unique problems that exceptional people face in their everyday lives. We hope that these human interest features will help you to develop positive attitudes toward the handicapped and gifted.

Glossary. Because we encounter a rather vast array of terminology in special education, we have included an extensive glossary at the end of the book.

Writing style. The diversity of special education dictates that a great deal of content be covered and we have attempted to deal with the breadth and depth of knowledge without overwhelming you with a tedious encyclopedic style of writing. We have written this text in a relatively informal style that we hope will make your reading of it an enjoyable, as well as educational, experience.

This text, covering an enormous amount of information, is the product of a concerted team effort. We, the editors, would like to thank our contributing authors for their cooperation and willingness to make this book successful. We again wish to thank our colleagues whose reviews were instrumental in developing the first edition: S. C. Ashcroft, George Peabody College of Vanderbilt University; J. W. Birch, University of Pittsburgh; Linda Blanton, Appalachian State University; Carolyn Callahan, University of Virginia; G. M. Clark, the University of Kansas; N. J. Fennick, University of Oregon; Albert Fink, Indiana University; Verna Hart, University of Pittsburgh; Herbert Prehm, Arizona State University; M. I. Semmel, University of California, Santa Barbara; and T. M. Skrtic, the University of Kansas. We also wish to thank professors who adopted the first edition and who answered our users' questionnaire and provided valuable insights into what needed to be changed for this second edition. In addition to users' comments we also benefited from the advice and ideas of our colleagues who read selected chapters or all of the second edition manuscript. They were: Bill Boomer, Wichita State University; Kenneth Kavale, University of California, Riverside; Gale Morrison, University of California, Santa Barbara; Gabriel Nardi, West Virginia University; Douglas Palmer, Texas A & M University; Chauncey Rucker, the University of Connecticut; Frank Rusch, University of Illinois at Urbana-Champaign; and Thomas M. Stephens, the Ohio State University. Again, as with the first edition, we wish to express a special note of recognition to Barbara Tymitz-Wolf, Indiana University, for her many recommendations.

We wish to extend our gratitude to Connie Fugate and Delores Henderson, who typed the manuscript and compiled the references, and Debbie Waites, who set up the chapter probe answer keys. Dan Otis helped us to convey our ideas clearly by making the writing style smooth and consistent. Our book editor at Little, Brown, Victoria Keirnan, carefully coordinated the many steps in producing the book from manuscript. We are particularly indebted to Mylan Jaixen, our editor at Little, Brown, who patiently taught us how to pull together a text of this scope into a comprehensive whole.

W.H.B.
A.E.B.

Brief Contents

Contents

Foundations of
Special Education

Over the past decade it has become clear that the similarities between regular education and special education are greater than their differences. Gone is the suspicion that the techniques, materials, and technology of special education cannot be used in other areas of education. Regular classroom teachers can no longer disregard the role and contributions of their colleagues in special education. Similarly, special educators can no longer isolate themselves from the mainstream of educational thinking. We now accept the premise that the same principles and procedures, with some modifications, can be used in the instruction of all children.

Special Education grew from the proposition that all children can reach higher levels of their potential given the opportunity, effective teaching, and proper resources. Because of this belief in the power of education, special education has indeed become an integral part of contemporary education. To appreciate what special education is and what it can offer, we begin our study by looking at the growth of the field, the issues and forces that

shaped it, and the emerging importance of early childhood education.

THE GROWTH OF SPECIAL EDUCATION SERVICES

In this chapter we discuss the terminology, origins, and development of special education. We will also describe the federal legislation that has had an effect on shaping the field as we know it today. Finally, we will describe the impact of systems and media technology and the special potential that microcomputers may have for the pupil with special learning needs.

ISSUES IN SPECIAL EDUCATION

The special issues that helped to create the field need to be understood by all educators. We describe the process of identifying children who can benefit from special education, and we analyze issues related to assessment. A vital element in special education is the normalization concept, and we look at it in relation to deinstitutionalization, mainstreaming, and the least restrictive environment. Additionally, we examine the major notions involved in individualizing instruction and accounting for cultural differences.

EARLY CHILDHOOD EDUCATION

The field of early childhood education has only recently become a generally accepted and mandated function in education. This recognition occurred in spite of the fact that research conducted years ago clearly showed that early educational experiences benefitted all children and was of critical importance for exceptional children. In this chapter we examine the rationale for providing special education services to young handicapped children and describe related issues and historical precedents. Of special importance is the discussion of normal child development, accompanied by illustrations of how various developmental milestones relate to exceptional children. Methods of identifying young handicapped children are also presented along with a description of the different methods of delivering special services to preschool children.

PART I   FOUNDATIONS OF SPECIAL EDUCATION

Bill of Rights for the Disabled

1. The right to prevention, early diagnosis, and proper care.

2. The right to a barrier-free environment and accessible transportation.

3. The right to an appropriate public education.

4. The right to necessary assistance, given in a way that promotes independence.

5. The right to a choice of lifestyles and residential alternatives.

6. The right to an income for a lifestyle comparable to that of the able-bodied.

7. The right to training and employment as qualified.

8. The right to petition social institutions for just and humane treatment.

9. The right to self-esteem.

1

The Growth of Special Education

A. Edward Blackhurst

A. Edward Blackhurst is a Professor and the Director of Graduate Studies in the Department of Special Education at the University of Kentucky. He has taught adolescents with mild mental retardation and was principal of a school for children with mild and moderate retardation. He is past president of the Association for Special Education Technology. He was instrumental in developing Teaching Exceptional Children, *a major journal for special education teachers published by the Council for Exceptional Children.*

Society's awareness of the needs and rights of people who have disabilities is evident in a number of tangible ways. For example, curb cut-outs, ramps, and buses with wheelchair lifts facilitate travel for people with physical disabilities. Elevators and room numbers in public buildings are frequently labeled in braille to assist those who have visual impairments. Sign language and printed captions are superimposed on the screen during many television programs so that people with hearing impairments can enjoy the programs. Activities such as the Special Olympics provide opportunities for people with mental retardation to engage in athletic competition.

Society is also responding to people with disabilities in many less tangible ways. Although less readily observed, they are probably more important than the visible accommodations mentioned above. For example, public schools are required to provide a free and appropriate education to all children who have been diagnosed as having a disability. Colleges and universities must admit people with disabilities and make the programs in which they are enrolled accessible to them. Furthermore, it is now illegal to deny employment to a qualified person because that person has a disability.

We wish we could state that society has always been responsive to the needs of people with disabilities. Sadly, such has not been the case. Most of the accommodations described above are the result of hard-won battles in court-rooms and legislatures. During the 1970s people with disabilities and those who served as advocates for them became extremely active in seeking legal remedies to the injustice and discrimination that existed at the time.

The "Bill of Rights for the Disabled" that appears at the beginning of this chapter reflects the results of these campaigns. These rights were codified by the United Cerebral Palsy Association and represent a mixture of moral, ethical, and legal responsibilities that society should assume in responding to the needs of people with disabilities. Special educators and other professionals who provide related services need to be aware of these rights and know how to respond to them. Chapter One will provide a basis for understanding the meaning of these rights. The impact of historical events, litigation, legislation, and technology on the growth and development of special education services will also be explained.

TERMINOLOGY AND PREVALENCE

You should be able to define terminology related to special education and report the number of children needing special education services.

If you asked a teacher or school administrator how schools should serve children, the response would probably include the comment that school programs should respond to the children's individual differences. Almost everyone thinks this is a desirable goal for a school system.

It is easy to state a goal. Achieving it can be another matter. If you think back to your elementary and secondary school career, you will undoubtedly recall many examples of individual differences. Some of your classmates were better than you in some subjects, while you were better in others. These differences *between* students are called *interindividual differences*. Similarly, you were probably better in some subjects than in others and enjoyed some more than others. These differences *within* students are called *intraindividual differences*.

How do schools respond to individual differences?

Your school probably responded to these differences by grouping in elementary school and by providing different electives and tracks in secondary school. In fourth grade, for example, you may have been a member of the Eagles reading group or the Buzzards math group. In high school you may have taken an academic rather than a vocational curriculum, and you may have taken several courses in subjects you were particularly interested in. Such arrangements are adequate to respond to the interindividual and intraindividual differences of most students.

For other students, however, these arrangements are not enough. Students who take longer to learn, who have severe difficulty in learning, who exhibit disruptive behavior, who have severe physical problems that interfere with learning, who are exceptionally intelligent or talented — all have needs that are not met by the general education program. They need programs designed to meet their needs individually. Special education exists to provide such programs.

Special education, then, is *instruction designed to respond to the unique characteristics of children who have needs that cannot be met by the standard school curriculum.*

A child's individualized education program is typically a modification of the standard school curriculum. The program may call for changes in content, methods of instruction, instructional materials, and expected rate of progress. It may also call for supportive services from speech pathologists, audiologists, physical and occupational therapists, psychologists, physicians, counselors, and others. Special education is delivered to each child according to an individualized educational program that has been developed for that child.

Special education can be delivered in a variety of settings, depending on the needs of a particular child. Some special children can be enrolled in regular classes where the teacher receives help from specialists. Some receive instruction for part of the day in resource rooms. Some require placement in a full-time special education class. Others need to be placed in homebound, hospital, or residential school programs. These options will be discussed in more detail later in this chapter.

TERMINOLOGY

The term most often associated with special education is "exceptional children." Many people believe this term refers only to very intelligent children, whereas others believe it refers only to the handicapped. Both beliefs are misconceptions; the term encompasses both groups.

Are the terms "exceptional children," "Impairment," "disability," and "handicap" synonymous?

Exceptional children are children who have physical, mental, behavioral, or sensory characteristics that differ from the majority of children such that they require special education and related services to develop to their maximum capacity. The category includes children with communication disorders, hearing disorders, visual impairments, physical disabilities, mental retardation, learning disabilities, behavior disorders, multiple handicaps, high intelligence, and unique talents. More precise definitions of these categories will be presented in the chapters that follow.

Several other terms are also used to refer to children who receive special education services. Although the use of varying terminology is quite common in special education, there are technical differences in meaning among a number of terms. In attempting to develop a system for classification of special education concepts, Stevens (1962) differentiated the following terms:

Impairment refers to diseased or defective tissue. For example, lack of oxygen at birth may cause brain damage or neurological impairment that will result in cerebral palsy. Similarly, a birthmark could be considered an impairment because it is different from the tissues that surround it.

Disability refers to the reduction of function, or the absence, of a particular body part or organ. A person who has an arm or leg missing has a physical disability. Similarly, someone who cannot control the muscles required for speech has a disability in communication. The terms *disorder* and *dysfunction* are frequently used as synonyms for disability.

Handicap refers to the problems that impaired or disabled people have when interacting with their environment. A Vietnam veteran who is confined to a wheelchair put it this way: "Sure I have a disability; but I'm not handicapped — until I try to get into a building that has a flight of steps and revolving door as its only entrance."

It should be noted that many people treat these terms as synonyms. In this book we will reflect the common practice of occasionally referring to impaired and disabled children as handicapped. This practice came about largely because

The Special Olympics provides a way for people with disabilities to participate in competitive athletic events.

federal legislation directs our public schools to provide special education to all "handicapped children."

Generally, however, there are distinct differences between impairment, disability, and handicap. A person can be handicapped in one situation and not in another. A boy with a birthmark on his face may be impaired, but he is not disabled. He may, however, be handicapped in getting dates. A musician may have a visual disability but not be handicapped when it comes to producing music. Consider the case of Kitty O'Neil described in *Parade* magazine:

> If Kitty O'Neil merely parked cars for a living instead of driving them at 600 mph and faster, she would still be a very unusual person. At one time or another, she has held 22 speed records. As a teenager, she was an Olympic class diving champion. She plays the cello and piano. And she's one of Hollywood's top stuntwomen.
>
> She also is totally deaf.
>
> *Parade* caught up with the 33-year-old Kitty at her home in Glendale, Cal. Communicating with her is easy. Her mother spent years teaching her to read lips and to speak. She does not know sign language and she doesn't need it.
>
> Kitty was raised in Wichita Falls, Tex., born to a part Cherokee Indian mother and an Irish father. At 4 months, she almost died from the simultaneous onslaught of chicken pox, measles and mumps — illnesses that robbed her of her hearing.
>
> At the age of 12, she began competitive swimming and diving, becoming an AAU Junior Olympic diving champion and earning a wallfull of medals. Obsessed with speed and motion — "I love to go fast and I love danger" — Kitty began racing in any vehicle she could climb onto or into: production sports cars, motorcycles, drag racers, speedboats, dune buggies and snowmobiles. She tried skydiving, scuba diving and hang gliding. At one time Kitty held the world's record for women's water skiing, zipping across the water at better than 104 mph. She tackled anything to prove that a stone deaf, 95-pound, 5-foot-3 slip of a woman could do as well as anyone, male or female. Eventually, she turned inward and began competing against herself. Her vehicle: the rocket car.
>
> At 38 feet long and developing 48,000 horsepower, the rocket car she drove was little more than an earthbound guided missile made principally of aluminum and fiberglass. After testing on the Bonneville Salt Flats in Utah, Kitty and her crew went to the Alvord Dry Lake in Oregon to try and beat the women's land speed record of 308 mph.
>
> On Dec. 6, 1976, she was strapped into the cockpit of the rocket car and attained an average speed of 512.7 mph. Later that day she made another run and hit an incredible 618.3 mph — just 4 miles an hour under the world record held by Gary Gabelich.
>
> Kitty supports herself these days as a movie stuntwoman [Satchell, 1979].

Does Kitty have an impairment? Probably. Her various childhood diseases probably damaged her auditory nerve or central nervous system. Does she have a disability? Yes. She cannot hear. Is she handicapped? Certainly not when she is racing or working as a stuntwoman. Yet she would be handicapped if she attempted to use a telephone.

It should be noted that even though a person has an impairment or disability, it does not mean that the person will be handicapped in all situations. Similarly, the severity of the disability may have little relationship to the severity of the ensuing handicap. The physical environment and psychological situation of the impaired or disabled person are crucial in dealing with these people. As Gearheart (1974) put it:

> The degree of the disability does not necessarily determine the degree of the handicap. Most children with special needs are more normal than abnormal and will likely spend most of their lives in a basically nonhandicapped world. They, therefore, must have programming that will help them to adjust to their social and physical environment and minimize the handicapping effect of their disability [pp. 22-23].

Terms have also been developed to refer to specialty areas of special education. Thus, children with speech and language problems are said to have "communication disorders"; those with visual problems are "visually impaired"; children in wheelchairs have "physical disabilities"; and those who are seriously mentally retarded with other physical problems are referred to as "severely [or profoundly] handicapped." The commonly used terminology is reflected in the chapter titles in this text.

PREVALENCE

To plan for the provision of special education services, it is important to know how many exceptional children there are at present and how many can be expected at a given point in the future. Accurate estimates can be used to get funds for programs and to determine how many teachers and other professionals will be needed to staff them.

How many exceptional children are there?
But the exact number of children who need special education services is difficult to determine. There are several reasons. First, there are many different definitions of the categories used to group children — especially those with learning problems. A child placed in one category by one authority might be placed in another by a different authority. For example, a child who has severe problems with academic subjects and who is very disruptive in class because of inability to do academic work may be classified as learning disabled by one diagnostician and emotionally disturbed by another. Second, categories often overlap. Children with more than one problem may be arbitrarily placed in one category or another. A child who has cerebral palsy, is confined to a wheelchair, and has difficulty reading may be classified in one school district as physically disabled, in another as learning disabled, and in a third as multi-

ply handicapped. Third, school officials simply have not identified all of the children who require special services.

Estimates of the proportion of school-aged children needing special education services have ranged from 10 to 15 percent. In 1976 the prevalence of handicapped children in the United States was estimated by the Bureau of Education for the Handicapped in the United States Office of Education. By surveying various special education organizations, the bureau was able to estimate the percentage of the population that had different types of handicaps. The estimate was that nearly eight million children under the age of 19 were in need of special education services.

In 1984, the United States Department of Education determined how many children aged 3 to 21 were actually being served in special education programs. These figures are displayed in Table 1-1.

You will note that the more recent figures indicate that only about 4.3 million students are receiving special education. Does this mean that the original estimate of eight million needing services was grossly in error? Not necessarily. The original estimate was indeed probably too high, but the more recent figures represent only those who are actually receiving services. The

Table 1-1
Number of Children Ages 3–21 Receiving Special Education Services during the 1982–1983 School Year

Category	Percentage of School Enrollment	Number
Learning Disabled	4.40	1,745,871
Speech Impaired	2.86	1,134,197
Mentally Retarded	1.92	780,831
Emotionally Disturbed	.89	353,431
Deaf and Hard of Hearing	.18	75,337
Multihandicapped	.16	65,479
Orthopedically Impaired	.14	57,506
Health Impaired	.13	52,026
Visually Handicapped	.07	31,096
Deaf-blind	.01	2,553
TOTAL	10.76	4,298,327

Note: Figures based upon reported school enrollment for preschool through twelfth grade children and special education enrollment for children ages 3-21.

Source: *Sixth Annual Report to Congress on the Implementation of Public Law 94-142: The Education for All Handicapped Children Act*. Washington, DC: U.S. Department of Education, 1984.

newer figures do not include those who need special education but have not yet been identified. The true prevalence figure probably lies somewhere between the eight million estimate of 1976 and the 4.3 million being served in 1983. But because of difficulties in identifying children, we may never know the actual number who need services.

It is estimated that there are also approximately 1.5 million gifted and talented children in the United States. Adding this figure to those mentioned above, we can probably safely assume that somewhere between 5.8 million and 9.5 million children need special education services.

A word of caution is in order about the use of the percentages listed in Table 1-1. Those percentages apply to the population as a whole. The actual prevalence for a particular population may vary according to the sex of the children being studied, the population's ethnic makeup and geographical region, and many other factors. For example, we frequently find more males than females being identified as having behavior disorders because there is a lower tolerance for deviant behavior in males. Often, more children need special education services in remote rural areas or inner cities where impoverished living conditions exist. Conversely, fewer special education students are found in upper-middle class and upper class communities where better health care is available and where parents place a premium upon education for their children. In addition, many children raised in non-English speaking homes are placed (often inappropriately) in special education programs. Reasons for such variations will be explained in greater detail later in this book.

Because variations such as these exist, prevalence figures should be used primarily for the early stages of planning. To project service needs accurately, the exceptional children in the area to be served must actually be located. Estimated projections of prevalence often differ considerably from the number of people who actually need services.

PROBE 1-1
Terminology and Prevalence

1. What is your definition of special education?

2. T   F   The term "exceptional children" refers primarily to the gifted and talented.

3. Differentiate between "disability" and "handicap."

4. Between _____ million and _____ million children are in need of special education services.

5. T   F   School officials should be wary of using national prevalence figures for estimating special education needs in their school districts.

HISTORICAL DEVELOPMENTS

> **You should be able to describe the effects of historical developments on special education.**

A knowledge of history helps one understand present practices and plan improvements. When we examine the historical forces that have influenced special education, we realize that the programs, practices, and facilities established at any given time reflect the prevailing social climate. People's attitudes have been particularly important; as attitudes have changed, so have the services that have been provided. For example, when people believed the mentally retarded were a genetic threat to the future of the human race, there was a dramatic increase in the practice of sterilizing the retarded. Similarly, when the prevailing attitude was that it was wrong to deny physically disabled people access to buildings, legislation to require the removal of architectural barriers was developed. Efforts to foster positive attitudes toward exceptional people are crucial in improving the services provided them. The history of these attitudes and the developments they reflected can be divided into distinct periods.[1]

EARLY PRACTICES: 1552 B.C.–1740 A.D.

We know little about how early cultures dealt with the handicapped. The significance of the few reports that are available has been exaggerated. Saint Nicholas Thaumaturgos, for example, has been described as a champion of the mentally retarded. Kanner (1964) pointed out, however, that although "he may well have put in a good word for them now and then, . . . he is also regarded as the patron saint of *all* children, of sailors, and — of pawn brokers; the fact that at a much later date he was made to serve as the prototype of 'Santa Claus' certainly does not qualify him to figure in the chronicles of mental deficiency" (p. 3).

What has been the plight of the handicapped across the centuries?

An Egyptian papyrus dated 1552 B.C. (known as the therapeutic Papyrus of Thebes) contains the first known written reference to the handicapped. Other references entreating people to care for the handicapped are found in the Bible, the Talmud, and the Koran, but at the time those works were written many were forced to beg for food and shelter.

Treatment had not improved in classical times. The ancient Greeks and some of the Romans thought the handicapped were cursed, and sometimes drowned them in efforts to preserve the strength of their races. At other times

---

[1] The events examined in this section were drawn from the following authorities: Doll, 1962; Kanner, 1964; Nazzaro, 1977; Payne, Kauffman, Patton, Brown, and DeMott, 1979.

those who could not care for themselves were simply allowed to perish. Some Romans did employ the handicapped in high positions — as "fools" who performed for the elite.

During the Middle Ages, the handicapped were viewed with a mixture of fear and reverence, because they were thought to be somehow connected with the unknown. Some were wandering beggars, whereas others were used as jesters in castles.

The Renaissance and the Reformation brought a change for the worse. Exorcism, demonology, and persecution of the handicapped flourished. Martin Luther and John Calvin, for example, accused the mentally retarded of being "filled with Satan," and many were put in chains and thrown into dungeons.

By the early 1600s, however, there were indications that attitudes toward the handicapped were beginning to change. A hospital in Paris began to provide treatment for the emotionally disturbed. The first manual alphabet for the deaf was developed. John Locke became the first person to differentiate between persons who were mentally retarded and those who were emotionally disturbed.

Change occurred slowly. In colonial America people with mental disorders that made them violent were treated as criminals. Those who were harmless were generally treated as paupers. The retarded, for example, were subjected to one of three treatments. They were (1) kept at home and given partial public support, (2) put in poorhouses, or (3) auctioned off to the bidder who would support them at the lowest cost to the community in return for whatever work the bidder could extract from them. The last practice was eventually halted by public outrage. The retarded were then put in poorhouses, where conditions were often worse than those provided by the person who had won the bid for their services.

THE MOVEMENT FOR TRAINING: 1798–1890

What were the contributions of special education pioneers?

One of the first persons to investigate methods of educating the exceptional child was the French physician Jean Marc Itard. Itard's initial contribution was the result of his effort to alter the wildly uncivilized behavior of a boy who had been found living naked and alone in the woods near Aveyron, France, in 1799 (Itard, 1932; Lane, 1976). Although Itard did not consider his efforts completely successful, the techniques he documented and promoted gave the initial impetus to the movement to train the mentally retarded.

Itard's investigations exerted a strong influence on special educators working in the United States in the early 1800s. Two of the most important are Thomas Hopkins Gallaudet and Samuel Gridley Howe. In 1817 Gallaudet founded the first school for the deaf in Hartford, Connecticut. Howe, a physician turned political and social reformer, was instrumental in founding the Perkins School for the Blind in Watertown, Massachusetts, in 1829.

During the middle of the 1800s major contributions were made by two special educators, Jacob Guggenbuhl and Edward Seguin. In the 1840s Guggenbuhl opened, in Switzerland, a facility for the mentally retarded with thyroid conditions (cretins) that was to become world-famous. Although he was later discredited and drummed out of business, he is acknowledged as the originator of institutional care for the retarded.

Seguin was a student of Itard's who emigrated to the United States in 1848. After completing his medical training in 1861 he worked with Howe, Gallaudet, and other American educators and continued to develop Itard's scientific techniques. Seguin's text, *Idiocy and its Treatment by the Physiological Method,* was published in 1866.

By the 1870s the movement to establish institutions had begun. An organization that urged the establishment of institutions was formed in 1876, with Seguin as its president. This organization, originally called the Association of Medical Officers of American Institutions for Idiotic and Feeble-minded Persons, later became the American Association on Mental Deficiency.

Although they were designed to be used for education, institutions during this period came to be used primarily for custodial care. By 1890 it was generally accepted that the states had the responsibility for providing institutional services for the handicapped.

MEASUREMENT AND SOCIAL CONTROL: 1890-1919

The first standardized test of intelligence was published in 1908 by Alfred Binet, a Frenchman. The test was developed to identify mentally retarded children. It was then standardized on American populations by Goddard and published in the United States in 1910. The intelligence quotient (IQ) was introduced by Terman in a 1916 revision of the test. IQ tests have been used ever since to identify persons with retarded or advanced intellectual development.

What was the impact of the IQ test?

Unfortunately, IQ tests have been subject to much abuse. Many people have ignored Binet's warning that the results of IQ tests are not to be trusted without taking into account other information about a child's performance. Abuses have led to federal legislation that prohibits the placement of exceptional children in special education programs solely on the basis of an intelligence test score.

Maria Montessori's work also began in the early 1900s. An Italian physician concerned with early childhood education, Montessori further developed Seguin's elaboration of Itard's techniques. Her methods text, published in 1912, detailed a sequence of instructional procedures for working with the retarded child. The so-called Montessori methods are still an important part of the curriculums of many regular and special preschool education programs.[2]

---

[2] Throughout this text, we will consider school-age children to be those between the ages of six and seventeen. Preschool children will be those aged five or under.

In 1912 a famous psychologist, Henry Goddard, published a study about the Kallikak family, which traced five generations of the offspring of a man who had fathered both a legitimate and an illegitimate child. A large percentage of the descendents of the illegitimate child were mentally retarded, whereas the descendents of the legitimate child were reported to have average or superior intelligence. Goddard's report led to the belief that mental retardation was an inherited trait and therefore a threat to the human race. The so-called Eugenic Scare that followed prompted many states to enact laws authorizing the sterilization of retarded people and criminals.

Other trends were more encouraging, however. At the same time that many of the mentally retarded were being institutionalized and sterilized, the number of special education programs in the public schools was gradually being increased. The first college programs for the preparation of special education teachers were also established in 1906 at New York University (Morsink, 1984).

EXPANSION OF SERVICES: 1920-1949

There were a number of new developments in the United States during the 1920s, 1930s, and 1940s. Many of them were good. Halfway houses were established to bridge the gap between institution and community; follow-up studies were performed to examine the relative effectiveness of various programs; out-patient clinics were established in hospitals; the use of social workers and other support personnel was increased; new diagnostic instruments were discovered; and comprehensive state-wide programs were developed.

The periods of progress proved to be of short duration in some areas, however. The number of special education programs begun in public schools increased fairly rapidly until 1930 and then began to fall. The impetus of the 1920s toward humane, effective treatment for the handicapped died out in the 1930s and 1940s. These decades were a period of stagnation, characterized by large-scale institutionalization and segregation of the handicapped from the rest of society. The economic depression was one cause. Another was the widespread dissatisfaction with poorly planned programs staffed by inadequately trained teachers.

During this period, attitudes were influenced by the "Progressive Education Movement." One such attitude was that any "good" teacher could teach handicapped children and that special education teacher preparation programs were unnecessary. Unfortunately, this idea proved to be wrong. The result was that many special education programs were poorly designed because school administrators were uninformed. The situation was further confounded because many teachers employed for these programs were not adequately prepared to teach children who had needs that could not be met by the standard school curriculum.

How did war affect special education services?

Even while the number and quality of services were being cut back, however, important changes in attitude and awareness were occurring. Cruickshank and Johnson (1975) point out that the massive screening of young men and women for service in World Wars I and II made it clear how many people were physically, mentally, or behaviorally handicapped or disabled. Few people had expected to find that such a large segment of the population had significant disabilities. The return of physically disabled soldiers from the wars also made the public more sensitive to the problems of the handicapped, and the acceptance offered them was extended to other groups in the population. The same phenomenon was to occur following the wars in Korea and Vietnam.

ADVOCACY AND LITIGATION: 1950-1974

Of all the factors that were significant in the rapid growth and expansion of special education during the period between 1950 and 1974, three stand out: (1) parent activism, (2) professional research on deviant human growth and development, and (3) changes in teacher education practices. The advocacy of parent activists and the effects of the litigation they instigated will be discussed in this section. More will be said about topics 2 and 3 later in the text.

What is NARC?

The majority of activities related to advocacy and litigation were intitated by parent groups and have been nurtured and supported by professional organizations. In 1950 the National Association for Retarded Children (NARC) was formed. This agency (later renamed the National Association for Retarded Citizens) pressured public schools to initiate programs for the moderately retarded and to expand other special education services. The next 25 years saw a rapid growth in services.

Residential institutions were also subjected to pressures, partly as a result of Burton Blatt's *Christmas in Purgatory* (Blatt and Kaplan, 1966). In this exposé of the squalid conditions in many American institutions for the handicapped, Blatt presented photographs of some of the most deplorable conditions imaginable and then contrasted them with photos of an institution in which humane treatment was provided. More than a decade later, Blatt and his colleagues reported a follow-up to the original study in *The Family Papers: A Return to Purgatory* (Blatt, Ozolins, and McNally, 1979). Unfortunately, many of the injustices that he found earlier still existed. (We recommend these works for a perspective on conditions and practices that continue to exist in many large residential institutions.)

How have lawsuits changed education practices?

A different tactic was used by a parents' group to fight for public support of services for severely handicapped children. In January, 1971 the Pennsylvania Association for Retarded Children filed a class action suit against the Commonwealth of Pennsylvania for failing to provide free and appropriate public education for all mentally retarded citizens residing in the state. *(Penn-*

sylvania Association for Retarded Children v. Commonwealth of Pennsylvania, 1972.) The plantiffs in this suit, which came to be known as the *PARC* case, were thirteen mentally retarded school-age children and all other school-age children of their class in Pennsylvania. The plantiffs contended that the state had not given them due process before denying them "life, liberty and property" (Fifth Amendment). It was also argued that they were not afforded equal protection under the law (Fourteenth Amendment). To support their position the plantiffs provided expert testimony regarding the educability of all mentally retarded children, regardless of the severity of their retardation.

Conceding defeat, the Commonwealth of Pennsylvania entered into a court-approved consent agreement with the plaintiffs. This agreement defined the Commonwealth's obligation to provide all mentally retarded children between the ages of six and twenty-one with a publicly supported, appropriate education, effective September, 1972. Included in the agreement were procedures for reevaluation, placement, and due process. Ages of attendance were established, as were regulations calling for homebound and preschool instruction.

The case of *Mills* v. *Board of Education of the District of Columbia* (1972) reinforced and extended the rights accorded exceptional children as a result of the *PARC* case. The *Mills* lawsuit, brought on behalf of seven children with handicaps of varying types and degrees, established the right to equal educational opportunities for all handicapped children, not just the mentally retarded. In this landmark decision, United States District Court Judge Joseph Waddy ruled (1) that all children, regardless of their disability, have the right to a publicly supported education, and (2) that the defendant's policies, which excluded children from educational services, denied the rights of the plaintiffs and their class due process and equal protection under the law (Weintraub and Abeson, 1976). The Board of Education claimed that it did not have enough money to pay for the services demanded in the lawsuit. In his ruling on the case, Judge Waddy stated that lack of money was no excuse for not providing services. He said:

> The District of Columbia's interest in educating children must clearly outweigh its interest in preserving its financial resources. If sufficient funds are not available to finance all services and programs that are needed and desirable in the system, then the available funds must be expended equitably in such a manner that no child is entirely excluded from a publicly supported education consistent with his needs and ability to benefit therefrom [Weintraub and Abeson, 1976, p. 9].

The *PARC* and *Mills* lawsuits served as an impetus for subsequent litigation designed to confirm the educational rights of all handicapped children. These suits included *The Kentucky Association for Retarded Children et al.* v. *Kentucky State Board of Education et al.* (1973) and *Maryland Association for Retarded Children* v. *State of Maryland* (1974). In the six-year period between 1969 and 1974, the following court decisions had a dramatic impact on special education programs and practices:

— Trainable mentally retarded children were not receiving a suitable education *(Wolf* v. *Legislature of Utah,* 1969).

— Mexican-American children were being inappropriately placed in classes for the mentally retarded *(Diana* v. *State Board of Education* in California, 1970).

— The constitutional rights of hospitalized mentally ill patients are being violated if they receive inadequate treatment or rehabilitation *(Wyatt* v. *Anderholt,* 1970).

— Adequate treatment is the right of mentally ill patients in state hospitals. This determination resulted in the setting of standards for treatment *(Wyatt* v. *Stickney,* 1971).

— The severely and profoundly retarded are entitled to a public school education *(Pennsylvania Association for Retarded Children* v. *Commonwealth of Pennsylvania,* 1972).

— No black student may be placed in a class for the educable mentally retarded solely on the basis of an IQ test *(Larry P.* v. *Riles,* 1972).

— Unjust transfers from one institution to another are prohibited *(Kessalbrenner* v. *Anonymous,* 1973).

— Non-English speaking students are entitled to bilingual special education *(Lau* v. *Nichols,* 1974).

In addition, 36 other "right-to-education" lawsuits had been filed in 25 states by 1974.

In the late 1970s and early 1980s, several court decisions appeared to provide a setback for some of the earlier gains. For example, in 1979, the Supreme Court ruled in the *Davis* case that a deaf student could be excluded from a program to prepare registered nurses. The ruling in *PASE* v. *Hannon* (1980) was that IQ tests are not necessarily biased against particular groups. In 1982 the appeal of a deaf girl for the services of an interpreter during the school day was denied by the Supreme Court in *Hendrick Hudson Board of Education* v. *Rowley* (Morsink, 1984). Each of these cases had features that were unique to the situation under question, however, and care should be taken not to generalize the decisions to all cases involving admission to higher education programs, use of IQ tests, or provision of interpreters.

These and other cases are reviewed in authoritative works on issues related to the right-to-education movement by Kindred, Cohen, Penrod, and Shaffer (1975) and Weintraub, Abeson, Ballard, and LaVor (1976). Turnbull and Turnbull (1978) have also written an interesting book about the effects of litigation and law on special education programs; the third printing of the text offers an informative appendix that updates case law through 1982. One of the most thorough references on litigation related to special education is the work edited by Burgdorf (1980). That book contains many of the actual texts of court decisions and judicial opinions about cases related to the legal rights of handicapped persons. The work was updated in a supplement by Burgdorf and Spicer (1983). These resources are recommended for those who are interested in obtaining a more comprehensive account of how handicapped people and their advocates have fought for legal rights.

TOTAL MOBILIZATION: 1975–PRESENT

The litigation mentioned in the last section, coupled with the passage of Public Law 94-142 (to be explained later in this chapter) has been most important in providing appropriate special education services. The concepts underlying the methods employed in providing these services, however, go back to the work of persons such as Itard, Seguin, and Montessori. These fundamental concepts include the following:

Which historical concepts are reflected in current special education practices?

1. Education should be provided for all exceptional children in order to maximize whatever potential for learning they may have.
2. Since handicapped children do have the potential to learn, they should be *educated,* not just cared for in residential institutions.
3. Exceptional children should be identified as early as possible, and their education should begin before they reach school age.
4. Special education programs should be individualized and should be based on the behavior each child exhibits.
5. Educational tasks should be stimulating and should progress from the easy to the difficult. The instructional environment should be carefully structured to increase the probability of success.
6. When children produce correct responses and exhibit appropriate behavior, they should receive rewards.
7. A major emphasis of special education should be preparation for gainful employment and social adjustment in the community.

One hundred years have passed since Itard published his first text, and seventy since Montessori first described her methods; the seven concepts listed above are widely recognized as fundamental. The challenge continuing to face special education is to ensure that these concepts are being applied in educational programs for exceptional children.

PROBE 1-2
Historical Developments

1. Match the item on the left with the appropriate name.

Contribution	Name
_____ First school for the deaf	a. Itard
_____ Preschool educational methods	b. Howe
_____ Worked with a "wild boy"	c. Gallaudet

_____ First school for the blind
_____ Brought special education to the
United States
_____ First intelligence test
_____ Introduced the IQ

d. Seguin
e. Montessori
f. Guggenbuhl
g. Terman
h. Binet

2. List four concepts developed by early contributors to special education that are relevant today.

3. T   F   There has been a steady, even growth in special education services since the early 1900s.

4. T   F   Institutions were originally set up for custodial purposes.

5. The name of the parent organization that fought for more public school services is the _____.

6. Contrast the PARC and Mills right-to-education cases.

LEGISLATIVE IMPLICATIONS

You should be able to describe the impact of legislation on special education practices.

The delivery of special education services in public schools is governed primarily by state laws. These vary from state to state. For example, some states mandate special education services for preschool children; others do not. Funding patterns for special education programs also differ considerably across the country.

What is the difference between laws, regulations, and policies?

Once laws are passed, regulations follow. They describe the procedures necessary to comply with the laws, and like laws they are not uniform among states. For example, all states have laws requiring teacher certification in special education, but the regulations that specify requirements for certification are not the same. This situation results from different philosophies about what is needed to be a special education teacher.

At the local level, boards of education handle direct delivery of special education services, and their policies reflect the state laws and regulations. Each board's policies are also a product of local attitudes and biases.

If you plan to become a special education teacher, you should be familiar with the laws, regulations, and policies that affect special education in your school district. You can obtain information from your state Department of Education or Department of Public Instruction, which includes a unit that administers programs for exceptional children. Regardless of where you work, you should also be aware of all federal laws that concern special education practices. Chart 1-1 describes some of this legislation.

Chart 1-1
Major Milestones in Federal Legislation for the Handicapped

1879	Funds to produce braille materials are granted to the American Printing House for the Blind (PL 45-186ª).
1918	Vocational rehabilitation services are authorized for World War I veterans (PL 65-178).
1920	Vocational rehabilitation services are extended to civilians (PL 66-236).
1936	Blind persons are authorized to operate vending stands in Federal buildings (PL 74-732).
1943	The mentally retarded and mentally ill become eligible for services under the Barden-LaFollette Vocational Rehabilitation Act (PL 78-113).
1958	Colleges and universities receive funds to aid in preparing teachers of the mentally retarded (PL 85-926).
1962	Provisions are made for production and distribution of captioned films for the deaf (PL 87-715).
1963	Funds are provided to train teachers for all disabilities; research and demonstration projects are established to study education of exceptional children (PL 88-164).
1965	Elementary and Secondary Education Act provides funds for local school districts to attack problems of educating disadvantaged and handicapped children (PL 89-10); support is provided to aid handicapped children in state institutions (PL 89-313); National Technical Institute for the Deaf is established (PL 89-36).
1966	Authorization is provided for establishing the Bureau of Education for the Handicapped and a National Advisory Committee on the Handicapped (PL 89-750); talking book services for the visually impaired are expanded to include the physically handicapped who are unable to handle printed material (PL 89-522).
1968	Experimental demonstration centers for preschool handicapped are established (PL 90-538); 10 percent of vocational education funds are earmarked for the handicapped (PL 90-576); provisions are made for deaf-blind centers, resource centers, and expansion of media services for the handicapped (PL 90-247).
1969	National Center on Educational Media and Materials for the Handicapped is authorized (PL 91-61).
1970	Facilities constructed with federal funds are required to be accessible to the physically handicapped (PL 91-205).
1972	Ten percent enrollment opportunities in Head Start must be available to handicapped children (PL 92-424).
1973	Rights of the handicapped in employment and educational institutions receiving federal funds are guaranteed through Section 504 of the Rehabilitation Amendments (PL 93-112).
1974	Due process procedures in placement, nondiscriminatory testing, and confidentiality of school records are guaranteed; programs for the gifted and talented are authorized (PL 93-380).

1975　　Free appropriate public education and other procedural guarantees are mandated for all handicapped children (PL 94-142).

1983　　PL 94-142 is amended to provide added emphasis on parent education and preschool, secondary, and post-secondary programs for handicapped children and youth (PL 98-199).

Source: Nazzaro (1977)

[a] The PL stands for "Public Law." The first two digits represent the number of the congressional session in which the law was passed. Thus, PL 94-142 was the 142nd law that was passed by the Ninety-fourth Congress.

Of the legislation mentioned in the chart, two acts have been of outstanding importance: Section 504 of the Vocational Rehabilitation Act of 1973, and PL 94-142, the Education for All Handicapped Children Act.

SECTION 504 OF THE VOCATIONAL REHABILITATION ACT OF 1973

> No otherwise qualified handicapped individual in the United States . . . shall, solely by reason of his handicap, be excluded from the participation in, be denied the benefits of, or be subjected to discrimination under any program or activity receiving Federal financial assistance.

This rather awkward sentence, Section 504 of the Rehabilitation Act of 1973, is perhaps the most important ever written regarding the handicapped. It is the first federal civil rights law that protects the rights of handicapped persons.

The language is almost identical to that of the Civil Rights Act of 1964, which applied to racial discrimination, and of Title IX of the Education Amendments of 1972, which dealt with discrimination in education on the basis of sex. The enactment of Section 504 reflects the realization that the handicapped, too, had been subjected to discrimination for many years.

Ending discrimination is an extremely difficult task; it took nearly four years to develop the federal regulations to implement this law. When he issued the regulations in 1977, Secretary of Health, Education, and Welfare Joseph Califano stated,

> The 504 Regulation attacks the discrimination, the demeaning practices and the injustices that have afflicted the nation's handicapped citizens. It reflects the recognition of the Congress that most handicapped persons can lead proud and productive lives, despite their disabilities. It will usher in a new era of equality for handicapped individuals in which unfair barriers to self-sufficiency and decent treatment will begin to fall before the force of law.

How has Section 504 influenced American life?

As a result of these regulations (Nondiscrimination on Basis of Handicap, 1977) the following changes have occurred:

— Employers are required to provide equal recruitment, employment compensation, job assignments, and fringe benefits for the handicapped.
— All new public facilities are required to be accessible to the handicapped.
— Handicapped children of school age are entitled to a free and appropriate public education.
— Discrimination in admission to institutions of higher education is prohibited.
— Discrimination is forbidden in providing health, welfare, and other social service programs.

As you can see, Section 504 opened up a whole spectrum of new opportunities for the handicapped. The next important step in ending discrimination was the enactment of PL 94-142, which provided for the education of all handicapped children.

PL 94-142: THE EDUCATION FOR ALL HANDICAPPED CHILDREN ACT

At about the time Section 504 was being enacted, Congress was investigating other aspects of the lives of the handicapped. In 1975 it reported that

— There are more than 8 million handicapped children in the United States.
— More than half of the handicapped children in the United States do not receive the educational services necessary to give them an equal opportunity.
— One million of the handicapped children in the United States are excluded entirely from the public school system and will not be educated with their peers.
— Many handicapped children have undetected handicaps that prevent them from being successfully educated.
— The lack of adequate services within the public school system often forces families to find services elsewhere, often at great distances from their homes and at their own expense.
— Developments in teacher training and in diagnostic and instructional procedures have advanced to the point that, given sufficient funding, state and local educational agencies could provide effective special education.

What responsibility does society have for educating handicapped children?

Congress also determined that state and local educational agencies have a responsibility to provide education for all handicapped children, even though present financial resources are inadequate. Finally, it determined that the national interest is served by the federal government's assisting state and local efforts to provide special education programs, thereby assuring handicapped children of equal protection under the law (PL 94-142, 89 Stat. pp. 774-775).

As a result of the congressional studies and pressures by advocacy groups,

PL 94-142 was passed and signed into law by President Gerald Ford on November 29, 1975. This law, commonly referred to as the *Education for All Handicapped Children Act,* establishes the right of all handicapped children to an education. It also explains the procedures for distributing federal resources to state and local agencies for the development and operation of special education programs. It is the most important federal mandate of services for children with special needs. The act is intended to

1. ensure that a free, appropriate education be made available to all handicapped children;
2. assist state and local education agencies in providing this education;
3. assess the effectiveness of these educational efforts; and
4. provide handicapped children and their parents with the assurances of due process.

The effect of PL 94-142 on both state and federal policy for special education service delivery was reviewed by Abeson and Ballard (1976). A summary of its provisions follows.

What guarantees does PL 94-142 provide?

Due Process. Handicapped children and their parents are guaranteed procedural safeguards in all matters related to identification, evaluation, and educational placement. This means that parents must be notified when their children are to be tested, and they must give permission for the test to be given. Parents must also be actively involved in any decision about the educational placement of their handicapped children.

Least Restrictive Environment. When appropriate, handicapped children are to be educated with children who are not handicapped. This provision has resulted in major changes in the organization of school programs for the handicapped. Many self-contained special education classes have been eliminated in favor of integrating mildly handicapped children into regular classes for much of the school day, with part-time instruction in resource rooms.

Nondiscriminatory Assessment. When children are tested to determine whether they are eligible for special education services, the tests and testing procedures must not be culturally or racially biased. Under this provision, all testing must be done in the native language of the child. In addition, no educational decisions can be made solely on the basis of a single test score. The use of a number of assessment techniques is required.

Individualization. An individualized educational program (IEP) must be developed for each child who is enrolled in a special education program. The plan is to be developed in consultation with the child's parents and based on the information obtained from assessment. The IEP must also be reviewed at least once a year and revised if necessary.

Confidentiality and Record Keeping. The confidentiality provision reiterates the provisions of the Family Educational Rights and Privacy Act (PL 93–380), also known as the Buckley Amendment, which guarantees parental control of school records. No one may have access to the records of handicapped children without specific written parental permission. In addition, the Buckley Amendment guarantees parents the right to examine all the school records of their children.

Parent Surrogate. If the parents or guardians of handicapped children are either unknown or unavailable, someone else can be appointed to work on behalf of the handicapped child. The parent surrogate is responsible for approving the testing and placement of the child. This person also serves on the committee that develops the individualized educational program. The parent surrogate is, in effect, an advocate for the child.

Categorical Priorities. The law determines priorities in the provision of services. The first priority is for handicapped children currently receiving no services. Second are those who are the most severely handicapped and who are receiving inadequate services. This means that schools must identify and serve handicapped children both in school and not in school. They must also identify those who are in an inappropriate educational program.

Federal law requires that all handicapped children receive a free and appropriate public education.

Age Levels. The law requires that all handicapped children between the ages of 3 and 21 be served. However, some states have mandatory school attendance laws that preclude preschool education. As a result of court cases, other states are not required to provide preschool programs. States that have such laws or court decisions are exempt from the requirement to serve handicapped preschoolers. Because early education is so important, though, special incentive grants are available to the states that do provide special education and related services to their preschool handicapped children.

Private Settings. Any child placed in or referred to a private school or institution by the state or local education agency must receive special education services at no cost to the parents. The agency receiving the child must also meet state and local education standards. In addition, the children served by these private agencies must be accorded the same educational rights they would have if they were being served by the public agency directly. Thus, all the conditions we are discussing in this section must be adhered to by private agencies that provide services under contract to local school districts.

Finances. The law establishes a formula according to which the federal government substantially increases its monetary contribution to state and local education agencies for their compliance with the act. Funds received by local districts must be used only for the extra costs of educating handicapped children. That is, a district must spend as much of its own revenue for educating a handicapped child as it does for educating a nonhandicapped child if it is to be eligible for PL 94-142 funds.

Planning. Each state Department of Education must submit to the United States Commissioner of Education a plan describing in detail how it proposes to provide a free and appropriate education to all its handicapped children. A similar plan must be submitted by local school districts to the state educational agency. These plans must be examined and revised annually. The plans are also subject to public review and comment prior to their submission.

In 1983, the Education for All Handicapped Children Act was amended by PL 89-199. Several significant changes were made as a result of the amendments. Additional financial assistance was made available to develop model early childhood projects to aid handicapped children and extend service levels from age three down to birth. New programs were also authorized in the area of secondary special education and services that would aid the transition of handicapped youth from school to the world of work or to post-secondary education. Increased support for information dissemination and training for parents of handicapped children was also provided. Greater emphasis on planning, evaluation, and accountability were also provided to further strengthen the provisions of PL 94-142.

The provisions of Section 504 and PL 94-142 have brought about tremendous changes. They put great pressure on schools to change their special education service systems.

As might be expected, the laws are controversial. Critics argue that the federal government should not meddle in what is essentially a local concern. In response, advocates for the handicapped point out that local school districts neglected the needs of the handicapped for years. Without federal legislation, they argue, most of the changes that have revolutionized life for the handicapped would not have occurred.

PROBE 1-3
Legislative Implications

1. What is the difference between a law and a regulation?

2. Circle the law that relates to each phrase:
   a. Civil rights for the handicapped   504   94-142
   b. Requires an IEP for all handicapped children   504   94-142
   c. Ensures due process safeguards   504   94-142
   d. Mandates building accessibility   504   94-142
   e. First to require a free, appropriate
      education for handicapped children   504   94-142
   f. Provides for a parent surrogate   504   94-142
   g. Prohibits discrimination in
      higher education   504   94-142
   h. Mandates fair employment practices   504   94-142
   i. Nondiscriminatory assessment   504   94-142

3. T F   All states must educate handicapped children between the ages of three and five.

4. Which of the following items established the right of privacy of educational records?
   a. Section 504
   b. The Buckley Amendment
   c. PL 94-142

THE IMPACT OF TECHNOLOGY

You should be able to describe the impact that the application of technology can have on special education programs.

The field of special education has benefited greatly over the years from advances in technology. For example, the development of the audiometer permitted a more accurate evaluation of hearing; the Perkins brailler enabled quick transcription of braille symbols for blind people; programmed instruction enhanced learning of students experiencing difficulty with academic subjects; machines that can produce speech sounds have helped facilitate communication with children who cannot talk; systematic approaches to classroom management have reduced problems encountered by students with behavior disorders; and specially designed keyboards have enabled people with physical disabilities to use the typewriter. These are only a few of the many benefits of technology.

Although there have been many advances, the potential that technology has for improving special education services and the quality of life of exceptional people has yet to be fully realized. It is becoming increasingly evident that special educators and related professional personnel will need to be aware of and know how to use various technologies if they are to be maximally effective in helping exceptional children. This section of the chapter will provide a foundation for the understanding of technology and its ramifications for special education programs.

Many people equate the term "technology" with hardware such as audiovisual equipment, teaching machines, and computers. The Commission on Instructional Technology (1970) pointed out in its report to the President and Congress, however, that technology is much broader than the use of hardware and software:

> Instructional technology is a systematic way of designing, carrying out, and evaluating the total process of learning and teaching in terms of specific objectives, based on research in human learning and communication, and employing a combination of human and nonhuman resources to bring about more effective instruction. (p. 199)

At about the time the Commission released its findings, Haring (1970) reviewed the application of instructional technology to special education design. He concluded:

> In the natural setting, educational technology is being applied in two ways: (1) through automated and non-automated media for display and measurement as part of the task of instruction, and (2) as a set of procedures which systematizes instruction. (p. 25)

How do media technology and systems technology differ?

Thus, today we hear discussions about the technology of teaching as well as computer technology. Some people refer to technology that includes machines as *media technology* and that which does not include machines as *systems technology*. In reality, however, the differences between the two are growing less distinct; for example, people working with media also stress systems procedures to guide their product development (e.g., Thiagarajan, Semmel, and Semmel, 1974). In the same way, those who work primarily with systems are using devices such as microcomputers to facilitate their efforts (e.g., Chaffin, Maxwell, and Thompson [1982]). Whether or not technological applications have involved the use of machines, systematic and integrated approaches to special education have been emphasized. Additional information can be obtained from reviews on the topic written by Lance (1973, 1977) and Blackhurst and Hofmeister (1980), from which much of this discussion is taken.

SYSTEMS TECHNOLOGY

How is the IEP related to technology?

Instructional Programs. In one bold move, the implementation of PL 94-142 placed systems technology on center stage. The major operational component of PL 94-142 is the Individualized Education Program (IEP), which was briefly described in the previous section. While the term "program" can be used in a variety of ways in education, the definition used in PL 94-142 resembles the concept of "program" developed in systems technology in the late 1960s (Corey, 1967). In fact, the process for designing IEPs was developed in accordance with the principles of systems technology.

What is an instructional package?

Instructional Packages. An instructional package is a systematically designed way of teaching. Most often, the term implies a self-contained and portable system. A package may consist of printed materials alone, but many include slides, cassette tapes, video tapes, films, and computer disks.

The approach to packaging that is having the greatest influence on special education stresses the use of relatively low-cost printed materials that give precise practical instructions for teaching specific skills to given populations of special education students. A good example is a manual that describes how to construct teaching aids for the classroom (Mercer, Mercer, and Bott, 1984). Twelve different formats for instructional materials are included. Each format is designed so that the student learns immediately whether a response was correct or the right answer if it was incorrect. Examples are provided to show how the materials can be used in a variety of content areas.

What are the features of direct instruction?

Direct Instruction. Systems technology has been used to develop a highly structured approach to the instructional process. Direct instruction has been described by Thomas (1983) as a teaching method that uses a model-lead-test format in the presentation of material. The process is interactive and very systematic, with the teacher demonstrating new information (modeling), providing controlled student practice in using the information (leading), and then evaluating student mastery levels (testing).

In addition to modeling, leading, and testing, teachers apply a number of principles to guide their teaching behavior. A high degree of teacher activity in the instructional process is required. Teachers actively define instructional goals and make frequent presentations to the students. High levels of student involvement with academic learning tasks are also required, so the teacher applies classroom management skills that increase student involvement with tasks and decrease off-task behaviors. Material is presented in small units, and teachers use a number of cues and signals to help focus students' attention on what is to be learned. Students are given many opportunities to respond, and they receive considerable feedback about the correctness of their responses. Instruction is designed to provide a high level of student success. The *DISTAR* reading materials are a good example of the application of the principles of direct instruction (Englemann and Bruner, 1969).

Direct instruction is a very systematic way of teaching, but it should not be used for teaching all subjects. It is particularly effective in teaching basic skills in reading and math, but it would be inappropriate for teaching such topics as art, social studies, or inquiry skills. According to Peterson (1979), direct instruction is particularly appropriate for students who have difficulty learning. More information about direct instruction can be found in the work of Becker and Carnine (1980, 1981).

Applied Behavior Analysis. One of the most promising instructional technologies to evolve during the 1970s and 1980s is applied behavior analysis. This is a structured, systematic approach to teaching and behavior management that employs direct observation and charting of student behavior. Teachers who use applied behavior analysis carefully analyze the tasks they want their students to learn, break these tasks down into small units of instruction, carefully sequence their teaching, use systematic reinforcement procedures, and continuously monitor student performance.

How do teachers use applied behavior analysis?

In teaching a student how to tell time, for example, the teacher studies the different tasks that a student must learn, such as identifying the numbers from 1 to 12, differentiating between the big and little hands, counting by 5's to 60, and so on. Those tasks that the student could perform are determined and recorded. Instruction then follows the sequence selected by the teacher, with care being taken to reward correct responses. Progress is recorded on the student's record in order to evaluate the effectiveness of instruction. This also provides feedback to the teacher about whether a change in instructional procedures is necessary in the event that those being used are ineffective.

Applied behavior analysis is a very powerful instructional tool in the hands of a well-trained special educator. It can be used to improve academic skills in direct instruction, to develop appropriate social behavior, and to reduce inappropriate behavior in students. Additional information about this topic is given in Section III of this text, which deals with individual differences in learning and behavior.

Competency-Based Teacher Education. The 1970s saw many states develop teacher certification standards based upon observed teaching competencies. A number of states now require that people demonstrate teaching competence before receiving a teaching certificate. In addition, the ongoing assessment of teacher competence as a means of periodic performance review is receiving more emphasis.

This emphasis upon teacher competence has resulted in the Competency-Based Teacher Education (CBTE) movement. CBTE is one of the most significant forces to affect the preparation of special education teachers in many years. Many colleges and universities have completely redesigned their programs as a result of studying the competencies needed by special education teachers and the curriculum that is required to develop those competencies.

What has been the impact of CBTE?

CBTE technology is based on several principles. Competencies that are required for any professional preparation program should be publicly stated. Specific objectives for the various educational experiences in a teacher education program should be explained and the criteria for evaluating when these objectives have been met should be made clear to students. When possible, alternative learning activities should be made available to students, and time for completing instructional activities should be variable while level of achievement is kept constant. Both instructors and students should share accountability for performance. More information about CBTE can be found in an earlier work by the author of this chapter (Blackhurst, 1977).

You will notice that this textbook incorporates a number of the principles associated with CBTE systems technology. At the beginning of each major section, we have listed a competency we want our readers to develop. We have also placed questions in the margins of the text to emphasize some of the more important objectives associated with each competency. *Probes* are provided to test whether the objectives and competencies are being met, and criteria, in the form of correct answers to the probes, appear at the end of the text. In addition, we have listed in the task sheets at the end of each chapter some alternative activities to facilitate learning.

MEDIA TECHNOLOGY

Educational Media. Educational media are the nonhuman resources that can be used for instructional purposes. The category has three components: hardware (the equipment), software (the materials, such as computer programs, that are used with the hardware), and content (the messages transmitted by the software and hardware).

We are all familiar with devices such as film projectors, tape recorders, slide-tape programs, and television in education, so these will not be reviewed here. Several other technologies, however, have significant implications for education. Because microcomputer technology is so important, a separate section will be devoted to that topic later in the chapter.

What is the potential of video disc technology?

One relatively new technology that will have tremendous impact on education is the video disc. Video disc systems present a dramatic change in storage capacity and flexibility over video systems such as video tape and video cassette because they can store single images in addition to the typical moving pictures that we see on our television screens. It is possible to quickly find and play back a single image or a segment of a program recorded on the disc. For example, a single, inexpensive disc can record and store the entire contents of the *Encyclopaedia Britannica* using only a small percentage of its available capacity.

One can store 54,000 single images, such as slides or photos of pages on one side of a video disc, and be able to gain quick access to each of them. One side of a disc can store 30 minutes of video programming. A disc's visual images can also be stored with more than one audio track, which would greatly facilitate education for bilingual children. Ronald Thorkildsen and his colleagues (Thorkildsen, Bickel, & Williams, 1979) at Utah State University are experimenting with video disc applications for special education populations.

Telecommunications Systems. The most readily available telecommunications system is, of course, the nation's telephone system. This can be used to transmit lectures and data, conduct interviews and audio teleconferences, and perform many other functions. Telephone systems have been very useful in providing instruction to homebound students. Parker (1977) concluded that classroom instruction conducted via telephone is at least as effective as face-to-face instruction.

How effective is instruction transmitted via telephone?

In-service training has been effectively conducted by telephone (Hershey, 1977). Tawney (1977) demonstrated that telephones could be used to link various instructional devices located in the homes of severely handicapped infants to a central computer control station. Computer-assisted instruction has also been transmitted over telephone lines.

Other telecommunications systems that have been used for educational purposes include open-circuit audio and video broadcast systems such as educational television and public radio. For special education, the best use of these media is the broadcast of programs that educate the public about the handicapped and gifted. The use of TV courses can also enhance teacher education. Donaldson and Martinson (1977) showed that video and audio programming can also influence adults' attitudes toward people with handicaps.

Although expensive to use, communications satellites have considerable potential for specialized communications. For example, the Council for Exceptional Children relayed portions of the First World Congress on Special Education from Scotland to the United States, enabling people who could not afford to attend the conference to participate in its activities from remote sites. The author of this chapter directed a project in which a NASA satellite was used in conducting a conference among special educators separated by approximately 2,500 miles. Other applications, such as remote diagnosis of physical problems by medical specialists, have demonstrated that satellites can be used to eliminate the need for travel and to solve communications problems in unique ways.

Assistive and Adaptive Devices. A number of devices have been developed to facilitate the physical functioning of people who have vision and hearing impairments, physical disabilities, and communication problems. Brief descriptions of just a few of these devices are given below to provide an overview of the scope of available products. Descriptions of other devices will be presented in later chapters.

How can assistive devices aid people with disabilities?

Communication aids include closed-circuit television systems that magnify print for people who have difficulty seeing, television programs with special captions for deaf people, communication boards that use symbols to permit people who cannot talk to communicate, and speech synthesizers that electronically generate vocal speech. These devices open new worlds for their users.

Numerous devices have been developed to aid those with visual impairments. A hand-held battery-powered calculator that speaks the name of each key as it is pressed is inexpensive and widely available. The Optacon converts printed materials into tactile images that can be read with the fingers, while the Kurzweil reader can convert print into spoken language. An electronic

This visually impaired student is using a device that enlarges text generated by the computer.

"paperless braille" machine uses audio cassettes to store braille information, which is then converted into tactile images. A special tape recorder can compress speech so that blind people can listen to recorded materials at a faster than normal rate. These and other devices will be explained in greater detail in the chapter on visual impairments.

Many devices are also available to help people overcome physical disabilities. Special keyboards for typewriters and computers that permit operation with fewer keystrokes have been developed. Those who have poor hand and finger movement can use switches manipulated by other parts of their bodies to control devices. Switches have been designed to be controlled by straws that the person sips or puffs. There are even switches that can be controlled by eyebrow movements. Systems to activate computers by voice commands are now available as well.

These and many other devices are described in Foulds and Lund (1976), Skinner (1977), American Foundation for the Blind (1978), and Vanderheiden (1978).

THE SPECIAL POTENTIAL OF MICROCOMPUTERS

Although they are rightly considered a form of media technology, we provide a separate section on microcomputers because of their importance and because their use epitomizes the blending of systems and media technology. No technological innovation has more potential for improving the quality of life and education for exceptional people than the microcomputer, which was developed in the late 1970s by Steve Wozniak and Steve Jobs, founders of the Apple Computer Company. The microcomputer and the programs and equipment that can be used with it have already been applied in many different ways in special education, and new applications are constantly being developed. We will describe some of the ways they are being used in both general and special education.

Drill and Practice. New concepts are usually not presented to students when the computer is used for drill and practice. Programs generally permit practice and reinforcement of concepts that are already learned or are in the process of being learned.

What is the major criticism of computers in education?

Perhaps the greatest single criticism of microcomputers in education is that their use is too frequently restricted to routine drill and practice. Unfortunately, this criticism is often justified. On the other hand, *meaningful* drill and practice *used appropriately* are important parts of the educational process with many children, and they can be delivered very effectively by computer.

One assumption about teaching children who have learning difficulties is that repetition facilitates their learning. A major challenge facing special education teachers who must use drill and practice with their students is to provide meaningful activities that contribute to learning and yet are varied enough to keep their students motivated.

Microcomputers have some unique qualities that make them particularly well suited for drill and practice. Taking an anthropomorphic view, one could say that these devices have infinite patience, provide opportunities for intense on-task engagement, offer varied and novel tasks, provide feedback and correction, and do not get frustrated with incorrect responses. In fact, for many drill and practice applications, it is quite likely that they can perform better than teachers or traditional drill activities such as work sheets.

Some excellent, highly motivating drill and practice programs are being developed. For example, Jerry Chaffin, of the Department of Special Education at the University of Kansas, spent time watching youngsters playing arcade games to see what they enjoyed and then developed a series of math and language arts drill and practice programs based on arcade game formats. He calls these "Arcademic Programs." Some of these are especially useful for students who have limited physical abilities since they can be operated by pressing a single key on the computer keyboard.

Tutorial. When the computer is used for tutorial purposes, new concepts are taught. Some drill and practice exercises might be included in a tutorial program, but the focus is on the initial teaching of concepts. One of the computer's real strengths, the ability to branch, can be used to advantage in tutorial programs. Branching is the process by which, on the basis of a student's response, the computer moves the student to the appropriate part of a program. For example, it might repeat a certain section or teach in a different way concepts that have not been learned. Similarly, branching can be used to bypass portions of a program that a student has already mastered.

Why is the computer's ability to branch so important?

Although a number of tutorial programs are being advertised, the development of many high-quality programs is just beginning. Authoring languages are computer programs that teachers can use to develop instructional programs for their students without having to learn a complex computer programming language. A number of good computer-assisted instruction (CAI) authoring languages are now available to facilitate the development of computer-assisted instruction efforts. One of the most powerful authoring languages for microcomputer users is PILOT (Programmed Inquiry, Learning, or Teaching). Versions of PILOT are available for most microcomputer systems.

Tutorial programs are being widely used in public schools. Other applications also have merit, however, and bear watching (e.g. Cartwright, 1984). For example, Philip Cartwright of the Pennsylvania State University developed a PILOT program for an introductory special education course that is being offered to students at various campuses throughout Pennsylvania.

Simulation. In simulation, the computer is used to model experiments or real-world events. Simulation programs sometimes resemble laboratory assignments. For example, a program might allow a student to manipulate variables in a theoretical science experiment and then observe the different results. Students are often given information and then required to use it to solve a particular problem.

Although simulation programs can benefit many types of students, they are especially valuable to gifted students. A number of interesting and very sophisticated simulation programs are beginning to appear on the educational market. These include simulations of nuclear disasters, election politics, strategic planning, science experiments, and the free enterprise system, to mention just a few.

For which children are computer simulations particularly beneficial?

Reinforcement. As noted earlier, a major area of interest to special educators is applied behavior analysis. Much research has been conducted on the use of reinforcement in learning. We know that positive reinforcement of desired responses will increase the likelihood of the reoccurrence of that response. Special education teachers must design ways to collect data about student performance to be used in making instructional decisions, develop ways to increase the frequency of positive reinforcement, and locate effective reinforcers. Permission to use microcomputers and computer games are very good reinforcers for some students.

How can computers be used for reinforcement?

Lewis Polsgrove, Herbert Reith, and their associates at Indiana University have been examining these issues for a number of years (Polsgrove & Reith, 1985). Their research shows that microcomputers can be used successfully in these areas in public school programs for children who have learning and behavioral problems.

Information Management. The implementation of PL 94-142 has placed considerable demands on public schools. Highly specific due process procedures must be followed in locating, testing, and placing students in special education programs. In addition, individualized educational programs (IEPs) must be developed for each child who receives special education services. Detailed reports must also be prepared to verify compliance with the federal law.

There are several microcomputer programs that can help school administrators manage such information, and others are being developed. For example, David Lillie of the University of North Carolina has developed a computer program that will facilitate the generation of IEPs (Lillie & Edwards, 1984). A number of similar programs are also being developed to help maintain student records. Many school systems are designing their own data management systems, using data management programs that are available for general use.

Ted Hasselbring, at Peabody College, Vanderbilt University, has also developed a valuable microcomputer program to manage information (Hasselbring & Hamlett, 1984). This program accepts data about a child's performance and provides graphs that help the teacher decide when to change the instructional methods and materials being used with the child.

TECHNOLOGY IN ACTION

Patty Burger teaches children who are both deaf and blind in a medium-sized school district in Indiana. She is the only person with this type of teaching assignment in her school district. Unlike other teachers, she does not have colleagues to turn to for advice about different instructional approaches for her students or for support when she encounters difficulties. Thanks to SpecialNet, however, the frustration of her situation has been considerably reduced.

Twice each week, Ms. Burger travels to the central school office after classes to use an Apple IIe computer that is connected to the telephone. After loading a telecommunications program into the computer, she types **DIAL** and a list of phone numbers appears on the screen. She selects the one for SpecialNet, and the computer begins to dial the telephone. It dials a local phone number, which is tied into a telecommunication system called TELE-NET. This eliminates the long-distance charges for hooking into the computer, which is located in Virginia.

A message appears on the screen, asking for the code for the type of computer she is using. She types **D2,** the code for the Apple IIe. An @ then appears, after which she types **MAIL.** The screen then displays the prompt **USER NAME?** She types **INDY.SE,** the name her school system selected to identify itself to other SpecialNet users. The screen responds with **PASSWORD?** and she enters a secret combination of letters that only users in her school district know. This prevents unauthorized access to the system.

This message then appears: **WELCOME TO TELEMAIL! YOUR LAST ACCESS WAS TUESDAY, FEBRUARY 24 AT 4:12 P.M.** The computer informs her that there is a message for her from Lee McNulty, a teacher of deaf-blind children in San Francisco, who has been corresponding with her electronically for the past six weeks. Each had placed a message requesting information about instructional materials for deaf-blind children on the EXCHANGE electronic bulletin board. After seeing her request, Mr. McNulty left a message for Ms. Burger, and they began corresponding about

mutual problems and concerns. Several other teachers of deaf-blind children periodically communicate via this system as well.

McNulty's message contains information about a new instructional game he has been using with his students. He includes the reference of the book that has a description of the game. Ms. Burger presses the **CONTROL** key and the **A** simultaneously, and that message is recorded on her disk. The computer then displays the prompt **ACTION?** to which she responds **ANSWER.** She types a note to McNulty, expressing her appreciation for the information; also, she promises to send him some information on a new diagnostic test she is using after she has finished evaluating it.

Next, she types **CHECK DEAFBLIND,** which is the name of one of more than a dozen electronic message boards that deals with different topics. She has not checked this board for a week, so she types **SCAN SINCE FEB. 17.** Four items are listed as having been posted since that date. Each has its own number, the date posted, the name of the sender, a brief description of the contents of the message, and the number of lines in the message.

Three of the messages don't appear to be relevant to her current interests, but message number 3 is labeled **NEW PRODUCT ANNOUNCE-MENTS.** She types **READ 3** and the message appears. It lists ten new products for children with multiple handicaps, several of which look like they have some merit for her children. She stores the message on her computer disk. She then checks the bulletin boards on **DEAFNESS, MULTIHANDICAPPED, ASSISTIVE-DEVICE, CEC.NEWS, VISION,** and **EXCHANGE.** Nothing else appears to be relevant, so she types **BYE** and the computer disconnects the telephone.

After hanging up, she commands the computer to print the information she had stored so she will have a paper copy of the message and the new product information. She was on-line a total of 13 minutes and found some very useful information.

On some of her "electronic visits," Ms. Burger enters information; on others she is primarily a recipient. Some days bring no information. The important thing to Ms. Burger, however, is that SpecialNet enables her to exchange easily information with other teachers of deaf-blind children throughout the country. Through the bulletin board system, she also learns many things that improve her professional skills.

What is SpecialNet?

The National Association of State Directors of Special Education (NASDSE), located in Washington, D.C., maintains a very useful service for the dissemination and exchange of information. This service, called "SpecialNet," provides electronic bulletin boards for displaying information about a variety of topics and a system for contacting any individual subscriber or the entire membership of the network. What is unique about SpecialNet is that all of this is done electronically, using a computer hooked up to a telephone line. Judith Wilson at the University of Kansas worked with the Kansas Department of Education to link the Directors of Special Education throughout Kansas via SpecialNet. Following is an example of how an individual teacher might use SpecialNet.

Communication. SpecialNet is obviously a communications system; however, its focus is on information exchange. Microcomputers can also be used to facilitate communication for those who have physical disabilities that hinder normal communication.

How can a speech synthesizer be useful?

It is now possible to add relatively inexpensive accessories to microcomputers that will produce synthetic speech. These amazing devices can be set up actually to pronounce whatever is typed into the keyboard. For example, the phrase "Please get me a drink of water" would actually be pronounced as a complete sentence after it was typed. The implications of such equipment for a person with severe cerebral palsy who could not speak intelligibly should be obvious. Similarly, a blind person handicapped by the inability to use ink print could have new career opportunities in areas such as computer programming because the computer can now "talk."

Samuel Ashcroft and his colleagues of George Peabody College at Vanderbilt University are conducting interesting research which couples microcomputers with devices that store braille on audio cassettes (Ashcroft & Bourgeois, 1980). His research is discovering optimum ways to use a variety of new technologies with blind people.

Assistive and Adaptive Equipment. Microprocessors are being used in conjunction with a variety of devices to aid people with physical disabilities. Some of these devices simply facilitate physical functioning, while others provide control over the environment. For example, people confined to their beds can operate equipment such as television sets, telephones, and word processors through environmental controls. Greg Vanderheiden of the Trace Center at the University of Wisconsin is quite active in developing devices to facilitate physical functioning.

Michael Behrmann of George Mason University is conducting interesting research on the use of computers with multiply handicapped babies. He is also exploring the use of robots with other multiply handicapped populations.

How may computers eventually be used with paralyzed people?

The work of Jerrold Petrofsky of Wright State University has attracted considerable attention in this area (see Chapter 7). He has been experimenting with computer controlled electronic stimulation of the leg muscles of paralyzed people to elicit movement of the paralyzed limbs. One of his subjects, a college student paralyzed in an automobile accident, walked ten steps to receive her diploma at graduation. This landmark research suggests that someday we may be able to implant in the body devices resembling heart pacemakers that will enable paralyzed people to walk.

Readers interested in additional information about the application of microcomputers in special education programs may want to consult the text on that topic edited by the author of this chapter (Blackhurst, 1985).

Because technology's impact on special education is so pervasive, we have provided a series of vignettes, such as the one you read about SpecialNet, throughout this book. Each chapter includes a vignette, titled "Technology in Action," that illustrates how technology is being applied to the topic of that chapter. Space limitations do not permit a more thorough exploration of technology, but the vignettes should give some indication of its great potential. As you read these brief accounts, you will note that we have provided examples of both systems technology and media technology.

What is ASET?

If you are interested in becoming involved in the fascinating topic of technology in special education, you may consider joining one of the professional organizations devoted to the study of this topic. The Association for Special Education Technology (ASET), established in 1973, was developed, in part, to stimulate the development of new technologies for special education and to foster cooperation among special educators and educational technologists. In 1978, this group started the *Journal of Special Education Technology* as a vehicle for disseminating information about technology. Membership information may be obtained by writing to ASET at Utah State University, UMC 68, Logan, Utah 84322.

As this chapter was being written, a special interest group on Technology and Media (TAM) was being developed within the Council for Exceptional Children (CEC). (Additional information about CEC is presented in Chapter 2). Interested readers can write CEC at 1920 Association Drive, Reston, Virginia 22091, to obtain information about TAM.

By affiliating with groups such as ASET and TAM, you will be kept apprised of the latest developments in special education technology. You will also learn about the availability of interesting jobs that involve applying technology to special education problems. Such jobs can provide excellent career options for those who are interested in this topic.

PROBE 1-4
The Impact of Technology

1. What is the difference between systems technology and media technology?

2. A teacher who is using a model-lead-test format is engaged in the process of

   _____.

3. CBTE stands for _____.

4. T   F   Research has shown that instruction via telephone is not as effective as conventional face-to-face instruction.

5. Name three types of assistive devices.

6. What is the difference between a drill and practice program and a tutorial program?

7. T   F   Drill and practice computer programs should not be used with special education students.

8. What does branching do in a computer program?

9. T   F   Computer games have no value in educational programs.

10. The electronic bulletin board system for special educators is called _____.

11. _____ is the abbreviation of an organization for special educators who are interested in technology.

SUMMARY

1. Special education is individually planned instruction designed to respond to the unique characteristics of children who have needs that cannot be met by the standard school curriculum.

2. In addition to the gifted and talented, the category of exceptional children includes those with communication disorders, hearing disorders, visual impairments, physical disabilities, mental retardation, learning disabilities, behavior disorders, and multiple handicaps.

3. Handicaps are the result of a person's interaction with the environment. A child with an impairment or disability may be handicapped in some situations but not in others.

4. It is estimated that between 10 and 15 percent of the children under the age of 21 need special education services. Thus, there are about 1.5 million gifted children and between 4.3 and 8 million handicapped children in the United States.

5. In the past the handicapped have sometimes been cared for and sometimes abused and persecuted. The development of genuinely beneficial programs began in 1950 with the founding of the National Association for Retarded Children.
6. Litigation has resulted in court determinations that affirm the right of all handicapped children to a publicly supported education.
7. Section 504 of the Rehabilitation Act of 1973 prohibits discrimination against the handicapped in employment, access to facilities, education, and other social services. It is essentially civil rights legislation for the handicapped.
8. Public Law 94-142 guarantees a free and appropriate public education to all handicapped children.
9. Systems technology and media technology are having a profound effect on the provision of special education services.
10. Microcomputers are being used to provide drill and practice, tutorial programming, simulations, reinforcement, information management, and communications in special education programs.
11. The Association for Special Education Technology and the Technology and Media Division of C.E.C. are organizations for special educators interested in applications of technology to the education of exceptional children.

TASK SHEET 1
Simulation of Disability

Select one of the following simulations of disabilities and perform the required tasks for a minimum of three hours. *Do not* spend the majority of this time resting or studying, or you will defeat the purpose of the simulation.

1. *Hearing Impairment:* Wear a pair of foam rubber ear plugs. During this simulation you should attempt to communicate with someone. Also try to watch part of a TV show with the sound turned off. Spend a portion of your time outdoors.
2. *Blindness:* Blindfold yourself so that you can see no light. Try to perform several routine tasks, including grooming, dressing, and eating. Make a brief venture out of doors, but take a companion with you to protect you from injury.
3. *Physical Disability:* Do *one* of the following:
   a. Wrap your hands so that you cannot use your fingers.
   b. Use a pair of crutches.
   c. Spend several hours in a wheelchair.
   d. Restrain your dominant arm by tying your wrist to your belt or waist.
   During the above simulations, attempt tasks that you perform every day, such as preparing food, eating, dressing, grooming, performing your job, studying, and so on.

Following this experience, write a brief report. It should include descriptions of the following:

1. The disability you selected.
2. The activities you engaged in during the simulation.
3. The things you could do without difficulty during the simulation.
4. The problems you encountered and how you attempted to solve them.
5. The feelings you had while simulating the disability.
6. The effect this experience had on you.

Freddy had difficulty with reading from the time he started first grade. When he entered second grade, he was reading at the beginning first-grade level. School officials told his parents that he was just a "late bloomer" and not to worry. They said that he would catch up as he matured. At the end of second grade, Freddy's father, who was in the Marines, was transferred.

At his new school, Freddy's reading problem was diagnosed as a "learning disability," and it was recommended that he receive part-time reading instruction from a special education teacher in a resource room. Following another transfer 2 years later, the psychologist in his new school diagnosed Freddy as being "educable mentally retarded" and suggested full-time placement in a special education class.

As he entered sixth grade, Freddy was still behind in reading. By that time, his inability to read was having adverse effects on his performance in other subjects. In an effort to draw attention away from his academic problems, he began to create disturbances in the classroom. He became known as the "class clown." His behavior also became more aggressive, and he began to get into fights with other students. After his father's next transfer, Freddy's unacceptable behavior led to further testing, which resulted in his being labled "emotionally disturbed."

As a seventh grader, Freddy was referred to a special school in which he received intensive reading instruction in a highly structured environment. This enabled him to bring his behavior under control. After 6 months at that school, he was transferred back to public school, where he entered a work-study program designed to develop prevocational skills.

By the time Freddy was ready to enter high school, he had a 2-inch thick set of records. He had been tested and retested by educational diagnosticians, psychologists, and psychiatrists, who had applied at least three different diagnostic labels. He could read at about the fifth grade level. At age sixteen, Freddy dropped out of school and obtained a job driving a cement truck for a local construction company.

2

Issues in Special Education

A. Edward Blackhurst

A. Edward Blackhurst is a Professor in the Department of Special Education at the University of Kentucky. He has directed special education instructional materials development and dissemination projects, scholarship programs for special education teachers, special education administrator training projects, and a project to prepare special education microcomputer specialists. He is past president of the Teacher Education Division of the Council for Exceptional Children.

Unfortunately, Freddy's educational career is not an isolated case. Too many "Freddys" have met a similar fate in our nation's school systems. Why is this so? Did Freddy have some innate characteristics that caused him to fail at reading? Did school officials misdiagnose the nature and cause of his problems? How many of Freddy's problems were caused by his parents' frequent moves? Was Freddy placed in inappropriate school programs? Were his educational needs ignored by school personnel? Did he get incompetent instruction? Could his problems have been prevented by earlier identification and treatment? What was the quality of the special education services he received? Did they help him or did they further aggravate his problems?

We will never know the answers to these questions. Perhaps only one of these factors was the primary cause of Freddy's educational problems. In all likelihood, however, several of the factors interacted to contribute to his problems and make them worse.

One thing is fairly certain with the Freddys of the world, however, and that is that school personnel can do very little about the characteristics that students bring to school. Teachers cannot control the environmental factors that influence a student outside of school. They typically have little impact on child rearing practices and what happens to the child in the home and community.

The primary way that school personnel can help students such as Freddy is to manipulate the variables under their control to ensure that they get the highest-quality education possible. These variables involve assessing the nature and severity of any educational difficulties that may exist, selecting an appropriate educational placement, providing individualized instruction that is specifically targeted to improve performance, being sensitive to the influence of cultural diversity, treating students humanely, and manipulating the environment to ensure that students are integrated into the mainstream of society.

A number of issues involved in providing special education and other services in these areas will be discussed in this chapter. We begin each section by posing a number of questions associated with the topic. As you will see in the discussions that follow, we do not have definitive answers for all of our questions. Some of the conclusions we draw must be considered the best professional judgement available at the time we wrote this chapter. One of the biggest challenges facing special educators today is to develop research projects that will yield empirical data that can be used to make more informed decisions about the issues we discuss here and elsewhere in this book.

Diagnostic labels are applied to children as a result of testing — often with unfortunate consequences.

STUDENT IDENTIFICATION

> **You should be able to describe how students are identified as being in need of special education services.**

Many students who receive special education services are identified before they enter school. This is particularly true of those who have severe problems such as blindness, deafness, or physical disabilities. Other students are placed in special education programs as a result of an accident or disease that occurs after they enter school. Still other are identified through the formal screening programs conducted in the schools on a regularly scheduled basis.

The great majority of special education students, however, have mild to moderate disabilities that go unnoticed until they are in school programs. These are students who, like Freddy, have trouble learning or adjusting to school situations. Most frequently, these students are first identified by regular classroom teachers.

These teachers usually notice that a student is having difficulty mastering a particular academic task. After trying to remedy the problem, the teacher may refer the student to the appropriate school officials, who start the process of conducting a thorough assessment to determine the child's particular difficulty. These procedures must follow the due process guidelines set out by the rules and regulations of PL 94-142.

How are students labeled? If assessment indicates that the child has a significant problem that could be solved through special education services, the child receives a diagnostic label. The child may be labeled as "educable mentally retarded," "learning disabled," "speech impaired," "physically handicapped," or be placed in one of a number of other diagnostic categories. This label is required to document the delivery of special education services in the schools. Assigning children to categories is also used as the basis for obtaining funds for special education teachers, program facilities, and related services.

Many questions can be raised about the assessment and labeling process. Among the most important are these:

— How reliable and valid are the tests used in the assessment?
— Do the tests discriminate against children from culturally diverse backgrounds?
— Are test results used appropriately?
— How does labeling affect the children labeled?
— How does labeling affect the people who work with labeled children?
— Are there any alternatives to labeling?

Issues associated with these questions will be explored in the following pages.

ASSESSMENT

The many methods of assessing the educational performance of exceptional children can be divided into two categories, informal and formal.

Informal assessment relies on (1) teachers' observations of children's varying skills in different areas, which may be recorded in what are called anecdotal records; and (2) teacher-constructed tests designed to determine whether a child has learned what is being taught.

Formal assessment relies on tests developed by test publishers. These may include achievement tests to measure academic attainment, intelligence tests to estimate level of ability, and parent interviews to obtain information about social skills. Language, personality, creativity, physical ability, vocational interest, and other tests may also be warranted.

Most of the tests available from test publishers are *standardized*. This means the test has been given to a large number of people under identical conditions: All people received the same instructions and had the same amount of time to complete the test. In addition, all the tests have been scored the same way. According to test publishers, the test must be administered and scored precisely as the directions indicate for the results to be useful.

How do norm-referenced and criterion-referenced tests differ?

Some tests are *norm-referenced,* whereas others are *criterion-referenced*. Norm-referenced tests are those that compare a particular student's performance to that of the norm group, the group of people on whom the test was standardized. For example, a score at the 2.0 level in reading on an achievement test indicates that the child reads about as well as most children at the beginning of the second grade. Most of the achievement tests you took in school are norm-referenced tests.

A criterion-referenced test, on the other hand, does not compare one child's performance with that of other children. Instead, the child's performance is compared to some standard, called a criterion. For example, a teacher giving a multiplication test on the sevens tables is interested only in whether a child can correctly multiply the numbers 0 through 10 by 7. The criterion would be 100 percent correct responses. Criterion-referenced tests are used to determine whether a child can peform a particular task, and not how well his or her performance compares to other children's.

All tests have a certain degree of *validity* and *reliability*. A test is valid when it actually measures what its authors say it will measure. If a test designed to assess reading ability accurately measures a child's ability to read material written at different grade levels, the test has a high degree of validity. Reliability is the consistency with which a test measures a particular trait. If we administered the same test to a student twice within a short period of time and got the same results, the test would be considered reliable.

Standardization alone does not ensure validity or reliability. Furthermore, the norms upon which the standardization was developed may not be appropriate for your purposes. If the types of children you are testing were not represented in the norm group, interpreting test results according to the standardized instructions may be inappropriate.

Many tests with poor reliability and validity and inappropriate norms have been used to make educational decisions about exceptional children. For example, Thurlow and Ysseldyke (1979) found that out of 30 tests widely used in programs for children with learning disabilities, only five had appropriate norms, ten had adequate reliability, and nine had sufficient validity. Clearly there is much potential for abusing test results. Those who test or use test results should use great caution to ensure that appropriate tests are administered and that appropriate decisions are made on the basis of their results. The test administration manual for publisher-made tests usually includes information about test norms, reliablity, and validity. Additional information about assessment can be found in the very informative text by Salvia and Ysseldike (1981).

The assessment of most exceptional children requires the use of formal and informal techniques, standardized and teacher-made tests, and norm- and criterion-referenced tests. Children are assessed for two primary purposes: (1) for identification, to determine who needs special education services; and (2) for teaching, to determine what and how a child should be taught.

Assessment for Identification. For most children in school, assessment for identification begins with the regular classroom teacher. If the teacher notices a child is doing very poorly or especially well in a particular area, the child may be referred to a specialist for in-depth assessment. The specialists are selected on the basis of the child's suspected problem and may include educational diagnosticians, psychologists, physicians, speech-language pathologists, or others.

What is screening? Many schools and health agencies prefer not to rely exclusively on teachers to discover exceptional children; there is always a chance that someone will be missed. As a result, systematic procedures to *screen* children have been developed. The vision screening program most schools conduct is a good example. In this program children are given a quick, easy eye examination every 2 years or so. When the results show that a child may have a problem, the child is referred to a vision specialist. The best identification programs rely on a combination of teacher observation and screening.

Whereas a child's visual acuity, hearing, physical ability, and speech can be measured fairly accurately, traits such as intelligence, personality, emotional stability, academic achievement, social adjustment, and creativity are very difficult to assess. One reason is that many of the tests used to identify them are imprecise. Tests are sometimes used inappropriately as well. For example, the administration of an English IQ test to a child whose primary language is Spanish may produce a very low IQ score, one that does not accurately reflect the child's ability to perform academic tasks. The use of inappropriate tests and testing practices such as this has resulted in laws forbidding the identification and placement of children on the basis of a single test score. Ideally, assessment for identification should be based on the results of a number of tests, in combination with the anecdotal records of teachers, the observations of parents, and the findings of physicians and other professionals who come in contact with the child.

Assessment for Teaching. The purpose of assessment for teaching is to provide information useful in planning what to teach (content) and how to teach it (methods).

What kinds of tests are most useful to teachers?

In this kind of assessment, teacher-made tests and observations are generally more helpful than the more sophisticated standardized tests. Teachers are more likely to use a teacher-made or commercial criterion-referenced test than a norm-referenced test. This may surprise you, but which would help you *teach* a child best — an hour-long IQ test or a five-minute session in which the child was asked to identify the initial consonants of words presented on flash cards? The IQ score would indicate the child's intellectual ability relative to that of a group of children of the same chronological age. The flash card test, on the other hand, would indicate which consonants the child could pronounce and which needed to be taught. What's more, by paying careful attention to the types of errors the child makes, the teacher should get some insight into how the consonants the child didn't know should be taught.

Effective teachers generally assess children regularly, not just at fixed times of the year such as at the beginning and end of the grading period. It is best to adopt the "test-teach-test" principle, according to which a concept is assessed, taught, and then reassessed. If the concept has been learned, the teacher can move on. If not, the concept is taught again — perhaps using different methods after the teacher has determined why the child did not learn during the first instructional sequence.

Once again we want to emphasize that the teacher should not rely solely on formal test data to make educational decisions. Although the data may provide insight into a child's strenghts and weaknesses, they can also be imprecise and inaccurate. They should be considered only in conjunction with observations of the child in the classroom. Ideally, the assessment process should result in an individualized education program such as the one discussed later in this chapter.

LABELING

Consider the image you see when you visualize the following terms:

idiot	spastic
bookworm	epileptic fit
cripple	crazy
deaf and dumb	vegetable

If you are like most people, each of these terms conjures up an image of a person who has a certain physical appearance or who is behaving in a certain way. Generally, the images are negative and stereotypical. We learn them from television, literature, and other media. For example, a person who does something unusual is called "crazy"; a bright child is often portrayed as a frail individual who wears glasses; stories sometimes have a "village idiot" as a character; an umpire may be referred to as "blind." The stereotypes that result are reinforced by daily conversations and the attitudes of the people we grew up with.

Labels of a different sort have been used for many years to categorize handicapped children. Children have been identified, diagnosed, and labeled as emotionally disturbed, learning disabled, and educable mentally retarded, for example. It was argued that placing children in categories helped in the effective delivery of instruction. Further, labeling was helpful in obtaining funds.

Today the tend is to reduce diagnostic labeling, particularly of children with mild disabilities. In addition to the obvious humanitarian reasons, there

Many handicapped children can be "mainstreamed" into regular classes.

are some very pragmatic ones. Gillung and Rucker (1977), for example, found that regular educators and some special education teachers had lower expectations for children who were labeled than for children with identical behaviors who were not labeled. A label can thus become a self-fulfilling prophecy. Even if the label were incorrectly assigned, children might eventually behave as the label said they would, simply because people expected them to. Although research on the effect of labeling on children has yielded mixed results, this at least seems clear: Most people tend to view a labeled person differently than a nonlabeled one.

What are the arguments for and against labeling?

Controversy about labeling reached such proportions in the early 1970s that the eminent psychologist Nicholas Hobbs was commissioned to begin a study called the Project on Classification of Exceptional Children. In his summary report, Hobbs (1975) described some problems with current diagnostic categories. His conclusion included the following points: (1) labels are applied imprecisely; (2) labeled children are stigmatized; (3) labels yield too little information for planning; (4) the classification of children with multiple problems in terms of a dominant set of attributes leads to the neglect of other conditions; (5) classification tends to be deviance-oriented; (6) classification systems are insensitive to the rapid changes that take place in children; (7) classification of a child can result in the disregard of important etiological (causative) factors.

In favor of labeling, one could argue that administrators need to be able to categorize children in order to qualify for state financial support. Labels can also help focus public attention and legislation on a particular problem. One could argue further that if one set of labels were eliminated it would soon be replaced by another, and that labels are useful in discussing children with similar characteristics.

As much as we might like to do away with them, the use of labels is almost inevitable. Labels and categories are used whenever something is being organized. For example, we organized the information in this text into categorical areas to present it in the most efficient manner.

The important thing to remember is that labeling can have bad effects if used incorrectly. Labels should be used only when necessary. The focus of attention should always be an individual, not a group or class. For special educators the crucial question is, "How should this particular child's strengths and weaknesses influence the teaching strategy I've devised?"

PROBE 2-1
Student Identification

1. T F   Standardized tests always have good reliability and validity.

2. T F   Most exceptional children are identified prior to entering school.

3. Give an example of an informal and a formal assessment technique.

4. _____ is the extent to which a test measures what it purports to measure.

5. _____ is the consistency with which a test measures what it is attempting to measure.

6. Differentiate between norm-referenced and criterion-referenced tests.

7. The two major types of assessment are assessment for _____ and assessment for _____ .

8. Give three reasons why labels should be de-emphasized.

9. Give one of the arguments in favor of labeling.

NORMALIZATION

You should be able to discuss the principle of normalization and its effect on exceptional people.

Normalization can be defined as the philosophy that all handicapped people should have the opportunity to live lives as close to the normal as possible; patterns and conditions of everyday life as close as possible to the norms and patterns of the mainstream of society should be made available to them (Nirje, 1969). This philosophy evolved in the late 1960s and early 1970s as a result of parental dissatisfaction with the placement of their handicapped children. Many were being placed in isolated residential institutions or in programs in public schools that were segregated from the nonhandicapped.

Normalization has resulted in the greater integration of the handicapped population into business and social activities. Its greatest influence on special education, however, has been the promotion of two practices, deinstitutionalization and mainstreaming.

A number of questions have been raised about the normalization principle. Chief among them are these:

— Should all large residential institutions for handicapped people be closed?
— What effect will group homes have on the communities in which they are located?
— Should we do away with self-contained special education classes?
— How is normalization related to mainstreaming?
— Who should be mainstreamed?

These questions and others will be addressed in the following pages.

DEINSTITUTIONALIZATION

Deinstitutionalization refers to the movement to eliminate large institutions, particularly those for the retarded. Wolfensberger (1972), an early advocate of normalization, proposed that long-term, total life care institutions be replaced by small, community-based group homes that would permit residents to participate in local activities and be closer to their families. The establishment of group homes is being encouraged by many parents and special education professionals.

Deinstitutionalization has its problems, however. It is often difficult to find qualified staff for group homes. States that have invested large sums to build or renovate institutions are reluctant to support moves to other facilities. What is more, the establishment of some group homes is opposed by the communities in which they hope to locate. Such community attitudes have prompted articles such as this:[1]

> Despite current-day myths about community resistence to group homes for mentally retarded there's much more community support *for* them than most of us realize.
>
> That's the surprising finding of a study of the myths and facts about community acceptance of group homes, conducted by three researchers from Texas Tech University and reported in a recent *Journal of Rehabilitation*.
>
> Here are highlights of four myths and some facts:
>
> *Myth One*
> Handicapped people in group homes are likely to engage in criminal activities. Therefore, keep them out.
>
> *The Facts*
> A 2-year follow-up of 105 group homes with nearly 2,000 developmentally disabled residents showed that fewer than one percent had ever run afoul of the law.
> A study of a community home for retarded juvenile offenders disclosed not a single event that disturbed the neighborhood.
>
> *Myth Two*
> If a group home moves into a community, surrounding property values will go downhill.
>
> *The Facts*
> A study of Washington State group homes showed that property values actually rose — because of superior care given to the group homes.
> The Crofton House study showed "no significant change" in the asking price of surrounding homes sold before or after the group home opened.
> In Stockton, Cal., 200 neighbors of community homes for elderly people

[1] Source: Blue Grass Association for Retarded Citizens Newsletter, July, 1979.

were asked whether the homes would have an adverse impact on housing prices. Eighty-four percent thought not.

Myth Three

Group homes create upheavals in neighborhood lifestyles. Everybody's living comfortably in single-family units and along comes this group home. . . .

The Facts

The California Department of Planning found that 93 percent of neighbors of foster homes for elderly people reported no traffic problems; 80 percent, no restrictions on children's play; 75 percent, no unusual activity in the neighborhood.

A Fresno, Cal., study of 20 community homes for mentally retarded people showed that 96 percent of the area's residents had no difficulties at all with their retarded neighbors.

Myth Four

People living near group homes will never come to like their mentally retarded neighbors, no matter how long they live together.

The Facts

A national study of group homes for developmentally disabled people showed that in 89 percent of the cases community opposition decreased after the homes opened.

A Fresno, Cal., study concluded that "once mentally retarded residents have lived in a neighborhood, they tend to be accepted."

A Warning

Utopia still isn't here for mentally handicapped people in group homes. It isn't even around the corner.

But these studies, and others like them, are rays of hope.

What appears to be happening to large residential institutions?

Some authorities, such as Blatt, Ozolins, and McNally (1979), advocate closing all residential institutions and moving toward smaller community-based facilities. The fact that large investments of money have been made in the physical plants of large institutions makes this unlikely, however. It is more likely that smaller facilities will be built as the larger ones become obsolete. These facilities will probably have slightly different missions than strict residential care, however. For example, in 1982 the Kentucky Association for Retarded Citizens went to court to prevent the rebuilding of an obsolete residential facility. The judge ruled that the institution could be rebuilt, but its size was drastically reduced. In addition, however, he ruled that the facility should provide space for emergency temporary care of mentally retarded people when their parents or legal guardians had to travel or pursue business that would be impossible if they had to maintain responsibility for the people in their charge.

Additional information about deinstitutionalization will be presented in Chapter 8, which deals with mental retardation.

MAINSTREAMING AND THE LEAST RESTRICTIVE ENVIRONMENT

The second aspect of normalization that relates to special education is a reflection of a provision of PL 94-142. The provision stipulates that handicapped children be educated in "the least restrictive environment." This means that handicapped children are to be educated with nonhandicapped children whenever possible, in as nearly normal an environment as possible. This process is known as *mainstreaming*.

The term "mainstreaming" (which does not appear in PL 94-142) was originally coined to describe the process of educating handicapped students in the least restrictive environment. Through common usage, however, mainstreaming now refers to the practice of integrating handicapped children into regular classes for all or part of the school day. The least restrictive environment, on the other hand, refers to the educational placement of students in a setting as close to the regular classroom as possible. For some children, the least restrictive environment might be placement in a regular class. For others, it might mean education in a self-contained special education class or homebound instruction.

What is the least restrictive environment concept?

Placement decisions are made at the time that the individualized education program is planned and should be based upon the child's unique needs. The options are illustrated in Figure 2-1. These options are frequently referred to as the "continuum of special education services" or the "cascade of services" (Deno, 1973). You will note that there are ten educational settings listed. The

The integration of handicapped and non-handicapped children in educational activities is beneficial to both groups of children.

Figure 2-1
Continuum of Special Education Services

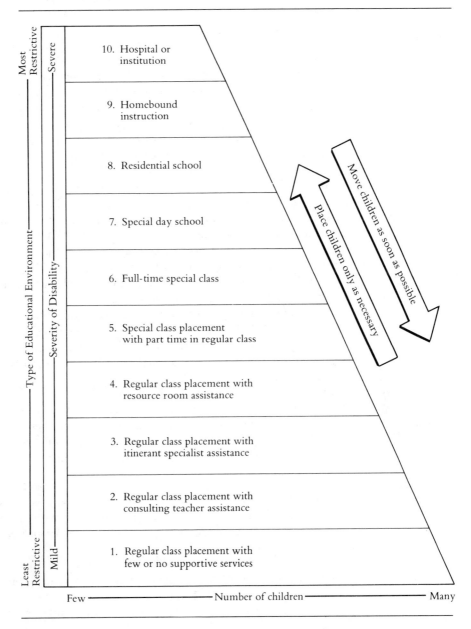

least restrictive setting is at the bottom, and the most restrictive is at the top. The arrows on the right illustrate that children should be placed in a more restrictive setting only if it is to their educational advantage; they should be moved to a less restrictive setting as soon as they are capable of being educated in that environment. You should also note that, in general, the more restrictive environment will have fewer children, and these will have more severe disabilities.

Educational environments 1 through 4 are all variations of the regular class. Environment 1 is a class that resembles the one you probably attended. In environment 2, specialists provide consulting services to the regular class teacher but do not work directly with children. In environment 3, itinerant specialists such as speech therapists and mobility instructors for the blind assist children directly. In environment 4, children leave the regular classroom for part of the day to obtain direct instruction individually or in small groups from a resource teacher. The resource teacher usually provides consultation help to the regular class teacher as well.

Although mainstreaming and placement in the least restrictive environment result in more appropriate education for most children, these concepts can cause problems. Unfortunately, some school administrators have interpreted the least restrictive environment provision of PL 94-142 to mean that handicapped children can be placed in regular classes without being provided the support services they or their teachers need. Others have terminated self-contained classes and have attempted to integrate all special education students into regular classes — often with drastic results.

We think the phrase "most facilitative environment" more clearly embodies the intent of PL 94-142. The use of that phrase alone would not eliminate the problem, of course; however, its more positive tone underscores the need to maintain a variety of educational environments for children who have different needs.

Who should be mainstreamed?

One of the most difficult tasks facing educators is to determine which students to place in regular classes for what subjects and for what amounts of time. Firm guidelines are not yet available to aid in these difficult decisions; but Schubert and Glick (1981) made seven suggestions following a study of successful mainstreaming practices common to a number of schools. To be mainstreamed,

— students should be capable of doing some work at grade level.
— students should be capable of doing some work without requiring special materials, adaptive equipment, or extensive assistance from the regular classroom teacher.
— students should be capable of "staying on task" in the regular classroom without as much help and attention as they would receive in the special classroom or resource room.
— students should be capable of fitting into the routine of the regular classroom.
— students should be able to function socially in the regular classroom and profit from the modeling or appropriate behavior by their classmates.

— the physical setting of the classroom should not interfere with the student's functioning (or it should be adapted to their needs).

— it should be possible to work out scheduling to accommodate the students' various classes, and the schedules should be kept flexible and be easy to change as students progress.

Students who cannot meet these criteria should probably not be placed in regular classes. They should instead be educated in one of the other types of educational arrangements, such as the self-contained special education class. A major goal for such students, however, should be to develop the skills needed to function in the regular class. In addition, as their skills develop, efforts should be made to integrate them into the regular class for short periods. This will give them opportunities to practice skills so they may eventually spend longer periods in the more normalized environment as they learn and mature.

Mainstreaming will not be effective if teachers and administrators reject the concept and believe that it will not work. One of the leading authorities on mainstreaming conducted a series of interviews with school personnel and identified six attitudes that appeared to be most conducive to successful mainstreaming (Birch, 1974, p.94):

1. Belief in the right to education for all children.
2. Readiness of special education and regular class teachers to cooperate with each other.
3. Willingness to share competencies as a team in behalf of pupils.
4. Openness to include parents as well as other professional colleagues in planning for and working with children.
5. Flexibility with respect to class size and teaching assignments.
6. Recognition that social and personal development can be taught, and that they are equally as important as academic achievement.

If these attitudes are prevalent among school personnel, mainstreaming seems likely to be successful. Of course, something more than good attitudes is needed. Classroom teachers also need to have specific competencies related to mainstreaming. These are described in considerable detail in the text by Stephens, Blackhurst, and Magliocca (1982). Additional information about mainstreaming can also be found in books by Lewis and Doorlag (1983) and Morsink (1984).

Probe 2-2
Normalization

1. Two concepts associated with normalization are _____ and _____.

2. T   F   Property values decline in neighborhoods around group homes.

3. T   F   Finding staff is one of the major problems in establishing more group homes.

4. Number the following settings with 1 being the least restrictive and 10 being the most restrictive:
   _____ Special Day School
   _____ Regular Class with Consulting Teacher Help
   _____ Hospital or Institution
   _____ Regular Class with no Support Services
   _____ Residential School
   _____ Regular Class with Resource Room Help
   _____ Full-time Special Class
   _____ Regular Class with Itinerant Help
   _____ Homebound Instruction
   _____ Special Class with Part-time Regular Class Placement

5 Define mainstreaming as the term is commonly used.

6. T   F   Mildly handicapped students should always be educated in regular classes.

INDIVIDUALIZED INSTRUCTION

You should be able to describe the components of the Individualized Education Program that is legally required for all handicapped students.

You should recall from Chapter 1 that an Individualized Education Program (IEP) is required for all handicapped students who have been admitted to a special education program. Several questions have been raised about the IEP and the process for developing it:

— How should the IEP be developed and what should its format be?
— Who should be involved in the development of the IEP?
— How can the myriad details associated with the IEP process be managed efficiently?

The IEP is the foundation on which the handicapped child's education is built. The IEP requirements generally do not apply to gifted students unless they also have a disability. However, West Virginia and some other states have regulations that require the development of IEPs for gifted children as well as those who have disabilities.

The development of the IEP is one part of the due process requirements of PL 94-142. Many people believe that it is the most important part, because it specifies in detail the nature of the special education and related services that will be delivered to a particular student. It is a written document developed by a committee of school personnel and at least one of the child's parents. Parent surrogates can be appointed to represent the child when necessary. In addition, the law provides that the student participate in the IEP deliberations if he or she is willing and able.

Who attends IEP meetings?

The school principal (or a designate) generally chairs the meeting at which the IEP is developed. The child's parents must always be included, but the composition of the rest of the IEP committee will vary considerably, depending on the nature of the child's problems. The psychologist or diagnostician who performed the assessment is often present. The teacher who referred the child and the teacher in whose program the child may be placed are often present as well. A variety of other professionals may attend, including a teacher consultant, speech–language pathologist, audiologist, physical therapist, occupational therapist, social worker, guidance counselor, and medical personnel.

IEP REQUIREMENTS

What should be included in the IEP?

At the IEP meeting, discussions center around the nature of the child's educational needs and the best type of program to meet these needs. PL 94-142 requires that at least eight pieces of information be included in the IEP:

1. The student's *present levels of performance*. Typically, this information is presented in a statement of educational strengths and weaknesses based on the results of the assessment.
2. *Annual goals* for the student's program. These are broad, general statements that help to focus on the general areas in which individualized services will be provided.
3. *Short-term objectives* associated with each goal. These focus on the specific things that the student will learn during the time the IEP is in effect.
4. The *special education and related services* to be provided to the student. The services are described and the names of the people responsible for providing them are included.
5. The *extent of the child's participation in regular education*. This requirement helps the IEP committee address the normalization concept described earlier.
6. The projected *date for initiating services*. This is given so that all parties will know when to begin implementing the IEP.
7. The anticipated *duration of services*.
8. *Objective evaluation procedures*. These provide specific criteria for determining when the objectives have been reached. The procedures to be used in the evaluation and the schedules for conducting the evaluation are included. The IEP must be reviewed at least annually.

To document that due process procedures have been followed, a number of other items typically appear on the IEP. These include the meeting date, the people who attended, the date that consent for testing was provided, the native language of the parent, the child's primary language, the rationale for the least restrictive environment placement recommendation, the annual review date, the birth date and ethnicity of the child, and the parent's signature indicating approval of the IEP.

An excerpt from an IEP is illustrated in Figure 2-2. To conserve space, only the first and last pages have been included. The complete IEP from which Figure 2-2 was derived also had goals and objectives in home economics, physical education, social competence, and reading. If you take the time to examine Figure 2-2 closely, you will be able to pick out the eight required

Figure 2-2
An Excerpt from an Individualized Education Program

INDIVIDUALIZED EDUCATION PROGRAM

A. Student Information

Name: Barbara T.
Birthdate: May 9, 1969
Language Spoken in Home: English
School: Blanton Senior High
Current Placement: Regular Business Education Class

Date: September 26, 1985
Gender: Female
Ethnicity: White
Grade: 11

B. Present Level of Functioning

Math Strengths

Barbara is able to recite all of the number facts. She can perform addition and subtraction problems with regrouping. She can successfully compute two- and three-digit multiplication and division problems.

Math Weaknesses

Barbara is unable to use a checkbook.

C. Annual Goals

Math

Barbara will learn how to write checks and balance a checkbook.

D. Short-Term Objectives

1. Given 10 completed checks, Barbara will state their date, monetary value, the signator, recipient, and the bank name with 100% accuracy.
2. Given 20 sets of dates, monetary values, and recipients, Barbara will correctly complete blank checks.
3. Given an initial balance of $750 and 20 checks of various denominations totaling $670, Barbara will be able to compute correctly a running balance in her checkbook.
4. Given a check register with 20 entries and a bank statement with five outstanding checks and a service charge, Barbara will be able to reconcile her check register correctly.

components described above and most of the supplementary items that were described in the previous paragraph.

From the teacher's perspective, the most important part of the IEP is the list of goals and objectives because they provide direction for what should be taught. Tymitz (1980) studied objectives written by teachers for inclusion in a hypothetical IEP and discovered many weaknesses. In some cases, the objectives were nothing more than restatements of the goals, or they were descriptions of activities. In others, the objectives were incomplete. To be most useful, objectives should include a description of the performance required of the child, the conditions under which such performance should be demonstrated, and the criterion to be used to determine whether the objective has been met (Mager, 1962). The usefulness of IEPs is significantly reduced when they include objectives that do not have these three features. Being able to

Figure 2-2 *(Cont.)*

E. Educational Services

Barbara will receive the services of a resource teacher for math instruction one hour each day. These services will commence on October 15 and continue until the objectives have been met. Ms. Ima Whizz will provide the resource room instruction. Barbara will spend the remaining 5 school periods in the regular Business Education program pursuing the secretarial science curriculum. Given her current levels of achievement, her career aspirations, and these goals and objectives, this placement is in Barbara's best interests.

F. Evaluation Procedures

Each of the 3 math objectives will be evaluated by a teacher-constructed simulation that will present Barbara with a hypothetical income, a list of expenditures that must be paid by check, blank checks, and a bank statement which she must reconcile. The evaluation will be performed four weeks after instruction on the use of a checkbook is initiated.

This Individualized Education Program will be reviewed in September, 1986.

G. Approvals

This Individualized Education Program was discussed in a meeting held at Blanton High School on September 26, 1985, with the following people in attendance:

Mary Ann Sunshine, Principal (and Committee Chair)
Justin Inkblot, School Psychologist
Ima Whizz, Resource Teacher
Lizzie Fingers, Business Education Coordinator
Mr. T., Barbara's father

I have had the opportunity to participate in the development of my daughter's Individualized Education Program and agree with its provisions.

Parent's Signature

write good instructional objectives is a major skill required of special education teachers. A checklist for determining the adequacy of IEP goals and objectives can be found in the work of Tymitz-Wolf (1982).

It is important to note that the parents should be active participants in the development of the IEP. Although school officials typically make a presentation to explain their findings and recommendations, parents are encouraged to make recommendations based upon their knowledge of the child and their perceptions of what would be in the child's best interest.

On occasion, parents disagree with the plan that is suggested and an impasse results. Parents may signify their disapproval by refusing to sign the IEP. When this happens, the due process procedures described in PL 94-142 are set in motion. Although negotiations about the IEP are preferred, parents do have the right to a due process hearing conducted by an impartial third party. If this course is taken, a recommendation is made by the hearing officer, which is subject to still further appeals by both the parents and school officials if disagreements remain. In the event that appeals and hearings are conducted, the child has the right to remain in his or her current educationl placement. The implementation of special education services cannot commence until the issues related to the IEP are resolved.

IEP MANAGEMENT

It should not be a surprise that the development of the IEP is a complicated and time-consuming process. In addition to the time required for assessment, considerable staff time and paperwork are needed to develop a draft of the IEP, participate in the meeting, finalize the IEP, maintain the necessary records, and conduct annual reviews.

The cost of developing an IEP will vary with the complexity of the case and the number of professionals involved. A California study by Enell and Barrick (1983) found that the cost of professional time involved in the preparation of IEPs using conventional manual methods ranged from $35 to $720 per case. This did not include clerical time or other costs such as transportation for parents, supplies, parent time, or interpreter service. Costs for annual IEP reviews ranged from $76 to $156. It is no wonder that school districts are interested in finding more efficient ways to manage the entire IEP process.

It should be noted that the information given above reflects only one computerized IEP system. In 1983, the authors of that report listed information about 30 different computer-based IEP systems that were available. Many of those systems were used with large mainframe computers, some of which contained data banks of more than 10,000 objectives, as opposed to microcomputer systems, which have much less storage capacity.

Enell and Barrick (1983) went on to conduct a study of five California school districts that used computers in the IEP process. These researchers were interested in determining whether districts using computers had different costs

TECHNOLOGY IN ACTION

Hesperia School District serves 234 special education students. It is using an IEP computer program, *Unistar I Pre-IEP,* developed by Microsystems Inc., of North Carolina. The program is available for use on the Apple or TRS-80 computers with 48K memory. The basic equipment needed for this system consists of a microcomputer, two floppy disk drives, a monitor, and a printer. The system produces a proposed IEP.

The Individualized Education Plan is divided into three major sections. These sections are (1) student data, (2) the assessment data, and (3) the goals and objectives. The computer program records the student data and then pre-selects a range of goals and objectives using the assessment data. The IEP team selects the goals and objectives from this range.

The student section has three subsections. The first is the school system information — school system name and school address. The second section is student identification — name, birth date, grade, student number, dominant language, etc. The third subsection is information for the Individual Education Plan — the type of meeting, meeting date, implementation date, etc.

The assessment section lists the scores on 17 dif-ferent tests of academic, motor, intellectual, speech, and other functioning. The scores entered are the age equivalent or grade equivalent scores. Judgments are recorded for adaptive behavior, mobility, vision and hearing, and other areas. A graphic profile of present functioning is presented using the scores and judgments. . . .

[The computer determines whether there are discrepancies between the student's actual and expected scores.] When discrepancies are found, goals and objectives may be preprinted by the computer in any of the following areas: written expression, reading recognition, reading comprehension, math computation, math reasoning, social/emotional, fine motor/gross motor, listening comprehension, visual discrimination, oral/expressive language, and spelling.

Paperwork flows to the district psychologist. A secretary enters the student data and test scores into the microcomputer and the Proposed Individual Education Plan is printed. Since the district serves 234 special education students, the number of IEPs entered each day is few. Estimated time for data entry and printing for one student is 45 minutes.

Reprinted from a report by Enell and Barrick (1983, p. 34–35).

Are computerized IEP systems effective?

than those that did not. A more important goal, however, was to find out whether there were differences between the acceptability and usefulness of the resulting IEPs. They interviewed school officials and parents to obtain their information. Here is a summary of some of their findings:

— When computers were used, nearly 30 minutes were saved at each annual review meeting, and varying amounts of time were saved during initial placement meetings. Compared to those who used manual methods, those who used computers saved 18 percent of the costs for personnel.

— Parents and teachers found the computerized IEPs more legible and easier to understand. Parents believed that assessment information and the IEP meeting were helpful, and they found the IEP a useful reference. They felt involved in the process, even though objectives were pre-selected. Most people believed that the computer-generated objectives were better written.

— Teachers were able to adapt to the computerized systems without difficulty. They did not object to its use and reported that the IEP systems had many advantages and few disadvantages.

It appears that the use of information processing systems has considerable merit for managing the IEP process. Two major caveats should be noted, however. First, it is imperative that users of such systems learn how to write objectives and become knowledgable about IEP development *before* they use an automated system. Such knowledge is needed in order to evaluate critically the IEP that is generated. One should always view the computer output in light of what is known about the child and what is known about sequencing of instruction. We have seen several computer-generated IEPs that listed objectives that were either inappropriate for the age of the child, poorly stated, or recommended in sequences that were not educationally sound.

Second, whether generated manually or by computer, the initial IEP should be viewed only as a draft to be used in the IEP meeting. The IEP should not be made final until the child's parents have a chance to react and propose modifications.

PROBE 2-3
Individualized Instruction

1. T   F   Parents are required by law to participate in the development of their child's IEP.

2. List the eight required components of an IEP.

3. T   F   Parents have a right to disagree with school officials about their child's IEP and proposed special education placement.

4. T   F   Teachers find the use of computerized IEP systems offensive and are opposed to their use.

5. T   F   Parents find computerized IEPs easier to read and understand than those that have been prepared manually.

CULTURAL DIVERSITY

You should be able to describe the implications of children's diverse cultural backgrounds for special education practices.

In 1954, racially segregated systems of public education were declared unconstitutional by the United States Supreme Court in the landmark case *Brown v. Topeka Board of Education* (347 U.S. 483, 1954). Since that time, schools have made progress toward integrating students of various cultural and ethnic backgrounds. Unfortunately, however, we continue to find a disproportionately large number of children from minority groups in special education programs.

How many minority children are in special education programs?

A 1980 study conducted by the Office of Civil Rights (OCR) of 40 million students found that 15.7 percent were black and 6.7 were Hispanic. At the same time, however, blacks constituted over 38 percent of the educable mentally retarded, 27 percent of the trainable mentally retarded, and 24 percent of the seriously emotionally disturbed school population. They also represented only 10 percent of the children who were being educated in programs for gifted students (Killalea Associates, 1980).

Although national data on Hispanic representation in special education reflected the percentage of Hispanics in the general population, the OCR study found major regional differences. Classes in western and southwestern states had disproportionately higher placements of Hispanics in classes for the educable mentally retarded and lower placements in programs for the gifted.

The rest of this chapter will address issues related to these findings. Questions that can be raised include the following:

— Are minority children more frequently handicapped than other children?
— Why do we find statistics like the ones just cited?
— What can be done to rectify inequities in placement and improved education for children from culturally diverse backgrounds?

Baca and Chinn (1982) have addressed these questions and a number of other issues related to cultural diversity in special education programs. The information presented below is organized around the major issues these authorities raise and draws heavily from their work.

IDENTIFICATION, ASSESSMENT, AND PLACEMENT

One of the major reasons we find more minority children in special education programs is improper assessment techniques. It was mentioned earlier, for example, that many students were placed in special education programs because they did not perform well on standardized tests administered in a language they did not fully understand. This is one of the reasons federal legislation requires that tests for special education placement be given in the child's native language. It was also the reason for banning the use of IQ tests for placing black students in classes for the educable mentally retarded in California (*Larry P. v. Riles*, 1972).

What is SOMPA?

There are now efforts to develop and use assessment techniques that consider the child's ethnic and environmental background as well as the more traditional factors such as intellectual performance. Examples of this approach are the System of Multicultural Pluralistic Assessment, commonly referred to as SOMPA (Mercer, 1979) and the Kaufman Assessment Battery for Children (Kaufman and Kaufman, 1983). SOMPA norms are being developed for white, black, Mexican American, and Navajo children, ages five to eleven. In addition, procedures such as peer nomination are being used to identify gifted culturally different children (Blackshear, Sullivan, Ewell, and Rogers, 1980).

Activities such as these are steps in the right direction, but much remains to be done. Extra care is especially important in interpreting test data on children not represented in the group on which the test was standardized. For example, if there were no Chicano children in the norm group of a reading test you are using, you should view with caution the test scores of any Chicano children in your class. If you use criterion-referenced tests, you should be certain your assessment is not biased by conflicts between the criterion you establish and the culture of the child being tested.

ATTITUDES OF STUDENTS AND TEACHERS

Unfortunately, many minority students also come from impoverished backgrounds. Thus, some special education students are in triple jeopardy: They are handicapped, belong to a minority, and are poor.

Most authorities agree that people from such backgrounds have different attitudes toward education than those in the middle class. For example, the middle class traditionally places a high value on education. This may not be the case in impoverished minority cultures. In fact, some minority parents have become disillusioned by education. This attitude can carry over into the attitudes of their children, which makes teaching them very difficult.

How do cultural assimilation and cultural pluralism differ?

Teachers also may have widely differing attitudes about the education of minority students. Some are proponents of cultural assimilation, the view that America is a melting pot and that the job of the schools is to foster the development of similar cultural patterns and lifestyles, regardless of the cultural background of the students. Cultural-assimilation extremists would actually deny the importance of cultural diversity and fail to recognize its worth. Most members of minority groups find such positions offensive.

The more widely accepted view is called cultural pluralism. Those who endorse this concept acknowledge that there is no single "model American" and recognize the unique contributions different cultural groups make to enrich our society. As Baca and Chinn (1982, p. 38) pointed out, "The teacher who supports the concept of cultural pluralism is more prone to recognize individual needs and differences among culturally diverse children and more likely to work toward providing for their needs appropriately."

TEACHING PRACTICES

The topic of multicultural education is so important that the National Council for Accreditation of Teacher Education (NCATE) adopted a standard in 1979 requiring a multicultural component in all teacher education programs. Bes-

What competencies should special education teachers have to teach culturally different students?

sant-Byrd (1981, pp. 94-103) proposed that people preparing to teach minority students in special education programs should be able to

— demonstrate knowledge of the role of a value system and evalute its influence on behavior.
— demonstrate knowledge of the philosophy of various cultures and exhibit an interest in expanding that knowledge.
— use relevant information and materials characteristic of both traditional and contemporary life styles of various cultures.
— understand different patterns of human growth and development within and between cultures.
— recognize potential cultural and linguistic biases in the composition, administration, and interpretation of existing assessment instruments.
— demonstrate the ability to provide a flexible learning environment which meets individual needs of learners from various culture groups.

LANGUAGE DIFFERENCES

Perhaps the most serious consequences occur when students and school personnel from different cultural backgrounds have language differences. When exceptional students speak a foreign language, it may be necessary to provide bilingual special education programs. You may want to review the work of Omark and Erickson (1983) for additional information about bilingual special education programs.

How should teachers deal with language differences in students?

In other cases, students' language patterns differ from the standard middle class language used in schools. When this happens, there is considerable potential for difficulties to arise. Taylor (1973, p. 39) suggested some questions a teacher should consider when dealing with the language of some black students:

— Is language used to make inaccurate statements about cultures and miseducate children?
— What is the mismatch between the language accepted by schools and the language that a substantial portion of black children bring to schools?
— What is the impact of language diversity on the performance of black children on standardized tests?
— How does language diversity affect the attitudes of teachers?
— Is an awareness of language diversity reflected in educational materials?
— [To what extent are] inaccurate diagnoses . . . related to an ignorance of the unique linguistic features of large numbers of blacks?

In summary, it is important to realize that when a child's cultural orientation differs from that of the school's personnel, the potential for a cultural conflict exists. When such conflicts occur, the child is usually the loser.

Probe 2-4
Cultural Diversity

1. T F Minority children are overrepresented in programs for handicapped children.

2. _____ is the acronym for an assessment procedure that attempts to take a child's cultural background into consideration.

3. What is the triple jeopardy that handicapped minority students frequently find themselves in?

4. Circle the preferred attitude toward cultural differences:
   a. Cultural assimilation   b. Cultural pluralism

5. T F The National Council for Accreditation of Teacher Education requires that all teacher education programs provide multicultural education.

6. The most serious consequences for culturally different students occur when their _____ differs from that used in the schools.

DESIGNING A PROFESSIONAL DEVELOPMENT PROGRAM

You should be able to design a personal program of professional development in special education.

The purpose of this text is to serve as an introduction to the terms, definitions, concepts, and ideas needed to understand the field of special education. Some readers may be interested in the text simply to expand their knowledge, but most will use it as a foundation for further study with an eventual goal of assuming a special education teaching career.

If you are among this majority, you should be competent to begin teaching when you complete your formal education. You should realize, however, that you will have to continue to develop your professional skills throughout your career. The field of special education is changing so rapidly that teachers must work diligently to keep up with new information, diagnostic instruments, instructional materials, and teaching methods.

In 1983, the Council for Exceptional Children (CEC) adopted a set of ethical standards to guide professionals who work with exceptional children. One of these guidelines reads as follows (Code of Ethics and Standards for Professional Practice, 1983, p. 208):

Special education professionals systematically advance their knowledge and skills in order to maintain a high level of competence and response to the changing needs of exceptional persons by pursuing a program of continuing education including but not limited to participation in such activities as in-service training, professional conferences/workshops, professional meetings, continuing education courses, and the reading of professional literature.

Several important questions can be raised about the topic of professionalism and professional development:

— What are the ethical responsibilities of special educators?
— What are the steps for designing a professional development program?
— What resources are available to support professional development activities?

In this section we discuss professional responsibilities and describe procedures that can be used to develop a personal program of professional development. The ideas that follow should be useful to both beginning special education students and practicing professionals. Teachers can use the information to plan for future professional growth, and students can use it to analyze their abilities and the quality of the education that they are receiving.

What steps should be followed in developing a program of professional development?

Much of the professional development of teachers occurs in a rather haphazard fashion. Although almost all special educators are members of professional organizations and attend in-service training programs, they may participate only when it is convenient or when attendance is required by school administrators. Few professionals systematically appraise their needs and develop a plan to meet them. The pressures of work, home, family, and social obligations often relegate professional development to a position of low priority. Although almost everyone has said, "I must learn how to do this" or "I must learn more about that topic," the time and the initiative are frequently lacking.

One reason for this desultory approach is that the subject of professional development is seldom approached systematically. To use time and resources efficiently, it is necessary to design a specific plan and carry out its activities. In the following pages, we will describe seven steps you can use to develop and implement such a plan. You should note, however, that the success of your plan will depend on three suppositions: (1) that you will apply the principles described in a systematic fashion; (2) that you will analyze your abilities and needs; and (3) that you will maintain the initiative to conduct the required activities. If these three rules are followed, you should be able to develop a program of professional development that will meet your needs.

STEP ONE: DEVELOP AND MAINTAIN A PHILOSOPHY

The first step involves developing a personal philosophy. A "philosophy" can be defined as "an integrated personal view that serves to guide the individual's conduct and thinking" (Good, 1959, p. 395).

The development of a philosophy is very important: as the definition implies, it can serve as the conceptual foundation for all professional activities. In most teacher education programs, however, little attention is paid to it. Although many programs expose students to a variety of philosophical viewpoints, and attempts are often made to encourage students to adopt the philosophy held by the program's faculty, little emphasis is usually placed on students' developing their own philosophy.

Neither students nor professionals are often asked to articulate their philosophy of special education. As Tymitz (1983) found in her research, the results of such inquiries are not very encouraging. She studied the philosophies of 40 special education teachers. There was general agreement among the teachers that teaching effectiveness is enhanced when one operates with a clearly formulated philosophy; unfortunately, however, most of those interviewed were unable to articulate one. As a result of her study, Tymitz recommended that increased attention be devoted to this important topic in teacher preparation programs.

It is very difficult to design guidelines for the development of a philosophy, because so many variables are involved. A person's philosophy is a reflection of his or her values, ethics, logic, aesthetics, and perceptions of knowledge, reality, and truth. There are, however, four criteria that can be used by everyone in the development of a philosophy, regardless of their philosophical orientation:

1. Develop your philosophy to the point where you can articulate it concisely for other professionals. You should also be able to explain it to parents and other people who may not have training in special education.
2. You should be able to defend your philosophy. This entails understanding which aspects of the philosophy can be supported with logic and facts and which aspects are derived from your values.
3. Be flexible. You should be receptive to new information and be willing to modify your philosophy in light of new experiences.
4. Demonstrate your philosophy by applying it in your personal and professional life.

How can a person develop a philosophy of special education?

If you meet these criteria and share with other special educators a commitment to improving the quality of life for exceptional children, your particular philosophical orientation is of no great importance.

In analyzing your philosophy, the following questions may help you focus on some of the basic issues:

—What are the responsibilities of society in providing for exceptional children?
—What are the responsibilities of the professionals concerned with the welfare of exceptional children?
—What should the relationship be between the special and general educator? How should they interact?

—What are the goals for the group of exceptional children I am working with?

—What theories of learning and instruction do I subscribe to and use in working with exceptional children?

—What is my position on issues such as normalization, human rights, institutionalization, mainstreaming, sterilization, individualized instruction, intelligence testing, genetic counseling, abortion, behavior modification, professional accountability, etiologies, labeling, and other contemporary issues?

—What is my rationale for doing each of my professional activities in one way rather than another?

Many other questions could be posed about the roles of schools and other agencies, about the education profession, and about specific teaching techniques. If you cannot answer a question or are dissatisfied with your answer, you should involve yourself in experiences that will permit you to develop or refine your thoughts about the subject of the question.

Experience shows that the most competent special educators are those who have a well-developed philosophy. They are the most effective teachers, they have the most self-confidence, and they are the most comfortable and secure in their professional activities. The first priority of those who do not have a solid philosophical base should be to develop one. The information in this book should give you a good start in developing your philosophy of special education.

One point deserves to be reemphasized: It is not enough merely to be able to articulate your philosophy; you must be able to demonstrate it in your life as well. It is hypocritical to articulate one philosophical position and act according to the dictates of another, but unfortunately some people do just that.

STEP TWO: DEFINE PROFESSIONAL ROLES

What roles are generally performed by special education personnel?

The second step in designing a professional development program involves defining the roles and functions of the special educator. In a provocative article that examined special education as a profession, Birch and Reynolds (1982) described special education roles at five different levels. According to these noted authorities, the first level consists of teachers in the regular grades who teach exceptional children integrated into their classes. Second level personnel are special educators and paraprofessionals who work full-time in individual schools in a variety of settings, including self-contained special classes and resource rooms in which exceptional children spend a portion of their days. These specialists frequently collaborate with the regular class teachers. At the third level are the specialists who perform their roles on a school district-wide or regional basis. These personnel serve as supervisors, administrators, psychologists, educational diagnosticians, parent educators, behavior analysts, consultants on learning problems, teachers of braille, physical therapists, and in many other capacities. Fourth-level personnel work at the college and university level to prepare the personnel at all of the other levels. Finally, fifth-level personnel are those who engage in research and development activities that generate new knowledge and procedures for the improvement of special education services.

At this point in your education, you may have decided which levels are your short-term and long-term career goals. Typically, undergraduate students plan to teach children at level one or two. A master's degree student may hope to become a resource teacher or diagnostic-prescriptive specialist at level two or three, while a doctoral candidate might express interest in the roles at level four or five.

Even though students know which role they want to assume when they graduate, they frequently pay too little attention to the specific functions involved in that role. It is not uncommon for students about to graduate to express concern about their ability to assume the role they have been preparing for. Part of the reason for their concern, of course, is that they are suddenly faced with reality. Of equal importance, however, is that they never really took the time to analyze the specific tasks or functions that they would be required to perform after they assumed a new position. The student who has made the effort to identify the reponsibilities required will not be caught unprepared to assume these responsibilities.

Let us assume that you are interested in becoming a resource teacher for children with mild learning and behavior disorders. One of your most important activities would be to identify the tasks you must be able to perform to do your job successfully. You could do this in a number of ways. You could talk to resource teachers and experts, and observe resource teachers at work. You could research the job in the library. The result might be a list of the tasks the resource teacher must be able to do, such as this one (Blackhurst, McLoughlin, and Price, 1977):

— Assess learner behavior.
— Design and implement instructional programs.
— Select and use instructional materials.
— Manage the learning environment.
— Provide for the needs of children with sensory and physical impairments.
— Initiate resource teacher programs.
— Implement due process safeguards.
— Work effectively with parents.
— Maintain student records.
— Demonstrate appropriate professional behavior.

Although this list might not apply to all resource teaching arrangements, it does provide a general guideline for the job's responsibilities. If you were already a resource teacher and planned to stay in that position, you would simply list your job's responsibilities.

STEP THREE: SPECIFY NEEDED COMPETENCIES

Once the responsibilities of the job are defined, you should ask yourself two questions: (1) Which responsibilities am I completely unprepared for? and (2) In which do I need additional experience? The answers would provide the general topic areas for your professional development program.

The next step is to determine what competencies are needed in each of the topic areas. As part of this process you would also discover more detailed information about the general responsibilities identified in the previous step. This would be accomplished by determining what competencies are involved in each general area of responsibility. To continue with the example begun in the previous section, let's examine some of the competencies associated with each of the functions required of a special educator serving as a resource teacher. A complete list of these competencies can be found elsewhere (Blackhurst et al., 1977).

What competencies should special education resource teachers have?

Assessing Learner Behavior. Special educators must be able to use assessment procedures to identify exceptional children. They must also be able to use in-depth diagnostic procedures to identify the educational strengths and weaknesses of children in each major area of instruction. Because many published tests are inappropriate for exceptional children, special educators must also be skilled in informal assessment and in direct observation of student behavior.

Designing and Implementing Instructional Programs. Once the child's educational needs have been assessed, the special education teacher must design the child's instructional program. Objectives must be written, and the instructional tasks to be performed must be analyzed. Instructional methods must be selected and implemented, and student performance must be monitored.

Selecting and Using Instructional Materials. The variety of instructional materials available has grown dramatically in recent years. The quality of these materials varies considerably, however, and the special education teacher must be able to evaluate them and select the most effective. Teachers must know how to use a variety of instructional materials and audiovisual equipment.

Managing the Learning Environment. A major responsibility of the special educator is to provide individual instruction. To do so, the teacher must be able to manipulate the many variables in the learning environment. The teacher also needs to develop rapport with students and use such management techniques as preventive discipline, behavior modification, active listening, contingency contracting, verbal and nonverbal signals, and precision teaching.

Providing for the Needs of Children with Sensory and Physical Impairments.
Special educators frequently work with children who have impaired vision,
hearing, speech, or physical functioning. They must be able to modify their
instructional approaches to accommodate the special needs of these children.
For example, they need to know how to use special assistive and adaptive
equipment, how to lift and transfer physically disabled children safely, how
to deal with seizures, and how to provide emotional support.

Implementing Resource Teaching Programs. Because exceptional children are
increasingly being educated in the regular classroom, the resource teacher
must be able to advise the regular classroom teacher on ways to modify
instructional programming to improve these children's integration into the
regular class. Assistance in sharing materials, approaches, equipment, and
ideas is also required. The ability to coordinate schedules and the services of
ancillary personnel is also an important skill.

Implementing Due Process Safeguards. Special education teachers and school
systems are considered legally responsible if the rights of exceptional children
or their parents are violated. It is therefore important to have a firm understanding of local, state, and federal laws, regulations, and guidelines that affect
special education programs. Great care should be exercised in protecting student and parent rights, and special educators should carry liability insurance
to cover them in the event of an inadvertent violation. Such insurance is
available through professional organizations such as The Council for Exceptional Children.

Working Effectively with Parents. Good parent-teacher interactions are especially important in the education of exceptional children. Children can be
educated more efficiently if parents reinforce what happens at school, or they
may progress slowly if parents and teachers work at cross-purposes. Therefore, it is necessary to keep communication channels with parents open and
maintain a good rapport. Parent conferencing skills are particularly important.

Maintaining Student Records. Accurate, up-to-date records are an important
tool in the development of the IEP required by federal law. Teachers should
be able to collect, organize, and maintain records of academic performance. It
is especially important to maintain a system for evaluating student performance using direct measurement and behavior charting. Teachers must also
respect the confidentiality of student records.

Demonstrating Appropriate Professional Behavior. Special educators should
be able to develop an educational philosophy and demonstrate it in their

professional activities. They should be able to facilitate the activities of others in a sensitive, humanistic fashion. They should also be flexible and receptive to educational change. Furthermore, they should conduct their professional activities in an ethical fashion. These general principles provide the foundation for effective teaching.

Most of the competencies just discussed would be equally applicable to general education teachers. Just as exceptional children resemble other children in more ways than they differ from them, special education teachers resemble general education teachers in many of their responsibilities. Special educators generally have a greater depth of knowledge and more specific skills because they are more highly educated. In addition, they may have responsibilities such as operating resource rooms and providing consultation services, and they have been trained to teach children who present more difficult educational problems.

The development of a competency checklist to analyze your ability to perform various competencies is explained in *Teaching Mainstreamed Students,* a text on integrating handicapped children into regular classrooms, by Stephens, Blackhurst, and Magliocca (1982). You might find it interesting to set up a competency checklist to keep track of progress during your educational career. Such a checklist could also be used to analyze the extent to which your formal courses are helping develop these competencies. If deficiencies are found, you might be able to design independent studies to rectify them.

STEP FOUR: DEVELOP OBJECTIVES

Once you have determined which competencies you need to work on, you should develop objectives to guide further your professional development efforts. Some competencies will have been stated clearly enough in the previous step that it will not be necessary to make them more specific. For example, a competency involved in working effectively with parents is "Be able to conduct parent conferences." This description alone might be explicit enough to direct activities for some people. For others, however, it may still be too general, in which case it would be necessary to break it down into more specific areas of interest. One might ask questions such as these:

How can priorities for professional development activities be established?

1. How can one establish rapport with parents?
2. Are there general rules for what one should or should not do in conferences?
3. What are some of the common concerns of the parents of exceptional children?
4. How can one make constructive criticisms of parents without being threatening?

5. What should be done when parents obviously disagree with each other about what should have been done with their child in a particular situation?

Such questions can be used to develop very specific program objectives. Some people require more specific objectives than others. More experienced persons typically prefer to use relatively general objectives, because they are familiar with the task and with their own educational strengths and weaknesses. What is most important is that the list of objectives be specific enough to provide an orientation for future activities. Once the list is defined, you can then set priorities for accomplishing each.

It is also important not to overlook development in areas for which objectives are difficult to establish, such as affective development or experiential learning. An example of an experiential development activity would be sitting in on another teacher's classes or observing an interdisciplinary meeting to assign staff to a particular student. Activities of this sort might provide insight into personal behavior or into the circumstances that affect an educational situation.

STEP FIVE: IDENTIFY CONTENT AND RESOURCES

Once the professional development program's objectives have been identified and priorities have been established, it is necessary to identify the materials needed to attain the objectives.

An obvious source of information is other people, including colleagues, supervisors, people from related professions, university professors, and librarians. There are also many state and local agencies that can provide information, including those concerned with health and mental health, education, rehabilitation, and welfare. Private agencies such as associations for retarded citizens, sheltered workshops, and clinics are also valuable sources. A list of agencies you can get in touch with for information is included at the end of each chapter in this book.

A number of federal agencies can provide valuable information, particularly about the federal resources available to support services to exceptional children. These include such agencies as the President's Committee on Mental Retardation, the President's Committee on Employment of the Handicapped, the Secretary's Committee on Mental Retardation, the National Institute of Mental Health, the Office of Child Development, and the Office of Special Education Programs in the federal Department of Education.

Another source of information is the reference section of most college libraries. References relevant to working with exceptional children include *Exceptional Child Education Resources; Mental Retardation Abstracts; Deafness, Speech, and Hearing Abstracts; Language and Language Behavior Abstracts; Psychological Abstracts; Education Index; Current Index to Journals in Education;* and *Dissertation Abstracts.*

This teacher is using a microfilm machine to read a document located while researching a topic in the ERIC files.

What is ECER?   Of the above sources, *Exceptional Child Education Resources, (ECER)* is probably the best starting place. *ECER* is part of the *Educational Resources Information Center* (ERIC), which supports a number of information clearinghouses, each dealing with a different educational subject. *ECER* is a journal that contains abstracts of literature on special education. It has a number of interesting features that permit rapid searches for information. By using *ECER* and its abstracts, you can quickly determine which articles contain information that is of greatest concern to you. Customized searches with a computer can also be performed to very rapidly scan the large amount of information in *ECER* to locate literature relevant to a particular inquiry. Most major university libraries store the ERIC documents, and many will conduct computer searches for a nominal fee.

A number of "on-line" data bases are available by subscription to people who have microcomputers. One gains access to these data bases via telephone lines that are hooked into a computer. Searches on topics ranging from special education literature to evaluations of microcomputer software can be conducted. The reference department at a college or university library should be able to provide information about such services.

Whatever source you use to find information, it is important that you know exactly what you are looking for. Librarians and people who work in agencies are best able to deal with specific requests. An important tool in making specific requests is the *Thesaurus of ERIC Descriptors,* which is available in most college libraries. This publication lists and defines many terms, some very broad and some very specific. These terms, or *descriptors,* are used in most organizations and reference works to organize and retrieve information. The use of appropriate descriptors will increase the speed and improve the results of most searches for information.

As an aid to locating information, a list of professional journals dealing with specific special education categories has been provided at the end of each chapter in this book.

STEP SIX: IMPLEMENT PROFESSIONAL DEVELOPMENT PROGRAM

The implementation of your professional development program will depend on your objectives and personal circumstances and will, as a result, be highly subjective. There are, however, general guidelines that apply to everyone.

First, professional development activities should be approached systematically. If you have carefully followed the previous steps, you should know what the results of each activity will be. This will be helpful in planning a program of coursework, in selecting in-service or continuing education programs, and in developing independent enrichment or study activities.

Second, you should join the appropriate professional organizations, most of which publish journals, conduct training courses, and provide other benefits. These organizations have been responsible for many of the recent improvements in the education of exceptional children through legislation, litigation, and professional negotiations.

What is CEC?   Although there are many specialized professional organizations that cater to different special educators, there is one that cuts across all categories: The Council for Exceptional Children (CEC). This organization has a membership of approximately 50,000 professionals and students preparing for special education careers. Founded in 1922, CEC serves professionals in the United States and Canada who work with exceptional children and adults. In 1984, there were 989 local chapters, 46 student associations, 58 state and provincial federations, and 12 divisions in the organization. Every CEC member receives two major journals. *Exceptional Children* is the official journal of the Council. It is published six times each year and contains articles, position papers, research reports, and other material related to the state of the art and the future of special education. *Teaching Exceptional Children* is published four times each year and contains articles related to the actual instruction of exceptional children.

CEC provides a number of other services to its members. These include national and special topical conferences and searches of the ERIC data base. The group also has a strong voice in the legislative arena on issues facing special education.

Most CEC members join one or more of the thirteen divisions that focus upon specific exceptionalities or a unique aspect of special education. These divisions are

— Council of Administrators of Special Education (CASE)
— Council for Children with Behavioral Disorders (CCBD)
— Division on Career Development (DCD)
— Division for Children with Communication Disorders (DCCD)

— Division for Early Childhood (DEC)
— Council for Educational Diagnostic Services (CEDS)
— The Association for the Gifted (TAG)
— Division for Learning Disabilities (DLD)
— Division on Mental Retardation (CEC-MR)
— Division for Physically Handicapped (DPH)
— Teacher Education Division (TED)
— Division for the Visually Handicapped (DVH)
— Technology and Media Division (TAM)

Each of these divisions also publishes its own professional journal, newsletter, or both. Student memberships are available at reduced rates. It is a good idea to join CEC and become active in the organization as a student. Not only will you receive the professional journals, you will be eligible to participate in the other benefits of the organization. Membership in an organization such as CEC also indicates to potential employers that you are actively engaged in professional activities.

Another benefit of belonging to a professional organization is related to mental health. Special education teaching is difficult work, and it provides different challenges than teaching in the regular classroom. For example, teachers of the severely and profoundly handicapped must often be content with small improvements in their students' skills, and they must have a high tolerance for repetitive teaching and for working with children who may have very limited language skills. What is more, the special education teacher frequently works without interacting with other special education colleagues. As a result of these factors, the teacher often becomes frustrated and depressed. The author knows of a number of teachers and administrators who have reported feeling "burned out" after a few years of work in this type of situation. Participation in a professional organization can provide you with opportunities to interact with colleagues who may have similar problems, to share ideas, discuss alternative methods of dealing with situations, and receive support for your efforts.

STEP SEVEN: EVALUATE, REVISE, AND REFINE

A program of professional development should be flexible. This means that the professional must continually evaluate his or her activities and plans and make modifications when necessary. But how does one engage in self-evaluation? Two procedures can be suggested. The first involves examining each of the competency statements in this chapter and asking yourself how well you can do the task and whether you should learn how to do it better. You could also obtain the forms used to evaluate student teachers or regular school teachers and assess your performance in each of the areas mentioned.

Although the emphasis has been on self-evaluation, you can also benefit by enlisting the assistance of colleagues. CEC Professional Guideline 2.4.2 states:

"Professionals participate in the objective and systematic evaluation of themselves, colleagues, services, and programs for the purpose of continuous improvement of professional performance" (Code of Ethics and Standards for Professional Practice, 1983, p. 208). Some school systems have successfully implemented a system of peer assistance in planning and evaluating professional development programs. Such a system provides mutual support and fosters greater objectivity in evaluating the elements described in this chapter.

CONCLUSION

The best special educators engage in an ongoing program of professional development. They become involved in their professional organizations, participate in continuing education programs, and constantly look for ways to improve their professional performance. To begin an effective development program, one must analyze one's strengths and weaknesses, locate the necessary resources and information, and efficiently manage time, energy, and personal resources.

Is there a code of ethics for special educators?

Above all, special educators should subscribe to the code of ethics established by the Council for Exceptional Children to govern the professional behavior of its members. The eight points of this Code are listed below (Code of Ethics and Standards for Professional Practice, 1983, p. 205).

Special education professionals:

1. Are committed to developing the highest educational and quality of life potential of exceptional individuals.
2. Promote and maintain a high level of competence and integrity in practicing their profession.
3. Engage in professional activities which benefit exceptional individuals, their families, other colleagues, students, or research subjects.
4. Exercise objective professional judgment in the practice of their profession.
5. Strive to advance their knowledge and skills regarding the education of exceptional individuals.
6. Work within the standards and policies of their profession.
7. Seek to uphold and improve where necessary the laws, regulations, and policies governing the delivery of special education and related services and the practice of their profession.
8. Do not condone or participate in unethical or illegal acts, nor violate professional standards adopted by the delegate assembly of CEC.

The steps described in this chapter represent a practical approach to professional development. The use of these steps accompanied by adherence to the CEC ethical standards, will produce highly competent professionals. The ultimate benefit, of course, will be improved services to exceptional children and adults.

PROBE 2-5
Professional Development

1. T   F   Traditionally, the professional development of special educators has proceeded in a highly systematic fashion.

2. The first step in designing a program of professional development is to develop a _____.

3. List the five levels of roles performed by special education personnel.

4. T   F   The competencies needed by special education teachers are significantly different from those needed by teachers in regular education.

5. The specification of _____ follows the identification of competencies in the steps for designing a professional development program.

6. The most useful reference journal for special educators is _____.

7. _____ is the most comprehensive professional organization for special education personnel.

We are continuing to make progress in arriving at solutions to the issues discussed in this chapter, but we still have a long way to go with many of them. As a person who may enter the field of special education, you may someday be in a position to contribute to their resolution. It is our hope that this book will provide the foundation necessary to make this possible. If you are interested in further reading on this topic, you may enjoy the text *Critical Issues in Special and Remedial Education* by Ysseldyke and Algozzine (1982).

SUMMARY

1. Most students assigned to special education services are not identified until after they start to attend school.
2. Both norm-referenced and criterion-referenced tests are used to assess children for purposes of identification and instruction.
3. Poor educational decisions are often made about children on the basis of assessment information from tests with poor reliability and validity and inappropriate norms.
4. In addition to test results, teachers should use other techniques such as direct observation and samples of children's work in making instructional decisions.
5. Assigning labels to exceptional children can lead to improper practices and should be avoided whenever possible.
6. Deinstitutionalization and mainstreaming are efforts to provide the handicapped with opportunities and environments similar to those that are normal for the nonhandicapped.

7. Exceptional children are educated in a variety of environments, including regular classrooms, resource rooms, special schools, residential facilities, homes, and hospitals. It is best to place the child in the least restrictive educational environment that meets the child's needs.

8. When placing a special education student in a regular class for a portion of the school day, it is important that the student be able to work at the same level as some of the other students in the class, work without much extra effort on the part of the teacher, handle the routine of the regular class, stay on task, and adapt socially.

9. Appropriate attitudes among teachers and principals toward mainstreaming are as important as the actual teaching competencies needed for successful mainstreaming.

10. An individualized education program must be developed for every handicapped child enrolled in a publicly supported educational setting.

11. Computers can be used effectively to assist in the development of IEPs.

12. Special educators should be particularly sensitive to the unique characteristics and needs of exceptional children from minority cultures.

13. Special educators have a responsibility to design educational programs that continue to develop their professional competence after they have completed their formal education.

14. A well-developed philosophy serves as the foundation for success as a special educator.

15. Professional development efforts are most successful if they are approached on a well-planned and systematic basis.

16. The seven steps in designing a professional development program are to develop a philosophy; define your professional role; specify competencies needed to perform that role; develop and rank objectives for meeting the competencies; identify content and resources related to the objectives; implement the program; and evaluate, revise, and refine your efforts.

17. Special educators should become active members of their professional organizations and abide by the standards and ethics of their profession.

18. The major professional organization for special educators is the Council for Exceptional Children.

TASK SHEET 2
Issues in Special Education

Philosophy of Special Education

This text has been designed to help you begin the development of a philosophy of special education. Start a notebook that you can use to jot down ideas about your philosophy as you progress through the book. Be prepared to write your philosophy of special education when you reach the end of the book. Refer to the section on philosophy in this chapter if you need some ideas about how to get started on this assignment.

CEC Membership

Join the Council for Exceptional Children. Write to CEC at 1920 Association Drive, Reston, VA 22091 for a membership application. If you are a student, you can join at reduced rates.

Select one of the following and perform the assigned tasks:

Assessment Observation

Get in touch with a school psychologist or the director of a special education diagnostic facility in your community and see if you can observe the administration of a psychological or educational test. (You may have some difficulty with this because of right to privacy regulations. Some agencies have observation facilities that permit unobtrusive observation. Agency policies may preclude such activities, however.) Record your observations and prepare a three-page report that describes what you observed and your reactions to the visit.

Professional Interview

Arrange to visit a school principal, special education teacher, director of special education, diagnostician, or school psychologist. Inquire about the topics that were discussed in this chapter. In a three-page report, answer the following questions:

1. Whom did you talk with and what did you ask the person?
2. What were the person's reactions to the issues you raised?
3. What problems did the person encounter in implementing special education programs?
4. What did you learn from this experience?

Interview with a Parent

If possible, visit with a parent who has gone through the IEP process. Ask the parent to describe his or her experience and reactions. Find out if the parent felt that he or she was permitted sufficient say in the development of the IEP. In a three-page paper describe your interview and your personal reactions.

Library Study

Locate three articles in the library related to the issues raised in this chapter. Write a one-page abstract of each, concluding with a paragraph about your reactions to the article. Here are the names of some journals in which you can find articles about these topics:

> *Exceptional Children*
> *Journal of Special Education*
> *Remedial and Special Education*
> *Teacher Education and Special Education*
> *Teaching Exceptional Children*

Design Your Own Field Experience

If you know of a unique experience you can have that is related to the topics covered in this chapter or do not want to do any of the listed options, discuss your alternatives with your instructor and complete the task that you both agree on.

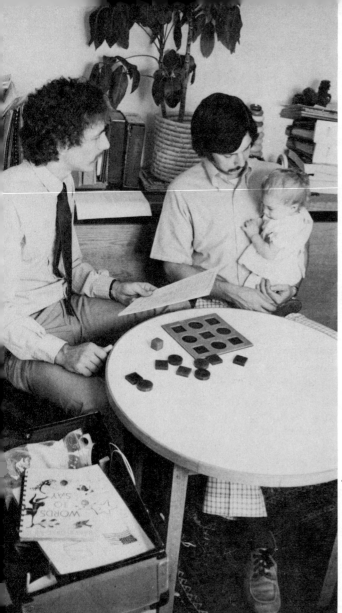

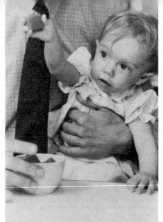

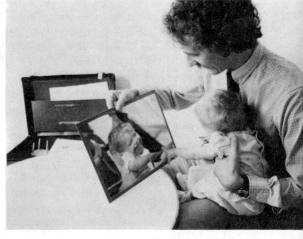

Early identification of children's problems greatly increases the chances of correcting them through education or medical treatment. From birth, this sixteen-month-old girl had feeding problems that resulted in her very small stature. Her parents were concerned about whether other areas of development were also affected.

Here, the examiner is administering tasks from the Bayley Scales of Infant Development. The tasks assess psychomotor development, social responsiveness, gross and fine motor functioning, language development, and conceptual abilities.

The child's performance was compared to norms for infants and toddlers between two and thirty months old. Although she was physically small, it was found that her psychomotor skills were developing normally. Had her performance been significantly below the norms, suggestions would have been made for activities to stimulate her development.

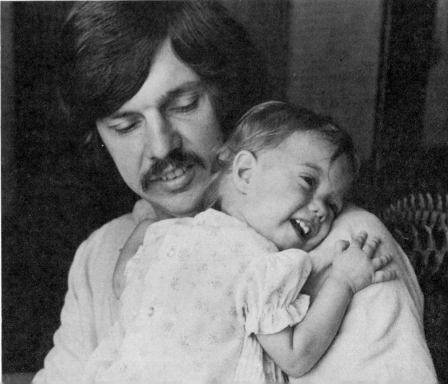

Robbie's mother first noticed his hearing impairment when he was ten months old. At the mother-infant class at the preschool for the hearing impaired, she learned to work with Robbie at home. From the time he was a year old, Robbie wore two hearing aids. He learned to understand and use language. When Robbie entered kindergarten, he had a vocabulary of about 300 words.

Ann was hospitalized for meningitis at age three. After she returned home, she was more quiet. Instead of full sentences, she now used fragments. Six months later, her language had all but disappeared. Her parents bought her a hearing aid, but they never learned to work with her. Ann did not talk to her parents, and they believed she did not listen. After Ann tried to flush her hearing aid down the toilet, her parents took it away from her. When she entered kindergarten, Ann had no speaking vocabulary.

During Paige's birth, brain damage occurred, resulting in cerebral palsy. As Paige developed, she appeared to understand events in her environment, but she did not speak clearly and had great difficulty grasping and moving. Paige was enrolled in a preschool program operated by the local Easter Seal Society, where she was taught self-help skills and given physical therapy and special speech instruction. Although she continued to have difficulty speaking and moving, she was enrolled in kindergarten, where she was able to succeed with the support of continued physical therapy and special education.

Scott was diagnosed as having Down's Syndrome. His parents desperately searched for services for him, but their small town could not provide assistance. Scott's parents placed him in a residential institution for the mentally retarded. Scott was confined to a crib and received very little stimulation. The parents noticed during visits that Scott was becoming increasingly less communicative. He had no speech or language, no bowel or bladder control, and spent most of his time rocking back and forth, biting his fingers, and screeching.

3

Early Childhood Education

Susan M. Kershman

Susan M. Kershman is an Associate Professor at the Pennsylvania College of Optometry. Her college teaching experience includes coordinating programs in early childhood education of the handicapped and education of the visually handicapped. She is an experienced teacher of the deaf and of the blind and former program director of a deaf-blind early intervention program.

The education of exceptional children in the age range from birth to five or six has undergone great changes in the last 30 years. Like Robbie and Paige in the anecdotes on the previous pages, more young exceptional children and their families are receiving services than ever before. These services are more diverse and widespread than they have ever been. Unfortunately, however, there are still many like Ann and Scott, who do not receive appropriate services. In fact, approximately two thirds of the disabled preschoolers who need services do not receive them (Gallagher, 1979).

Why are so few disabled preschoolers served? There are several reasons: funds are lacking, trained personnel are scarce, and decision makers are often badly informed. Public attitudes are also important; for example, it used to be widely believed that all young children should be kept at home with their mothers rather than being placed in day care or educational settings. In the last three decades, however, our understanding of the effectiveness of early intervention has grown tremendously. There is now no doubt that exceptional children can benefit from educational intervention begun as soon as a problem is diagnosed. Model programs, public and private infant and preschool projects, and researchers have demonstrated the effectiveness of early education for handicapped, at-risk, and disadvantaged children. As a result, additional funds have been made available for the growth of many new services; person-nel are being educated and in some states certified to work specifically with exceptional preschoolers. Although great strides have been made, problems persist. The political climate threatens to undo recent gains in access to services for very young children. More than ever before, the impact of early education programs on children, families, schools, and society must be broadly under-stood; without this firm basis on which to build, there won't be universal support for the education of exceptional children in their first few years of life.

INTRODUCTION TO EARLY CHILDHOOD EDUCATION

You should be able to define "early childhood special education" and tell why it is important to children, families, schools, and society.

In the first chapter, special education was defined as instruction designed to respond to the unique characteristics of children who have needs that cannot be met by the regular school curriculum. Having been through it ourselves, we are all familier with the regular curriculum for children of school age. However, for very young children, there is little universal agreement about what the "regular curriculum" should be; in fact, the very purpose of educa-tion for very young children has been questioned by some authors (Spodek, 1977).

DEFINING EARLY CHILDHOOD SPECIAL EDUCATION

A single, customary curriculum for children younger than "school age" sim-ply does not exist. Many different curricula, based on diverse philosophies of early childhood education have been developed and implemented. Some of these have concentrated on play or social and emotional skills; others have been based on Piaget's theory of early cognitive development or Montessori's methods. Still others have been quite structured and focus on pre-academics. Some early childhood education programs have included disabled children in the classes with nondisabled children; others have kept the disabled children together in their own group. Given this kind of diversity in curriculum, in philosophy, and in target population, how should one define special education when it is applied to children younger than the usual age for school entry?

Early childhood education is generally considered to be the education of children who are in the age range from birth to eight or nine years (Hayden, 1978). Falling under this general definition are the following subcategories: *Infant* education deals with children under the age of 2 years. *Preschool* education is concerned with children who are between approximately 2 and 5 years. In federal legislation, infancy includes the third year of life and is distinguished from the preschool period, which covers children between ages 3 and 5 (Behr and Gallagher, 1981). The age at which children enter *kindergarten* differs from one state to another, but is usually between 5 and 6 years. *Primary* classes in public and private schools usually serve children from 5 to 9 years of age. These different age groupings hold true for nondisabled children as well as for those who have disabilities.

What is the goal of early childhood special education?

The goal of special education, when it is applied in the early childhood years, is to provide instruction during the early development years from birth to age six in order to prevent or minimize the handicapping effects of a

While early education helps all children, it is particularly important for children with disabilities because it can help reduce the handicapping effects of their disabilities.

disability or an impairment. As we will explain, the instruction may be provided directly to the infants or young children involved, or to parents, who, in turn, teach their infants or young children. In some instances, early childhood special education services are directed toward young children who have a high probability of manifesting developmental disabilities or school-related problems in later childhood (Linder, 1983). *Early childhood special education,* then, may be defined as either direct or indirect instruction designed to respond to the unique characteristics of young children who have needs that cannot be met by the curriculum established for the nondisabled.

In the twentieth century, the education of young children has undergone several periods of growth and change. The two fields of special education and early childhood education have merged during the most recent growth period, resulting in the new field of early childhood special education. From early childhood education has come the realization that all children, including those with disabilities, are essentially equal in their rights to education. From special education has come the need for increased acceptance and normalization in the lives of young disabled children. The emergence and growth of this new field is based on the fundamental view that preschool exceptional children have the same basic needs, desires, and problems in growing up as other children, but they also have additional difficulties to overcome.

The growth of the field has been influenced by many factors, including broad social changes, new trends in the structure and functioning of the modern family, the philosophies and practices of many prominent thinkers, and changes in legislation and litigation that have spawned the development of new services in early childhood special education. A comprehensive review and discussion of this new field is beyond the scope of this chapter; for more information, the reader is referred to texts in early childhood special education (Allen, Holm, and Schiefelbusch, 1978; Fallen and McGovern, 1978; Jordan, Hayden, Karnes, and Wood, 1977; Linder, 1983; Meisels, 1979; Safford, 1978).

HISTORY AND IMPORTANCE OF EARLY CHILDHOOD EDUCATION

Why is early education so important for handicapped children?

In this century, the idea that educating children at a very young age can be important to the children, their families, schools, and society has gained increasing popularity and support. The most powerful support for this concept has come from research that has demonstrated two major points: (1) early learning can correct or reduce environmental or developmental deficits; and (2) particularly in cases of special need, failure to provide appropriate opportunities for early learning can lead to "cumulative deficits" that are much more difficult and more costly to remedy at a later time.

One way of studying the behavior and learning of the young is through animal research. This resource in psychology suggests that early learning or deprivation may have profound effects on later development. For example, the research of Lorenz (1971) suggested that animals have a "critical period," a time span before which they are not "ready" for learning, and after which learning becomes more difficult or impossible. Harlow's (1974) research showed the profound effects of maternal deprivation in monkeys. The effects of early sensory experience or deprivation, diet, and a variety of forms of stimulation have also been investigated in animals (Linder, 1983). This research suggests that human infants who do not receive adequate treatment in their early years may experience serious developmental setbacks.

Interest in the early development of human infants and young children began to grow in the early part of this century. Psychological studies of human infants became popular as the universities began to open nurseries and child study laboratories around the United States. When the Clinic of Child Development at Yale University opened in 1911, Arnold Gesell, a physician and psychologist, became the director. Gesell collected filmed observations of thousands of children. By studying these films he was able to describe the behaviors of young children and the ages at which they appeared. This work resulted in his *Schedules of Development* and many other publications.

Gesell believed that the early years were the most important biologically and mentally, since they laid the foundation for all subsequent development (Gesell and Ilg, 1943). Probably because of his medical training and background, he also believed that genetic endowment and biological maturation were responsible for both the changes or "unfolding" of children in their early years and their ultimate achievement and IQ levels.

The Depression and the two World Wars were later periods of growth for nurseries, day-care, and kindergarten programs. Because many mothers were needed to work in the war industries and could not stay home with their young children, more children than ever before were enrolled in preschool programs. During these periods, it became more socially acceptable for children to be away from their homes in their early years.

By the 1950s, the work of Jean Piaget, the Swiss psychologist, was gaining popularity and esteem in the United States. Like Gesell, Piaget derived his theory from observing children. At the core of his theory is the idea that all children progress through the same sequence of stages of cognitive development. When and how these stages are reached depends on the quality of learning opportunities in the child's environment (Flavell, 1977).

By the mid-1950s, the Russian launching of Sputnik and international competition brought about an effort to examine and improve American education. Jerome S. Bruner was one of several influential writers and educators concerned with the process of education. He emphasized that information should be presented to children in the sequence most appropriate for the child's level of understanding (Bruner, 1960). Like Piaget, he felt that the environment could be arranged either to enhance or to retard cognitive growth.

Benjamin Bloom's *Stability and Change in Human Characteristics* (1964) was an important comprehensive review of child development research. Bloom suggested that experience has its greatest effect during periods of rapid change, such as in the first few years of life. As a result, he argued, stimulating and enriching experiences have the strongest influence on the very young child. Bloom's book had great impact on the fields of psychology and education. One of his most striking statements was that 50 percent of intelligence, as measured at age 17, is fully developed by the age of 4 (Bloom, 1964). This is currently interpreted to mean that 50 percent of the variance in adult intelligence can be predicted by age 4.

Like Bloom, J. McVicker Hunt also published an analysis of then-current research. In his book *Intelligence and Experience* (1961), Hunt took issue with the idea that intellectual development is genetically fixed. He argued that the individual's environment and experience can largely determine the rate and final level of intellectual achievement. The result of Hunt's work was a popular reinterpretation of the concept of intelligence. Hunt drew public attention to the early years of life and became known as a strong advocate for preschool enrichment programs for the poor to ensure equality of opportunity (Braun and Edwards, 1972).

By the middle of the 1960s, President Johnson had begun his "War on Poverty." In psychology, the importance of the early years had been popularly recognized. The concept of intelligence was in transition; it was no longer considered to be an inflexible quantity from birth onward. It was an optimistic period in which early intervention was proposed as a way of improving the nation's psychological health and educational achievement levels. It was in this milieu that Head Start began.

How effective is Head Start?

Head Start legislation was passed in 1964 as part of the Economic Opportunity Act; its stated purpose was to provide preschool education to children from disadvantaged environments. But as a part of the War on Poverty, its goals were even more broad-based. They included provisions for nutrition, medical and dental examinations, and parent involvement in the development of the local programs. Early studies of the effectiveness of Head Start were not encouraging; the academic gains of the children seemed to "wash out" by the time they reached second grade. More recently, however, several long-term follow-up studies of Head Start participants have supported the value of this program. Lazar and Darlington (1979) collected test and interview data from children between ages 9 and 19 at the time of the follow-up study and compared with data from children who had not been in preschool programs. The findings included the following:

1. Among school-age children, the number assigned to special education or retained in grade was significantly lower for the group who had attended preschool.
2. At the fourth-grade level, the group who had attended preschool had significantly higher scores in math achievement tests and somewhat higher scores in reading tests.

3. On the Stanford Binet IQ test, low-income children who had attended preschool had higher scores for up to three years after the preschool programs ended.
4. Mothers who had attended preschools had higher vocational aspirations for their children than the children had for themselves.

These results suggest that Head Start had a significant positive influence on its participants.

Another research study that showed the long-term effectiveness of an early education project was conducted by Schweinhart and Weikart (1981). Their study followed 123 children from ages 3 to 19 in order to evaluate the effects of their participation in the Perry Preschool Project compared to a control group, which received no early education program. The results indicated superior scholastic achievement for the preschool group, even 10 years later. This group showed higher motivation, fewer placements in special education, fewer retentions in grade, and less delinquent behavior than the controls. The parents of the preschool group were called in to school less often to talk about their children. They also had higher aspirations for their children than the control group and were more satisfied with their children's achievements than the parents of the control group. An important feature of this study was the examination of the cost-effectiveness of early education. By calculating the mothers' released time when the children were in preschool, the money saved by the public schools for fewer special education placements and fewer retentions in grade, and the lifetime earnings for each child, the benefits far outstripped the cost of the early education program. The authors reported a 248 percent return on the original investment!

In summary, recent research has demonstrated the value of early education for young disadvantaged children, their families, the schools, and society. The developmental consequences of being born into a low-income disadvantaged environment, previously thought to be inevitable, have been shown to be modifiable. At the same time that these studies were conducted with disadvantaged children, similar research questions were being asked in special education.

RELEVANCE TO SPECIAL EDUCATION

As public attitudes toward the importance of the early years were changing, several investigators tried to apply the new ideas to children with disabilities. The slow process of transforming public opinion concerning the handicapped progressed as research that bridged both special education and early childhood education was begun.

What does research tell us about early education for the handicapped?

One of the most dramatic studies of the long-range effectiveness of early intervention was designed by Skeels and Dye (1939) and followed up by Skeels (1966). The plan for the study came from an accidental discovery of IQ gains in two young, "hopeless" children institutionalized with older retarded women who cared for them and played with them. An experimental group of 13 young children was transferred from an orphanage to the institution, while a control group of 12 babies in the same age and IQ range remained at the orphanage. The older retarded women on the ward stimulated and cared for the young children in the experimental group. A year and a half later, the IQs of the experimental group children had gained about 28 points. Those of the control group had lost about 26 points. At the time these results were published, the Skeels and Dye study was severely criticized, but it is recognized today as one of the earliest empirical studies of the effectiveness of early intervention.

Many years later, Skeels reported on what had happened to the two groups of children. Of the experimental group of 13, all were self-supporting adults. Their median level of education was twelfth grade. Four persons from this group had attended one or more years of college, and one had graduate training. Of the original control group of 12, four were still wards of an institution, and one had died in adolescence. The median level of education for the control group was third grade. Of the 50 percent employed, all but one were unskilled laborers.

Another important study was conducted by Kirk and reported in 1958. For this study, two groups of mentally retarded institutionalized children between 3 and 5 years of age were compared. The children's IQs were between 40 and 60. The experimental group was given 2 years of preschool training, while the control group was not trained. Both groups were retested 2 years after the preschool training had ended. The trained group had improved in mental and social maturity, but the control group's scores had dropped on all tests.

These studies demonstrate the importance of early experiences on children's development. Failure to provide early stimulation can lead not just to a developmental standstill but to actual regression. In both studies, children in the control groups did not remain at the level of achievement they started with but actually grew worse in comparison with other children of the same age.

As professionals who worked within each of the "categories" of special education became aware of the importance of the early years for later achievement, efforts were made to begin educating children with disabilities at younger and younger ages.

Hearing Impairment. By far the most serious effect of early significant hearing impairment is that it limits language development. The early years are a critical period for language learning; if hearing impairment is not detected and special education not begun, the handicapping potential of hearing impairment is compounded. Young hearing-impaired children who do not learn to use and understand language have retarded intellectual and educational growth (Horton, 1976). Simmons-Martin (1981) has shown that with an early education program, the language development scores of children with significant hearing impairments can increase consistently, through the early childhood years.

Visual impairment. Infants who are blind from birth often have problems relating to adults and to objects. Blindness also delays control of the hands and gross motor development. Researchers have found that blind children who received early education services show smaller developmental delays than other blind children (Adelson and Fraiberg, 1975; Fraiberg, 1975).

Physical Disabilities. Scherzer (1974) noted that, although cerebral palsy is a difficult condition to diagnose in infants, it is no longer acceptable to adopt a "wait and see" policy before planning intervention. Both parents and physical therapists need to be included in the educational programs for such children. The value of such programs was demonstrated by Koch (1958), who did a follow-up study of cerebral palsied children who had participated in a nursery school program. His results showed that better long-term results were achieved by children who had early treatment than by those for whom treatment was postponed.

Mental Retardation. LaCrosse (1976) stated that sending mentally retarded children to nursery school can encourage them to enter group activities at a time when their differences from the normal group are not very distinct or severe and when society is more willing to accept them. Parent-child relationships are likely to improve as young mentally retarded children become less dependent, less fearful, and less burdensome.

The early studies of mentally retarded children (Kirk, 1958; Skeels, 1966; Skeels and Dye, 1939) provide convincing evidence of the effectiveness of early education in raising IQ scores and improving social behavior. More recently, the multidisciplinary preschool program for Down's syndrome children at the University of Washington has provided a model of effective early childhood educational practices for children whose mental retardation stems from an organic cause. In this program, children served as their own controls, with their current performances being compared to their earlier progress. This permits all identified children to participate fully. The mean developmental lag was reduced from 21 to 5.6 months for children in the program, and participating children mastered certain designated tasks as well (Hayden and Dmitriev, 1975). In 1977, Hayden, Morris, and Bailey reported that 34 percent of the program's graduates were doing well in their regular public school classes. This program has clearly established not only the effectiveness of early and continuous education, but also its cost effectiveness and efficiency in terms of the children's later placements.

Learning Disabilities. Although it has been argued that identifying learning disabled children at an early age may lead to unnecessary labeling and stigmatizing (Hayden and Edgar, 1977), there have been efforts to define the characteristics of this population and begin early intervention (Keogh, 1970). Learning disabilities are suspected when a child's written or spoken language problem has no obvious cause such as deafness or mental retardation. Most young children are not expected to read, spell, or do arithmetic, but their problems may be no less apparent in their thinking, talking, or listening (Wallace and McLaughlin, 1975).

Early childhood education may eliminate or reduce the severity of specific learning disabilities before children are required to learn academic subjects (Wallace and McLaughlin, 1975). But despite the need for services, especially for children with severe problems, programs for children with early symptoms of learning disabilities are quite scarce.

Behavior Disorders. Children who have behavior disorders present particular difficulties at home. For this reason, early education programs for these children place a special emphasis on the role of parents. One such program is at the Rutland Center in Athens, Georgia. In this program, parents are given information about the children's progress and needs and assisted in implementing complementary home programs (Shearer and Shearer, 1977). Of the graduates from this program, 65 percent were placed in regular elementary classes and the remainder were placed in nurseries, kindergartens, and special classes (Karnes and Zehrbach, 1977a).

Multiple Handicaps. Appell (1977) reported that deaf-blind children are extremely vulnerable to developmental delay. Without early diagnosis and intervention most will never achieve their full potential. Despite the expense and

Young children with social and behavioral problems can be helped through early childhood special education programs.

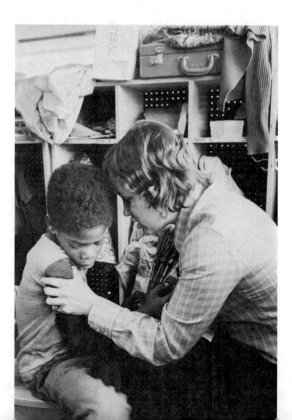

other requirements of early instruction, Appell stated, "Saving an infant and family in crisis from further deprivation, dissolution, and disruption more than justifies the cost and the effort expended" (p. 163).

Giftedness. Efforts to help gifted children achieve to the extent of their abilities are just as important as efforts to help other exceptional children. Because children establish their individuality and a strong, healthy identity in their early years (Torrance, 1974), educational services should begin as soon as children reveal their distinctiveness. Gifted children among the handicapped may be particularly hard to identify, but the results of serving them may be outstanding.

In addition to functioning in the ways described above, early childhood education for exceptional children also provides assistance and support to the parents. They can receive emotional support from other parents, models for working with their own children, and specific suggestions for ways to assist in the education of their children. Positive changes in parental attitudes towards their child are often correlated with their child's progress (Sandler, Coren, and Thurman, 1983).

Thus, the importance of the early years has been underscored by research showing the impact of successful early learning experiences for disabled children. The value of systematic instruction to minimize or prevent the handicapping effects of disabilities or impairments has been demonstrated in every area of special education.

LEGISLATION

As public awareness of the value of early education has increased, interest in and demand for services for young disabled children and their families have grown. Federal and state governments have had a major role in supporting and initiating new programs and services. Because state legislation varies considerably, only federal legislation will be discussed in this section.

Head Start. In 1974, Head Start legislation was amended (PL 93-644) to require that at least 10 percent of the enrollment opportunities in each state be made available to handicapped children. As a result, many handicapped preschoolers have been placed in programs that were previously unavailable to them. In 1981, DeWeerd reported that over 41,000 preschool children with disabilities were being served by Head Start.

What is the purpose of the HCEEP Act?

First Chance. The Handicapped Children's Early Education Assistance Act (PL 90-538) was passed by Congress in 1968. The purpose of this act, which came to be known as the First Chance Program, or HCEEP, was to develop experimental demonstration projects for preschool handicapped children. The program called for the possible replication of projects that proved to be successful. There are now First Chance Programs or local programs based on practices developed in First Chance Programs in every state in the country. The federal law required that each of these projects educate parents and decision makers as well as the enrolled children. As a result, awareness of the importance of early education for the handicapped has increased.

An amendment of HCEEP in 1974 (PL 93-380) established funding for State Implementation Grants. These grants were to be used by State Departments of Education to develop comprehensive plans for the education of young handicapped children.

Section 504 and PL 94-142. In Chapter 1, PL 94-142 and Section 504 of the Rehabilitation Amendments were discussed. Under the provisions of these laws, it is illegal to discriminate against the handicapped in the area of education. Several provisions of these laws, however, relate specifically to early education. These are summarized below.

What are the legal requirements for early special education?

—If a state provides education to any preschool nonhandicapped children, then similar services must be made available to preschool handicapped children.

—Any state that provides services to preschool handicapped children is eligible for a special incentive grant from the federal government for each child who is enrolled. Although this program was only partially funded, the law authorizes up to $300 for each child per year.

—Although the provisions of PL 94-142 include handicapped children down to age three, a state that has a law or court order excluding children of preschool age from educational services is not required to provide such services.

—Preschool children receiving special education under the provisions of PL 94-142 are entitled to the same benefits as school-age children (due process, Individual Education Plans, nondiscriminatory testing, parent involvement in planning, and so on).

Developmental Disabilities Act. The Developmental Disabilities Act (PL 95-602) was passed in 1978. To fall under the act, the disability must originate before the child is 18 years old and must be substantial enough to threaten the child's ability to function normally in society. There is no lower limit to the age at which children may receive services; thus, children under age three, who may not be old enough to qualify for educational services from the public school, may be served by Developmental Disabilities funding.

In conclusion, it is clear that despite the unevenness of the development of educational opportunities for young children with disabilities, significant progress has been made. Although some requirements of these legislative acts, such as parental involvement and diagnostic evaluations, originated in legislation designed for young children, they are now accepted practices for all exceptional children. The future of these legislative efforts may now be uncertain. It is unlikely, however, that having developed strong communications and organizations, parents will permit a return to the indifferent attitudes and lack of concern about civil liberties that prevailed before the legislation.

PROBE 3-1
Introduction to Early Childhood Education

1. What are the chronological ages associated with each of the following?
   a. Early childhood education
   b. Infancy
   c. Preschool
   d. Kindergarten
   e. Primary school

2. List six reasons for establishing broader educational opportunities for disabled children of preschool age.

3. T F Young disabled children who do not attend early childhood education programs are more likely to show declining achievement over time than other children of their age.

4. Matching

   _____ 1. Gesell   a. Developed major theory of cognitive development
   _____ 2. Bruner   b. Believed that most intelligence is fully developed by age four
   _____ 3. Piaget   c. Provided evidence to challenge the idea of fixed intelligence
   _____ 4. Hunt   d. Studied the effects of drugs on intelligence
   _____ 5. Bloom   e. Developed schedules of child development
                               f. Was concerned about the way information was sequenced and made appropriate for learning

5. _____ was the first law designed to provide educational services to children who were disadvantaged.

6. What percentage of enrollments in Head Start should be available to handicapped preschoolers?

7. The First Chance Program was designed to _____ .

8. T F State Implementation Grants were designed to provide funds to states to develop comprehensive plans for services to the preschool handicapped.

9. T   F   If a state does not provide services to 3- and 4-year-olds because they are excluded from the mandatory attendance law, then the provisions of PL 94-142 do not apply to handicapped children of the same age.

HUMAN GROWTH AND DEVELOPMENT

You should be able to describe the principles of human growth and development and how sequences of milestones in the major areas of child development are related to educational programming for young disabled children.

Development theory is based on the assumption that individuals change throughout their lives. Some of the most obvious changes in infants and young children are changes in physical size and proportions. For example, during the first year of life, infant growth is very rapid; infants increase typically about 50 to 55 percent in length and 180 to 200 percent in weight. After the first year, average increases in overall body length are greater than increases in length from head to buttocks (Garwood and Fewell, 1983). Thus, the head grows more slowly than the trunk after the first year. Growth may be defined as an increase in physical size of the whole or any of its parts.

Changes in size, however, produce corresponding changes in function. These changes in function are often referred to as development. But the exact definition of the term "development" varies depending on the type of development that is being described. For example, motor development is an increase in skill and complexity of movement. Cognitive development, on the other hand, is the process of gaining abilities related to knowing, perceiving, and recognizing. Development results from both growth and learning. The terms "growth" and "development" do not mean the same thing, but they are obviously related. For our purposes, development will be regarded as a continuous, cumulative process.

Neither growth nor development is a smooth, uniform process. Each is characterized by spurts of rapid change, periods of apparent rest or "plateaus," and even, at some stages, decline. For example, in old age growth becomes insufficient to replace lost cells and the body may become inefficient. Similarly, certain behavioral skills may decline as other skills are learned. The various physiological systems of the body change at different but related rates, too. For example, the reproductive system of the young child changes very slowly during the first three years, whereas the motor system changes very quickly.

What are milestones?

Specific behaviors that typically occur at certain ages are called milestones. These have been identified by studying different children representing each age level (called *cross-sectional research*) or by examining the behaviors of the same individuals at different ages (called *longitudinal research*). The milestones usually represent a particular behavior, such as walking without assistance, which is characteristic of young children at a certain level of development. Sample milestones of development are presented and summarized in the charts and figures in this chapter.

The average ages at which milestones occur are called norms. It should be emphasized, however, that wide variations of age for any given milestone should be expected. For example, a child who does not pull up to a standing position using furniture for support at exactly eleven months is not necessarily retarded in this area. Individual variations in the appearances of milestones may simply mean that the child's rate of development is different from the average. Nevertheless, greater variations from norms are found among disabled than nondisabled children.

Information on normal development is based on the fact that sequences of early development milestones are *uniform* and *universal*. Remarkable though it may seem, the sequences described by Gesell, Piaget, and others are found in numerous cultures around the world, and children everywhere move through them in about the same way.

PRINCIPLES OF NORMAL DEVELOPMENT

Normal early development involves a myriad of behaviors and changes in behaviors. Unless one understands the principles of normal development, it is impossible to work effectively with children who are developing abnormally. Several general principles are associated with developmental change:

How do children grow and develop?

1. The sequence of development is, in general, the same for all children, but individual children develop at their own rates and to their own ultimate levels (Meier, 1976).
2. Rates of growth and development vary between individuals and between different developmental areas within the same individual.
3. Progress in development is often uneven; the rate of change in one skill area may vary while other skills are being learned.
4. Individual differences are apparent in young children at a very early age; they also tend to remain apparent over time (for example, see Neilon, 1948).
5. Early development proceeds by processes of increasing *differentiation* and *integration*. When newborns are startled, their whole bodies tense in reaction. This mass activity is gradually replaced by more specific activity; startled 3-year-old children show tension only in their shoulders and neck

muscles, and they blink their eyes rapidly shut. Thus, early mass responsiveness has become differentiated into responsiveness that is more localized and specific. Furthermore, as development proceeds, small units of behavior (for example, hand movements) are combined and integrated into larger, functional behaviors (for example, reaching for and grasping objects).

6. Children progress step by step in orderly sequences of development. Each accomplishment prepares the way for the next one. Regardless of chronological age, the mastery of later milestones generally depends on the achievement of earlier ones. One such early example is head control, which is used later in walking.

7. Motor development progresses in a *cephalocaudal* and *proximodistal* direction. This means that control of voluntary movement in the infant proceeds from the head downward and from the trunk outward, respectively. This is illustrated in the following summary of early motor development (Adapted from Gesell and Amatruda, 1947, p. 10):

> In the first quarter of the first year, infants gain control of the six sets of muscles that move their eyes; in the second quarter, the muscles that support their heads and move their arms. They reach out for the objects they see. In the third quarter, the controlled use of their hands improves; in sitting, they grasp, transfer, and manipulate objects. In the fourth quarter, they stand on legs and feet. Using forefinger and thumb, they poke and pluck. In the second year, they walk and run.

8. There are times during which children show that they are "ready" for new learning. During these times particular kinds of learning may be cultivated or damaged relatively easily. Before or beyond this point (referred to as a sensitive or "critical" period), learning a particular skill or process may be more difficult.

9. Children (including very young infants) give those taking care of them subtle behavioral cues about their needs, rhythms, and readiness for new learning. Professionals and parents can be taught to recognize these cues. Progress is best when the stimulation provided matches the child's readiness to learn.

10. As children develop increasing capacities for learning and doing, they tend to use these abilities. Conversely, especially with regard to the senses, what one does not use, one loses.

11. All areas of development are interrelated. Although we often speak of motor development or conceptual development as separate entities, in the normal child all areas are related to each other.

12. The process and outcome of development are influenced by children's genetic inheritances, their social and cultural backgrounds, and their families.

13. Development results from both growth and learning, each of which con-

tinually influences the other. The challenge of education is to provide the influences necessary to achieve the child's full potential.

USES OF DEVELOPMENTAL NORMS

Why should teachers be aware of child development norms?

Information about normal development is used in many educational settings for many different purposes. The purpose of *screening* is to identify children who may have problems, so that, if appropriate, special education services can be provided. Developmental norms are also considered in the educational *assessment* of a child's strengths and weaknesses. This information is used to plan instruction that uses the child's areas of strength to compensate for, or help build up, areas of weakness.

The milestones identified in developmental norms are also used as the basis for *curriculum development* in preschool programs. Unlike school-age subject matter, which is neatly divided into such disciplines as reading, writing, arithmetic, geography, and history, the skills and content that should be taught in early childhood have never been widely agreed upon. Nevertheless, while early education programs differ in almost every respect, in programs for exceptional children there is general agreement on the value of a developmental approach as a basis for planning instructional objectives (Bagnato and Neisworth, 1981). To use a developmental approach, teachers of young children must be familiar with the milestones and norms of early development. Young exceptional children are viewed first as needing instruction that promotes adequate developmental progress. The instruction developed to meet this goal is then adjusted to meet the special needs created by the child's disability.

MAJOR AREAS OF CHILD DEVELOPMENT

The behavioral changes young children go through can be categorized into distinct but related areas of development. Seven areas will be discussed in this chapter:

1. *Gross motor development* deals with reflexes, postures, locomotion, and other whole body movements.
2. *Fine motor development* is concerned with the sequence of milestones in reaching for, grasping, and manipulating a variety of objects.
3. *Perceptual development* includes milestones related to the use of vision and hearing.
4. *Conceptual development* is concerned with the sequence of milestones in the following areas: relating to objects, imitation, classification, knowledge of time and gender, and making analogies and comparisons.

5. *Social-emotional development* involves children's increasing attachments to persons and objects; it also involves their expanding abilities to differentiate between feelings, the different levels of play, and the emergence of independence.
6. *Communication* is divided into receptive and expressive areas. More will be said about these in the next chapter.
7. *Self-help* consists of eating, dressing, bathing, grooming, and toileting.

What is parallel development?

The normal child generally develops at about the same rate in all these areas. This is sometimes called *parallel development*. It is important to recognize the relationships between milestones and skills in different areas of development to form an integrated picture of the whole child. Consider, for example, some of the milestones typical of 2-year-olds. In the area of gross motor skills, the average normal child can walk well and go up and down stairs alone. In the fine motor area, the child can turn doorknobs that are within reach and hold a pencil well enough to make vertical and circular strokes or dots. Visually, most 2-year-olds are able to look for missing objects. In the realm of auditory perception, they respond to simple sound patterns and may enjoy nursery rhymes. Conceptually, they may be able to give a single-word correct answer to the question: "What do you do with a key?" Socially, most 2-year-olds possess only rudimentary social graces. They may enjoy having others present, but their play is usually parallel or even solitary rather than actively involving another child or person. In communication skills, they may combine three words to make a sentence, although they understand a vocabulary of about 200 to 400 words. In the area of self-help, 2-year-olds use a spoon well in eating, but they can only assist in dressing themselves; they can wash their own faces and hands, but not very well. Although they may stay dry at night if taken to the bathroom, 2-year-olds are rarely toilet trained in our culture.

While the normal child progresses across all seven areas of development at approximately the same rate, the exceptional child often shows uneven progress. For example, while orthopedically handicapped 2-year-old children may not have sufficient motor development to climb the stairs independently, they may be able to verbally express their independence or their desire to be independent. Similarly, blind children's visual-perceptual skills will not parallel their achievements in communication. It is unlikely that a crayon would hold the interest of a totally blind 2-year-old for very long, but the child's communication skills may be at or above the norms. The early childhood educator must be able to determine when the cause of a child's inability to do a task is merely the child's age, and when the cause is a disability or impairment. To do this the educator must know the behaviors appropriate for various ages, and the effects of various disabilities.

In the following discussions of the seven areas of development, several important milestones in normal development sequences will be described. We

Figure 3-1
Gross Motor Development

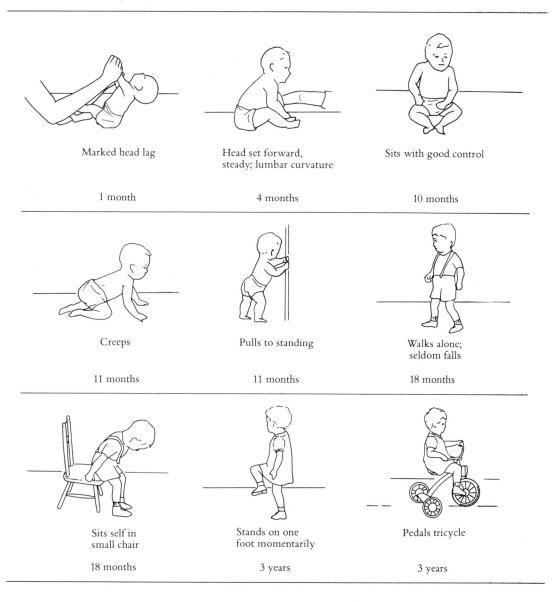

Marked head lag	Head set forward, steady; lumbar curvature	Sits with good control
1 month	4 months	10 months
Creeps	Pulls to standing	Walks alone; seldom falls
11 months	11 months	18 months
Sits self in small chair	Stands on one foot momentarily	Pedals tricycle
18 months	3 years	3 years

will also illustrate how these sequences relate to the education of exceptional children. Unfortunately, space limitations do not allow for the inclusion of a complete list of skills in each area of development. References are provided in each section for those who want to obtain additional information.

GROSS MOTOR DEVELOPMENT

Some of the sequences of gross motor development are described in Figure 3-1. These sequences illustrate how the large muscles of the body gradually come under increasing control.

In a study of the emergence of milestones related to movement (Pikler, 1971), it was reported that without any urging from adults, children changed their postures (turning to prone, turning back, rising on all fours, kneeling, sitting up, standing, and getting down from all these positions) an average of 53.3 times in 30 minutes. These changes were most frequent in children in the developmental periods between sitting up, kneeling up, and standing up. This means that the normal young developing child moves and changes position almost twice every minute with no particular adult inducement to do so. (Having read that, try sitting perfectly still for as long as you can. It is more difficult to be still than you may realize.) Normally developing young children are remarkably active creatures, a fact many parents sorely regret. You may have heard the anecdote about the professional athlete who tried to imitate the movements of a toddler — he collapsed halfway through the day. Even before children begin to walk, they are into everything; they can become a danger to themselves as well as to their environments, particularly if their surroundings have not been babyproofed.

Chart 3-1, an excerpt from a gross motor development checklist, illustrates the range of milestone behaviors that children can exhibit in an 18-month period. From the time they begin to change positions voluntarily, normal developing infants are learning many things. Aside from what they learn about the environment through exploration, they learn how to use their own bodies, how to move in a coordinated fashion, how it feels to touch different textures and surfaces, and how their movements can lead to new explorations. As you can see, motor development is related to the development of concepts.

Chart 3-1
Sample Gross Motor Milestones

19 mo.	stairs: walks down, one hand held, two feet per step
	walks fast, runs stiffly
20 mo.	walks, carrying large objects
	climbs on furniture
	walks, pushing toy
21 mo.	stairs: walks up alone, two feet per step
	stairs: creeps down backwards
22 mo.	raises self from sitting position with hips first, then head
	walks with stability
23 mo.	when walking, makes short turns and sudden stops

2 yrs.	runs well without falling
	kicks ball without overbalancing
	stairs: goes up and down alone, two feet per step
	jumps from first step without help, with one foot leading
	walks with heel-to-toe gait
2 ½ yrs.	jumps with both feet in place
	walks on tiptoes briefly
	picks up objects from floor
3 yrs.	stairs: goes up, one foot per step, and down, two feet per step
	stands on one foot for one second
	runs and gallops; takes short running steps on his toes
	rides a tricycle
	jumps from bottom step with both feet together

Why do children put themselves through the trouble of learning to walk when crawling and creeping seem so much easier and efficient? Reinforcement by parents is probably of secondary importance. What the child probably enjoys most is the ability to see new levels of the adult world. Walking also frees the hands to manipulate an ever-increasing number of items within reach. With increasing motor skills, shifts in attention become more rapid and more diversified.

How can poor motor development affect learning?

For children with motor impairments, this learning is altered or limited. If the ability to explore is limited, so is the number of new experiences available to the child. What is more, handicapped children have less success and fewer rewards when they try. This may decrease their motivation to keep active. As you can see, problems in the development of motor skills have implications for other areas of development as well. Children who can't walk see only what others put in front of them, and they have trouble investigating the sources of sounds. Although their language development may appear to be normal, closer examination often reveals that the concepts behind the words they use are not the same as for children with normal motor functioning.

Because children with motor impairments are generally imprecise or restricted in their movements, their parents often feel they need to be protected. As a result, many children who can move around somewhat are prevented by their parents from developing these abilities. This attitude is common in the parents of young children with many disabilities. Although the attitude is understandable, parents should be made to understand the importance of exploration, or the child will be further handicapped by the lack of experiences.

Real limitations in self-help skills are often seen in children with spina bifida and cerebral palsy, when bowel and bladder control are impossible or late in developing. Motor impairments may also affect the child's level of independence, as seen in dressing and self-feeding skills.

According to Finnie (1975), one of the foremost authorities in early intervention for cerebral palsied children, those who cannot move by themselves should not be left in any one physical position for more than 20 minutes, In current intervention practices, appropriate handling, positioning, and movement are emphasized in order to inhibit abnormal movement patterns, to facilitate the development of more mature patterns, and to prevent stiffness or contractures in the physically handicapped young child. This often means that teachers spend part of their day moving children from one position to another, feeding, and changing diapers. It should be remembered, however, that these services are just as important to the overall welfare of the child as any teaching the teachers may wish to do. By carrying out the appropriate techniques of physical management, teachers help to minimize the long-range effects of physical disability.

FINE MOTOR DEVELOPMENT

Some of the most important milestones of fine motor development are in grasping (prehension) and releasing objects. Obviously, children who have difficulty with these fine motor skills will also have difficulty in other skills, such as feeding, dressing, and writing. An excellent article by Erhardt (1974), written from a physical therapist's perspective, provides practical suggestions for activities teachers can use to stimulate the development of prehension skills.

Grasping develops well before release. This sequence of skills begins with the reflexive grasp present at birth. The infant can grasp objects during the first 7 or 8 months, but at this age grasping does not include the thumb — objects are held with the fingers against the palm of the hand. The pincer grasp (forefinger against the thumb) typical of adults does not usually appear until about 11 months of age. Voluntary release begins to appear at about 9 months. At this age, infants get objects out of their hands by pressing the object against a firm surface. Parents should know that voluntary release is usually clearly established only when the child is around 11 months or one year of age. Parents who demand objects from a child who has not yet developed voluntary release may interpret the child's apparent reluctance as misbehavior.

In addition to grasping and release, a host of other fine motor skills is developed by young children. Chart 3-2 illustrates those typically developed between the ages of two and five years.

How concerned should preschool teachers be with fine motor control problems?

It is important for teachers not to jump to conclusions when a child is delayed in reaching a milestone. Particularly where there is no preschool, many children enter nursery school, kindergarten, or the first year of academic work with only a minimum of experience with books, pencils, and crayons, and with hardly any idea of how they should behave. For the child with poor

Chart 3-2
Sample Fine Motor Milestones

2 yrs.	turns pages of a book one at a time
	places two or more objects neatly in a row
	can string large beads with shoelace
	turns door knob, unscrews lids
2½ yrs.	overgrasps and overreleases
	holds object (pencil) in hand instead of fist
3 yrs.	closes fist and wiggles thumb
	can fold a piece of paper lengthwise and crosswise along a dotted line
	exhibits good wrist rotation
	snips with scissors
3½ yrs.	moves fingers with agility
	completes two-piece puzzle
	brings thumb into opposition and touches thumb to two or four fingers on the same hand
4 yrs.	brings thumb into opposition with each finger on both right and left hands
	completes three-piece puzzle
	cuts with scissors fairly well
4½ yrs.	completes seven-piece puzzle
5 yrs.	can pluck a dozen pellets, one by one, drop into a bottle with speed and accuracy, usually with preferred hand
	can wind thread on a bobbin
	can manipulate clay into balls and other shapes

fine motor control, the teacher must ask, "How much opportunity and experience has this child had in these activities?" The lack of hand dominance, for example, is not necessarily an early predictor of learning disabilities.

The child who has problems with tasks requiring fine motor development may try to avoid them if the teacher does not give enough opportunities to do them successfully. Such children may also prefer to do tasks requiring gross motor skills, sometimes to the extent that they are labeled hyperactive or learning disabled.

Children with fine motor development problems should be screened for vision problems. A child with poor visual acuity from birth will not be aware of or communicate the problem but may show it in specific fine motor behaviors. For example, the use of utensils, drinking from a cup or glass, pouring from a pitcher, unbuttoning and buttoning, zipping, snapping, lacing, and tying shoes all require eye-hand coordination as well as control and strength for fine motor movements. As with other skills, fine motor skills are integrated with the growth and development of the whole child.

PERCEPTUAL DEVELOPMENT

Perceptual development is related to vision and hearing. Because a separate chapter is devoted to each of these topics, this section will be relatively brief.

Vision. Knoblock and Pasamanick (1974) stated that seeing cannot be isolated from children's postures, manual skills, coordination, intelligence, or even their personalities. Several of the most significant milestones in the early development of vision will be discussed below.

What are amblyopia and strabismus?

One of the most important of these milestones is the coordinated movement of both eyes at 6 months (12 weeks, according to Knoblock and Pasamanick, 1974). If the two eyes fail to move in coordination, they may appear to be crossed (one or both looking in toward the nose) or divergent (one or both looking out to the side). This condition is usually called *strabismus*.

Because the brain receives two uncoordinated visual images, one from each eye, most children with strabismus see "double" (two of everything). The brain will not tolerate double vision for long, and it suppresses the image being sent by the weaker eye. This is called *amblyopia* or "lazy eye blindness." The result is the loss of depth perception. At 12 months, children without depth perception may persistently fail to come in contact with the object they are reaching toward. Although these children tend to learn other ways to compensate for the lack of depth perception, they may fall down very frequently in learning to walk. At a later age, this vision problem may cause the child to miss the cup when pouring water from a pitcher or walk into the door frame instead of through the doorway. These problems are not always recognized as visual.

Typically, the young child with strabismus can be helped; surgery, eye exercises, patching, or prescriptive lenses may be recommended, depending on the cause of the condition. These remedial techniques, however, become progressively less effective the longer treatment is postponed. The longer suppression goes untreated, the more difficult the restoration of normal visual functioning. Reinforcement of bad visual habits can eventually reduce the chances for attaining full vision and straight, fully coordinated eyes (Windsor and Hurtt, 1974).

Strabismus is both identifiable and preventable in the early years. The National Society to Prevent Blindness, Inc. (79 Madison Avenue, New York, NY 10016) will send you a Home Eye Test for Preschoolers free of charge on request. It is intended for use by parents. Screening for strabismus is even less demanding than writing a letter. One need simply be aware of the 6-month milestone for conjugate eye movements.

Most newborn babies cannot see well. About 80 percent of all babies are born *hyperopic* (farsighted), 5 percent are *myopic* (nearsighted), and about 15 percent have normal visual acuity (Vaughan and Asbury, 1980). As babies grow, their eyes grow and change shape, too. As a result, visual acuity changes may be very rapid in the early years of life.

The development of blind and visually handicapped children who do not receive early education shows us that vision problems can affect the development of other skills. The areas most seriously affected by early lack of vision are gross and fine motor development. Specifically, the related actions of reaching out to objects and attaining independent locomotion are significantly delayed in blind babies. One reason is that they cannot see behaviors being performed by others and as a result cannot model their own movements.

In her work with blind infants, Fraiberg (1975) described efforts to substitute sound cues for visual cues to elicit reaching out and mobility. Theoretically, locating something by sound operates by allowing the listener to interpret very subtle differences in the times at which sounds coming from the left or right reach each ear. However, when sound sources are directly in front or directly behind a listener, their precise location cannot be detected without the additional cues provided by head movement. Similarly, neither distances nor azimuth (up-down) positions can be detected without head movements, even by normal individuals. As a result, the sound-making toys that may be used to induce reaching out and movement by blind infants are of limited use and may take a long time to provide the desired effect.

Adelson and Fraiberg (1975) reported that blind babies in their early intervention program achieved postural milestones (elevation on arms in prone position; sitting and standing) within the norms established for sighted children. However, the blind infants were characterized by delays in initiating their own mobility. Interestingly, hand regard, which appears at approximately 4 months of age, is noted in blind as well as sighted infants (Bower, 1977; Illingworth, 1972). Hand regard is the process in which infants hold their hands in front of their faces and appear to be studying all aspects of the fingers and hands. It does not apparently require visual stimulation, however. Like the early babbling of infants, this behavior is "built-in."

Vision also helps develop the body image, a central aspect of the child's self-concept. Through vision, infants and young children achieve coordination and control of their movement (Barraga, 1978). Because blind babies are not reinforced by seeing their own movements, they often become quiet, passive, and undemanding; these behaviors are often mistakenly interpreted by parents as qualities of a "good" baby. Understandably, parents of blind infants are also often overprotective, which leads to deficits in experience and to immature social-emotional development.

Research has shown that blind children often have severe delays in cognitive development (Stephens, 1978). Much of our learning really depends on vision. For example, some of the important early milestones of cognitive development are based on the knowledge that objects continue to exist even when they are out of sight (object permanence). The appropriate manipulation of objects, the mimicry of domestic activities, and other forms of manipulation and imitation depend very heavily on being able to see.

A further example of how much learning depends on vision is the early development of social-emotional skills. Mothers of blind infants do not experience eye contact with their infants and may have difficulty reading their infants' responses. At the same time, blind infants do not have access to their mothers' smiles and visual responses. Recent research (Rogers and Puchalski, 1984) has documented the differences between the mother–child interactions of sighted and visually impaired infants. These differences show the need for early childhood educators to help both the mothers and their infants to develop strong and positive patterns of interaction.

What are "verbalisms"?

Problems in communication skills are also often noted in the visually handicapped population. Cutsforth (1932) coined the term "verbalism" to describe the use of words for which blind children could not have a firsthand understanding — color words, for example. Young blind children typically learn these verbal associations by rote memorization; they learn that sighted people label the grass as green, the sky as blue, the sun as yellow, and so on. However, teachers must be aware that blind children can develop excessive dependence on verbal learning if they aren't given opportunities for concrete experiences with their other senses.

> In John's first-grade class at the school for the blind, the topic of discussion was nature. As was often the case, John seemed to be more advanced than his classmates in his knowledge of vocabulary related to the topic. While other children reviewed terms such as "grass," "trees," "shrubs," and "leaves," John recited a long list that included the words "bark," "branches," "trunk," and "stems."
>
> At lunchtime John's teacher asked him to accompany her to another building to collect some materials for the afternoon. As they walked, John recited the directions for their walk and the number of stairs they encountered. Basing her actions on a suspicion, the teacher led John off the normal route, through the grass and toward a large tree. She placed his hands on the tree trunk and asked John what he was touching. John could not answer the question. He had apparently learned his advanced vocabulary without ever actually exploring a tree with his hands!

In dealing with blind children, teachers often depend heavily on verbal explanation and description. The value of providing blind children with firsthand experiences, which give information via the senses of touch, hearing, taste, and smell, cannot be overestimated. On the other hand, the use of language or concepts that are visually oriented (e.g., "Do you see what I mean?") should not be limited in teaching visually handicapped children. As Warren (1977, p. 161) suggested, "The goal should be to bring the blind child to the point of maximal use of the language used by the surrounding culture so that language can aid in meaningful and useful social interaction, in behavioral self-direction, and in progress in the educational system."

Hearing. What young normal children hear around them determines in large part what language they will produce. If, as infants, they hear French spoken, then French is the language they will gradually begin to speak. If they hear English, they will speak English. If what they hear is muffled and unclear and makes no sense to them, they will gradually stop paying attention to sound. This causes a serious delay in the development of language skills. Without early intervention efforts, young profoundly deaf children often cease babbling entirely and become quite silent. The same principle that applied to amblyopia applies here: What you don't use, you lose.

Some of the most important milestones in the development of auditory perception in the first 2 years contribute to normal development in several other areas. For example, auditory *localization* skills develop during the first year. The ability to identify correctly the source of sound helps the child learn associations between the sound and events in the environment. By 3 months of age, infants turn their heads and eyes in the general direction of a sound source. By 4 months of age, infants who hear the sound of the spoon in their bowls anticipate being fed. These single and combined skills improve gradually; an awareness of them can help parents and others identify children whose problems would not otherwise be noticed until the children fail to talk at the usual time. Normal-hearing infants localize at 7 months using a curving arc. That is, they turn their heads in a two-stage motion, first to the side, and then up or down. By 8 months they can without hesitation turn diagonally and directly to a sound source. The associations built in this way are the basis on which later cognitive and communication skills are learned. By 15 months of age, children combine their newly acquired motor skills with their auditory localization skills to actively seek out and investigate sounds.

The infant's own movements produce sounds, as do the actions of others. The normally developing infant experiments with producing sounds by using his or her voice and by using objects. These produce auditory as well as social consequences. By the age of 18 months, young normal-hearing children swing rhythmically with their whole bodies in response to music (Knoblock and Pasamanick, 1974). Later, children can recognize melodies, sing songs and parts of songs, match and grade tones and sound blocks, and participate in rhythmic play. As a result, their rapport with their social environment is strengthened. When a child cannot hear, some of these activities may be imitated through vision, but their meaning and association to sounds may not be recognized.

Young children with significant hearing impairments may also show subtle problems in gross motor development. This is caused partly by the loss of association between sounds and movement and partly by the loss of auditory feedback on their own movements. Moreover, the problems that cause hearing loss often affect the semicircular canals as well, which can affect the body's ability to balance.

What skill is most affected as a result of a hearing impairment?

Communication is the area of development most seriously affected by hearing impairment in the early years. Methods have been developed to help young deaf children develop communication skills. These include the use of appropriate amplification devices to allow deaf children to use their residual hearing. For reviews of these educational programs and methods, see the

TECHNOLOGY IN ACTION

Five-year-old Tracy Husted doesn't really care that she has made medical history. She is too busy enjoying her escape from a prison of silence. Two years ago Tracy lost her hearing after a meningitis infection destroyed sensitive hair cells in both inner ears. Doctors told her parents that she would never be able to hear again.

Tracy's happy, talkative, bright childhood began to crumble. Unable to hear her own voice, the most important reinforcement for normal speech, her words became unintelligible. She lost interest in her surroundings and withdrew into her silent world.

But 6 months later she became the youngest person to receive a cochlear implant, the closest thing yet developed to an artificial ear. With electrodes implanted in the inner ear to take the place of the destroyed hair cells, the device electrically stimulates the hearing nerve, sending out signals that the brain interprets as sounds.

Now Tracy can hear such sounds as her dog barking and her cat meowing. . . . She plays with other children, and she attends pre-kindergarten classes at a regular school. . . . Most importantly, Tracy will turn around when someone calls her name, and she recognizes a number of spoken words, her mother said.

Although doctors at the House Ear Institute in Los Angeles, where the device was implanted, had warned Mrs. Husted that Tracy probably would not be able to understand speech, she does understand some phrases, even when she is not facing the speaker, Mrs. Husted said. "The implant has helped her tremendously," she said. "Tracy doesn't act like a deaf child. She wants to learn to play the piano."

The device is a single-channel stimulator that stimulates the hearing nerve at one point, enabling a patient to hear many different environmental noises, such as sirens, running water, alarms, footsteps, and ringing telephones. Although the patient cannot easily recognize speech he or she can hear sounds produced by voices, which is an invaluable aid in helping someone to lip read.

Some of the newer implants have 4 to 12 simulator channels. Because of the ability to stimulate the hearing nerve at more than one site, a wider range of sounds can be produced, especially sounds that can make many spoken words understandable. Cochlear implants are so promising that the American Medical Association passed a resolution endorsing them as an acceptable procedure for people who are profoundly deaf. "Cochlear implants are unquestionably one of the most important developments in ear surgery in this century," said Dr. Brian McCabe, chief of otolaryngology at the University of Iowa Hospitals and Clinics.

From an article by Ronald Kotulak in the Lexington Herald-Leader, *February 8, 1983.*

articles by Horton (1976), Moores (1976), Northcott (1973a, b), and Simmons-Martin (1981).

Along with the delay or lack of communication skills in young hearing-impaired children come problems in conceptual, social-emotional, and self-help skills. The meaning of sounds in the environment is often misunderstood or missed completely by young children with impaired hearing. Furthermore, because they cannot express themselves through language, they often resort to physical means to express their desires. Teachers of hearing-impaired preschool children are frequently asked whether their students are also emotionally disturbed. This reaction highlights the importance of teaching deaf children the language necessary to express their moods and feelings. The lack of adequate language for understanding and expression, combined with the common overprotective attitudes of parents, can cause serious problems in the development of independence and self-help skills in young hearing-impaired children. (For a developmental model applied to problems of deafness, see Schlesinger and Meadow, 1972.)

CONCEPTUAL DEVELOPMENT

A concept can be a thought, an opinion, an idea, or a mental image. The word "concept" can also be used to refer to the attributes a class or group of things have in common (Good, 1959). Red, yellow, and blue, for example, have in common the fact that they are all colors. There are other kinds of concepts, too. The concept of *object permanence* is the knowledge that objects continue to exist even when they can no longer be seen (Wadsworth, 1978). The concept of *motor meaning* is the knowledge that an object is usually used for a particular purpose, such as cups for drinking or hair brushes for grooming.

Concepts are useful because they help us bring order to the things in our environment (Sigel, 1975). They reduce the ambiguity in our lives and allow us to function more efficiently, because we do not have to relearn something when we first encounter another member of that class or concept.

Concepts are associated with and expressed in observable behaviors. For example, infants suck, look around, listen, make noises, grasp, and move their trunks and limbs. Between the ages of 4 and 8 months, they learn that their actions can produce effects. They can, for example, make the mobiles over their cribs move by hitting them or shaking their cribs. As a result, the concept that they learn is *cause and effect* (Sigel, 1975).

The acquisition of object permanence can usually be seen in infants between 9 and 12 months of age. They are able to find an object that they have seen previously even after it has been completely covered.

Infants who have the concept of motor meaning (also usually in the last quarter of the first year) go through the appropriate motions (such as shaking head or arms) on seeing an object (such as a rattle). In the first half of the second year, the child learns a more advanced behavior representing the concept of motor meaning and attempts to activate a mechanical toy after seeing it demonstrated. In the second half of that year, children try to activate mechanical toys even before they see a demonstration. At the same time, they imitate absent models, as when they sweep the floor or try other domestic activities in playing house.

Matching activities also illustrate the acquisition of concepts. Some of the milestones in the sequence of matching skills in early conceptual development are (1) matching familiar objects, such as two balls; (2) matching objects by their use, such as a toy baby bottle and a baby doll or a key and a door; (3) matching colors; and, finally, (4) matching pictures. This sequence can be helpful in designing instructional activities for young children and those who are having problems in matching activities.

Why is the "range of reaction" so important?

As a result of studies of the ages at which children from different cultures achieved object permanence, Hunt, Paraskevopoulos, Schickedanz, and Uzgiris (1975) introduced the concept of "range of reaction." The range of reaction is the span between the highest and the lowest average ages at which children raised under different conditions achieve a particular milestone. For example, the range of reaction in achieving object permanence is 109 weeks, or over 2 years. An understanding of range of reaction helps one develop some perspective on development. Inherent in range of reaction are the assumptions that environmental conditions and intervention can hasten or retard the accomplishment of conceptual milestones and that some children develop concepts sooner than others.

A relationship between conceptual and social development was demonstrated by Bell's (1970) research, which introduced the notion of *person permanence*. Bell's study showed that for most babies, person permanence, the knowledge that people continue to exist even when they are out of sight, precedes object permanence. Thus, the quality of parent-infant interactions contributes significantly to the infant's acquisition of early conceptual milestones. Bell's findings also illustrate the relationship between milestones in different areas: Person permanence could just as easily be categorized as a social milestone as a conceptual one.

Teachers who work with young children should be aware that matching colors is easier than naming colors, as evidenced by the fact that at 3 or 3½ years of age, children can match several colors but can name only one or two. Similarly, counting by rote is easier than counting objects. Three-year-old children can usually count by rote to ten. But it is not until they reach about 4 or even 4½ years that they can count four objects and tell how many. An excellent description of the warning signs of academic difficulties is in Simner's (1982) article updating the profile of the kindergarten child at risk for later academic failure.

Problems in conceptual development have been reported in brain-injured children and children with communicative disorders (Johnson, 1975), in deaf children (Hicks, 1975), in learning disabled children (McCarthy, 1975), in visually handicapped children (Stephens, 1978; Umsted, 1975), and in children with mental retardation (Moss and Mayer, 1975). Safford (1978) reported that the mentally retarded children he studied proceeded through the same developmental progression as nonretarded youngsters, although their rates of progress and their levels of highest attainment were different.

Students interested in additional literature on concept development should examine the works of DeVries and Kohlberg (1977), Furth (1970), Kamii (1973), Sigel (1975), and Wadsworth (1978).

SOCIAL-EMOTIONAL DEVELOPMENT

Children's social behaviors are developed through interactions with people and other parts of the environment (Corter, 1977). The components of these behaviors that the child internalizes are referred to as "feelings" (Lewis and Rosenblum, 1978). As young children develop, so does their ability to think and to use language to interact with other people in their environment. Thus, conceptual development and communication skills are often closely linked with social-emotional development. In fact, those who find parenting difficult often express frustration precisely because their infants cannot use language to communicate their thoughts and feelings.

Following are some of the major milestones in the social-emotional development of young children.

At about one month of age, newborns stop crying when they see their mother or hear her approaching. At 2 months, they smile in response to a smile, a voice, or physical care. By 4 or 5 months, they react positively to being placed in a sitting position; their gross motor development has not allowed much sitting before this age. At 5 months, the infants begin to show emotional responses closely tied to the situation; for example, the infant may vocalize displeasure if a toy is taken away or if insufficient attention is given. By 7 months, distress has become differentiated into fear, disgust, and anxiety, while delight has evolved into elation and affection. At 9 months, infants play games of give and take; at 10 months, peek-a-boo is very popular.

One-year-olds may compete with others for parental attention; they also repeat performances that are laughed at or praised. At 15 months, they begin to claim possessions and to differentiate between "yours" and "mine." Children in our culture usually engage in parallel play at age 2 and imaginative play (make believe) at age 3. They begin social or cooperative play at 3½, the same age at which they become less attached to favorite objects. At 4 they often begin to participate in dramatic play and organized or competitive games. At this time, they seem to become more interested in playing with others. Four-year-olds will share their toys, although sometimes it is only with their imaginary friends; they may also tell stories (or fabricate them) and go on errands outside home. While four-year-olds are not yet fully socialized, they are far from the infants they once were in their ability to interact in socially acceptable ways (Cooper and Holt, 1982).

What difficulties are encountered in evaluating social-emotional development?

The social-emotional area of development is the most difficult one to evaluate objectively. It is very difficult to define "normal" social-emotional behavior, notwithstanding the generalizations discussed above.

Definitions and descriptions of the different levels of play have been changing in recent years (e.g., Garwood, 1982) and more research has focused on the patterns of play in groups of handicapped and nonhandicapped children (e.g., Field, Roseman, De Stefano, and Koewler, 1982; Rogers and Puchalski,

1984). In addition, there is much controversy surrounding the ages of achievement of many social-emotional milestones.

Because of the often conflicting definitions and descriptions, special educators working with children who may be socially or emotionally disturbed are faced with an especially difficult task. On the one hand, they do not want to apply a label such as "emotionally disturbed" or "socially maladjusted," prematurely, because such a label can become a self-fulfilling prophecy. On the other hand, children with real problems need to be diagnosed and labeled before they can receive special services.

Behavioral problems in young handicapped children often result from frustration caused by another problem. The behavioral problems can often be relieved by eliminating the frustration. For example, teaching young deaf children the language they need to express themselves may help keep them from acting inappropriately.

Safford (1978) described several symptoms that could indicate a social or emotional problem. Each symptom could be temporary or could indicate a serious problem. Safford emphasized the need for preschool teachers to record behaviors objectively if they are to develop effective intervention strategies. Symptoms that may indicate problems are (1) great difficulty in separating from parents, (2) extreme withdrawal, (3) extreme aggressive behavior, and (4) infantile patterns of behavior. Beginning school may cause a child to behave mildly abnormally in any of these areas. For example, nursery school teachers often notice regressions in toilet training of children separated from their parents for the first time. In this area, as in others, teachers need to be able to observe and systematically document children's behaviors; they must also be acutely aware of how their responses reinforce or discourage a behavior. The most obvious approach to take is simply to tell the child what is expected of him or her.

Additional information related to this topic is covered in Chapter 10, in Garfunkel's (1976) review, and in Enzer and Goin (1978). An excellent resource for information on play and development is the October (1982) issue of *Topics in Early Childhood Special Education*.

COMMUNICATION

Communication may be defined as "the passing of meaning from one source to another" (DuBose, 1978). Subjects considered under this general heading are receptive language (understanding), expressive language (speaking), and speech (the articulation of specific speech sounds). It is important to understand the distinctions among these three areas to identify accurately young children's problems.

Major milestones in the early normal development of speech and language and in communication disorders will be presented in detail in the next chapter. For this reason, only a few fundamental concepts will be discussed here.

Receptive language development precedes and exceeds expressive language development. By the time children begin to use their first words, they have already been listening for approximately 10 to 12 months. This "listening age" (Northcott, 1972) is important because of the number of skills that must develop before the child begins to use words. Several skills, such as auditory localization and auditory association, were described earlier as occurring in the period before the appearance of the first word.

Additional processes also support the early development of language. The infant must be skilled in *auditory discrimination,* the ability to distinguish between the sounds heard, including very subtle differences in speech sounds; and in *auditory memory,* the ability to remember sequences of auditory events, both at the level of individual speech sounds ("dog" versus "god") and at the level of entire sentences. As you can see, the comprehension and interpretation of language are complex receptive processes, and the rate at which they develop helps determine when the child begins to speak.

When children have problems in expressive language, their teachers should be able to analyze their difficulties by referring to the normal milestones of development. The following questions should also be considered: (1) Is the child's language adequate in quantity, considering the child's chronological age? (2) Is the child's intelligibility appropriate with respect to chronological age? If the teacher cannot understand a child's utterances, the problem may be the teacher's limited experience with children of this age and development, and not with the child's manner of speaking. A reasonable third question is: How familiar am I with the speech and language of children of this age?

How can disorders in communication affect other skills?

Disorders in communication are common accompaniments to other disabilities. Communication problems may in turn adversely influence the development of other skills in a variety of ways. For example, for most instruction, children need to be able to understand and follow verbal directions. When children begin school, their ability to understand language and concepts becomes increasingly important. They may become socially isolated while other young children who do not have communication problems become more and more verbal in their play.

When children fail to acquire language normally, their families often begin speaking to them less frequently. The substitution of gestures and nonverbal forms of communication might help, but many of the same children who don't understand oral language also have difficulty interpreting nonverbal symbols such as facial expressions and vocal inflections (Johnson, 1975). As a result, such children may not be able to go on errands that involve verbal requests or the use of a telephone. All of these problems tend to retard the growth of the communication-impaired child's independence from the family. As was true of the other areas of development, a problem in developing communication skills affects all aspects of a child's development.

SELF-HELP SKILLS

The ability to care for oneself is fundamental in achieving independence and self-sufficiency. The collected norms for self-help skills have been divided into those related to eating; dressing, bathing, and grooming; and toileting. These will be discussed in three sections.

Eating. The earliest self-help behaviors are those related to feeding and eating. When the cheek is lightly touched, normal newborns turn their head toward the stimulus and purse their lips (rooting reflex). Normal newborns also have sucking and swallowing reflexes. The sucking reflex is lost when spoon or cup feeding is begun (Knoblock and Pasamanick, 1974). The sight of food or the sounds of food preparation produce excitement and anticipation in the normal 4-month-old. By 6 months of age, biting and chewing begin to replace the earlier mouthing of objects or foods (Knoblock and Pasamanick, 1974). Finger foods are usually introduced when the child can sit and grasp objects (see Chart 3-3).

Chart 3-3
Milestones for Eating Skills

Birth	reflexes: rooting, sucking, swallowing, gagging
2 mo.	sucks and swallows liquids from spoon
4 mo.	anticipates on sight of food or sound of food preparation
6 mo.	feeds self cracker, begins to bite and chew
8 mo.	chews small lumps
10 mo.	finger feeds self part of meal with ease
1 yr.	holds cup, two hands
14 mo.	chews table food
15 mo.	grasps spoon, inserts into mouth, uses wrist rotation, spilling much
1 ½ yrs.	manages spoon well, a little spilling
	uses cup (two hands), drinks without spilling
21 mo.	replaces cup after use
23 mo.	requests food when hungry, water when thirsty
2 yrs.	holds and uses small glass, one hand
	uses spoon well, no spilling
3 yrs.	uses fork for spearing
	spreads butter/jam on bread with knife
4 yrs.	uses knife for pulling meat apart
	helps set the table
	pours from pitcher
5 yrs.	cuts with knife
6 yrs.	sets table without help

According to Knoblock and Pasamanick, the movements of eating (biting, chewing, control of salivary overflow, swallowing with a minimum of air) and drinking (command of lips, tongue, and jaws) are well differentiated and well coordinated by 18 months of age. By 5 years, children can handle a knife and fork quite well, although they may need occasional help.

During the second or third year of life, the rapid growth that characterized early infancy declines. Children gain weight at a slower rate, and their metabolic rates decline. Many children begin to refuse to eat at around this time, and it is during this period that behavior problems often begin (Lowrey, 1973). These problems can be exacerbated by excessive parental concern over the child's decreased appetite. Although not clearly established, there is some evidence that learned attitudes about food can cause overweight and obesity, which in turn can affect the development of gross motor skills and social acceptance by peers. In addition, overweight children often have weight problems as adults (Powell, 1981).

Dressing, bathing and grooming. Dressing, bathing, and grooming skills begin to develop in young normal children at about 2 years of age. At this age, children begin to assume more responsibility for themselves, although they are still somewhat dependent on their care givers. Their earlier passiveness begins to be replaced by more active participation in bathing and getting into and out of their clothing.

Norms for these areas of development are among those most influenced by

Many early childhood special education programs provide instruction on the use of eating utensils.

cultural context. Keep that fact in mind as you read the following summary of early milestones in the development of dressing, bathing, and grooming skills.

Undressing is easier than dressing. As early as 3 months of age, infants begin to tug at their clothing. They pull off their socks at 18 months, their shoes at 2 years, and pullover garments at 4 years. In contrast, they put their socks, pants, and shoes on at 4 years, and pullover garments at 5 years (Bleck, 1982). Similarly, unfastening appears before fastening. Buttons on the front and side can be undone at 3 years of age, and in the back at 5½. In comparison, a series of buttons on the front can be fastened at 3½ years of age. In the back, buttons can be fastened by the time the child is a few months past 6 years. The norms associated with fastening and unfastening zippers are very similar to those for buttons (Bleck, 1982).

Bathing independently requires some skills from other areas of development. For example, turning faucets on and off requires wrist rotation, listed in Chart 3-2 as characteristic of 3-year-olds. Thus, although many children cooperate in washing themselves once they are in the bath, preparing a bath is not usually done by the child before age 3 or 3½. By the time children are 4½ years old, they should be washing and drying their hands and faces well. Also by this time, they should be able to brush their teeth. By 6 years of age, they blow their noses without assistance, and by 7 they brush their teeth routinely. Most children comb their hair by age 7½; by 8 years of age, they wash their ears and bathe independently (Bleck, 1982).

When should toilet training start?

Toileting. Although wide variations appear in the literature, children are considered physiologically capable of inhibiting bowel and bladder release by the time they are approximately 15 months old. By 18 months of age they can indicate that their pants are wet. They use their newly developed ability to express themselves to tell about the product of urination or a bowel movement after the fact. Gradually they begin to associate internal sensation with language; at approximately 2 years they tell as they perform the act. The next stage is to tell before they act, but not soon enough to be taken to a toilet. Finally, they tell of a need for the toilet in advance. The level of maturity for toilet training can be estimated by measuring and recording the length of time between one bowel movement or urination and the next. After a few days a pattern will emerge. Children are ready for toilet training if they are dry for periods of 2 hours or more. Unless they are dry for at least 2 hours at a time, they will not have a sensation of relief as they use the toilet. Some of the milestones in toileting are summarized below.

For the first 4 or so months of life, infants may not show any delay between feeding and elimination. By around 7 months of age, they may stay dry for one- or two-hour intervals, and by 10 months, they may remain dry after a short nap. By approximately 18 months of age, children may respond verbally when asked if they want to go to the toilet. By about 2 years of age, they may stay dry at night if taken to the toilet. By 3 years of age, they use routine times for elimination, and by 3 ½, they attempt to wipe themselves, usually without success. Considering the milestones in dressing, you can see that by 4 years of age, children are able to manage their own clothes; at this time, they go to the bathroom alone. Five-year-olds toilet themselves, have few accidents, may still need reminding during the day, and have only one bowel movement a day.

Disturbances in toilet training may appear with the beginning of school attendance or during other periods of anxiety or excitement. The progress of toilet training may be slowed if the child finds it is more rewarding not to be toilet trained because of the play and social interaction surrounding the changing of diapers (Hart, 1974).

Since toilet training is as much a parental activity as a child's, parental readiness should also be assessed. This may be done by exploring parents' attitudes about past toilet training efforts, the advantages of toilet training, the time investment required, and the convenience. Toilet training can be accomplished more quickly and easily if both parents and child are ready, as determined by the criteria we have mentioned.

For exceptional young children, the appearances of milestones of development in each of the seven areas we have described may not proceed on schedule. Although achievements in one area may progress normally, a handicapping condition may affect achievements in other areas. Bearing in mind that the ages for attaining milestones are to be considered guides, not exact criterion ages, both parents and professionals can identify children with developmental delays be being familiar with the sequences of normal early development. If children are identified early, services can be provided to overcome the developmental delays and minimize their ill effects.

When parents know their child has a handicap, they often alter their expectations of the child's progress in ways that are detrimental to the child's attaining full potential. Both parents and professionals can learn to differentiate between what exceptional children are unable to perform because of their age and what they cannot do because of their impairment. A knowledge of normal early development and familiarity with the effects of a variety of handicapping conditions form a solid basis for working with exceptional young children.

PROBE 3-2
Human Growth and Development

1. T F All children develop at the same rate.

2. T F Developmental information:
   _____ may be used to screen children.

_____ may be used to assess handicapped children.

_____ may be used to build preschool curricula.

_____ is not observable or measurable.

_____ is incompatible with professions other than early education.

_____ may be applied to low-functioning children.

3. T F Learning to walk upright is not only socially reinforcing, it also opens new horizons and brings countless new objects within easier reach of the young child.

4. T F The coordinated movements of the two eyes are normally established by 6 months of age.

5. T F Beginning to attend school is often sufficient cause for mild forms of abnormal social-emotional behaviors.

6. T F Disorders in communication are uncommon in young handicapped children.

7. T F The child's refusal to eat during the second or third year of life is caused by a change in his temperament at this time.

8. T F All children reach the physical maturity required for toilet training at the same time, 12 months of age.

IDENTIFYING YOUNG CHILDREN WHO NEED SPECIAL SERVICES

You should be able to define and give examples of activities used to identify young children who need special services: casefinding, screening, diagnosis, and assessment.

As services for young exceptional children and their families are expanded, many states are involved in efforts to locate and identify this target population. However, these efforts present some unique problems and furthermore, there is often confusion about the terminology used in these efforts. The following definitions and descriptions may provide helpful clarification.

CASEFINDING, CHILD FIND, AND EARLY IDENTIFICATION

How do case-finding and child find differ?

The term *casefinding* refers to the activities designed to make initial contact with a target population and increase the public's awareness of the services that are available (Cross, 1977). Casefinding activities can include circulating brochures, presenting radio or television announcements, preparing newspaper articles, sending notes home with children already in programs, making personal contacts with agencies (including health, civic, religious, and community organizations), and door-to-door canvassing. The relative effectiveness of each of these approaches depends on a variety of factors, but it is crucial that the target population be defined (ages of children, types of handicapping conditions, geographic boundaries) before casefinding efforts begin. Zehrbach (1975) reported that no one approach is effective in all areas.

The term *child find* is applied to many of these same activities when they are implemented by states and local educational agencies as a result of federal legislation requiring that all handicapped children be identified and served (Safford, 1978). Each state has its own definitions of handicapping conditions and ages of eligibility for services. Thus, child find efforts and activities, particularly those related to very young children, vary from one place to another.

Identification is the process of establishing an awareness that a problem exists (Hayden and Edgar, 1977). Certain kinds of problems or potential problems can be identified very early. For example, certain conditions such as Tay-Sachs disease and Down's syndrome may be detected during pregnancy by *amniocentesis*. This procedure involves testing the amniotic fluid surrounding the fetus to determine whether a problem exists. Another example of early identification is *genetic counseling*, which may make prospective parents aware of risk factors indicated by their own genetic makeup or histories. Using this information, prospective parents can decide whether or not to risk the birth of a child who may be disabled.

Beck (1977) stated that 6.8 percent of all handicapped children could and should be identified at birth or shortly after birth. Examples of conditions identifiable at birth are genetic disorders such as galactosemia and phenylketonuria (PKU), which are identified by urine tests. (These will be explained in greater detail in Chapter 8.) The harmful effects of these two conditions can be avoided by special diets for the infants.

Some children develop disabilities through accidents, illnesses, or poisoning. Many young children have handicapping conditions that go unnoticed.

In the period between birth and school age, there are procedures to identify children who need special services, but they are not universally applied (Kakalik, Brewer, Dougherty, Fleischauer, and Genensky, 1973). Pediatricians (when they are consulted) often lack the time or techniques to notice developmental problems (Hayden, 1978). Thus, many children who could benefit from early identification do not receive the services they need. Suggestions to remedy this situation have included the establishment of a national registry for all births (Caldwell, 1976), the maintenance of "high risk" registries (Conference on Newborn Hearing Screening, 1971), and the use of public information programs and mass mandatory screening programs (Karnes and Zehrbach, 1977b).

SCREENING

Screening is the testing of a large number of children to identify those most likely to exhibit disabilities. The children who are identified as possibly having disabilities are then referred to a professional for a more in-depth assessment. Ideally, screening should be accomplished by administering a standardized, quick, easy-to-administer, and efficient assessment test (or tests) to the population being screened. This keeps the screening effort as economical as possible. It is also helpful if the screening instrument is acceptable not only to the professionals who do the follow-up, but also to parents and the general public. One example of a screening procedure is the urine test for PKU, mandated by law in many states. For young children a variety of screening instruments have been developed; one of the most well known is the *Denver Developmental Screening Test* (Frankenburg, Dodds, and Fandal, 1975). Lists and reviews of screening instruments are available elsewhere (Fallen and McGovern, 1978; Frankenburg and Camp, 1975; Garwood et al., 1979; Hayden and Edgar, 1977; Lerner et al., 1981; Safford, 1978).

What issues are involved in conducting screening programs?

There are several important issues to consider in developing a screening program. Prior to the passage of PL 94-142, some used to argue that if the necessary diagnostic follow-up personnel and educational services are not available to help suspected or identified children, the screening effort should not be undertaken. On the other hand, current screening efforts are supported by legislation based on the notion that if the number of children needing services is not known, funds for their services are not likely to be allocated.

Particular attention should be given to the accuracy of the instruments selected for use in a screening program. Obviously, if the screening instrument does not accurately select the target group from the larger population, it will not provide accurate data on the number of children needing services.

Other important factors that help determine the value of a screening effort are (1) whether the condition being screened for improves with treatment, (2) whether early treatment improves the prognosis more than treatment at the usual time, and (3) whether the condition can be adequately diagnosed through the use of further tests. It is important to remember that when children are selected through the screening process (that is, they fail the screening test), their parents should be made aware of the need for further diagnosis before decisions are made about their suspected problems. If this is not done and the other factors we have mentioned are not considered, parents may be caused unnecessary anxiety. Screening should not result in the application of a label without further diagnostic study.

In 1967 the Early and Periodic Screening, Diagnosis, and Treatment (EPSDT) program was established by an amendment to Title 19 of the Social Security Act. The purpose of this legislation was to make these services available to all children eligible for Medicaid, up to age 21. The program began in 1972; in 1976, it was reported that of the 12 million eligible children, about 4.5 million were enrolled in EPSDT. There were wide variations from state to state in how this program was being run and in its quality (Special Report: Public Policy, NAEYC-EPSDT, 1976). The Child Health Assessment Act represents a more recent legislative effort to provide preventive health care services to children other than those from low-income families.

DIAGNOSIS

The major purpose of screening is to select those children in need of additional services. The next services needed for the child identified in a screening effort are diagnostic. The purposes of diagnosis are (1) to determine whether a problem exists and if it is serious enough to require remediation, and (2) to clarify the nature of the problem.

How should a diagnosis be performed?

Diagnosis is best carried out by a multidisciplinary team selected on the basis of the child's suspected problem. The team may include doctors, psychologists, social workers, teachers, and other education personnel. In performing the diagnosis, members of the team collect data in various ways about the child in question and examine the collected data to develop a comprehensive interpretation (Lerner et al., 1981). The exact diagnostic instruments used by members of the team, and the extent and duration of the process, are determined by their own decisions. Thus, the entire process is highly individualized and cannot be accomplished in a uniform way for all children. Also, teams differ in the extent to which they involve parents in the diagnostic process. The ultimate purpose of diagnosis of suspected educational problems is to determine what is hindering the development of the child and how best to help. Once the relevant information on the child's problem is collected and analyzed, a conference should be arranged with the parents to discuss placement and treatment options.

ASSESSMENT

After a child is placed in a program, educational assessment is used to determine (1) specific strengths and weaknesses in the child's abilities; (2) the child's level of functioning in a number of developmental areas, and (3) the child's learning characteristics. This information allows teachers to plan specific instructional objectives in the child's curriculum. The use of assessment (including diagnostic) information ensures that a child's overall program is based on consideration of individual needs, strengths, and weaknesses. An adequate educational assessment should examine observable behaviors in a comprehensive manner, using several different devices and approaches from a variety of sources. Adapting assessment items to suit the child's needs is another way to minimize the distortion of results (Bagnato and Neisworth, 1981).

Assessment can involve the use of criterion-referenced measures, norm-referenced measures, Piagetian devices, anecdotal records, daily logs, observational records, and video tapes.

How should teachers be involved in early identification?

The importance of identifying exceptional children as early as possible has been emphasized throughout this chapter. Teachers of young children in early childhood programs should be a part of this early identification process. According to Safford (1978) teachers should (1) be familiar with normal developmental processes, (2) know the symptoms of specific handicapping conditions, (3) be skilled observers and recorders of individual children's behaviors, (4) be able to use informal procedures to diagnose educational problems, (5) be familiar with and able to use resource persons in the community and the school, and (6) be able to communicate effectively and continuously with parents. Teachers of young children see them longer and more continuously than other professionals, such as pediatricians or psychologists; although they cannot make final diagnoses, their efforts to identify children with problems are very important. In many cases, their efforts to develop curricula that suit the special needs of handicapped children have proven effective.

PROBE 3-3
Identifying Young Children Who Need Special Services

1. Describe five methods of casefinding.

2. How may certain disabilities be identified before or at the time of birth of the child?

3. T F The purpose of screening young children is to complete diagnoses of their disabilities; this may be done through the screening procedures.

4. Give one reason why the accuracy of the screening instrument is an important consideration.

5. Give one example of a condition that may be screened for at the preschool level. What are the benefits to the identified children?

6. Why are teachers in a good position to screen the children in their early childhood programs?

7. Name 3 assessment procedures commonly used with early childhood screening programs.

EDUCATION AND TREATMENT OPTIONS

You should be able to describe various educational provisions for young exceptional children.

The process of casefinding, screening, diagnosis, and assessment culminate in the preparation of individual educational programs (IEPs) for young exceptional children. These programs are implemented and delivered to children and their families in many different ways. Only three of the most prevalent alternatives are discussed in the following section. For more detailed information, you are referred to texts by Allen, Holm, and Schiefelbusch (1978); Bagnato and Neisworth (1981); Far West Laboratory for Educational Research and Development (1980); Jordan, Hayden, Karnes, and Wood (1977); Lerner et al., (1981); Meisels (1979); and Tjossem (1976).

CENTER-BASED SERVICE DELIVERY

What are the benefits of Center-based services?

Among educational programs developed for young children, center-based models (those in which services are provided in a central location) are the most numerous. The advantages of this method of providing early education services include exposure and access to a wide variety of toys, materials, other children, observation opportunities, specialized therapies, and other parents. Programs of this type also afford parents some time away from their handicapped child, and thus some respite from the problems involved (Linder, 1983). Among the existing programs, many tend to be for preschool children rather than infants. Center-based programs are particularly appropriate for those with relatively severe or multiple disabilities, who benefit most from the specialized equipment and personnel assembled at the central location (Karnes and Zehrbach, 1977a). Although staff members may only rarely visit the children's homes, parent participation at the center is considered important, and parents are encouraged to use at home what they've learned.

One example of a center-based program is the Model Preschool Center for

Handicapped Children at the University of Washington, mentioned earlier. This program serves children with Down's syndrome and other handicapped children of all ages, including the newborn and the very young. The Preschool Center is part of the Experimental Education Unit of the College of Education and the Child Development and Mental Retardation Center. Children in this program may be placed in one of several classrooms, depending on their needs and levels of functioning. Individual instruction is based on initial and ongoing assessment and behavioral information. Parents and staff work together to formulate each child's objectives (Hayden and Haring, 1976).

Another center-based program for young exceptional children and their families is the UNISTAPS Project in Minneapolis, Minnesota. This program serves hearing-impaired children in the public schools from birth onward. Parent involvement is also one of the strengths of this program (Freedman, Warner, and Cook, 1973).

CENTER- AND HOME-BASED SERVICE DELIVERY

Many programs provide services coordinated between an instructional center and children's homes. Parents may receive training at the center as well as home visits from teachers who conduct parent conferences, observe parent-child interactions, and educate parents about appropriate teaching methods. DeWeerd (1981) reported that in the last few years, many HCEEP model programs have added home-based components to their services.

The PEECH (Precise Early Education of Children with Handicaps) Program at the University of Illinois is a combined home- and center-based service delivery system. In Illinois, services to handicapped children from the age of 3 years are mandatory, so the program must meet state requirements for certification, size of class, length of school day, eligibility criteria, teacher-pupil ratio, and length of the school year. This program serves children who are mildly to moderately multiply handicapped.

The PEECH Program uses several different classrooms, each with a maximum of ten handicapped and five normal children, who act as models. This "reversed mainstreaming" model program is staffed with educators, psychologists, speech and language therapists, and social workers. Parents are encouraged to teach at home, attend parent group meetings, use the parent library and toy-lending library, speak at public gatherings, work with other parents, construct instructional materials, and make policies (Karnes and Zehrbach, 1977a and b).

The PEECH Program has been replicated in many states since it began. Research (Karnes, Kokotovic, and Shwedel, 1982) has shown that replication sites utilized a higher percentage of classroom components than family or administrative components. However, the progress of the children in the replication sites was essentially as good as for those in the demonstration site.

Another combined home- and center-based model is the Early Education Project at the Central Institute for the Deaf in St. Louis, Missouri. Here, a home demonstration center permits parents to simulate their normal daily routine and also meet with professionals for guidance. This program combines some of the advantages of the home-based with the center-based models of service delivery.

Other examples of combined center- and home-based programs include the Rutland Center in Athens, Georgia, the Chapel Hill Training Outreach Project in North Carolina, and the Preschool and Early Education Project (PEEP) in Starkville, Mississippi. More complete descriptions of these and other programs may be found in the text by Jordan, Hayden, Karnes, and Wood (1977), and in *Educational Programs That Work* (Far West Laboratory for Educational Research and Development, 1980).

HOME-BASED SERVICE DELIVERY

When are home-based services most valuable?

Home-based programs are particularly well suited to rural sparsely populated areas and clusters of small towns. They do not necessarily serve only those with relatively uncommon disabilities, such as hearing or visual impairment or severe multiple disabilities. Home-based services have several advantages. The child's learning takes place in a natural environment, minimizing the need to teach transfer or generalization of skills. Teaching objectives can be realistic and functional and can take the family's cultural background into account. More members of the family can become involved in the child's program, which increases the likelihood that the child will maintain new learning. Many home-based programs begin between birth and age 3.

Home-based early education programs augment the parent's natural role as teacher of the infant or child. In fact, the practice of involving parents in their children's educational programs as teachers and central advocates for their children is probably the greatest strength of home-based early education service delivery. When parents are interested in enhancing their children's development, the children are more likely to gain from the early intervention program. Furthermore, the gains made by the target child often have beneficial effects on the child's siblings (Klaus and Gray, 1968). Parents have filled a number of other roles in early intervention programs, acting as administrators, disseminators, staff members, recruiters, curriculum developers, counselors, assessors of children's skills, evaluators, and record keepers. But perhaps in home-based early education programs more than in other types of programs, parents are viewed as their children's first, most enduring, and most influential teachers. In these programs, professionals or paraprofessionals provide instruction and demonstrations for parents on a regular schedule of home visits.

One of the most well-known examples of a home-based program is the

Portage Project. This program, originally funded by HCEEP, has developed 70 replication sites to serve children with a wide variety of disabilities from birth to age 6. The program was originally developed for the large rural area surrounding Portage, Wisconsin. Soon after the original First Chance funding, the program gained support from the local schools and the State Department of Public Instruction.

Children in the Portage program initially had a mean IQ of 75. They gained 15 months in developmental age over an 8-month period as measured by the Cattell Infant Test and the Stanford/Binet. Families involved in the program received home visits by teachers. The children thus taught by their parents showed greater gains in mental age, language, academic, and socialization skills than children receiving only classroom instruction. Each full-time home visiting teacher served approximately 14 children. The cost per pupil averaged $650 for a 9-month school year (DeWeerd, 1981).

Other examples of home-based programs with unique approaches include REACH Project (Rural Early Assistance to Children) in Northampton, Massachusetts, where special provisions are made to include fathers in the project activities. In the Williamsburg Area Child Development Resources Program of Lightfoot, Virginia, an instrument called the *Skills Inventory for Parents* is used to assess parental skills in several different areas that may need improvement. More information on these and other programs may be found in *Early*

Most preschool special education programs involve the child's parents. Here a father is being taught how to help his child develop motor and conceptual skills.

Childhood Education for Exceptional Children, edited by Jordan, Hayden, Karnes, and Wood (1977), and in *Educational Programs That Work* (Far West Laboratory for Educational Research and Development, 1980).

In addition to the three alternatives for service delivery just described, many programs provide a sequence of home-based instruction for children under a certain age (usually 2 or 3 years), followed by center-based preschool. Yet another alternative is provided by the itinerant (traveling) consultant or resource teacher. These teachers provide assistance to children or to other preschool teachers who have identified exceptional children in their classrooms. The purpose of the consultant teacher is to help with the integration of young exceptional children in classes with nondisabled children. As mentioned earlier, many thousands of preschool children with disabilities are now being served in Head Start and other "mainstreamed" settings. An excellent resource on the topic of mainstreaming young exceptional children is Guralnick's (1978) text, *Early Intervention and the Integration of Handicapped and Nonhandicapped Children.*

INFANT PROGRAMS

What is the primary goal of infant intervention?

Some of the most exciting changes in the practices of early childhood education programs in recent years have been in programs for disabled infants. Several authors (Bronfenbrenner, 1975; Caldwell, 1971; DeWeerd, 1981) have suggested that the earlier intervention begins and the longer it continues, the better are the results. For infants, many services such as newborn intensive care units are now available, and more interest has been directed toward *preventing* developmental disabilities (for example, see Ramey and Bryant, 1982). Although there is general agreement about the principle of early intervention, there is no consensus on who should deliver services to young children (Behr and Gallagher, 1981). Studies have shown that most people prefer that the public school undertake this responsibility, and in some places, infants are being successfully served by public school programs. However, the need for many more programs persists.

Several excellent resource texts describing the issues and strategies for providing exemplary services for infants are *Infant Education: A Guide for Helping Handicapped Children in the First Three Years* (Caldwell and Stedman, 1977); the *Program Guide for Infants and Toddlers with Neuromotor and Other Developmental Disabilities* (Connor, Williamson, and Siepp, 1978); and *Educating Handicapped Infants* (Garwood and Fewell, 1983). For a recent survey of this field, interested readers should consult the June, 1982, issue of the *Journal of the Division for Early Childhood Education,* which is devoted to the topic of intervention programs that begin in the first two years of the infant's life.

PROBE 3-4
Education and Treatment Options

1. Describe the advantages of center-based programs. Give one example of this type of program.

2. Give one example of a combination center- and home-based program for young exceptional children. Describe this program.

3. Under what circumstances are home-based services for young exceptional children appropriate? Name one such program.

SUMMARY

1. Many researchers have demonstrated the importance of providing early education for exceptional children. Children with special needs who do not receive early education may actually decline in their development.
2. Preschool exceptional children have the same needs, wants, and problems as all other children, but they also have additional difficulties to overcome.
3. The intellectual, social, and academic achievement levels previously thought to be the unavoidable consequences of low-income disadvantaged environments have been shown to be flexible and modifiable.
4. Ten percent of the vacancies in Head Start programs for the disadvantaged must be made available to the handicapped.
5. Special incentive grants are available to states that serve preschool handicapped children. Other federal legislation provides funds for experimental demonstration projects for the young handicapped.
6. Exceptional children go through the same developmental stages as other children.
7. Developmental norms are useful in screening, assessing, and developing curricula for young exceptional children.
8. The areas of development most important in young exceptional children are gross motor, fine motor, perception, conceptual, social-emotional, communication, and self-help.
9. State and local officials are involved in casefinding, child find, and early identification projects. The purpose of these projects is to identify young disabled children who need services.
10. Screening is the testing of a large number of children to identify those who need additional in-depth diagnosis and assessment; these activities can result in the provision of special services.
11. Services are most frequently delivered to young disabled children in cen-

trally located service delivery centers, in the children's homes, or in both centers and the children's homes.
12. There is a trend to develop and offer infant intervention projects for very young children to reduce the effects of disabilities on later development.
13. It is extremely important to involve parents in the education programs for their young handicapped children.

TASK SHEET
Field Experiences in Early Childhood Special Education

Select one of the following and complete the assigned tasks.

Program Visitation

Visit a preschool program for exceptional children. This could be a center-based program, a kindergarten, or a home-based program. Describe in a paper of no more than three pages the program that you visited, the curriculum that was being used, the interaction that you had with the staff or the students, and your general reactions to the program.

Professional Interview

Arrange to visit a professional who works with preschool exceptional children. This could be a teacher, pediatrician, physical therapist, or director of a preschool. Discuss the job with the person you choose and write a paper that answers the following questions.

1. Where did you visit?
2. Whom did you interview?
3. What were the responsibilities of the person being interviewed?
4. What types of training were necessary to enter the profession?
5. What types of problems does the person encounter?
6. What are the rewards that the person receives?
7. What did you learn from this experience and what was your reaction?

Parent Interview

Interview the parents of a preschool exceptional child. Using great tact, inquire about the types of services that they have received for themselves and their child, and the types of problems and rewards of being the parent of an exceptional child. In a paper of no more than three pages, summarize your findings. Include your reactions and a description of what you learned from this experience.

Home Inventory

Obtain the inventory included in the following article and evaluate your home. Then, summarize your evaluation and indicate what you would need to do in order to make it safe for a young child.

Wolinsky, G.F. and Walker, S.A. Home Safety Inventory for Parents of Preschool Handicapped Children, *Teaching Exceptional Children,* 1975, 7(3), 82-86.

Library Study

Select three articles from your library that relate to the education of preschool exceptional children. Write a one-page abstract of each. Two journals that contain articles are:

Journal of the Division for Early Childhood
Topics in Early Childhood Special Education

Design Your Own Field Experience

If you know of a unique experience you can have with young exceptional children, or do not want to do any of the above alternatives, discuss your alternative with your instructor and complete the tasks that you agree on.

Communication and Sensorimotor Disorders

An understanding of the principles, issues, and forces that underlie current special education practices serves as a base for studying the various categories of exceptionality. In Part II we consider children who have impairments that affect their ability to communicate, hear, see, or move about in their environment. Communication problems are commonly labeled communication disorders, and problems with hearing, vision, and mobility are jointly referred to as sensorimotor disorders.

Communication and sensorimotor disorders are usually easier to identify and can be measured more precisely than learning problems. For example, while a child's visual acuity or hearing loss can be measured accurately, it is far more difficult to assess such internal characteristics as intelligence or learning ability. It does not automatically follow, however, that the needs of children with communication and sensorimotor disorders are easier to meet. While these disorders do not necessarily affect chil-

dren's intellectual abilities, the great majority of these children can learn and do school work as well as their peers. We trust you will remember this throughout your professional career.

Although communications and sensorimotor disorders are presented in separate chapters, you should be aware that children often have more than one type of disability. Determining the nature and intensity of the disability, which is the first step in developing educational and treatment programs, is often difficult. Assessing and educating children with communication and sensorimotor problems can involve a number of specialists who must be able to work together as a team. The teacher's role is supplemented by the expertise of speech and language pathologists, who do diagnostic evaluations; audiologists, who evaluate hearing; peripatologists, who offer mobility training to the blind; physical therapists, who assist in the rehabilitation of the physically handicapped; and medical personnel, such as orthopedic surgeons, psychiatrists, and nurses. Special education teachers themselves must also have highly specialized skills. Teachers of the deaf, for example, may have to know sign language, and teachers of the blind must be able to use braille. Decisions about the education and treatment of a child with cerebral palsy may involve a physician, special education teacher, speech-language pathologist, physical therapist, nurse, principal, and the child's parents.

As you no doubt will see, cooperation among specialists is very important. It has been our experience, however, that some special education teachers, particularly those who are just beginning their careers, occasionally feel intimidated by physicians and other specialists. You should remember that just as physicians are specialists in the treatment of children's physical needs, teachers are specialists in meeting children's educational needs. A professionally well-prepared teacher has no reason to feel intimidated.

In the next four chapters, we take up the study of communication and sensorimotor disorders.

COMMUNICATION DISORDERS

More children are potentially affected by communication disorders than by any other type of disability. We begin this chapter by defining and differentiating speech and language development. Then, we describe four types of language disorders and three types of speech disorders. We close with a discussion of the roles of the speech-language pathologist and classroom teachers in providing therapeutic services to children with communication disorders.

HEARING DISORDERS

In this chapter we consider the nature of sound and how we hear. Five conditions that can lead to hearing loss are also explained, and the procedures used by audiologists to measure hearing loss are described. We discuss the effects of hearing loss and examine the treatments and classroom techniques used with the hearing impaired. Finally, the roles of the different professionals who work with the hearing impaired are described, and the operation and maintenance of hearing aids are discussed.

VISUAL IMPAIRMENTS

At the outset of this chapter we describe the characteristics and identification of visual impairments. We analyze six disorders of the visual system and consider their implication for classroom practices. At the end of the chapter, we describe some current educational programs and methods used to teach the visually impaired, including braille and other aids.

PHYSICAL AND HEALTH-RELATED DISABILITIES

The physical and health-related disabilities encountered in schools are described in this chapter In our discussion of the disabilities that affect children's health, we place particular emphasis on cerebral palsy and epilepsy. The significance of architectural barriers and the ways to eliminate them are explained, and a description of the equipment used to help children adapt to their disabilities is also included.

PART II COMMUNICATION AND SENSORIMOTOR DISORDERS

Brian, six, was repeating words and phrases. He was certain that he couldn't talk like everyone else. The children at school teased him unmercifully. He began to develop "stomachaches" and "headaches." His parents, in an attempt to help, suggested to Brian that his stuttering handicap was something he had to learn to live with. It certainly did not affect their love for him or make him a lesser person. After three months of speech therapy, Brian was speaking normally. He was looking forward to school each day and could demonstrate to his classmates and his parents that he could talk just like everyone else.

Martha, six, could not move her tongue, lips, and jaws on command to talk. Even though she clearly understood all that was said and could gesture or point to appropriate responses, she was unable to use spoken language. Her IQ when tested with instruments that did not require speech placed her in the average to bright group. Much to her parents' concern and after many futile attempts to train Martha to use spoken language, her speech pathologist introduced an electronic communication device that Martha could program to say for her some of the things she could not say for herself.

Walter's mother spent countless hours training him to repeat the letters of the alphabet, name body parts, and identify colors, hoping that he would be placed in a class with normal seven-year-olds. Walter learned his letters and words but repeated them in a parrotlike way with no understanding of their meaning. He could not understand simple directions or even use his memorized words appropriately. A speech-language pathologist counseled Walter's family and helped them to realize that before his language could be meaningful, Walter had to learn what words meant. Currently Walter is in a class for mildly retarded children where the teacher in cooperation with the speech-language pathologist is providing him with the enriched experiences he needs to learn how to use language.

4

Communication Disorders

Richard Culatta and Barbara K. Culatta

Richard Culatta is Associate Professor of Speech-Language Pathology and Audiology at the University of Kentucky. Current areas of interest are disfluency in children and adults and clinical supervision. Dr. Culatta has functioned as a speech-language pathologist in public schools, hospitals, rehabilitation centers, and university clinics. Barbara K. Culatta is Associate Professor at the University of Rhode Island. Currently the coordinator of an early childhood program for handicapped children, Dr. Culatta has developed several language intervention programs. Her primary research interest is the relationship between perceptual and linguistic deficits in hyperactive and autistic children.

The three children and their communication disorders described on the facing page represent success stories in the diagnosis and treatment of speech and language problems. Unfortunately, these success stories are not nearly as common an occurrence as we would like to see. Most of us can speak as easily as we breathe. Our children can tell us quite clearly of the worlds they are discovering as they grow. Although we may have to struggle for words occasionally, and sometimes we can't express precisely what we would like to, we can almost always make someone understand what we are trying to say.

For more than 20 million people in this country, about 10 percent of the population, communication is much more difficult (Human Communication and Its Disorders: An Overview, 1969). Some people have mild disorders, sources of occasional embarrassment and annoyance. Others have problems so severe that it is impossible for them to live normal lives, especially in a society like ours that places great emphasis on the ability to communicate.

This chapter is about the processes of communication and the causes and effects of communication problems. When you are finished, you should know how to tell the difference between speech and language; how speech and language are acquired; how to define a "communication problem"; what the characteristics of some common speech and language disorders are; and what the responsibilities of the speech-language pathologist are.

It is important to remember that communication problems, like the other disorders discussed in this book, cannot be considered in isolation. The ability or inability to communicate can have an effect on every other area of development. You should always regard a child's problem in the context of the whole child.

BASIC CONCEPTS OF SPEECH AND LANGUAGE

You should be able to define speech and language, differentiate between them, and describe how each develops.

WHAT IS A COMMUNICATION PROBLEM?

There have been many attempts to describe what constitutes a communication disorder. According to Van Riper (1978), a person has a communication problem when that person's speech differs from the speech of others to the extent that it calls attention to itself, interferes with the intended message, or causes the speaker or listener to be distressed. More concisely, impaired speech is conspicuous, unintelligible, or unpleasant. Perkins (1977) adds that speech is impaired when it is ungrammatical, culturally or personally unsatisfactory, or injurious to the speech-producing mechanism. Johnson (1967) stresses the importance of listener reactions and the speaker's feelings.

How can you tell when a person has a speech problem?

Perhaps the best way to determine whether a person has a speech problem is to ask yourself the following questions:

1. Can I understand this person? This is the simplest judgment you will have to make. If you cannot understand or can understand only with difficulty what someone is saying, that person has a communication disorder.
2. Does this person sound strange? If you can understand someone, but that person doesn't sound the way you'd expect, there is a problem. An adult who sounds like Elmer Fudd, a 200-pound adult male who sounds like a nine-year-old girl, and a person who has a flat, expressionless manner of speaking all have communication problems.
3. Does this person have any peculiar physical characteristics when speaking? A person who has distracting mannerisms that interfere with messages has a problem. These mannerisms might include unnecessary or unexpected movements of the lips, tongue, nostrils, arms, legs, or posture.
4. Is the communication in a style inappropriate to the situation? We do not expect the president of the United States to greet Congress before his

annual State of the Union address by saying, "Hey, baby, what's happenin'? It's cool at my pad, what's goin' down here?" Nor do we expect a baseball manager to confront an umpire with "I strenuously object to the judgment process in which you have recently indulged. It would be to our mutual benefit if you would reconsider your opinion and its ramifications." Our point is that we normally shift our style of communication to fit a given situation. A speaker unable to do this may have a problem.

5. Do I enjoy listening to this speaker? This is a judgement we all feel comfortable making. If the reason we don't enjoy a speaker is that we don't like the message, the speaker doesn't have a problem. If, on the other hand, we don't enjoy a speaker for one of the reasons mentioned here, there probably is a communication problem. It is said that a true diplomat can tell you to go to hell in such a way that you'll look forward to the trip. Speakers who can alienate people merely by introducing themselves need help.

6. Is this person's speech mechanism being damaged? Like most other parts of the body, the organs used in communication can be misused. Although diagnoses of physiological abuse can be made only by specialists, listeners can often detect signs of strain in a speaker. Teachers should always refer to professionals any children they think may be injuring their voices. An unnecessary referral hurts no one, but overlooking a symptom can have disastrous consequences.

7. Does the speaker suffer when attempting to communicate? This is difficult to judge, because a listener cannot usually determine how a person feels about his or her efforts to communicate. Many people considered normal communicators by their peers suffer emotionally as a result of shortcomings they imagine. Communication problems such as these that do not have obvious symptoms are among the most difficult to treat.

As you've probably realized, many speakers with problems will have more than one of the characteristics in this list. As always, your emphasis should be on the speaker as a whole, and not exclusively on a particular behavior.

THE DIFFERENCE BETWEEN SPEECH AND LANGUAGE

What is language?

Speech and language are related, but they are not the same thing. Speech is the physical process of making the sounds and sound combinations of a language. Language is essentially the system according to which a people agree to talk about or represent environmental events. Once a group of people agree on a system for representing objects, events, and the relationships among objects and events, the system can be used to communicate all their experiences. The language system consists of words and word combinations.

What is speech?   Whereas the meaning of language is contained in its words and word combinations, it is speech that permits the transmission of meaning. Speech sounds are not meaningful in themselves, of course. They acquire meaning only if the speaker or listener knows their relationship to real events. To state it very simply, speech sounds are a medium for carrying messages.

Language, however, does not have to be transmitted via speech. Gestures that have some agreed-on relation to environmental events, such as the American Sign Language used by the deaf, can also be used to transmit messages. Similarly, words can be transmitted in writing. People cannot learn to interpret written words, however, unless they know what objects, actions, or events the words stand for. The distinction between the sounds used in words and the meanings of words is very important. The ability to make speech sounds is worthless unless we understand the meaning of the sounds. A parrot can be taught to produce words, but it cannot be taught to communicate with them.

We must remember that speech is a purely expressive activity, whereas language has both a receptive component and an expressive component. Our ability to receive language develops before our ability to express it. Furthermore, we all understand more language than we can say; we've all been unable to pronounce or define a word that we feel quite comfortable reading. In fact, our receptive skills, the ability to process and derive meaning from language, are a necessary prerequisite for expressive language. The person who cannot develop a receptive language will not produce an expressive one.

SPEECH MECHANISMS

How do we produce speech sounds?   Our ability to speak involves the coordination of three physical systems: the respiratory system, the sound-production system, and the articulatory mechanism.

The respiratory system permits us to draw air into our lungs. As this air is slowly exhaled, it encounters the sound-producing structure, the larynx (Figure 4-1). The larynx, a complex arrangement of cartilages, ligaments, muscles, and membranes, guards the passage to the lungs and contains a pair of soft tissue folds called the vocal folds. These folds can be brought together over the trachea; sound is produced when air rushes past and vibrates them. You can feel this vibration if you place your fingers beside your Adam's apple and say "ZZZZZZ." Sounds that require the vibration of the vocal cords are said to be *voiced*.

The sound produced in the larynx is then acted upon by the third speech-producing system, the articulatory mechanism (Figure 4-1). This consists of the throat (pharynx), the mouth (oral cavity), the nose (nasal cavities), the jaw (mandible), the soft palate (velum), the lips, and the tongue, each of which affects the sound.

Figure 4-1
The Sound-Producing Structure

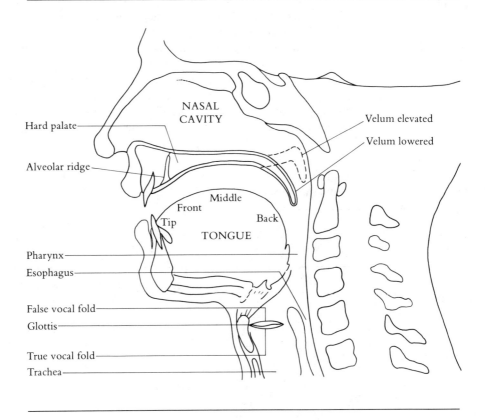

Hard palate

NASAL CAVITY

Velum elevated

Velum lowered

Alveolar ridge

Middle

Front

Tip   Back

TONGUE

Pharynx

Esophagus

False vocal fold

Glottis

True vocal fold

Trachea

These complicated systems are all coordinated by the neurological system. Damage to the brain or nerves can drastically affect how they function, as we will discuss in the section on cerebral palsy.

Detailed accounts of the working of the physical systems used in speech can be found in James Curtis's *Processes and Disorders of Human Communication* (1978).

THE THREE TYPES OF SPEECH SOUNDS

There are three basic types of sounds in our language: vowels, diphthongs, and consonants. Examples of these sounds and examples of words in which they appear are listed in Table 4-1.

You will notice the strange symbols in Table 4-1. These symbols represent the sounds of the English language that are found in the International Phonetic Alphabet. It is important that speech-language pathologists know the symbols of the International Phonetic Alphabet and the sounds that they represent. When diagnosis of a speech problem is made, the sounds that are mispronounced are indicated on the diagnostic report, separated by slashes. Thus, if you saw a report that said, "The client substituted the / ʃ / for the / s / sound," you would know that words such as *kiss* were pronounced "kish."

If you ever see a diagnostic report with symbols such as this, you will know to check the International Phonetic Alphabet to see how those sounds are pronounced. If you plan to become a speech-language pathologist, you

Table 4-1
Phonetic Symbols

Vowels		Diphthongs		Consonants	
Symbol	*Key*	*Symbol*	*Key*	*Symbol*	*Key*
i	be	eɪ	paid	p	pill
I	lip	aɪ	time	b	ball
e	chaos	aʊ	couch	t	tip
ɛ	bed	ɔɪ	boil	d	down
æ	fad			k	kick
u	ooze			g	go
ʊ	took			tʃ	charm
o	odor			dʒ	judge
ɔ	ball			f	fall
a	ought			v	vast
ɝ	girl			θ	thank
ə	ago			ð	this
ʌ	up			s	kiss
				z	zipper
				ʃ	shoe
				ʒ	usual
				h	hot
				m	mild
				n	never
				ŋ	bring
				l	light
				w	wish
				r	rule
				j	yesteryear

will take coursework in phonetics that will enable you to learn the symbols of this alphabet and how to use them.

How do we produce vowel sounds?

Vowels are speech sounds that require voicing (the vibration of the vocal folds) and shaping by the tongue and lips without any part of the tongue or lips touching. For example, compare the vowel in *be* with the one in *pool*. The *e* is made with the tongue tip and the lips in a grin. (This is also the vowel sound in "cheese," which is why we smile when we say that word for a photographer.) By contrast, the vowel in *pool* is made with the lips rounded and the airway modified by the back of the tongue.

What are diphthongs?

Diphthongs (pronounced as if spelled difthongs) are combinations of two vowels in a single syllable. Like vowels, they require voicing. Compare the single vowel in the word *hall* to the diphthong in the word *toil*. Can you hear the difference? Try saying the following diphthong words aloud, listening carefully until you hear the two-vowel combinations: *paid, time, couch,* and *boil.*

How are consonants produced?

Consonants can be made with or without voicing. They are produced by specific movements of the articulators. Three factors determine how consonants sound. They are : (1) the release of the exhaled air; (2) the major places where the articulators come in contact; and (3) whether the sound is voiced or not.

THE DEVELOPMENT OF SPEECH

When do children develop different speech sounds?

We don't learn all the sounds of our language at the same time. Some estimates suggest that many children are still acquiring the sounds of speech after the age of seven. Some sounds, however, are generally learned much earlier.

As with all developmental skills, articulation skills normally develop within an age range. As a general rule /p/, /m/, /h/, /n/, /w/ should be produced by age three. The sounds /b/, /k/, /g/, /d/, /f/, /y/ should be normally produced by age four. By age five children should produce /t/ and /ð/. The sounds /r/ and /l/ come in by age six, while /tʃ/, /ʃ/, /j/, and /θ/ arrive by age seven. The latest developing sounds /s/, /z/, /v/, /ð/ and /dʒ/ arrive by age eight. These are the uppermost limits. For most children, sounds will arrive much sooner. Although individual sounds develop as the child matures, most children should be easily understood between the ages of three and four.

THE DEVELOPMENT OF LANGUAGE

Like speech, language takes a long time to acquire. There is a well-defined pattern that children go through in the acquisition of language.

At what ages do children develop different language concepts?

Children usually begin to attach meaning to words when they are eight to ten months old. At this age children probably do not know the meanings of individual words, but they may associate whole phrases with whole experiences. They might, for example, anticipate going to bed when they hear the phrase "night-night time." Children at this stage also associate words or phrases with specifically taught gestures. For example, they may begin waving when they hear "Wave bye-bye" or begin clapping when told "Patty cake."

At about 10 to 12 months, children begin to comprehend what people say to them if they have environmental information to help them figure it out. A child might, for example, respond to the request, "Give me your shoe" if the shoe is in sight. The same child, however, would probably not respond to the same request if it were heard just before dinnertime or if the shoe were not in sight. At this stage the child learns language by using the knowledge of the event being experienced to figure out the meanings of the words and word combinations heard.

At about the same time, children begin to produce their own first words. The first words learned generally refer to specific familiar people or objects — *mamma* or *doggie,* for example. The child of this age does not generalize words to new situations. The child may, for example, produce an approximation of "Water" to request a drink from the kitchen faucet, but it may be some time before *water* is used when it is seen in a bird bath, toilet, or water fountain.

Between 12 and 18 months the child begins to use words to refer to classes of objects and events instead of just specific events. Concrete words like *hot, more, go,* and *shoe* may be used in a variety of contexts.

Until approximately two years of age, the child usually uses single words and may acquire a fairly large single-word vocabulary. However, some single words will probably be used inappropriately. A child may, for example, overgeneralize and apply the same words to different people or events, calling all animals "doggie" or all men "da-da." Overgeneralization indicates that the child is trying to figure out the relationship between words and experiences. It also indicates that the child knows that words stand for classes of events and not just specific events. When children reach this point they can begin to use words to communicate in any situation.

At two years, children begin to learn to combine words. Their very first attempts are simple two-word phrases in which the words are combined, not at random, but in an organized manner that indicates they have begun to understand the importance of word order. The child now begins to signal relationships between people, actions, and objects, with phrases or sentences like "Daddy go," "Mommy eat," or "eat cookie."

At two and a half to three years, the child begins to use three-word combinations. At this stage, more than one relationship can be specified in a single phrase. By saying "Get my cookie," the child is not only requesting a cookie but also pointing out the child's relationship to the cookie. These children can combine words in all sorts of creative ways. With an increasing vocabulary and knowledge of how to signal relationships among people and objects, a child can even talk about events never before experienced.

After learning to specify most basic meanings in simple word combinations, the child begins to include some of the less crucial parts of speech in sentences. For example, at about three years the child begins to add words such as *is, the,* and *an.* The child begins to speak in very simple, grammatically correct sentences. The process of adding grammatical parts of speech such as word endings continues gradually until the age of five or six.

While acquiring rules for combining words into sentences, the child is continuing to develop vocabulary. In fact, vocabulary development is a never-ending process. By two years of age a child learns words that stand for familiar objects, actions, and simple events, such as *car, get, cup, milk, shoe, no, more, all gone, put away, pick up, bear, chair, look,* and *come.* The three-year-old learns words for less common actions. For example, the words *press* or *scatter* might be added to the child's vocabulary. The three-year–old child also begins to add words that describe particular aspects of experiences, such as *same* or *soft.*

By the time most children are five or six years old, they have mastered language well enough to produce grammatically correct sentences like those used by adults.

It should be emphasized that the ages quoted may vary considerably with a particular child. Some children pass through these stages slower or faster and still develop normal speech and language. The norms we mention are generally accurate, however, and any child who develops at a rate significantly different from them should be closely monitored by trained professionals. There is no penalty for unnecessarily checking a pattern of development that turns out to be normal, but ignoring a real problem can have serious consequences.

Language development is a fascinating and complex subject. If you'd like to develop a greater understanding of it, we suggest Lois Bloom and Margaret Lahey's *Language Development and Language Disorders* (1978).

PROBE 4-1
Basic Concepts of Speech and Language

1. _____ percent of the population of the United States have communication disorders.

2. T F Only people who sound unusual have communication problems.

3. A sound is called a voiced sound when there are _____.

4. We speak on air that is _____ .

5. We produce the different vowels of our language by changing the shape and position of our _____ and _____ .

6. *Matching*

Linguistic Event		*Age*
_____ three-word combination		a. 8–10 months
_____ use of words		b. 10–12 months
_____ two-word combinations		c. 12–18 months
_____ comprehension of sentences		d. 24 months
_____ meaning attached to familiar words		e. 30–36 months

7. T F Speech and language are essentially the same.

8. T F Speech is part of language.

9. T F Language is part of speech.

10. T F Speech is acquired prior to language.

11. T F Language and speech are developmental processes.

12. T F By age six, children should be producing adult-like sentences that are grammatically sound.

13. T F Language develops at the same rate for all children.

LANGUAGE DISORDERS

You should be able to describe the components of a language disorder.

How many people have language disorders?

Of all the communication problems we will discuss, language disorders are the most complex and the most serious. Between 1 and 5 percent of this country's population have language disorders — perhaps as many as 12 million people (Perkins, 1977).

Language disorders vary as much as the people who possess them. They may occur in every population discussed in this book. To understand thoroughly a language disorder, we must know the child's levels of language and nonlanguage functioning, physical and perceptual skills, and what aspects of language the child is not able to use. The purpose of this section is to give you the background necessary to develop the ability to make such determinations. We will discuss the nature and assessment of language disorders and specific methods of remedying them.

TYPES OF LANGUAGE PROBLEMS

Children have language problems when they cannot adequately receive and send messages about their world. Such children do possess knowledge of themselves and their environments, but they cannot talk about them meaningfully or understand when other people do.

When does a language problem exist?

A language problem does not exist if the child's level of language functioning equals the level of nonlanguage functioning. For example, a six-year-old child who functions developmentally at the level of a three-year-old should be expected to have the language development of a three-year-old. This does not mean that developmentally delayed children cannot benefit from language teaching; rather, it means that their expected level of achievement should be commensurate with their nonlanguage functioning. Parents of retarded children often correctly believe that their child's other problems would be less handicapping if they could just speak. They sometimes don't recognize, however, that these other problems are what keeps the child from speaking.

How do language problems differ?

There are three major types of language disorders that result from differences between language and nonlanguage functioning. These are receptive, expressive, and mixed receptive and expressive.

Receptive Language Problem. A child has a receptive language problem when the child's ability to comprehend questions and commands is below his or her mental age. In other words, such children's knowledge of world events is at a higher level than their ability to comprehend descriptions of those events. In addition, a child with a receptive language problem has a greater age-level ability to solve problems without language than to comprehend problems presented in language. For example, at 30 months, a child may show his or her level of development by recreating familiar events in play, such as feeding or fixing toys. The child may also throw away broken or dirty objects, put things where they belong, match objects, or give people things that belong to them. If the same child does not understand age-appropriate words and sentences, such as "Show me your shoe," "Throw away the paper," or "Give Baby some milk," he or she may have a receptive language problem.

Expressive Language Problem. Adults as well as children understand more words than they can produce. But when children's ability to send messages is significantly below their ability to receive them, they may have an expressive language problem. For example, a child with a three-year level of receptive skills and a one-year level of expressive skills would have an expressive language problem.

Mixed Receptive/Expressive Problems. Children may show both a receptive and an expressive language delay. This is indicated when their receptive language age is below their mental age and their level of expressive language is lower still. An example would be a child who functions as a four-year-old while doing nonlanguage tasks, who understands language at the two-year-old level, and who expresses language at the level of a one-year-old. This child would understand simple language such as "Get your coat" and "Do you want more milk?" but be able to say only a few single words, such as "Milk," "Mama," or "Go."

REQUIREMENTS FOR LANGUAGE LEARNING

What factors can contribute to language problems?

Problems such as those just described can result from deficits in the physical processes necessary to learn or from an inadequate language learning environment. The language learning processes include sensorimotor and cognitive skills. The environmental processes include exposure to language and responsive listeners.

Sensorimotor Processes. The problems of the deaf and hearing impaired will be discussed in Chapter 5. Suffice it to say that the child who does not hear will have a language problem that requires intensive treatment. A child must be physically able to send messages to have normal language. Even if he or she knows words and syntax, a child will not be able to communicate verbally without the physical capability to shape and transmit sounds. This type of language disorder will be explained more thoroughly later in this chapter.

How does auditory perception contribute to language?

Cognitive Skills. To learn language, a child must be able not only to hear but to associate aspects of the environment with specific sounds. This process is called *auditory perception*. A child who cannot recognize the word *"rough"* each time it is heard, for example, will not be able to learn to associate the word with coarse textures. A child who cannot detect distinctions in sounds may have difficulty recognizing them in different contexts. A child who cannot distinguish between the words *"ball"* and *"doll,"* for example, may have difficulty comprehending the words if the objects are not present.

Children with auditory perceptual problems have difficulty understanding what is said when their language model does not speak clearly, when the message is distorted, or when sentences are presented rapidly. Their understanding tends to rely on information present in the context of the situation. A child with an auditory perceptual problem will have trouble understanding what is said in less than ideal circumstances, such as a noisy classroom.

How can memory deficits affect language?

Memory deficits can interfere with language learning and use in two ways. First, memory is necessary for the child to learn relationships between words and the events they stand for. For example, to learn the word *chair* a child must remember that the word *chair* is associated with the object the child sits on at dinner. If the child remembers hearing the word *chair* in reference to his or her high chair, then he or she will be more likely to recognize the word again in another context. The storing of words in memory allows the child to build knowledge of what the words mean.

Memory deficits can also interfere with the child's ability to comprehend language in natural contexts. If a child is presented with an explanation in class, he or she must remember the first part of the message while trying to attach meaning to the subsequent words in the message. If the child is told a pen won't write if you hold it upside down, the child must conduct a search of the memory for the meaning of the word *pen* and hold that meaning in memory while trying to remember the meaning of the word *won't*.

What is conceptual knowledge?

A child who has inadequate knowledge of environmental events will have difficulty learning words for those events. *Conceptual knowledge* is a child's understanding of the environment. This understanding can occur without comprehension or production of words. For example, a child may have the conceptual ability to judge spatial relationships but may not know the word *above*. The reverse process is not possible: a child cannot know the meaning of the word *above* without the concept that objects can be placed above each other. Children cannot learn the meanings of words if they do not have conceptual knowledge of the events they stand for.

Children must also possess *retrieval skills* to develop language normally. Retrieval is the ability to summon words from our memories. Children with retrieval problems have trouble selecting appropriate words, even though they may understand the word they are seeking. Such a child might be unable to recall the word *break* when trying to describe a broken pencil, but recognize and understand the word "break" when it is spoken.

What is the role of the environment in developing language skills?

Environmental Processes. Children cannot acquire language unless they hear the words, phrases, and sentences for the things they experience. Children who are talked to frequently have a greater opportunity to figure out how language works and to make additions to their knowledge of language. These *language models* are more effective if they are not too complex for the child to comprehend. If the child produces and comprehends simple statements such as "Your face is dirty," the parent can make slightly more complex statements. The parent could say, "Yes, your face is dirty. You got some egg stuck on it. Let's pick it off." or "We'll try to scrub it off. We'll scrub it off. We'll wash your face real hard."

To learn language, children must not only hear language they can understand, they must have their communication needs and desires fulfilled. Children must receive responses to their attempts to communicate regardless of the lack of sophistication of their sentences. Children learn language by being exposed to alternate, more complex ways of conveying their communication intentions. A child who says "Sticky" may want his listener to acknowledge that he's got gum stuck on his hands or may want the listener to remove the gum. Children whose needs or desires are not acknowledged have little reinforcement or motivation to use language or to listen to better speech models.

ASSESSMENT AND INTERVENTION PROCEDURES

What is the difference between a language disorder and a language delay?

Children with language disorders have problems with different aspects of language. Before a particular child can be helped, the child's knowledge of language (receptive skills) and use of language (expressive skills) must be assessed. By comparing the child's receptive and expressive language levels to his or her mental and chronological ages, we can differentiate between a language disorder and a developmental delay. A six-year-old child with a four-year-old's knowledge of the world would have a specific language disorder if language skills were at the two-year-old level. This same child would be considered mentally or developmentally delayed if language skills and mental abilities were both at the four-year-old level.

Intelligence tests that are language based are of little use in differentiating language delays caused by mental retardation from those caused by deficits in perception or retrieval. A child who does not know the meanings of words and who has difficulty following directions and understanding explanations will do poorly on verbal intelligence tests regardless of mental abilities.

How are semantics, syntax, and pragmatics assessed?

There is no shortcut to an effective language assessment. A child's facility with each of the three components of language (semantics, syntax, and pragmatics) must be assessed. *Semantics,* the content expressed in language, is evaluated by determining what words and meaningful relationships among words the child knows and can use. For example, does the child know the difference between "Mary hit John" and "John hit Mary"? *Syntax,* the rules for combining words in sentences, is evaluated by determining the complexity and number of language rules the child can use to produce or comprehend sentences. *Pragmatics,* the communicative functions that language serves, is evaluated by observing how the child uses language to achieve needs and desires. Each of these skills must be thoroughly understood and the results of testing carefully considered before appropriate goals and intervention strategies can be selected. In establishing goals and planning intervention, however, it is important that all three components be assessed together. A child who sees water running from the sink must have the ability to use meaningful words, produce them in well-formed sentences, and use them to alert someone that a pipe is broken.

Observations of responses to verbal instructions can indicate a child's receptive language age. Properly recorded samples of how the child uses language to communicate are useful in evaluating a child's expressive language abilities.

How is treatment planned for language disorders?

Once a child's language skills have been assessed, the selection of treatment objectives and strategies depends on several factors. Objectives are established to meet the individual child's needs and depend primarily on the nature of the language deficit. If the child has a receptive language deficit, the objective is to increase the child's language comprehension. If the child has an expressive deficit, the objective is to increase the child's ability to convey experiences.

Objectives also depend on the child's level of functioning. If a six-year-old child's language is like that of a four-year-old, the goals would be those at the four-and-a-half-year-old level. Language rules and skills are selected at the next step in the developmental sequence, independent of the child's chronological age. The particular words or grammatical rules selected should be those that the child does not know but that are close to the child's current level of language complexity.

While strategies for teaching language vary depending on the nature of the deficit (receptive, expressive, or mixed) and the child's current language abilities, there are some fundamental principles for teaching language. It is critical that people frequently expose the child to words and sentences that convey the child's own needs and interests. The language addressed to the child should not be too complex and should pertain to what the child is immediately experiencing. It is also essential that the child's own attempts to communicate be acknowledged and reinforced. Good language models and frequent communicative interchanges aid the acquisition process.

RELATIONSHIP BETWEEN LANGUAGE AND LEARNING PROBLEMS

How can language disorders relate to other learning problems?

Language problems can occur in all populations of handicapped children. The presence of a specific language deficit may help differentiate mentally retarded from learning-disabled children. Language is often the primary handicapping condition in learning-disabled children because their language skills are below their mental abilities. Despite certain mental abilities, a learning-disabled child will be capable of using only language skills already acquired to perform successfully in school.

Children with mental handicaps are often not considered to have a specific language disorder because their mental abilities are often no better than their language abilities. Mentally handicapped children have reduced language skills because they have reduced conceptual knowledge of the world. These children benefit from intensive language training. Mentally handicapped children can often make great strides in learning if they are trained in language.

APHASIA

What is a cerebral vascular accident?

Unlike the disorders we've already described, aphasia generally affects adults who have already mastered language. It is usually caused by a stroke (a cerebral vascular accident, or CVA) or by direct destruction of brain tissue through trauma. A CVA occurs when the flow of blood to the brain is suddenly interrupted by a blocked or burst blood vessel. Without oxygen, the brain tissue is very quickly destroyed. If the CVA occurs in an area of the brain that deals with communication, a language disorder may result. Car accidents, gunshot wounds, and other sources of cranial impalement can also destroy brain tissue and result in aphasia. Many war veterans have aphasia as a result of their wounds.

What is aphasia?   Aphasia is a general term used to describe a variety of problems. According to Darley and Spriestersbach (1978), "Aphasia is a disorder of language function — a disturbance of the ability to recognize and use the symbols by means of which we relate to our surroundings and other people . . . Questioning and testing will probably reveal the language difficulty is both receptive and expressive in nature." Aphasics may have difficulty expressing themselves or understanding what is said to them; they may hear well enough but not understand the meanings of words. Their situation is somewhat analogous to what yours would be if you had to communicate using a foreign language you understood very poorly. This analogy is not completely appropriate, however, because you would be able to trust your understanding of the words you could communicate with, whereas an aphasic person, because part of the brain is damaged, cannot.

Aphasia can be predominantly expressive or predominantly receptive. Expressive aphasics have difficulty in using language symbolically. They do not lack the physical ability to speak; rather, they have trouble formulating and editing what they are trying to say. They may have trouble recalling specific words and grammatical constructions necessary to convey messages.

Receptive aphasics have trouble understanding spoken and sometimes written language. This often leads to an inability to talk coherently.

Aphasic people are not retarded; they are just as intelligent as they were before they became aphasic. IQ tests cannot be administered to them, of course, because most of these tests are based on verbal skills.

Aphasia, caused by cranial impalement or CVAs, is rarely found in children. Thus, aphasic children are infrequently encountered in schools.

PROBE 4-2
Language Disorders

1. The three types of language disorder are._____ , _____ , and _____ .

2. T F   Children are not perceived as having language problems if their language functioning is equal to their mental age.

3. Receptive language is to expressive language as understanding is to _____ .

4. T F   Deaf children automatically have language problems.

5. Name the four cognitive skills necessary to learn language.

6. The content expressed in language is referred to as _____ .

7. _____ represents the rules for producing language.

8. The communicative function that language serves is known as _____ .

9. The first step in treating language problems is to develop _____ .

10. CVA stands for _____ .

11. What are two ways a person might become aphasic?

SPEECH DISORDERS

You should be able to describe different types of speech disorders.

Speech disorders can disrupt a person's ability to communicate as seriously as language disorders. It should be emphasized that speech and language disorders are not necessarily separate entities. Children often have severe language problems complicated by speech disorders. The focus of attention should always be on the whole child.

What is the difference between organic and functional speech problems?

Speech disorders can be either *organic* or *functional*. Organic problems are caused by a physical or neurological abnormality. Functional problems are not the result of physical problems; they can be caused by improper learning.

Organic problems can be regarded as having three components. First, there is the symptom — what we hear. With the child who says, "shoup" for "soup", we hear "sh" substituted for "s." Second, there is a physical explanation for the symptom. The child saying "shoup" is using an inappropriate tongue position. Third, there is an underlying neurological or physiological reason for the symptom's physical explanation. In this case, it might be cerebral palsy, resulting in poor muscular control.

Functional problems also have symptoms that have physical explanations, but they lack an underlying physiological cause.

The difference between these two kinds of problems affects how we attempt to remedy them. Obviously it would be pointless to ignore a serious organic problem when planning speech therapy since uncorrected physiological problems might make correction impossible. The types of speech disorders we will discuss are (1) articulation disorders (speech sound production), (2) voice disorders, and (3) fluency disorders.

ARTICULATION DISORDERS

What are the four types of articulation disorders?

People with articulation problems tend to make four kinds of mistakes when speaking. These are substitution, omission, distortion, and addition. The acronym SODA may help you remember them.

Substitution is the replacement of one sound for another. For example, a person who says "thoup" for "soup" is substituting a voiceless "th" for "s." Saying "wabbit" for "rabbit" is another example. *Omission* is leaving a sound out altogether, saying "oup" for "soup" or "abbit" for "rabbit," for example. *Distortion* is the replacement of an acceptable sound with one that doesn't exist in our language. The slushy Daffy Duck kind of /s/ sound is a good example of a distortion. *Addition* is the addition of a sound that doesn't normally occur in a word, saying "athalete" for "athlete" or "atpple" for "apple," for example.

The speech of some speakers with problems such as those described above is obviously disordered; when this is true, it is easy to diagnose a speaker as having an articulation problem. Effective guidelines for diagnosing less conspicuous cases have been provided by Tomblin (1978):

> Even the most careful speakers will occasionally misarticulate sounds. Therefore, we cannot reasonably propose that a person making any error in articulation has an articulation disorder. Although no definition exists that is universally accepted by speech pathologists, we propose that a disorder of articulation involves the following characteristics:
>
> 1. There must be rather frequent and recurring misarticulations of one or more speech sound units.
> 2. The sound units considered to be in error must be elements of the phonemic system of the person's linguistic community.
> 3. It is reasonable to expect that the misarticulated sound elements would be articulated acceptably by most persons of the same age.
>
> Even if these characteristics are not met, individuals could be considered to have an articulation problem if their articulation causes them to believe that they are inadequate speakers.

How are articulation problems identified?

Once it has been determined that a person has an articulation problem, a speech sample must be obtained and analyzed before treatment can be planned. The method that seems most obvious, listening to a person speak for a while, is not very effective. The examiner must listen to content to determine what the person is saying, and he or she must also listen to the pronunciation of specific sounds. To do both at once is very diffcult. Therefore, an examiner would have to listen to a speaker for a long time to be certain all the sounds of our language were produced.

To overcome such problems, articulation tests that require the person being tested to say specific sounds have been developed. Most of these tests rely on easily recognizable pictures of objects that contain the target sound. The person being tested is asked to name the objects, and the examiner listens for specific sounds. Generally the same sound is tested three times — once at the beginning of a word, once in the middle, and once at the end. Thus, for the sound /s/, a person might be shown pictures of a s̲aw, a ba̲seball, and a glas̲s̲.

By going through sounds and sound combinations in this way, the examiner can discover errors. After this, an attempt can be made to assess a sample of spontaneous communication, because the examiner will know what sort of errors to listen for. It is important to listen to a sample of conversational speech, because we say words differently in sentences than we do when we pronounce them individually. As you can see, correctly administering an articulation test takes a good deal of skill and practice.

Organic Causes. Among the most common organic causes of articulation disorders are *cleft palate* and *cerebral palsy*. A severe hearing impairment will also affect a child's ability to learn to articulate correctly. This will be discussed in detail in Chapter 5.

What causes cleft palate?

Cleft palates can actually be of three types — clefts of the lip only, clefts of the palate only, or clefts of both the lip and the palate. They are caused by the failure of the lip or palate to grow together during the child's fetal development. It is uncertain why this happens. It occurs during the first three months of pregnancy in one of every 600 births in the United States.

As you can see in Figure 4-1, the palate forms the roof of the mouth and the bottom of the nasal cavity. The front two-thirds is called the hard palate, and the back third is called the soft palate, or velum. All but three of the sounds in our language ("m," "n," and "ng") require that the soft palate contact the throat, thereby sealing off the nasal cavity. Many children with cleft palates cannot do this; as a result their speech may be excessively nasal, breathy, and difficult to understand.

Lip clefts usually involve only the upper lip. A cleft may appear on either side of the nose or on both sides. Figure 4-2 shows a unilateral cleft of the lip.

What is the treatment for cleft palate?

Treatment of clefts and the resulting articualtion disorders is a long-term, coordinated effort made by a team of speech-language pathologists, doctors, and dentists. The repair of physical structures is undertaken by surgeons. Surgery for cleft lip is usually performed when the child is one-and-a-half to three months old. Surgery for cleft palate problems is postponed until the surgeon is certain that it will not alter facial growth. Figure 4-3 shows the result of surgery to the boy in Figure 4-2.

A child may be fitted with a prosthesis that closes the opening in the palate during the period before surgery. A prosthesis is illustrated in Figure 4-4.

Articulation disorders are found much more frequently among those with cleft palates than cleft lips. Unfortunately, surgery alone does not usually lead to normal articulation. In addition to having excessive nasality, those with cleft palates may have trouble making sounds that require the damming up of air pressure, such as /p/, /b/, /t/, /d/, /k/, /f/, /z/, and /s/. They need to be taught to take full advantage of the tissue they do have or to use their prostheses effectively. With effective education a child can be taught to reduce excessive nasality and develop the air pressure necessary to produce sounds. Postsurgical muscular training may also help improve speech.

Figure 4-2
A cleft lip

Figure 4-3
Two years later, following surgery

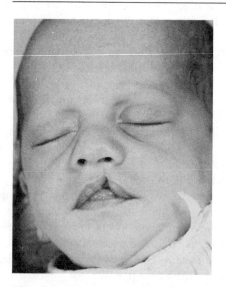

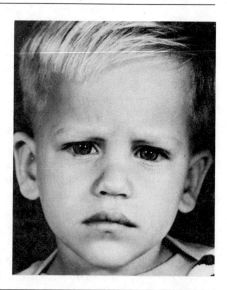

Some articulation problems are the result of the soft palate's inability to reach the throat rather than the complete absence of soft palate tissue. When this is the case, the adenoids (tissue located where the back of the throat and the nasal cavity join) are sometimes used to fill the gap. Before the adenoids are removed surgically, it is very important to determine their role in closing off the nasal cavity. Careless removal of adenoidal tissue can result in articulation problems that could have been avoided.

Additional information on cleft palates is sometimes available from university and teaching hospitals, many of which maintain cleft palate teams.

Why does cerebral palsy cause articulation problems?

Cerebral palsy, like cleft disorders, is not itself a communication problem; it is, rather, the cause of one. Its severity is related to the extent of the brain damage that causes it. This brain damage impairs the ability to control the articulators (the tongue, lips, soft palate, and so forth), which results in an articulation disorder.

People with cerebral palsy are likely to have slow, labored speech, to articulate words imprecisely, and to slur sounds together or omit them completely. They may also expel air too quickly or not be able to exhale enough air to speak smoothly. One effect of these factors is a distortion of the rhythmic patterns we associate with normal speech. Until one becomes familiar with these distorted patterns, a cerebral palsied person's speech may be unintelligible.

Figure 4-4
A Velo-pharyngeal Prosthesis and How It Is Fitted

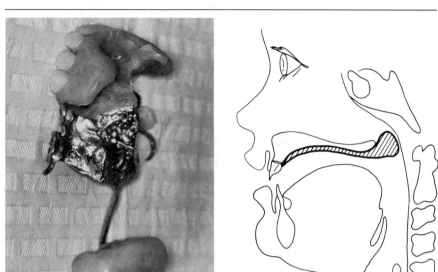

The reason people with cerebral palsy speak as they do is basically their inability to bring together the complex movements necessary for speech with the speed needed to speak normally. Normal speakers make the rapid adjustments necessary to travel from one sound to another without having to think about them. In fact, we make these adjustments so quickly that we must "cheat" a little to keep up with our thoughts. For example, try saying the /p/ sound, as in "pay," and then the /p/ sound in "play," paying close attention to the different positions of the tongue. You will notice in the latter case that your tongue has anticipated the next sound almost before you had finished the first. These rapid movements can be seen clearly in x-ray motion pictures of the mouth. If you have access to a cleft palate team, you should ask them to show you a sample film.

How can people with cerebral palsy compensate for poor articulation?

Although the effects of cerebral palsy cannot be reversed because brain tissue will not regenerate, it is possible to teach a person to compensate for deficits. Most cerebral palsied people can be helped to become more intelligible, although few will develop normal articulation. For some, oral communication will be impossible, and tools such as microcomputers, communication boards, or picture cards may be the best option.

When microcomputers are used, they may be programmed with a dictionary of messages. By choosing a key that corresponds to a particular word or phrase, children can have their messages printed by computers. Microcomputers may also be used with speech synthesizers, which produce speech electronically rather than displaying typed messages.

Communication boards and picture cards may involve scanning devices activated when the child tilts his or her head. With the press of one key, a switch activates a light that scans a sequence of words or pictures; the handicapped person uses the switch to stop the light when it reaches the correct word, message, or pictorial representation of a common event.

Other aspects of cerebral palsy will be presented in Chapter 7.

What causes functional articulation problems?

Functional Causes. Between 2 and 20 percent of all articulation disorders are classified as functional rather than organic in origin. The higher percentage is for children in primary grades, whereas the 2 percent figure is for those in or beyond secondary school. Functional articulation disorders, as you will remember, are those that have no identifiable organic cause. They may be the result of improper learning, short auditory memory span, problems in phonetic discrimination, and many other factors. Unlike organically caused articulation disorders, functional disorders can often be completely cured. Effective diagnosis and remediation efforts usually result in normal articulation.

Additional information on this subject can be found in Charles Van Riper's *Speech Correction: Principles and Methods* (1978). Chapter 6 of that text deals with disorders of articulation; pages 173-216 explain how to remedy them and where to find more information.

VOICE DISORDERS

How can you determine that a person has a voice disorder?

A voice disorder exists when the pitch, loudness, quality, or flexibility of a voice differ from the voices of others of similar age, sex, and cultural group (Aronson, 1980). Approximately 1 percent of the population of this country, or more than 2 million people, have voice disorders (Perkins, 1977). Although some are organic in origin, the result of changing tissue or structural inadequacies, most problems are caused by abuse of a normal voice. However, if a normal mechanism is misused, it may show physical signs of abuse. These signs can be seen as the organic result of functional misuse.

What are the different types of pitch disorders?

Pitch Disorders. The sound you hear when people laugh or clear their throats is their *optimal pitch,* the sound they can produce most efficiently. Ideally, optimal pitch is the same as *habitual pitch,* the pitch we use most frequently. When one's optimal pitch differs severely from one's habitual pitch by being too high, too low, or lacking in variation, a pitch disorder is indicated.

TECHNOLOGY IN ACTION

Art has a severe form of cerebral palsy. The portions of his brain that control many of his voluntary muscles were damaged during a very difficult birth. He is confined to a wheelchair because he cannot walk. His speech is almost impossible to understand, and he has great difficulty controlling the movement of his hands and arms.

There is nothing wrong with Art's intelligence, however. In fact, his teachers believe that he is quite bright. In spite of his difficulties, he learned to read at the same time as other children. Academically, he is at the sixth-grade level, which is normal for his age. Art has good receptive language skills; and he understands just about everything that is said to him. Although his expressive language appears to be good, he has a great deal of difficulty communicating because of his poor speech.

Until recently, Art communicated with his teacher by using a specially equipped typewriter. The typewriter had a template over the keyboard with holes in it that corresponded to the positions of the keys. Art hooked his fingers over the holes in the template and pressed the keys. The template kept him from accidentally pressing a wrong key because of the uncontrollable muscle movements in his hands and arms. Although Art was able to type messages this way, it was a difficult and time-consuming process for him. He often typed messages that indicated his frustration with the limitations of this method of communication.

Art's special education resource teacher, Ms. Duke, recently attended a conference on electronic equipment for people with physical disabilities. Upon her return, she persuaded the school to purchase some equipment that was to dramatically improve Art's life.

The school purchased an Apple IIe microcomputer with a disk drive and video monitor, a printer, an Echo II speech synthesizer, and a computer software program called the Microcommunicator. A template, similar to the one Art used with the typewriter, was also obtained for the computer. After installation, the Echo II software disk was placed in the disk drive and the computer was turned on. A mechanical voice clearly spoke the words, "Hello. I am an Echo II speech synthesizer. I can take normal text and turn it into speech."

After presenting a demonstration of its features, the computer asked Art to type in anything and then press the **RETURN** key. Art slowly typed, "Hello. I am Art and I can talk." He pressed the **RETURN** key and, amazingly, those words flowed from the speaker.

Art quickly learned that some words had to be typed phonetically in order to be pronounced correctly. Most words, however, only had to be spelled correctly. Any word or sentence that Art could think of could be typed into the computer and "spoken" by the speech synthesizer.

The Microcommunicator program was slightly adapted so that the entries could be "pronounced" by the speech synthesizer. The Microcommunicator permitted Art to store several hundred words, phrases, and sentences that he frequently used. These could be called up and pronounced by a single keystroke, so Art didn't have the laborious job of retyping items that he used frequently. These could also be printed on the printer so that he could compose short messages and notes to his friends. A simple word processor program, called Bank Street Writer, was added to the system so that he could print out his written school assignments.

Art's newly acquired skills have opened immense new vistas for him. Although it takes a little time, he is now able to communicate orally with his teachers and fellow students. His parents have purchased a similar system for use at home. Not surprisingly, Art's grades have improved and his intellectual potential is beginning to be fully realized. When asked about his future, Art recently said (via his speech synthesizer), "I am going to go to college and study computer science. I want to learn how to develop other ways that computers can be used to help people with physical disabilities."

In our society, men with very high voices and women with very low voices may pay severe social penalities. Although these disorders are sometimes organic, they are generally functional, the result of improper use. In men the disorders usually begin during adolescence, when, for reasons ranging from psychosexual fixation to poor learning, their voices fail to change and they retain the high-pitched voices of youth. This condition is generally remediable.

A related disorder is pitch breaks. These are the sudden shifts in pitch that occur primarily in the voices of pubescent males. Pitch breaks are associated with growth spurts and rarely occur for more than six months. Although a period of pitch breaks is normal, the condition may have destructive effects if it becomes chronic or if a person develops bad vocal habits in an effort to disguise or avoid them. A person who has pitch breaks for more than six months should be referred to a speech-language pathologist.

People whose voices lack the variation in tone we expect from a normal speaker may also have pitch disorders. Pure monotone or monopitch voices are very rare, but there are many people who alter their tone very little, or alter it in a predictable pattern. This condition can be caused by hearing loss or by the use of a habitual pitch level that doesn't permit pitch variation. It can also be caused by emotional problems, when, for example, a person tries to hide powerful emotions by speaking in a flat, calm, controlled voice. This behavior is sometimes appropriate, but when it becomes the dominant manner of speaking, it indicates a problem. As you can see, a person's voice is frequently an accurate indicator of psychological condition; how a person presents a message can be as important as the message itself.

Loudness Disorders. Inappropriately loud or soft voices are another type of voice disorder. Some loudness problems are caused by the lack of control that results from impaired hearing or cerebral palsy. In some cases, however, an excessive loudness is the result of a family's communication problem. For example, children who have to shout to get attention from their parents may also speak very loudly at other times. If this continues over a long period, the

What are "screamer's nodes?"

child may develop "screamer's nodes," growths on the vocal cords that lead to a harsh-sounding voice. It is usually the family that needs treatment in these situations, and not only the child.

Weak or very soft voices are also usually the result of psychological or environmental problems, rather than organic disorders. A person who is frequently punished when speaking or drawing attention to himself or herself may learn to speak in a barely audible voice. At times, of course, this is appropriate, but a person who tries to be unobtrusive by rarely speaking or speaking inaudibly has a serious problem. As was true of loudness problems, the child may not benefit from treatment unless the situation leading to the development of the habit is changed.

How may voice quality vary?

Problems with Voice Quality. Voice quality defects are among the most common and most difficult to describe. Four of the most common are excessive or insufficient nasality, breathiness, harshness or stridency, and hoarseness.

Nasality problems result from the inability to control the flow of air into the mouth and nasal cavity. As we described in the section on cleft palates, excessive nasality is usually an organic problem best controlled by a team of doctors, dentists, and speech-language pathologists. Sometimes, however, it results from improper learning and can be cured without surgical intervention.

Insufficient nasality is the cause of the sounds we associate with having colds, allergies, or enlarged adenoids. These blockages and swollen tissues hamper normal resonance and result in a flat-sounding voice.

To clarify the difference between the two nasality disorders, try saying "time and tide wait for no man" first with excessive and then with insufficient nasality.

People with nasality problems that persist after their organic causes have been remedied should be referred to speech-language pathologists.

Breathiness can be caused by a number of organic and functional disorders. It is the result of the vocal folds not coming together correctly, which allows air to rush past them without vibrating them as it does in normal speakers. This can be the result of callus-like nodes developing on the folds, caused by chronic vocal abuse, or it can be caused by vocal fold paralysis. Breathiness can also result from functional problems and poor vocal habits.

The voices of people with breathiness problems have a whisper-like quality because of excessive air flow. This can be very distracting to a listener. Except when caused by paralysis or irrevocable tissue damage, it can usually be cured.

Harshness is usually the result of tension or strain. Some speakers develop harsh voices because they have to strain to be heard where they work; others have personality conflicts. The condition can also have organic causes. If eliminating the source of stress does not resolve the problem and a medical examination reveals little or no pathology, a psychological examination may be appropriate.

Hoarseness is familiar to everyone. It is usually the result of cheering or shouting too loudly. Another common cause is laryngitis, a swelling of the area around the larynx. Hoarseness should last for only a few days. If it lasts longer, a physician should be consulted; hoarseness is the first symptom of a number of potentially dangerous disorders.

What is a laryngectomy?

Disorders Resulting from Laryngectomy. The final voice disorder we will discuss is that of the person whose larynx has been removed, generally to keep cancer from spreading (Figure 4-5). This procedure involves changing the position of the trachea, which normally carries air from the nose and throat to the lungs. During surgery, the trachea is redirected to a stoma, or

Can people with laryngectomies talk?

opening, in the lower part of the neck. It is through this stoma that the person breathes.

When the larynx is removed, the vocal folds are removed as well; as a result, a laryngectomized person can no longer speak with vocal fold vibrations. These people, generally older adults, can be rehabilitated, however. The easiest way for them to produce understandable speech is to use a substitute sound generator, commonly called an electrolarynx. This instrument is placed beside the neck, and the speaker articulates the buzz that the device produces (Figure 4-6).

Although the device is easy to use, many people find the sound produced by an electrolarynx highly artificial and unpleasant. A method known as *esophageal speech* is a preferred alternative. The esophageal speaker forces air from the mouth into the area where the pharynx and esophagus join. This area, known as the PE segment, vibrates when the air is released, and the articulators are used to shape sounds. Esophageal speech takes a relatively long time to learn, but the resulting speech is closer to normal than that produced by the electrolarynx devices.

Additional information on alaryngeal speech is available in "Voice Disor-

Figure 4-5
After Laryngectomy

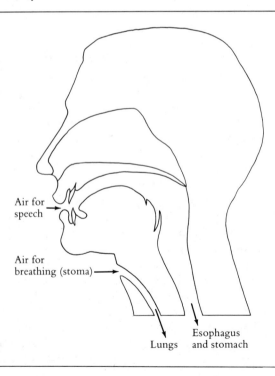

Air for speech

Air for breathing (stoma)

Lungs

Esophagus and stomach

Figure 4-6
How the Electrolarynx Is Used

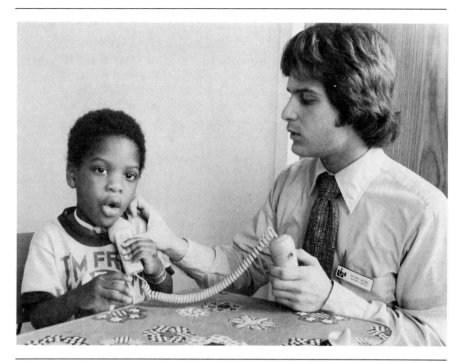

ders," by Paul Moore, in *Human Communication Disorders,* edited by Shames and Wiig (1982) and in *Clinical Voice Disorders* (1980) by Arnold Aronson.

The Role of the Physician. Because many voice disorders are caused by changing tissue, it is very important that a person with symptoms of a problem get a medical examination before vocal rehabilitation is attempted. An examination by an Ear, Nose, and Throat (ENT) specialist, more formally called an otorhinolaryngologist, can determine whether the patient has a serious degenerative disease. As we mentioned earlier, vocal disorders are sometimes symptoms of diseases that can lead to serious disabilities or even death.

What is an otorhinolaryngologist?

Treatment of Voice Disorders. Voice therapy can be thought of as the attempt to return a person's voice to normal or near normal. Not everyone can have a normal voice after treating a voice problem. How close to normal a person's voice can be after therapy depends upon the destruction done by the disorder, the person's age, and the success of therapy.

How are voice disorders treated?

Although the specific techniques for each of the disorders mentioned in this section may vary, Wilson (1979) suggests ten steps to modify voice disorders.

(1) The client learns to recognize the defective vocal behavior when it is demonstrated by the clinician. (2) The client learns to recognize an inappropriate voice in others and (3) an appropriate voice in others. (4) The client learns to recognize his or her own incorrect vocal behavior and (5) modification of vocal behavior. At this point, clients can modify their vocal production. (6) Situations are then described where the client's vocal behavior is inappropriate and (7) where it may be appropriate. Finally Wilson states the client must use this normal voice outside therapy (8) some of the time, (9) most of the time, and ultimately (10) all of the time.

For more information on speech disorders in general, we recommend Charles Van Riper's *Speech Correction: Principles and Methods* (1978).

FLUENCY DISORDERS

What is disfluency?   *Disfluency,* the preferred term for stuttering, is a disorder that begins and usually ends in childhood. The age of onset is typically between two and seven years, with its highest incidence occurring among two-and-one-half- to three-and-one-half-year-olds. It affects about 1 percent of the total population (Milisen, 1971).

Disfluent adults who did not begin stuttering during childhood are quite rare. Most experts agree that it is a learned disorder that results from the continuation of the disfluency many children experience as part of their verbal development.

Normal and Developmental Disfluency.[1] A child's first words are almost always free from disfluency. They are usually a source of pride for both child and parents. However, when children begin to combine words and learn the rules for sequencing words while selecting them, they hesitate in order to edit and revise the intended message. Adults also pause to revise and edit their speech; such pauses in a speaker's verbal flow are considered normal disfluency.

Normal disfluency differs from developmental disfluency in several respects. In the former case, the speaker pauses or inserts a phrase or a sound such as "uh." Developmental disfluency, on the other hand, is characterized by the *repetition* of words, parts of words, or phrases during editing time (Davis, 1939). They also differ in that developmental disfluency may begin suddenly, without apparent explanation, and without the child's being aware of the altered speech. Distinctions such as these are sometimes hard to make, however, and the boundary between the normal and the abnormal is hard to define precisely. The speech of either kind of disfluent is relaxed and appar-

[1] Parts of this segment are reprinted from "Stuttering as an aftereffect of normal developmental disfluency" (Rubin and Culatta, 1974).

ently effortless. The speaker is, in effect, saying, "Don't interrupt me. I'm not finished yet."

The period of developmental disfluency normally lasts from a few weeks to a few months. Parents can be assured that it is normal behavior, the result of a child's not knowing the conventional methods of gaining time to organize words. The child hasn't learned to say "let me see" or "you know" yet; the easiest way to hold the floor is to continue saying a word already uttered fluently. For example, the child might say, "Can, can, can, can I go with you?" Most children go through the disfluent stage at about the same period of language development, one that is characterized by many inconsistent displays of disfluency.

Adult disfluency can grow out of the normal developmental disfluency of childhood. Each instance of disfluency can be the occasion for parents to react unusually to the child's speech. Any acknowledgment a parent makes of a child's disfluency may make the behavior more likely to appear again. This acknowledgment need not be anything obvious. For example, a parent who stops raking leaves or fixing lunch when the child is disfluent but not during fluent speech may draw the child's attention to the unusual speech. Even parents who are not worried about their child's disfluency, but are merely trying to help by saying "Slow down" or "Think before you speak," can affect a child's verbal behavior. Ideally, parents should react in the same manner when the child is fluent and disfluent.

What causes disfluency?

Stress-Induced Disfluency. Shames and Florence (1982) make a distinction between normal disfluency, which results from editing, and disfluency caused by environmental pressure. If the child has unconsciously recognized during a period of developmental disfluency that being disfluent serves a purpose, the child may revert to disfluency when making requests, answering direct questions, and during other stressful situations. If the child's parents reinforce this behavior, it may become ingrained in their child. However, both the child who stutters and the parents who reinforce stuttering are unconscious of the effect of their behavior.

Purposes for Disfluency. A child may use disfluency for three possible purposes: to secure attention, to express hostility, and to control the behavior of others.

Securing Attention. Disfluency draws attention to itself. A child who is not getting enough attention may prefer even negative comments to no attention at all. Disfluency is no longer normal if a child has learned to use it to gain parental attention.

How can parents contribute to the development of disfluency in their children?

Parents who are unaware that a period of disfluency is frequently part of a child's normal language development are especially susceptible to apprehension about their child's disfluency. This apprehension may take the form of worry, empathy, or sympathy — all forms of caring that the child may be seeking.

Adults may also feel threatened by a child's disfluency, imagining that it reflects on their ability as parents. These feelings may be reinforced by the social embarrassment they suffer if they are subjected to unsolicited and unhelpful comments from friends and relatives. As a result, parents may be irritated with their child, sometimes to the point of anger; they may even punish the child if they believe his or her behavior is willful. More frequently, however, parents regard their child's disfluency as beyond volitional control, and sublimate their irritation into feelings of concern.

Expressing Hostility. Any child who faces restrictions and controls will be frustrated and sometimes angry at the parents who are in control. If the child cannot express anger through name-calling or physical aggression, he or she may express it indirectly. If the child is already disfluent and the parents are unduly concerned, the child may become more disfluent to elicit further concern.

Every child faces restrictions, of course, and can be expected to rebel against them occasionally. Disfluency may result only when the child cannot express frustration, and when parents are made uncomfortable by the child's speech problem. Even relatively secure children may be so hesitant to antagonize an adult that they may habitually use their disfluency to irritate, inconvenience, frighten, embarass, or intimidate threatening adults. Neither parent nor child is usually aware that the disfluency is being used aggressively.

Controlling the Behavior of Others. Once a child's disfluency is labeled (i.e., identified by both the parents and the child), it undergoes a rapid series of changes. It ceases to be a relaxed repetition of words, syllables, and other sounds, and becomes very tense (Johnson, 1959). The child may have periods when no sound is uttered, repetitions may become very tense; and pitch and loudness may vary frequently. The child generally begins to show signs of anxiety as well. The child may circumlocute, substitute some words for others, or go to the extreme of avoiding speaking altogether. In addition, disfluency is likely to become more predictable in certain situations, although the child may retain fluency when not under stress — while alone, with other children, or while singing, for example.

Once a child's disfluency becomes habitual, parent and child alike begin to anticipate and prepare for it in the situations where it has appeared most consistently. The child is identified as different from other children and treated accordingly. Even those who struggle to speak fluently will probably lack confidence in their ability to change. Parents who regard their child's problem as organic in origin rather than caused by the environment are likely to begin adjusting to it rather than trying to eliminate it. Because they believe they themselves can do nothing to cure the condition, parents often turn to a specialist for advice.

What is the treatment for disfluency?

The Treatment for Disfluency. Unnecessary parental concern about disfluency and the pressure on children that often results from it can frequently be eliminated by informing parents that a period of developmental disfluency is normal.

Those who tend to worry excessively or who have already labeled their child as disfluent, however, should seek professional help as quickly as possible. The longer a child is disfluent, the harder the condition is to cure. Early diagnosis and treatment are also important because the environmental factors that cause disfluency are harder to control once a child has started school. Because it is difficult for parents to assess their·effect on a child's behavior objectively, they should be referred to a speech pathologist.

Some speech pathologists prefer to work exclusively with parents, basing their strategies on restructuring the child's environment rather than the child. Others view disfluency as a family problem and prefer to involve the child in treatment along with the parents. The speech pathologist may also have to impress parents with the fact that disfluency is acquired and explain that environmental changes are crucial if their child is to speak normally.

An understanding of the circumstances that perpetuate a child's disfluency often provides the insights necessary to change a child's speech. An analysis of the child's home, and of the circumstances during which a child is most fluent and disfluent, can be very helpful. Once parents understand what may have been very subtle and confusing environmental influences, they can help adjust the home invironment to change their child's speech.

For example, they may decide not to ask questions or otherwise encourage speaking in situations where their child has been consistently disfluent. Conversely, the child should be encouraged to speak in situations where consistent fluency is typical. If family members have to compete for speaking time at the dinner table, they might adopt a policy that allows time for everyone. If the child's schedule creates pressure, it should be changed. Because at this age children spend most of their time in the home, parents can manipulate much of what their children experience and can provide occasions for fluent speech.

Disfluent Adults. Although we have stressed childhood disfluency in the preceding section, there are many disfluent adults as well. A great deal can be done to help them. Whether their speech problem is caused by improper learning, psychic trauma, or one of the other factors that we discussed earlier, it can be treated effectively.

What cautions should be observed in seeking treatment for disfluency?

When discussing the treatment of disfluency, caution is always advised. Stuttering has been "cured" many times over by charlatans and quacks. Since many people who stutter can modify their speech in distracting situations, it is not uncommon to find that fluency "tricks" resolve the problem for a time.

Everything from pebbles in the mouth to speaking while listening to white noise has been proposed as a "cure" for stuttering. Most of these techniques only bring temporary relief and eventual devastating failure, however.

It is always wise to question the credentials and professional standing of those who purport to have a cure for stuttering. Unfortunately, there is currently available no quick, successful technique that will carry over to a person's real-life speaking situations.

For further information on disfluency, we recommend the chapter titled "Stuttering," by Dean Williams, in *Processes and Disorders of Communication* (1978), and Oliver Bloodstein's *A Handbook on Stuttering* (1981). The latter book, an inexpensive paperback, is the most comprehensive available on the subject of disfluency. The author writes so clearly that even the most complex theories are easily understandable.

Other works of interest are Williams (1957), Kent (1961), Rubin and Culatta (1971), Culatta and Rubin (1973), and Culatta (1976).

PROBE 4-3
Speech Disorders

1. List three characteristics of a speech problem. Put an asterisk next to one item that is not a characteristic of a functional problem.

2. Name the four types of articulation disorders, using the acronym SODA.

3. The most common communication problem with speakers who have cleft palates is _____ .

4 What is a cleft palate prosthetic device?

5. How might cerebral palsy cause an articulation disorder?

6. How can a functional voice problem become an organic voice problem?

7. People with hay fever may sound _____ whereas a person who is unable to block off the nasal cavity will sound excessively _____ .

8. What does ENT stand for?

9. What does an otorhinolaryngologist do?

10. How does a laryngectomized person breathe?

11. T   F   Occasional pitch breaks in adolescent males should be a cause for concern.

12. Four voice quality defects are _____ , _____ , _____ , and _____ .

13. List 5 of Wilson's ten suggestions for modifying voice disorders.

14. Why is disfluency called a disorder of childhood?

15. Most children pass through a stage called normal developmental disfluency at approximately _____ to _____ years of age.

16. What are three purposes disfluency may serve for a young child?

17. T F Adults who are disfluent cannot be helped because their problem is so deeply ingrained in them.

PROVIDING EDUCATIONAL SERVICES: THE ROLE OF THE TEACHER AND SPEECH PATHOLOGIST

> **You should be able to describe ways for teachers and speech-language pathologists to cooperate in providing educational services to children with communication disorders.**

Educating the child with a communication disorder entails a coordinated effort by the teacher and speech-language pathologist. The team approach begins with identification of children whose communication problems interfere with their education, and it continues through goal selection and remediation.

Teachers may share the responsibility with the speech-language pathologist for identifying children who need speech or language services. The teacher should ask the seven questions presented at the beginning of the chapter when evaluating a child's speech and language. The teacher should be particularly alert in identifying children who do not follow novel directions or understand explanations. The child who watches others and who relies on gestures to comprehend may not be able to use language as a way to acquire new skills or information.

What is the most critical variable in classroom instruction?

Devising an educational program for children with communication disorders entails individualizing objectives. Since language is the medium of instruction, the most essential aspect of coordinated programming is to ensure that the child has the necessary language and communication skills for appropriate classroom performance. A child must know all the words heard in the classroom and be able to follow classroom instructions and understand explanations. The objectives should be to train the child to comprehend and use the sounds, words, and sentence types necessary to communicate ideas related to classrooom activities. If the complexity of the communication demands are beyond the child's abilities, then a treatment program should be initiated that will probably include strategies to both facilitate strengths and remedy deficits.

How can teachers and speech-language pathologists work together?

While treatment entails coordinating the approaches of the classroom teacher and speech-language clinician, the role of the two professionals may differ. Several approaches may work. One is for the speech-language clinician to model treatment strategies in the classroom. Another approach is for the clinician to begin teaching new skills in a therapy environment and having the classroom teacher attempt to integrate the skills into real contexts. When the classroom teacher knows what words, sounds, or information the child is learning, he or she may be able to identify situations in which these skills can be incorporated into daily events.

In addition to teaching particular skills, speech clinicians and teachers can facilitate communication in all contexts. Communication is facilitated first by giving the child many opportunities to use language skills to obtain information or to convey ideas. The classroom teacher may also reduce the complexity of the language the child hears, repeat directions, and provide visual aids. When aware of the child's new skills, the teacher can encourage the child to use them. The teacher can reward attempts at adequate communication and reduce the penalities the child might suffer because of inadequate communication. The actions of the teacher as facilitator can go a long way toward ensuring that behavior mastered in therapy will be maintained and used effectively by the child.

Because communication encompasses all aspects of the educational program, therapy will not be effective unless the prescribed program is carried out in the child's regular environment. The speech-language pathologist will accomplish little without the active involvement of parents and teachers.

This child is receiving speech therapy from a speech-language pathologist.

SUMMARY

1. Communication is disordered when it deviates from accepted norms such that it calls attention to itself, interferes with the message, or distresses the speaker or listener.
2. Speech results from many organs of the body working cooperatively to produce sound.
3. The three major types of sounds in our language are vowels, diphthongs, and consonants.
4. The sounds of our language may be characterized by the manner in which they are made, and the primary place in the oral cavity where they are articulated.
5. Speech and language are developmental processes acquired over time.
6. Language disorders are the most complex and most serious of all communication problems.
7. Most speech disorders involve problems with speech sound production, voice, or fluency.
8. Speech problems may have an organic cause, or they may not. Problems of the latter type are called functional problems.
9. Speech-language pathologists are professionals trained to deal with communication disorders.
10. The classroom teacher has an important role in the early identification of communication disorders.
11. Gains made in therapy sessions must be reinforced in the home and classroom for speech therapy to be effective.

TASK SHEET 3
Field Experiences with Communication Disorders

Select *one* of the following and complete the required activities.

Program Visitation
Arrange to visit a program that provides diagnostic or therapeutic services to children with communication disorders. In no more than three pages, describe the program you visited and what you observed. If you saw children being treated, describe the treatment that was being administered and the problem it was intended to help cure. Describe your general reaction to the program.

Professional Interview
Interview one of the people listed below and determine his or her job responsibilities, the training necessary for the job, the problems encountered, and the rewards of the work. If observation facilities are available, ask to observe the person working with a client.
   a. Speech-language pathologist
   b. Director of a speech clinic at a hospital or private clinic

c. Member of a cleft palate team at a hospital
d. An otorhinolaryngologist

Interview with a Communication-Disordered Person

Using great tact and discretion, either interview or observe a person who has a communication disorder. This may be someone who has had a stroke, a member of The Lost Cord Club (for laryngectomized speakers), a stutterer, or a person with a cleft palate, cerebral palsy, or an articulation problem. In your interview or observation, pay particular attention to the person's communication. Describe your experience and your reaction to it in no more than three pages.

Speech and Language Analysis

Do one of the following:

a. Ask a child of nursery school age (2½–3½) to tell you a story such as *The Three Bears,* and then ask a child who is two or three years older to tell you the same story. Aside from linguistic sophistication, note the difference in the fluency of the speakers. Compare the number of repetitions of words, hesitations, and false starts for the two children, and describe your conclusions and reactions.

b. Locate two children of different ages, tell them a fairly complex story, and then ask them to retell it to you. Describe the differences in the children's linguistic development, especially differences in sentence length, sentence complexity, embellishments of the story, vocal inflection, and general storytelling ability. It may be helpful to tape-record the stories.

Agency Investigation

Request information from the following agencies about the services they provide in the area of communication disorders. Write a three-page paper summarizing these services and how you might use them if you were a professional working with children who have speech or language problems.

American Speech-Language
Hearing Association
10801 Rockville Pike
Rockville, MD 20852

Information Center for Hearing,
Speech and Disorders of Human
Communication
310 Harriet Lane Home
Johns Hopkins Medical Institute
Baltimore, MD 21205

Library Study

Select three articles concerning communication disorders and write a one-page synopsis of each. Conclude by writing your personal reaction to each article. You can find articles about communication disorders in the following journals:

Journal of Speech and Hearing Disorders
Journal of Speech and Hearing Research
Language Speech and Hearing Services in the Schools
ASHA
Journal of Childhood Communication Disorders

Design Your Own Field Experience

If you know of a unique experience you can have with children or adults who have a communication disorder or do not want to do any of the listed alternatives, discuss your alternatives with your instructor and complete the task that you agree upon.

In 1934, a handsome fifteen-year-old boy was brought to school in Danville for the first time. His parents explained that they had been unable to part with him when he became old enough for school and thus he had grown up entirely uneducated and had never learned to obey, or live under restrictions of a regular school.

The school administration had to admit this boy, but foresaw the difficulty of training him, also teaching him.

They got an older boy to be his "Big brother" and help keep him in line. This proved quite difficult, since the new boy was powerfully built and showed great distaste for the life at school.

Despite the difficulties encountered, most of the school population were of the opinion that the new pupil would gradually adjust to the new life and surroundings.

One Saturday afternoon, the older boys were allowed to attend the movies in town and took this boy with them in hopes he would have a good afternoon. By some . . . ruse, the boy gave his big brother and the other boys the slip and disappeared in the darkened theatre.

It was later discovered that he had left the theatre, unobserved and gone to the bus station. Since he couldn't read or write he, in some unexplained way, had bought a ticket to a town where they had recently had a bank robbery, arriving at midnight.

The boy got off the bus and being in a strange darkened town, made for a lighted window. This happened to be the bank where a guard was stationed. . . .

The boy banged on the bank door seeking admittance. This alarmed the guard who drew his gun. . . .

Seeing the guard with his gun pointed at him, the boy took flight and was shot to death when he failed to halt when ordered to do so.

Identification was easily established because in his coat pocket was a letter to him at the school by his mother, in which she told him to be a good boy and do as he was told.

This is only one of the many tragedies attributed to deafness which could be recounted in our history, but is a true story and explains why our educators are so determined in getting young deaf children in school.

Source: From J. B. Beauchamp, "A Tragedy of Deafness," *The Kentucky Standard,* Danville: Kentucky School For the Deaf, February 1979, Used by permission.

5

Hearing Disorders

William W. Green

William W. Green is Professor of Neurology, Pediatrics, and Special Education, and is also Director of the Neurosensory and Communicative Disorders Program at the University of Kentucky. Current areas of interest include audiological evaluation of infants, noise induced hearing loss, and environmental hearing conservation.

The tragedy described on the facing page is, of course, an exaggeration of the dilemma most deaf persons are confronted with, an invisible handicap that the public can easily misunderstand and react to inappropriately. The interpersonal disabilities that hearing disorders often bring about are staggering when one considers the high rate of oral language used in most societies. Helen Keller, renowned author, educator, and advocate for the deaf and hard of hearing succinctly describes the multiple dilemmas of being deaf:

> I am just as deaf as I am blind. The problems of deafness are deeper and more complex; if not more important than those of blindness. Deafness is a much worse misfortune. For it means the loss of the most vital stimulus — the sound of the voice that brings language, sets thoughts astir, and keeps us in the intellectual company of men [Keller, 1933].

That statement was made by Helen Keller when she was asked to describe the effects of her problems of deafness and blindness. It might surprise you: many of us assume that a loss of vision would have a deeper and more disruptive influence on our daily lives than a loss of hearing. One reason we make that assumption could be that vision problems are relatively easy to imagine — almost everyone has played games that involve being blindfolded or tried to maneuver in the dark. But how many people have ever tried to function without hearing, even for a little while? Almost no one. We generally take our hearing for granted, and we often remain unaware of the subtle and the not-so-subtle ways we are affected by the sounds that pervade our environment.

By the end of this chapter you should have an increased understanding of the importance of hearing. Specifically, we will discuss normal hearing and hearing disorders, particularly as they relate to the education of children. In addition, we hope to motivate you to seek more information to help you to better understand hearing and to enhance your abilities as an educator.

SOUND AND HUMAN HEARING

You should be able to describe the nature of sound and the different ways we use our hearing.

Unless you are reading in a soundproof room, it is almost impossible for you not to be hearing something. If you stop for a moment, close your eyes, and just listen, you may hear a number of simple and complex sounds: a clock ticking, a bird chirping, the hum of a light or heater, wind rustling through the trees, rain hitting the window, the radio or television, traffic noise, people talking, and so on. Our environment is filled with sounds. We are accustomed to them; they are part of our feeling of well-being or annoyance, of our participation in a world full of life.

THE NATURE OF SOUND

Before we discuss hearing and hearing disorders, it is important that you understand what a sound is. Although physicists and acoustic engineers refer to different aspects of sound in many different and often complicated ways, a simple description best serves our purposes. The basic parts of a sound system are identified in Figure 5-1. This configuration is called the TMR system.

How is sound generated, transmitted, and received?

A sound is created by the vibration of an object, a transmitter (T). It may be a string, reed, or column of air, as in a musical instrument, or it may be metal, wood, or some other object. The human vocal folds consist of highly specialized vibrating tissue. Vibration, however, becomes sound only if there is a surrounding medium (M) that can carry it. The most common carrying medium is air, but it is also possible for water, metal, or other substances to carry the vibration. The final link in the sound system is something to receive the sound. This receiver (R) may be electronic in the case of radio or TV, but one of the most sensitive receivers is the ear.

Figure 5-1
A Sound System

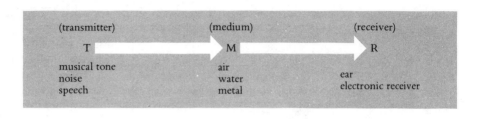

HOW WE USE OUR HEARING

What are Hertz and decibels?

A normal, healthy human ear can hear sounds over a remarkable range of frequencies and intensities. Frequency and intensity are two of the measurable physical characteristics of sound. Pitch is the ears' perception of frequency, and loudness is the ears' perception of intensity. A good way to understand the difference is to regard the lowest and highest keys of a piano keyboard as somewhat representative of the range of frequencies and pitches that the ear can hear, while the intensity and loudness of the sounds are related to how hard the keys are pressed.

The frequency of sounds is expressed in a unit called the Hertz (abbreviated Hz). This is an internationally recognized notation and replaces the use of cycles per second that has predominated in the United States. The human ear can generally hear sounds ranging from 20 to 20,000 Hz, but most sounds in our environment fall between 125 and 8000 Hz. The frequencies of speech sounds fall in the range from 300 to 4000 Hz; it is especially important that the ear be able to hear in this range. Frequencies above 8000 Hz are not crucial to hearing speech, but we do use them to enjoy live and reproduced high fidelity music.

The intensity of a sound is directly related to the energy or force of the vibration that caused it. Since the human ear is capable of responding to an enormous range of sound energy, a ratio scale is used to describe intensity. The unit of intensity is the decibel (dB). Zero dB represents the intensity of the softest sound that the normal young adult ear can hear, and 140 dB represents a level so loud it is painful. The intensity range of the human voice is between 40 dB and 60 dB. Figure 5-2 displays the intensity and frequency ranges for some common environmental and speech sounds.

Levels of Hearing. As we mentioned in the opening paragraphs, most people do not understand how much they depend on their hearing. Ramsdell (1970)

Figure 5-2
Typical Sound Frequencies and Intensities

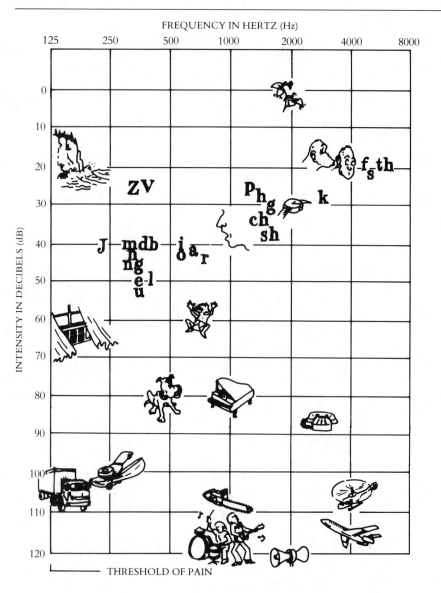

describes hearing as having three psychological levels: (1) the *symbolic level,* (2) the *signal* or *warning level,* and (3) the *auditory background* or *primitive level.*

**What is the
difference
between the
symbolic, signal,
and auditory
background levels
of hearing?**

An understanding of these three levels will enable us to appreciate the practical implications of hearing loss and the psychological changes that accompany it.

The symbolic level of hearing is the level we use to understand words, which are the symbols of objects and concepts. Good hearing is essential for learning speech and language.

The second level is used as a signal or warning system. We constantly rely on hearing to signal us of changes in our environment and to warn us of approaching danger (e.g., a car horn, a train whistle, or an approaching storm). Our use of this level is generally unconscious, but nevertheless it is important. A loss of hearing places an additional burden on the other senses, which sometimes cannot compensate adequately.

Finally, the ear functions on a so-called primitive or background level by constantly monitoring sounds in our environment, thereby keeping us in touch with it. People who have lost the ability to hear background noises often experience almost overwhelming feelings of isolation. These feelings and the frustration that accompanies them can have serious psychological consequences.

We might also consider these levels of hearing from the perspective of the special education teacher. Many mentally retarded, learning disabled, and emotionally disturbed children have delayed speech or language development. Although this delay may not be the direct effect of a hearing loss, it can result from central auditory perceptual or processing problems. These children are likely to have trouble with the symbolic level of functioning.

These special children may also have problems with the signal/warning level or the background level. They are often easily distracted and have trouble adjusting to sudden environmental changes. They may, for example, be distracted or even alarmed by the ringing of the bell to signal class changes, or by the public address system. As a result, the special education teacher may have to control background noises and signal/warning-level sounds.

**PROBE 5-1
Sound and Human Hearing**

1. What are the three basic components of a sound system?

2. How would you define sound?

3. Two measurable aspects of sound are _____ , which is measured in _____ , and _____ , which is measured in _____ .

4. What is the intensity range for average conversational speech?

5. List Ramsdell's three psychological levels of hearing.

HOW WE HEAR

> **You should be able to describe how we hear.**

ANATOMY AND PHYSIOLOGY OF THE EAR

To understand hearing disorders, it is necessary to understand the structures and processes involved in normal hearing. It is helpful to consider the ear in three parts, *the outer ear, the middle ear,* and *the inner ear.* The parts of the human ear are illustrated in Figure 5-3.

Outer Ear. The outer ear consists of the pinna or auricle (the cartilagenous structure on the side of the head) and the external auditory canal. Since the pinna is the only outwardly visible part of the ear, many people think it is more important than it actually is. The function of the pinna is to collect sound waves arriving at the ear and direct them into the auditory canal. If you have a dog or a cat, you have probably noticed that they can move their pinnae to improve their hearing. Humans retain only a vestige of this ability. We must turn our entire head to focus the ear on a particular sound.

What is the function of the outer ear?

The auditory canal protects the sensitive internal structures in the ear from damage and foreign objects. It is one to two inches long and has stiff hairs at its outer edge to help keep objects from entering. In addition, the skin lining the outer third of the canal secretes a bitter-tasting wax called cerumen that traps foreign material and keeps the ear canal and eardrum from drying out. Earwax is not dirt, and the process of removing it can sometimes result in irritation and infection. The old adage that you shouldn't put anything smaller than your elbow in your ear is still good advice. A doctor should be consulted if you have a problem with wax buildup.

How do the structures of the middle ear operate?

Middle Ear. The outer and middle ear are separated by the eardrum. The eardrum is a membrane that vibrates when it is struck by sound waves; the vibration is then transmitted by a series of three small bones, the malleus (hammer), incus (anvil), and stapes (stirrup). These bones, which are named for the objects they resemble, carry the vibration across the middle ear cavity to the entrance to the inner ear.

Another important structure generally considered part of the middle ear system is the eustachian tube, which extends between the back wall of the throat and the middle ear cavity. This structure opens and closes to equalize the air pressure on the inside of the eardrum with that on the outside. The eustachian tube is the structure that relieves the feeling of pressure or stoppage we feel when descending in an airplane or swimming under water. By swallowing, yawning, or using normal muscle action, we cause the tube to open,

Figure 5-3
The human ear. The pathways for sound waves to be transmitted to the inner ear are shown.

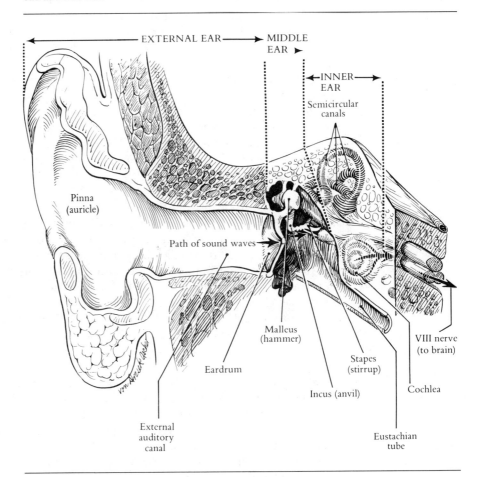

which allows air to enter the middle ear cavity (Davis and Silverman, 1970; Newby, 1972).

Inner Ear. The inner ear is a remarkably intricate structure. The cochlea of the inner ear contains thousands of hair cells (12,000 in the human ear). The two major structures of the inner ear can be differentiated by their function. The vestibular mechanism, consisting of the semicircular canals, is used for balance; the cochlea is used for hearing. Both structures are filled with fluid and are joined by the vestibule, the open area into which sound waves enter from the middle ear.

The vestibular mechanism is the structure that enables us to maintain our balance. It consists of three loop-like structures, the membranous semicircular canals. The angles of the loops correspond to horizontal, vertical, and lateral planes. The canals and two other structures, the utricle and the saccule, relay information about head movement, body movement, and acceleration to the brain, which then adjusts the body to maintain balance (Martin, 1975; Newby, 1972).

What is the cochlea?

The cochlea, which lies just below the semicircular canals, is important for hearing. This organ, which is shaped like a snail shell, contains the endings of the auditory nerve (Cranial Nerve VIII) in a central channel called the cochlear duct. The movements of the stapes in and out of the opening to the inner ear create waves in the fluid in the cochlea. These waves then stimulate the nerve endings of the auditory nerve, which sends an electrical impulse to the brain (Davis and Silverman, 1970; Martin, 1975).

These structures are all considered part of the peripheral hearing mechanism, to distinguish them from the central auditory mechanism, which consists of those parts of the brain involved with sound. The peripheral hearing mechanism serves as an extremely efficient sound transmitter. To repeat the steps: a transmission starts with a vibration in air (sound wave), which travels down the auditory canal and causes the eardrum to vibrate. This vibration is then carried across the middle ear cavity mechanically by the three bones of the ossicular chain, to the opening of the inner ear. There the vibration is transferred to a fluid movement that travels through the cochlea. The fluid, vibratory energy is finally changed to electrical energy by the stimulation of the nerve endings of the auditory nerve.

Central Auditory Processing. The operations involved in the central processing of auditory signals are far too complex to discuss in detail in this text. You need only understand that sounds in the form of electrical energy travel along the auditory nerve through several complex lower brainstem areas to the cortex, which is the covering of the brain. One area of the cortex is adapted to manage sound; it is there that the interpretation and perception of sound take place. This area, called the auditory cortex, is responsible for the gross and fine discrimination necessary to understand speech and language. (Ades, 1959; Northern and Downs, 1974).

What is the purpose of the auditory cortex?

The function of the auditory cortex and the rest of the central auditory system is roughly comparable to that of a computer. It interprets and analyzes the sounds that are fed into it, organizing them into a pattern that we can understand and use as a language. The analogy is only partially accurate, however — only humans can interpret the emotions, subtleties, and intentions expressed in speech.

You may be surprised to learn that a five-month-old human fetus can hear sounds. At birth, the newborn has been hearing, albeit passively, for four months. After the child is born, he or she begins learning the basic building blocks of language. Children gradually refine their cooing, gurgling, and babbling by listening to his or her own sounds and the sounds of those around them, a process known as an "auditory feedback loop." Children with normal hearing usually produce their first words at about one year old, and language develops very quickly thereafter. This process is delayed by several years in deaf children, and the words these children learn must be acquired by means other than hearing.

As you can see, learning is a complex process that takes place formally and informally throughout our lives. It depends on the senses, particularly vision and hearing. These senses are so basic that problems with any component in their complex arrangement can interfere with learning.

Auditory learning requires an intact peripheral auditory mechanism. The hearing losses that result from problems at this level preclude the processing of raw data (sounds). A partial hearing loss can retard auditory learning, and complete deafness stops auditory learning altogether and requires a heavy emphasis on visual skills. If the peripheral hearing mechanism functions as it should, the central auditory system is the crucial mechanism in auditory learning and speech/language development.

PROBE 5-2
How We Hear

1. Match each item on the left with the appropriate selection on the right.

        _____ 1. incus   a. cerumen
        _____ 2. sense organ of hearing   b. malleus
        _____ 3. outer ear   c. stapes
        _____ 4. ventilation   d. semicircular canals
        _____ 5. balance   e. anvil
        _____ 6. earwax   f. pinna
        _____ 7. transmits sound to brain   g. eardrum
        _____ 8. hammer   h. cochlea
                                                  i. auditory nerve (VIII)
                                                  j. eustachian tube

2. T   F   Earwax is dirt and should be cleaned from the ears.

3. Trace the pathway of sound through the structures of the ear.

4. The part of the brain most important to hearing is the _____ .

5. The human ear begins responding to sound at what age?

HEARING LOSS

> You should be able to define hearing loss, describe its prevalence among children, and know its major classifications and causes.

DEFINITION AND CLASSIFICATION

Many different systems have been proposed to define and classify hearing loss. Some of these systems are physiologically oriented and focus only on the measurable amount of hearing loss, whereas others focus on the extent to which the hearing loss affects speech/language development, educational achievement, and psychological adjustment (Myklebust, 1964; Newby, 1972). Another consideration is the age at which the hearing loss occurred. Very early loss of hearing affects a child's development more than a later loss (Myklebust, 1964). A classification system designed to aid teachers and counselors of the hearing impaired must take into account all of these factors.

An important distinction must be made between the term "deafness" and other more general terms such as "hearing loss," "hearing disorder," and "hard of hearing." *Deafness* means a hearing loss so great that hearing cannot be used for the normal purposes of life, whereas the other terms are used to describe any deviation from normal hearing, regardless of its severity. For the educator of deaf or hard-of-hearing children, the definitions proposed by the Conference of Executives of American Schools for the Deaf can be used effectively. This group first proposed definitions in 1938, as follows (Davis and Silverman, 1970):

How do the terms "deaf" and "hard of hearing" differ?

1. *The deaf.* Those in whom the sense of hearing is nonfunctional for the ordinary purposes of life. Based on the age at which the deafness occurred, the deaf were grouped into two distinct classes:
   a. The *congenitally deaf.* Those who were born deaf.
   b. The *adventitiously deaf.* Those who were born with normal hearing but in whom the sense of hearing became nonfunctional later through illness or accident.
2. *The hard of hearing.* Those in whom the sense of hearing, although defective, is functional either with or without a hearing aid.

These definitions were more recently refined to reflect the importance of hearing in language acquisition, as follows:

Hearing Impairment — A generic term indicating a hearing disability that may range in severity from mild to profound. It consists of two groups, the *deaf* and the *hard of hearing:*

A *deaf* person is one whose hearing disability precludes successful processing of linguistic information through audition, with or without a hearing aid.

A *hard-of-hearing* person is one who, generally with the use of a hearing aid, has residual hearing sufficient to enable successful processing of linguistic information through audition (Report of the Ad Hoc Committee to Define Deaf and Hard of Hearing, 1975).

The educator should be very careful not to classify a child as deaf or hearing impaired until his or her hearing has been thoroughly assessed. Even after assessment, professionals should remain flexible about a child's classification. New evidence about a child's ability to hear or speak with proper stimulation, education, or amplification may dictate that he or she be reclassified (Silverman, 1971).

PREVALENCE

What is the prevalence of hearing impairment?

It is estimated that approximately 8 percent, or some 17.4 million Americans, experience some degree of difficulty hearing or understanding speech (Punch, 1983). Table 5-1 provides a further breakdown of hearing impairment by age group and suggests that almost 100,000 preschool-age children have hearing loss. School children in the elementary and junior high school age categories have approximately 600,000 hearing-impaired classmates, while 900,000 high school and college-age students have some degree of hearing loss (National Center for Health Statistics, 1982).

Table 5-1
Prevalence rates of hearing impairment, per 100 persons, in the civilian, non-institutionalized population of the U.S. Rates are based on 1977 interview data.

Age Group In Years	Number	Prevalence Rate (%)
<5	96,034	0.63
5–14	592,595	1.63
15–24	922,012	2.32
25–34	1,380,760	4.29
35–44	1,344,130	5.82
45–54	2,269,974	9.79
55–64	3,095,322	15.35
65–74	3,430,852	24.10
75–	3,087,095	38.55
All	16,218,774	7.64

Source: NCHS, 1982.

CAUSES OF HEARING LOSS

Up to this point we have considered the nature and process of hearing and its importance in the development of speech and language and of auditory learning. Those of us with normal hearing pay little attention to the complexities of these processes. The complexities are more difficult for a person with a hearing impairment to ignore. Hearing losses can result from a number of conditions and illness. There are five major types: conductive, sensorineural, mixed, functional, and central.

Conductive Hearing Loss. A conductive hearing loss results from problems with the structures in the outer or middle ear, generally a blockage in the mechanical conduction of sound. Sounds must be amplified to overcome the blockage.

What is otitis media?

The leading cause of conductive hearing loss is middle ear infection, or otitis media. This condition usually results from a malfunction of the eustachian tube. If this organ does not allow enough air into the middle ear to equalize the air pressure on the outside of the eardrum, the oxygen in the air trapped in the middle ear is gradually absorbed by the middle ear cavity tissue. This causes a partial vacuum, which pulls the eardrum into the middle ear cavity. Next, the tissues of the middle ear secrete fluid to fill the void created by the absorbed oxygen. This fluid may become infected. If the condition is unchecked, the fluid may build up sufficiently to rupture the eardrum.

Children have smaller, more horizontal eustachian tubes than adults and more frequent colds and allergies, which affect the eustachian tube openings. As a result they have more eustachian tube problems and much more frequent middle ear infections. Teachers should be aware that this is a common problem. Children who appear to be daydreaming or don't understand assignments may have mild hearing losses caused by ear infections.

Another cause of conductive loss is the blockage of the auditory canal by excessive earwax or a foreign body. If the ear canal is completely blocked, a mild conductive hearing loss can result. Earwax buildup is not as common a problem as many people think, however; even a tiny opening through a plug of earwax is sufficient for relatively normal hearing. Often a condition assumed to be caused by earwax has an entirely different cause. Children may have a mild hearing loss as a result of putting a foreign object, such as a bean or part of a toy, in the auditory canal.

What is otosclerosis?

Another cause of conductive hearing loss is a condition called otosclerosis. This results from the formation of a spongy-bony growth around the stapes, which progressively impedes its movement and causes gradual deterioration of hearing. This condition can often be overcome by a surgical procedure called a stapedectomy.

Conductive hearing losses are usually temporary, and the amount of hearing loss varies depending on the medical condition that causes it. These losses are seldom severe enough to prevent one from hearing speech entirely, but they can cause a child to miss sounds and words and delay the development of speech and language. Most conductive hearing loss can be successfully treated with medicine or surgery. Specific treatments will be discussed later in this chapter.

Sensorineural Hearing Loss. Sensorineural hearing losses result from damage to the cochlea or the auditory nerve. This damage is caused by illness or disease. Sensorineural hearing losses are usually greater than those caused by conductive disorders, and they require extensive treatment.

What are the major causes of sensorineural hearing loss?

Viral diseases are a major cause of hearing loss, particularly in children. These can occur either before or after birth and may cause problems ranging from mild hearing loss to deafness. There is a high probability that a pregnant woman who contracts rubella (German measles) during her first three months of pregnancy will give birth to a child with some sensorineural hearing loss. It is estimated that 10,000 to 20,000 children were born deaf as a result of the rubella epidemics of the early and mid 1960s (Northern and Downs, 1974). Severe hearing loss or deafness can also result from infectious meningitis, mumps, measles, chicken pox, and influenza. Viral conditions may also result in malformed body parts, retardation, nervous system damage, and congenital heart disease.

Rh incompatibility is the cause of impairment in about 3 percent of the children who have hearing loss (Northern and Downs, 1974). This condition, called erythroblastosis fetalis, is the result of the destruction of fetal Rh positive blood cells by maternal antibodies. The condition kills some of the afflicted infants during the first week of life. Of those who survive, 80 percent have partial or complete deafness. Like viral diseases, Rh incompatibility can cause other problems, such as cerebral palsy, mental retardation, epilepsy, aphasia, and behavioral disorders.

Other hearing problems are caused by ototoxic medications, medicines that destroy or damage hair cells in the cochlea. Kanamycin, neomycin, gentamycin, streptomycin, and vancomycin are some of the drugs known to be ototoxic. These drugs can cause partial or complete hearing loss when taken by the child or the pregnant mother. The fetus is particularly susceptible during the first three months of its development, especially the sixth and seventh weeks. The use of drugs by expectant mothers and young children should be carefully controlled.

Hereditary factors can also cause hearing loss. Proctor and Proctor (1967) report that hereditary deafness occurs in one of 2,000 to one of 6,000 live births. In many cases hearing loss is only one of several symptoms of a genetic problem. A specific group of symptoms may be classified as a syndrome, which may be identified by facial appearance, physical anomalies, mental retardation, sensory deficit, and motor weakness. Alport's syndrome, Treacher-Colling syndrome, and Down's syndrome are examples of genetic conditions that may result in hearing loss. The child with a hereditary deficit often presents complex multiple problems that challenge the background and resourcefulness of the special educator.

Can exposure to noise affect hearing?

Although we have emphasized conditions that result in sensorineural hearing loss in children, two other important causes of sensorineural loss should be mentioned — exposure to noise, and aging. The recognition that noise can damage hearing has led to government regulation of acceptable noise levels in industry and the environment. Most of us can expect our hearing to deteriorate as we grow older. Both aging and excessive noise initially affect our ability to hear high-frequency sounds; the loss may gradually progress until we have problems understanding speech.

Unlike conductive hearing losses, sensorineural losses are not medically or surgically treatable. They are usually quite severe and require long-term rehabilitation efforts, which will be discussed later in this chapter.

What is a mixed hearing loss?

Mixed Hearing Loss. A mixed hearing loss is one caused by both sensorineural and conductive problems. Such losses can create particularly serious problems for schoolchildren: a physician may focus on the conductive, medically treatable part of the loss, and be unaware of the sensorineural component. As a result, a child may not receive proper treatment for a problem that affects his or her classroom performance.

Most hearing losses are caused by conductive, sensorineural, or mixed problems. However, all three types of problems may affect only one ear or may affect one ear more severely than the other. When this is the case, the child relies on the better ear and may turn that ear toward the speaker; the child also has trouble determining the source of a sound. Generally, however, a child with good hearing in one ear acquires speech and language without difficulty.

What causes functional hearing loss?

Functional Hearing Loss. Functional problems are those that are not organic in origin, as you will remember from the last chapter. Functional hearing losses are generally affected to (1) gain attention, (2) explain a poor performance, (3) avoid a responsibility, or (4) collect insurance money. In some cases, functional hearing loss may be psychosomatic or hysterical in origin, and the person may not be conscious of the assumed loss.

Among children, functional hearing losses occur most frequently between the ages of 9 and 13. The losses are usually discovered in hearing tests given in school. It is not unusual to discover that a child with a functional loss is upset or unhappy. There might, for example, be a new baby in the family who diverts parental attention; there may be a divorce or friction between the child's parents; there may be problems with the child's siblings or peer group; or the child may be receiving poor grades. Any of these conditions could cause a child to assume a hearing loss. Once the loss was assumed, it would be awkward and threatening to admit that it was all a game:

Sonja was an attractive, alert nine-year-old child from a Middle-Eastern country who was brought to the clinic by her aunt. She had been seen by a local otologist whose tests showed moderate hearing loss. The otologist could find no ear pathology, however. The aunt explained that Sonja had failed one subject, dictation, and under the educational system in her country she was required to repeat the entire year. Her family was upper class and ambitious, and when Sonja was questioned about the failure, she stated that she could not hear the teacher. This triggered a chain of events that led to a trip to America to visit her aunt for medical treatment and/or a hearing aid. The first test in the clinic showed a moderate loss, but after considerable counseling and with the aunt's help, testing finally revealed normal hearing. Sonja then admitted that she failed dictation because she didn't like the teacher, not because she didn't hear her. Once she had fallen into the trap of having a "hearing loss," she couldn't find a comfortable way out. Apparently, no one wondered why she had trouble hearing one of her teachers and not the others.

Among adults, functional hearing loss is often consciously intended, and can generally be considered malingering. The purpose is usually to make money, from an automobile or industrial accident, for example. When there was a military draft, it was not uncommon for a hearing loss to be "faked" to avoid induction. There were also attempts to obtain disability payments at discharge by assuming a hearing loss. There are functional hearing losses that are not intentional, of course. A functional loss can result from emotional or psychological problems. Most adult losses, though, are intentionally assumed. Audiologists have several tests designed to detect malingering.

What is a central auditory disorder?

Central Auditory Disorders. Central auditory disorders are those in which there is no measurable peripheral hearing loss. Children with this type of disorder may display problems with auditory comprehension and discrimination, auditory learning, and language development. These disorders are the result of lesions or damage to the central nervous system, but specific causes are hard to pinpoint. Children with central auditory disorders have trouble learning and are often considered learning disabled. Interest in children with these disorders is growing. They have serious long-term problems and are difficult to treat effectively.

PROBE 5-3
Hearing Loss

1. A person who had a hearing loss severe enough that he or she cannot learn language through hearing is classified as _____ .

2. As many as _____ preschool-age children have some degree of hearing loss.

3. List the five major types of hearing loss.

4. Otitis media is the most common cause of _____ hearing loss. Other possible causes for this condition are _____ and _____ .

5. When a "hearing loss' is assumed to explain poor school performance, the "loss" would be termed _____ .

6. When there is damage or deterioration of the cochlea or VIII nerve, the hearing loss is termed _____ . A major cause of this type of problem is _____ disease. One of these diseases, _____ , is a major cause of deafness in children.

7. When a child displays weakness in auditory skills and yet shows no measurable hearing loss, a _____ should be suspected.

EVALUATING HEARING LOSS

You should be able to discuss how hearing loss is identified and evaluated and be able to read an audiogram.

The hearing problems of children are identified at different ages and by a variety of different people. Children are generally referred first to a physician or otologist, who may in turn refer the child to an audiologist if there is no obvious problem that can be resolved medically or surgically. The audiologist can perform many different types of tests to determine whether a child has a problem, what kind of problem he or she has, and how it should be remedied.

As is true of other types of disorders, hearing disorders are treated most effectively if they are discovered early. In fact, there is sometimes concern about a child's hearing before birth, if there is a hereditary factor predisposing the child to a hearing problem or if the mother has had an illness such as rubella or meningitis. There may also be concern if the mother has taken ototoxic drugs or had a traumatic accident, or if there is Rh incompatibility. Hearing evaluations are sometimes difficult to perform with very young children, but evaluations must be begun early to give the child every possible advantage.

Hearing problems are often discovered when the child is older, however. Parents may notice that a child does not react to loud sounds, does not turn his or her head when hearing a voice, does not engage in vocal play, or is delayed in speech and language development. Hearing problems may also be identified in hearing screening programs offered through health departments, speech and hearing centers, or school systems. Attentive teachers who notice that a child doesn't pay attention or frequently asks to have things repeated sometimes uncover hearing problems as well. However a problem is discovered, it should be promptly and thoroughly evaluated.

This evaluation is generally medical and audiological. The pediatrician or otologist takes a thorough medical history of the child and does a complete examination of the auditory canal and eardrum with a small light called an otoscope. If the child has an obvious middle ear infection, the doctor may be able to cure the problem. Audiometry may be requested to determine the effects of treatment. If the doctor cannot find the cause of the problem, the parents and child should be referred to an audiologist.

AUDIOMETRIC EVALUATION

Special educators should have some knowledge of the means and purposes of audiometric testings and should be able to read an audiogram. A thorough discussion of audiometric testing can be found in Newby (1972) and Martin (1975).

Some types of hearing evaluation that yield gross information do not require the use of sophisticated equipment. Observations by parents and doctors provide some information, as do the child's medical history and otoscopic examination. Even something as simple as the child's reaction to loud noises such as hand clapping and rustling paper can help determine the need for further evaluation. The relatively refined methods of formal audiometric test-

This student's hearing is being tested with an audiometer.

ing, some of which are described in this section, are necessary to determine the precise extent of the hearing problem and the best methods of auditory rehabilitation.

What type of audiometric evaluation is most frequently done in schools?

Pure Tone Audiometric Screening. Pure tone audiometric screening is usually a child's first encounter with formal hearing testing. Most school systems provide a regular schedule of hearing screening through the school speech-language pathologist or school nurse. Group hearing screening tests (Newby, 1972) offer the advantage of testing more than one child at a time, but they are less susceptible to control and less reliable than individual tests.

Pure tone screening of individual students, often referred to as sweep testing, is performed with a pure tone audiometer (Newby, 1972). In this test the child is presented with pure tones over the frequency range from 250 Hz through 8000 Hz, and at a set intensity level of 20 or 25 dB. The child is asked to respond if he or she hears a tone, usually by raising a hand; children who cannot hear sounds at two or more frequencies are referred for more extensive evaluation.

Pure Tone Threshold Audiometry. Pure tone audiometry is a testing method that requires a child to raise a hand or push a button each time he or she hears a tone. The audiologist gives the child tones of different frequencies, ranging from 125 Hz to 8000 Hz, and determines the lowest intensity the child can hear, the threshold, at each frequency. This testing is done through earphones (air conduction) or through a vibrator placed on the mastoid bone behind the ear (bone conduction). The air conduction (AC) test reveals the presence of hearing loss and shows the amount of the loss. Bone conduction (BC) testing measures the response of the sensorineural mechanism of the inner ear, by-passing the outer and middle ear systems. A comparison of air conduction and bone conduction thresholds reveals the loss as conductive, sensorineural, or mixed as follows:

How are the results of air conduction and bone conduction audiometric tests used?

Conductive loss is indicated when AC testing reveals some loss of hearing in the outer or middle ear, but BC testing shows normal hearing because the auditory nerve is functioning properly.

Sensorineural loss is indicated when AC and BC testing show the same amount of loss, which signifies that the outer and middle ear are intact and the inner ear is affected.

Mixed loss is indicated when BC testing shows a loss resulting from a sensorineural problem, and AC testing shows further loss resulting from a middle ear problem.

What is the speech reception threshold?

Speech Audiometry. Speech audiometry is a technique used to determine a child's ability to hear and understand speech. The threshold for speech (that is, the lowest intensity at which words are heard), is called the speech reception threshold, abbreviated SRT. The SRT is discovered by asking the child to repeat two-syllable words that he or she hears, while the audiologist reduces the intensity of the words until they are barely heard. To determine how well the child can understand or discriminate among words heard at a comfortable loudness level, the child is presented with a recorded list of one-syllable words and asked to respond. The child is expected to respond to all words whether the child understands them or not. The purpose of the test is to determine how many correct responses the child makes in a given word list (usually 24 or 50 words). The number of correct responses is converted to a percentage score, and this is the speech discrimination score. Both the SRT and speech discrimination measures require the use of earphones.

In some cases it is necessary to keep one ear "busy" to test the other ear accurately. This occurs primarily when one ear is better than the other. This technique called *masking,* involves transmitting a constant hissing noise to the good ear to keep the good ear from hearing a sound being presented to the bad ear.

When are special audiometric tests needed?

Special Audiometric Tests. Pure tone and speech audiometry constitute the standard test battery used to determine what type of hearing loss a child has and how extensive it is. Both tests require that the person being tested understand the test instructions and give a voluntary response, such as pushing a button, raising a hand, or repeating words. Some children cannot be evaluated with these tests, however, because they are too young (less than two), have motor or emotional problems, are mentally retarded, or present other difficulties. For these children special tests and test variations have been devised.

If a child is too young to understand test instructions or is unwilling to wear earphones, hearing can be evaluated by observing the intensity levels at which the child responds to sounds broadcast through speakers. Using this method, sound field audiometry, the audiologist presents speech, noise, or pure tones, and notes whether the child pays attention to the sounds or consistently turns to determine the sound source. The speech reception threshold of very young children can sometimes be determined by asking them to point to pictures or parts of the body as they are named. The same method can also be used to get an impression of a child's ability to discriminate speech (Northern and Downs, 1974).

Various techniques can be used to entice a frightened or reticent child to participate in testing by setting up a game or challenge (Newby, 1972; Northern and Downs, 1974). Behavioral play audiometry involves the child in a series of activities that reward the child for responding appropriately to tone or speech. The game might involve putting a block in a bucket, activating a moving toy, turning on a light, or completing a puzzle.

The *impedance audiometer* is used to obtain information about the functioning of the middle ear system to assist the physician in treating otitis media and other middle ear problems. The two major impedance audiometry tests are *tympanometry,* which gives information about the compliance or resistance of the eardrum and *stapedial reflex testing,* which measures the reflex response of the stapedial muscle to pure tone signals. These tests do not require a behavioral response from the child and are therefore useful with very young and difficult-to-test children (Northern and Downs, 1978).

The *evoked response technique* requires the use of an electroencephalograph and a computer. It is used to measure the changes in brainwave electrical activity in response to sound. Like impedance audiometry, this type of testing does not require a behavioral response from the child; it can also be performed when the child is asleep or sedated. It is used with infants who are suspected of being deaf and with children who have multiple handicaps (Martin, 1975; Northern and Downs, 1974).

INTERPRETATION OF AUDIOGRAMS

What is an audiogram?

Pure tone air conduction and bone conduction results are generally charted on a grid, or audiogram, that has the frequencies tested noted at the top and the amount of loss in decibels noted down the side (see Figure 5-4). The type of test and the ear being tested are noted in symbols:

O — right ear, air conduction (△ when masking is applied to the left ear)
X — left ear, air conduction (□ when masking is applied to the right ear)
< — right ear, bone conduction ([when masking is applied to the left ear)
> — left ear, bone conduction ( ] when masking is applied to the right ear)

The extent of a hearing loss can be categorized as normal, mild, moderate, severe, or profound (Figure 5-4), based on the average pure tone air conduction loss at 500, 1,000 and 2,000 Hz (the frequencies on the audiogram most representative of the speech range) for each ear (see How We Use Our Hearing earlier in this chapter). The type of loss and its extent determine whether medical treatment or rehabilitation is necessary. Examples of typical audiograms are found in Figure 5-5A through 5-5E.

Figure 5-5A shows the test results for a six-year-old boy who has had a recurrent ear infection. His teacher thinks he doesn't pay attention, and he is having problems in school. This hearing test was requested by his pediatrician. It indicates a mild conductive hearing loss in both ears, which was treated with medication.

Figure 5-5B shows test results for the same six-year-old boy following his medical treatment. His hearing has returned to normal for both ears. His mother was urged to take her child to a doctor if she suspected a recurrence of the problem. The child's teacher was asked to seat him in the front of the classroom so he would not miss instructions if his problem returned.

Figure 5-4
Extent of Hearing Loss

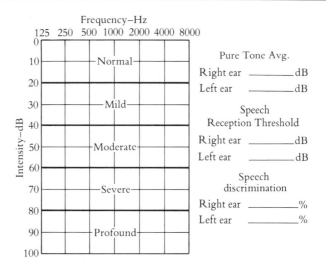

Figure 5-5C is the audiogram for a four-year-old deaf boy whose mother had rubella during the first three months of her pregnancy with him. His pediatrician sent him for testing at three months of age, and he has had several tests since. He was fitted with a hearing aid when he was fourteen months old. He was first enrolled in a preschool program for the deaf and later in a residential program, where he did very well.

Figure 5-5D represents the hearing of a nine-year-old girl who was referred for evaluation because a problem with her right ear was discovered in a school screening program. The family doctor found no medically treatable condition and sent her to an audiologist for a complete evaluation. The evaluation indicated that she had normal hearing in her left ear and a profound sensorineural loss in her right ear. Her mother was surprised to learn of the loss, because her daughter had had no trouble learning speech and language, got good grades in school, and was an able conversationalist. Her normal hearing in one ear accounts for these abilities. This child did, however, have trouble determining where sounds were coming from, because we rely on differences in the time of arrival of sounds at our two ears to determine their direction of origin. Favorable classroom seating was requested for this child. In her case favorable seating was on the front right side of the room, so her good left ear was toward the teacher.

Figure 5-5E is the audiogram for Sonja, the nine-year-old Middle Eastern child discussed earlier in this chapter. The pure tone responses labeled #1 are results of the first attempt to test; they represent the functional moderate-to-

Figure 5-5
Examples of Typical Audiograms

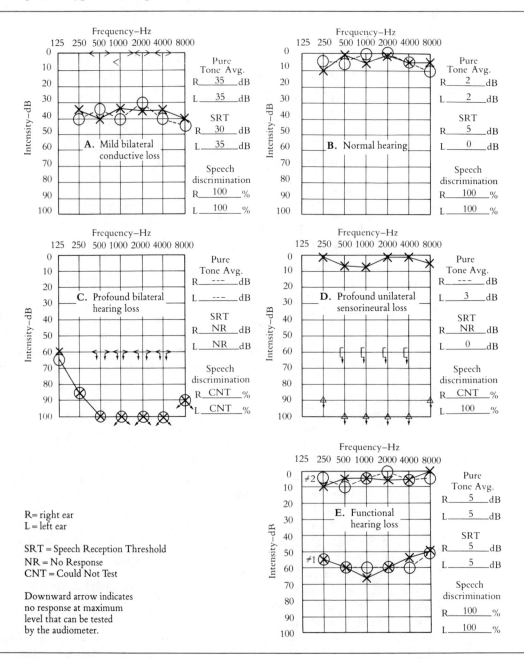

R = right ear
L = left ear

SRT = Speech Reception Threshold
NR = No Response
CNT = Could Not Test

Downward arrow indicates
no response at maximum
level that can be tested
by the audiometer.

severe "loss." The pattern labeled #2 represents the true responses, which show normal hearing. During all the tests Sonja took, her responses to speech were normal, and she had excellent understanding and discrimination. As with all functional hearing losses affecting children, it was necessary to resolve the problem that prompted the child to "need" the hearing loss.

PROBE 5-4
Evaluating Hearing Loss

1. What are four signs that might indicate a hearing loss?

2. A graphic portrayal of a person's hearing is called an _____ .

3. T F An otoscopic examination will determine whether a child has a sensorineural hearing loss.

4. List the different types of audiometric test.

5. T F Children's hearing cannot be tested accurately until they are six years of age.

6. Match the audiometric symbol on the right with the correct category listed on the left.

   _____ 1. right ear, bone conduction   O
   _____ 2. right ear, air conduction (masked)   X
   _____ 3. left ear, air conduction   >
   _____ 4. right ear, air conduction   <
   _____ 5. left ear, bone conduction (masked)   △
   _____ 6. left ear, air conduction (masked)   □
   _____ 7. right ear, bone conduction (masked)   ]
   _____ 8. left ear, bone conduction   [

7. The speech frequencies on the audiogram are _____ , _____ , and _____ Hz.

8. Match the amount of average loss on the right to the descriptive word on the left.

   _____ 1. mild   0–20 dB
   _____ 2. profound   20–40 dB
   _____ 3. moderate   40–60 dB
   _____ 4. normal   60–80 dB
   _____ 5. severe   80+ dB

9. The audiometric test that measures a person's ability to understand speech is called _____ .

THE EFFECTS OF HEARING LOSS

> **You should be able to discuss the effects of hearing loss.**

A hearing loss is a major sensory deficit, and it can affect many different abilities. Its effects vary depending on a number of factors, including the severity of the loss, the age at which it occurred, and the hearing-impaired person's determination to adapt. Those who teach and treat the hearing impaired must consider the extent of the handicap that results from the hearing loss, and whether the handicap is exclusively the result of the loss, or of societal expectations and pressures as well. In this section we will discuss some of the issues that relate to the development and adjustment of the hearing impaired.

INFLUENCE OF AGE OF ONSET AND SEVERITY OF HEARING LOSS

Myklebust (1964) stressed the importance of the age of onset and severity of hearing loss on the personality development and emotional adjustment of the hearing impaired. These factors are also crucial in developing language and speech skills, in educational achievement, and in vocational, social, personality, and emotional adjustment. Tables 5-2 and 5-3 summarize some of the effects of these variables. You should refer to them as we discuss the characteristics and needs of the hearing impaired.

LANGUAGE AND SPEECH DEVELOPMENT

One of the most serious consequences of a hearing loss is the effect it can have on the development of speech and language. Language is crucial to personal and societal development. As Northern and Downs put it,

> All the progress that man has made, if one can call a highly technologic society progress, is due to sophistication in the manipulation of language. . . . It follows that language deprivation is the most serious of all deprivations, for it robs us of a measure of our own human-ness. Whether caused by sensory deprivation, by experimental deprivation, or by central disordering, in some degree it keeps one from the complete fulfillment of one's powers [1978, p. 264].

To understand the effects of a hearing loss, you must understand normal speech and language development. The role of hearing in this process was discussed in Chapter 4. For our purposes it is sufficient to reiterate the importance of the auditory feedback loop. As you will remember, an auditory

Table 5-2
Hearing Loss: Effects of Age of Onset

Age of Onset	Speech/Language Development	Educational Adjustment	Vocational Adjustment	Social Adjustment	Personality and Emotional Adjustment
birth to 2 yrs.	Deafness prevents normal development of speech and language. Hearing loss may retard speech/language and may require some therapy.	Deafness requires early special education. Parents need counseling. Child with hearing loss may be held back by early influence of loss.	Not crucial at this age, except for deaf whose vocational future is limited.	Child may begin to notice he is different and environments restricted.	Feeling of isolation, frustration, and fear may begin to develop. Problems mostly at signal level.
2-6 yrs.	Deaf child will need therapy to develop speech/language. Hearing-impaired child will need therapy for speech/language development delay.	Deaf child should attend daily special preschool. Hearing-impaired child will need some preschool special services.	Deafness will restrict later vocational choices. Not crucial for mild to moderate hearing-impaired.	Children may tease or be impatient with the deaf child. Adults may lack the necessary patience. Child with mild loss may not be affected.	Continuation of problems identified above. Problems mostly at signal and symbolic levels.
6-18 yrs.	Deafness/hearing loss may not affect already developed speech and language; therapy may be needed to prevent regression of speech/language skills.	Deaf child may need day or residential school; young adult needs auditory rehabilitation and possibly vocational training.	Deafness restricts vocational choices. Moderate-severe loss may cause change in career goals.	Deaf child will have peer-group problems. Hearing loss may cause social withdrawal or affect marital status.	Deafness and severe loss may result in friendship and peer-group identity problems. Problems at signal and background levels.
18-60 yrs.	Same as for 6-18. Speech and language needs likely center on vocational and social concerns.	Deaf or hearing-impaired may need formal or informal education and job training.	Crucial vocational period for deafened or hearing-impaired. Hearing loss may require change in work setting or career goals.	Deafness or hearing loss may cause traumatic social changes, withdrawal, marital upheaval.	Basic personality may not change, but frustration, isolation, and insecurity may develop.
60+ yrs.	Same as for 18-60. Speech and language needs determined by social and family concerns.	Deaf or hearing-impaired may need informal education to understand hearing loss better and to help with social adjustment.	Person close to retirement age, so hearing loss may not affect vocation.	Deafness or severe hearing loss may cause withdrawal and isolation from family and friends.	Deafened and severely hearing-impaired may withdraw, feel isolated, or be insecure or bitter. Problems at background and signal levels.

Table 5-3
Hearing Loss: Effects of Degree and Type

Average Hearing Loss (500-2000 Hz)	Probable Causes	Ability to Hear Speech Without a Hearing Aid	Extent of Communicative Handicap	Auditory Rehabilitative Considerations
0-20 dB *Normal Range*	May have slight, fluctuating conductive loss. Child with central auditory disorder will show normal hearing.	No difficulty in any conversational setting. Child with central auditory disorder will seem to hear but not understand.	None, except for child with central auditory disorder or with speech/language disorders from other causes.	Probably needs no rehabilitative treatment. Child with central auditory disorder will need intensive therapy.
20-40 dB *Mild Loss*	Most likely conductive from otitis media. Sensorineural loss may result from mild illness or disease.	Hears in most settings, misses soft or whispered speech, will hear vowels but may miss unvoiced consonants, says "huh?" wants TV turned up loud.	Mild handicap, may have speech disorder or mild language delay, may omit final and voiceless consonants.	If conductive and medically or surgically treatable, needs favorable classroom seating. Child with sensorineural problem may need hearing aid, speech reading, and auditory training.
40-60 dB *Moderate Loss*	Conductive from otitis media or middle ear problem; maximum conductive loss is 60 dB. Sensorineural loss from ear disease or illness.	Hearing is a problem in most conversational settings, groups, or when there is background noise; hears louder voiced consonants, may need TV and radio up loud, and have difficulty on the phone.	Possible disorder in auditory learning, mild to moderate language delay; articulation problems with final and voiceless consonants; may not pay attention.	All of the above may apply. May also need special class for the hearing impaired or special tutoring.
60-80 dB *Severe Loss*	Probably sensorineural, although mixed is also possible. Rubella, meningitis, Rh, heredity are possible causes.	Misses all but very loud speech, unable to function in conversation without help, can't use telephone.	Probably severe language and speech disorder; learning disorder; may have no intelligible speech.	All of the above may apply. May need placement in school for the deaf.
80 dB or more *Profound Loss*	Sensorineural, or mixed with large sensorineural component. Rubella, meningitis, Rh, heredity, ear disease, etc. are causes.	Unable to hear speech except loud shout, does not understand spoken language, can't hear TV or radio, can't use the telephone.	Severe speech and language deficit, probably no oral speech, learning disorder, "deaf-like" speech and voice.	All of the above may apply. Will need placement in deaf-oral school or school for the deaf.

feedback loop is a process beginning at birth whereby the child monitors his or her own utterances as well as those of other people and is reinforced as he or she learns correct speech and language (Northern and Downs, 1974). This process may result in speech-like sounds when the child is two months old and in the first meaningful words at about one year. Although we never stop learning language, the early months and years are especially crucial (Lenneberg; 1967, Menyuk, 1972).

Why does hearing loss have such a negative effect on language?

The interruption of this vital auditory feedback loop, or its absence in the case of a child born deaf, can slow speech/language development or preclude it altogether. The earlier the onset and the more severe the loss, the greater the developmental deficit. A child with mild to moderate loss will probably develop speech/language skills slowly, but he or she can usually learn to speak and use language effectively with therapy and adequate amplification from a hearing aid (Holm and Kunze, 1969; Quigley, 1970). A child born deaf, on the other hand, generally grows up without acquiring adequate speech or language skills (Carhart, 1970).

Those who become deaf after even a brief exposure to speech and language are much more likely to develop communications abilities than those who were deaf at birth. According to Lenneberg (1967), "It seems as if even a short exposure to language, a brief moment in which the curtain has been lifted and oral communication established, is sufficient to give a child some foundation on which much later language may be based" (p. 239). Helen Keller, who became deaf and blind from meningitis at age two, is the classic example. The "lifting of the curtain" for the first two years of her life undoubtedly provided the basis for the excellent communication skills she later developed.

EDUCATIONAL ACHIEVEMENT

Most education systems use spoken and written language as the vehicle for learning. As a result, individuals with hearing loss, especially if it is severe or profound, are at a distinct disadvantage in the learning process. This is not because the education of the hearing-impaired has been consistently inadequate; on the contrary, there has been much progress in the field. There is, however, a tendency to judge inappropriately the hearing-impaired by the standards used to measure the achievement of their hearing peers. Similarly, some of the tecnniques used to teach those with hearing problems are variations of the methods used to teach those who hear normally. More innovative techniques would often be more effective.

The areas of greatest concern in educating the hearing-impaired are their intellectual ability and their ability to learn to read.

Intellectual Ability. The intellectual ability of hearing-impaired children has been the subject of controversy for many years. The question of the relation-

How does hearing loss affect intellectual ability?

ship between intelligence and deafness was first raised in a 1920 study by Pintner and Reamer. In that study it was concluded that deaf children were two years retarded mentally and five years retarded educationally as compared to their hearing peers. It also suggested that two years of the educational lag could be attributed to mental inferiority and three years to language handicap. The debate has continued ever since.

Myklebust (1964) pointed out that the conclusions of the early Pintner and Reamer study were biased by the nature of the test materials, which required verbal ability, and also by the fact that a group test was used. Pintner (1941) himself eventually concluded that education for the hearing impaired should stress motor skills. As test techniques have become more sophisticated, the reported differences between the intellectual abilities of deaf and normal-hearing individuals have been shown to be largely attributable to test error. Using more appropriate nonverbal tests, Vernon and Brown (1964) and Lenneberg (1967) have reported relatively insignificant intellectual differences between deaf children and their hearing peers. This view is further reinforced by the findings of the Annual Survey of Hearing Impaired Children and Youth of Gallaudet College, which reviewed the cases of almost 20,000 hearing-impaired children and found an average IQ close to the norm for normal-hearing individuals (McConnell, 1973).

Is reading achievement affected by hearing impairment?

Reading Ability. Over the past few decades there have been several studies of the reading skills of hearing-impaired children. Myklebust (1964) reported that deaf children had a much smaller reading vocabulary than their normal-hearing counterparts. Deaf children the age of high school seniors were reported to have reading vocabularies at the level of nine year olds — an eight- to nine-year lag in reading skills. A 1963 survey by Wrightstone, Aranow, and Moskowitz of hearing impaired students between the ages of 10.5 and 16.5 years indicated that the average reading achievement level was that expected of a third grader. The reading skills deficit indicated in this study is between three and eight years. Williams and Vernon (1970) reported on a study that included 93 percent of the deaf students over 16 years old in the United States and found that 60 percent were below grade level and 30 percent were functionally illiterate.

If one considers the direct relationship between speaking and reading abilities, these findings are not surprising. It is the underlying language problems of deaf people that cause their serious lag in reading skills. People with minor hearing losses can be expected to have reading levels closer to the norm than those with severe losses.

VOCATIONAL AND SOCIAL ADJUSTMENT

Most of the vocational and social adjustment problems of the hearing-impaired are the result of their having to live in a society that relies heavily on spoken and written language. This creates barriers, and as a group they experience more marital, social, and vocational problems than those with normal hearing (Meadow, 1975).

What is the most serious social problem for a person with a severe hearing loss?

Probably the most serious social problem for those with severe hearing loss is isolation. The young deaf child cannot communicate easily with his or her hearing peers or with most adults who have normal hearing. Many deaf people interact socially almost exclusively with other deaf people. Interaction with people who hear normally can be very demanding; it is much easier for the deaf to find social acceptance among people with similar disabilities.

Deafness also affects an individual's choice of vocation. The deaf are often restricted to manual jobs where there is relatively little verbal interaction. Williams and Vernon (1970) note that the vocational trend toward more white-collar jobs and greater technical knowledge and education requirements increasingly limits the job market for the hearing impaired.

PERSONALITY AND EMOTIONAL ADJUSTMENT

The loss of any sensory capability can result in emotional and personality adjustment problems. The emotional impact of a loss is not always directly related to the severity of the loss, but greater losses do tend to cause greater isolation and hence more serious adjustment problems. It has been suggested but not proven that those who are born deaf or lose their hearing early in life have fewer adjustment problems because they never acquired a dependence on hearing.

Isolation mentioned in the last section can cause emotional as well as social and vocational problems. Those who sustain severe hearing loss sometimes feel rejected and frustrated (Meadow, 1975; Myklebust, 1964). They also frequently report feelings in a "dead" world. The loss of the primitive or background sense of hearing may have a greater effect than the loss of the signal or symbolic levels.

Why do some people refuse to wear a hearing aid?

Many hearing impaired individuals could relieve their feelings of isolation by wearing a hearing aid. It is not unusual, however, for people to refuse to wear an aid because they feel it stigmatizes them. Adults are sometimes concerned that their aid will be considered a sign of old age, whereas children may be afraid of the reaction of their classmates. Both cases may require emotional adjustment.

PROBE 5-5
The Effects of Hearing Loss

1 What are some major areas of development and adjustment for those with hearing loss?

2. The average age at which children produce their first words is _____ .

3. T F   The normal child establishes an auditory feedback loop at three months of age.

4. T F   Deaf individuals are two to five years mentally retarded as compared to individuals with normal hearing.

5. T F   The reading skills of deaf individuals may lag as much as eight to nine years behind those of their hearing peers.

6. Severe language and speech disorders should be expected if a child's average hearing loss is greater than _____ dB and it occurs before age _____ .

7. A child whose hearing loss is greater than _____ dB is considered deaf.

TREATMENT FOR HEARING DISORDERS

You should be able to describe the various types of treatment for hearing loss.

There are many ways to treat hearing disorders. In some cases the appropriate treatment is medical or surgical; in others longer-term rehabilitative procedures are required. Although we cannot discuss all types of treatment in detail, we will describe some of the common, basic treatments, emphasizing those that are frequently used with children.

MEDICAL AND SURGICAL TREATMENT

In most cases conductive hearing loss in children can be overcome by appropriate medical or surgical treatment. The conductive component of a mixed hearing loss may also respond to this type of remedy. Children suffer from more conductive hearing disorders than any other age group. The most common cause is otitis media, or middle ear infection (Davis and Silverman, 1970; Newby, 1972; Paparella and Juhn, 1979). As you will remember, blockage of the external auditory canal and otosclerosis can also cause conductive loss, but these disorders are relatively uncommon.

What is the treatment for otitis media?

Otitis media can be cured with medication (Paradise, 1979). If the condition recurs frequently, the doctor may insert a small tube through the tympanic membranes, to act as a substitute for poorly functioning eustachian tubes, and to help ventilate the middle ear (Paparella, 1979). These tubes tend to work out of the eardrums every few months, and it is sometimes necessary to reinsert them. Physicians can also remove excessive earwax and objects that have become lodged in the auditory canal. Parents should not attempt this operation with cotton-tipped sticks because of the risk of damage to the ear canal.

Can sensorineural problems be cured?

Sensorineural hearing problems, on the other hand, are not yet medically treatable. There are some experimental efforts to implant surgically a small device resembling a hearing aid in the cochlea or auditory nerve, bypassing the damaged nerve area and thereby overcoming the sensorineural loss (Michelson, Merzenich, and Shindler, 1975; Porter, Lynn, and Maddox, 1979). This technique holds great promise, but it will probably not be perfected for many years.

AUDITORY REHABILITATIVE TREATMENT

Sensorineural losses and central auditory disorders are relatively complex and require long-term intensive treatment. Auditory rehabilitation can include the use of hearing aids as well as auditory training and speech reading (Davis and Silverman, 1970; Sanders, 1982). It is usually a team effort involving an audiologist, a speech pathologist, and a special teacher, as well as a psychologist and a social worker in many cases.

What is the goal of auditory rehabilitation?

The goal of all auditory rehabilitative treatment should be to develop an individual's communication skills. In the case of young children, language development is particularly important (Northern and Downs, 1974). This is done most effectively by using a variety of different techniques and approaches.

Hearing Aids. Hearing aids are electronic devices that make sounds louder to assist in communication (Northern and Downs, 1978; Rubin, 1976; Sanders, 1982). The use of a hearing aid does not result in normal hearing, but it often greatly improves communications skills. Hearing aids may be considered for children with mild to severe sensorineural losses. They may even help deaf children by allowing them to detect some environmental sounds.

In recent years technological advances have resulted in smaller, more powerful aids with improved sound quality and fidelity. There are many brands and types on the market. The very young child with a severe or profound hearing loss will probably first use a body hearing aid because it is both powerful and durable. The child may later be able to change to a strong-gain ear-level aid. The aid used most commonly is the over-the-ear or behind-the-ear model. There are also aids that are built into glasses or into an earmold that fits into the external auditory canal. These types of aids are illustrated in Chart 5-1.

What should a hearing impaired person do before seeing a hearing aid dealer?

Before they see a hearing aid dealer, it is important that adults and especially children receive a thorough audiological evaluation and medical clearance. This procedure is required by federal regulations and by many state laws as well. The different considerations in selecting an appropriate aid are too in-

Chart 5-1
The Hearing Aid

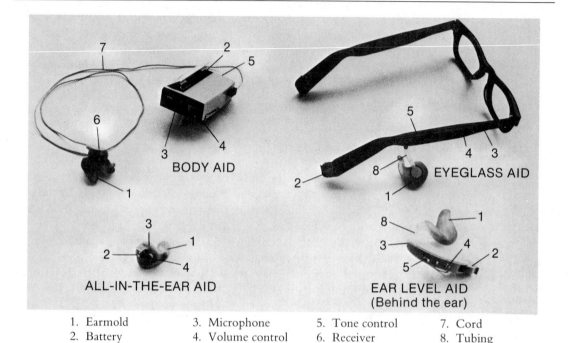

1. Earmold	3. Microphone	5. Tone control	7. Cord
2. Battery	4. Volume control	6. Receiver	8. Tubing

The Parts of the Hearing Aid

1. The *earmold* fits into the ear canal. In body aids, the earmold holds the receiver; in ear-level aids, it is connected directly to the rest of the aid through a piece of clear tubing. The earmold should fit snugly but comfortably. It should be checked immediately if the ear becomes sore or if the hearing aid squeals. The earmold should be cleaned at least once a week using lukewarm soapy water. A pipe-cleaner can be used to remove earwax.

2. The *battery* supplies the power that operates the hearing aid. When the battery is weak, the sound will be weak. Most hearing aids require only one battery. The battery must be put in such that its terminals line up correctly, or the hearing aid will not operate. The battery should be taken out of the aid when it is not going to be used for several hours.

3. The *microphone* is usually located on the front, tip, or sides of the case. Clothing that rubs the case of the body-type hearing aid can cause noises that interfere with hearing, so the aid is best worn outside the clothing.

4. The *volume control* is a wheel that can be turned to increase or decrease the loudness of sound. In some hearing aids this wheel also controls the on-off switch.

5. A *tone control* switch, not found on all hearing aids, allows the tone to be adjusted. The audiologist will recommend the best setting.

6. The *receiver* is the button that can be attached to the earmold on body-type hearing aids. It should fit the earmold tightly. If the hearing aid squeals when the volume is turned up, it usually means either that the receiver does not fit the earmold tightly enough, or that the earmold does not fit tightly enough in the

ear. Although the receiver is small, it is expensive to repair or replace.

The receiver of an ear-level aid is inside the instrument's case.

7. The *cord,* found only on body aids, connects the receiver with the hearing aid case. It should be cleaned frequently to make certain it connects correctly. The cord should be replaced if it becomes worn. The wires in a worn cord are likely to break, which may cause the sound to be transmitted intermittently or not at all.

General Suggestions for Hearing Aid Use

1. The parents or teacher should check the child's hearing aid every morning. They should know what the various controls do, where the battery is inserted, and how to fit the earmold properly in the child's ear.
2. The child should have spare batteries available at home and at school. Those who use body aids should also have at least one spare cord.
3. *Never* attempt major repairs on the hearing aid. Only the manufacturer can make them correctly.
4. Preschool children with impaired hearing should have annual audiological and hearing aid reevaluations. Older children should receive such checks at least once every two years.
5. It's important to remember that a child who wears a hearing aid does *not* hear normally. The aid's effectiveness will vary with the situation. Children with normal hearing may easily understand speech in a noisy environment; a child dependent on a hearing aid may find it impossible to understand speech in the same situation.
6. Teachers and parents must be sensitive to a child's needs to adjust socially and psychologically to a hearing aid. It is sometimes best to begin a child's hearing aid use in gradual stages, with the eventual goal of the child's using the aid during most of the time the child is awake. The child's classmates should be told about hearing loss and hearing aids to help them understand and accept the child.

Hearing Aid Problems and How to Solve Them

Problem

1. Squealing, or feedback, is a high-pitched noise that may occur when the child moves his or her head or may be constant. In the classroom this feedback can disrupt the work of other students. Although the hearing-impaired student may not hear the feedback, it usually means that the aid is functioning less efficiently than it should.

What to do about it

a. Be sure the earmold is placed correctly in the ear and is the proper size for the child and is not too loose. Arrange to get a new earmold made if it is loose or does not fit properly.

b. With body aids, check that the earmold is snapped firmly to the nub of the receiver.

c. With ear-level aids, be sure the hollow plastic tube from the earmold fits tightly over the receiver opening.

Problem

2. The hearing aid does not work or works only intermittently. This problem may be indicated if the child fails to respond or has an unusually hard time with assignments. The hearing aid can be checked by holding the earmold or receiver to the teacher's ear.

What to do about it

a. Replace battery.

b. Make sure that positive (+) and negative (−) ends of battery are placed correctly in

Chart 5-1 Continued

the battery compartment and that the battery is held firmly in its compartment.

c. Check for corrosion on battery contacts. This can be removed with a pencil eraser.

d. Be sure the canal of the earmold is not plugged with earwax.

e. If the aid is the body type, turn it on and wiggle the cord where it fits into the receiver and where it enters the case.

f. Be sure the aid is not switched to "telephone" position.

Problem

3. The signal is weak, distorted, or scratchy. This problem may come to light when the child reports it to the teacher, or the teacher may notice a reduction in the child's performance. It can also be checked by listening to the child's aid.

What to do about it

a. Change the battery, even if it is new or checks normal on battery tester.

b. With a body aid, try another receiver if one is available.

c. Turn the volume control up and down and listen for scratchiness or dead spot.

d. Make sure the tone control, if there is one, is set properly.

---

volved to discuss in this chapter; the reader who seeks additional information is directed to Northern and Downs (1974) and Rubin (1976).

Those who work with children who use a hearing aid should know the parts of the aid and how to take care of it (Chart 5-1).

A discussion of hearing aids would not be complete without mentioning some of the misconceptions that prevent people from trying amplification. Sanders (1982) and Northern and Downs (1974) discuss several. One such misconception is that people with sensorineural hearing loss cannot benefit from amplification. This misconception is based on the assumption that damaged nerves cannot be stimulated or regenerated, and amplification is therefore pointless. But most people with sensorineural losses retain the ability to hear some sounds through the parts of the auditory nerve that function correctly, and amplified sound can travel along these structures. In fact, over 95 percent of hearing aid users have sensorineural rather than conductive losses. Those with conductive hearing loss can, of course, benefit from amplification, because their auditory nerves are intact. These individuals can usually be helped medically or surgically, however, and they don't need hearing aids. Everyone with a sensorineural hearing loss should have an opportunity to try amplification.

How do hearing aids help their users?

A second misconception is that a hearing aid will restore hearing to normal. A hearing aid is an amplifying system that makes things louder. It does not heal the ear, and most hearing aid users initially report that the sound through the hearing aid is artificial. Hearing aid technology is improving, however, and with a reasonable effort the hearing aid user will adjust to the artificial quality of the sound.

Some people believe that a hearing aid will result in increased hearing damage. This misconception is derived from the understanding that very loud noise can damage the ear, particularly the sensorineural component that hears high-frequency sounds. It would be possible for damage to result from the use of an aid that was far too powerful. It is doubtful, though, that the hearing aid user would tolerate such overcompensation. The danger is further reduced by relying on the guidance of an audiologist.

Finally, it is believed that hearing aids do not help those with mild or severe losses. No hearing loss is so mild or so severe that hearing aid use should not be attempted. Although people with mild losses do not always find an aid helpful, many like to use them in school, at work, or in social settings. The profoundly deaf can also use aids to help them communicate. Although a hearing aid will not allow them to understand speech, it can be used to supplement their speech reading.

Auditory Training. Auditory training is intended to teach the hearing impaired to use their residual hearing to the greatest extent possible (Sanders, 1982). It is usually provided by an audiologist or speech pathologist in individual or group therapy sessions and reinforced in the regular classroom and at home. In auditory training, the child is taught to use and care for a hearing aid, to use environmental cues in conversation, and to sharpen the ability to discriminate among sounds and words. The goals of an auditory training problem include the following:

What are the goals of auditory training programs?

1. To familiarize the child and parents with the nature and extent of the loss. This involves explaining how the normal ear functions; describing how various types and amounts of hearing loss affect communication, and specifically how the loss will affect the child's communication; and explaining the child's audiogram.
2. To familiarize the child and parents with hearing aids and hearing aid maintenance. This involves explaining that hearing aids make things louder, not necessarily clearer; explaining the controls and settings of the hearing aid; and providing the child and parents with information on the care and maintenance of the hearing aid.
3. To familiarize the child and parents with the methods and goals of the auditory training plan. This includes developing an awareness of sounds and the basic meanings of sounds; teaching the child to discriminate among sounds; and encouraging the child to make full use of his auditory abilities.
4. To carry out the program designed to meet the individual child's needs. This requires regularly scheduled therapy sessions with an audiologist or speech pathologist; active involvement of the child's regular classroom or special teacher in reinforcing the auditory training; and active involvement of the parents in reinforcing auditory training in the home and family.

**How much speech
is visibly displayed
by lip
movements?**

Speech Reading. A child who has had a hearing loss naturally becomes more attentive to a speaker's lips and facial movements. Most hearing impaired people are not even aware that they are doing so. Such "lip reading" or "speech reading" can be a valuable skill, but it can be used only to supplement communication, not as a complete communication system. Only 30 to 40 percent of the sounds in our language are produced with visible lip movements, so the speech reader has many gaps to fill in.

Nevertheless, many hearing impaired children do benefit from formal speech reading training. It is typically provided by audiologists and speech pathologists in group or individual therapy sessions. These usually take place through speech and hearing clinics or in the school. Speech reading therapy is most effective when it is part of a rehabilitation program that includes auditory training and the use of a hearing aid. Speech reading lessons are most productive when they take advantage of the child's interests and experiences.

Some people cannot become good speech readers even with formal training. It requires considerable concentration to speech read successfully.

A communications system based on speech reading has the same components as the TMR system described in Figure 5-1. The transmitter is the person speaking, the receiver is the speech reader, and the medium is the environment in which the communication occurs. As with other communications systems, successful communication depends on the proper functioning of the three components, as we will now describe (Berger, 1972).

**What can people
do to make speech
reading easier for
a deaf person?**

Speech reading is usually easier if one is familiar with the speaker. Ideally, the speech reader should be able to see the speaker's entire face from the front. This allows the speech reader to distinguish both lip movements and facial expressions. As much of the speaker's body as possible should be in view of the speech reader, since body gestures are a part of communication. The speaker's lip movements are crucial. A lack of normal movement or exaggerated movement makes speech reading more difficult. Also, the speaker should speak at a normal pace.

The second component in our system is the environment. The distance between the speaker and the speech reader is very important. The greater the distance, the more difficult it is to speech read effectively. To speech read, one must be able to see the speaker's face. Therefore, good lighting is also important. Even when the speaker is clearly seen, however, it is sometimes difficult to read speech if the environment is filled with distractions.

The speech reader can also affect the quality of the communication and may be the most crucial component. Intelligence, age, and educational background do not appear to have a serious effect on the ability of an individual to speech read effectively. However, it is usually easier for younger people to learn speech reading than it is for older people, and the speech reader's attitude, ability to pay attention, and motivation are crucial. Good visual acuity is also necessary for successful speech reading.

PROBE 5-6
Treatment for Hearing Disorders

1. Small tubes may be inserted in the tympanic membrane to _____ the ear.

2. T F Hearing aids are electronic devices that always make sound clearer.

3. The young child with a severe hearing loss will probably require a _____ type hearing aid.

4. T F By law, medical clearance and an audiological evaluation are required before one can obtain a hearing aid.

5. What are four reasons that a child's hearing aid might squeal?

6. _____ consists of techniques that help a hearing impaired child use residual hearing as much as possible.

7. When a hearing impaired child watches a speaker's lip and facial movement, he or she is _____ .

8. T F Seventy to eighty percent of the sounds in our language are visible on the speaker's lips.

EDUCATIONAL NEEDS OF THE HEARING IMPAIRED

You should be able to describe the educational needs of hearing impaired children and the implications of mainstreaming practices.

IDENTIFICATION

What clues might alert parents to the possibility of a hearing loss in a pre-school child?

Many children are identified as having a hearing loss before they enter school, particularly if their loss is severe enough to delay speech and language development. The loss is generally first recognized by a doctor or by the child's parents. A doctor may be especially alert for hearing problems because of (1) a history of hereditary hearing loss; (2) infections or illnesses of the mother during pregnancy; (3) defects of the child's ears, nose, or throat; (4) low birth weight; (5) prematurity; or (6) infections, diseases, or accidents sustained by the child (Northern and Downs, 1974). Parents may discover a hearing loss by observing that their child does not respond normally to sounds. Children whose hearing problems have been discovered very early have probably undergone audiological evaluation and treatment before they entered school.

**What indicators
point to possible
hearing loss in
school children?**

Children with hearing losses that have not been discovered when they entered school are frequently identified by their teacher. One of the most common indications of a hearing problem is a child's failure to pay attention. Other signs that may indicate a hearing disorder include the following (Duffy, 1967):

— The child complains of frequent earaches or has a discharge from the ears.
— Articulation of speech sounds is poor, or consonant sounds are omitted.
— Easy questions are answered incorrectly.
— The child fails to respond or pay attention when spoken to in a normal manner.
— "Hearing" appears to be better when the child faces the speaker.
— The child often asks the speaker to repeat what was just said.
— When listening to the radio, TV, or other audiovisual equipment, the child turns up the volume to a level that is uncomfortable to those with normal hearing.

Although some of these signs may indicate problems other than hearing disorders, any child displaying them should be observed carefully. A child thought to have a hearing disorder should be referred to an audiologist.

Most school systems have regularly scheduled hearing screenings. They are usually conducted by the school speech pathologist, audiologist, or nurse, sometimes with the assistance of parent volunteers. In some schools, screening programs make use of university-based audiology training programs. Whoever staffs them, screening programs are an effective method of discovering undetected hearing problems.

EDUCATIONAL NEEDS OF THE CHILD
WITH MILD TO MODERATE HEARING LOSS

The treatment and educational requirements of a school-age child will depend on the nature and severity of the child's hearing loss.

Mild to moderate conductive losses that result from recurrent ear infection can often be successfully treated medically or surgically. Although most children with this type of disorder can function in a regular classroom, the teacher should not assume that the child requires no special attention. The child should at least be given favorable seating. The teacher should also know that recurrent otitis media may result in delayed speech and language development (Holm and Kunze, 1969; Lewis, 1976; and Needleman, 1977). If it does, the child will need regular speech and language therapy. Children with mild to moderate conductive losses will benefit from the use of a hearing aid only in the uncommon cases that are not curable.

Most children with mild to moderate sensorineural hearing loss can also function in regular classrooms. In fact, the school-related problems of these children are sometimes not thought to be the result of hearing loss, because they can usually hear and understand conversational speech. These children will probably need a hearing aid, preferential seating in the classroom, speech/language therapy, and possibly speech reading and auditory training therapy. In some cases the child with mild to moderate sensorineural hearing loss may benefit most from being placed in a special class. This is determined by audiological and educational assessment.

How can teachers meet the needs of hearing impaired students in their classes?

Suggestions for the Classroom Teacher. There are many children with mild to moderate hearing loss in regular classrooms. The following suggestions may help the teacher work with them effectively.

1. If the teacher generally teaches from the front of the room, the hard-of-hearing child should be seated in the front, preferably slightly off center toward the windows. This allows the child to hear better and read lips more effectively. Light should be directed toward the teacher's face and away from the speech reader's eyes.
2. If the child's hearing impairment involves only one ear, or if the impairment is greater in one ear than the other, the child should be seated in the front corner seat such that the better ear is toward the teacher.
3. The teacher should pay attention to the posture of the hearing impaired child's head. The habits of extending the head or twisting the neck to hear better can become firmly fixed.
4. The child should be encouraged to watch the face of the teacher whenever the teacher is talking to the child. The teacher should speak at the speech reader's eye level whenever possible.
5. The teacher should try to face the hard-of-hearing child as much as possible when speaking to the class. An effort should be made to give all important instructions from a position close to the child. It's best not to stand between the child and the windows, which may prove distracting.
6. The teacher should not speak loudly or use exaggerated lip movements when speaking to the hard-of-hearing child.
7. The hearing-impaired child should be encouraged to turn around to watch the faces of children who are reciting.
8. It is easy to overestimate the hearing efficiency of a child. It should be remembered that it takes a greater effort for a hearing-impaired child to hear than it does for a normal child. It may as a result be more difficult to hold the hearing-impaired child's attention.
9. A hearing loss of long duration can cause a person's voice to become dull and monotonous. It can also result in poor diction. The hearing-impaired child and the rest of the class should be encouraged to speak clearly and distinctly.
10. An interest in music and participation in vocal music should be encouraged.

11. Use of an overhead projector allows the teacher to write without having to turn away to write on the chalkboard. The overhead projector also helps to illuminate the teacher's face, thus making lip reading easier.
12. Key words, expressions, or phrases should be written on the chalkboard or shown on an overhead projector.
13. Supplementary pictures or diagrams should be used whenever possible.
14. Care should be taken not to talk with one's face either turned downward to read notes or hidden by a book or papers.
15. Since a hearing loss affects all the language processes, the child should be encouraged to compensate by taking a greater interest in reading, grammar, spelling, original writing, and other activities that involve language.
16. The hard-of-hearing child should be observed carefully to ensure that he or she doesn't withdraw or suffer emotionally as a direct or indirect result of poor hearing.
17. The hard-of-hearing child should participate actively in all plays and other activities that involve speech.

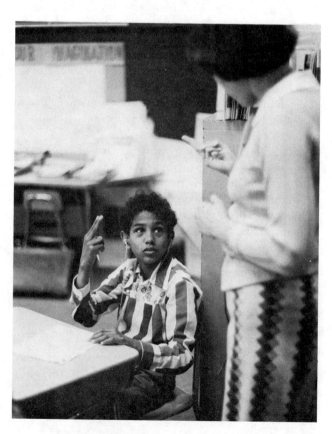

A deaf student communicating with his teacher using manual signs

TECHNOLOGY IN ACTION

In the 1970s several efforts were mounted to super-impose printed captions on television broadcasts so that deaf people could understand the programs. Unfortunately, studies found that hearing people claimed that the captions were distracting and detracted from their viewing pleasure. As a result, this practice was not widely implemented.

A ten-year research and development effort paid off in March of 1980, however. At that time a system of "closed captioning" was initiated. Television programs are transmitted so that a series of "lines" are eventually displayed on the screen, which result in the visual images that we see. In 1976, the Federal Communications Commission approved the use of television's line 21 for the purpose of closed captions.

With special encoding equipment, captions can be added to the program video signal in an invisible form that is broadcast to all receivers. With the use of a special device that is available from Sears department stores, deaf people can decode the signal so that the captions are visible on their TV set.

The National Captioning Institute operates a production service for captioning television broad-casts. It takes 25 to 30 person-hours to produce a captioned version of a one-hour broadcast. The cost for such encoding is approximately $2,500.

Over 35,000 homes in the United States are now equipped with the decoders. At the present time, ABC, NBC, PBS, and several Canadian companies provide closed-caption programming. CBS does not provide closed captioned programming at this time because it is experimenting with a system, called Teletext, which it claims will permit the storage and retrieval of larger amounts of information than are currently possible with closed captioning.

You probably have noticed a symbol in your TV viewing guide that looks like a little television screen inside a "cartoon balloon" or have seen this symbol at the beginning of a television program, accompanied by the words "Closed captioned for the hearing impaired." This means that the program you are watching can also be enjoyed by deaf people who have the TV decoders. By having captions available, they can "see" what other people hear.

— Adapted from an article by Tracy L. Harris, in *Counterpoint*, November, 1981.

---

18. Teachers should watch carefully for illnesses in hearing impaired children. Colds, influenza, throat and nose infections, tonsilitis, and other ailments should be treated as soon as possible.

19. The teacher should be able to assist the child who wears a hearing aid in the classroom.

EDUCATIONAL NEEDS OF THE CHILD WITH MODERATE TO SEVERE LOSS

A hearing loss in the moderate to severe range has a much greater effect on a child's education than a mild to moderate loss. Most of the more serious losses are caused by irreversible sensorineural problems present at birth or from a very early age. There are some moderate conductive hearing losses, but they are relatively uncommon and can usually be successfully cured.

What is a group auditory training unit?

Auditory Rehabilitative Considerations. The child with a moderate to severe sensorineural loss will probably use a hearing aid. The teachers of such children must be familiar with the information on aids presented earlier. These children may also need special therapy, reinforced by classroom drills. If there are several children with hearing loss in a classroom, the teacher may need to use a group auditory training unit. These units enable a teacher to speak to a large number of children through an amplifying device that is connected to earphones or the children's hearing aids (Davis and Silverman, 1970; Sanders, 1982).

The child with a moderate to severe loss may also need to learn speech reading. As mentioned earlier, most hearing-impaired people speech read to some extent without being aware of it and without having been taught (Berger, 1972). Formal training in speech reading will help the hearing impaired in general communication, in the classroom, and in maintaining speech.

Communicative Considerations. The techniques of auditory training and speech reading we have described are associated with what is known as the *oral approach* to teaching communication skills to the severely hearing impaired and the deaf. For the child with moderate hearing loss, oral speech and language skills can usually be taught through long-term, regularly scheduled auditory training sessions, speech reading, and speech-language therapy. When a child's hearing loss is in the severe to profound range, the development of oral speech and language is a more difficult process, and what is known as the *manual approach* may be considered most appropriate. These two approaches have historically been considered separate and mutually exclusive, and oralists and manualists have been debating the relative effectiveness of the two approaches for many years.

What are the arguments for and against the oral and manual approaches to communication?

Supporters of the oral approach focus their efforts on teaching the child to speak and speech read. The use of gestures is discouraged and manual signing is prohibited (Furth, 1973). Strict oralists contend that a manual system tends to isolate those who use it, arguing that the deaf child should adapt to our speech- and hearing-oriented society. Manualism has been the preferred method for a long time, but oralism began gaining popularity in Europe during the mid-nineteenth century (Sanders, 1982). The oral approach has worked very effectively for many people with severe impairments, but some have trouble learning it and never develop intelligible oral speech.

Proponents of the manual approach believe that sign language is the common, natural language of the deaf. Manualists contend that deaf children learn language best by using their vision. Garretson (1963) cites some of the other arguments for the manual approach:

1. Denying a child the use of fingers and hands in the communicative process can lead to anxiety and emotional stress.
2. The use of manual systems of signs and finger spelling in conjunction with speech enhances communication. The manual alphabet is illustrated in Figure 5-6.
3. Signs are clearer, larger, and more easily visible than lip movements.
4. Children's individual skills in oral communication vary widely. Finger spelling and signs are easier to learn. Thus, these manual systems might

Figure 5-6
The Manual Alphabet

The manual alphabet as the receiver sees it

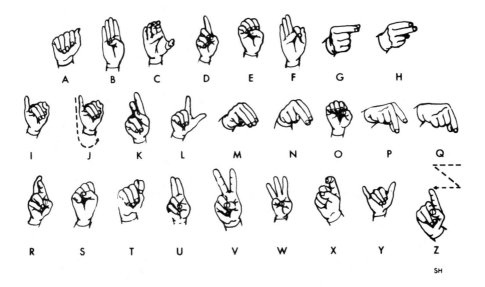

The manual alphabet as the sender sees it

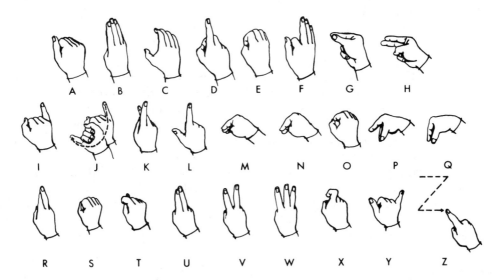

be considered less discriminatory, permitting children equal opportunity to participate in and learn from classroom activities.

What is the philosophy of total communication?

The realization that no single method is appropriate for all children has recently broken down some of the barriers between proponents of the two methods and given rise to a philosophy known as *total communication*. This increasingly influential philosophy advocates the use of every possible method to develop a base for language learning, including combinations of the oral and manual approaches (McConnell, 1973).

EDUCATIONAL SETTINGS FOR THE SEVERELY HEARING IMPAIRED

In what types of settings are hearing impaired students educated?

Children with severe to profound hearing loss have traditionally been placed either in *residential settings* or *day schools*. Most residential schools are state-supported and usually stress the manual approach, whereas most day schools are privately funded and emphasize oralism (Meadow, 1972). There is a current trend toward a philosophy of total communication in both settings. Since the late 1950s there has been a tendency to place children in day schools rather than residential settings (McConnell, 1973).

The contemporary emphasis on providing education in the least restrictive environment is reflected in several educational settings for the hearing-impaired. These include the *special class* and the *resource room*. In a special class with other hearing impaired children, a child is given training designed to permit eventual entry into a regular classroom. Once this step is made, the child may receive individual help for part of the day in a resource room. The goal is to integrate the child to the greatest extent possible into the "mainstream" of the educational process that children with normal hearing pass through.

Goals of Education for the Deaf/Severely Hearing Impaired. Regardless of the educational setting selected for severely hearing-impaired or deaf students, the educational goals remain the same. The educational setting should enable the deaf child to develop (1) adequate language skills, (2) intelligible speech, (3) ease of communication with peers, and (4) good mental health (Northern and Downs, 1974). The keystone to any program must be language development, and the method of training must focus on that need. With language as a base, it is possible for the child to develop some intelligible speech, and the combination of manual and oral skills will enhance the child's ease of communication with peers and others. These goals must be accomplished in an environment of acceptance to provide the proper framework for personal adjustment and good mental health.

Mainstreaming. The integration of severely hearing-impaired students into regular classrooms with hearing children is considered the most desirable system by many educators. This mainstreaming to the "least restrictive" environment seeks to change the practice of residential school training toward the utilization of local community programs and schools. The concept is becoming increasingly popular, but Northcott (1973) cautions that partial or full-time integration for hearing-impaired students into regular classrooms is not a realistic goal for every child. A study by Craig et al. (1976) indicated that 30 percent of residential schools, 65 percent of day schools, and 73 percent of regular day classes for the deaf offered their deaf students an integrated program. Overall, approximately 44 percent of all deaf children are integrated with hearing students for some part of their instructional day.

There is considerable controversy over the pros and cons of mainstreaming for the severely hearing impaired. Vernon and Pickett (1976) describe three traditional approaches that they feel are flawed:

1. "Dumping" deaf children into classes with normal-hearing children, giving them hearing aids, preferential seating, and occasional resource teacher assistance;
2. Providing self-contained classrooms for the deaf in the public schools and mainstreaming students only for limited activities such as lunch and physical education;
3. Placing the deaf child in a day school program with other deaf children for the elementary years and then "suddenly" mainstreaming the child in junior high or high school.

However, Birch (1976) contends that such practices are the exception, not the rule. He finds that mainstreaming of deaf children is typically done with more thorough and careful preparation. An outstanding program known as the Holcomb Plan has been implemented in Newark, Delaware (Holcomb and Corbett, 1975). This plan requires a total communication approach, and the deaf child is placed in a hearing classroom only when there is a tutor-interpreter available to translate what is said into sign language and finger spelling. This method bridges the gap from self-contained classes for the deaf to complete mainstreaming.

PROBE 5-7
Educational Needs of the Hearing Impaired

1. What are four reasons a physician might suspect a hearing loss in a newborn baby?

2. Name five signs of possible hearing loss that a classroom teacher should watch for.

3. T F Language and speech delay can result from recurrent ear infections.
4. T F Hearing aids are never appropriate for children with conductive hearing loss.
5. T F The classroom teacher should use exaggerated lip movement and speak loudly to assist the hearing impaired child.

6. T F The manual approach to communication stresses speech reading and auditory training.

7. Educators of the deaf who prohibit the use of gestures by the child are called
_____ .

8. Educational settings for the severely hearing impaired include the _____ , _____ , _____ , and _____ .

SUMMARY

1. A person with a substantial hearing loss at the frequencies in the 300–4,000 Hz range will be severely handicapped in hearing other people's speech.
2. The intensity, or loudness, of normal conversational speech at a distance of five feet is between 40 and 60 decibels.
3. In normal hearing, sound waves are collected by the outer ear and mechanically transferred by the eardrum to the hammer, anvil and stirrup bones of the middle ear. These bones carry the sound vibration across the middle ear to the inner ear, where fluid motion within the cochlea stimulates the auditory nerve. This nerve transmits electrical impulses to the brain, where they are interpreted.
4. One of the most serious consequences of hearing loss is that it can hamper the development of speech and language in young children.
5. Hearing losses are due to conductive, sensorineural, mixed, functional, and central auditory problems. The conductive loss, which is usually caused by middle ear infections, is the easiest to correct.
6. It is estimated that there are 49,000 deaf children and 328,000 hard-of-hearing children in the nation's schools.
7. The professionals who evaluate hearing by means of audiometric testing are called audiologists.
8. A hearing loss of between 20 and 40 decibels is considered mild. A loss of between 40 and 60 decibels is considered moderate. A 60- to 80-decibel loss is considered severe, and losses of more than 80 decibels are considered profound.
9. Hearing loss can affect speech and language development, and educational, vocational, social, and emotional adjustment.
10. Hearing aids make sounds louder. They do not make sounds clearer.
11. For educational purposes, children with hearing disorders are classified as either hard of hearing or deaf.
12. The philosophy of total communication makes use of both oral and manual procedures to teach deaf children.
13. Regular class teachers should be able to recognize signs that may indicate hearing disorders so that they can refer children for hearing evaluations.

Teachers can help keep children with hearing disorders in the regular classroom in many different ways.

14. Children with severe hearing impairment are best educated in a variety of settings, depending on the severity of their problem. These settings include the residential school, day school, special class, and resource room.

TASK SHEET 5
Field Experiences with Hearing Disorders

Select *one* of the following and complete the activities that are described. Do a report of no more than three pages on the alternative that you choose.

Professional Interview

Interview a professional who provides hearing services and answer the following:
1. Whom did you interview?
2. What services does this person provide?
3. What questions did you ask?
4. What did you learn from the interview?

Observation of an Audiometric Examination

Observe an audiometric testing of a child or adult and respond to the following:
1. Where did you observe the examination?
2. Describe the person being tested.
3. What did the tester do?
4. What tests were administered?
5. What problem was identified by the tests?
6. What follow-up was recommended?
7. Describe your reaction to the experience.

Observation of a Program for Hearing-Impaired Children

Visit an educational program for hard-of-hearing or deaf children and respond to the following:
1. Where did you observe?
2. Describe the physical setting.
3. Describe the activities that were being conducted.
4. Interview the teacher about the purposes of the program and what kind of problems are encountered.
5. Describe your reactions to the experience.

Library Study

Use the library to locate three articles related to a topic associated with hearing disorders. Write a one-page abstract of each.
Here are the names of some journals in which you can find articles:

American Annals of the Deaf
ASHA
Ear and Hearing
Journal of Speech and Hearing Disorders

Journal of Speech and Hearing Research
Language, Speech and Hearing Services in the Schools
Volta Review

Agency Investigation

Request information from three of the following agencies about the services they provide to people with hearing impairments. Write a three-page paper summarizing these services and how you might use them if you were a professional working with children who have hearing problems.

Alexander Graham Bell
Association for the Deaf
1537 37th Street, N.W.
Washington, DC 20007

American Organization for the Education of the Hearing Impaired
1537 35th Street, N.W.
Washington, DC 20007

American Speech Language Hearing
Association
10801 Rockville Pike
Rockville, MD 20852

Council on Education of the Deaf
Colorado School for the Deaf and the
Blind
Colorado, Springs, CO 80903

Council of Organizations Serving the
Deaf
Wilde Lake Village Green,
Suite 310
Columbia, MD 21044

Deafness Research Foundation
366 Madison Avenue
Suite 1010
New York, NY 10017

Gallaudet College
7th and Florida Avenues, NE
Washington, DC 20002

National Association for the Deaf
814 Thayer Avenue
Silver Spring, MD 20910

National Technical Institute for the Deaf
One Lomb Memorial Drive
Rochester, NY 14623

Design Your Own Field Experience

If you know of a unique experience you can have with hearing disabled persons, discuss your alternative with your instructor and complete the task that you agree on.

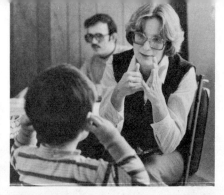

This little boy, pictured at age 2½, has a severe sensorineural hearing loss that was discovered when he was three months old. Almost totally deaf, he has been using sign language since he was two. His first signed word was "cookie" and his first spoken word was "mama." The entire family uses sign language and has participated in a speech and language development program for preschool deaf children.

The child is now enrolled in a communication disorders program that includes an evaluation of the effectiveness of his body hearing aid. Recent tests indicate that his language comprehension is appropriate for his age, his vocalizing is good, and his signing has improved. He has begun to speak in complete sentences, and his parents are thrilled at his progress.

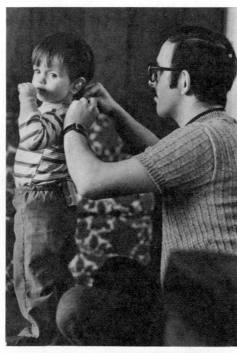

. . . JoAnn has been blind since she was born at Des Moines, Iowa. She went to special schools until her sophomore year in high school, when she was "mainstreamed" — put into a regular high school. There, she says, her biggest trouble was that "I didn't have a very good self-image."

That, she says, is the major problem of the nation's half-million people who are totally blind, and probably the million more Americans whose sight is so impaired they can't read.

Two years ago JoAnn was a student at a Des Moines School run by the Iowa Commission for the Blind, which she says operates "the best program for the blind in the country." The commission bought a Kurzweil Reading Machine for the Blind, the second such machine purchased in the nation. . . .

The Kurzweil machine has opened a new world to her. It is the world of books, of any printed material. Now, says JoAnn, "I want to be a lawyer."

The machine is described by its inventor, Raymond Kurzweil, 30:

"A camera scans the print. A small computer recognizes the letters, all type styles — that's the heart of the problem. The computer groups letters into words. A thousand linguistic rules and 1,500 exceptions to the rules are fed into the computer's memory. This enables the machine to change the letters to phonemes, the sounds of words pronounced phonetically. There are 64 phonemes, and these are fed into a speech synthesizer which produces speech."

Result: JoAnn Guidicessi now "reads" about 210 words a minute, faster than most sighted persons can read. . . .

The first Kurzweil machine was installed at the end of 1976. Since then about 50 have been installed and Kurzweil has orders on hand for another 100 from as far away as Sydney, Australia.

The U.S. Bureau of Education for the Handicapped picked up on the Kurzweil machine after its first installation. It funded research for its improvement and has ordered 64 of the new models. . . .

Source: From William Steif, Machine Can Open Reading World to the Blind. *The Albuquerque Tribune,* March 2, 1979. Reprinted by permission.

6

Visual Impairments

Hilda R. Caton

Hilda R. Caton is Associate Professor in the Vision Impairment Program at the University of Louisville and Director of Braille Projects at the American Printing House for the Blind. Dr. Caton has also worked as a resource and itinerant teacher of the visually impaired in elementary and secondary day school programs, as a special teacher of reading in a residential school for the visually impaired, and as a vision consultant in a State Department of Education. Current areas of interest are research and curriculum development for adventitiously blind persons and development of assessment instruments for the visually impaired.

Most of us who can see take our vision for granted. We watch television, read books and newspapers, use the library, walk from place to place without difficulty, and engage in a host of other activities that depend on our ability to see.

But think what your life would be like if you lost your ability to read. The information in newspapers, magazines, textbooks, even letters from your friends would be lost to you. For you the worlds described in poetry and fiction might not exist. A device such as the Kurzweil Reader described on the facing page could have an enormous effect on you. Whole realms of thought previously only partially available in the form of braille or audio tapes would be opened up. The extent of the handicap that results from blindness could be greatly reduced.

That is the goal of special education for the visually impaired — the reduction of vision-related handicaps to the greatest extent possible. In this chapter we will describe visually impaired children and the different degrees of visual impairment. We will explain the visual system and some of its common disorders and discuss the developmental characteristics of visually impaired children, as well as some of their educational alternatives. Finally, we will illustrate methods of educational assessment and describe some of the instructional methods and equipment used to reduce the effects of visual impairment.

HOW WE SEE

> **You should be able to identify the parts of the visual system and describe how we see.**

The most obvious characteristics of the visually impaired child is that his or her vision is in some way abnormal. Normal, or unimpaired, vision has four basic components: (1) the object to be viewed; (2) light that reflects from the object; (3) an intact visual organ (the eye); and (4) the occipital lobes of the brain, where visual stimuli are interpreted and "seeing" takes place (Chalkley, 1982; Kirk, 1981).

THE PHYSIOLOGY OF SEEING

The visual system consists of the eye and the parts of the brain responsible for seeing. The eye itself is a complex organ consisting of a number of structures. The structures are, however, closely related. The eye is illustrated in Figure 6-1. The discussion of the parts of the eye is based on the work of Allen (1963), Chalkley (1982), Vaughan and Asbury (1974), and Kirk (1981).

What parts of the visual system protect the eye?

The bony socket, sclera, eyelids, eyebrows, and conjunctiva are considered to be the *protective* part of the visual system. The bony socket provides a strong outer protection from severe blows, sharp objects, or other wounds. The sclera is the tough outer layer of the eyeball, which holds and protects its contents. The eyelids, eyelashes, and eyebrows trap dust and other particles and keep them from entering the eye, where infection and damage can occur. Further protection from dust and particles is provided by the conjunctiva, a thin, transparent layer that lines the eyelids and covers the front of the eye. The tears protect by washing out particles that have entered the eye. They also contain an enzyme that helps prevent infection.

What is refraction?

The cornea, aqueous, iris, lens, ciliary body, and vitreous are the *refractive* parts of the eye. They are responsible for making sure that light rays reach the exact point on the retina of the eye that will result in distinct vision. The cornea, aqueous, lens, and vitreous refract (bend) the light rays that enter the eye and direct them to that point. Part of the function of the iris, the colored part of the eye, is to screen out a portion of the entering light rays. The iris is controlled by muscles that contract to allow less light through the pupil or expand to allow more light.

The ciliary body has two parts and two functions. One part, the ciliary processes, produces the aqueous fluid. The other part, the ciliary muscle, changes the shape of the lens so that light is focused correctly on the retina.

Figure 6-1
Cross-section of the Human Eye

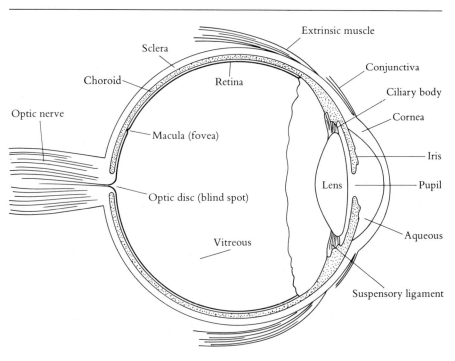

Where is light focused when it enters the eye?

The retina is the *receptive* part of the eye. It is often referred to as the "nerve-layer" of the eye. It consists of a thin layer of tissue and nerves that line the inside of the eyeball. It is actually an extension of the optic nerve, which enters the back of the eye, coming directly from the brain. For a person to have a clear, distinct vision, the light rays must strike a small spot on the retina called the macular area. When this occurs, nerve impulses are sent out of the eye through the optic nerve along another nerve system to the occipital area of the brain. There the visual stimuli are interpreted and "seeing" takes place.

The retina receives its nourishment from the blood vessels in the choroid, the layer of the eye between the sclera and the retina.

What is strabismus?

The movement of the eye is controlled by extrinsic, or external muscles. These muscles turn the eyes to enable them to focus simultaneously on specific objects. There are six external muscles, located on each side of the eyeball and above and below it. These muscles move the eye to the left, right, upward, and downward. The failure of the muscles to function promptly can result in crossed eyes (strabismus) and double vision.

THE PROCESS OF SEEING

Seeing is a complex process, with the efficient functioning of one part of the visual system often dependent on the efficient functioning of other parts. The process is illustrated in Figure 6-2.

Basically, the process of seeing involves the following sequence of events:

1. Light rays are reflected from an object and enter the eye.
2. The light rays pass through the cornea, which refracts, or bends, them.
3. The light rays, properly refracted, pass through the anterior, or aqueous, chamber, where they are again slightly refracted.
4. From the anterior chamber, the light rays pass through the pupil. The size of the pupil can be changed by the movement of the iris to allow more or less light as needed.
5. The light rays pass through the lens, the major refracting structure of the eye. The shape of the lens can be changed by the suspensary ligament to focus the light rays on exactly the right place in the eye. This process is called accommodation.
6. The light passes through the vitreous chamber. Its content, the vitreous humor, also has a slightly refractive effect.

What function does the fovea perform?

7. The light rays are focused on the fovea, a small spot on the macula that produces the clearest, most distinct vision.
8. Light energy is changed to electrical impulses, which are carried by the optic nerve to the occipital lobe of the brain, where "seeing" takes place.

Figure 6-2
The Process of "Seeing"

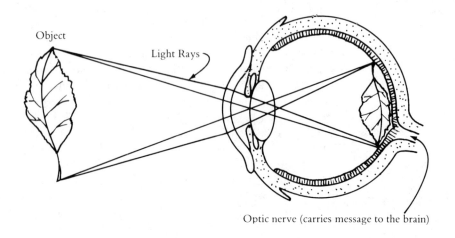

Object

Light Rays

Optic nerve (carries message to the brain)

PROBE 6-1
The Visual System

1. Indicate whether each of the following is a (a) protective part of the eye; (b) refractive part; or (c) receptive part, by placing the appropriate letter in the blank preceding each item.

_____ bony socket	_____ optic nerve
_____ retina	_____ tears
_____ cornea	_____ lens
_____ eyelid	_____ vitreous
_____ aqueous	_____ conjunctiva
_____ eyebrow	

2. Describe, in your own words, the process of "seeing."

DISORDERS OF THE VISUAL SYSTEM

You should be familiar with some common disorders of the visual system.

REFRACTIVE DISORDERS

Disorders of the refractive structures of the eye are among the most common encountered in children today. The so-called refractive errors are hyperopia (farsightedness), myopia (nearsightedness), and astigmatism. The physical state of the eyeball in each of these conditions is illustrated in Figure 6-3.

What is the difference between myopia and hyperopia?

Hyperopia, or farsightedness, occurs when the eye is too short and the rays of light from near objects are not focused on the retina. Myopia, or nearsightedness, occurs when the eye is too long and the rays of light from distant objects are not focused on the retina. The hyperopic eye can see objects more clearly at close range. Astigmatism is "blurred" vision caused by uneven curvature of the cornea or lens. This curvature prevents light rays from focusing correctly on the retina. Except in extreme cases, all of these disorders can be corrected with spectacles or contact lenses, so children with refractive errors are not often placed in special programs. These problems are found very frequently in regular classrooms, however, and can cause serious problems unless they are detected and corrected.

What are cataracts?

Cataracts, a common disorder of a refractive structure, often do result in the need for special education placement. Cataracts are not, as many believe, growths on the eye. They result, rather, when the semifluid substance in the lens gradually becomes opaque and the vision is obscured. Cataracts can result in severe visual loss. They are an especially serious problem in young children,

Figure 6-3
Refractive Errors of the Eye

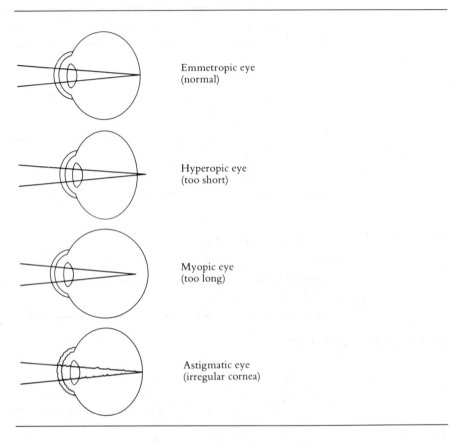

Emmetropic eye
(normal)

Hyperopic eye
(too short)

Myopic eye
(too long)

Astigmatic eye
(irregular cornea)

since the opacity prevents light rays from focusing on the retina. This can result in the retina's failure to develop. Surgical procedures for the treatment of cataracts are quite advanced, however, and visual losses can usually be prevented.

RETINAL AND OPTIC NERVE DISORDERS

Common problems of the receptive parts of the eye include degeneration of the retina and the optic nerve and detachment of the retina.

Although some forms of optic nerve degeneration result from infections, and some forms of retinal degeneration are linked to recessive gene traits, the cause in most cases is unknown. The severity of the visual loss varies widely, since the pace of the structure's degeneration is different for each person

Can degenerative visual disorders be treated?

affected. Total blindness occurs in many cases, but not in all. These degenerative conditions are extremely difficult to cope with, both medically and educationally: Little is known about their causes or rate of progress, and there is no known treatment for them. Children with these eye conditions are almost always placed in special educational programs.

Retinal detachment is a separation of the retina from the adjacent layers of the eye, the choroid and the sclera. This disorder is sometimes associated with extreme cases of myopia, or nearsightedness, where the eyeball becomes excessively long and pulls the retina away from surrounding tissues. Retinal detachments can also result from retinal degeneration, glaucoma, and other disorders. Although it is now possible to reattach the retina through various surgical techniques, this must be done immediately or extensive visual loss will occur (Chalkley, 1982). Children with retinal detachment are almost always placed in special education programs because of their visual loss and because they must be protected from sharp blows on the head, falls, and other actions that could cause further detachment.

MUSCLE DISORDERS

How can amblyopia be treated?

Disorders of the extrinsic muscles are very common in young children. They are usually the result of the muscles being imbalanced. As noted earlier, such an imbalance creates a condition known as strabismus, or crossed eyes. When this occurs, the eyes cannot focus simultaneously on the same object. As a result, the child sees a double image of the object. Normally, the brain reacts by suppressing the image in one eye, and when that eye is not used its vision is lost, a condition called amblyopia. Fortunately, amblyopia can be prevented if detected early and properly treated. The treatment sometimes consists of placing a patch over the unaffected eye to bring the affected eye into focus. A simple surgical procedure to straighten the muscles involved can also be used. Because muscle disorders are easily corrected and rarely impair vision severely, children who suffer from them do not often need special education.

GLAUCOMA

What causes glaucoma?

Glaucoma is a common disorder that is not related to one specific structure of the eye. It is caused by the failure of the aqueous fluid to circulate properly, which results in an elevation of pressure in the eye. This pressure very gradually destroys the optic nerve. The result can be total blindness. Glaucoma can be treated, however, and if the treatment occurs early, visual loss can be prevented. Because their eyes are not fully developed, however, young children are especially susceptible to harm from glaucoma, and many have severe visual losses. Those who do usually need special education.

RETROLENTAL FIBROPLASIA

How can RLF be prevented?

One of the most devastating eye disorders affecting young children is retro-lental fibroplasia (RLF). First observed in the early 1940s, this disorder affected only premature babies, usually weighing three pounds or less at birth. The disorder was characterized by what appeared to be an overgrowth of imma-ture blood vessels from the retina into the vitreous of the eye (Harley and Lawrence, 1977). The eye appeared to have fibrous growths in the vitreous. The disorder became progressively more prevalent for ten years, with the highest incidence occurring in 1952 and 1953. The medical profession was baffled about the cause until it was finally discovered to be the use of high concentrations of oxygen in the incubators of premature babies. After that, steps were taken to control oxygen concentrations, and the disorder almost disappeared.

When these children were first placed in educational programs, it was thought that only their vision was affected. Evaluations conducted when the children were 10 to 15 years old, however, indicated that many of them also had neurological and behavioral disorders, as well as some speech problems (Bender and Andermann, 1965). A related problem that has surfaced in recent years is that reduced levels of oxygen in incubators have caused cerebral palsy in some premature babies (Silverman, 1977). Problems resulting from the reduced oxygen levels have ultimately had an effect on the number of multiply handicapped, visually impaired children to be served in educational programs and has required the development of new techniques and materials for these programs.

Silverman (1977) presents a summary of the entire investigation and solu-tion to the problem of RLF for those who wish more detailed information. Stanley and Lanman (1976) have published a detailed report on the disorder which includes sections on modern premature infant care, particularly the use of oxygen.

DISORDERS CAUSED BY MATERNAL RUBELLA

What percent of children whose mothers had rubella have vision problems?

Women who have rubella (German measles) during the first trimester of pregnancy often have babies with severe multiple handicaps. Among these handicaps, visual impairment is very common. McCay, Grieve, and Shaver (1980) have estimated that at least 33 percent of children with congenital rubella syndrome have vision problems.

The major visual disorder among children with this syndrome is congenital cataracts. An associated visual disorder is glaucoma, a disorder that frequently occurs with cataracts.

The last major rubella epidemic occurred in 1964. Since that time significant medical advances, such as the development of a vaccine to help prevent ru-

TECHNOLOGY IN ACTION

Advanced computerized devices like "talking" clocks and speech-synthesized reading machines are helping the blind become more independent. However, these developments seem modest compared to the goal of research now under way to create an artificial eye that will give a totally blind person limited vision.

At the Institute for Artificial Organs, based in New York City, Dr. William H. Dobelle, chairman, and Dr. John P. Gervin, of the University of Western Ontario, are working on a so-called electronic eye controlled by a tiny microcomputer concealed in the sidepiece of an eyeglass frame.

Dr. Dobelle, a biophysicist and neurophysiologist, began research in artificial vision to restore sight about ten years ago. The technique, based on earlier experiments of two British scientists, focuses on direct electrical stimulation of visual areas of the brain cortex. In one of Dr. Dobelle's studies, a 35-year-old man blinded by a gunshot wound was surgically implanted with an arrangement of 64 platinum electrodes embedded in a piece of Teflon.

Using a stimulator powered by a conventional external computer linked to a video camera, researchers were able to send signals through the electrodes to the brain, causing the blind man to see changing patterns of white points of light, known as phosphenes. Such light sensations can vary in brightness depending on the level of electrical current sent to the cortex. Tests conducted during the experiment showed that the man was able to read a visual version of braille substantially faster than he could decipher tactile braille material.

Dr. Dobelle believes that by increasing the number of implanted electrodes, the blind will be able to see animation similar to the movement shown, for example, on the electronic scoreboard in Yankee Stadium. Certain physical characteristics, such as those differentiating the sexes, also could be visually perceived, he notes.

The ultimate goal of his research, Dr. Dobelle says, is use of phosphenes as the basis of a prosthetic, or artificial device. With his colleagues, the scientist is now creating such an "electronic eye" using two Teflon strips, each inlaid with over 200 electrodes, implanted on either side of the brain. Within the glass eye itself, a half-inch-size video camera will produce images stimulating the electrodes that are controlled by a microcomputer built into the glass frame.

The entire system, which could run on a battery pack also attached to the eyeglasses, would cost an estimated $3000 to $5000. It is now in prototype form and is expected to be available in about five years.

From Popular Computing, *April, 1984, p. 34.*

---

bella, seem to have prevented the occurrence of another such epidemic. However, educational advances for these children have not been as significant. Although some progress has been made in the establishment of educational programs for multiply handicapped visually impaired children, a great deal remains to be learned about how they function and what services are most appropriate for them.

PROBE 6-2
Disorders of the Visual System

1. If detected early, amblyopia can be corrected by either _____ or _____ .

2. T   F   Cataracts are growths on the eye.

3. Nearsightedness is to _____ as farsightedness is to hyperopia.

4. Two diseases that resulted in large numbers of multiply handicapped blind children are _____ and _____ .

5. _____ is the eye disorder caused by excessive oxygen in incubators of premature babies.

DEFINITIONS

You should know the definitions of visual impairment and the purposes for which they are used.

Definitions and descriptions of visually impaired children tend to vary considerably, depending on the purposes for which individuals or groups are being described. Generally, the term *visually impaired* includes all children whose vision is sufficiently impaired to affect their functioning in school (Scott, 1982). They need specially trained teachers, specially designed or adapted curricular materials, and specially designed educational aids in order to reach their full potential (Ashcroft, 1963).

Within this broad definition, visually impaired children are differentiated into two categories, the blind, and the partially seeing or low-visioned (Ashcroft, 1963). Two definitions are accepted for both blind and partially seeing children, one based on visual acuity, and one on the educational media to be used.

DEFINITIONS BASED ON VISUAL ACUITY

Definitions based on visual acuity are used for legal and economic purposes and for the allocation of federal funds to purchase educational materials. They are called the "legal" definitions of visual impairment.

What is the legal definition of blindness?

Legally blind children are defined as (1) those whose visual acuity is 20/200 or less in the better eye with the best possible correction, or (2) those whose field of vision is restricted to an angle subtending an arc of 20 degrees or less (American Foundation for the Blind, 1961). Partially seeing children are defined as (1) those whose visual acuity is between 20/200 and 20/70 in the better eye with the best possible correction, or (2) those who in the opinion of an eye specialist need either temporary or permanent special education facilities.

Although these definitions are useful for legal and funding purposes, they do not provide enough information to deliver effective educational services to visually impaired children. It is important to understand what the definitions can and cannot tell educators about these children.

The first factor to be considered in both definitions is the concept of visual acuity itself. Visual acuity is simply a means of describing the sharpness or clearness of vision. It does not describe the efficiency with which particular individuals use their vision, nor does it take into account the variety of ways in which vision is used in an educational setting.

What is a Snellen Chart?

The visual acuities used in the legal definitions are measures of distance vision. These are almost always obtained through the use of the Snellen Chart, illustrated in Figure 6-4. This chart is designed so that the top letter, when seen from a distance of 200 feet, seems to be the same size as the standard when seen from a distance of 20 feet. The test distance of 20 feet was used because rays of light reflected from objects at that distance are parallel. When light rays entering the eye are parallel, the muscles of the normal eye are at rest, and the visual acuity obtained does not reflect the accommodative power of the eye (the clear image on the retina). As a result, the visual acuity obtained at 20 feet gives a truer picture of the sharpness and clearness of vision than it would at other distances.

How is a 20/20 index of visual acuity interpreted?

Visual acuity is expressed as an index, such as 20/20, 20/70, or 20/200. This index does not represent the fraction of remaining vision, as some people think. The top number in the index represents the 20 feet the person being tested stands from the chart. The bottom number is the distance at which a person with normal vision can distinguish the letters in the line being viewed. For example, if a person being tested can read at 20 feet what the person with normal vision can read at 200 feet, his or her visual acuity is 20/200.

How useful to teachers is knowledge of a child's visual acuity?

Visual acuity actually tells educators very little about the child's ability to read or examine educational materials at close range. Barraga (1964) has illustrated that some children with visual acuities as low as 6/300 can learn to use their remaining vision quite efficiently. In educational planning, then, the causes of the visual loss as well as the efficiency with which the child uses remaining vision must be considered. For example, a child with corneal opacities (small opaque areas scattered throughout the cornea) would have an extremely low visual acuity (around 8/400) as measured by the Snellen Chart, because the child would be unable to see through the opacities when looking directly at the chart. The child might, however, be able to read relatively small print held close to the eyes if he or she turned the head to see around the opacities. Many illustrations of this kind could be given. The point is that the visual acuity alone is not an adequate measure of a child's ability to function in an educational setting. The limited value to teachers of definitions based on visual acuity should be clear.

Figure 6–4
Snellen Symbol Chart

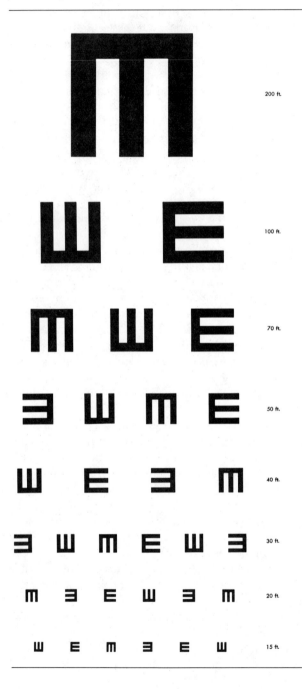

The second factor to be considered in these definitions is the visual field, or peripheral vision. Peripheral, or "side," vision is measured in degrees of visual arc. The procedure for measurement is to place the individual about 39 inches from a square black chart and ask the person to fix his or her eye on a central point on the chart. A round, white object is then moved in from the periphery of the chart in a circular pattern until the individual being tested can see it. The distance at which the stimulus can be seen is then measured. When the widest angle at which the stimulus can be seen is 20 degrees or less in the best eye with the best possible correction, the person is considered to be legally blind. Many educators would also consider the person educationally blind.

What is tunnel vision?

The field of vision is often reported on charts similar to those in Figure 6-5. A separate chart is provided for each eye. The dark lines in the center of the chart represent visual fields, in both eyes, of a person with a visual field loss of 20 degrees. If you examine the fields of vision represented on the charts, you will note that an individual with a field of vision of 20 degrees or less can see little more than what is directly in front of the eye. People with this restricted field of vision are said to have tunnel vision.

Tunnel vision causes problems in mobility as well as in reading. The lack of peripheral vision makes it difficult for a person to see objects not directly in front. This severely limits the person's knowledge of the area he or she is traveling through. Reading problems are caused by the inability to see more

Figure 6-5
Field of Vision Charts (O.S. = left eye   O.D. = right eye)

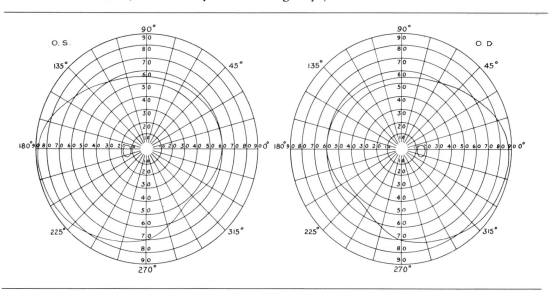

than one letter at a time or letters too large for the visual field. Even when the visual acuity in the very small visual field is good, the restriction in the field severely impairs the vision.

DEFINITIONS FOR EDUCATIONAL SERVICES

How do teachers differentiate between blind and partially seeing children?

Although definitions based on visual acuity and field of vision are helpful, definitions that describe children in terms of the type of education they receive are most appropriate for educational planning. This kind of definition, first proposed in 1957 (American Foundation for the Blind, 1961), is now widely accepted by educators of visually impaired children. Educationally defined, the blind child is one whose visual loss indicates that he or she should be educated chiefly through the use of braille and other tactile and auditory materials. The partially seeing child is defined as one who has some remaining useful vision and can use print and other visual materials as part of the educational program.

PROBLEMS WITH DEFINITIONS

Obviously, neither a definition based on visual acuity nor an educational definition should be used as the sole criterion for deciding how and in what programs a child should be educated. Such factors as (1) age of student, (2) age of onset of visual impairment, (3) level of achievement, (4) level of intelligence, (5) presence of other handicapping conditions, (6) nature (etiology) of the visual impairment, and (7) emotional stability must also be considered (Gearhart, 1980).

Why are knowledge of etiology and age of onset of visual impairment important?

The most important considerations are the etiology and age of onset. The etiology is crucial because some eye conditions require the use of a particular teaching method or set of materials. For example, children affected by atrophy of the optic nerve require a great deal of light and materials with good contrast. They might eventually need to learn braille. Children with visual losses from other causes might require different methods and materials.

The experience a child had before a loss of vision and the age at which the loss occurred are also important. An early visual loss obviously limits what was learned through seeing to a much greater extent than a later visual loss. The knowledge of how much a child knew when the vision became impaired can help a teacher decide what the child needs to learn and how it should be taught.

Intellectual ability and chronological age, though also important in determining how a child should be educated, are not as significant as the factors already discussed. They will be discussed in the section on the developmental characteristics of visually impaired children.

PROBE 6-3
Definitions

1. Define visually impaired children.

2. Visually impaired children are classified as either _____ or _____ .

3. With correction, a legally blind child has visual acuity no better than 20/200. A partially seeing child has visual acuity between _____ and _____ .

4. T F Visual acuity is a term for sharpness and clearness of vision.

5. Explain the meaning of an index of visual acuity that is stated as 20/150.

6. Field of vision is measured in terms of _____ .

7. From the perspective of educational definitions, how would you differentiate between a blind and partially seeing child?

IDENTIFICATION AND PREVALENCE

You should be able to describe the procedures used in identifying visually impaired children.

To plan for the education of visually impaired children, the children must first be identified. As was pointed out in the preceding section, a knowledge of visual acuity alone is of limited value. The children who actually need services can be discovered only by careful, systematic identification procedures such as those carried out by school systems. The planner must also know the numbers and types of visual problems to determine how many and what kinds of programs are needed.

IDENTIFICATION

Systematic identification procedures include coordinated preschool and school vision screening programs as well as national, state, and regional child-find programs. These programs are team efforts by teachers, doctors, and other people. A good identification program includes (1) comprehensive screenings, (2) referral for complete eye examinations of those who appear to have problems, and (3) follow-ups to ensure that the recommendations resulting from the examination are carried out. The eye specialist, and not the people doing the screening, makes the final diagnosis (Harley and Lawrence, 1977).

Ideally, every child should have a complete eye examination every year.

How does the National Society for the Prevention of Blindness help with vision screening?

Unfortunately, most children don't. As a result, preschool and school vision screening programs tend to be the most effective means of identification.

The agency most active in preschool and school vision screening programs is the National Society for the Prevention of Blindness. All across the United States its branches train volunteers, who then conduct the actual screening sessions. Their basic screening program consists of an annual test for distance visual acuity using the Snellen Chart and careful instructions to teachers describing symptoms that may indicate eye disorders (National Society for the Prevention of Blindness, 1980). The test for visual acuity is used because it has proven to indicate effectively which children have eye problems when they are later examined by ophthalmologists. The Society recommends that children be referred for an eye examination if they are unable to read the following lines on the Snellen Chart:

Three-year-olds	20/50 or less
Four-year-olds through third grade	20/40 or less
Fourth grade and above	20/30 or less

Very strict standards have been set up for the actual testing session. They must be followed exactly in order to obtain valid results. These standards are described in the Society's *Vision Screening in Schools* (National Society for the Prevention of Blindness 1980), which is available through the organization's national, state, and regional offices. Standards and procedures for correct screening are also illustrated in a film, *Before We Are Six,* which is available through the national office.

Observations by teachers, parents, and others closely associated with the children are also important in the identification of eye problems. Some symptoms that might suggest an eye problem are:

How could a teacher identify a possible vision problem in a student?

1. Clumsiness and trouble walking in a new environment.
2. Having to hold one's head in an awkward position or having to hold material very close to one's eyes, in order to see.
3. "Tuning out" when information is written on the blackboard or somewhere else a child might have trouble seeing.
4. Constant requests for someone to tell the child what is going on.
5. Being inordinately affected by glare or not being able to see things at certain times of the day.
6. A pronounced squint.
7. Excessive rubbing of the eyes.
8. Pushing the eyeballs with fingers or knuckles.
9. Obvious physical anomalies such as red, swollen lids, crusts on the eyes, crossed eyes, etc. (National Society for the Prevention of Blindness, 1980)

Children who exhibit any of these symptoms should be referred to an eye specialist.

Visually impaired children are identified through means other than vision screening programs, of course. Pediatricians and family doctors discover the problems in many children. In addition, school systems and states now have agencies whose major responsibility is the identification and appropriate referral of the visually impaired.

What is the difference between an ophthalmologist and an optometrist?

Once a child has been identified as possibly having an eye problem, he or she is referred to the appropriate eye specialist. Generally this is an ophthalmologist or an optometrist. The opthalmologist is a physician whose specialty is diseases and disorders of the eye. He or she can prescribe and fit eyeglasses and can also use drugs and surgery to correct eye defects. The optometrist is not a physician but a professional whose practice is limited to the prescription and fitting of corrective lenses and the treatment of optical defects without drugs or surgery. Other specialists are the optician, who grinds lenses or makes glasses, and the orthoptist, who provides eye exercises when they are prescribed by an ophthalmologist.

What does an optician do?

Because they are most familiar with all possible eye defects, it is generally best to refer a child who has vision problems to an ophthalmologist. All these eye specialists have important roles in eye care, however, and educators should acquaint themselves with the specific services that each of them provides.

PREVALENCE

It is very difficult to get an accurate count of the number of visually impaired children. There are several reasons for this. Definitions of visual impairment vary from state to state, as do the methods of collecting and reporting data. The accuracy of the data collected varies as a consequence. In addition, a national census of visually impaired children has never been taken. As a result of these factors, prevalence figures are usually estimates based on a variety of sources.

How many visually impaired children are there in the United States?

The most often quoted prevalence figures state that approximately one in every 1,000 school-age children, or about 0.1 percent, is either blind or partially sighted. This figure, arrived at independently by Jones and Collins (1966) and Meyen (1978) is considered fairly accurate. According to population estimates, then, there are about 55,000 visually impaired children in the United States today. This figure matches that projected by the United States Department of Education in 1971-1972, a fact that further argues for the figure's accuracy.

Another source of information regarding numbers of visually impaired children is the annual registration of legally blind children by the American Printing House for the Blind. Although this registration does not tell us what percentage of all children are visually impaired, it does give an accurate count of the legally blind children enrolled in school programs throughout the country. In 1982, a total of 38,249 legally blind children were registered (American Printing House for the Blind, 1982). Of these, approximately 15 percent had to use braille as their reading medium, and approximately 34 percent had sufficient vision to read large type. These percentages do not include children with visual acuities better than 20/70 and do not therefore reflect the overall prevalence of visually impaired children.

Even though the accuracy of these estimates is subject to disagreement, it is clear that visually impaired children make up one of the smallest groups of exceptional children. It should also be noted that more visually impaired children are partially seeing (read print) than blind (read braille). The most accurate prevalence figure, which states that 0.1 percent of the school-age population is visually impaired, is the one that should probably be used in planning educational services.

From this discussion it is obvious that a great variety of disorders can affect the vision of children. Unfortunately, there are no recent figures on the relative prevalence of specific eye disorders. The latest figures that are available are furnished by the United States Department of Health, Education, and Welfare (1976). These figures show that among visually impaired persons who are not legally blind the leading causes of impairment are cataract, refractive errors, and glaucoma. Among the legally blind and totally blind the leading causes of impairment are retinal disorders, glaucoma, and cataract. Most of the visually impaired children in special educational programs have one of these disorders.

PROBE 6-4
Identification and Prevalence

1. *Matching*

   Profession
   _____ ophthalmologist
   _____ optician
   _____ optometrist
   _____ orthoptist

   Function
   a. provides eye exercises
   b. physician specializing in the eye
   c. grinds lenses and makes glasses
   d. non-physician who prescribes glasses

2. The name of the most common instrument for screening visual impairments in children is the _____ .

3. List five symptoms that may indicate eye problems:

4. T F Visually impaired children constitute one of the smallest groups of exceptional children.

DEVELOPMENTAL CHARACTERISTICS

> **You should be familiar with the physical, learning, and social-emotional characteristics of visually impaired children.**

To plan effectively, persons concerned with the education of visually impaired children should be familiar with their physical, learning (mental, cognitive, etc.), and social-emotional characteristics.

There is little agreement on the effect of blindness on the physical, mental, and emotional development of children. On one end of the spectrum of opinion are Cutsforth (1951, p. 3), who states that "no single mental activity of the congenitally blind child is not distorted by the absence of sight," and Carroll (1961, p. 11), who states that when vision is lost "the sighted man dies." On the other end are Ashcroft (1963), Scholl (1973), and Scott (1982), who state that visually impaired children are like other children in many more ways than they are different from them.

The last statement is probably the most accurate. It is worth remembering in educational planning, because it points out that "other" children are not all alike; they are individuals, each with his or her own characteristics and developmental patterns. The statement that visually impaired children are more like other children than different from them simply means that they are not a homogeneous group that fits easily into a carefully delineated category. They are just as varied a group as sighted children, and their educational needs vary just as greatly. It is extremely important to keep this in mind during the discussion that follows, since the emphasis on aspects of development unique to these children may appear to set them apart from other children.

PHYSICAL CHARACTERISTICS

Are there any physical differences between blind and seeing children?

In general, the physical development of visually impaired children resembles that of children who see normally. They do not tend to be taller, shorter, fatter, thinner, and so on, than other children simply because they are visually impaired. However, visual impairment often does have indirect effects on their physical development (Scholl, 1973). This is true largely because the physical activity of many visually impaired children is severely limited.

Some visually impaired children are overly protected or neglected by parents and do not have the opportunity to move about and develop physical skills. When these children enter school, the overprotection or neglect may continue, because teachers and peers sometimes fail to understand that these children can do many of the same physical activities that normally seeing children do. As a result, the physical skills of these children may not develop at a normal rate. An additional problem results from these children's not being able to observe the physical activities of others. They cannot develop certain physical skill through imitation, as seeing children do.

To overcome these problems, the visually impaired must be allowed the freedom to move about in their environment and to participate in the physical activities normal for all children. They can be taught directly many of the physical skills normally learned through visual observation. When they are given this training and a rich, stimulating environment, their physical development will follow the same pattern as that of their seeing peers.

LEARNING CHARACTERISTICS

Because there is no generally accepted definition of learning, it is difficult to discuss the many factors that influence it. Most experts acknowledge, however, that a child's ability to learn is significantly affected by two factors: intelligence and the ability to develop concepts. Accordingly, our discussion will focus on these two qualities and how and why they affect the child's school achievement.

Intelligence. The results of research on the intelligence of the visually impaired must be viewed with caution for several reasons. First, the children studied have been enrolled either in segregated residential school programs or in special education programs in public schools. Second, most of the intelligence tests used were originally developed for use by children with normal vision. Third, a child's score on an intelligence test reflects not only intellectual potential but also the opportunities the child has had to develop that potential. Each of these factors could have an effect on a child's intelligence test score.

Does visual impairment affect intellectual ability?

Nevertheless, a number of studies of the intelligence of the visually impaired have been undertaken. Although the evidence is inconclusive, many studies indicate no significant differences between the intelligence of the blind and that of those who see normally. The small differences that are sometimes found are probably attributable to the three factors we have mentioned. Students interested in specific studies are directed to Dauterman, Shapiro, and Swinn, 1967; Davis, 1970; Goldman, 1970; Hammill, Crandell, and Colarusso, 1970; Hayes, 1941; Parker, 1969; Scholl and Schnur, 1976; Tillman and Osborne, 1969; and Warren, 1977.

Studies of the intelligence of partially seeing children are scarce, and most are not very recent. However, those conducted have yielded results similar to those for the blind. Livingston (1958), for example, found the average IQ of partially seeing children to be 98.6; and Pintner, Eisenson, and Stanton (1941) also found intelligence levels in the normal range. Other studies by Bateman (1963) and Birch, Tisdall, Peabody, and Sterrett (1966) came to the same conclusions.

It seems likely, then, that the intellectual development of children is not directly affected by visual loss. Intelligence quotients alone, however, are an inadequate measure of a child's ability to learn.

How can visual impairment affect concept development?

Concept Development. Like intelligence, concept development is affected by the restrictions that result from visual loss, rather than by visual loss itself. A visually impaired child has a smaller range and variety of experiences, has trouble moving about freely, and has a more difficult time interacting with the environment (Lowenfeld, 1973). Many visually impaired children have never visited a farm, a grocery store, a park, and many other places familiar to most of us, and thus have little understanding of spatial relationships, faulty impressions of distance, and little concept of form, size, position, and so on (Nolan, 1978). The visually impaired are further handicapped by their inability to learn through imitation of what they see. They must learn through direct experiences, which, as mentioned, they often don't have.

Visually impaired children do, however, progress through the same sequence of developmental stages as other children, albeit at a much slower pace. This is indicated by a number of studies that compared the performance of visually impaired children on Piagetian tasks with that of seeing children (Friedman and Pasnak, 1973; Gottesman, 1971, 1973, 1976; Higgins, 1973; Miller, 1969; Simpkins and Stephens, 1974; and Tobin, 1972). Piaget's theory of stages of development is based on the belief that a child progresses through active interaction with his or her environment. This argues further that it is the restricted environmental involvement of the child that causes his delayed conceptual development, and not his visual impairment itself. It should be noted that the age of onset of the loss of vision will significantly affect the child's concept development.

Is school achievement affected by visual impairment?

School Achievement. As you might expect, visually impaired children tend to lag behind children with normal vision in school. Children with partial vision are average in their grade placement and somewhat below grade level in academic achievement, according to studies by Bateman (1963) and Birch et al. (1966). The same pattern of achievements is found among blind students who read braille (Caton and Rankin, 1980; Lowenfeld, Abel, and Hatlen, 1969). The children studied in the Caton and Rankin research were from 2 to 4 years over age for grade placement and from 1½ to 2 years below grade level in reading achievement.

This does not mean that a vision impairment necessarily leads to underachievement in school. Ashcroft (1963) suggests that the academic lag may be the consequence of many factors, including the following:

1. Visually impaired children usually enter school at a later age than other children.
2. Many children with vision problems are educated in inappropriate programs.

3. Many children miss a great deal of school because of surgery or treatment for eye conditions.

4. Many do not have any opportunity to attend school.

5. All children with severe impairments must use braille or large-type editions of books, which retards their ability to gather information.

As you can see, then, school underachievement, too, is an indirect rather than a direct result of visual impairment.

Though we have considered only a few of the factors that can influence learning, we can draw two general conclusions: (1) visual impairment does not necessarily result in mental retardation; and (2) the delays that are found in the intellectual development of the visually impaired are the result of inadequate opportunities to explore the environment (Harley, 1973; Scott, 1982). It should be noted that these conclusions do not take into account visually impaired children who also have other handicaps.

SOCIAL-EMOTIONAL CHARACTERISTICS

What is the primary cause of social and emotional problems that visually impaired people might have?

The prevailing opinion is that most of the social and emotional problems of the visually impaired are caused by the attitudes and reactions of those who can see. Cutsforth (1951), in fact, stated that society's negative attitudes were entirely responsible for their social and emotional problems. A number of studies (Bauman, 1974; Cowen, Underberg, Verillo, and Benham, 1961; Gowman, 1957; Spivey, 1967) reveal that visually impaired children either accept the opinions and expectations conveyed to them by society or suffer isolation as a result of rejecting them. In general, children with partial visual impairment tend to be more isolated by their seeing peers than those who are totally blind. This appears to be true because less severely handicapped children do not elicit the sympathy accorded totally blind children. Harley (1973) suggests that this is at least partially due to the practice of placing the visually impaired in special schools and classes.

Another factor that causes persons with normal vision to react negatively toward the visually impaired is the lack of contact between the two groups. This results in misunderstanding by both groups and the formation of unrealistic ideas about the effects of visual impairment on children. For example, a typical attitude of seeing persons toward the visually impaired is that all persons with visual losses are totally blind and that, as a result, they are basically helpless and dependent. This is, of course, not true. It is this kind of misconception that causes social and emotional problems in visually impaired children.

It is possible to improve attitudes, however, as Bateman (1964) found when she studied the attitudes of seeing children who were enrolled in classes with visually impaired children. She found that these children had much higher estimations of the abilities of visually impaired children than children who had not had direct associations with them. Siperstein and Bak (1980) found similiar results when analyzing the results of a study to improve fifth- and sixth-grade sighted students' attitudes toward their blind peers. This implies that greater integration of the visually impaired into classes with seeing children and more training about the capabilities of the visually impaired for regular classroom teachers would result in improved attitudes toward the visually impaired and more appropriate educational planning and placement.

PROBE 6-5
Developmental Characteristics

1. T   F   Although blind children may have delayed physical development because of their inability to do some physical activities, they typically do not differ in physical ability from normally seeing children.

2. List three possible causes of apparent retardation in the intellectual development, school achievement, and concept development of blind children.

3. The most widely accepted reason for social-emotional adjustment problems in blind children is _____ . This can be overcome by _____ .

INSTRUCTIONAL METHODS AND MATERIALS

You should be familiar with the methods and materials used to educate visually impaired children.

Once a child has been placed in the most suitable educational environment, the educator must consider the curriculum that will best meet the student's needs. The term "curriculum" means "the total experiences a learner has under the supervision of the school" (Smith, Krouse, and Atkinson, 1961, p. 969). The curriculum includes the subjects to be taught and the methods and materials used to teach them. The educator must consider the needs that the visually impaired share with other children as well as the needs unique to the visually impaired.

What special skills should be taught to children with visual impairments?

Children with visual problems are usually taught the same sequence of subjects as children with normal vision because they need to master the same basic skills. Unlike children with normal vision, however, they will need to be taught additional special skills, such as how to orient themselves, how to attain mobility, and how to take care of themselves. Visually impaired children will also need to be taught certain skills to learn academic subjects —

how to read braille, how to use an Optacon (described later in this section), and how to use recording equipment, for example. Although the responsibility for implementing the total curriculum plan lies with the regular classroom teacher, the assistance of a specially trained teacher of the visually impaired will be necessary to teach children the special skills just mentioned.

Many educators believe that the methods of teaching the visually impaired should not differ from the methods of teaching those with normal vision. Others contend that the instruction of the visually impaired requires significantly different strategies (Hatlen, 1980). Both positions have some validity. When adjustments or adaptations are made, they involve changing the media and the manner in which material is presented.

The media through which visually impaired children obtain information are tactile, visual, and auditory. The selection of the appropriate medium for a particular child was mentioned earlier in this chapter. You will remember that a measurement of visual acuity alone does not provide enough information to decide which medium is best for a child. some children with extremely low visual acuity can use visual materials quite efficiently, whereas others will need tactile materials, and still others may be able to use both. Decisions about the best medium for a child should be made only after thorough assessment by specially trained professionals. This assessment can be accomplished with the use of a number of procedures described by Swallow (1981), Genshaft, Dare, and O'Malley (1980), Rabin (1982), and many others; the careful observations of teachers are also helpful. Once the primary medium for learning has been selected, teachers should keep in mind that some children can use both tactile and visual materials and that all children can and should use auditory materials. In other words, a "total communication" approach for visually impaired children should be employed.

SPECIAL SKILLS

Children with visual impairments need to learn certain special skills not included in the curriculum of children with normal vision. Broadly defined, the two most important such areas are orientation and mobility, and daily living skills.

Why are orientation and mobility training important?

Orientation and Mobility. The ability of children to move about in their environment and interact with it has important educational and social effects (Lowenfeld, 1971). Educationally, it allows them to develop realistic concepts about their environment and thus enables them to participate more fully in learning experiences with seeing children. Socially, it helps to dispel the notion that visually impaired persons are helpless and dependent and fosters the notion that they can become fully participating and contributing members of society. Thus, it is very important that schools provide orientation and mobility training for all children who need it (Welsh and Blasch, 1980). It is also important that properly trained orientation and mobility specialists provide this training.

Orientation training involves teaching visually impaired children to understand their environment and to recognize their surroundings and their relationship to them. Mobility training involves teaching the child to move efficiently from place to place in the environment (Welsh and Blasch, 1980). These types of training are generally taught by specially trained instructors, although some preliminary skills can be taught by the regular classroom teacher of the visually impaired. Orientation and mobility training should not be considered only for the child who is totally blind; many children with partial vision can also benefit from it. The training should begin as early as possible to avoid the formation of unrealistic concepts and attitudes.

How can technology help with mobility?

A number of new and exciting devices to aid in mobility training have recently been developed. Galton (1978) describes the laser cane, developed by Bionic Instruments of Lynwood, California. This cane uses beams of light to probe the environment, sending auditory and tactile signals to warn of obstacles, stairs, curbs, and so on. Wormald International Sensory Aids produces two electronic mobility devices for the visually impaired, the Mowat Sensor and the Sonic Guide (Figure 6-6). The Mowat Sensor is a hand-held electronic probe that uses vibration signals to indicate the distance to objects that fall within its narrow beam (Wormald International Sensory Aids, 1979). The Sonic Guide is an electronic aid in the form of spectacles, which emit sounds to convey spatial information (Wormald International Sensory Aids, 1979). Other electronic mobility aids continue to be developed. They hold great promise for the visually impaired.

How do children with visual impairment learn daily living skills?

Daily Living Skills. Daily living skills include such things as eating, bathing, toileting, dressing, grooming, and household chores. Most of these skills are acquired by seeing children through visual observation alone and are not directly taught in school programs. However, it is usually necessary to teach the skills directly to visually impaired children. Ideally, most of these skills should be acquired at home before the child enters school, but this doesn't often occur; thus, the responsibility for teaching the skills is left with the school. In most cases, the special teacher of the visually impaired provides the training, although regular classroom teachers can also do so with assistance from special teachers. To provide training in a particular daily living task, the task is analyzed and programmed lessons are developed leading the child through the task in steps, with the emphasis on the use of senses other than vision. Welsh and Blasch (1980) provide some guidelines for developing these skills for preschool children, and O'Brien (1976) includes a number of developmental scales in her study of preschool children. The latter are excellent references for planning lessons in daily living skills.

Figure 6-6
Electronic Mobility Devices. Left: Sonic Guide. Right: Mowat Sensor.

ACADEMIC SKILL DEVELOPMENT

In addition to the skills just described, visually impaired children need to learn how to use the techniques that have been designed to compensate for their loss of vision. These techniques involve the use of tactile, visual, or auditory media. Children with visual problems acquire information through reading and listening. The two media used for reading are braille and print.

What is braille?   *Braille.* The primary tactile medium used by visually impaired persons is the braille code, developed by Louis Braille in 1829 when he was a student at the Paris School for the Blind. The code is based on a braille "cell," which consists of six raised dots:

$$1 \bullet \bullet 4$$
$$2 \bullet \bullet 5$$
$$3 \bullet \bullet 6$$

Sixty-three combinations of these six dots are possible. With these 63 combinations, three braille codes have been developed — one for presenting literary material, one for mathematics and science, and one for music. Since the braille cell occupies a great deal of space (each cell takes up a quarter inch), the original code has been altered to make it more compact. For example, many of the single braille units that represent alphabet letters (see Figure 6-7) also represent whole words. Many words are also represented by abbreviations, shortened forms of words, and nonalphabetic symbols. The total number of meanings assigned to the 63 configurations is 263. All of the duplicate meanings of a single configuration were assigned to conserve space (American Printing House for the Blind, 1981).

The changes in the braille code designed to save space have created problems for children who must use the code to learn how to read. Most of the material used to teach reading to the visually impaired is transcribed directly from material designed to teach print reading. The problems unique to the braille code are not taken into consideration. For example, words sequenced in order of their difficulty for a child who can see may be sequenced inappropriately when transcribed into braille (Caton, 1979; Caton and Bradley, 1978-1979). To overcome these problems, the American Printing House for the Blind has now produced a complete basal reading program based on the unique characteristics of the braille code and the unique characteristics of visually impaired children (Caton, Pester, and Bradley, 1980-1983).

This program is entitled *Patterns: the Primary Braille Reading Program*. It consists of six levels: readiness, preprimer, primer, book one, book two, and book three. Each level has complete teacher's editions, which provide very detailed directions for teaching reading to children who use braille as their reading medium. Also included in each level are student texts, drill worksheets, review worksheets, and posttests. Children in either day school programs or residential school programs can use *Patterns* effectively. This program can be used as the only basic reading program for braille readers or in conjunction with print reading programs that have been transcribed into braille.

Figure 6-7
The Braille Alphabet

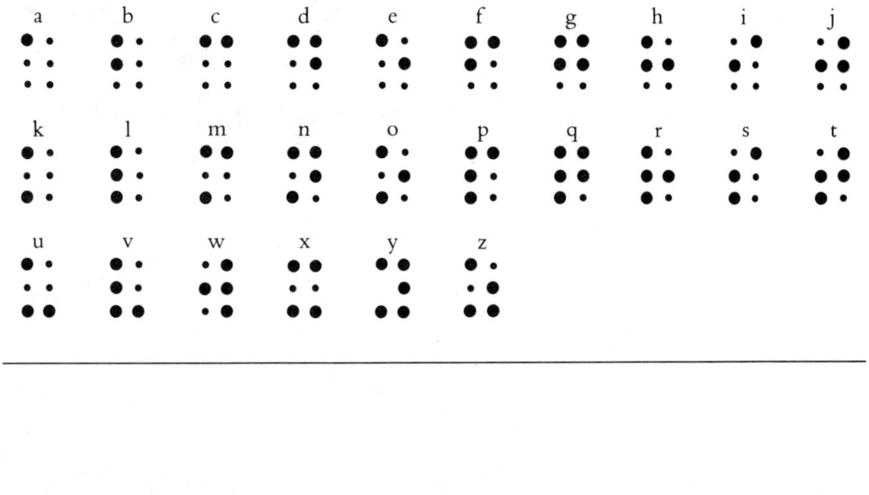

Because of the problems just discussed, it is absolutely essential that those who teach reading to children who use braille be well trained. When the basic skills of reading and the braille code have been mastered, most braille readers can participate successfully in reading classes with children who read print.

The "paperless" brailler is another innovative approach to the problems of braille readers (see Figure 6-8). The information for a paperless brailler is stored on small cassettes and can be projected onto displays. The different kinds print between 12 and 20 braille lines; some also have audio components, and one kind can index and place-find. Although these machines save the cost of books by storing large amounts of information on a small cassette, they are themselves expensive. There are other disadvantages, too. They are limited in what they can display, and they project short lines, which may affect the reading process. Nevertheless, their use in education has exciting possibilities.

Another braille machine that seems to be very effective is the Modified Perkins Brailler. It is not a paperless braille machine, however. It produces paper braille and can be used with several kinds of microcomputers. Most

What is the advantage of "paperless braille"?

Figure 6-8
The Telesensory "Paperless" Brailler

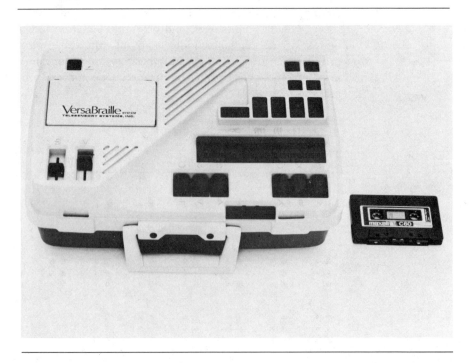

educators feel that the potential for using this machine in teaching children is very good.

Writing in braille is accomplished with a braille writer, illustrated in Figure 6-9, or a slate and stylus, illustrated in Figure 6-10.

The braille writer is a hand-operated machine with six keys, one to correspond to each dot in the braille cell. When a key is pressed, a dot is embossed on paper inserted in the back of the machine. The other parts of the machine are labeled in Figure 6-9.

Figure 6-9
The Perkins Brailler

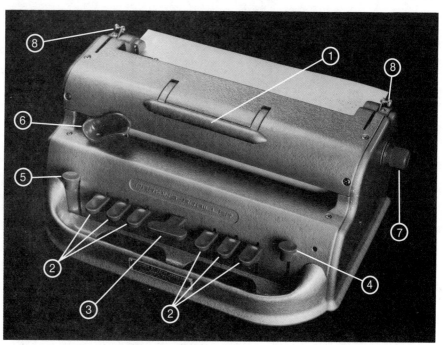

1. Handle
2. Keys
3. Spacing key
4. Back-spacing key
5. Line-spacing key
6. Embossing head lever
7. Paper feed knob
8. Paper release levers

Figure 6-10
Slate and Stylus

How does one operate a Slate and Stylus?

There are many different braille slates. The chief variation among the various types is in their size. All slates consist of a metal or plastic frame, which is sometimes mounted on a board. A pointed steel stylus is used to hand-punch braille dots. Each slate has two parts connected by a hinge on the left side. The bottom part has several rows of braille cells indented on its top. The top part has holes that correspond to the indentations. The paper is placed between the two parts, and the stylus is used to punch in the dots from the tops.

The braille writer and slate have been in use for many years. It has been only in recent years that microcomputers have been used extensively for braille writing. The access equipment necessary to accomplish this is described in the section on microcomputers in this chapter. With this equipment and one of several software programs now available, it is possible for persons who do not know braille to enter print into a microcomputer and produce braille. The development of programs of this type should have a significant effect on the writing and production of braille.

Print Reading. Children with partial vision can read print if it is presented to them appropriately. Such conditions as proper lighting, reduction of glare, print size, spacing, and the use of low-vision aids must be considered to ensure that the child is reading as efficiently as possible.

Is there an optimal size of type for partially seeing children?

The best print size for a particular child will probably fall between 12 and 24 points (⅙ to ⅓ inch from top of capital letters to bottom of descenders), although there is some evidence that normal-sized type is just as efficient if read with the proper optical aid (Peabody and Birch, 1967; Sykes, 1971). Similarly, the most effective print size will vary with the particular child. Studies have indicated that 18-point (¼-inch) type may be the most efficient size for most visually impaired children (Eakin, Pratt, and McFarland, 1961). Most of the larger-type books published by the American Printing House for the Blind are printed in this size. Examples of 12-, 18-, and 24-point type are illustrated in Figure 6-11.

Figure 6-11
Samples of Three Type Sizes

12 Point When darkness fell, the women began preparing a great heap of wood for the circle of ceremonial fires. Then Chanuka slipped into the river and swam silently

18 Point When darkness fell, the women preparing a great heap of wood circle of ceremonial fires. Then Ch slipped into the river and swam s

24 Point When darkness fell, th preparing a great heap circle of ceremonial fires slipped into the river an

What are optical aids?

When an optical aid is called for, the user may choose from among several types. These are (1) magnifiers attached to eyeglass frames or as part of the eyeglass lenses themselves; (2) stand magnifiers, which are mounted on a base to maintain a particular viewing distance; (3) hand-held magnifiers; (4) telescopic aids, which are used like binoculars; and (5) television viewers, which magnify print and project it onto a television screen. The type of aid selected will depend on the user's preference and the task for which the device is to be used. The strength of magnification is best determined by a professional in a low-vision clinic or by a suitably trained teacher (Harley and Lawrence, 1977; Kirk, 1981).

The child's reading environment is just as important to reading efficiency as print size and the use of optical aids. The chief environmental considerations are the brightness of the lighting and the contrast between the writing itself and its background (Harley and Lawrence, 1977; Kirk, 1981).

The amount of illumination required for comfortable reading will vary considerably from child to child. However, the best quality lighting is generally from fluorescent bulbs evenly distributed throughout the room. Children with optic atrophy will require intense illumination, whereas those with vision problems resulting from albinism will require less than normal illumination. In all cases, care must be taken to avoid glare.

How can teachers help partially seeing children with reading materials?

Children with partial vision are able to read most efficiently when the print they are reading contrasts sharply with the material on which the letters are printed. Most children read dark print on buff-colored paper best, but some prefer dark print on white paper. Buff-colored paper is used because it reduces glare. Contrast is also important when chalkboards are being used. White chalk on a black chalkboard provides the best contrast, but white chalk on a green board is acceptable for some children. In general, contrast is best when the background is clear and uncluttered and when the shade of the material to be viewed is sufficiently different to stand out clearly.

Most visually impaired children who read print do so at a much slower rate than children who see normally. Those who read large print typically read at less than half the rate of children with good vision. Those who use optical aids also read relatively slowly.

Several factors retard the rate of reading. Some eye disorders permit the reader to see only one or two letters at a time. The reading of large type is slower because it takes longer to pass the eye over larger letters and words. The use of an optical aid reduces the field of vision and requires that the aid be moved or adjusted frequently.

Once the many factors that influence how the visually impaired read have been considered, the child can be taught to read using normal instructional methods. Visually impaired children can usually be taught in the regular classroom if the teacher is assisted by a special teacher in setting up an appropriate environment.

**What is an
Optacon?**

Reading Machines. There are two new technological alternatives to the reading methods and techniques just discussed. They are called direct print reading systems and involve the use of machines — the Optacon, illustrated in Figure 6-12, and the Kurzweil Reading Machine, described at the beginning of this chapter.

The Optacon (Optical-to-Tactile Converter) "reads" print and reproduces the form of the print letters with a series of small wires. Detailed descriptions of the construction and operation of the Optacon are available from its developer, Telesensory Corporation, 455 N. Bernardo Ave., Mountain View, CA 94043. To use the Optacon, the reader fits one hand into an opening in the machine and touches the panel where the letters are formed by small wires. With the other hand the reader scans a page of print with a small camera. The print is converted into letter shapes made up of the small wires. To use the Optacon efficiently, the reader must have extensive training in its use. Specif-

**Figure 6-12
Reading with an Optacon**

ically, he or she must be trained to perceive tactually the shapes of print letters. In addition, he or she must be trained to read words and sentences made up of combinations of these letters. Many educators feel that not enough attention has been given to the teaching of reading with the Optacon. They feel that the major emphasis has been on the more technical aspects of operation and letter recognition. However, the Optacon has been especially useful to visually impaired persons who must read print for their jobs. It has also been used extensively with school children, but its educational effect has not yet been evaluated thoroughly.

The Kurzweil Reading Machine, introduced in 1975, converts printed words into synthetic speech. It provides access to a great deal of printed matter that was previously unavailable to the visually impaired.

Listening. There are, of course, means of acquiring information that do not involve reading. Listening is one of the most effective. Accordingly, listening skills have been increasingly emphasized in recent years. A number of guides to developing listening skills have been produced. One of the most valuable is available through the Illinois Instructional Materials Center, where it was developed (Alber, 1978). Listening is not a solution to all academic problems, but it is effective in such areas as literature and social studies. It is crucial in the education of children who can read neither print nor braille.

SPECIAL EDUCATIONAL AIDS

A number of instructional materials have been designed to meet the needs of the visually impaired. These include diagrams, charts, and maps available with large print or in tactile form; sets of materials to replace pictures or visual displays in textbooks; mathematics aids such as specially adapted abacuses and tactile graph boards; braille writers; special bold-line paper for writing both braille and print; and many others.

Most of these aids are available from the American Printing House for the Blind in Louisville, Kentucky. Federal funds for purchasing materials produced by the American Printing House for the Blind are available to children who meet the legal definition of blindness given at the beginning of this

How does the American Printing House for the Blind serve the visually impaired community?

chapter. These children must be registered at the American Printing House for the Blind by the first Monday in January of each year. Specific information about registration and ordering procedures can be obtained from special education departments, state departments of education, state residential schools for the blind, or the American Printing House for the Blind.

Organizations other than the American Printing House for the Blind have developed materials to be used in teaching specific subjects to the visually impaired. The MAVIS program (Social Science Education Consortium, 1978) is used to teach social sciences, for example, and the SAVI program (Lawrence

Hall of Science, 1978; Social Science Consortium, 1978) describes activities to be used in teaching science. In both cases the materials are adaptations of curricula originally designed for children with normal vision.

The work of Dr. Natalie Barraga (1964) has had a strong effect on the materials and planning procedures used to educate the visually impaired. Dr. Barraga's work has demonstrated that visually impaired children can be trained to use their residual vision to a much greater extent than was formerly thought possible, even if the impairment is very severe. A set of materials based on Dr. Barraga's work is available through the American Printing House for the Blind. These materials have recently been revised and are now entitled *Program to Develop Efficiency in Visual Functioning*. They include a diagnostic assessment procedure, a set of lessons, and a vision sourcebook (Barraga, 1980).

Another set of materials that appears to have potential to affect significantly the education of visually impaired children is *Patterns: The Primary Braille Reading Program* (Caton, Pester, Bradley, 1980-1983), described previously in this chapter. Initial inspection of data collected on children using the program indicates that these children have made signficant progress in learning to read and that the majority are reading at grade level or above. A survey of the reading level of braille readers (Caton and Rankin, 1978), which was conducted prior to the development of the *Patterns* program, indicated that most braille readers were reading below the expected grade level based on their age and number of years in school. At the present time, all available information indicates that the program, which is based on the braille code, has enabled braille readers to learn to read at a rate comparable to children who read print.

The use of special methods and materials alone will not adequately compensate for a child's loss of vision. Regardless of the subject being taught, the child must, whenever possible, be given the opportunity to learn through direct experience with the environment. These experiences should be accompanied by thorough verbal explanations by the teacher. In addition, visually impaired children should be encouraged to interact with seeing members of their environment. A child who is given these opportunities and who makes appropriate use of the methods and materials discussed previously can be regarded as having a completely developed curriculum.

MICROCOMPUTERS

How can microcomputers be used in the education of children with visual impairments?

The use of microcomputers in all areas of education has increased dramatically in recent years, and most school-age children now receive some form of computer instruction. Special educators have begun to provide this instruction to exceptional children, including the visually impaired. The process for these children has been slower than for others, however. In 1980, only 3 percent of the visually impaired were learning about computers; a year later, the figure was 23 percent (Young and Ashcroft, 1981). The trend toward providing training in microcomputers to the visually impaired will probably continue as microcomputers are made more accessible to this group.

Because of their visual losses, most visually impaired students need additional equipment to translate computer information into a form they can read. Ruconich, Ashcroft, and Young (1983) provide an excellent description of the types of equipment now being used for this purpose and discuss the advantages and disadvantages of each type:

1. Electronic braille — These include "paperless" braille machines such as the Versabraille machine pictured in Figure 6-8 and "paper" braille, which can now be provided by the Modified Perkins Brailler. The major advantage of electronic braille devices is that they can both send and receive information. Disadvantages are that the machine can display only one short line at a time and that some print extremely slowly.
2. The Optacon — Described earlier and shown in Figure 6-12, The Optacon allows visually impaired students to read print by using a small camera. The device can be used to read a variety of printed material, but for most students the reading is very slow.
3. Synthesized speech — Speech synthesizers enable the computer to talk and give visually impaired persons the information from the computer orally. Synthesized speech is quick, but most of the equipment has limited review capabilities.
4. Enlarged print — Microcomputer displays of large print can be used by a majority of the visually impaired. A disadvantage is that computers usually have only one size, which may not be appropriate for all persons; in addition, the Optacon cannot read all sizes.

A major disadvantage of all these types of equipment is their cost. Although the prices of some have been reduced, they are all expensive (Ruconich, Ashcroft, and Young, 1983). Nevertheless, they can be extremely valuable to visually impaired students, and the future of microcomputer use with this population looks bright.

A number of exciting research projects are underway and the results look promising. As Ruconich, Ashcroft, and Young (1983) have stated, the major concern is the development and use of equipment that can provide visually impaired students access to computers. The equipment exists now. Some of it needs to be refined, and some is still too expensive for most users. However, visually impaired students do appear to be well on the way to becoming successful users of microcomputers.

The majority of information in this section was taken from articles by Ruconich (1984), and Ashcroft (1984). Others have written on the subject. Interested readers should consult articles by Fullwood (1977), Ryan and Bedi (1978), Pera and Cobb (1978), Schofield (1981), Ashcroft and Bourgeois (1980), Brunken (1984), and Sanford (1984).

PROBE 6-6
Instructional Methods and Materials

1. T F Visually handicapped children are usually taught the same sequence of subjects as children with normal vision.

2. T F Many instructional procedures that are effective for children with normal eyesight are also effective for visually impaired children.

3. List some optical aids that can be used by partially seeing children to assist them in reading.

4. The most important areas included in the curriculum of the visually impaired but not in the curriculum of those with normal vision are _____ and _____ .

5. The media through which visually impaired children obtain information are _____ , _____ , and _____ .

6. Technological advances have resulted in the development of a number of exciting new devices for the visually impaired. List three devices related to reading that blind people can use.

7. The major concern in teaching visually disabled students to use microcomputers is _____ .

8. Name the four types of access equipment needed by visually impaired students when using microcomputers.

9. T F Visually impaired students need only one type of access equipment to use microcomputers.

EDUCATIONAL PROGRAMMING

You should be able to describe the implications of PL 94-142 for educating visually impaired children in the least restrictive environment.

To understand current practices in educating visually impaired children, it is necessary to understand their history and development.

The first formal educational program for visually impaired children was a residential school, primarily for totally blind children, established by Valentin Hauy in Paris in 1784. Hauy was extremely influential in the development of educational programs for the visually impaired in Europe. Residential schools for the blind were eventually begun in several European cities.

The first educational programs for the visually impaired in the United States were also residential schools. These schools were designed for totally blind children, but children with partial vision were eventually enrolled in them as well. The earliest schools, which both opened in 1832, were the Perkins School for the Blind in Boston, and the New York Institute for the Blind in New York City. In 1833 the Pennsylvania Institution for the Instruction of the Blind was opened in Philadelphia. This later became the Overbrook School for the Blind. Other residential schools were gradually established in other states.

The first local day school classes for blind children were set up in Chicago in 1900, followed by a day school program for those with partial vision in Roxbury, Massachusetts, in 1913. As you can see, the practice of separating blind and partially seeing children in local day school classes was established early. It has continued in some areas until the present. The current trend, however, is to combine programs for the blind and partially seeing children with those for normally sighted children. Today there are a variety of types of programs in the U.S. for visually impaired children, including the residential school and five types of administrative plans in local day schools.

RESIDENTIAL SCHOOLS

How has the role of residential schools changed in recent years?

The residential school has traditionally provided a total educational program for visually impaired children. This program usually has a complete range of grades from kindergarten through twelve, and teaches the same curriculum taught in other schools in the state or region. Most residential school students do not attend classes integrated with children with normal vision, although some residential schools have an agreement with the local school system that allows some visually impaired students to attend regular classes.

The role of the residential school has changed during the past decade. Some residential schools now function as educational resource centers for the visually impaired. They may provide activities that involve the visually impaired with sighted children outside the school and services to local school programs that serve visually impaired children. These services can involve storing materials and resources and developing special summer programs to train children in orientation and mobility, daily living skills, and other special skills.

Other residential schools serve as centers for visually impaired children with additional handicaps. These schools offer extensive support services, such as physical therapy, occupational therapy, and speech therapy for severely handicapped children, as well as regular education programs. This use of residential programs for the multiply handicapped reflects the current trend of placing children in local day schools whenever possible and reserving space in residential programs for those who cannot function successfully in other environments. The effectiveness of such residential programs cannot be assessed until they have been in operation for a longer period of time.

LOCAL DAY SCHOOLS

What educational alternatives are available in day schools?

Local day schools for the visually impaired are currently run according to one of the five basic administrative plans. These are as follows:

1. The special class plan. Students are enrolled in a special class for the visually impaired and receive most of their instruction in that class. They may participate in some nonacademic activities with sighted children, but they usually do not receive academic instruction outside the special class.
2. The cooperative class plan. Students are enrolled in a special class for the visually impaired in a public school. They do some of their academic work in this room and some in the regular classroom. They also participate in nonacademic activities in the regular classroom.
3. The resource room plan. Students are enrolled in the regular classroom and come to a special classroom for the visually impaired for special help in difficult academic areas. They spend as much time as possible in the regular classroom and leave only when help is necessary.
4. The itinerant teacher plan. Students are enrolled in the regular classroom, and a specially trained teacher of the visually impaired, who most often serves several schools, provides them with special instruction and materials.
5. The teacher-consultant plan. Students are enrolled in regular classrooms and receive basically the same services as those offered under the itinerant teacher plan. The major difference between the teacher-consultant plan and the itinerant teacher plan is that the teacher-consultant spends a greater part of his or her time working with the regular classroom teacher or other school personnel to assist them in providing appropriate services (Hatlen, 1980).

All of these plans require a specially trained teacher of the visually impaired as well as special equipment and materials for both blind and partially seeing children. The major differences among them involve their administrative organization and the instructional duties of the teachers. In the special class plan, for example, the child is enrolled in a special classroom, and the teacher of the visually impaired is responsible for most of the academic instruction and grading. In the resource room, itinerant teacher, and teacher-consultant plans, on the other hand, the child is enrolled in the regular classroom, and the regular teacher is responsible for most of the instruction and for grading. Under these plans the teacher of the visually impaired assists the regular teacher in obtaining materials and provides instruction in subjects in which the child is having difficulty.

The resource room, itinerant teacher, and teacher-consultant plans are preferred today because they permit greater integration of visually impaired children into regular classrooms. In actual practice, many school districts use combinations and adaptations of the plans to suit their needs. This is desirable, of course, since the goal of all educational programming is to provide each child with a program that will meet his or her individual needs. It is very important that program planning remain flexible. The selection of the least restrictive alternative should not be based on existing administrative plans. It must be based on the needs of the individual child.

SELECTING THE LEAST RESTRICTIVE ENVIRONMENT

What factors should be considered in selecting an educational program?

PL 94-142 requires that the least restrictive environment for a particular child be selected by a committee that includes the child's parents. The committee must be furnished with a variety of evaluation data, including (1) an eye examination report, (2) a medical report, (3) a developmental and social history, (4) reports of behavioral observations by parents and teachers, and (5) any other information that might be helpful. The committee reviews the data and then decides the type of educational environment best suited to the child's needs.

The decision to place a child in a particular program should be based on the child's level of independence and the kind of services the program makes available. Generally speaking, the more independent the child, the less structured the program needs to be. A high school student who can travel independently and succeed academically with only occasional help from the special teacher may do best in an itinerant teacher program or with the help of a teacher-consultant. Young children who are acquiring basic skills will probably require daily contact with a teacher of the visually impaired and may be best educated under the resource room plan. Children who have severe impairments or handicaps in addition to blindness will probably function best under the special or cooperative class plans. For some students, residential school placement may be most appropriate.

Because children's needs change as they develop, it is important to remain flexible in determining what program best fulfills a child's needs. A program well suited to a six-year-old child may be inappropriate for the child at age eight. As Taylor (1947, pp. 118-120) states, "The facility should be selected which fulfills a particular need, at the time of the need, and for only as long as — in light of the total situation — it is fulfilling this need." Children should be educated as much as possible in the classes they would be attending if they were not visually impaired, and they should spend as much time as possible in classes with children who have normal vision.

There are several other important factors to be considered in choosing the program best suited to an individual child's needs. The most important is that the child's parents should be made familiar with all the data on their child and should play an important role in selecting the child's program. Even though the final decision on a child's placement rests with the Admissions and Release Committee of the local school system, parental consent for such placement is required by law. Parents must also consent to the collection of evalution data (Abeson, Bolick, and Haff, 1976).

It is also very important that placement recommendations be based on all the available information on a child. All too frequently a measurement of the child's visual acuity is used as the primary criterion for placement. Although visual acuity is important, it should be considered in conjunction with other information about the child's level of functioning.

Finally, the availability of appropriate programs should be considered. Unfortunately, there is sometimes a shortage of programs for the visually impaired, particularly in sparsely populated areas. Federal legislation states, however, that the fact that no program exists in a particular community does not relieve the school district of the responsibility to provide such a program. This means that the recommendations of the placement committee should be based solely on the needs of the child, and not on the availability of a particular program. In some communities, however, it may be impossible to provide the full range of programs that are available in major population centers.

PLANNING FOR DIRECT INSTRUCTION

In addition to selecting the best program for a child, the Admissions and Release Committee is responsible for developing an Individual Educational Program (IEP) for each child who is referred to it. The IEP is used as the basis for planning direct instruction. To plan effectively, the teacher must be familiar with the characteristics of visually impaired children and know what types of assessment tools are available and how to interpret their results.

Characteristics Relevant to Educational Planning. Persons involved in assessment should pay particular attention to the effect of visual loss on the formation of concepts. A visually impaired child whose ability to interact with the environment is restricted will not perform well on tests that assess concepts usually formed visually. The child's formation of visual concepts is also affected by the age at which the loss of vision occurred, whether the loss occurred gradually or suddenly, and, of course, the severity of the loss. The severity of loss will influence what reading medium the child uses, how efficiently the remaining vision is used, and whether optical aids are needed (Scholl and Schnur, 1976).

What assessment information is needed for program planning?

Assessment Data Needed. Visually impaired children vary as much as other children. Thus, the data used to plan their education should be derived from a variety of formal and informal assessment techniques. DeMott (1974) suggests that information in the following areas be included in any educational assessment of the visually impaired.

1. Visual efficiency — the use the child makes of any remaining vision.
2. Sensory abilities — the ability to use hearing, touch, taste, and smell to acquire information.

3. Other impairments — the identification of impairments in abilities other than vision that might affect the child's ability to learn.
4. Motor performance — the ability to move about to gain information.
5. Language — the ability to use speech and listening skills to learn.
6. Intelligence — the intellectual ability to learn.
7. Achievement — academic progress and ability.

Bauman (1974) suggests that the child's personality, social competency, vocational interests and aptitudes, and readiness to learn be assessed as well. Areas of assessment have also been discussed by Swallow (1981).

Assessment Instruments. There are three basic types of assessment instruments available for visually impaired children:

1. Those developed specifically for the visually impaired.
2. Those developed for a seeing population but adapted for use by the visually impaired.
3. Those developed for a seeing population and used in their original form by the visually impaired.

Assessment instruments are described by a number of authors, including Bauman (1974); Chase (1951); Scholl and Schnur (1976); Spungin and Swallow (1977); Swallow, Mangold, and Mangold (1978); and Swallow (1981). The American Foundation for the Blind and the American Printing House for the Blind can also provide valuable assistance in selecting assessment instruments.

Interpretation of Assessment Data. Although the interpretation of assessment data is too complicated a topic to cover adequately in this chapter, the student should be familiar with two general guidelines.

1. Assessment data should be interpreted only by specially trained persons who are familiar with the characteristics of the visually impaired.
2. Information about norms (i.e., standard scores based on the population used to establish standards for a test) should be used with caution. If the norm data were based on a sample of visually impaired children, it is important to know whether the children were enrolled in public schools or in residential school programs. Most of the children in residential schools today have multiple handicaps, and norms based on such children may not be valid for children with visual impairment alone. Norm data based on a sample of children with normal vision will not be valid for the visually impaired unless the data have been modified for an adapted form of the test.

When should teachers be cautious about interpreting test results?

The most important considerations in providing the best education for a particular child can be summarized as follows: The least restrictive environment consists of the program in which the child can learn best. Generally, this should be the one the child would normally be placed in if he or she were not visually impaired. As much as possible, visually impaired children should be educated with children who have normal vision. However, they may need to spend part of their day with the vision teacher. Ideally, there should be a continuum of services so that a child can be moved from one program to another as needs change. The educator should never regard a child's placement as final; he or she should, rather, be willing to move the child to a different program if the child's needs change.

PROBE 6-7
Educational Programming

1. The first schools established for the visually impaired in Europe and the United States were _____ schools.

2. T F The residential school traditionally follows the same curriculum as other schools in the same state or region.

3. How has the role of residential schools changed in recent years?

4. List the five types of local day school programs provided for visually impaired children.

5. T F Under PL 94-142, the school principal makes the decision about the type of program that a visually impaired child should be placed in.

6. List three types of information that are used to make placement decisions for visually impaired children.

7. T F Under PL 94-142, parents must consent to the collection of evaluation data and to the placement of their visually impaired child in a particular program.

8. Persons involved in assessing visually impaired children should pay particular attention to the effects of the loss of vision on _____ development.

9. DeMott suggests that information about a number of areas be included in the educational assessment of the visually impaired. List four of these areas.

10. What three types of testing instruments are used to assess visually impaired children?

11. T F Normative data provided for standardized tests are appropriate for use with visually impaired children.

SUMMARY

1. Normal, or unimpaired, vision has four basic components: (a) the object to be viewed, (b) light that reflects from the object, (c) an intact visual organ (the eye), and (d) the occipital lobes of the brain, where visual stimuli are interpreted and "seeing" takes place.

2. The leading causes of visual impairment among those who are not legally blind are cataracts, refractive problems, and glaucoma. Among totally blind persons, the leading causes of blindness are retinal disorders, glaucoma, and cataract.

3. Definitions of visual impairment based on visual acuity are used primarily for legal and economic purposes, and for the allocation of federal funds for the purchase of educational materials.

4. Educational definitions of visual impairment are based on the media through which the child learns rather than on visual acuity.

5. The incidence of visually impaired children in the school-age population is generally considered to be one in every 1,000.

6. Most visually impaired children are not totally blind. Approximately two-thirds of all visually impaired children have some remaining vision.

7. The physical characteristics of visually impaired children other than vision are the same as those of children who are not visually impaired.

8. The intellectual development of children is not directly affected by visual impairment or blindness.

9. Because the loss of vision leads to restrictions in the child's range and variety of experience, ability to get about, and interaction with the environment, the visually impaired child has problems in concept development.

10. Visually impaired children tend to lag behind their seeing peers in school achievement.

11. The most widely accepted view is that the social/emotional problems of visually impaired children are the result of the attitudes and reactions of persons with normal vision and not the result of the loss of vision itself.

12. The curriculum for programs for the visually impaired is usually the same as that for the other school programs in a particular state or region.

13. In considering basic instructional methods for visually impaired children, it is important to remember that many of the techniques and strategies that are effective with seeing children are also appropriate for the visually impaired.

14. Visually impaired children do have some unique instructional needs and will require help from special trained teachers of the visually impaired in some academic areas.

15. In the United States, visually impaired children are educated in residential schools and a number of different types of programs in local day schools.

16. Those involved in educational planning should remain flexible in their approach to placement.

17. It is important to remember that the most appropriate, least restrictive environment for visually impaired children is the one in which they learn best. They should be educated to the greatest extent possible with children who are not visually impaired.

TASK SHEET 6
Field Experience Related to the Visually Impaired

Select *one* of the following and perform the assigned tasks.

Program Visitation

Visit a residential school, a local day school (self-contained) program, or a resource program for the visually impaired. In a paper of no more than three pages, describe the program you visited, the curriculum that was being used, the interactions you had with the staff and students, and your general reactions and impressions of the program. How did it differ from programs for normally seeing children?

Professional Interview

Arrange to visit one of the following professionals, and discuss his or her job: ophthalmologist, optometrist, optician, orthoptist, teacher of the visually impaired, rehabilitation counselor for the visually impaired, or director of a facility for the visually impaired. In a paper of no more than three pages, answer the following questions:

1. Where did you visit?
2. What were the responsibilities of the person you interviewed?
3. What type of training was necessary to enter this profession?
4. What types of problems does the person encounter?
5. What did you learn from this experience, and what was your reaction to it?

Interview with a Visually Disabled Person

Interview a visually impaired person or the parents of a visually impaired person and determine the types of problems the person encounters, as well as his or her attitude toward the disability and toward people with normal vision. Describe your findings and the feelings you had during the interview.

Agency Investigation

Write to three of the following agencies, requesting information about the services they provide to people with visual impairments. Write a three-page paper synthesizing your findings and indicate how you might use these services if you were a professional person working in this area.

American Foundation for the Blind
15 West 16th Street
New York, NY 10011

American Printing House for the Blind
1839 Frankfort Avenue
Louisville, KY 40206

American Optometric Association
7000 Chippewa Street
St. Louis, MO 20852

AAWB/AEVH Alliance
206 N. Washington Street
Suite 320
Alexandria, VA 22314

Department of Education
Division for Blind and Visually
Handicapped
330 C. Street, SW
Washington, DC 20202

Helen Keller International
15 West 16th Street
New York, NY 10011

Howe Press of Perkins Schools for the
Blind
175 North Beacon Street
Watertown, MA 02172

National Association of Parents of the
Visually Impaired
P.O. Box 180806
Austin, TX 78718

National Braille Association
422 Clinton Avenue So.
Rochester, NY 14620

National Institute of Neurological
Diseases and Blindness
National Institutes of Health
Bethesda, MD 20014

National Society for the Prevention
of Blindness
79 Madison Avenue
New York, NY 10016

Recording for the Blind, Inc.
20 Roszel Road
Princeton, NJ 08540

Science for the Blind
221 Rock Hill Road
Bala-Cynwyd, PA 19004

Library Study

Read three articles related to some aspect of visual impairment. Write a one-page abstract of each article, concluding with your personal observations about the article and its value. You can find articles in the following professional journals:

Education of the Visually Handicapped
Heldref Publications
4000 Albermarle St., N.W.
Washington, DC 20016

*Journal of Visual Impairment
and Blindness*
American Foundation for the Blind
15 West 16th Street
New York, NY 10011

Journal of Special Education
Grune and Stratton
111 Fifth Ave.
New York, NY 10003

The New Beacon
Royal National Institute for the Blind
224 Great Portland Street
London WIN 6AA
ENGLAND

. . . Five years after an accident left her paralyzed, paraplegic Nan Davis rose from her wheelchair and walked 10 feet to receive her college diploma — with a book-size computer telling her numbed legs what to do.

"This is a special day for all of us," she said . . . when she reached the podium at the University of Dayton Arena to receive her bachelor's degree in elementary education from Wright State University.

. . . "The last time she walked in public . . . was in high school, and she wanted to walk in her college graduation," said Dr. Jerrold Petrofsky. He is executive director of Wright State's National Center for Rehabilitation Engineering and developer of the computer system that helped Miss Davis to walk.

Miss Davis, 23, rose from her wheelchair and was accompanied by Petrofsky and colleague Dr. Chandler Phillips. They held her arms as her legs moved to the commands of the computer carried by Petrofsky. . . .

Her first computer-aided walk required a huge stationary computer that selectively activated small electrodes on her skin to make selected leg muscles contract.

The computer she used at Saturday's commencement was about 4 inches by 6 inches and less than an inch thick.

Petrofsky's subjects, including Miss Davis, first undergo 6 to 12 months of physical therapy to improve their muscular, bone, and cardiovascular strength. That is necessary, he said, because the bones, muscles, and cardiovascular systems atrophy in paralyzed people, increasing the danger of such things as bone fractures during even mild exertion.

. . . What are the next steps in the research? "We will be looking at further miniaturization of the portable walking system and at implanting the electrodes in the body over the next few years," Petrofsky said. . . . "We will be working on achieving more sophisticated movement with our walking systems, while continuing to run extensive tests on the systems. These are just some of the areas we hope to tackle."

But for Nan Davis, at least one dream has already been realized: She walked up to accept her college diploma on her own two feet.

Adapted from an article by Dale Leach, Computer Made Graduation Special. *The Lexington Herald-Leader,* June 13, 1983, and information provided by Wright State University, Dayton, Ohio.

7

Physical and Health-Related Disabilities

Donald P. Cross

Donald P. Cross is Associate Professor, Chairperson of the Department of Special Education and Director of the Educational Assessment Clinic, Department of Special Education, University of Kentucky. Dr. Cross is a member of the Division for Physically Handicapped (DPH), the Division for Learning Disabilities (DLD), and the Teacher Education Division (TED) of the Council for Exceptional Children, and a member of the Council for Learning Disabilities (CLD).

The story about Nan on the facing page illustrates another of several dramatic types of change that have occurred recently in the care of the physically disabled. Recent developments in computer technology have led to an increasing application in areas that yesterday were only imagined in futuristic fiction. The evolution of educational programming has been more subtle, but great progress has been made since the turn of the century. Consider the following statement, written in 1878:

> Inherited physical deformity means mental deformity, particularly when the former is an affection of the cerebral or sensory nerves, or even of the motor organism. So positively has this been demonstrated that in the treatment of feebleminded and insane children, as well as of adults, physicians attempt to correct physical disorder first. With the normal physical functions restored, mental equilibrium also ordinarily returns [Taylor, 1898, p. 184].

As this statement indicates, children with visible disabilities were perceived at that time as being mentally defective, and it was thought that the mental problem could be cured by correcting the physical problem.

At the beginning of the twentieth century, children with physical disabilities either stayed at home or were institutionalized. Gradually, however, educators began to admit the physically disabled into the schools, and special schools and hospital classes were developed. Later, programs for the physically disabled were incorporated into public schools through the establishment of self-contained special classes, but they were frequently housed in substandard facilities, such as church basements or old houses.

Like children with other disorders, the physically disabled are typically grouped in categories. In this chapter we will discuss children who are grouped according to their abilities to function in a particular area, and children who are grouped according to a medical diagnosis. The functional categories are *ambulation,* which refers to the child's ability to move from place to place, and *vitality,* which refers to the child's health and ability to sustain life. In the medical category, we will discuss convulsive disorders. We will also discuss architectural barriers and devices that are designed to assist the physically disabled.

Categories are useful in grouping children for education, funding, and research. At the same time, however, children who have been placed in a category for the physically disabled tend to be isolated from other children. The current trend is to eliminate categorical labels that can prevent the physically disabled from attending regular education programs.

DEFINITIONS

> **You should be able to define physical disabilities and related terminology.**

For our purposes, a physically disabled child will be defined as *one whose physical or health problems result in an impairment of normal interaction with society to the extent that specialized services and programs are required.* This group does not include persons with visual or hearing impairments or persons who can be labeled severely or profoundly handicapped.

The disabilities we will discuss in this chapter are presented separately, and each of them is described separately in medical literature. This does not mean, however, that children with one type of disability should be separated from children with a different type or from children who have no disability. Children with disabilities resemble one another in more ways than they differ from one another. Particular disorders are discussed separately simply because that is the most efficient method of presenting the material relevant to each of them.

TERMINOLOGY BASED ON ANATOMY

Most of the terms used to describe physical disabilities are based on medical usage, which is itself derived from Greek and Latin. Areas of the body are

What are the different "plegias"?

frequently designated with prefixes, whereas suffixes are used to designate conditions of the body. For example, the prefix "hemi" refers to one side of the body, whereas the suffix "plegia" refers to paralysis or the inability to move (Johnston and Magrab, 1976). Thus, the term "hemiplegia" refers to the paralysis of one side of the body. The serious student of physical disabilities is advised to take a class in medical terminology.

Other common terms are listed here:

Term	*Body Area Involved*
Monoplegia	One limb
Hemiplegia	Both limbs on the same side of the body
Paraplegia	The lower limbs
Diplegia	All four limbs, but the lower limbs more seriously than the upper
Triplegia	Three limbs
Quadriplegia	All four limbs
Double hemiplegia	Upper limbs more seriously affected than the lower
Anterior	Front
Posterior	Back
Medial	Nearest the middle
Lateral	Farthest from the middle
Superior	Nearer to the head
Inferior	Farther from the head

There are a number of other terms used to describe the physically disabled. The terms *proximodistal* and *cephalocaudal* are used to describe the growth of children. The term *proximodistal* is used to describe the sequence of development that begins with the child's gaining control of muscles close to the trunk (proximo) and progresses gradually until the child gains control of muscles located farther away (distal). For example, a child can control shoulder and elbow movements before controlling finger movements. The term *cephalocaudal* refers to the maturation of the nervous system, which begins at the head (cephalo) and progresses down the trunk to the more distant parts of the body to the tail, or anterior end (caudal). Thus, a child can control head movements before arm movements (Johnston and Magrab, 1976).

Other terms and concepts will be explained as they are used. For those who would like further reading, Bleck (1982a, pp. 1-16) is a good source of information on terminology, growth, and anatomical structure. Nealis (1983b; 1983c) also presents basic information on human anatomy and neuroanatomy. The Johnston and Magrab text presents an excellent description of normal motor development and cerebral palsy (Johnston and Magrab, 1976, pp. 15-55), as does the chapter by Capute et al. (1983).

PROBE 7-1
Definitions

1. T F The term "proximodistal" is used to refer to the process whereby the child gains control of the muscles in the trunk before gaining control of muscles in the fingers.

2. The suffix that means paralysis, or inability to move, is _____ .

3. In the illustration below, write the appropriate word in the space next to the part of the figure that it represents.

Anterior   Monoplegia
Cephalad   Paraplegia
Caudal   Posterior
Hemiplegia   Quadriplegia
Inferior   Superior

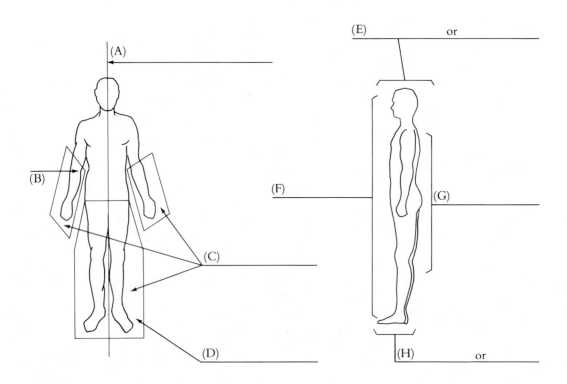

DISORDERS THAT AFFECT AMBULATION

You should be able to describe disabilities that affect ambulation.

Physical disabilities that prevent a child from entering a building, traveling easily from room to room, using toilet facilities, moving from one floor to another, or traveling in a crowded hallway all cause serious problems. It is this type of impairment that has restricted the physically disabled to special schools and modified self-contained classrooms. We cannot discuss all of the disabilities that affect ambulation but must restrict ourselves to those most commonly encountered in the classroom. Some ambulatory problems that result from other disabling conditions will be discussed in other parts of this chapter.

CEREBRAL PALSY

Cerebral palsy is caused by damage to the brain. It is a nonprogressive disorder (that is, it does not become progressively more debilitating) that affects gross and fine motor coordination. It is often associated with convulsions, speech disorders, hearing defects, vision problems, deficits in measured intelligence, or combinations of these problems. Cerebral palsy was originally called "Little's Disease," after the English surgeon who first described it. The condition was first called cerebral palsy by Sir William Osler (Wolf, 1969), and the name was brought to common usage by Dr. Winthrop Phelps, a doctor who studied cerebral palsy in the 1930s and demonstrated that cerebral palsied children can be helped.

Prevalence. Although the individuals with cerebral palsy have never actually been counted, figures suggest that it affects 1.5 per 1,000 persons of all ages (Hallahan and Kauffman, 1978). The different types of cerebral palsy are classified according to the physiological, topographical, and etiological characteristics they exhibit (Keats, 1965). Bleck's citation of a statement by Phelps is useful in placing cerebral palsy in perspective:

> Seven children per 100,000 are born with cerebral palsy. Of those seven, one dies the first year. Of the remaining six, two are so severe as to require institutional treatment. Of the four left for treatment, one will receive only home care or day care center treatment. Two are moderately involved and benefit from treatment while the remaining one is so mild that no special treatment is required [Bleck, 1982b, p. 60].

What is the prognosis for children born with cerebral palsy?

Today, however, the description would be somewhat different, largely because of deinstitutionalization and the current emphasis on services for the multiply handicapped. Many of those who would once have been placed in institutions or kept at home are now being educated in public schools, and many children who would once have died are now being saved. These factors could result in an increase in the measured prevalence of cerebral palsy, but improved medical care has reduced the number of children stricken by cerebral palsy. As you can see, a definitive prevalence rate is difficult to establish.

Classifications of Cerebral Palsy. Persons with cerebral palsy can be classified and described in several different manners. One way is to describe the limbs that are affected, as discussed in the previous section. The most frequently used classification system, the physiological system, is based on the person's body functioning. According to this system, there are six types of cerebral palsy.

What are the different types of cerebral palsy?

1. *Spastic.* The spastic type is characterized by a loss of voluntary motor control. Without this control, the extensor muscles, which are used to extend the arm, and the flexor muscles, which are used to pull the arm toward the body, contract at the same time. This causes movements to be tense, jerky, and poorly coordinated. The spastic may be easily startled by sudden noises or movements, which can cause rigid extension or flexion of the muscles. As a result, the spastic child may become fixed in a rigid position, which gradually relaxes as the child regains composure. As the child grows, the spastic muscles become shorter, which can cause limb deformities. For this and other reasons it is important that the spastic child receive physical therapy. Spastic characteristics are found in about 40 percent of the cerebral palsied population.

2. *Athetosis.* Athetoid cerebral palsy is characterized by involuntary, purposeless movements of the limbs, especially at the extremities. Fluctuating muscle tone affects deliberate muscle exertions, which results in uncontrolled writhing and irregular movements. The throat and diaphragm muscles are also affected, which causes drooling and labored speech. The hands are affected most frequently, followed by the lips and tongue, and then the feet. Excitement and concentrated efforts to control movement generally result in increased tension and spasticity; by contrast, athetoid movement stops during relaxation or sleep. There are at least two major types of athetosis, tension and nontension. The tension athetoid's muscles are always tense, which tends to reduce the contorted movement of the limb. The nontension athetoid has contorted movements without muscle tightness. Athetosis affects 15 to 20 percent of the cerebral palsied population. It is not uncommon for spasticity and athetosis to be found in the same individual.

3. *Ataxia.* Ataxia is caused by damage to the cerebellum, which results in balance problems. Ataxics have poor fine and gross motor movements, poor depth perception, slurred speech, and a staggering gait. They frequently fall. About 25 percent of the cerebral palsied population is ataxic.

4. *Rigidity.* Rigidity cerebral palsy has been described as a severe form of spasticity (Bleck, 1982b). It is characterized by continual, diffuse tension of the flexor and extensor muscles. This "equal pull" of the two muscles renders

the limb rigid and hard to bend; once a limb is bent, it tends to stay in that position, like a lead pipe. The words "lead pipe" are frequently used to describe this type of cerebral palsy.

5. *Tremor.* Tremor cerebral palsy is characterized by the shakiness of a limb, which may be evident only when one is attempting a specific movement. This is called intentional tremor. The shakiness of the limb is caused by alternating contractions of the flexor and extensor muscles. Tremor cerebral palsy is differentiated from athetoid by the extent of the limb movement: athetoid motor movements are large and changeable, whereas tremor movements are small and rhythmic.

6. *Mixed.* Most cerebral palsied individuals have more than one type of palsy; they are labeled according to the predominant type. A typical combination involves spasticity and athetosis.

What causes cerebral palsy?

Etiology. Cerebral palsy can be caused by a number of disorders, which can arise before birth (prenatal), during birth (perinatal), or after birth (postnatal). Prenatal causes include German measles (rubella), prematurity, Rh incompatability, lack of oxygen to the brain of the fetus, and metabolic disorders such as maternal diabetes. Perinatal causes include prolonged labor, breech (feet first) delivery, asphyxia of the fetus, and some obstetric procedures. After birth, cerebral palsy can be caused by infections such as encephalitis, lack of oxygen, and injuries to the head. Postnatal causes are said to be "acquired," whereas those present at birth are "congenital."

Certain types of cerebral palsy are caused by damage to the pyramidal, extrapyramidal, and cerebellar tracts of the brain. Damage to the pyramidal tract, located between the motor and sensory areas of the cortex, affects the nerve cells that initiate motor impulses to the muscles. Damage to the extrapyramidal system, located in the basal ganglia in the midbrain, results in athetosis, rigidity, and tremor in varying degrees. Damage to the cerebellum affects the ability to maintain balance and coordinated movement; it can also cause ataxia. More information on the physiology and anatomy of cerebral palsy is found in Capute (1975, pp. 151-156), Denhoff (1966, pp. 24-77), and Jones (1983, pp. 41-58).

Associated Conditions. Many people with cerebral palsy have problems in a number of areas. These include disorders in communication and sensory systems, intellectual disabilities, and convulsive disorders. These associated disorders can sometimes have effects as serious as the cerebral palsy itself.

Other than the physical disability, what is the most common problem associated with cerebral palsy?

1. *Communication disorders.* Disorders in speech are found in 70 percent of the cerebral palsied population. Studies indicate that speech defects are found in 88 percent of persons with athetosis, 85 percent of those with ataxia, and 52 percent of those who are spastic. Most of the speech problems are caused by problems controlling the muscles used to make speech sounds (dysarthria).

Delayed speech may also be caused by either mental retardation or the cerebral dysfunction. Other communications problems are voice disorders, stuttering, and aphasia.

2. *Sensory disorders.* Jones (1983) states that from 25 to 30 percent of the cerebral palsied population have hearing defects. Hopkins et al. (1954) reported a lower figure, ranging from 7 percent in those with spasticity to 22 percent in those with athetosis. Athetoids were affected more frequently because athetosis was often caused by Rh incompatibility, which also caused hearing disorders. Current medical treatment can reduce the Rh incompatibility problem.

Vision defects in the cerebral palsied vary according to the type of disorder. Hopkins et al. (1954) reported an incidence rate ranging from 42 percent in ataxics to 27 percent in spastics and 20 percent in athetoids. Jones (1983) indicates that 50 percent of the cerebral palsied population has ophthalmological problems. This includes eye muscle incoordination and imbalance.

3. *Intellectual ability.* Studies indicate that 50 percent of the people with cerebral palsy have IQs below 70 (Hohman and Freedheim, 1958; Hopkins et al., 1954). It is important to recognize that accurate measures of the intelligence of the cerebral palsied are difficult to achieve. Motor and communications problems interfere with the administration of the tests, and tests such as the Stanford Binet and the WISC are not standardized on a cerebral palsied population. Although it has been reported that adaptations of tests to accommodate a physical disability do not significantly affect test scores (Allen and Jefferson, 1962), the skill with which the test is adapted and the expertise of the examiner may influence the outcome. If a child does better in the classroom than an IQ score leads one to expect, the IQ score should be disregarded in favor of more reliable data about the child's performance.

4. *Convulsive disorders.* Estimates of the percentage of the cerebral palsied population that have convulsive disorders vary considerably. Denhoff (1966) estimates 30 to 60 percent, Jones (1983) reports 30 percent, while Keats (1965) reports that 86 percent of the spastic population and 12 percent of the athetoid population have convulsive disorders.

As you can see, cerebral palsy can cause a wide variety of problems, some very serious, some relatively easy to adapt to. Those who have cerebral palsy can be expected to attend school in regular classrooms, in classes for the orthopedically handicapped, or in programs for the severely or multiply handicapped. Cross (1983) found that 26 percent of the cerebral palsied children reported in a state-wide survey were placed in classes for the multiple handicapped. Sixteen percent were placed in classes for the trainable retarded or in a program identified as a variation plan; 13 percent of the cerebral palsied were receiving educational programming in classes for the orthopedically handicapped; and 8 percent were receiving homebound instruction. These children may need physical, occupational, and speech therapy. Some will need minimal extra attention, whereas others will need a great deal of assistance to develop to their full potential.

MUSCULAR DYSTROPHY

Muscular dystrophy is a disease in which the voluntary muscles progressively weaken and degenerate until they can no longer function. The age of onset can vary widely; cases have been identified in people ranging in age from one through eighty. There are several types. The Duchenne type, which is the most common, affects young children. It is transmitted to male offspring by the mother, who is the carrier of the condition. Some children are afflicted when there is no family history; this is thought to be caused by gene mutation. The Duchenne type of muscular dystrophy usually appears first between the ages of three and six. Growth and development are normal before the initial onset.

Progression. Muscular dystrophy progresses slowly. In the early stages it is painless and its symptoms are nearly unnoticeable. The first symptoms can include delayed muscle functioning; difficulty walking and climbing stairs; abnormal gait, in which the trunk sways from side to side; difficulty rising from a sitting position; frequent falling; and difficulty in running (Bender, Schumacher, and Allen, 1976). Another early symptom is known as "Gower's Sign," the name given to the practice of placing the hands on the knees and thighs and literally "walking up" the leg. To do this, the child must bend the upper body; because the back and stomach muscles are also affected, the child may have trouble straightening up again. The child may also grasp something to pull the body up into a vertical position, or place the hands on top of the desk to push the body up. The child may also "tiptoe," a symptom caused by the weakening of the muscle that pulls the feet up to a level position.

In the disease's second stage the child has more difficulty rising from the floor after falling because of muscle degeneration in the calves, front thigh muscles, and the dorsiflexors of the feet. The child will also probably have a sway back and protruding abdomen (lordosis). The calf muscles will appear large and healthy (pseudohypertrophy; false enlargement).

During the third stage the child can no longer walk independently and gradually becomes completely confined to a wheelchair. Those who have Duchenne muscular dystrophy usually have reached this stage by age ten.

During the final stage, the child is bedridden and totally dependent. Some children grow obese, which complicates the process of taking care of them. In other cases the muscles atrophy and the child becomes very thin. As the muscles weaken, contractures (shortenings of the muscles) occur, which can result in disfigurement and the loss of limb functioning. Death is caused most often by heart failure, when the heart muscles become weak, or lung infection due to the weakening of the muscles involved in breathing.

How is muscular dystrophy treated?

Treatment. There is no cure for muscular dystrophy. The primary treatment is physical therapy designed to control contractures. Bleck (1982c) indicates that positioning the joints with sandbags or other equipment is more helpful than stretching or exercise. He also describes group games designed to promote good breathing and increase the limb's range of motion. Bracing can be used to prevent contractures, but it is rarely used after the child becomes confined to a wheelchair. Surgery can be used to correct deformities in some cases; treatment will vary from child to child.

Educational Implications. The goal of a school program for the child with muscular dystrophy should be to keep the child as active as possible. The child should remain in the regular classroom as long as feasible. When necessary the child may be moved to a special class or receive homebound instruction. Despite reported IQ scores in the 80s (Bleck, 1982c), and the fact that the child will not live beyond the second decade, the child should be given instruction appropriate to his or her level of functioning. The child, teacher, and the child's family may need counseling about the nature of the illness and the poor prognosis for improvement.

SPINAL MUSCULAR ATROPHY

Spinal muscular atrophy affects the spinal cord and may result in progressive degeneration of the motor nerve cells (Koehler, 1982). It may be associated with a number of diseases (see Ford, 1966, pp. 188-312; Goldberg, 1983, pp. 147-156). The degeneration can cause problems ranging from slight weakness to symptoms similar to those of muscular dystrophy. The primary characteristic is the progressive weakening and atrophy of the proximal (trunk) muscles. This may cause delayed motor skills acquisition, and the child may be easily fatigued and appear clumsy. The atrophy of muscles may cause muscle tightening and joint contractures. Bone substance may be lost because of muscle and joint disuse.

What is the cause of Spinal Muscular Atrophy?

Spinal muscular atrophy is known to be inherited. If both parents are carriers of the defective gene, there is a 25 percent chance that the offspring will have spinal muscular atrophy and a 50 percent chance that the child will be a carrier of the defective gene.

Although there is no cure for spinal muscular atrophy, therapy is used to prevent or reduce joint contractures and other bone complications. Surgery is frequently used to reduce scoliosis (curvature of the spine). Physical therapy is very important. Respiratory infections and aspiration of food must be carefully avoided.

Children with this disorder have normal intelligence but little or no motor strength. Some children are severely affected, whereas others are affected relatively mildly. In school, tasks that do not require muscular skill or strength should be emphasized. If the child's condition stabilizes, vocational training may be required.

POLIO

Poliomyelitis (infantile paralysis) is a viral infection that affects or destroys the anterior horn cells in the spinal cord. When these cells are destroyed, the muscles that they serve eventually die or become paralyzed. The paralysis may affect the entire body or just parts of the body. Some persons are kept alive only through the use of a lung machine that helps the person breathe. Many people with polio are bedridden, confined to wheelchairs, or dependent on braces and crutches for ambulation.

What was Jonas Salk's contribution to society?

Polio was once a greatly feared disease that affected thousands of people each year, but the development of the Salk polio vaccine has almost eradicated it. Unfortunately, an increasing number of children are not being vaccinated, and they are extremely vulnerable to the disease. Although polio is not a major disabling disease today, it could become one again if children are not vaccinated.

SPINAL CORD INJURIES

Spinal cord injuries are most often caused by auto accidents, sports accidents, and accidents at work. In the past most of the victims have been male, but the increasing participation of women in hazardous sports and occupations may increase the number of women with spinal cord injuries. An injury may result in quadriplegia or paraplegia. Depending on the damage that occurs, the injured person may recover completely or not at all.

If a person who has been in an accident complains of neck or back pain or can feel nothing in the legs, he or she should be treated on the assumption that the spinal cord has been injured. The person should be required to lie flat and not be allowed to turn the head or rise to a sitting position. The injured person should be moved without bending or twisting.

Medical care and physical therapy both play a part in the treatment of spinal cord injuries. Most children with injuries of this type will be served in hospital schools and homebound education programs. Some may be able to return to the regular classroom, whereas others will be placed in classes for the ortho-

These are pictures of Nan Davis, whose remarkable accomplishments were described at the beginning of this chapter. The picture on the left shows her in the experimental laboratory, practicing walking under her own muscle power with computer assistance. Nan was paralyzed from the waist down as the result of an automobile accident on her high school graduation night. The picture on the right shows her getting ready to walk to the podium to receive her bachelor's degree from Wright State University. The computer that controls her movements is contained in the bag under the arms of the system's designer, Dr. Jerrold Petrofsky.

pedically impaired, depending on the extent of the child's recovery. Intelligence is not affected by a spinal cord injury.

How is intelligence affected by spinal cord injury?

Computer technology is now being applied to the treatment of spinal cord injuries. The story of Nan, which precedes this chapter, is a very recent example of the work being done by the Wright State University National Center for Rehabilitation Engineering. The solution is not yet found, but a good start has been made.

SPINA BIFIDA

Spina bifida is a congenital defect that results when the bones of a part of the spine fail to grow together. The defect, the cause of which is unknown, occurs during the first 30 days of pregnancy (Bleck, 1982d). The gap in the spine can appear anywhere, but it is usually found in the lower part, the lumbar-sacral area. It can cause paraplegia and loss of bowel and bladder control.

What is a myelo-meningocele?

There are three types of spina bifida. The most severe is called myelomeningocele (or meningomyelocele). In this type, part of the spinal cord protrudes through the gap in the bones of the spine into a sac-like structure that surrounds the gap, causing a neurological problem (see Figure 7-1). If the sac contains cerebrospinal fluid but the spinal cord does not protrude and there is no neurological impairment, the condition is called meningocele. The least severe form is called spina bifida occulta. The only evidence of this form is a growth of hair covering the area of the defect. Myelomeningoceles are four to five times more common than meningoceles (Bleck, 1982d).

Peterson (1972, p. 252) states that spina bifida is the third most common disability found in long-term education settings. Its incidence is estimated to be between 0.1 and 4.13 cases per 1,000 live births (Bleck, 1982d). The prevalence rate is somewhat lower than the incidence rate because some of the children die shortly after birth. Recent medical advances have decreased the mortality rate, but spina bifida is still a dangerous condition frequently accompanied by several other chronic disorders.

One of the most common is hydrocephalus, or "water on the brain." This condition occurs when the drainage of cerebrospinal fluid is blocked. The buildup of pressure that results can cause serious brain damage, including mental retardation. Kidney infections caused by poor urinary drainage are another condition associated with spina bifida. If untreated, these infections can lead to kidney failure. Pressure sores are a problem that results when the blood supply to an area of skin is cut off. Persons with normal feeling experience discomfort when this happens and shift their position to allow the blood to circulate normally. Those who are paralyzed, however, do not feel the discomfort. Pressure sores are very difficult to heal. Other disorders that may accompany spina bifida are dislocation of the hip, club foot, and when the

Figure 7-1
A Myelomeningocele

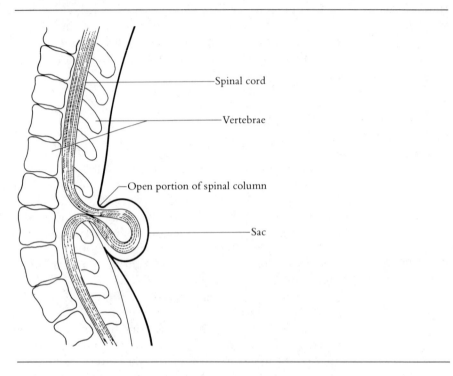

Spinal cord

Vertebrae

Open portion of spinal column

Sac

child is older, scoliosis (spinal curvature), kyphosis (humpback), and lordosis (swayback).

Treatment. The initial treatment of spina bifida is surgery for the outpouch (sac) and hydrocephalus, if that is also a problem. Surgery for hydrocephalus involves placing a shunt to drain excess cerebrospinal fluid to the atria of the heart or to the abdominal cavity. When successful, there is no brain damage. Surgery for the outpouch frequently takes place during the first week after birth. Sharrard (1968) reports less paralysis and a lower mortality rate among those who receive surgery within 48 hours. Bleck (1982d), however, reports that early surgery does not diminish paralysis.

Most people with spina bifida, particularly those with myelomeningocele, use crutches or wheelchairs, which may be a problem in school. A more serious problem is the lack of bowel and bladder control. In some cases, physical, occupational, and speech therapy will be part of the school program. Most cases require continual medical monitoring.

OSTEOGENESIS IMPERFECTA

Osteogenesis imperfecta is also known as *brittle bone disease*. The bones of children with this disorder break very easily; the many fractures cause the limbs to be small and bowed. The disorder is inherited and affects both male and female children. The bones of those with osteogenesis imperfecta have been described as being immature, like the bones of a developing fetus. Many children with this disorder are hard of hearing because of defects in the bony structure of the ossicles.

What is the treatment for osteogenesis imperfecta?

There is no cure for this disorder. Surgery and bracing are used to straighten the legs and aid in ambulation. Many use a wheelchair as well. Since the intelligence of these children is normal, their educational prognosis is good. Great care must be exercised in working with these children, however, because their bones can be broken very easily — even when helping them change position in a wheelchair. The physical activity of these children will of course be severely restricted.

MULTIPLE SCLEROSIS

Multiple sclerosis is a progressive disorder in which portions of the myelin sheath (tissues surrounding the spinal cord) are damaged and replaced by scar tissue, resulting in a short-circuiting of nerve impulses to muscles. This demyelination process does not occur in any systematic order. Some persons may experience mild attacks and recover completely. For others, the disease process involves a series of attacks and then periods of remission. With each attack, or active state of the disorder, more damage to the myelin sheath occurs. The initial symptoms may consist of visual disturbances and mild motor incoordination problems. As the disorder progresses, more and more damage occurs, and the person may become blind or severely visually impaired, have a speech disorder, lose bowel and bladder control, and become partially or totally paralyzed in the extremities. At various times during the disorder, the person may be confined to a wheelchair but later, as remission occurs, may ambulate normally or with the aid of crutches.

How does multiple sclerosis affect the body?

There is no known cure for this disorder. However, two promising experimental treatments have been reported (Clark, 1983). Both treatments view the cause of multiple sclerosis as a defect in the body's immune system in which the white blood cells, not bacteria, attack the myelin. The treatment is aimed at periodically suppressing the immune system. Despite the fact that there is no known cure for this disorder, most persons who have multiple sclerosis live a normal life span. Physical therapy is important in the treatment program. Rehabilitation counselors should also help implement other treatment programs and aid in securing transportation.

JUVENILE RHEUMATOID ARTHRITIS

What are the symptoms of juvenile arthritis?

According to the Arthritis Foundation, there are five common forms of arthritis: rheumatoid, osteoarthritis, ankylosing spondylitis, rheumatic fever, and gout. Rheumatoid arthritis is the most common among school-age children. The first signs of the disease are general fatigue, stiffness, and aching of the joints as they swell and become tender. It is a chronic condition, but 60 to 70 percent of those affected are free of the disease after ten years (Miller, 1982). During the active phase, children experience severe pain whenever the affected joints are moved. If the condition first appears in childhood, most children recover completely. Those who first acquire the condition as adults have a much smaller chance of a permanent remission.

Arthritis cannot be cured. Aspirin is used to reduce the pain, and rest and exercise are also important parts of the treatment. The most severe (but infrequent) complication of juvenile rheumatoid arthritis, occurs when the heart muscle becomes inflamed, which can be fatal (Miller, 1982). Less severe complications are temporary hearing loss, which is caused by taking aspirin, and permanent damage to the joints, which can restrict their mobility. Some types of therapy have proven to have more harmful consequences than the disorder itself. Cortisone, for example, when administered frequently to children can halt growth, reduce resistance to infection, and cause obesity and brittleness of the bones.

In school, arthritic children may have difficulty remaining in one position for long periods of time. The child may also need extra time to get from one place to another.

OTHER MUSCULOSKELETAL DISORDERS

How do scoliosis, lordosis, and kyphosis differ?

A problem in one part of the body frequently causes problems in another part. Children who have cerebral palsy, spina bifida, muscular disorders, or other disorders frequently have back problems as well. Muscles that pull too hard or that are unequally balanced can cause such disorders as scoliosis, lordosis, and kyphosis. Inadequate muscle tension sometimes results in the complete collapse of the skeletal system.

Scoliosis is lateral curvature of the spine. A person with scoliosis will appear to have an s-shaped spinal column when viewed from behind. *Lordosis* is a condition in which the spine is curved inward, resulting in a swayback and protruding abdomen. *Kyphosis* is a condition in which the area surrounding the shoulders is rounded. These disorders are treated with physical therapy, bracing, and in some cases, surgery. If not properly treated they can cause severe physical deformity and can threaten breathing and other life-sustaining functions. They may also increase pressure on a number of the body's organs.

A *club foot* is a disorder that can appear by itself or in conjunction with another problem. Children with this disorder are born with one or both feet turned down and in. The condition can be corrected with surgery, bracing, and casts, and children who have club feet learn to walk in the normal fashion. They are indistinguishable from their normal peers by the time they reach school age.

Amputation is another important disability. It can be partial or complete. Most amputations are necessary because of accidents, but some are required because of life-threatening physiological disorders and diseases.

Limbs may also be missing as the result of disruptions in the early fetal development of the limbs. This sometimes occurs randomly, but it can also be caused by drugs such as *thalidomide,* which was taken by pregnant women as a relaxant. Depending on the time at which it was taken during the first trimester of pregnancy, it can cause a variety of congenital deformities, including extremely short or missing limbs (phocomelia). In this disorder, the hands and feet, which are deformed themselves, are attached directly to the torso and may resemble "seal flippers." Several thousand children with this deformity were born in Germany, where the drug was routinely prescribed in the late 1950s and early 1960s. Once the effects of the drug were established, the drug was taken off the market. Special schools for thalidomide children have been established in Europe. The United States Department of Health did not approve the medication, so the problem in this country was relatively uncommon. Some American women who did obtain thalidomide gave birth to children with birth defects. This tragedy underscores the fact that pregnant women must be very careful not to take drugs that may harm the fetus.

PROBE 7-2
Disorders That Affect Ambulation

1. T F Cerebral palsy is caused by brain damage.

2. *Matching*

   _____ Tense and jerky movements   a. Athetosis
   _____ Involuntary, writhing movements   b. Rigidity
   _____ Staggering gait   c. Spastic
   _____ "Lead pipe" stiffness   d. Tremor
   _____ Shakiness   e. Ataxia

3. _____ -natal means before birth, _____ -natal means during birth, and _____ -natal means after birth.

4. T F There is a higher incidence of speech disorders, sensory disorders, and mental retardation in the cerebral palsied population than in the "normal" population.

5. T F Cerebral palsy is rarely accompanied by convulsive disorders.

6. T F   Cerebral palsied children do not attend public schools.

7. *Matching*

    _____ Meningocele   a. Polio
    _____ Brittle bones   b. Spina bifida
    _____ Salk vaccine   c. Multiple sclerosis
    _____ Degeneration of the myelin sheath   d. Osteogenesis imperfecta
    _____ Curvature of the spine   e. Scoliosis
    _____ Inflammation of joint   f. Muscular dystrophy
    _____ Progressive muscle deterioration   g. Juvenile rheumatoid
                                   arthritis

8. _____ is a drug that caused numerous congenital deformities of the extremities of children in Europe and elsewhere.

9. T F   Most children with osteogenesis imperfecta have normal intellectual ability.

10. Which type of supportive service is used to minimize muscular deterioration in children with diseases such as muscular dystrophy, spinal muscular atrophy, and polio?

11. T F   Children with muscular dystrophy generally recover.

DISORDERS THAT AFFECT VITALITY

You should be able to describe disabilities that affect the vitality of children.

Children with disabilities that affect vitality are frequently placed in special classes or programs. Although all of these disorders are life-threatening, some are more dangerous than others. All children with these types of disorders will need special assistance from a primary care worker or teacher, and special educational, social, and vocational training as well.

CONGENITAL HEART DEFECTS

The symptoms exhibited by persons with congenital heart defect are shortness of breath, cyanosis (blue apperance of the skin), and low tolerance for exercise (Myers, 1975). Most congenital heart problems, which are generally recognized at birth or early childhood, are mechanical in nature (i.e., they do not involve infection or inflammation). They can frequently be repaired surgically.

What should teachers be aware of with children who have heart defects?

Because these children are often restricted physically and have usually spent a lot of time in hospitals, they have not had the opportunity to participate in many of the normal activities of children. Although the intelligence of most of these children is in the normal range, they may not function academically at the level of their peers. The child's classroom activities may be restricted by orders from his or her physician, and the teacher will have to watch the child carefully for signs of overexertion. At the same time, however, the teacher should be aware that the child may try to use the condition as an excuse not to participate in activities that he or she is capable of participating in. The care and education of children with this disorder require careful cooperation among the child's parents, teacher, and physician.

CYSTIC FIBROSIS

Cystic fibrosis is a chronic genetic disorder that affects the pancreas, the lungs, or both. When the lungs are affected, the mucus normally found in the lungs does not drain properly, and when it builds up, it blocks the passage of air to and from the affected area. When the pancreas is affected, digestion is impaired and the child may suffer from poor nutrition, even if he or she eats what would normally be an adequate amount of food. The disease, which is hereditary, is usually fatal in childhood. It is estimated that one in every twenty-five Caucasians carries the defective gene. It is the most common cause of death from a genetic disorder in the United States (Harvey, 1982b). Proper treatment may slow the progress of the disease, however, and some children live to adulthood.

Why is percussion used with children who have cystic fibrosis?

In school, the child may cough frequently, have an increased appetite, and have low physical stamina. Treatment typically combines medication with percussion. Percussion is a process designed to dislodge mucus. The child is placed in a position designed to enhance lung drainage while the chest is vigorously clapped and vibrated (Harvey, 1982b). These children have normal intelligence; they will need special attention only for periods of treatment and restrictions in their physical activities.

DIABETES

Diabetes is an inherited metabolic disorder. The diabetic does not produce enough insulin to absorb the sugar in the blood stream. The disorder is treated with a special diet and injections of insulin, administered by the diabetic on a prescribed schedule. If properly treated, the condition can be adequately controlled. If too much insulin is taken, however, blood sugar may be consumed too readily, and the diabetic may go into insulin shock. When this occurs, the child must be given some form of concentrated sugar, such as a sweet hard

What should a teacher do if a diabetic child begins to go into insulin shock?

candy or sweetened fruit juice, immediately. If the diabetic does not have enough insulin, he or she will go into diabetic coma.

Hypoglycemia, a related disorder, is caused when the body produces too much insulin. This may cause a condition similar to insulin shock, although it is usually not as severe.

The diabetic or hypoglycemic child may need to eat snacks during class time. Hypoglycemic children need to reduce their intake of carbohydrates, as well. Cooperation between the teacher and the child's parents is very important in dealing with these disorders effectively.

ASTHMA

What might precipitate an asthma attack?

Asthma is a chronic condition characterized by wheezing or labored breathing, which is caused by the constriction in the individual's air passages and by excessive secretion in the air tubes of the lungs. The decrease in the size of the air passage makes breathing — particularly exhalation — difficult (Harvey, 1982a). The causes of the condition are not fully understood, but allergic reactions to foods (ingestants) or to particles in the air (inhalants) appear to precipitate it. Excessive emotionality is not considered a primary cause, although it is thought to influence the conditions that may bring on an asthmatic attack.

Asthma tends to run in families. The severity and duration of asthma attacks vary considerably. Harvey reports that it is the fifth most common reason for a child to see a physician in the state of Washington. It is similarly prevalent in other states.

The treatment of asthma involves removing ingestants and inhalants from the child's environment. The child may also be given injections to increase resistance to allergic reaction. Breathing exercises and mechanical drainage of the lungs may also be helpful. During an acute attack, medication can be used to relax the bronchial tree.

The treatment of asthma is a long-term process. The teacher should find out from the parents whether the child's environment or physical activities need to be controlled and whether the child needs other special attention. Aside from these considerations, the asthmatic child should be treated like any other.

PROBE 7-3
Disabilities That Affect Vitality

1. A condition characterized by low tolerance for exercise is _____ .

2. Children with asthma typically have difficulty _____ .

3. Diabetes is controlled through _____ .

4. T F Most children with cystic fibrosis die during childhood.

CONVULSIVE DISORDERS

You should be able to identify and treat symptoms exhibited by children with convulsive disorders.

Epilepsy is caused by brain damage that impairs the brain's ability to control its normal electrical activity. This can perhaps best be understood through an analogy: The electrical activity of the brain can be compared to a glass of water filled to just above the brim. The water may bulge slightly over the top of the glass, but it will not spill unless the surface tension is broken by a pin prick, a movement of the glass, or some other disturbance. When the brain has been damaged, electrical energy flows over the brain, and control of the resultant overload can be lost as a result of a minor disturbance. When control is lost, electrical energy stimulates many different parts of the brain at the same time, and the individual has a seizure. About 1 percent of the population has epilepsy. It affects males more frequently than females.

Epilepsy has been a recognized disorder for thousands of years. Hippocrates was the first to suggest that seizures were caused by brain malfunctions. The term "seizure" itself, which is used to describe the active motor states of epilepsy, is derived from Greek and Latin and means "seized by the gods." The Romans called epilepsy "the sacred disease."

Today, epilepsy and seizures are categorized under the general heading of *convulsive disorders*. Epilepsy can occur in anyone at any age. Young children may have convulsions during high fever, but these are considered "febrile seizures" rather than epilepsy. Prolonged high fever can cause brain damage that results in epilepsy, however. Epilepsy can also be caused by injuries when the child is being born, or later by head injuries. Epilepsy that has no apparent cause is called "idiopathic" epilepsy.

TYPES OF EPILEPSY

There are many types of epilepsy. The three major types will be discussed in this section. The different types of epilepsy are actually classified medically under four categories: partial seizures, generalized seizures, unilateral seizures, and unclassified seizures (Epilepsy Foundation of America, 1977). This classification system is primarily used for medical diagnosis; we will use the traditional classifications and terms in common use that are described within this classification scheme. More information on epilepsy can be found in Berg (1982) and Nealis (1983).

How do petit mal, grand mal, and psychomotor seizures differ?

Petit Mal. The petit mal seizure frequently goes unnoticed. It lasts 5 to 10 seconds, and its only visible symptoms are staring, a momentary suspension of activity, a "frozen" posture, and perhaps a slight fluttering of the eyelids. The child may appear to be daydreaming or going to sleep. Petit mal seizures may occur as often as 10 to 15 times a minute, or they may occur only occasionally.

The main effect of a petit mal seizure is a momentary lapse of consciousness. It can be compared to a radio that has a short in its system such that only parts of the broadcast can be heard. The child may miss portions of the classroom instruction. Even when teachers notice that a child is behaving oddly, they may not realize what is happening. It is important that parents and teachers collect accurate data on the seizures to aid the doctor in prescribing treatment.

Grand Mal. The grand mal seizure is much more conspicuous. It is this type of seizure that is referred to by the uninformed as a fit, spell, attack, or convulsion. The child may fall to the ground, become stiff (tonic stage), begin to jerk or thrash (clonic stage), and cry out or make noises. The child may hurt himself from falling or biting his tongue, or by hitting objects when thrashing on the floor. The child may also lose bowel and bladder control momentarily. Grand mal seizures may last from a few seconds to 5 minutes or more. As the seizure progresses, the child's movements gradually slow and finally cease. When the epileptic regains consciousness, he or she will not remember the seizure or anything that happened during it. The child may also be confused and very tired, particularly if the seizure was a severe one. In some cases, however, the child simply gets up and continues activities.

Grand mal seizures may be preceded by a warning, or aura, of some kind. An aura can be a sensation, a sound, a light perception, or some other indication. If the child is aware that he or she is about to have a seizure, the child should be quickly taken to as safe a place as possible.

Psychomotor. The psychomotor seizure is characterized by automatic, stereotyped movements, which may be purposeless, inappropriate, or both. This type of seizure progresses through the following stages: suspension of activity, repetitions, automatic movements, incoherent or irrelevant speech, possibly followed by a display of rage or anger. Persons who have this type of seizure are often identified as emotionally disturbed or as having a temper tantrum. When the seizure is over, the individual will be confused.

FACTORS THAT CAN PRECIPITATE SEIZURES

Seizures are most likely to occur one to two hours after a person falls asleep or one to two hours before awakening. Physicians use this knowledge to help diagnose epilepsy by comparing the results of electroencephalogram (EEG) testing, which is used to record brain wave activity, with observed abnormal motor activity.

What can precipitate seizures?

Seizures can also be caused by *emotional disturbance* and *stress*. They are more common among women during the menstrual period. Drug withdrawal, hyperventilation, fever, photic stimulation (such as sunlight glittering through leaves or on water), television, and fluorescent lights have also been known to precipitate seizures. If an individual's seizures tend to be precipitated by a certain kind of environmental event, the seizures can sometimes be controlled by avoiding the events that precipitate them.

The following newspaper article illustrates some of the misconceptions held by the general public about epilepsy and the consequences of these misconceptions for the epileptic.

> A young man wakes up from his epileptic seizure to find a woman bystander dancing over him, trying to exorcise what she believes is a devil that has possessed him. . . .
>
> Quoting from a national survey about charitable causes to which the public is most likely to contribute, the board president of the financially ailing Epilepsy Association of Kentucky says: "We're right down at the bottom, just one notch above venereal disease."
>
> Welcome to the uncertain, somewhat secret world of the epileptic.
>
> They are suffering — or have suffered sometime — seizures ranging from dramatic convulsions to brief lapses of consciousness. More than that, they have suffered from public ignorance and uneasiness over the ailment. . . .
>
> "The average citizen is not hostile to epilepsy. It's just they don't know very much about it, and sometimes they're scared about it," said E. Wayne Lee, a 27-year-old epileptic. . . .
>
> Greater understanding in the schools can prevent some of the embarrassment and ridicule faced by students who suffer from epilepsy.
>
> This embarrassment sometimes prompts teen-age epileptics not to take their seizure-preventing drugs in an attempt to prove they really are like everyone else. . . . [Peirce, 1979].

TREATMENT OF EPILEPSY

What is the primary treatment for epilepsy?

Epilepsy is treated primarily with chemotherapy, the administration of drugs. The drugs are used to prevent seizures or to reduce their frequency. Many of them have serious side effects, which vary with the child and the medication being taken. Dilantin, for example, causes a condition known as gingival hyperplasia, in which the gums become swollen and tender and grow over the teeth. The gums also bleed easily and are susceptible to infection. Other side effects of concern to the classroom teacher are lethargy and restlessness.

Another part of the treatment program involves classroom adjustment and efforts to ensure that the epileptic is accepted by the teacher and the child's peers. Children are much more likely to accept the epileptic child if seizures have been explained to them. The teacher may also have to control classroom activities that regularly precipitate grand mal seizures. If, for example, the child regularly has a seizure after heated classroom discussion, the discussion may have to be toned down, or the child may have to be occupied with another activity. The teacher should also know how drugs affect the child's schoolwork.

How to Deal with Seizures. Although seizures can generally be controlled with medication, the teacher may occasionally have to manage seizures in the classroom or elsewhere. Petit mal seizures are more difficult to control than grand mal seizures. The teacher who has children who experience petit mal seizures may have to repeat instructions several times to be certain they are clearly understood. The teacher should also realize that the child is not merely daydreaming.

A child who experiences an aura or warning that precedes a grand mal seizure should be taken immediately to as safe a place as possible. If the child falls to the floor, these instructions should be followed:

1. Give the child room to thrash. The immediate area should be cleared of children and objects on which the child could be hurt.
2. Allow the child to remain on the floor. The child should not be moved, restrained, or held during the seizure.
3. Protect the child's head by cradling it in your hands. Do not restrain head movement, however. Move with the child.
4. When possible, turn child's head to one side. This allows saliva to drain. If it flows back into the throat, the child may choke. Turning the head to one side also keeps the child from choking on the tongue, which may be caused by gravity forcing the tongue to the back of the throat if the child is lying face-upward.
5. Don't put your fingers in the child's mouth. The child could bite and seriously injure them. Tremendous strength is exerted during a seizure. Do not force anything between the teeth.
6. Don't lay the child on his or her stomach; to do so will impair breathing. When possible, the child should be turned on one side.
7. Loosen tight clothing.
8. Get down on the floor with the child. Do not stand up and look down at the child.
9. Allow the child to remain lying down for a while after regaining consciousness.

10. Talk to the child in a calm voice. Acknowledge the seizure but don't make a major issue of it.
11. When the child is ready, help the child to stand.
12. Allow the child to lie down or sit at a desk with the head down. The child should be permitted to go to sleep.
13. Unless instructed otherwise, you need not call the physician. You should report the seizure to the parents and principal and note its severity and duration in the anecdotal seizure record.
14. Children near the child should be assigned the task of moving tables, chairs, and other objects away from the child, because they are closer than the teacher. Other children should be instructed to go on with their work.
15. Children in the classroom should be prepared for the event. Discuss the appropriate procedures for dealing with seizures with the child's parents, and obtain parental and school permission to discuss seizures with the class. A discussion can perhaps be related to health instruction. After the child has regained consciousness, appropriate reactions (do not stare, do not avoid the child) should be discussed with the class.
16. Above all, try to remain calm.

Psychomotor seizures should generally be treated in the same way as grand mal seizures. It is important to recognize the emotional component and when necessary clear the room or take the individual from the room. The individual may resist attempts to be moved, however; if this occurs, the child should be allowed to remain.

What is status epilepticus? If the child is still convulsing after five minutes, or seems to go from one seizure right into another, the child's parents and the physician (or school nurse if one is available) should be consulted immediately. This is a condition, called status epilepticus, which can cause death if allowed to continue. This condition requires treatment by a physician (Nealis, 1983a).

EDUCATIONAL IMPLICATIONS

Children with epilepsy will be found in the regular classroom and in the special class. Epilepsy alone is not sufficient reason to place a child in a special class or program, but it is often found in conjunction with other disabilities, such as mental retardation and cerebral palsy. The teacher must watch for the side effects of medication and adjust the classroom to reduce the effects of the seizure on both the child and other students. The teacher should collect data on side effects and the incidence, duration, and severity of seizures, which should be reported to the child's physician to aid in monitoring the child's disorder. Epilepsy is not a progressive disorder, nor does it cause mental retardation. It is not contagious. As noted, the child will require some adaptations and adjustment but otherwise should be treated as normally as possible.

PROBE 7-4
Convulsive Disorders

1. A temper tantrum may sometimes be confused with what type of seizure?

2. A child who falls to the ground, thrashes around, and loses bladder control may be suffering from a _____ seizure.

3. The type of seizure that often goes unnoticed is a _____ .

4. T F Epilepsy is treated primarily through chemotherapy.

5. T F In treating a person having a grand mal seizure, one should place one's fingers between the teeth to prevent swallowing of the tongue.

6. When is it necessary to call in professional help for a child having a grand mal seizure?

EDUCATION AND TREATMENT OF CHILDREN WITH PHYSICAL DISABILITIES

You should be able to describe education and treatment procedures for children with physical disabilities.

CHILD ABUSE AND NEGLECT

How can teachers identify abused or neglected children?

In Section 3 of the Child Abuse Prevention and Treatment Act (PL 93-247), child abuse and neglect are defined as "the physical or mental injury, sexual abuse, negligent treatment, or maltreatment of a child under the age of eighteen by a person who is responsible for the child's welfare under circumstances which indicate that the child's health or welfare is harmed or threatened thereby." Some symptoms that might indicate abuse or neglect have been described by Kline (1977) and are shown in Chart 7-1. (He also published a checklist worth examining if you want to develop a program to combat child abuse and neglect in a school system.) It is important to note that only nonaccidental or deliberate injuries are considered abusive.

Approximately 1 million children are abused, neglected, or sexually molested each year, according to the National Center for Child Abuse and Neglect. The causes are hard to determine. Child abusers come from all income levels, geographic areas, family settings, religious backgrounds, ethnic groups, and residential environments. They do not necessarily use drugs or alcohol.

There is one factor that seems related to child abuse: Many child abusers were themselves abused as children. And, although a cause-effect sequence has not been demonstrated, Kline has reported a clear relationship between child abuse and handicapping conditions. His research found that of children judged to be abused or neglected, 27 percent were subsequently enrolled in special education classes. Many of these children had symptoms resembling those of behavior disorders. PL 94-142 programs designed to locate handicapped children will probably indentify a number of children who have been abused or neglected.

Chart 7-1
Symptoms of Abuse and Neglect

Symptoms of Abuse	Symptoms of Neglect
Evidence of repeated injury	Clothing inappropriate for weather
New injuries before previous ones have healed	Torn, tattered, unwashed clothing
Frequent complaints of abdominal pain	Poor skin hygiene
Evidence of bruises	Rejection by other children because of body odor
Bruises of different ages	Need for glasses, dental work, hearing aid, or other health
Welts	services
Wounds, cuts, or punctures	Lack of proper nourishment
Scalding liquid burns with well-defined parameters	Consistent tiredness or sleepiness in class
Caustic burns	Consistent, very early school arrival
Frostbite	Frequent absenteeism or chronic tardiness
Cigarette burns	Tendency to hang around school after dismissal

Obviously, cases of child abuse should be identified and reported as soon as possible to treat existing injuries and to ensure that the child is protected from further injury. Teachers have not only humane and professional responsibilities to report possible cases of abuse; in at least 36 states they have a legal responsibility as well. In the other states, persons and institutions providing social services are similarly obliged. Failure to report a suspected case is a misdemeanor in nearly half the states (Kline, 1977).

You should note, however, that providing proof of abuse is not the responsibility of the teacher; that is done by the agency that receives the report. In fact, every state except Oklahoma provides immunity from civil or criminal liability to those who report cases in good faith (Kline, 1977).

The effects of some disabilities may be confused with child abuse. A child with osteogenesis imperfecta (brittle bones disease) will frequently and easily break bones. One who is alert to child abuse but not aware of the physical disorder could make a mistake. The person working with the physically disabled should be alert to potential child abuse yet be aware that many children with physical disabilities will show conditions that resemble physical abuse.

A CHECKLIST FOR TEACHERS

What should teachers be aware of when teaching a child with physical disabilities?

Children with physical disabilities can frequently be educated in the regular classroom with the help of some of the devices mentioned in the next section. Depending on the severity of the child's disability and the extent to which he or she requires special attention, the child might be placed in any of the environments described in Chapter 1. If a child with a physical disability or a health problem is assigned to your school program, you should contact the child's parents and those who have worked with the child in the past, and obtain answers to the questions in the following areas.

Medical Concerns

— In addition to the child's primary disorder, does the child have additional problems such as seizures or diabetes? Does the child have any sensory disorders?
— Does the child take medication? How frequently, and in what amounts?
— If medication is taken, is the school authorized to administer the medication during school hours?
— What are the expected side effects of the medication? What are the other possible side effects?
— What procedures should be followed in the event of a seizure, insulin shock, diabetic coma, or other problem, with regard to contacting the child's parents or medical personnel?
— Should the child's activities be restricted in any way?

Travel

— How will the child be transported to school?
— Will the child arrive at the usual arrival time?
— Will someone need to meet the child at the entrance to school to provide assistance in getting the child on and off the vehicle?
— Will the child need special accommodations to travel within the school building or the classroom?

Transfer and Lifting

— What methods are used to get the child on and off the school bus?
— What is the preferred way to lift and transfer the child out of a wheelchair and onto the school seat?
— What cautions or limitations are there regarding transfer and lifting?
— How much help does the child really need with movement and transfer?

Communication

In addition to finding answers to the following questions, the teacher of a child with a communications problem should consult a speech/language pathologist.

—If the child does not communicate verbally, what particular or unique means of communication does the child use?

—Does the child have a speech or language problem?

—Does the child use gestures? If so, what are they? Is a pointer used? Does the child use the same signal consistently for *yes, no,* or other common words?

—Can the child write? Type? How?

—Is an electronic communication aid used? If so, are there any special instructions necessary for the child to use it or for the teacher to understand and maintain it? Are fresh batteries or a charger needed?

—Can the child make his or her needs known to the teacher? How?

Self-Care

—What types of help does the child need with self-care activities such as feeding, dressing, toileting, etc.?

—What equipment, such as a special feeding tray, does the child need?

Positioning

If possible, the physical therapist should be involved in conversations with parents about this area of concern.

—What positioning aids or devices (braces, pillows, wedges, etc.) does the child use?

—What particular positions are most useful for specific academic activities? What positions for resting?

—What positions are best for toileting, feeding, dressing, and other activities?

—Are there any other special aids or devices that I should know about?

Sources of information about providing architectural accessibility include Aiello, 1976; Kliment, 1976; and Mace and Iaslett, 1977. Additional information on principles useful in mainstreaming the physically disabled is available in Cathey and Jansma (1979).

ASSISTIVE AND ADAPTIVE EQUIPMENT

There are many devices available to help the physically disabled overcome problems of everyday living. The story of Nan at the beginning of this chapter is an example of one of the more recent applications of modern technology. Medical science has been using assistive and adaptive equipment for a number of years: skin grafts; veins for heart bypass surgery; pacemakers to enable the heart to beat at a given pace; body organs such as kidneys, livers, and, most dramatically, the heart. Modern technology has enabled the nonspeaking to speak, the nonhearing to hear, and the nonseeing to see. One has only to attend a convention for professionals who work with the disabled to recognize

TECHNOLOGY IN ACTION

Inventor Donald Dattilo says the idea for his latest creation came to him while he was watching an old science-fiction movie. "This guy was sitting in a game room with electrodes attached to his forehead to make things happen," he recalled. "I got to thinking maybe that sort of thing wasn't all fictional anymore."

He assembled his thoughts on a drawing board and four months later had an experimental neuro-muscular processor ready for testing. The device resembles a headband. It has four sensors in it and wires that run to a control box.

Datillo's invention reads muscle movements on a person's forehead and translates them to electrical impulses to operate machinery. He built it to help quadriplegics steer motorized wheelchairs.

Paul Piet, who lost use of his limbs in a 1971 auto accident, was the first person to test the head-band. . . . [A] small earphone fed four different tones, one for each direction, into his right ear. Within five minutes he had learned to use the unit.

Each time he would flex his jaw muscles he would cause an electronically perceptible movement in his forehead. A tone would sound and the wheelchair would begin moving. He soon was able to hold a tone to keep the chair on course.

Datillo said the sensors capture bioelectric energy transmitted through the contraction of small muscles. "There is a whole mess of random signals put out by muscle movements," he said. "This device can unscramble the mess by directing the signals from specific muscles." . . .

The device has many potential uses. . . . "In this age of robotics we could do all sorts of things. We could have a robot moving around a room, lights and appliances switching on and off, and a bed that moves up and down. All of the actions would depend on movement of facial muscles," he said.

From the Associated Press, Lexington Herald-Leader, *January 3, 1984.*

---

the dramatic increase in the application of modern technology to adaptive-assistive devices for the handicapped.

In the realm of communications, for example, devices are already used extensively. Some devices enable one to communicate using only a sip or puff on a straw-like device. Voice synthesizers attached to microcomputers enable persons who could not speak to have a voice. Persons who cannot normally open a door, turn on a radio or TV set, or flip on a light switch can now do so with vocal commands such as "Open the door." In these instances a microcomputer is literally trained to recognize the person's voice (and only that person's voice) and to activate a motor connected to a door or a light switch when it hears the right command. The motor performs the desired function. One must keep abreast of new technological developments if one works with the physically disabled.

What is the difference between an orthosis and a prosthesis?

There are also many less highly technical devices used by the physically disabled to overcome problems of everyday living. *Prosthetic* devices such as artificial arms and legs are used to replace missing body parts. *Orthotic* devices are attachments, such as a leg brace or a splint, that assist a body function. Other types of adaptive equipment, such as wheelchairs, machines that turn pages, and long forceps used to reach objects that would otherwise be out of reach, are also available.

Not all disabilities result in handicaps.

In a survey of public school special classes that contain physically disabled children, Cross (1983) found that providing for communication disorders was the most common adaptation. Adaptations for self-care activities such as feeding, toileting, and dressing were also frequently reported, as were devices relating to travel. Surprisingly, instructional adaptations were not among the most frequently reported provisions for the physically disabled.

Although adaptive-assistive devices may be beneficial to the disabled, they should not be recommended without a careful examination of their potential effect. In some cases the use of a device may lead to a dependency that adversely affects the disabled person's remaining physical functions. Those who do not use adaptive aids may become more independent and thereby prevent or slow their physical deterioration. Some prosthetic devices actually hinder body functioning or motor movement, and tasks may be accomplished more efficiently without them. In some instances, careful evaluation of body positioning and support must be made before adaptive techniques are implemented. This may involve a visit to a clinic such as the Trace Center in Madison, Wisconsin. Questions about the use of a particular device should be referred to the appropriate specialists or to the physical or occupational therapist if no specialists are available.

The many devices used to help the handicapped have been classified in a variety of ways. The Veterans' Administration (U.S. Government Printing Office, 1982) provides an excellent list of devices entitled *Directory of Living Aids for the Disabled Person*. This directory provides alphabetical lists of product living aids, living aids manufacturers, and product living aids by state. Alternatively, Melichar (1977, 1978) has designed an information storage and retrieval system called the Information System for Adaptive, Assistive, and Rehabilitation Equipment (ISAARE). Under this system, *adaptive* equipment is defined as that which helps one adapt to the environment through the use of supportive devices or materials. *Assistive* equipment is described as items designed to help people increase their functional capability by providing support or replacing the lost capability. *Rehabilitation* equipment is that used in physical therapy or in rehabilitating people who are trying to regain physical functioning they have lost. Under the ISAARE system, equipment is divided into six categories, according to the purpose for which it is used. These categories are *existence, communication, in situ motion, travel, adaptation,* and *rehabilitation*. These categories and an example of a piece of equipment in each are described in the following list. The examples are taken directly from the ISAARE manual.

Existence. Items in the existence category provide support, stabilization, and protection. They allow the disabled person to pursue activities necessary to sustain life. Aids in this category are used for feeding, elimination, bathing, grooming, sleeping, fastening clothing, and so on.

Dorsal feeding splints provide assistance for independent feeding to the person who lacks wrist extension and flexion and who is unable to grasp. The dorsal feeding splints are structured to support the palm, wrist, and forearm. An 8-inch long band of lightweight metal or rubber with soft underpadding extends lengthwise on the dorsal side of the individual's forearm; three adjustable leather or Velcro straps are attached to the band winding around the user's palm, wrist, and mid-forearm. An adaptable utensil holder is usually inserted or otherwise attached to the palmar strap (Figure 7-2).

Communication. Communication devices are used in the reception and expression of information. Included are specialized typewriters, hearing aids, braille writers, magnifiers, and machines that help dial telephones. Devices not included in the ISAARE system are the more recent electronic applications of microcomputer technology as well as the use of Bliss Symbols and other non-oral symbols. Bleck (1982e) and the Fountain Valley School District (1980) are among a number of excellent sources that provide excellent information in this area. The Trace Center (Vanderheiden, 1982) also provides a listing of microcomputer applications currently available.

Automatic page turners (Figure 7-3) are devices that enable the patient with impaired upper extremity function to turn magazine or book pages automati-

Figure 7-2
Dorsal Feeding Splint

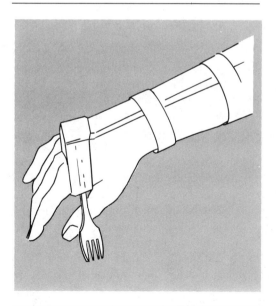

Figure 7-3
Automatic Page Turner

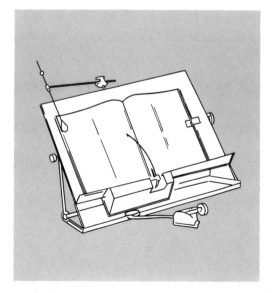

cally. The device operates to turn pages with a slight momentary touch or movement of a sensitive switch mechanism by any part of the body.

The automatic page turner accommodates all sizes of magazines and books and adjusts to hold positioned materials at any angle, depending on the reading position of the patient.

The automatic page turner is available in two models: a model that turns pages forward and backward, and a model that turns pages in only one direction.

An able-bodied person is required to set the machine for an individual book or magazine, and it takes some time to get the correct amount of pressure on the automated arm.

In Situ Motion. Equipment related to in situ motion is designed to support a person's body. It can either stabilize the body so that it remains immobile (a splint, for example) or add support to facilitate movement (a brace).

Institutional relaxation chairs allow the person with no sitting balance and a severely involved trunk area to sit comfortably. These chairs are used in therapy units to accommodate patients who are too handicapped to use a conventional chair or wheelchair.

The chair is made of wood, plastic, or metal with two solid sides enclosing the user from the armrests to the base; a solid back extends from the headrest to the base with a bench-like seat. This chair tilts on a metal rod at the back of the platform on which the chair rests. The chair may be adjusted to a 30-degree angle; the seat tilts to a full jackknifed position; the padded headrest is contoured; and the platform is on casters (Figure 7-4).

Travel. Devices in the travel category help a person to move either vertically or horizontally. A wide variety of items are included in this category: wheelchairs, hoists, canes, walkers, and crutches. Not included in the ISAARE system are microcomputers that enable paraplegics to walk, such as that used by Nan. Wright State University, Dayton, Ohio, is very much involved in developing and furthering the application of microcomputers to enable paralyzed persons to ambulate.

Stairclimbing wheelchairs provide greater mobility to the user than standard wheelchairs, as they will negotiate stairs. The stairclimbing wheelchair creeps along on caterpillar treads, is battery operated with push-button controls, and has a tilting seat so the occupant is always in an upright position (Figure 7-5). On floors and level areas the chair rides on two power-drive front wheels with two trailing casters; the tracks are stationary and clear the ground. Both the tracks and wheels are driven in negotiating curbs; the rear wheels are retracted in climbing stairs.

Figure 7-4
Institutional Relaxation Chair

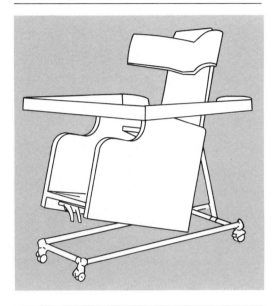

Figure 7-5
Stairclimbing Wheelchair

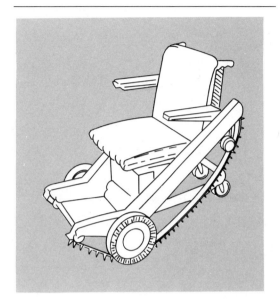

Adaptation. Included in this category are such things as cooking utensils that can be used by someone with one hand, aids for doing housework, and driving accessories. Devices not included in the ISAARE system include the more recent voice-operated applications of microcomputer technology, which enable one to command that a door be opened, a light turned on, a TV turned off, etc.

Drive control units basically consist of a hand lever, usually positioned on the left side and directly behind the steering wheel, which has been connected by long rods to the brake and accelerator (Figure 7-6). There are various types of mounting; some are attached to the steering column, some to the lower portion of the dashboard. Also located on the hand control is a headlight dimmer switch.

The hand control is operated by pushing it downward, toward the floor, to brake; and pulling it back in the direction of the lap of the driver to accelerate. In some models it is possible to brake and accelerate simultaneously, as would be necessary in starting on a hill.

Figure 7-6
Drive Control Unit

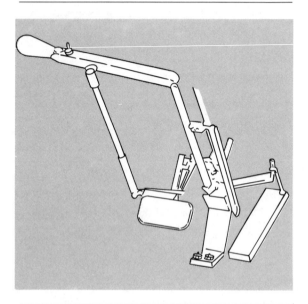

Figure 7-7
Finger Shoulder Ladder

Rehabilitation. The rehabilitation category includes devices and equipment used by medical personnel and physical therapists. Included are items that are used to exercise various body parts and to measure physical functioning.

Finger shoulder ladders are therapeutic devices used to increase range of motion of the shoulder joint. The ladder is constructed of wood, 1½ × 2½ × 89 inches with grooved steps for the fingers to climb. It is mounted on a wall and may be positioned at a convenient level (Figure 7-7).

If you are interested in finding out more about the ISAARE system, you might read the article by Melichar (1978) or obtain a copy of the ISAARE retrieval system manual (Melichar, 1977).

ARCHITECTURAL BARRIERS

People with physical disabilities are frequently faced with architectural barriers that prevent them from using facilities easily accessible to people without disabilities. There have been several important laws passed by Congress, however, that are designed to reduce or eliminate architectural barriers, and it is now illegal to build with federal funds facilities inaccessible to the handicapped

(PL 90-480). Another piece of legislation, the Urban Mass Transportation Act of 1964, was amended in 1970 to require that federally supported transportation be barrier-free. The Architectural and Transportation Barriers Compliance Board was created to monitor building and ensure that the intent of legislation on accessibility is being followed (PL 93-112).

What are the ANSI Standards?   A set of standards and specifications for making facilities accessible to the handicapped has been developed by the American National Standard Institute (ANSI). These standards, followed by planners and builders, describe specifications for (1) parking and approaches to building entrances; (2) travel within hallways and on elevators and stairs; (3) services such as public telephones, water fountains, and rest rooms; (4) hazardous places, gratings, and alarms; (5) special rooms, such as kitchens; (6) schoolrooms, such as lecture halls, libraries, and physical education facilities; and (7) other buildings, such as churches, restaurants, and stadiums.

Useful resources for planning facilities for handicapped children have been published by the Council for Exceptional Children (CEC), the state of North Carolina, and the Rehabilitation Services Administration (Aiello, 1976; Kliment, 1976; Mace and Iaslett, 1977). The drawings and specifications in the following section are from these sources.

Access to the Community. Most of us can do everyday things like open doors, climb stairs, answer the phone, and use the lavatory without giving it a thought. But consider the problems you would face in these situations:

— You are blind and must find a certain office or house number.
— You are in a wheelchair and must get into a building that has only stairs and revolving doors, or you are in an elevator and cannot reach the button for the floor you want.
— You are on crutches and can't carry your groceries or push a grocery cart.

As you can see, tasks most of us accomplish easily can present impenetrable barriers to the handicapped. Some obstacles cause just minor inconveniences — being late for an appointment, perhaps. Others can have grave consequences. What if you are deaf and can't hear the fire alarm in your apartment building?

The situation is improving, however. As we mentioned earlier, Section 504 required that buildings built in part with federal funds be accessible to the handicapped. Colleges and universities, too, are prohibited from discriminating against the handicapped; many are renovating their physical plants to give the handicapped access to previously inaccessible facilities.

With respect to school programs, it is important to remember that *all parts* of all buildings need not be accessible; rather, all *programs* must be accessible. Thus, access to a second-floor science class need not be provided to a student in a wheelchair. The science class may, however, have to be moved to the first floor to make the science program accessible to all.

Curbs Can Be Hazardous
To Your Health

Especially if you are in a wheelchair, on crutches, have a heart condition, or suffer from other conditions such as the ageing process which hamper your mobility.

In an attempt to eliminate the hazardous conditions that curbs present this segment of the community, the Kentucky Department of Transportation has developed a design for curb ramps which is both safe and efficient, and meets all the requirements of the curb ramping laws.

Copies of these designs are available through the Department of Transportation, Division of Design, Frankfort, Kentucky 40601.

Mobility. A basic law which cannot be violated.

Poster funded by Department of Transportation, Office of Highway Safety Programs; Picture courtesy of Canadian Rehabilitation Council for the Disabled.

The Council for Exceptional Children publishes a useful resource for planning facilities for handicapped children (Aiello, 1976). In it are listed a number of other resources that deal with barrier-free environments.

Heightened sensitivity to the needs of the handicapped is also reflected in the use of the international symbol of access for the handicapped (Figure 7-8A). You've probably seen it along highways, where it is used to indicate restrooms equipped for the disabled. You may also have seen the signs in Figure 7-8B and C, which indicate the route a handicapped person should take to enter or leave a building. The sign in Figure 7-8B means "straight ahead," whereas the one in Figure 7-8C means "turn right."

What do you think the signs in Figure 7-9 represent? The first indicates a ramp; the second, a telephone; the third, parking; and the fourth, an elevator accessible to the handicapped.

Although few people would argue that access for the handicapped is undesirable, it is controversial because it is so expensive. For example, Wieck (1979) reported that it cost $15,000 to outfit a bus with a lift or ramp. High costs such as this influenced the National Council of Mayors' decision to state their preference for alternative services, such as dial-a-van. Some groups of handicapped have gone to court to force full access to buses.

Wieck also reported that there were 404,000 people in wheelchairs in urban areas in 1979 and that the Department of Transportation estimated the cost of providing full access to buses, subways, railcars, and trolleys at $1.7 billion. This figure was challenged by the American Public Transportation Association, which claimed it would cost $3-6 billion just to adapt the subway systems of nine major cities. Whichever figure one accepts, the cost of providing access is staggering.

Figure 7-8

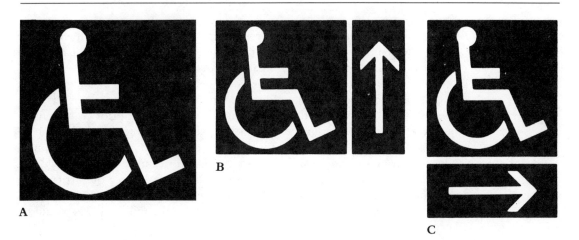

A

B

C

Figure 7-9

The following narrative describes some of the barriers you might encounter on a trip to the dentist if you were in a wheelchair. The standards that should be met to overcome these barriers are also discussed.

As you can see, a building designed to be accessible to the handicapped is significantly different from a traditional building in a number of respects. It is not necessary, however, that every building constructed prior to the enactment of access legislation be renovated. Section 504 requires only that all *programs* be accessible. For example, every dormitory on a college campus does not have to be accessible, but some dormitories must be. Similarly, the entire building housing a math department need not be free of barriers, but the math program must be available to handicapped students. The expense of making accessible all buildings constructed before the middle 1970s would be enormous.

A TRIP TO THE DENTIST

Walkways

You will need to travel on sidewalks in order to get to the building. A walkway is defined as a predetermined, prepared surface that leads to or from a building and is on the same level as the adjacent ground. Walks should be at least 48 inches wide, and should have a continuous surface that is not interrupted by steps or abrupt changes of more than one-half inch. Larger vertical changes than this may obstruct the small wheels on wheelchairs and trip people who have trouble walking.

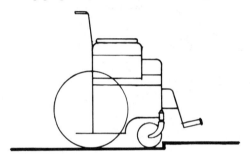

Ramps

You must get from the walk up the stairs to the entrance of the building. To do so, you must use a ramp. A ramp is a sloping walkway that enables one to move from one floor elevation to another without encountering any obstruction. Ramps should be at least 4 feet wide and should have a slope of not more than 8.33 percent, which is a drop of one inch in every 12 inches.

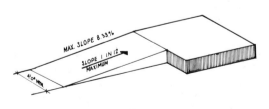

Doormats and Grates

After wheeling up the ramp, you encounter a grate that has been installed in front of the doorway to trap snow and sand. The grate should have grid openings of no more than three-eighths of an inch square. Larger openings will create hazards for those who use canes and will make wheelchair travel difficult.

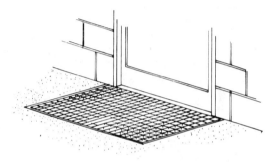

After you have traveled across the grate, you come to a door mat. Thick, bristly doormats of hemp or plastic bunch up under the small wheels of chairs and make the wheelchair difficult to push. Door mats more than one-half inch thick should be recessed into the surface, or thin mats of woven rubber should be used.

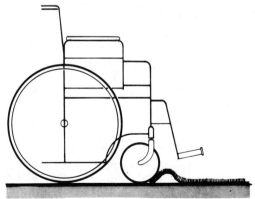

Entrances

You are successful in maneuvering over the grate and door mat and are now ready to open the door to the building. Revolving doors and turnstiles should have accessible doorways placed immediately beside them. The threshold at an exterior door should be beveled and have a maximum edge height of three-quarters of an inch so that you can get your chair over it without difficulty. You should be able to open the door with one hand, and the passageway with the door open should be at least 32 inches wide. An adult wheelchair is approximately 27 inches wide, so a 32-inch doorway allows 2½ inches on each side for the hands as they are used to turn the wheels.

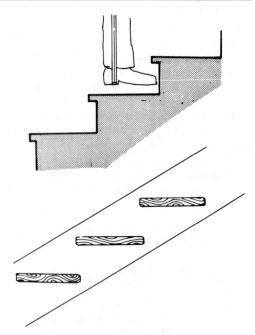

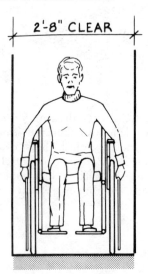

Acceptable stairs have either vertical or slanted risers. They could be used by someone who had to lift her legs straight up or drop them straight down without risk of the person's catching her toes on the top of each step. Two types are shown below.

Stairways

Now you are in the building. Ideally, there would be an elevator to take you to the second floor where the dentist's office is located. If there were no elevator and you could ambulate with crutches or leg braces, you would have to use the stairs. Open riser stairs are attractive, but they are hazardous to a person wearing leg braces. People who wear braces also have a difficult time climbing stairs that have abrupt or square lips that stick out over the stair riser. The following two side views are examples of unacceptable stairs.

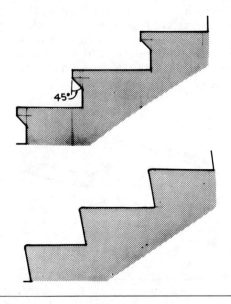

The handrails of stairways should also be modified to make it easier for someone with limited grasping power to hold on to them.

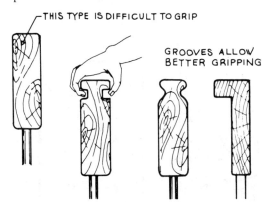

After arriving at the dentist's office, you must move from the wheelchair to the dental chair. You have of course chosen a dentist who has been trained in lifting and transfer techniques. He straddles one of your knees, places his wrists under your arms, and, bending his knees, leans you forward. Then, using his legs for lifting, the dentist pivots you 90 degrees so that you are seated in the chair. The same procedure is used to get you back in the wheelchair after the dentist informs you that you have no cavities.

Rest Rooms

If you need to go to the rest room after your visit to the dentist, you may encounter obstacles there as well. Most rest rooms have self-closing doors that can make toilet facilities inaccessible. Time-delay door closers and automatic, power-operated doors that slide or pivot should be used at major entrances, doorways, and rest rooms.

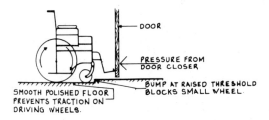

After you have gotten through the door, you must still gain access to the stall. Standards now require that one toilet room for men and one for women be accessible to the handicapped on every floor that has a rest room. Each rest room must have at least one accessible toilet as well. There are three basic techniques for transferring from a wheelchair to a toilet in a stall. The first two methods, used in ordinary stalls, are difficult or impossible for many people who have not had extensive training. You have probably seen the grab rails that have been installed in some stalls to assist the physically disabled with their toileting.

Method 1

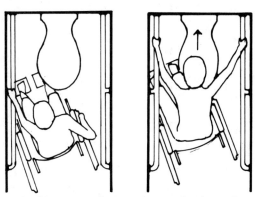

1. (Left) *Enters stall, turns at an angle, placing footrests and feet to one side of the water closet.*

2. (Right) *Leans forward, placing hands on rails near wall, and pulls torso forward, sliding onto seat in sideways position.*

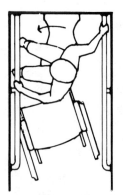 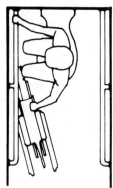

Method 2

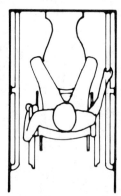 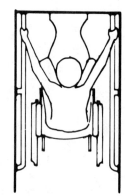

3. (Left) Switches right hand from right rail to left, arriving in side seated positon as in 4.

4. (Right) Maintains balance with right hand while using left to fold chair or push it back.

1. (Left) Enters stall straight in and pulls chair up to seat, placing legs to each side of water closet.

2. (Right) Leans forward, placing hands on bars near wall. Pulls torso forward, sliding onto seat.

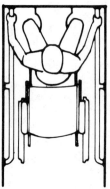

5. With chair folded or pushed back, swings legs around to front, switching left hand to opposite rail.

3. Remains in "backward" position facing wall.

Method 3

This side-approach method can be used by most people in wheelchairs. Stalls that allow space for this method are preferred.

temperature of the water should not exceed 120 degrees Fahrenheit. Exposed hot water pipes should be insulated to avoid burning people who have no feeling in their legs.

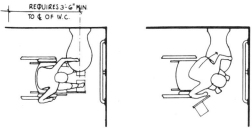

1. (Left) *Approaches water closet from side.*

2. (Right) *Removes arm rest and swings foot rest to side. Places one hand on seat or grab bar and other on chair.*

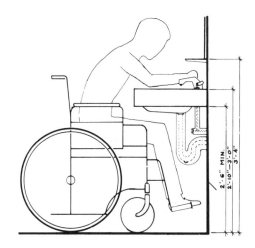

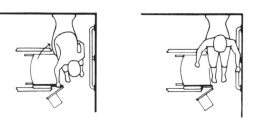

3. (Left) *With a lifting and sliding motion shifts torso onto seat.*

4. (Right) *Maintains balance by using grab bar and wheelchair.*

If the rest room contains mirrors and shelves, one of each should be placed above the sink for the handicapped. The shelf and the bottom of the mirror should be no more than 40 inches from the floor. The operating mechanisms (cranks, coin slots, buttons) of towel racks, dispensers, disposal units, vending machines and other appliances should be within 40 inches of the floor as well.

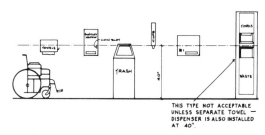

To complete your use of the rest room, you will need to wash and dry your hands. Each rest room should have a sink no more than 34 inches from the floor. There should be a space of at least 29 inches between the floor and the bottom of the sink so that a wheelchair can be pushed close to it. The

PROBE 7-5
Education and Treatment

1. List 3 symptoms of child abuse.

2. List 3 symptoms of child neglect.

3. Describe the conditions under which you would recommend that children be placed in the regular classroom for their education.

4. What criteria would you propose for selecting physically disabled children for placement in a self-contained special class?

5. List one question you should ask a physically disabled child's parents in each of the following areas to help develop procedures for caring for the child.

   a. Medical
   b. Travel
   c. Transfer
   d. Communication
   e. Self-care
   f. Positioning

6. *Matching*
   Place the letter of the category into which each piece of equipment would fit in the blank that precedes the name of that equipment.

Equipment	*Category*
_____ Exercise stairs	a. Existence
_____ Arm sling	b. In-situ motion
_____ Adjustable head pointer	c. Rehabilitation
_____ Bus wheelchair lift	d. Adaptation
_____ Self-threading needle	e. Travel
_____ Drinking straw holder	f. Communication

7. Differentiate between a prosthesis and an orthosis.

8. When would it be inappropriate to recommend an assistive or adaptive device for use by a person with physical disabilities?

9. Standards for the elimination of architectural barriers have been developed by an organization called _____ .

10. Doorways should be at least _____ inches wide to accommodate wheelchairs.

11. Ramps should be at least _____ feet wide.

12. T F A lavatory stall can be made accessible to all persons in wheelchairs by placing grab bars at convenient heights.

13. T F Thick door mats should be used in front of doors to give wheelchair travelers better traction on wet days.

14. T F Open-riser stairs are particularly well suited for persons who are wearing braces.

15. Lavatory towel dispensers and other appliances should be mounted no more than _____ inches above the floor.

16. Obstructions on walkways should not be more than _____ high or they may cause travel problems.

17. T F Although there may be architectural barriers in a given school, all programs must be accessible to the handicapped.

SUMMARY

1. Physically disabled children are those whose physical or health problems result in an impairment of normal interaction with society to the extent that specialized services and programs are required for them.
2. Cerebral palsy is caused by damage to the brain. It is characterized by impaired motor coordination. There are several types of cerebral palsy, including spastic, athetoid, ataxic, rigidity, tremor, and mixed.
3. Muscular dystrophy is a progressive weakening and degeneration of the voluntary muscles.
4. Other disorders that affect ambulation are spinal muscular atrophy, poliomyelitis, multiple sclerosis, arthritis, osteogenesis imperfecta, and spinal cord injuries.
5. Spina bifida is a congenital defect caused by the failure of the bones of the spine to grow together completely.
6. Thalidomide, a drug taken by pregnant mothers, caused a large number of children to be born with physical defects in the late 1950s and early 1960s.
7. Some of the disabilities that can affect the vitality of children are congenital heart defects, cystic fibrosis, diabetes, and asthma.
8. There are many abused and neglected children in special education programs. Teachers need to be particularly alert for signs of child abuse and neglect.
9. Epilepsy is caused by uncontrolled electrical discharges in the brain. The three primary types of seizures that result from epilepsy are grand mal, petit mal, and psychomotor seizures. Epilepsy can usually be controlled with medication.
10. Standards have been developed to aid in the elimination of the architectural barriers encountered by the physically disabled. Federal law now requires that buildings built in part with federal funds be barrier-free.

11. Many types of assistive and adaptive equipment have been developed to help physically disabled children in their day-to-day existence, travel, adaptation to their environment, and communication.
12. The great majority of physically disabled children can be educated in regular classrooms with the use of assistive equipment and special teaching aids.

TASK SHEET 7
Field Experiences with the Physically Disabled

Complete *one* of the following alternatives:

Building Accessibility Survey

Acquire a copy of the Accessibility Compliance Checklist included in Kliment's (1976) work, another appropriate checklist, or develop your own. Select a public building in your area and survey it for accessibility. Try to select a building that has been constructed relatively recently, since buildings constructed prior to the mid-1970s are less likely to be in compliance with accessibility standards. If you find areas out of compliance, try to talk to the building owner or supervisor. What was his or her reaction, and what problems did you encounter in your survey?

Program Visit

Arrange to visit an education program for the physically disabled. Describe the type of program that you visited, the physical setting, the assistive and adaptive equipment that was being used, the modifications that were made in the physical environment to adapt to the needs of the children, the type of lesson that you observed, and your general reaction to the program. If possible, interview the teacher and ask what types of problem are encountered in teaching children with physical disabilities. Describe what you learned and how you felt about the experience.

Professional Interview

Interview one of the following professionals: physical therapist; occupational therapist; orthopedic surgeon; prosthetist; orthotist; director of a facility serving the physically disabled; affirmative action officer or person responsible for supervising accessibility at the public school, university, or hospital; or anyone else who works with physically disabled people. Describe whom you interviewed, the person's responsibilities, the problems encountered in performing the job, the type of training needed, what you learned from the interview, and how you felt about it.

Interaction with the Physically Disabled

Arrange to help a physically disabled person with a routine daily task such as traveling, shopping, etc. Describe whom you helped, the activities you helped with, where you went, the problems you encountered, the adaptations that had to be made, and what you learned from the experience.

Agency Investigation

Write to three of the following agencies, inquiring about the services that they provide to people with physical or health related disabilities. Write a three-page paper describing what you learned and how you as a professional might use their services.

Allergy Foundation of America
801 Second Avenue
New York, NY 10017

American Academy for Cerebral Palsy
% Mrs. James E. Bryan
1255 New Hampshire Avenue, N.W.
Washington, DC 20036

American Heart Association
44 East 23rd Street
New York, NY 10010

American Occupational Therapy
Association
6000 Executive Blvd, Suite 200
Rockville, MD 20852

Architectural and Transportation
Compliance Board
Switzer Building
Washington, DC 20201

Arthritis Foundation
1212 Avenue of the Americas
New York, NY 10036

Easter Seal Research Foundation of the
National Easter Seal Society for Crippled
Children and Adults
2023 W. Ogden Avenue
Chicago, IL 60612

Epilepsy Foundation of America
1828 L Street, N.W.
Washington, DC 20036

International Society for Rehabilitation
of the Disabled
219 East 44th Street
New York, NY 10017

Juvenile Diabetes Foundation
23 East 23rd Street
New York, NY 10010

Library of Congress
Division for the Blind and Physically
Handicapped
1291 Taylor Street, N.W.
Washington, DC 20542

Little People of America
Box 126
Owatonna, MN 55060

Muscular Dystrophy Association of
America
810 7th Avenue
New York, NY 10019

National Association of the Physically
Handicapped
76 Elm Street
London, OH 43140

National Congress of Organizations of
the Physically Handicapped
7611 Oakland Avenue
Minneapolis, MN 55423

National Cystic Fibrosis Research
Foundation
521 Fifth Avenue
New York, NY 10017

National Easter Seal Society for Crippled
Children and Adults
2023 W. Ogden Avenue
Chicago, IL 60612

National Foundation of Dentistry for the
Handicapped
1121 Broadway
Suite 5
Boulder, CO 80302

National Foundation of the March of
Dimes
Box 2000
White Plains, NY 10602

United Cerebral Palsy Association
66 East 34th Street
New York, NY 10016

Library Study

Select three articles concerning children with physical or health related disabilities and
write a one-page abstract of each, concluding with your personal impressions about
the value of the article. Here are some journals in which you can find articles:

American Journal of Physical Medicine
American Journal of Nursing
American Journal of Occupational Therapy
Archives of Physical Medicine Rehabilitation
DPH Journal
Electronics
Engineer
Exceptional Children
Human Factors
Rehabilitation Literature
Physical Therapy

Design Your Own Field Experience

If you prefer, design your own field experience and after discussing it with your
instructor, perform the designated tasks.

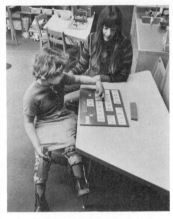

This ten-year-old girl was born with spina bifida and has no feeling below her thighs. She wears braces and walks with the aid of crutches, although she sometimes uses a wheelchair. She often vacillates between wanting to use the wheelchair, which gives her speed, and wanting to use the crutches, which she perceives as giving her more social approval.

She attends public school classes and receives physical therapy once each week at a cerebral palsy center, doing follow-up exercises daily at school. (At times she balks at doing her exercises.) Her physical therapist believes that she may eventually be able to get along with only one crutch.

After a period of adjustment she has developed a very positive self-image and is well liked by the other children. As these photographs demonstrate, she is an active participant in school activities.

Individual Differences in Learning and Behavior

In the section on communication and sensorimotor disorders, many of the characteristics we described were shown to have educational implications. For example, a child who is legally blind and cannot read print will probably use braille, and a child with a profound hearing loss may use sign language. Among the disabilities discussed in this section, however, the category in which children are placed does not automatically have implications for their education. What is important is how the child performs in an educational setting. A child who cannot differentiate among initial consonants, for example, will be taught with the same techniques whether that child is labeled educable mentally retarded, learning disabled, or mildly behaviorally disordered. In fact, many children with sensorimotor disabilities will respond to generic teaching techniques, once their impairments have been corrected to the greatest extent possible.

Despite such educational commonalities across the various handicapping conditions, there are three reasons for dividing our coverage into separate categorical chapters. First, classification is a process scientists go through to organize and systematize information, permitting them to make useful statements about the phenomenon being classified. Thus, we have chosen to follow the common practice by presenting the material in these categories. We do try, however, to limit the use of a number of terms one frequently hears in special education circles, such as "neurotic," "psychotic," "dyslexic," "minimal brain dysfunction," "developmental retardation," and so on.

Secondly, most public school programs use categories in their special education programs. For example, there are classes for the educable mentally retarded, resource rooms for the learning disabled, and programs for the behavior disordered. Also, we find in the state and local levels that categorization is used because it is traditional ("We've always done it this way"); because of funding ("You have to label the kids to get the money"); and because of certification practices ("I'm certified to teach the emotionally disturbed"). Fortunately, placing children in categories is becoming more flexible in public schools. The current trend in state funding is to permit groupings based on educational variables. In addition, some states have moved to teacher certification that is noncategorical, or generic.

Third, many colleges and universities are still training teachers in categorical areas. Consequently, if we don't include chapters on the various categories, it is doubtful that anyone would adopt this text for use in their program. We hope that by the time future editions of this text are published, special education will have advanced to the point where we will not have to include categorical chapters.

Throughout the chapters you are about to read, we have tried to focus on specific behavior and learning characteristics that have relevance for education, yet the material has of necessity been organized into categories. You will notice in the ensuing chapters that there is considerable overlap among the characteristics of children who have been categorized as mentally retarded, behavior disordered, learning disabled, or severely developmentally disabled. We believe this repetition will reinforce some of the major concepts that are presented.

A BEHAVIORAL ORIENTATION

The authors of the chapters in this section subscribe to the behavioral approach to instructing exceptional children. The word "approach" is difficult to define, but it has to do with a way of thinking about a phenomenon, the kind of theory used, and the techniques or methods employed when teaching or providing other services. Although there is wide support for the behavioral approach, there are other paradigms espoused and used by researchers and special education teachers. Many teachers draw on different parts of several approaches, depending on the demands of the task they are trying to accomplish. They do this in part because there are little data to support the contention that one approach is conclusively better than another. There is evidence that each of these approaches can be applied successfully, especially when used by devoted and resourceful teachers.

The Humanistic Approach. Advocates of this approach believe that children's problems are caused by psychological or emotional conflicts that interfere with the ways in which they try to understand or cope with their feelings and emotions. Many humanists also assert that children so affected cannot learn in traditional school settings and recommend that alternative school environments be developed. The school environment should be "open," with many opportunities for self-directed activity. Humanists believe that the teacher should be a friend to the students and should serve as a facilitator for the students' self-directed activities. More information on this approach is available in the work of Peter Knoblock (1973).

The Psychodynamic Approach. The psychodynamic approach is based primarily on the work of Sigmund Freud. Adherents to this philosophy believe that a person's actions are governed by unconscious impulses that were formed by the emotional atmosphere in which the person was reared. Problems that arise are considered the result of conflicts the individual went through during a previous stage of development. Psychodynamically oriented teachers would create a permissive atmosphere in which children could act out their impulses. Accordingly, teachers would not try to change the behavior of children directly; rather, they would attempt to uncover the symbolic meaning of the behavior and help the children work through their conflicts. Bruno Bettelheim (1950, 1967) provides additional information on the psychodynamic approach.

The Psychoeducational Approach. This approach is an outgrowth of the psychodynamic model. Proponents of both approaches search for the causes of behavior; but advocates of the psychoeducational model strive for a balance between psychiatric and educational concerns. Teachers who subscribe to psychoeducational thinking focus attention on the cognitive processes involved in learning and use diagnostic and educational techniques designed to evaluate and remediate these processes. Moreover, they favor structure in academics and set up highly individualized instructional programs. Carl Fenichel (1966) has written on how the psychoeducational approach can be applied in classrooms.

The Ecological Approach. Ecologists are concerned with how organisms interact with their environment. They contend that children with learning or behavior problems are out of balance with their ecosystem and believe that an imbalance in one part of the system affects all the other parts. The design of education or treatment programs must reflect, therefore, conditions in the family, school, community, and all other systems of which the child is a part, as well as the child's classroom. As will be seen in chapters later in this section, the ecological approach can be combined with other approaches to education. More information about the ecological approach is available in the work of Nicholas Hobbs (1966, 1974).

The Behavioral Approach. The behavioral approach is based on the work of B. F. Skinner. Behaviorists believe that all behavior is learned and that searching for the psychological causes of behavior is futile; instead, they focus their attention on behaviors that can be observed, measured, and recorded. Educational programs developed by behaviorists emphasize the modification of children's behavior by the manipulation of their environment, especially through altering the effects of particular behaviors. Because in recent years the influence of behaviorism on special education has perhaps been greater than that of any other approach, it is useful at this point to explore a bit more intensely the salient principles of behaviorism. You can find additional information in books by Frank Hewett (1968), and Norris Haring and Richard Schiefelbusch (1976), all of whom provide good examples of the application of the behavioral approach in special education.

PRINCIPLES ASSOCIATED WITH THE BEHAVIORAL APPROACH

In describing the field of applied behavior analysis, Kerr and Nelson (1983) have listed several principles that are basic to its understanding and application. Principle number one is that behavior is controlled by its consequences. Some consequences increase or decrease the frequency of behavior while others maintain behavior. The other principles are as follows: behavior is strengthened by either positive or negative reinforcement; behavior is weakened by punishment and by removing consequences that have been associated with it; consequences must be applied consistently and immediately following the behaviors they are meant to influence; and modeling can strengthen, weaken, or maintain behavior.

Using behaviorism in special education is generally accomplished through intervention, therapy, or instruction — often collectively referred to as behavior modification or applied behavior analysis. There are many behavior modification procedures, and O'Leary and O'Leary recommend that they be considered in two groups: those which are intended to increase performance or behavior, and those which are intended to decrease performance or behavior (1972, p. 26). This dichotomy is somewhat arbitrary, but it does bring to the array of available procedures an order that allows the teacher to find an appropriate procedure quickly. Ready access to a proven procedure can be very important to teachers who have children with severe behavior problems.

PROCEDURES USED TO "INCREASE" BEHAVIORS

Let us look at the procedures identified by O'Leary and O'Leary that are used to "increase" behavior (1972, pp. 26–31).

Praise and Approval. A positive response by the teacher to a desired student behavior can increase the frequency of the behavior. The response could be verbal praise, gestures, giving the student a star, or some other expression of approval.

Modeling. Showing or demonstrating the desired behavior and then having the student repeat the behavior is an effective teaching technique. The results of modeling can be enhanced by using praise and other expressions of approval. Modeling can be done either by the teacher or by another pupil.

Shaping. A teacher using a shaping procedure rewards successive approximations of the desired behavior, rather than waiting for the student to make a completely correct response. By rewarding successive approximation, the teacher helps ensure repeated success and keeps learners aimed in the right direction.

Passive Shaping. A passive shaping procedure is often used with children who cannot or will not imitate or model behavior. The teacher demonstrates the desired behavior and then actively helps the student imitate the behavior.

Token Reinforcement. This process involves the systematic use of either tangible reinforcers, such as food, tokens, or grades, or intangible reinforcers, such as a smile or praise from the teacher to reinforce behaviors. Generally, a token reinforcement system, or "economy," involves (1) rules specifying which behaviors will be rewarded and which will not; (2) a system for issuing the tokens that does not disrupt the activity that is occurring; (3) a system for exchanging the tokens for tangible items, like prizes, or for special privileges.

Self-Specification of Contingencies. Allowing children to participate in the selection of backup reinforcers in a token economy can significantly improve the economy's effectiveness. This procedure can also help the teacher determine what a particular child enjoys doing, and the teacher can often use this knowledge to encourage the child to do something he or she does not enjoy. For example, if reading is a low preference for a child, but listening to records with earphones is a high preference, the teacher can make listening to records contingent on the child's reading appropriately. This is called contingency contracting.

Programmed Instruction. Under this practice several rather discrete steps are involved. The student is presented with relatively brief segments of content, is required to respond actively, and is given immediate feedback about performance on each step. The steps are progressively sequenced from lesser to greater difficulty, and the feedback information can be used in the next level task. Instruction using programmed instruction and task analysis has revolutionized some types of special education.

Self-Reinforcement. As the student becomes familiar with the token economy and the effects of appropriate behavior, behavior will gradually become influenced more by self-reward than by rewards from others. In addition, the student often begins to model the behavior exhibited by authority figures. If those figures have clearly defined high standards of performance, the student will often adopt similar standards. Although self-reinforcement is often thought of as the end result of successful behavioral programming, it does require specific attention on the part of the teacher.

Establishing Clear Rules and Directions. In all the behavior modification procedures described it is important that rules and directions be stated clearly. The relationship between expectations and conditions for reward must be understood by both teachers and students. Developing "contracts" between teachers and students is common in many special education settings, because contracts permit classroom rules and directions to be altered to meet individual children's needs. Contracts can also be made with the entire class to help establish an effective learning environment.

PROCEDURES USED TO "DECREASE" BEHAVIORS

Now we examine some procedures for "decreasing" behavior described by O'Leary and O'Leary (1972, pp. 32–38).

Extinction. The extinction procedure involves selectively ignoring inappropriate behavior. Extinction has been used effectively in a wide variety of settings: It is especially effective when coupled with the reinforcement of appropriate behavior. However, some inappropriate behaviors (self-mutilation, aggressive acts) cannot be safely ignored.

Reinforcing Behavior Incompatible with Undesirable Behavior.
Reinforcement is often used with extinction. Basically, it involves analyzing the undesirable behavior to determine what behaviors would decrease the probability that the undesirable behavior would occur. For example, children being out of their seats without permission is undesirable. The teacher can generally decrease the frequency with which they leave their seats by (1) reinforcing the children when they remain seated, and (2) ignoring the children when they are out of their seats.

Soft Reprimands.
Often, teachers use unobtrusive reprimands in conjunction with extinction. By keeping the reprimand between the teacher and the child, the teacher reduces the chances that the child will be reinforced by increased class attention.

Time-Out.
This technique involves removing students to a position in which they cannot be reinforced in any way for a specified period of time. Time-out procedures may involve removing the child to an isolation room, changing the child's seat to a remote area of the classroom, or seating the child in a carrel or cubicle. The specific technique used is often determined by school policy and the availability of other resources.

Relaxation.
Children who are easily frustrated, agitated, or angered often benefit from being taught how to relax. A relaxed child will often exhibit fewer symptoms of emotional or behavioral disorders than one who is not relaxed.

Gradual Presentation of Fearful Stimuli in Vivo.
A gradual process is frequently used to decrease or eliminate unrealistic fears or phobias. For example, a child who has a fear of school might at first be placed in real-life *(in vivo)* situations that don't resemble school and then systematically brought into increasingly comparable situations and reinforced for appropriate behavior at each step along the way.

Desensitization.
This procedure consists of completely relaxing individuals and then asking them to talk about situations that arouse anxiety. It has been found that after repeated sessions clients are able to control anxiety or fears and maintain their relaxed state. The desensitization procedure is not commonly used with young children, but it has been used with considerable success with young adults and older individuals.

Response Cost.
Commonly used in contingency management or token economy programs, the response cost procedure involves establishing rules for removing or deducting tokens or rewards for inappropriate behavior. This type of system helps the children understand that a behavior can have either a positive or a negative consequence. Students quickly learn the effects of a particular behavior and begin to control ensuing acts.

This list of applied behavior analysis methods does not include all the procedures currently in use, but it does feature those most important in special education. These procedures, along with increased use of educational technology, have had a great impact on special education as it is practiced today.

Applied behavior analysis is a powerful tool for teachers. Because it is easy to misuse these techniques, all teachers should make sure they understand the princples and implications of behavioral methods. Applied behavior analysis is *not* used solely to eliminate undesirable behavior, as many people seem to believe. Rather, these techniques can be used quite effectively to help improve academic and social skills.

OVERVIEW

Mental Retardation.
In Chapter 8 we look at the nature of retardation, genetic and environmental causes, and major methods of prevention and treatment. New information on etiology and genetic counseling reflects current research. We also examine the learning characteristics of persons with mental retardation and describe contemporary educational and service programs. We conclude the chapter with a discussion of a new model for services.

Learning Disabilities. Children with learning disabilities are the largest group currently receiving special education services. We begin Chapter 9 with an introduction to the controversy surrounding the definition of learning diabilities and to the process of identifying children with learning disabilities. More detailed attention is then given to the academic subject disorders and to the psychological process disorders, social-emotional disorders and to motor skill disorders. We conclude with a stimulating look at the trends in the field and new theories about causes and treatments.

Behavioral Disorders. As with learning disabilities, controversy surrounds the definition and labeling of children with behavioral disorders. After examining the characteristics of behavior disorders, we go on to describe the classification and diagnosis of children. Causes of behavior disorders are examined from both the biophysical and environmental perspectives. Educational and treatment options are our final topics.

Severe Developmental Disabilities. Placing children with severe developmental disabilities in public schools is a relatively recent phenomenon that was brought about largely by federal and state litigation and legislation. In Chapter 11, we begin with a discussion of the diversity of characteristics of persons with severe developmental disabilities. The major issue of their educability is analyzed, and we devote attention to the process of educational assessment. We conclude the chapter with a look at contemporary service delivery options.

Gifted and Talented. The education of the gifted and talented has long been neglected. The reasons for this neglect and many of the misconceptions about the gifted and talented serve as a basis for our discussion. Our look at characteristics and identification procedures of the gifted leads to a comprehensive description of educational provisions, trends in gifted education and barriers to achievement. Of particular interest to special education teachers is the discussion of gifted handicapped children.

After returning from a two-week vacation, I was met by Bernie, a 55-year-old former resident of the BGAMR group home. During my absence he had graduated from our program and along with another former resident moved into an apartment in the community. With a smile from ear to ear he shook my hand and said, "I'm out, you know. I have an apartment and I want you to come sometime for dinner. I'm happy." . . .

Bernie, unfortunately, spent 47 years of his life in one institution or another because there simply was no place else for him. When he was referred to us in February 1976, we were told by a state official that we were wasting our time. . . .

"Chalk one up for Bernie," I thought. . . . If one restricts an individual to his home, school or work with little or no time for recreation, responsibility, challenges or the dignity of risk and trying new things, then surely the mind is not being exercised and stimulated to its full potential and will probably remain dull.

After 47 years of institutionalization, Bernie arrived at the group home, still unable to write the first letter of his name. Since this time, 2 years and 3 months later, Bernie has learned to write his name by attending adult education classes. Bernie has learned to budget his money on a week-to-week money management system. He makes up his own menus using a pictorial cookbook, does his own laundry and grocery shopping, prepares his own meals and tends to all his own personal hygiene needs. . . .

Bernie was adjudicated incompetent when he was a child and after forty-seven years, on December 20, 1977, he was restored complete citizen rights by a Fayette County judge.

Bernie has held the same job as a kitchen helper at a local hotel for nearly five years. . . . Bernie has earned his dream — respect, trust, faith, and above all his freedom and the right to be a human being just like each of us. . . . He has paid a tremendously unfair price for being mentally retarded and a little different, when all he ever needed was . . . a little faith and someone who really cared. . . .

Source: From the *Blue Grass Association for Mental Retardation News, June-July,* 1978. Reprinted by permission.

8

Mental Retardation

William H. Berdine

William H. Berdine is an Associate Professor and Coordinator of the certification program for teachers of the trainable mentally handicapped at the University of Kentucky. He has taught classes for the mentally retarded in both elementary and secondary settings. Current areas of interest are the design and implementation of community-based education programs for low-incidence handicapping conditions.

The vignette about "Bernie" on the preceding page reflects a new advocacy position for community-based services for persons with mental retardation. This position, which has evolved slowly over the past 20 years, reflects a shift in the emphasis of programs and services from the mildly retarded to the more severely and profoundly retarded person. The process has not necessarily been an easy one for anyone involved. Both professional and lay persons have had to make difficult decisions concerning where to spend rapidly dwindling funds. Often decisions meant that some who would have been served in the past would not be as well served in the future. Out of this process, it is to be hoped, the person with mental retardation, regardless of educational classification, has gained a broader, more normalized and humane continuum of services.

The shift of emphasis to the severely retarded can be attributed in part to federal legislation. For example, the preface to the Rehabilitation Act of 1973 (PL 93-112) states that there should be a "special emphasis on services to those with the most severe handicaps." The same act also states that those with the most severe handicaps should be served first. The highest priority of PL 94-142 is on serving unserved children and the most severely handicapped who are underserved. More recently, the Comprehensive Rehabilitation Services

Amendments of 1978 (PL 95-1780) add, "Comprehensive services [should be provided] to handicapped persons who may not be ready for vocational rehabilitation" (Haywood, 1979, p. 430). The intention of recent legislation is clearly to bring the severely handicapped into programs they were previously ineligible for.

DEFINING MENTAL RETARDATION: PROBLEMS AND ISSUES

> **You should be able to define mental retardation.**

Why has a satisfactory definition of mental retardation been difficult to develop?

The development of a satisfactory definition of mental retardation has proven difficult for several reasons: There is little agreement about the criteria that should be used to assess intelligence and adaptive behavior; measuring instruments are often not as precise as we want; and the needs of the different professional groups concerned with the mentally retarded vary widely. Each professional group considers the problems of the mentally retarded from a different perspective, and the groups rarely share a common training philosophy or similar goals. Because the interests and orientations of professional groups differ, it is unlikely that a universally acceptable definition will be developed. For the educator, a useful definition of mental retardation should offer clear criteria that can be used to identify retarded children who need special education services.

What are three criteria for a definition of mental retardation?

According to MacMillan (1982), a definition of mental retardation should meet three criteria. First, the conditions that must be met before an individual is classified as retarded should be specifically stated. Second, every retarded person must share the elements described in the definition. Third, those who are not classified as retarded must fail to exhibit at least one of the elements of the definition.

CONTEMPORARY DEFINITIONS OF MENTAL RETARDATION

Two definitions of mental retardation are currently being widely discussed. These are the behavioral definition and the definition proposed by the American Association on Mental Deficiency (AAMD).

A Behavioral Definition. The articulation of the behavioral definition is generally attributed to Bijou (1966, p. 2), who stated that "a retarded individual is one who has a limited repertoire of behavior shaped by events that constitute his history." In his definition Bijou emphasizes observable behavior and pays little or no attention to nonobservable internal mental processes.

What are the problems with the behavioral definition?

The behavioral definition of mental retardation quite often presents problems to special educators who have not been trained in applied behavioral analysis. Neisworth and Smith (1978) point out that a major shortcoming is its failure to quantify what is meant by a limited behavioral repertoire. In other words, the definition does not describe the point at which the limitations in a person's repertoire of behaviors indicate that he or she is retarded.

MacMillan and Forness (1973) point out that this model does not take into account some of the more widely accepted concepts regarding human growth and development that were pioneered by Piaget and other developmental psychologists. Nevertheless, the behavioral approach has important implications for teaching retarded children, and many educators subscribe to it.

The American Association on Mental Deficiency Definition.

The revised 1983 AAMD definition has found the widest acceptance of any, but even this definition is not universally accepted. The AAMD definition has been revised frequently over the past two decades (Grossman, 1973, 1977, 1983; Heber, 1959, 1961). In its current form it represents a compromise between the needs of those who require statistical objectivity (e.g., IQ test scores) and those who require environmental performance data (e.g., adaptive behavior assessment). This is the 1983 AAMD definition of mental retardation:

> Mental retardation refers to significantly subaverage general intellectual functioning resulting in or associated with concurrent impairments in adaptive behavior and manifested during the developmental period.

What are the key aspects of mental retardation as defined by the AAMD?

The key terms in the 1983 AAMD definition are defined by Grossman (1983) as follows:

— General intellectual functioning is operationally defined as the results obtained by assessment with one or more of the individually administered standardized general intelligence tests developed for that purpose.
— Significantly subaverage is defined as an IQ of 70 or below on standardized measures of intelligence. This upper limit is intended as a guideline and could be extended upward depending on the reliability of the test used. This particularly applies to children in schools and similar settings whose impaired behavior is clinically determined to be due to deficits in reasoning and judgment.
— Impairments in adaptive behavior are defined as significant limitations in an individual's effectiveness in meeting the standards of maturation, learning, personal independence, and/or social responsibilities that are expected for his or her age level and cultural group as determined by standardized clinical assessment scales.
— Developmental period is defined as the period between conception and the eighteenth birthday. Developmental deficits may be manifested by slow,

arrested, or incomplete development resulting from brain damage, degenerative processes in the central nervous system, or regression from previously normal states due to psychosocial factors.

What are the implications of the AAMD's upper limit for IQ scores?

The IQ Controversy Continues. Why have IQ scores been retained among the diagnostic criteria for mental retardation despite the professional controversy concerning both the use of the term and the tests from which it is derived? As Grossman (1983, p. 18) explains, "The 1983 classification system is based on empirical and scientific evidence and reflects the state-of-the-art on relevant issues." In previous AAMD manuals, an equivalent but slightly different upper limit IQ for identifying persons with mental retardation was recommended, namely, an IQ under two standard deviations below the mean test score. This arrangement unfortunately resulted in different upper limits, because not all assessment instruments use the same standard deviation figure.

The AAMD's change toward a more liberal interpretation of an upper limit for an IQ classification of mental retardation is a significant change for educators. As Grossman (1983, p. 23) points out, "treating the IQ with some flexibility permits the inclusion of persons having higher IQs than 70 who truly need special education or other programs." Educators must develop procedures to ensure that this new flexibility of interpretation is not used to place children inappropriately in special education programs.

PROBE 8-1
Definitions of Mental Retardation

1. What is Bijou's behavioral definition of mental retardation?

2. For the special educator, what is the principal value of a behavioral definition?

3. What is one criticism of the behavioral definition?

4. The most widely accepted definition of mental retardation is that of the

   a. APA   d. CEC
   b. AAMD   e. ABS
   c. AMA

5. Write the current definition of mental retardation proposed by the American Association on Mental Deficiency.

6. The developmental period is the period between the child's _____ and age _____ .

INTELLIGENCE AND MENTAL RETARDATION

> **You should be able to discuss intellectual assessment as it relates to the identification of mentally retarded children.**

Defining the nature of "intelligence" is a central concern of most educational endeavors for the mentally retarded. Over the years numerous definitions of intelligence have been suggested (e.g., Bruner, 1964; Cattell, 1971; Guilford, 1956; Hebb, 1942; Piaget, 1950). These definitions have ranged from the simplistic "intelligence is what is measured by intelligence tests" to the complex conceptualization of Guilford (1956), who proposed a structure that describes 120 types of intelligence.

What considerations are important in defining intelligence?

For the special education teacher it seems appropriate to define intelligence in terms of children's interactions with their environment: how well they meet the demands made on them by their school, family, community, and other social institutions. A person who is consistently unable to meet those demands without some form of special assistance is generally considered mentally retarded. To be classified as mentally retarded, a child must be unable to demonstrate behavior based on intellectual functioning that is appropriate for that person's age or social situation (Salvia, 1978). To put it another way, the mentally retarded are incompetent in behaviors that their society believes to be indicative of intellectual functioning.

It is important to distinguish between intellectual incompetence and other forms of behavioral incompetence. For example, blind children may be incapable of performing some academic or motor tasks at the age considered normal for seeing children, but this is because of their visual impairment, not an intellectual defect. Mentally retarded children may be willing to perform a task and have all of the necessary senses but be unable to perform it even with additional training. The concept of incompetence is also important in distinguishing the mentally retarded from those with deviant behavior. For example, mentally retarded children may be willing to perform tasks appropriate for their age but be unable to perform the tasks. Incompetence in adapting to the demands of the environment is another factor to be considered when distinguishing retarded children from those with normal intelligence.

How is intellectual incompetence different from sensory impairment or behavioral deviancy?

ASSESSMENT OF INTELLECTUAL RETARDATION

What is a standardized test?

For educational purposes, mental retardation is generally considered a child's inadequacy in performing certain behaviors that society values and that are appropriate for the child's age group. Intelligence tests are used to assess the intellectual ability that theoretically determines whether a person can perform educational tasks. The forms of different intelligence tests vary widely, but the majority are *standardized*. As noted in Chapter 2, a standardized test is one that was developed and tried out on a group of children who all received the same instructions, who took the test under the same conditions, and whose responses were all interpreted the same way. The test items, which are devised by the test developers, are designed to determine the level of some aspect of intellectual functioning. If a particular culture believes that the test measures qualities that are important for that culture, the tests become a generally accepted means of measuring intellectual functioning in that culture.

The most frequently used intelligence tests yield two types of scores, an intelligence quotient (IQ) and a mental age (MA). Most of the commonly used IQ tests are designed such that the average IQ is 100. In theory, this means that if a test such as the Stanford-Binet Intelligence Scale (Terman and Merrill, 1973) was administered to a large number of children, the test scores would range from very low to very high, but the average, or mean, score would be 100. If the scores were plotted on a graph, the result would be a bell-shaped curve, called the *normal curve* (see Figure 8-1). A statistical computation yields a figure known as the *standard deviation* (SD), which can be used to determine where a person's score falls in relation to others in the population. For example, the standard deviation for the Stanford-Binet is 16. If you look at Figure 8-1, you will see that one SD below the mean is 84. A person who receives a score of 100 on the Stanford-Binet is average; about 50 percent of the population scored below that average and 50 percent scored above it. Between each pair of SD cutoff points is written the percentage of the population that falls between them. By starting at the left of the normal curve, you can estimate the number of people who fall below a particular score by adding the percentages. Thus, the child who scored 84 would have a score that was higher than about 16 percent of the population and lower than about 84 percent. Conversely, a person who scored 116 would have a score that was higher than about 84 percent of the general population and lower than approximately 16 percent.

The scores shown in Figure 8-1 represent plus or minus 4 standard deviations from the mean. In theory, however, the scores could go into infinity, because intelligence does not have absolute limits. Intelligence is viewed by most developers of intelligence tests as a continuum of abilities and not really a discrete or finite entity.

The determination of a score below which children are considered retarded is an issue of great social, political, and educational concern. As mentioned earlier, intellectual ability — behavior considered socially valuable and appropriate — is defined by the predominant cultural group, which as a result determines what will be considered normal intelligence as well. In special education, the IQ score of 70 adopted by the American Association on Mental Deficiency (Grossman, 1983) is generally considered the score below which children are described as exhibiting mental retardation. Some variation in cutoff scores is found among different intelligence tests. For example, the

Figure 8-1
The Normal Curve

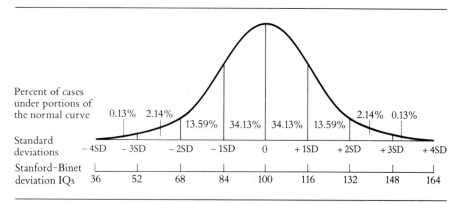

standard deviation for the Wechsler Intelligence Scale for Children (WISC) is 15, and the cutoff for retardation is 69 (Wechsler, 1974). Table 8-1 illustrates the cutoff scores established by the American Association on Mental Deficiency (AAMD) for different levels of mental retardation. Notice that the scores are different because of variations in the test's standard deviations.

PROBLEMS WITH USING IQ SCORES

The use of IQ test scores in education presents a number of problems.

1. To provide useful scores a test must have been tried out on a large enough normative group to reflect the cultural, social, and economic variables that affect the children in a given classroom.

Table 8-1
Level of Retardation Indicated by IQ Range

Level of Retardation	*IQ Range*
Mild mental retardation	50–55 to approx. 70
Moderate mental retardation	35–40 to 50–55
Severe mental retardation	20–25 to 35–40
Profound mental retardation	Below 20 or 25
Unspecified classification	

Adapted from Grossman, H. *Manual on Terminology and Classification in Mental Retardation.* AAMD, 1983, p. 13.

2. The items in a particular test may measure a relatively small variety of behaviors. The IQ score derived from such a test should be considered in the context of the test items and the norm group.
3. A test score may be inaccurate and may not reflect a person's actual level of intellectual functioning.
4. An IQ score should be considered only in conjunction with information about the child's chronological age and home life, the resources of the child's school, and other environmental variables.
5. An IQ score is not very useful for planning the education of a particular child. The knowledge that one pupil has an IQ score of 70 and another has an IQ score of 75 does not help a teacher develop appropriate instruction.

How are the IQ scores of retarded children used?

Teachers should not overemphasize the importance of IQ scores. The major function of determining the IQs of retarded children is to identify them, place them in special programs, and obtain the funds necessary for operating the programs.

In spite of the limitations in their use, intelligence test scores are one of the most reliable types of data on children's performance, and they will probably continue to be used in the assessment of mental retardation. Today, however, most professional organizations such as the American Association on Mental Deficiency require the IQ test scores be corroborated with assessment information on adaptive behavior.

MEASURING ADAPTIVE BEHAVIOR

What is adaptive behavior?

The importance of adaptive behavior in determining whether a person should be diagnosed as mentally retarded has been recognized by the AAMD since 1959 (Grossman, 1983). The AAMD defines Adaptive Behavior as the quality of everyday performance in coping with environmental demands (Grossman, 1983, p. 42). The AAMD qualifies its definition by stating that "the quality of general adaptation is mediated by the level of intelligence. . . ." (Grossman, 1983, p. 42). This qualification clearly indicates that the two terms, adaptive behavior and intelligence, have a functional relationship. When the two terms are used by educators, it should always be kept in mind that the term Adaptive Behavior ". . . refers to what people do to take care of themselves and to relate to others in daily living rather than the abstract potential implied by intelligence" (Grossman, 1983, p. 42). Few researchers question that intelligence and adaptive behavior are related. The relationship is not, however, very well understood. Grossman (1977) noted that people at the same level of intellectual functioning may be at different levels of adaptive behavior. In 1983, Grossman also noted that "although there is some variability in level of competence on different dimensions of adaptive behavior, patterns of skills tend to develop or be performed with a fairly high degree of consistency" (Grossman, 1983, p. 46). All diagnoses of mental retardation should take into careful account both current intellectual functioning and adaptive behavior.

What are the four levels of impairment in adaptive behavior?

The AAMD recognizes four levels of adaptive behavior impairment: mild, moderate, severe, and profound. You will notice that these degrees of impairment are described with the same terms as intelligence. Adaptive behavior impairment is generally considered the result of problems in maturation, learning capacity, and social adjustment. Most assessment scales examine areas that special education teachers are familiar with, such as self-help (e.g., dressing), language and communication skills (e.g., writing a letter), self-direction and responsibility (e.g., doing a chore reliably), and relationships with others (e.g., playing with other children) (Helton, Workman, and Matuszek, 1982).

What are the problems in assessing adaptive behavior?

While the use of adaptive behavior assessment scales has become fairly routine for educational classification and placement purposes, their use is a subject of considerable debate among educators and persons involved in testing and test development. For example, one of the most widely used adaptive behavior assessment scales is the American Association on Mental Deficiency's Adaptive Behavior Scale (ABS) (Nihira, Foster, Shellhaas, and Leland, 1974). Both the reliability and validity of its Public School Version (ABS-PSV) (Lambert, Windmiller, Cole, and Figueroa, 1975) have been severely questioned (Helton, Workman, and Matuszek, 1982; Salvia and Ysseldyke, 1981). The appropriateness of the ABS-PSV for classification purposes has also been questioned. Helton et al. (1982) recommend the ABS-PSV only for educational program planning, and Salvia and Ysseldyke (1981, p. 443) appear to question its use outside of California, where its "norms appear representative." The criticisms leveled at the ABS-PSV are representative of criticisms of most of the other adaptive behavior scales. The major components of the AAMD's ABS are outlined in Table 8-2.

With the legal mandate to provide adaptive behavior as well as intelligence data for classification purposes in the area of mental retardation, better scales are needed. The 1983 revision of the Vineland Social Maturity Scale (VSMS) appears to have better reliability and validity and to have improved provisions for a representative norm population (Helton et al., 1982).

What is SOMPA?

One problem with both intelligence tests and adaptive behavior instruments concerns whether their norm populations are adequately representative of the general population and specifically of smaller subcultural and cultural groups. The System of Multicultural and Pluralistic Assessment (SOMPA) was designed by Mercer (1979) to compensate for any possibility of cultural discrimination. SOMPA attempts to provide nondiscriminatory assessment of public-school-age children (chronological ages 5 to 11) by collecting information on three different dimensions — the child's medical circumstances, social system, and "pluralistic" abilities. The medical dimension is concerned with data relevant to pathology, disease, or any other body system dysfunction that might account for the person's behavior during the data collection. The social system dimension is concerned with the extent to which the person is currently meeting the expectations of the social system of which he or she is a member. The pluralistic dimension is essentially a measure of the person's

Table 8-2
Components of the AAMD Adaptive Behavior Scale

Part One	Part Two

I. Independent Functioning
  A. Eating
  B. Toilet Use
  C. Cleanliness
  D. Appearance
  E. Care of Clothing
  F. Dressing and Undressing
  G. Travel
  H. General Independent Functioning
II. Physical Development
  A. Sensory Development
  B. Motor Development
III. Economic Activity
  A. Money Handling and Budgeting
  B. Shopping Skills
IV. Language Development
  A. Expression
  B. Comprehension
  C. Social Language Development
V. Numbers and Time
VI. Domestic Activity
  A. Cleaning
  B. Kitchen Duties
  C. Other Domestic Activities
VII. Vocational Activity
VIII. Self-Direction
  A. Initiative
  B. Perseverance
  C. Leisure Time
IX. Responsibility
X. Socialization
	I. Violent and Destructive Behavior
	II. Antisocial Behavior
	III. Rebellious Behavior
	IV. Untrustworthy Behavior
	V. Withdrawal
	VI. Stereotyped Behavior and Odd Mannerisms
	VII. Inappropriate Interpersonal Manners
	VIII. Unacceptable Vocal Habits
	IX. Unacceptable or Eccentric Habits
	X. Self-abusive Behavior
	XI. Hyperactive Tendencies
	XII. Sexually Aberrant Behavior
	XIII. Psychological Disturbances
	XIV. Use of Medications

Source: ABS Manual (Fogleman, 1975, pp. 6-7).

ability to solve problems as such; it is intended to determine a person's potential for learning or current level of intelligence. The SOMPA is of interest to special educators working with Hispanics, blacks, and Caucasians, who were represented in the SOMPA norm population.

What data sources should be utilized in determining mental retardation?

Of particular interest to special educators conducting adaptive behavior assessment is the social-system model data collection instrument, the Adaptive Behavior Inventory for Children (ABIC). Salvia and Ysseldyke (1981) and Helton et al. (1982) question the overall reliability of SOMPA and its use outside of California, but the reliability of the ABIC alone is reported to be within acceptable limits. ABIC is essentially an interview instrument, where either parents or other persons knowledgeable about the child being assessed are questioned about 242 items covering six adaptive behavior areas — family, community, peer relations, nonacademic school roles, earner/consumer, and self-maintenance. The classroom teacher is not intended as the primary source of information but could certainly be involved in either all or part of the interview process of ABIC. Helton et al. (1982) cite the length of time it takes to administer ABIC, its restricted age range, and its lack of information on educational programming as the instrument's major weak points. The 1980s will offer many opportunities to validate further adaptive behavior assessment instruments such as ABIC and the new version of VSMS. It is to be hoped that they will add to the credibility of adaptive behavior data as meaningful components of the educational assessment process.

Neither an intelligence test score nor an adaptive behavior assessment score is comprehensive enough to be used as a sole criterion for determining that a child is mentally retarded. Not only would the use of a single measure be unwise professionally, but also it is illegal under the provisions of PL 94-142. The best procedure is to use data from a variety of sources, including assessments of intelligence and adaptive behavior, anecdotal records from teachers, an analysis of the home and family situation, direct observation of the child's behavior in the classroom, and measures of school achievement.

PROBE 8-2
Intelligence and Mental Retardation

1. T F A diagnosis of mental retardation should never be made solely on the basis of an intelligence test.

2. The popularly used tests of intelligence generally report a summary of performance in the form of an _____ score.

3. The AAMD requires that a child's _____ and _____ be considered in diagnosing mental retardation.

4. What is the range of IQ scores for each of the following levels of retardation, according to the AAMD? (Do not use a particular IQ test as a referent.)
   a. Mild
   b. Moderate
   c. Severe
   d. Profound

5. T   F   The AAMD's Adaptive Behavior Scale (ABS) is the only adaptive behavior instrument that research has documented as being both reliable and valid for use with persons exhibiting mental retardation.

6. T   F   All IQ tests have a mean score of 100 and a standard deviation of 16.

7. List four problems involved in the use and interpretation of IQ tests.

8. T   F   A special education teacher could not teach if he did not have the IQ scores of the mentally retarded children in the class.

9. Define adaptive behavior.

10. What is a problem encountered in measuring adaptive behavior that is not encountered in measuring intelligence?

11. List four components of adaptive behavior.

12. The adaptive behavior scale that is a part of SOMPA is:
    a. ABS
    b. ABIC
    c. AAMD
    d. VSMS

CLASSIFICATION AND PREVALENCE OF THE MENTALLY RETARDED

You should be able to describe the different systems used to classify mentally retarded children.

Over the years a number of systems have been used to classify mentally retarded children. Several of these systems have been alluded to in previous sections of this chapter, where terms such as mild, moderate, severe, and profound were used to refer to diagnostic categories.

Gelof reported in 1963 that 23 classification systems were being used in English-speaking countries alone. Classification is necessary because the retarded are such a heterogeneous group. Placing those with common characteristics in categories makes communications among professionals more productive. It is also assumed that appropriate classification leads to placement in appropriate treatment and educational programs.

There have been three primary systems of classification: according to etiology, clinical type, and severity of symptoms.

CLASSIFICATION ACCORDING TO ETIOLOGY

What is an etiological classification system?

It has at different periods been fashionable to classify mentally retarded children according to the cause (etiology) of their retardation. A number of etiological classification systems simply divided the children into two groups: those for whom a cause of the retardation could be identified and those for whom a cause could not be identified. Some of the terms used during the past 50 years to classify known and unknown etiologies are given in Table 8-3.

These early etiological classification systems were useless for educational purposes and were often considered offensive by parents. Imagine being told that your child had "garden-variety mental retardation," or that his or her retardation was "familial in nature."

What is the interaction hypothesis?

The cultural-familial classification, while not widely used by educators, is still used by some psychologists and social workers who believe that mental retardation is often caused by a combination of environmental and hereditary factors. This belief, called the interaction hypothesis, is based on the assumption that mental retardation of unknown origin is caused by a combination of biological weaknesses and environmental deprivation. Almost all cases of cul-

Table 8-3

Known Etiology		*Unknown Etiology*	
Extrinsic	Tredgold, 1937	Intrinsic	Tredgold, 1908
Pathological	Lewis, 1933	Subcultural	Lewis, 1933
Exogenous	Strauss & Lehtinen, 1947	Endogenous	Strauss & Lehtinen, 1947
		Garden Variety	Sarason, 1953
		Cultural-familial	Zigler, 1967

Source: Donald L. MacMillan, Mental Retardation in School and Society, 2/e, Tab. 2-2 copyright: © 1982, Donald L. MacMillan.

tural-familial retardation are found in severely economically depressed communities, and many professionals attribute them to the effects of malnutrition and other dietary problems in combination with the psychological effects of poverty. The results of research into the effects of sociocultural factors on intellectual performance are inconclusive. The data do show that environmental factors such as poverty can seriously affect the intellectual development of children, and there is some evidence that heredity sometimes limits intellectual development. The environment a child grows up in clearly influences whether he or she achieves maximum hereditary potential, a fact that has significant implications for early childhood and parent education.

Retarded children are still classified according to etiology by physicians and psychologists. The 1983 AAMD *Manual on Terminology and Classification in Mental Retardation* lists ten medical classifications, including those based on the following causes: infections and intoxicants, trauma (injury), metabolism or nutrition, brain disease, conditions due to unknown prenatal influence, chromosomal abnormality, gestational disorders, psychiatric disorders, environmental influences, and others. Many of these causes will be explained in the section of this chapter on etiology.

CLASSIFICATION ACCORDING TO CLINICAL TYPE

Retarded children are also classified according to the clinical type of their retardation. In this classification system an attempt is made to separate the symptoms of the retardation from its causes. Like etiological classifications, clinical type classification systems are used primarily by physicians.

The cause of a particular clinical type of retardation may or may not be known. What is more, it is possible that within a given clinical classification the causes of some children's retardation will be known and the causes of the retardation of others unknown. For example, some types of cretinism (a thyroid deficiency) are caused by genetic problems and other types are caused by a lack of iodine in the diet. Children with both types exhibit similar symptoms, making the identification of the cause difficult.

What is a syndrome?

The word *syndrome* is often used in discussions of classifications according to clinical type. A syndrome is a cluster or constellation of symptoms. Perhaps the most common with respect to mental retardation is Down's syndrome, which will be discussed in the section on etiology.

Systems that classify children according to clinical type are of little use to educators. The wide variety of conditions and behaviors that characterize mentally retarded children make it impossible to fit them neatly into classifications made in this manner. Most children for whom this classification system is appropriate have distinct physical symptoms that are readily observable by the physician or diagnostician.

CLASSIFICATION ACCORDING TO SEVERITY OF SYMPTOMS

The earliest system that classified retardation according to the severity of its symptoms was developed by the American Association for the Study of the Feebleminded (later to become the American Association on Mental Deficiency) at the turn of the century. This organization used the term *moron* to denote those with IQ scores between 50 and 75, *imbecile* for those with IQs between 25 and 50, and *idiot* for those who had IQs below 25. Although this derogatory terminology has been eliminated from the professional literature, retarded children are still classified according to the severity of their deficits in intellect and adaptive behavior. You will remember that the AAMD classifies people's levels of retardation as mild, moderate, severe, and profound according to their IQ scores and their levels of adaptive behavior.

What is the most widely used classification system for the mentally retarded?

The classification system of the AAMD is the system currently used most widely by diagnosticians, and a system of educational classification that parallels the AAMD categories has evolved. Smith (1971) describes these categories as *educable mentally retarded, trainable mentally retarded,* and *severely/profoundly retarded.* (The term *handicapped* is frequently substituted for the term *retarded*.) The mildly retarded are called educable and the moderately retarded, trainable. The severely and profoundly retarded categories are the same under both systems.

What is the major difference between EMR, TMR, and S/PR?

Although IQ scores are usually one of the criteria used to differentiate the educable mentally retarded (EMR), trainable mentally retarded (TMR), and severely/profoundly retarded (S/PR), the major difference among these groups for special educators is in their educational needs. Children in different categories require different types of educational programs. As a result, schools set up separate classes and programs for children in different classifications, and teachers are trained and certified to work with children at a particular level of functioning. This classification system is currently the most useful one for special education programming.

PROBLEMS WITH CLASSIFICATION SYSTEMS

Each of the classification systems just discussed presents problems. For example, Smith (1971, pp. 12-13) described three problems encountered in attempts to classify mentally retarded children: "First, one is never able to gain total agreement between people on which dimensions or factors should be classified. . . . A second problem . . . is that of deciding on upper and lower boundaries within subgroups . . . A third . . . is in the assignment of individuals to a category."

What are some of the differences in programs for EMR and TMR students?

Problems in deciding what program a child should be placed in are particularly difficult when a child is near the cutoff point between the EMR and TMR classifications. Distinctions between the TMR and the S/PR are generally easier to make, but these too can present problems when one is dealing with children in the upper range of the S/PR classification and the lower range of the TMR classification.

It could be argued that it shouldn't matter what category a child is placed in, because the goal should always be to raise the child to a higher level of functioning. As a practical matter, however, it does make a difference, because almost all special education programs provide different kinds of education to those who have been classified as EMR and those who have been classified as TMR. Programs for the EMR generally focus on academic skills such as reading, arithmetic, language, and vocational training. These basic skill areas are taught to prepare the EMR child for independent living. The program for TMR children, on the other hand, generally focuses on the development of self-help skills and the survival skills needed for communication and coping with the demands of a community. The TMR child is prepared for living in a supervised environment and employment in facilities such as sheltered workshops. Placing a child in a program for the trainable mentally retarded would be a grave error if the child was capable of functioning in a program for the educable mentally retarded.

As you will have noticed, it is extremely important that decisions about the classification of retarded children be made cautiously. Children should be classified only when classification leads to the development of an appropriate educational program that will meet the needs of the child involved.

PREVALENCE OF MENTAL RETARDATION

See Chapter 1 for definitions of prevalence. It is important to know the number of retarded children in our society to plan for the provision of services, to obtain funding, and to estimate the number of teachers and other professionals needed to serve them.

What are some of the problems in determining prevalence?

The prevalence of mentally retarded individuals in our society is difficult to determine accurately. An actual census would be prohibitively expensive. The process of obtaining accurate figures is complicated by differing definitions, public apathy, and the reluctance to label a child as mentally retarded. As a result of these problems, estimates are based on studies of various communities; the results are extrapolated to cover the entire population. Many geographical, cultural, and social factors influence estimates. Finding a population that is sufficiently large and that reflects the composition of the entire population is a problem. These many variables have resulted in prevalence estimates varying from 0.6 percent to 15 percent of the population.

Current Estimates of Mental Retardation. Although the actual number of mentally retarded individuals in the population is not known, the consensus is that the prevalence is 1 percent (Tarjan, Wright, Eyman, and Kiernan, 1973). This means that about 1,000 people in a city of 100,000 are mentally retarded. The 1 percent prevalence estimate has been corroborated in studies conducted by Birch, Richardson, Baird, Horobin, and Illsley (1970); Heber (1970); and Mercer (1973), who actually conducted a census of a city of 100,000 people. Mercer (1973) noted that a one-dimensional definition of mental retardation (e.g., IQ scores only) might yield a prevalence rate approaching 3 percent. The use of multidimensional definitions that include both IQ and adaptive behavior, however, yields a prevalence rate of roughly 1 percent.

What is the traditional ratio of EMR to TMR to S/PR?

Traditionally, the ratio of EMR to TMR to S/PR is estimated to be 12:3:1 (or 75:20:5 in terms of percentages). This means that of a hundred identified mentally retarded children in the population, 75 can be expected to be in the educable range, 20 would be in the trainable range, and 5 would be in the severely/profoundly range. This ratio was fairly well confirmed by Mercer (1973) in her study of the community of 100,000 people.

PROBE 8-3
Classifications and Prevalence of the Mentally Retarded

1. List the three major systems used to classify mentally retarded children.

2. *Matching*
   _____ Severely/profoundly retarded   a. EMR
   _____ Moderately retarded   b. TMR
   _____ Mildly retarded   c. S/PR

3. Cite two problems in the use of classification systems for retarded children.

4. List the three categories in the classification system that are most useful for special education programming.

5. What is a syndrome?

6. T F   Retarded children should be classified only when classification leads to the development of an appropriate educational program.

7. The "traditional" prevalence of persons with mental retardation is _____ percent.

CAUSES AND PREVENTION OF RETARDATION

You should be able to describe the major causes of mental retardation.

For teachers, the cause of retardation in a particular child is of little importance. The teacher should be concerned more with the child's behavior and other characteristics than with the causes of his or her retardation. Why, then, have we included a discussion of causes? There are at least two reasons. First, as a teacher you will encounter a number of the terms and diagnostic labels in diagnostic reports, particularly medical ones. Second, you should be able to answer the questions of parents and other lay people. A knowledge of causes will make you a better rounded professional, even if the information is not directly applicable to teaching.

More than 250 causes of mental retardation have been indentified. It's hard to believe, but these causes account for only about 10 percent of the cases of mental retardation. In the remaining 90 percent, the physical or medical cause of the retardation cannot be pinpointed (Maloney and Ward, 1979).

GENETIC IRREGULARITIES

A review of some of the basic concepts of genetics is in order before we proceed to our discussion of retardation caused by genetic problems.

What is the functon of genes?

Genes are the basic units of heredity. They direct and control the processes of growth and development that occur in each of our cells. A defect in a gene can interrupt the biochemical processes that occur in the cells, which can in turn affect certain physical and mental characteristics.

The genes are located in *chromosomes,* of which every body cell has 46. At the moment of conception, 23 chromosomes from the sperm cell and 23 from the egg cell are combined to form a new cell of 46 chromosomes, which then begins to divide and ultimately forms a new human being.

When does a recessive gene determine a characteristic?

The genes are arranged along the chromosomes almost like matched strings of beads. When the chromosomes pair up at conception, the genes from both parents that relate to eye color, hair color, etc., are matched up with one another. A *dominant* gene generally determines a characteristic, regardless of the gene that it is matched up with on its paired chromosome. A *recessive* gene determines a characteristic only when it is matched up with a similar recessive gene on its paired chromosome. If two recessive genes do not match up, the offspring will not exhibit the trait that they are responsible for; in that case, however, the offspring will be a "carrier" of the trait and will have the potential of passing it on to future offspring if the recessive gene does match up with a recessive mate. Additional information on genes is available in the work of Gottesman (1963), from which this account has been taken.

What is a "carrier" of a genetic trait?

Dominant Gene Defects. Fortunately, mental retardation caused by single defective dominant genes is quite rare. Conditions such as tuberous sclerosis and neurofibromatosis are caused by dominant genes and result in severe retardation. These conditions are rare because the parents have the disorder themselves, and they frequently cannot pass on the traits because of sterility or lack of opportunity (Telford and Sawrey, 1977).

What are some of the problems that can be caused by recessive genes?

Recessive Gene Defects. A number of retarded children are born to seemingly normal parents. This is often the result of the inheritance of matching recessive genes from the child's parents. Recessive genes can cause problems in metabolism, endocrine disturbances, and cranial anomalies, any of which can result in retardation. These conditions are relatively rare, however.

Phenylketonuria (PKU) is a recessive gene disorder that affects the metabolism of proteins. PKU can be identified in infants by a simple blood test that should be routinely administered shortly after birth. The probability that the disorder will result in retardation can be reduced through a diet low in phenylalanine, one of the amino acids. There are several conditions that affect the metabolism of proteins (Robinson and Robinson, 1976).

Another recessive gene disorder is *galactosemia,* a condition that affects the metabolism of carbohydrates. If the disease is detected before brain damage has occurred, retardation can be prevented with a milk-free diet. Several other disorders of carbohydrate metabolism can also cause retardation (Telford and Sawrey, 1977).

Tay-Sachs disease affects the metabolism of fats; it is most prevalent in Jewish families. This disease can cause paralysis, blindness, and convulsions; it usually causes death by the time the child is three years old (Robinson and Robinson, 1976).

Cretinism, a disorder of the endocrine system, is characterized by lack of the thyroid hormone. Although this condition is sometimes caused by recessive genes, it can also be caused by a diet that is deficient in iodine. Early treatment with thyroxin can prevent some of the physical symptoms associated with cretinism, but persons with this disorder are almost always retarded (Robinson and Robinson, 1976).

Microcephaly is one of several cranial disorders that can be caused by recessive genes. Microcephalic children are generally short and have small skulls, curved spines, and rather severe retardation. This condition can also be caused by nongenetic factors such as exposure of the mother to excessive dosages of x-rays during pregnancy (MacMillan, 1982).

What is the most common condition involving chromosomal aberrations?

Chromosomal Aberrations. Retardation is also caused occasionally by improper cell division, which can result in cells that have an abnormal structure. The most common condition involving chromosomal aberrations is *Down's syndrome.* (The term *syndrome,* you will remember, means a constellation or cluster of symptoms.) Down's syndrome used to be called *mongolism,* primarily because children with this syndrome have almond-shaped eyes that slightly resemble those of the Mongol race. Down's syndrome children have three number 21 chromosomes (called trisomy-21). Children with Down's syndrome constitute about 10 percent of the moderately-severely retarded population. The risk of having a Down's syndrome child is related to the age of the mother. Between the ages of 20 and 30, the risk is one in 1,500; *amniocentesis* can determine whether a pregnant woman is carrying a child with Down's syndrome or other chromosomal aberrations. In this test, a small portion of the amniotic fluid that surrounds the fetus is examined.

A recently identified chromosomal aberration, *Fragile-X Syndrome* (fra [X]), has been diagnosed as a cause of mental retardation (Giraud, Aymes, Mattei, and Mattei, 1976; Harvey, Judge, and Wiener, 1977; Turner and Opitz, 1980; Brown et al., 1981; Bishop, 1982). The syndrome is inherited in the same fashion as a recessive gene defect. This is because males have only one X chromosome (XY) and females have two (XX), and the syndrome affects the X chromosome. This means that the syndrome is typically exhibited only in males. Epidemiological studies give an estimated incidence of 0.92 per 1,000 males (Herbst and Miller, 1980), making it the second leading genetic aberration resulting in mental retardation, Down's syndrome being the leading cause.

What is fragile-X syndrome?

Behaviorally, fra (X) typically results in moderate to severe mental retardation. Research reports from the New York State Institute for Basic Research in Developmental Disabilities (Brown et al., 1981) indicate that affected males have no strikingly abnormal features except for long faces and large ears. Adults often have abnormally large testicles. Prenatal diagnosis is possible with amniocentesis. Fragile-X has also been linked to cases previously diagnosed as autism (Brown et al., 1982). (See Chapter 10 for a discussion of autism.) A full understanding of fra (X) remains in the future, but the initial breakthrough linking it to persons with mental retardation is significant and has direct implications for those concerned with the prevention of mental retardation.

Genetic Counseling. The advances of contemporary science in the area of human heredity and genetic research have opened new vistas for understanding prenatal growth and development. It is estimated that existing prenatal genetic analysis procedures can be used to detect at least 1,364 genetic disorders (McKusick, 1978). Once these modern medical techniques become generally available to all persons from all segments of society, it will be easier to provide all would-be parents with accurate genetic counseling.

What should be the function of genetic counseling?

The function of genetic counseling should be twofold; first, to inform interested persons of their genetic makeup as individuals and as parents; and second, if pregnancy occurs, to offer parents, in a nondirective manner, information about the probable genetic predisposition of their unborn child. In most segments of American society this form of genetic counseling is generally available only for those known to be at risk. For example, the children of a father with Huntington's Chorea would be in the at-risk category for producing offspring who would be classified either as carriers of the disease or who would actually exhibit the disorder in middle age. This genetic disease is characterized by progressive neuromotor disability (cerebral palsy), chorea (spasmodic movement) of the limbs and facial muscles, speech dysfunction, and mental deterioration.

In 1983, Gusella et al. reported a major breakthrough in regard to Huntington's Chorea, the identification of the fourth human chromosome as the etiological location of disease (Gusella et al., 1983). With this information, it will be possible to develop a predictive test for families with a history of Huntington's disease. Currently, families with a history of Huntington's have to wait for the disease to exhibit its symptoms. Typically, the symptoms do not become readily evident until middle age, so a predictive test would be a great asset in counseling at-risk families.

What is chorionic villi sampling?

Another genetic defect diagnostic procedure that has great significance for pregnant women at risk for producing a defective child is *chorionic villi* sampling. Unlike amniocentesis, which is typically performed after the sixteenth week of pregnancy, chorionic villi sampling can be performed optimally any time between the eighth and tenth weeks of pregnancy (Cowart, 1983). The procedure also differs from amniocentesis in that it does not require puncturing the womb to collect an amniotic fluid sample for genetic analysis. Chorionic villi sampling involves collecting a sample of approximately 30 milligrams from the chorion tissue surrounding the developing fetal placenta. The sample is obtained by passing a "16 cm plastic catheter with a 1.5 mm flexible aluminum obturator through the vagina into the uterus and up to the chorionic villi under ultrasound guidance" (Cowart, 1983, p. 1,249). Figure 8-2 illustrates the procedure and the location of the chorionic villi.

While it is not really possible to determine the exact number of genetic disorders that have mental retardation as a concomitant condition, it is known that each year more than 250,000 American babies are born with physical or mental defects of varying severity, in more than 7 percent of all births (March of Dimes, 1984). The increasing availability of genetic counseling and prenatal genetic diagnostic techniques adds a new and important aspect to efforts to prevent mental retardation.

PROBLEMS DURING PREGNANCY

During what trimester of pregnancy can prenatal factors have the most serious consequences?

A number of factors that can cause retardation can affect a woman during pregnancy. These prenatal factors have the most serious consequences during the first three months of pregnancy, although some factors can endanger the fetus at any point during gestation.

A number of prenatal factors that can (but sometimes don't) cause retardation have been described by Berlin (1978). Maternal disease such as serious *kidney disease* or *diabetes mellitus* is one such factor. It can cause a number of complications during pregnancy. Certain drugs, exposure to large doses of radiation, and poor maternal nutrition can also harm the fetus.

Infections are also a major cause of retardtion. *Rubella,* or German measles, in the first trimester of pregnancy can have disastrous consequences. Rubella can now be prevented with vaccinations. *Syphilis* is another infectious disease that can injure the fetus.

Figure 8-2
Chorionic Villi Sampling

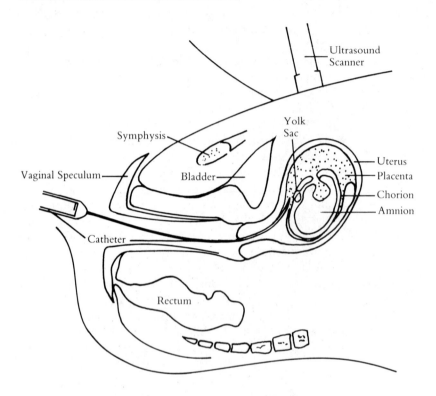

Source: Journal of the American Medical Association, Sept. 9, 1983, Vol. 250, No. 10, p.1249.

What is Rh incompatibility?

Rh incompatibility can also have serious consequences. A woman with Rh negative blood who is impregnated by an Rh positive male has a chance of producing a fetus with Rh positive blood. When this occurs, the mother's body produces antibodies that attack the fetus as they would attack a foreign substance that has entered the body. Rh incompatibility rarely affects a first-born child; a vaccine called RhoGam has been developed that prevents Rh factor problems in later pregnancies. In some cases it is necessary to give the child a blood transfusion to eliminate antibodies that are damaging to the child's tissues.

There is also some evidence that LSD, heroin, and cigarette smoking can negatively affect the fetus (MacMillan, 1982). Pregnant women should limit their use of tobacco and use only those drugs that are recommended by a physician.

What impact can alcohol have on a developing fetus?

The effect of alcohol on the developing fetus has been the subject of much concern and research. There is a definite link between Fetal Alcohol Syndrome (FAS) and mental retardation. Research by Ouellette et al., (1976, 1977) indicates that FAS may be the third most common cause of mental retardation. Furey (1982), citing reports from Sandmaier (1978), Kaminski, Rumeau-Rouquette, and Schwartz (1978), and Hanson, Streisguth, and Smith (1978), suggests that an average daily consumption of 89 ml (approximately 3 ounces) or more of absolute alcohol (the equivalent of three "hard" drinks) per day presents high risks to the fetus. Scientists studying FAS are not certain about the amount of alochol consumption acceptable without risk to the fetus, but the following observations seem to reflect a consensus concerning daily consumption of absolute alcohol:

Up to 1 ounce . . . . . . Little risk
1 to 2 ounces . . . . Moderate risk
2 ounces or more . . . Significant risk

Until we are more certain about the effects of alcohol on the developing fetus, it would seem appropriate to warn all women not to drink any alcohol during pregnancy. Additionally, the early identification of FAS children and determination of their educational needs should become a priority with special educators. As Umbreit and Ostrow (1980) note, there is little longitudinal research on the FAS child; such research must be undertaken if adequate educational services are to be provided.

PROBLEMS AT BIRTH

A number of problems that can result in retardation can occur during labor and delivery.

What is asphyxia?

Although there is no direct cause-effect relationship between prematurity and retardation, premature babies are more susceptible to disease and more fragile than full-term babies, and are as a result more susceptible to retardation (MacMillan, 1982). Brain damage can be caused by prolonged or difficult labor, by difficult forceps manipulation, and by problems related to a mother's small pelvis. *Asphyxia* (also referred to as *anoxia*), the deprivation of oxygen, may be caused by compression of the ubilical cord or other problems (MacMillan, 1982). This is probably the major cause of cerebral palsy.

Treatment for some genetic disorders must be begun shortly after birth. Children born to mothers with Rh antigens must be monitored to ensure that high levels of bilirubin do not result in brain damage. The blood sugar levels of infants born to diabetic mothers should be monitored to determine whether the child needs treatment. PKU and galactosemia tests should also be conducted, and treatment should be initiated if it is warranted. Surgery may be necessary in cases of spina bifida, as mentioned in the chapter on physical disabilities. Hydrocephaly, a related condition, can also be identified shortly after birth. This condition is characterized by the buildup of cerebrospinal fluid in the skull. If untreated, the head will expand, which results in severe brain damage. Surgical procedures have been developed where a shunt can be inserted to drain the fluid into the general circulatory system.

PROBLEMS AFTER BIRTH

What are some of the causes of mental retardation after birth?

Mental retardation can also be caused by problems occurring after the child is born, including head injuries, brain tumors, infectious disease such as mengitis and encephalitis, hunger and malnutrition, and some food additives. Lead and mercury poisoning can also cause retardation, as can complications arising from childhood diseases such as whooping cough, chicken pox, and measles.

PSYCHOSOCIAL FACTORS

Most of the causes of retardation discussed thus far have involved damage to the central nervous system. The causes of most of these cases can be identified. As mentioned earlier, however, these causes account for only about 10 percent of the mentally retarded population. What is more, the children affected by this type of disorder generally have retardation in the moderate to severe range. What is the cause of the remaining cases of retardation, most of which are relatively mild?

What percentage of mentally retarded children come from poverty areas?

The President's Committee on Mental Retardation (1976) concluded that 75 percent of our mentally retarded children come from urban and rural poverty areas. Although the causes already discussed affect children from poverty areas too, most cases are of unknown origin. We can only speculate on why so many mildly retarded children come from impoverished environments.

What are "psychosocial" factors relating to mental retardation?

It seems reasonable to assume that malnutrition, inadequate medical and prenatal care, disease-producing conditions, and other health hazards associated with poverty all contribute to lowered intellectual functioning. In addition, it appears that a number of other less readily observable factors help produce mental retardation. These are related to child rearing practices, the home environment, family structure, and similar factors. Causative factors of these types are known as "psychosocial" factors.

The American Association on Mental Deficiency (Grossman, 1982) uses four criteria to determine whether a child's retardation can be attributed to psychosocial disadvantages.

1. Intelligence and adaptive behavior are at retarded levels of functioning.
2. There is retarded intellectual functioning in the immediate family and usually the larger family circle as well.
3. There is no clear evidence of brain damage in the child.
4. In most instances, the home environment is impoverished.

Mild retardation caused by psychosocial factors is almost always difficult to identify in young children. Most of the youngsters in this category appear to develop fairly normally; they are generally only slightly slower than their nonretarded peers. Most of these children are not identified until they reach school age, when it is discovered that they have difficulty with educational tasks.

Most authorities on mental retardation do not believe that intelligence and other characteristics of the personality are caused exclusively by either genetic or environmental factors. The current belief is that these traits result from the interaction of genetic and environmental variables. It is believed that intelligence can be limited to a certain range by genetic factors, but within that range an individual's intelligence will be determined by environment. This means that children who have the genetic potential to be only mildly retarded may have a much lower level of intelligence if they are raised in a very poor environment. As you can see, it is important that children be raised in as rich and stimulating an environment as possible.

PREVENTION

The chances of preventing mental retardation improve every time a cause is identified. A number of preventive measures are already known. Among these are:

— Vaccination against rubella
— Surgical procedures to correct hydrocephaly
— Amniocentesis to detect chromosomal aberrations in the fetus
— Use of drugs to control the effects of childhood illnesses
— Blood transfusion of Rh-factor babies and vaccination of Rh-sensitized mothers
— Laws that prohibit the use of lead-based paint on baby toys and furniture
— Dietary treatment of PKU and galactosemia
— Improved maternal nutrition and prenatal health care
— Genetic counseling for persons who are carriers of potential genetic defects
— Enrichment of impoverished environments

Educating the public about the causes of mental retardation and the methods of preventing it is one of the major challenges facing the special educator today

PROBE 8-4
Causes and Prevention of Retardation

1. T F A knowledge of the causes of retardation can be very helpful to a teacher in the actual instruction of retarded children.

2. T F The causes of most cases of mental retardation cannot be clearly identified.

3. List the four criteria used by the AAMD to identify mental retardation due to psychosocial disadvantage.

4. Describe current beliefs about the roles of genetic and environmental factors in determining intelligence and other personality characteristics.

5. *Matching*

_____ Dominant gene defect   a. Down's syndrome
_____ Preventable with diet   b. Cretinism
_____ Treated by blood transfusion   c. Cerebral Palsy
_____ Thyroid deficiency   d. Rh Factor
_____ Trisomy-21   e. Tuberous Sclerosis
_____ Small skull   f. Hydrocephalus
_____ Correctable with surgery   g. PKU
_____ Asphyxia a major cause   h. Microcephaly

6. List five methods of preventing mental retardation.

EDUCATING INDIVIDUALS WITH MENTAL RETARDATION

You should be able to describe the major education and learning characteristics of mentally retarded individuals.

Individuals with mental retardation often have educational characteristics similar to those of normally developing children, although they may differ in their rate of skill acquisition, ability to attend to task, memory, generalization and transfer of recently acquired skills, and language development. The development of retarded individuals appears to parallel that of normal children although it is somewhat slower, and the final level of skill mastery may not be as refined (Woodward, 1959; Inhelder, 1968). As more research is done on cognitive develoment, we are learning more about specific learning characteristics of mentally retarded individuals.

LEARNING CHARACTERISTICS

In the following section we discuss the so-called intellectual or learning characteristics that have substantial implications for educators and others who develop skill-building programs to facilitate retarded persons' entrance into the community.

Attention. Many mentally retarded individuals have trouble attending to relevant cues while performing tasks. They do not appear to differentiate the more significant aspects of the situation from those that are less useful (Zeaman and House, 1963b, 1979). Retarded learners also have a tendency to focus on specific cues rather than shifting attention to new cues (Lovass, Schreibman, Koegel, and Rehm, 1971). This overselectivity, or perseveration, may hinder learning. Mentally retarded individuals have a narrower breadth of attention. They do not simultaneously attend to as many dimensions of a given task as normal individuals do. Retarded learners require more frequent and lengthier opportunities to practice a task before they can master it. Once a task is mastered, however, retarded persons can perform it at a rate similar to that of nonretarded persons. Zeaman and House (1979) suggest that discrimination problems can be reduced through (1) using three-dimensional objects; (2) sequencing of tasks from the easy to the more difficult; (3) emphasizing the relevant aspects of tasks; (4) increasing the novelty of the negative and positive stimuli; (5) avoiding failure; and (6) establishing a "set" to attend to relevant dimensions, e.g. providing opportunity to practice attending to specific dimensions so that when confronted with task situations, the learner will discriminate relevant versus irrelevant stimuli prior to attempting to complete the task.

What is meant by overselectivity or perseveration?

How many discrimination problems can be reduced?

Memory. Mentally retarded individuals often perform poorly on nonserial short-term memory tasks such as memorizing numbers out of rote order. This problem occurs because their use of strategies is limited. For example, they may lack spontaneous rehearsal techniques and not practice unless they are specifically directed to do so (Belmont and Butterfield, 1971; Butterfield, Wambold, and Belmont, 1973). Given lists of words or pictures to recall, mentally retarded individuals do not appear to cluster items according to recognizable categories (Jensen and Fredrickson, 1973). The clustering that does occur is most often idiosyncratic. Many mentally retarded individuals have trouble recognizing recurring patterns or redundancy in stimuli (Spitz, 1973).

It has been demonstrated that mentally retarded individuals retain less information in sensory storage and iconic memory (memory involving symbolic images that have inherent meaning such as ↑ for "up" and ↓ for "down" [Pennington and Luszcz, 1975]). Research seems to indicate that mentally retarded individuals are slower to transfer information from sensory storage to short-term memory. This deficit increases as the amount of information increases (Baumeister, 1979). Many of these memory deficits respond to training and educational intervention strategies.

What is generalization and transfer training?

Generalization and Transfer. The ability to generalize or transfer recently learned skills to new situations is another problem area for the retarded, and training in this area is an important part of their education programs. In programs for the moderately and severely retarded, it is not unusual to require the pupil to demonstrate mastery of a skill (1) in reaction to, or in the presence of, at least three different persons; (2) in at least three different natural settings; (3) in response to at least three different sets of instructional materials; and (4) in response to at least three different appropriate language cues (Brown, Nietupski, and Hamre-Nietupski, 1976).

In what areas of language development do retarded children demonstrate delay?

Language. Language learning is closely tied to cognitive development. A language deficit is very often a criterion for the definition of mental retardation. Most researchers suggest that retarded children develop language at a slower rate but in a similar manner to normal children (Evans and Hampson, 1968; Lackner, 1968; Ryan, 1975). Retarded children are delayed in such areas as sentence length, sentence complexity, speech sound discrimination, and percentage of nouns in the vocabulary (Spreen, 1965). Delays may be caused in part by delayed development of the prerequisite cognitive structures required for meaningful communication (Bowerman, 1976).

A higher incidence of voice and articulation defects is found among retarded individuals, in part because of delays in motor development (Edwards and Edwards, 1970). The delayed development of language and its crucial role in social and cognitive development make this a major area of concern for those working with mentally retarded pupils. The real value of research in this area of learning is its utility in the development of curricula and behavior change or teaching strategies.

CURRICULAR IMPLICATIONS

What impact have community-based services had on curricula for the mentally retarded?

The curricula designed for the three most commonly used educational classifications of mental retardation (educable mentally retarded, trainable mentally retarded, and severely/profoundly mentally retarded) differ in both the difficulty of skills taught and the actual skills or subjects covered. The educational needs of pupils with mental retardation vary so greatly that it is not feasible to utilize just one curricular approach for even a single educational classification. The recent emphasis on community-based services and program delivery options has necessitated that parents and educators give more emphasis to the development of skills that will facilitate the mentally retarded person's integration into the community. Skills such as using public transportation, purchasing from store clerks, using pay telephones, and attending to traffic signals are curricular areas that institutional or residential programs could ignore. Today's emphasis on community-based programs cannot leave these and myriad other "functional skills" out of the mentally retarded person's educational training options.

In what ways are curricula for the mentally retarded similar to those used with normal children?

Instructional techniques and rates of progress for mentally retarded pupils may differ from those for nonretarded students, but learning sequences, skill hierarchies, and other spects of human growth and development are the same for all pupils. The major curricular efforts in the preschool and early childhood education of mentally retarded pupils closely approximate those offered in regular education programs. The emphasis in curricula for very young mentally retarded persons is on early intervention, including infant stimulation and including the child's home in the programming as much as possible. See Chapter 3 for a detailed examination of special education programming for the young handicapped person.

A useful model for developing secondary curricula for use by teachers of severely handicapped pupils has been suggested by Brown et al. (1979). The model could readily be applied by any teacher working with mentally retarded pupils. In this model, the educator uses six steps in establishing a curriculum. The steps are:

1. Organize the curriculum into four performance or skill domains:
   a. Daily Living
   b. Leisure/Recreational
   c. Community Functioning
   d. Vocational
2. With a specific pupil in mind, identify the natural environments in which the pupil currently functions (e.g. natural home, school) and may eventually function.
3. Further divide the pupil's natural environments into specific sub-environments, i.e., natural home subdivided into bathroom, dining room; school subdivided into classroom, lavatory, gymnasium.
4. Make an inventory of the typical activities that occur in the sub-environments in which the pupil may be a participant.
5. Identify the skills needed to participate successfully in the activities identified in #4.
6. Write goals and objectives for instructional programs that teach the skills identified in #5.

How does the "top down" approach differ from more traditional approaches?

This approach to curriculum development is often referred to as a "top down" approach because it starts with where you expect the pupil to be when you are finished with your formal instructional activities. The more traditional approach is often referred to as a "developmental" or "bottom up" approach.

TECHNOLOGY IN ACTION

Libby Holmes is a resource teacher for educable mentally retarded students in a junior high school. She has recently become acquainted with the many uses of microcomputers in planning her weekly instructional methods. Ms. Holmes does not know the first thing about programming the computer; she has, however, learned to use software programs designed specifically for teachers, gearing them to the individual needs of her students.

One of her students, Edna, is having difficulty adding numbers with carrying. This skill is necessary in the Home Ec class that she is attending. Ms. Holmes knows that Edna can add with carrying. She suspects that Edna has forgotten this skill, and that a review would be all that is needed to rectify the problem.

She selects a computer program that enables her to generate four different sets of 45 addition problems that require carrying. The first is to be used as a diagnostic test, the second as a work sheet following instruction on the ones that are missed, the third is to be used as a homework assignment, and the fourth as a test to check how she did. To use the program, Ms. Holmes simply follows the instructions that appear on the screen. She is asked to indicate the type of problems that she wants. After selecting addition from the menu, she is asked for the number of digits, whether carrying is wanted, and the number of problems. Following her answers, the computer pauses for a brief moment and then indicates that it is ready to print. She turns on her printer and a page of problems is printed, followed by a second page with the answers to the problems, so that she can quickly check Edna's answers. No two pages are identical.

Ms. Holmes then selects a program that constructs word searches. She has been working with Dave, who is learning to spell the days of the week and the months of the year. This programs asks her whether she wants the words to go left to right, up and down, diagonally, or all three. She selects left to right and enters the days and months. The computer mixes these up, and then adds letters to fill a 40 by 40 matrix. It then prints a square of 1,600 letters. Dave will have to find the words and circle them. Again, the computer prints an answer key to enable Ms. Holmes to check Dave's answers quickly.

Five of the students who come to Ms. Holmes's room are learning how to type. They are using a computer program that is designed to improve their speed and accuracy. Ms. Holmes loads that program into her computer, enters a special code, and is shown a record of each student's performance during the previous week. She then makes a decision about which students need additional work.

A program that generates crossword puzzles is used to develop a crossword puzzle for Scotty, who is studying internal combustion engines in his science class. Ms. Holmes enters 20 words into the computer, each followed by a brief definition. The computer generates a crossword puzzle and puts the definitions at the bottom of the page. Again, an answer sheet is printed for her reference.

Ms. Holmes then stores grades from the papers she had corrected over the weekend onto a computer disk that is used with a grade book program. She keeps all of her student records on the computer.

She previews a new English textbook that the school is considering purchasing for her use. Using another computer program, she types in three 100-word passages and the computer analyzes the reading level. She determines that the reading level is too high for most of her students.

Finally, using a word processor, she writes a brief note to the parents of one of her students. She had previously recorded several paragraphs that related to items of classroom business that occurred on a frequent basis. She calls several of these paragraphs up for use in the letter. She then adds information that is unique to that piece of correspondence. This procedure has enabled her to communicate more frequently with the parents of her students, who have reported that they appreciate the extra contact.

Ms. Holmes completes her work in a little more than two hours. Previously, if she had attempted to do all of these things by hand, it would have taken her most of the day. She is convinced that the availability of the microcomputer is helping her to become a better teacher.

In the latter, curriculum is designed based on assessment of where the pupil is currently functioning. The assessment data are then compared to developmental norms to determine if the pupil is progressing as typically expected or not. If not, the curriculum should indicate the skills that were not properly mastered and where to begin the pupil in the curriculum. The remainder of the pupil's instruction follows the developmental sequence of the curriculum. The "top down" curricular approach has the advantage of permitting individualization of instructional programming. Its principal disadvantage is its cost in terms of staff time for development and monitoring. The advantage of the "bottom up" curriculum is ease of system-wide use and monitoring. The principal disadvantages are loss of individualization for the pupils involved and loss of direct input by the teacher responsible for the instructional program implementation. The selection of a curriculum for use in a given educational program should reflect the needs, interests, skills, and resources of both the education agency delivering the curriculum and those receiving it, both parent and pupil, as defined by the IEP. See Chapter 11 for a more in-depth examination of educational programming for severely handicapped persons.

PROBE 8-5
Educating Individuals with Mental Retardation

1. T F There is higher incidence of voice and articulation defects among mentally retarded individuals.

2. List five ways the development of retarded individuals differs from that of normally developing children.

3. List three attending problems often exhibited by mentally retarded individuals.

4. Generalization and transfer training for mentally retarded pupils requires responses across what four performance domains?

5. T F Many memory deficits of the mentally retarded will not respond to training.

6. List two ways that curricula designed for the "EMR," "TMR," and "S/PR" pupil often differ.

7. T F Individuals with mental retardation often demonstrate educational characteristics similar to normal children.

8. T F Language deficit is often included when defining mental retardation.

EDUCATIONAL AND SERVICE DELIVERY OPTIONS

> **You should be able to describe the implication of PL 94-142 for educating mentally retarded children in the least restrictive environment.**

The implications of normalization were discussed in Chapter 2. The impetus in the drive for normalization came from parents and professionals concerned about the practice of placing the mentally retarded in large residential institutions that were little more than warehouses for human beings. Because the normalization movement was started by people concerned with the welfare of the mentally retarded, it is not surprising that the most striking changes that have resulted from normalization involve individuals with mental retardation. Important changes have occurred in the care of children in public school programs as well as in institutional and residential care settings. Some of the currently available options that have resulted from normalization are discussed in the following pages.

EDUCATIONAL SERVICE OPTIONS

What considerations are important in determining educational placement?

The continuum, or cascade, of educational services was described in Chapter 2. It may be helpful to refer back to Figure 2-1 to refresh your memory about the educational provisions currently available to children with mental retardation. When considering educational options for the retarded, it is important to keep in mind that (1) educational placement should be based on the child's needs; (2) the child should be placed in the most facilitative (or least restrictive) environment; and (3) placement should be flexible enough that a child could be moved to a different setting if the situation warrants it.

The Regular Classroom. You will recall that there are several options available for children placed in the setting at the least restrictive end of the continuum — the regular classroom. EMR children are much more likely to be placed in regular classrooms than TMR children, and most EMR children will require support services. These may involve itinerant teachers who work directly with the child on a part-time basis (e.g., with a child who needs speech therapy), consulting services for the regular classroom teacher, or part-time attendance in a separate resource room staffed by a special education teacher, where the child is usually given extra help in a basic subject such as reading or mathematics.

Which "type" of retarded child would be most successful in the regular class?

EMR children in the upper range of the classification are likely to be most successful in the regular classroom. Those with lower intellectual and adaptive behavior levels require more special services. The child with a low level of adaptive behavior is especially likely to present problems in the regular classroom.

When should a
special class
placement be
made?

The Special Class. There are two special class options in the continuum of educational services: part-time placement and full-time placement. Only those whose academic and adaptive behavior problems preclude placement in the regular classroom should be placed in the special class. It may be best for EMR students with severe academic problems but good adaptive behavior to remain in the special class for academic work and join their regular classmates for physical education, art, music, shop, home economics, and other activities in which academic skills are not crucial. Full-time placement in a special class is warranted only for those children who need intensive instruction in academic areas and adaptive behavior. Some children who have relatively good academic skills but poor adaptive behavior are placed full-time in a special class. When this is the case, every effort should be made to improve the child's

Being capable of purchasing well balanced and nutritious groceries and safely preparing them for eating are important skills taught in many group home settings.

adaptive behavior so that he or she can be moved to a more facilitative environment.

Most TMR and S/PR children will be educated in full-time, self-contained special classes. The emphasis in the TMR classroom is on self-help skills, basic communication skills, and vocational skill development that will eventually permit the child to be employed in a supervised or sheltered job site. Although most TMR people require supervision throughout their lives, it is not unusual for a TMR individual to acquire in school all the life-care skills needed to live independently or in a group home.

Because the full-time pupils in a special class are segregated in their education, it is important that they be allowed other opportunities to participate in the social and nonacademic life of the school. Both EMR and TMR children benefit from social and leisure time interaction with nonhandicapped children. In fact, these children interact most frequently with nonhandicapped children when they are not in school. School personnel should try to foster such interactions and should attempt to provide the retarded with skills that will permit them to interact successfully.

The Special Day School. The special day school is rapidly disappearing. At one time it was common practice to house all education programs for handicapped children in special schools. Such facilities still exist, but they are generally quite specialized and are appropriate only for children who cannot profit from integration in regular public schools. These schools are generally found only in large metropolitan areas, where the population of severely and profoundly handicapped individuals is large enough to justify the operation of a separate educational facility.

Homebound Instruction. Homebound instruction for the mentally retarded is uncommon. This type of instruction is generally provided only to those who cannot attend school because of a medical or physical problem, as when a child requires complete bed care. Most homebound instruction is short-term, provided only while the child is recuperating from a temporary illness or disorder. The cascade-of-services model requires that the child be moved back into the least restrictive environment as soon as feasible.

When are children placed in facilities such as hospitals and residential institutions?

Hospitals and Residential Institutions. Children are placed in facilities such as hospitals and residential institutions only when they have a medical problem or are severely retarded. Unless they have severe or dangerous behavioral problems, EMR children should not be placed in such settings. The placement of a TMR child in such a facility would be justified only after placement in school and community-based programs had proved ineffective. Although S/PR children are found more frequently in these setting, they, too, should be placed there only after other options have been tried and found inexpedient.

As a result of PL 94-142, S/PR children are being served more frequently in public schools. Program options for the S/PR child will be discussed in more detail in Chapter 11.

In summary, the cascade-of-services model has been found to be a workable alternative to the exclusion and segregation of the retarded from public school programs. The success of several derivative or adaptive models has been documented (Adamson, 1970; Taylor and Soloway, 1973; Van Etten and Adamson, 1973). As Deno (1970, p. 233) points out:

> The cascade system is designed to make available whatever different-from-the-mainstream kind of setting is required to control the learning variables deemed critical for the individual case. It is a system which facilitates tailoring of treatment to individual needs rather than a system for sorting out children so they will fit conditions designed according to group standards not necessarily suitable for the particular case.

AN ERA OF ADVOCACY

> **You should be able to describe the changes in advocacy for community-based services for all persons with mental retardation.**

The slow change toward a mandate for community-based services is just one of several shifts that have occurred in the provision of special services for persons with mental retardation. In the area of mental retardation, the focus of the 1960s was on providing additional services to the mildly and moderately retarded. By the latter half of the 1970s, however, the focus had shifted to the provision of services to the severely and profoundly retarded. Indeed, this shift of attention was so great that it led some professionals (e.g., Haywood, 1979) to wonder, "What happened to mild and moderate retardation?"

THE IMPACT OF LEGISLATION

The new emphasis can be attributed in part to federal legislation. Amendments to Medicaid provided additional funds for institutions, for example, and PL 94-142 gave its highest priority to serving unserved children and the most severely handicapped who were underserved. The Rehabilitation Act of 1973 (PL 93-112) stated that there should be a "special emphasis on services to those with the most severe handicaps." These provisions and others all tended to bring the more severely handicapped into programs for which they were previously ineligible.

THE IMPACT OF LITIGATION

What were some of the changes in the treatment of institutionalized persons brought about by court cases in the 1970s and 1980s?

Federal court decisions have also brought changes, particularly in the area of institutional reform. During the 1970s, the population of persons with mental retardation being served in large residential facilities decreased significantly and more community-based services were provided. Between 1970 and 1980, despite population increases, the number of mentally retarded residents in state-administered institutions fell by 63,747 (Scheerenberger, 1982). Court cases influencing the treatment of persons in institutions included the following:

— *Wyatt* v. *Stickney* (1972), which established minimum standards for state-administered schools and established independent monitoring committees to ensure that the law was implemented.
— *Lesard* v. *Schmidt* (1972), which guaranteed persons with mental retardation the right to a trial to determine if their best interests were being served or to challenge the decision to institutionalize.
— *Souder* v. *Brennan* (1973), which established a precedent that persons with developmental disabilities could not be compelled to provide free labor to operate the very institutions in which they were receiving treatment.
— *Halderman* v. *Pennhurst State School and Hospital, et al.* (1982), which recognized for the first time that residents of institutions for the mentally retarded have constitutional rights to habilitation and freedom from unnecessary restraint.

Changes such as these have brought great benefits to a part of the population that was long denied equal services, but the change in emphasis has resulted in reductions in study and research concerning the mildly and moderately retarded. This is an alarming and unfortunate trend, in part because the size of the mildly and moderately retarded population is much larger than that of the severely retarded, as Haywood pointed in 1979 (pp. 430-431):

> On a population base of 222 million persons [in 1980] we shall have 110,000 persons with IQs less than 20, and 444,000 with IQs between 20 and 50, but we shall have 6,693,940 individuals with IQs between 50 and 70. Thus, in 1980 there will be more than 12 times as many mentally retarded persons in the IQ 50 to 70 range as there will be with IQs less than 50.

With the new advocacy come new responsibilities. The emphasis on developing programs and services for the severely/profoundly mentally retarded person may also inadvertently create problems for that population in the 1980s. Switzky, Haywood, and Rotatori (1982), in an interesting corollary to Haywood's 1979 question concerning the plight of the mildly handicapped, ask, "Who are the severely and profoundly mentally retarded?" The authors comment, "the diagnostic categories of severe and profound mental retardation are presently blurred and used in idiosyncratic ways by both researchers and practitioners. A review of the literature shows that severely and profoundly mentally retarded persons actually have distinctly different characteristics that may form functional subcategories of individual differences related to programs of education and training" (p. 268). With today's economic uncertainties, the educational endeavors that will remain in the forefront of public interest cannot afford to be seen as applying educational classification and terminology in "idiosyncratic" ways.

During the 1980s, efforts should be made to balance distribution of efforts more evenly without sacrificing any of the benefits acquired during the 1960s and 1970s.

COMMUNITY-BASED RESIDENTIAL SERVICES

What has replaced large residential institutions?

During the past two decades, especially the 1970s, a movement has grown to provide services to the mentally retarded in their home communities. This is a dramatic change from the former practice of isolating the mentally retarded, particularly the moderately and severely retarded, in large, self-contained residential institutions that offered little or no contact with the outside community.

A change in the general public's perception about the mentally retarded is largely responsible for a more humane and realistic approach to the delivery of services. Wolfensberger (1972) suggests that the mentally retarded should be regarded as developing individuals. This view emphasizes that their behavior is caused by developmental retardation, that their behavior can change, and that they are capable of growth and development. As a result of Wolfensberger's work, a shift away from residential services characterized by large institutional "warehouses" for the retarded has occurred (Wolfensberger 1971, 1976).

Principles of normalization in the delivery of services to the retarded are reflected in the following suggestions of Menolascino (1977, pp. 79–83):

1. Programs and facilities for the mentally retarded should be physically and socially integrated into the community. . . .
2. No more retardates should be congregated in one service facility than the surrounding neighborhood can readily integrate into its resources, community social life, etc. . . .
3. Integration of the mentally retarded can best be attained if the location of services follows population density and distribution patterns. . . .
4. Services and facilities for the retarded must meet the same standards as other comparable services and facilities for the nonretarded. . . .
5. Staff personnel who are working with retarded persons must meet at least the same standards as those who are working with comparable nonretarded individuals. . . .

6. The retarded must have maximal exposure to the nonretarded population in the community. . . .
7. Daily routines for the mentally retarded should be comparable to those of nonretarded persons of the same age.
8. Services for retarded children and adults should be physically separated as they are in the mainstream of society. . . .
9. The retarded should be dressed and groomed like other persons their age, they should be taught a normal gait, normal movements, normal expressive behavior patterns, and their diets adjusted to assure normal weight.
10. As much as possible, the adult retardate, even if severely retarded, should be provided the opportunity to engage in work that is culturally normal in type, quantity, and setting. . . .

One of the more critical tests of the 1980s will be whether the public will continue to pay for the expanded array of community-based services. This test will be especially critical in the area of services for the severely retarded adult for whom the public has historically placed greater emphasis on institutional or life-care residential service provisions. The 1970s saw an evolving array of services for adults with mental retardation that closely resembled those available for their normally developing peers. While the principle of normalization has enjoyed popular appeal among both professional and lay persons, and services have definitely expanded, continuation of the expansion, and perhaps even its maintenance, is not guaranteed.

A NEW MODEL FOR SERVICES

Singleton (1981) and Skarnulis (1980) described a community-based services delivery strategy called "Core Home and cluster of services." The Core Home attempts to alleviate the community reentry and relocation difficulties that many persons with retardation exhibit when moved from one residential setting to another. Cohen et al. (1977) state that this "relocation syndrome" is characterized chiefly by withdrawal from the environment and that "short-term deterioration in adaptive behavior may be viewed as one of the many risks of relocation of mentally retarded persons." The Core Home is used to facilitate transition from one setting to another and to ease the stress inherent in the move. During the short-term stay in the Core Home the client is assisted in exploring the community's cluster of services, adapting to its demands, and gaining access to its opportunities. (See Figure 8-3 for an example of a Core Home and cluster model.) The Core Home serves as a focal point for the coordination of community-based services, with responsibility for the following:

What is the role of the Core Home?

1. Management, to provide support and supervision for the cluster of services in the community

2. Intake procedures, for all new clients, to assess their needs
3. Training, for new clients and service delivery staff
4. Respite care, for families with children exhibiting handicaps, crisis support for homes in the cluster and for other clients who need such services
5. Community advocacy, providing a focal point for local services

The concept of normalization of services for people with mental retardation may be one of the most stridently debated issues in the field of mental retardation in the 1980s. Within that context, the problems of the person with mental retardation adjusting to community-based service delivery and the community's acceptance of persons with mental handicaps must be a focus of critical attention if the gains of the 1970s are to be enhanced or even maintained.

The continuum of adult residential services illustrated in Figure 8-3 represents an evolving service array that will continue to change as economic and community attitudes shift. These services are described in the following section.

What mentally retarded persons might be appropriately placed in an unsupervised personal residence?

Unsupervised personal residence. Living in one's own home or apartment has traditionally been a goal of young adults. This least restrictive residential living environment offers at once the greatest degree of personal freedom, expression of individuality, and personal and social responsibility. Historically, persons with mental retardation have not typically been permitted this expression of freedom. Professionals in the field of mental retardation generally agree that anyone exhibiting responsible behavior commensurate with that of age peers ought to have equal access to the benefits of responsible behavior. If a person with mental retardation can cope with the demands of making a life independent from family, state, or community agency supervi-

Figure 8-3
Core Home and Cluster of Residential Services

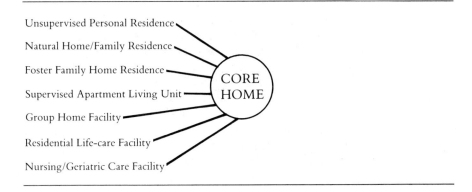

sion, then that person ought to be permitted to exercise a free choice in selecting a residential life style. The economic benefits of adding contributing members to a community far outweigh the alleged additional expense of providing community-based services. The institutional service model is both more expensive and less effective in providing habilitative and rehabilitative services (Conley, 1979; Center on Human Policy, 1979; McCormick, Balla, and Zigler, 1975). This does not warrant a wholesale abandonment of all institutional services for mentally retarded persons.

What are the traditional problems with family residence for the mentally retarded?

Natural Home/Family Residence. For many families with mentally retarded children, living at home with parents or members of one's extended family has for a long time been the only alternative to institutions. Traditionally, the problem with this form of residential service has been the lack of community-based supportive services such as vocational or prevocational training, recreation, or even respite care. The effect of a person with a handicapping condition on the family will be described in greater detail in Chapter 14. Current research indicates that with readily available support services, a person exhibiting retarded development can be a positive addition to the family milieu. The Core Home model mentioned earlier is a good way to provide the support base believed necessary for families to provide in-home residential care. The Core Home can also serve as a transition arrangement whereby the person with retardation makes the move from family residence to independent residential living.

What are ALUs?

Foster Family Homes. To develop adaptive behavior skills, it is extremely important that the retarded child and adolescent grow up in a family. Alternative living units (ALUs) are generally defined as any form of residential setting other than a person's natural family setting. Most foster family arrangements are regulated by state and municipal licensing boards. In most cases, foster parents receive fees, but they do not usually receive training. Supervision of foster care homes is usually less rigorous than it is for group homes or other alternative living units. The Eastern Nebraska Community Office of Retardation (ENCOR) program has a "Developmental home" plan similar to the foster home plan. In this program, however, the participating parents are trained to work with persons classified as mentally retarded, and planned supervision of their care is provided.

Supervised Apartment Living. Apartment living arrangements are less common than group homes, but they are expected to grow more popular as the ALU arrangement becomes more familiar to the public. In some programs the apartment ALU begins with the supervisor living with the client in an apartment, or clients may live in a "cluster" of apartments in a separate part of the same building as the supervisor. As the individuals acquire the skills necessary to live independently, they are encouraged to move into an apartment of their own or to share an apartment with an acquaintance. Supervisors drop by at regular intervals. In most ALU programs, clients with mental retardation attend a training program that helps them develop vocational and independent living skills. The clients should have their recreation and work independent from agency staff but remain part of life-care and counseling programs.

What is often the first living arrangement after leaving an institution?

Group Homes. Typically, in group homes, from six to twelve people live together, share household responsibilities, work, and recreation in the immediate community. Both males and females may live in the group home, but cohabitation is generally not permitted. The group home is usually staffed full-time by live-in personnel who rotate shifts.

In many cases the group home is the first arrangement the person with retardation lives in after leaving an institution. It is also a good first step outside the immediate family for adults leaving home for the first time. Whether moving from home or from an institution, the individual with mental retardation should be moved to a different living arrangement, such as an apartment, as soon as he or she demonstrates the ability to function more independently.

The Eastern Nebraska Community Office of Retardation (ENCOR) was one of the earliest community-based organizations to advocate the use of group homes and of alternative living units designed to house six or fewer clients. Many effective, community-based, residential service programs have been designed around similar models. The McComb/Oakland Regional Center (MORC) in Mt. Clemens, Michigan, is another notable example of a community-based service delivery agency with a contemporary array of residential alternatives. These programs highlight the notion that community-based service delivery is in its infancy, rapidly growing, continuing to change, and a challenge to all involved.

Residential Care Facilities. When federal funding became available for residential construction, many private corporations were formed to sponsor construction of residential facilities designed to house 50 to 100 persons. These facilities, known as Intermediate Care Facilities for the Mentally Retarded (ICF/MR), are regulated by the federal government. Most ICF/MRs are designed to provide total care for retarded clients throughout their lives.

It is sometimes difficult to operate a profit-making corporation and at the same time provide a normalized service delivery system to persons with mental retardation. There has been some litigation by advocates claiming that services are sacrificed for the sake of profit. Just as there were major court cases during the 1970s involving large institutions for persons with mental retardation, it seems likely that there will be cases during the 1980s involving claims that the civil rights of persons with mental retardation in ICF/MRs are being violated.

What types of
living
arrangements are
appropriate for
the older retarded?

Nursing or Geriatric Care Facilities. Attention has only recently been focused on providing care for the elderly retarded. With today's emphasis on community-based facilities, services for the 5 percent of the mentally retarded population who are over fifty is becoming a major issue. Schapiro and Eigerdorf (1975) describe nine types of arrangements that are appropriate for the older retarded:

1. Older Adult Apartments: any apartment complex built or modified to serve the elderly.
2. Alternative Living Units: two- or three-bedroom apartments with supervision within the apartment.
3. Rural Living Arrangements: provisions for rural housing for the elderly provided under HUD's Housing Rural Development Act.
4. Mobile Home Living: resembling any other mobile home park, but providing supervision and assistance to the elderly retarded.
5. Congregate Housing: supervised existing public housing.
6. Nursing Homes: public or private; the retarded should be integrated with "normal" elderly patients.
7. Institutions: may include hospitals with units designed to provide long-term life care.
8. Extramural Care: care provided in the home.
9. Sheltered Housing: a situation in which assistance in managing daily activities is provided in the client's own home; not a nursing home or apartment setting.

Living arrangements available to the elderly retarded person ought to resemble in quality of living those typically made available in the community for their nonretarded peers. The ultimate goal is to provide an array of services that assures the elderly person with retardation a quality of health care programs throughout life that we would want for ourselves.

PROBE 8-6
Educational and Service Delivery Options

1. What characteristics should an EMR child exhibit to be considered for placement in some variation of the regular classroom?

2. T F Most TMR children will be educated in self-contained special classes.

3. Under what circumstances might an EMR child receive homebound instruction?

4. T F Special day schools for the retarded continue to be a popular educational option.

5. What role perception of the mentally retarded has been suggested by Wolfensberger?

6. List four principles of normalization.

7. List three living alternatives to institutional placement.

8. What is a major criticism of foster family care for the retarded?

9. What type of facility sometimes takes on the characteristics of large institutions for the retarded?

10. T   F   The Core Home is a long-term residential arrangement for use with "hard-to-place" persons with mental retardation.

11. Over the decades of the 1960s and 1970s, emphasis on services changed from _____ to _____ .

12. List three reasons/causes for this change in emphasis.

13. During the current decade, what aspect of services should be attended to by professionals in the field?

SUMMARY

1. There is a new advocacy stressing community-based services.
2. The impact of federal legislation and litigation has caused a new emphasis on providing services to the severely and profoundly retarded.
3. To be diagnosed as mentally retarded, a person must be significantly subaverage in both intelligence and adaptive behavior.
4. Mental retardation is defined as significantly subaverage general intellectual functioning resulting in or associated with concurrent impairments in adaptive behavior and manifested during the developmental period (Grossman, 1983, p. 5).
5. A child's level of adaptive behavior is determined by comparing his or her performance to the standards of independence and social responsibility that are expected for his or her age level and cultural group. Adaptive behavior is very difficult to measure.
6. IQ scores should be considered in diagnosing mental retardation, but they are of little use in teaching a retarded child.
7. Classification systems related to etiology and clinical type are of little use in education. The classification system based on severity of symptoms, which identifies children as educable mentally retarded, trainable mentally retarded, and severely/profoundly retarded, is the system of greatest utility.
8. Children should be classified into diagnostic categories only when classification will lead to the development of an educational program that will meet their needs.

9. The estimated prevalence of mental retardation is about 1 percent.

10. Genetic irregularities, problems during pregnancy, problems at birth, problems after birth, and psychosocial factors can cause mental retardation, but the causes of most cases are unknown.

11. In many cases, mental retardation can be prevented with proper care.

12. Mentally retarded individuals often demonstrate intellectual characteristics similar to those of the normally developing child, although they may differ in the rate of skill acquisition, ability to attend to task, memory, generalization and transfer, and language development.

13. The recent emphasis on community-based services has necessitated a greater emphasis on functional living skills in programs for the retarded.

14. EMR children with good adaptive behavior skills can often be successfully integrated into regular classes.

15. TMR children are usually educated in special classes.

16. It is best to regard retarded people as "developing individuals" who are capable of growth and development that can lead to favorable changes in their behavior.

17. Living arrangements such as group homes and alternative living units located in the local community are preferable to large residential institutions.

TASK SHEET 8
Field Experiences in Mental Retardation

Select any one of the following alternatives and complete the assigned tasks.

Program Visitation

Visit a program that serves the mentally retarded, such as a public school, group home, any form of ALU, sheltered workshop, or rehabilitation center, and respond to the following:
1. Where did you visit?
2. Describe the physical setting.
3. Describe the activities you observed.
4. Interview one of the professionals at the facility about the program and some of the problems typically encountered in that setting.
5. Describe your reactions to the experience.

Professional Interview

Interview a professional who provides services to persons with mental retardation. Describe whom you interviewed, the services this person provides, the questions you asked, the person's responses and what you learned from this experience. (If you prefer and can make the necessary arrangements, interview a parent of a child with mental retardation.)

Reading

Read *Christmas in Purgatory*, by Burton Blatt, and write a 150-word report on your reactions to the book and its photo essay.

Agency Investigation

Write to and request information from one of the following agencies about the services they provide in the area of mental retardation. Write a three-page, double-spaced paper, summarizing these services and how you might use them if you were a professional working with persons with mental retardation.

American Association on Mental
Deficiency
5201 Connecticut, N.W.
Washington, DC 20015

National Association for Retarded
Citizens
2709 Avenue E., East
Arlington, TX 76011

American Academy on Mental
Retardation
Development Center
Maimonides Medical Center
4802 Tenth Avenue
Brooklyn, NY 11219

Library Study

Select three articles concerning mental retardation and write a one-page synopsis of each. Conclude by writing your personal reaction to each article. You can find articles about mental retardation in the following journals:

American Journal on Mental Deficiency
Exceptional Children
Education and Training of the Mentally Retarded
Mental Retardation
Teaching Exceptional Children
Exceptional Parent

Design Your Own Field Experience

If you know of a unique experience you can have with children or adults with mental retardation or do not want to do any of the listed alternatives, discuss your alternative with your instructor and complete the task that you agree upon.

Tony was a ten-year-old boy with bright eyes and a beautiful smile. Until he started school, his parents never imagined that he had a learning disability. He could carry on an adult level conversation and loved to listen to stories, although he showed little interest in looking at books.

Yes, his mother said, it was hard for him to learn to ride a bike and to zip his coat, and he did wear her out with all of that activity — he was touching, poking, tapping something all the time and never wanted to take a nap.

In kindergarten and first grade he scribbled on the color sheets, wouldn't copy lines or circles, refused to try to print his name. He wouldn't sit still while others looked at little books in reading circle, and at the end of the year he still couldn't recognize any of the words the other children knew.

When Tony was tested, the psychologist said his vision and hearing were normal, his intelligence was above average, but that he had something called a "learning disability."

9

Learning Disabilities

Catherine V. Morsink

Catherine V. Morsink is a Professor and Chairman of the Department of Special Education at the University of Florida. Dr. Morsink's professional experience includes teaching special classes for learning disabled and mentally retarded children and a regular third-grade class in which several mildly handicapped children were mainstreamed.[1]

"Learning disabled" (often abbreviated LD) is a label applied to children who, because of problems in specific areas of learning, are eligible for special education services. As can be seen from the case on the facing page, the student exhibiting a learning disability can be easily misunderstood by teachers and parents. Learning disabilities are extremely varied and complex; they include specific difficulties in learning to read, write, calculate, comprehend — even, in the broadest sense, to find places on a map or to tell time. To understand and help learning disabled individuals, you should be familiar with current identification procedures and the LD definition. You should also be able to discuss the disorder's characteristic behaviors, its controversial issues, and future trends.

[1] The contributions of Kate Algozzine to the review of literature are gratefully acknowledged.

DEFINITION AND INCIDENCE OF LEARNING DISABILITIES

> **You should be able to cite the current definition of the label "learning disabilities" and to estimate how many students are affected by this condition.**

CREATION OF THE TERM

Who coined the term "learning disability"?

The term "learning disabilities" was created in the early 1960s by one of the pioneers in this field, Dr. Samuel Kirk. The description of its creation (Kirk and Gallagher, 1979, p. 287), indicates that "The term learning disability became popular when the Association for Children with Learning Disabilities (ACLD) was organized under the name in 1963."

Created by parents who were concerned that their children were not learning in school, and yet were not eligible for special services, the ACLD organized its own special schools. These schools "were called by different names such as schools for the neurologically handicapped, brain-injured, aphasoid, dyslexic, and perceptually handicapped" (Kirk and Gallagher, 1979, p. 287).

Kirk, addressing the ACLD in 1963, advised that the term "learning disability" might be preferable to currently used terms (e.g., cerebral dysfunction or brain injured), since it was more related to teaching or learning. Shortly after that time, the term was adopted as a new category of exceptionality.

MOST RECENT DEFINITIONS

Students who meet the federal or state criteria for learning disabilities are eligible for special education services. There has been a great deal of controversy over the federal definition, and there are some variations of this definition among the different states. There is a need for a definition that is more nearly "operational"; that is, one that can be more useful in identifying LD students and in providing them with services.

The LD definition adopted by the federal government in December 1977, to provide guidelines for funding programs under PL 94-142, reads as follows (Federal Register, December 29, 1977, p. 65083):

> "Specific learning disability" means a disorder in one or more of the basic psychological processes involved in understanding or in using language, spoken or written, which may manifest itself in an imperfect ability to listen, think, speak, read, write, spell, or to do mathematical calculations. The term includes such conditions as perceptual handicaps, brain injury, minimal brain dysfunction, dyslexia, and developmental aphasia. The term does not include children who have learning problems which are primarily the result of visual, hearing, or motor handicaps, or mental retardation, or of environmental, cultural, or economic disadvantage.

During 1978 these guidelines were widely discussed, expanded, and modified. Final guidelines for the learning disabilities definition in PL 94-142 were not agreed on until January 1979, although the law was passed in 1975. The original guidelines and definition were so controversial that changes were required.

What are the criticisms of the federal definition of learning disability?

The controversy persists. According to Hammill, Leigh, McNutt, and Larsen (1981), the major areas of dissatisfaction include the following:

— The word "children" is too limited; it misleads readers to believe that LD doesn't occur in older students or adults
— The list of labels, such as perceptual handicap and developmental delay, is confusing and controversial
— The "exclusion" clause leads to the misconception that learning disabilities can't be present in persons who also have other kinds of handicaps.

Hammill et al. (1981) stated that the representatives of six major organizations involved in the National Joint Committee for Learning Disabilities (NJCLD) met in 1981 to resolve this controversy by agreeing on a new definition. It is as follows (Hammill et al., 1978, p. 336):

Learning disabilities is a generic term that refers to a heterogeneous group of disorders manifested by significant difficulties in the acquisition and use of listening, speaking, reading, writing, reasoning, or mathematical abilities. Those disorders are intrinsic to the individual and presumed to be due to central nervous system dysfunction. Even though a learning disability may occur concomitantly with other handicapping conditions (e.g., sensory impairment, mental retardation, social and emotional disturbance) or environmental influences (e.g., cultural differences, insufficient/inappropriate instruction, psychogenic factors), it is not the direct result of those conditions or influences.

This new definition is more easily understood and is becoming more widely accepted, even though the federal definition of 1977 is still used as the basis for funding LD programs.

What are the elements common to most definitions of learning disability?

Many professionals disagree about precisely what constitutes a learning disability, but there is general agreement about some of the disorder's basic dimensions. These dimensions might be summarized as follows:

1. *Discrepancy.* There is a difference between what these students should be able to do and what they are actually doing.
2. *Deficit.* There is some task others can do that an LD child can't do (such as listen, read, or do arithmetic).
3. *Focus.* The child's problem is centered on one or more of the basic psychological processes involved in using or understanding language.
4. *Exclusions.* These problems are not the direct result of poor vision or hearing, disadvantage, or retardation, but these students still aren't learning.

In some states the criteria for classifying a student as LD are changing. Often the reason for the change is that too many students are being classified as LD, while the identification procedures are inconsistent among local districts.

There is a trend for states to focus on more specific criteria, which can be used for program planning (Liles-Whitehurst, 1982). These criteria include the following:

— discrepancy between IQ and academic skills achievement, based on comparisons of standard scores
— evidence that other educational alternatives (behavior management, remedial reading/math, modified teaching techniques, tutoring, etc.) have been tried and are not effective.

In some states the criteria include evidence of a visual, auditory, motor, or language "process" disorder, while in others they do not.

Earlier in the history of LD, there was even less agreement in definitions among states. Vaughan and Hodges (1973) reported 38 different state definitions. Mercer, Forgnone, and Wolking (1976) surveyed 42 state departments of education and also found considerable variation. Some states, for example, indicated that the LD student's IQ had to be above average, while others specified that it had to be above the range for mental retardation. In a recent survey, Mercer, Hughes, and Mercer (in press) found that 44 percent of the states are now using the 1977 federal definition without modification, while an additional 28 percent are using it with slight variation; 24 percent of the states use other definitions; and 4 percent do not use an LD definition at all.

INCIDENCE AND PREVALENCE IN SCHOOL POPULATION

How many children have learning disabilities?

There is a wide range of estimates on the number of students who meet the criteria for classification as LD, according to these various definitions. Initially, the incidence was predicted to be about 2 percent. Lerner (1981) suggests that the *prevalence* ranges from 1 percent to 30 percent of the school population; Wallace and McLoughlin (1979) estimate the prevalence from 1 percent to 28 percent; Tucker, Stevens, and Ysseldyke (1982) indicate that the prevalence may be between 9 and 70 percent.

By 1982–1983, the number of children ages 3 to 21 classified as LD and served under PL 89-313 and PL 94-142 was 1,745,891 (see Table 1–1, p. 11) (U.S. Department of Education, 1980). These figures indicate that though the incidence — the percent expected — should not have changed, the prevalence — the number and percent of students classified and labeled as LD — has risen. Tucker (1980) stated that, in one state, the percentage of special education students classified as LD rose to almost 44 percent between 1970-1977.

The increase in the number of students classified as LD is felt to be the result of at least two factors, according to Tucker (1980). First, the schools have made an effort to provide services for the larger number of students who are experiencing academic difficulties. Second, there is a need to avoid misplacing minority students in classes for the mentally retarded; LD is a more socially desirable category.

ISSUES RELATED TO DEFINITION

Why are definitions important?

If agreement on a definition is so difficult, and labeling so controversial, why have a definition at all? The primary reason is that defined categories are required by the legislation that funds services. The federal definition is used to identify learning disabled children and to fund their educational programs.

The second reason definition is important is presented by Grossman (1978), who discusses the observations of science historian Thomas Kuhn. Kuhn has observed that there is a pattern to the development of definitions. Once definitions are accepted, all new data are measured against them. This is the form of quality control that separates astronomy from astrology and chemistry from alchemy. The accepted definitions, then, need to be specific enough to exclude the absurd yet flexible enough to accommodate the creative thought that generates new knowledge. The federal definition seems to contain elements of both specificity and flexibility. That it is controversial and tentative reflects our present state of knowledge: Nobody knows exactly what a learning disability is!

PROBE 9-1
Definition and Incidence of Learning Disabilities

1. Federal guidelines indicate that LD means a disorder in _____ spoken or written, which may manifest itself in imperfect ability to _____ . It excludes children whose learning problems are primarily the result of _____ .

2. On what four dimensions of a learning disability do professionals agree?

3. Explain why the prevalence of LD is so high.

IDENTIFICATION OF STUDENTS AS LEARNING DISABLED

You should be able to describe how students are identified as eligible for special services due to a learning disability.

THE REFERRAL PROCESS

When a classroom teacher, parent, physician, or other professional — or the student — suspects a learning disability, a referral for testing is made. It is important that certain things occur before this referral to be sure that the problem is more likely to be a learning disability than any number of other causes of school failure. For example, it is important that:

What should occur before a referral is made?

— a conference be held with the student's parents, the school's administrator, or both to discuss the problem.

— observations of the student's behavior be made in the classroom — by someone other than the teacher — to rule out environmental causes of the learning problem.

— the student's vision, hearing, speech, and language be checked to determine if any of these are contributing causes.

— the student's records be reviewed to assess the impact of possible related factors such as medical problems, excessive absenteeism, etc.

— some alternatives be tried with the student in the classroom setting (for example, individual tutoring or special management plans to change inappropriate behavior).

These preliminary steps determine whether the problem can be handled without the expensive process of referral, assessment, and placement in a special program. Classroom teachers are especially important in the referral process. It is often possible for them to modify certain aspects of the curriculum, the instructional materials, or the way they present instruction, and, as a result, to minimize the student's learning difficulties.

In all cases, the pre-referral activities are designed to determine whether a referral is actually warranted. If, after careful consideration of the above, it appears that the student should be referred for assessment of a possible learning disability, the referring person should follow the school district's referral procedures, a copy of which should be available from the building principal or special education teacher.

ASSESSMENT OF STUDENTS

Once a learning disability is suspected, the necessary pre-referral procedures are conducted, and parental permission is obtained, the student is given a series of tests. If the results of these tests indicate that the student meets the criteria specified in the definition, he or she is eligible for special services. It is important that teachers be aware of these procedures, and also that they understand the limitations of assessment.

Why is assessment important?

Assessment procedures. The tests given to a student suspected to have a learning disability are designed to (1) provide data on the student's overall intelligence level and academic strengths and weaknesses; (2) summarize the student's approach to the learning process; and (3) rule out other factors (visual, hearing, or motor disorders; low intelligence; environmental disadvantage) as primary causes of the problem.

Evidence of academic strengths and weaknesses are typically determined by achievement tests. Although the scores on group tests might be used for screening, they are not adequate for identification of LD. The achievement tests should be those specifically designed to be individually administered by a qualified professional. They might be norm-referenced tests, such as the *Wide Range Achievement Test* or the *Peabody Individual Achievement Test,* which provide scores comparing the student's performance to others at a particular grade level. Or they might be criterion-referenced tests, such as the *Basic Educational Skills Inventory,* which indicate which of a set of sequential skills the student has mastered. The academic areas of reading, math, and spelling are always evaluated. When necessary, the other areas in which the disorder may be manifested — listening, thinking, talking, writing — are also explored through testing. The examiner tries to discover whether the student's academic achievement is significantly below the level of expectation for students of similar ability, age, and grade level, and also whether the student has a pattern of academic strengths as well as weaknesses.

The examiner also tries to determine whether the referred student shows any signs of disorder in the "psychological processes" involved in understanding or using spoken or written language. An individually administered IQ test is used here, in an effort to determine whether the student's level of intelligence is significantly higher than performance in academic achievement. Often, other tests are given — for example, the *Bender Visual-Motor Gestalt Test,* a test of ability to copy designs; or the *Detroit Tests of Learning Aptitude,* which include 19 subtests to assess psychological/language processes such as auditory-visual association and verbal expression. There is a great deal of controversy over the meanings of these mysterious "psychological processes"; yet there is general agreement that unless a learning disability can be related to such a basic disorder, every student whose performance is below average could be labeled as LD. Since there is so much question about the use of standardized tests to document a "process disorder," most examiners also include data collected through classroom observations of the student's performance and an analysis of their work samples (types of errors and organizational skills) in the documentation of the process disorder.

The examiner also tries to rule out other factors as primary causes of the learning problem, as specified in the definition's "exclusion" clause. For example, there should be evidence that visual acuity is better than 20/70 (see the chapter on visual impairments) in order to rule out poor vision as the cause of inadequate performance on tasks that require vision. There should be evidence that loss of auditory acuity is not greater than 30 decibels in the better ear unaided (see the chapter on hearing impairments), to rule out hearing impairment as the primary cause of difficulty on tasks that involve listening. Similarly, motor handicaps resulting from identifiable conditions such as cerebral palsy should be ruled out when the learning disability manifests itself in poor visual-motor coordination. And, if the intelligence testing indicates an overall low level of cognitive functioning and achievement commensurate with potential, the label "mental retardation" would probably be more appropriate than "learning disability."

The assessment process is complex and lengthy, involving the judgment of many professionals as well as careful documentation of the evidence. Even so, the assessment of learning disabilities is controversial and imperfect.

Limitations of Assessment Procedures. We explained earlier that the LD definition varies among states and school districts and that the criteria for labeling are not always objective and clear. Identifying a student as LD is often a function of the operational formula or definition. The results of testing may be differentially biased, depending on the match between the school's curriculum and the tests used (Jenkins and Pany, 1978). The manner in which diagnostic personnel compute test scores also makes a difference in whether a given student is classified as LD (Epps, Ysseldyke, and Algozzine, 1981). Further, there may not be real test score differences between students who are low achievers and those labeled LD (Ysseldyke et al., 1982).

Many specialists have questioned the reliability and validity of the tests used in assessment for LD. Arter and Jenkins (1979) and French and Cozzi (1981) suggest that many of these tests are unreliable, that they lack criterion validity with respect to academic skills, and that they do not have diagnostic validity. Some of the tests commonly used may be technically inadequate (Ysseldyke and Algozzine, 1979); as a result, it may be that up to 40 percent of the students in a given school population may be misclassified (Ysseldyke, Algozzine, Shinn, and McGue, 1982). Coles (1978) has analyzed the problem further. He indicates that the tests used in representative LD assessment batteries have not demonstrated that students diagnosed as LD are neurologically impaired. Also, there is difficulty in determining the construct validity of the tests; often there is a discrepancy between what the test authors claim and what LD specialists believe these tests measure.

IMPORTANCE OF COMPREHENSIVE REVIEW

The diagnosis of learning disabilities is so complex that it requires a comprehensive review of all possible factors that may contribute to the student's learning problem. This review should include (and is required by law in some states) observations of the student in the school setting. Also, input from parents and from a professional team should be considered carefully prior to labeling the student as LD.

Need for ecological perspective. One of the proponents of the ecological approach is Hobbs (1978, p. 495), who defines the term this way: "The term ecology or ecosystem considers the total life circumstances of the child." One of the most important parts of this "ecology" is the classroom environment — the instructional program and the teacher's interactions with students.

In an early definition, Money (1962) stated that students could not be said to have a learning disability unless they had at least been exposed to conventional instruction. Samuels's (1970) definition of the disabled reader also includes the requirement that the child not have learned "despite adequate instruction." Reynolds and Birch (1977, p. 351) have stated the essence of the problem of instructional factors: "Most pupil behaviors called learning disabilities and behavior disorders are best acknowledged as the consequences of failure to provide enough high quality individualized instruction."

How can inappropriate instruction contribute to learning disability?

Of course it is difficult for teachers who have large classes to provide this high-quality individualized instruction. It is also difficult to state specifically all the dimensions of good instruction, since there are a number of theories of learning and a variety of effective techniques. But there are some general guidelines. You can perhaps understand them better if you can imagine a situation in which you are required to learn something new and very difficult. If you fail repeatedly, your teacher's patience may naturally wear a little thin. The difficulty of the subject, combined with the teacher's intensified efforts and your increasing feelings of frustration, may make you feel like a disabled learner, even though you're not. Try the simulation exercise in Chart 9-1 and see if you can explain the relationship between learning difficulties and instructional factors which occur in the student's ecological environment.

Chart 9-1
Teaching Disability Simulation

You have been selected for the high reading group, the "Eagles." You are to try to learn this new code. Pay special attention to the directions on this task sheet, and complete all activities carefully.

Learn these new words and phrases:

MKC	—Kansas City, Missouri
FA	—weather report
Ø4	—fourth day of the month
1852	—time in Greenwich. This is the same as 1252 in Kansas City, 1152 in Denver, or 1052 in Los Angeles.
IA KANS NWRN MO	—Iowa, Kansas, Northwestern Missouri
NEB EXCP PHNDL	—Nebraska except the panhandle
KTS	—knots
8–15 ⊕	—800–1500 feet, complete overcast

AGL   — above ground level
5HND   — 500
R–F   — light rain and fog
①   — scattered clouds
⊖   — broken clouds

Now learn this rule: Words in this code are spelled by their main consonant sounds. For example:

FLWG   — following
SPRDG   — spreading
CNTRD   — centered
PHDL   — panhandle

Of course there are exceptions, like WX = weather, and V = variable, but you'll just have to learn them separately.

Now that you know the rules, try this little test: How do you think you would write the following words in this code?

Evening _____ Kansas _____ Monday _____

Did you say EVNG, KNS, MNDY? Wrong! It should be EVE, KANS, MON.

If that was too hard for you, try the easier task given to the slower group, the "Robins": *Look at these words and compare them with the code symbols to see what is left out:*

CSDRBL   — considerable. These letters are left out:
                                 C-NS-D-R-BL-.
VSBY   — visibility. These letters are left out: V-S-B----Y.

Not bad. Now try a harder one. What is CIGS? _____ Did you say cigars?

Cigarettes? Wrong!!! This is a weather code. CIGS means ceilings — the distance of the clouds above the ground. You'll have to concentrate better than that.

Well, *try one more.* You won't have to move down to the slowest group, the "Sparrows," if you get this one right. What is ① V ⊖? Come on, we had all that before! You just weren't paying attention, were you? It's variable scattered to broken clouds. Sorry, you blew it!

So you have a learning disability, do you? The code you were trying to learn is not unlike the English code, with its inconsistent, confusing rules, and symbols that are hard to tell apart. That was part of the problem. But the way the lesson was presented made the code even harder to learn. Describe two of the instructional factors (i.e., what the teacher did and how the material was presented) that exacerbated your problem.

This task is a modification of a two-part simulation prepared for use in teacher training. The original includes all instructions and a second example of a more effective presentation of the same material. See Morsink, C., LRNG to Read, *Journal of Learning Disabilities,* 1973, *6,* 479-85.

Need for team decision. The complexity of assessment and the need to consider ecological factors make it imperative that the diagnosis of LD be a team decision. In most school districts, this team includes persons such as:

— the student's parent(s) or guardian(s)

— The school administrator or a representative of the administration

— an LD specialist

— the student's teacher(s)

— a person qualified to give individual intelligence tests

— others as needed (speech pathologist, school counselor, physician, LD teacher, etc.).

What is the role of the placement team?

The team may determine that a student has a learning disability if the assessment and observational reports indicate that criteria for the district's LD definition have been met. The team prepares a written report on the student's learning strengths and weaknesses, develops an individual educational plan (IEP), and agrees upon the type of school setting (regular class, resource room, special school, etc.) most appropriate for the student. Several studies have indicated that teams make more accurate placements and fewer misplacement decisions than do individuals (Vautour, 1976; Pfeiffer, 1981; Pfeiffer, 1982). Since the team concept is relatively new, however, there are still some difficulties with implementing the process, and one of the members — usually the school psychologist — may be most influential in making the placement decision (Pryzwansky, 1981). It is increasingly important, according to Deno, Marston, Shinn, and Findal (1983), that teachers become actively involved in this process.

Parents are particularly important members of the placement team. McAfee and Vergason (1979) have summarized the current problems in parental involvement in special education programs, indicating that when the goals and values of parents and professionals differ, there must be some means of reaching agreement and of ensuring parental support. Many special educators have resisted complete and meaningful parental involvement in educational planning (Yoshida, Fenton, Kaufman, and Maxwell, 1978), yet parents of LD students can, with special help, become active and supportive participants in their children's programs (Margalit, 1982). The important ways that parents must be involved in determining their child's placement and program have been summarized by Adelman and Taylor (1983). These include notification for evaluation, placement or change in placement, the right to an independent evaluation, the right to examine the student's records, the right to participate in placement and programming meetings, and the right to an impartial hearing if they disagree with the school's program for their child. Parents, like professionals, are important members of the LD student's team.

RECOMMENDATIONS FOR IMPROVING IDENTIFICATION

A number of specialists have attempted to improve the process of identification in learning disabilities. Suggestions for observation and evaluation of the classroom environment and documentation of instructional alternatives have been described previously and will not be repeated here. New assessment instruments are also being developed. One of these is the *Kaufman Assessment Battery for Children* (Kaufman and Kaufman, 1983). Unlike tests that measure "verbal" and "performance" IQ, this test attempts to measure what happens in problem solving between input and output of information. It assesses sequential information processing (one aspect at a time) and simultaneous information processing. It has, in addition, a separate score for achievement (knowledge in academic skills) and a special nonverbal scale for use with non-English speaking children and those who have hearing impairments and speech or language disorders. The authors intend that the test results be used more for problem solving than for labeling.

What should be included in an assessment?

Most of the recommendations for improving assessment and identification procedures focus on the assessment of the learning task and the instructional program rather than on the student. This means that the task to be learned should be assessed in order to provide more appropriate instruction. Lovitt and Fantasia (1980) propose a direct approach to evaluation — one that measures the learner's rate of correct and incorrect responses. Blankenship and Lilly (1981) are among those who recommend "curriculum-based assessment" — measurement of the student's performance on the specific tasks required in the curriculum. Wallace and Larsen (1978) have urged regular classroom teachers to become involved in the evaluation of students with learning problems, using both formal tests and informal assessment procedures.

Adelman and Taylor (1983) state that presently we do not have assessment procedures that result in differential diagnosis and related prescriptions. They recommend that "person-assessment" and test procedures should not be overemphasized; assessment of the environment and teacher-student interactions should be included, and alternative assessment procedures should be developed.

PROBE 9-2
Identification of Students as Learning Disabled

1. T F The teacher who suspects a student may have a learning disability should make an immediate referral for testing.

2. In what areas does the professional conducting the assessment of the referred student gather data? What does this person also try to rule out?

3. T F The LD definition and criteria for labeling are the same in every state.

4. List two important factors in providing a comprehensive review of learning problems.

5. Tell how assessment for learning disabilities can be improved.

CHARACTERISTICS OF LEARNING DISABILITIES

> **You should be able to recognize some of the characteristics of learning disabilities and to distinguish them from simple learning difficulties.**

HISTORICAL PERSPECTIVE AND CURRENT VIEWS

Early in the development of the learning disability concept, researchers studied neurologically impaired children and described LD characteristics that were similar to those found in brain-injured adults. Learners with disabilities were observed to have difficulty recalling the orientation and sequence of letters, a phenomenon that the neurologist Orton (1937) termed "strephosymbolia," or twisted symbols. Strauss and Lehtinen (1947) noted that neurologically impaired children tended to perceive fragmented parts rather than integrated wholes, that they were distracted by extraneous details, and that they did not perceive figures as distinct from their backgrounds. Strauss and Lehtinen also discussed their students' difficulty in relating temporal patterns (sounds) and spatial patterns (the letters in a word that the sounds represent). They suggested that their students had a tendency to perseverate (repeat the same response over and over again) or to respond impulsively. In a 1961 report based on observations of brain-injured and hyperactive children, Cruickshank and his colleagues (Cruickshank et al., 1961) reported that hyperactive children without evidence of brain damage exhibited learning characteristics similar to those of the neurologically impaired.

Most current studies of LD characteristics focus on the components of learning disabilities described in the federal definition. These components are described in the following manner. First, the LD characteristics related to learning basic academic subjects (reading, math, language) are summarized. Second, the characteristics that describe disorders in the learning process (cognition and attention) are presented. Third, the LD student's related social and emotional characteristics are described. Fourth, characteristic disorders relating to motor skills are described. Finally, the current view that learning disabilities characteristics are a continuum ranging from mild difficulties to severe deficits is discussed.

BASIC ACADEMIC SUBJECT DISORDERS

Disabled learners are characterized most often by their difficulties in learning the basic school-related skills. Research has focused on characteristics in the three academic skill areas that have received the most emphasis: reading, mathematics, and language.

Reading. Reading problems characterize a large number of students labeled LD. Kirk and Elkins (1975) reported that reading difficulty was the primary focus for two-thirds of the 3,000 LD students served in the 24 federally funded Children Service Demonstration Centers. Several others have indicated that students with reading disabilities represent the largest subgroup in the LD category (Erb and Mercer, 1979; Mercer and Mercer, 1979; Silberberg and Silberberg, 1977).

What problems occur in children with reading disabilities?

In an earlier review, Morsink (1977) summarized the educationally relevant problems of students with severe reading disability. They are:

1. Attention difficulty
2. Perceptual problems
3. Poor motivation or attitude
4. Poor sound-symbol association
5. Memory problems
6. Language deficits
7. Transfer difficulties

These problems may be related to some underlying difficulties in processing information. On the surface, the disabled reader's problems are lack of ability to decode words and/or to comprehend the meaning of words, sentences, and passages. The disabled reader may read in a slow, halting manner, have a short attention span, and have difficulty remembering what is read (Morsink, 1977). Pflaum and Bryan (1980), studying the oral reading behaviors of elementary students with learning disabilities, also discovered that the LD group was less effective in using context for decoding. They self-corrected less frequently and made decoding errors that changed meaning more seriously.

Disabled readers aren't all alike. Some have extreme difficulty in figuring out new words (decoding) but are able to understand very well when someone reads the information to them. Others can recognize words but seem unable to comprehend their meanings or to analyze and apply information. The presence of the two groups has led to a lot of controversy about whether LD students should be taught to read through phonics or whole-word methods.

A number of researchers have investigated in greater depth the question of whether, for disabled readers, context provides better decoding clues than does letter-sound correspondence. The results indicate that there are individual differences in the ability of disabled readers on these tasks. Reisberg (1982), studying the ability of 20 reading-disabled 8- to 12-year-olds, found that as a group they read words significantly better in context than in isolation, though three individuals made consistently fewer errors when reading isolated words. He stressed the importance of recognizing individual differences. Ganschow, Wheeler, and Kretschmer (1982), questioning whether decoding and comprehension are independent processes, suggested that if they were, disabled readers could be poor in one while adequate in the other. In a total sample of 48 students, they compared 13- to 15-year-old disabled readers to both age-matched normal readers and achievement-matched younger readers on four tasks involving decoding and explaining the meanings of words presented in isolation and in context. They found that context facilitated the performance of all three groups. The disabled reader's performance was:

1. uniformly inferior to that of same-age good readers;
2. similar on meaning tasks to that of younger normal readers;
3. inferior on decoding to that of younger normal readers.

When the performance of individual disabled readers was examined, the investigators found that there were two with decoding strength and meaning weaknesses (both in context and on isolated words) and two with meaning strength and decoding weakness (again, both in context and on isolated words). They supported Reisburg's inference that there are individual differences in disabled readers; different students learn in different ways.

There is some evidence that special teaching methods can help disabled readers improve their reading performance. This can be done both for comprehension (Pflaum, et al., 1982; Wong, Wong, and Lemare, 1982) and for word attack (Morsink and Otto, 1977; Trembley, 1982) by providing specific instruction on reading objectives and subskills. It may be that the most important teaching methods are those that actively involve the learner in the reading task (Wong, 1979, 1982; Bos, 1982). Wong has done this by developing questioning strategies to aid retention of main ideas, while the research of Box has involved repeated readings to increase reading fluency. Much of the research on reading disability suggests not only that this failure of the learner to be involved actively is a characteristic of LD, but also that reading disability is a symptom of more pervasive deficits in the learning process.

What are the two primary mathematics disorders?

Mathematics. Although there is not as much research on mathematics as on reading as a characteristic of LD, the research findings with this subgroup also suggest that severe math deficits may be symptomatic of underlying cognitive disorders. Johnson and Myklebust (1967) were among the first to study the mathematical disorders of LD students. They hypothesized that there were two main types of disorders: those related to difficulty in processing auditory or visual information and those characterized by an inability to perform arithmetic calculations. More specifically, they indicated that LD students were often unable to:

— understand 1-to-1 correspondence
— count meaningfully
— associate auditory and visual symbols
— learn both cardinal and ordinal counting systems
— visualize clusters of objects within a larger group
— grasp the principle of conservation of quantity
— perform arithmetic operations

TECHNOLOGY IN ACTION

A talking computer in Phoenix, used by children who already know how to talk, but who are having trouble with reading and writing, is producing dramatic results. Dr. Teresa Rosegrant, a developmentalist in early childhood education and linguistics, designed her word-processing system so that the computer can say each letter, word and sentence a child types. The child chooses what it is to say.

One of the children Dr. Rosegrant worked with was a frustrated, mischief-maker in second grade who could barely read and write. He was in danger of being held back. "No one knew what to do with Kevin," Rosegrant says. "When I met him, I found he was incredibly interested in machines, so the first day he came in we opened the computer lid and talked about interface cards and how impulses went to the printer.

"It was pretty tough for him to use the keyboard," Rosegrant recalls. "It was hard for him to coordinate what his hand was doing with his eyes, and to scan the lines of print. But we started talking about dirt bikes, which he just loved. I told him I thought other kids would be interested in what he knew about dirt bikes.

"The next session Kevin came in with his title 'All About Dirt Bikes,' and started writing: 'There are many ways that you can start a dirt bike. You can turn on the key, kick the peg, or hotwire it. Dirt bikes come in many sizes. They have many chain lengths. Some chains are 23 inches long and some chains are 48 inches long.' It was his first story on the word processor. It grew to eight sentences, and took him five days. Hearing what he typed helped him stay with it."

When it was printed, Kevin carried the story away with delight, only to return three days later looking exasperated. "When you write books, you don't put the whole thing on one page," he griped. "I can't make a book out of this one page!" Rosegrant sat him down at the computer. "I'll show you the next level of word processing," she explained. "You decide what is page one and I'll show you how to move the rest down to page two." Kevin was awed. He figured out where to break up the story, printed three pages and left happy.

Five minutes later he came back. "The title should be on its own page," he said. The chastised educator watched her budding author create a title page.

As his motor coordination and confidence improved, Kevin started teaching other second-graders how to use the word processor. But he doesn't get to use it by himself any more. Now in third grade, he is no longer regarded as learning disabled.

From an article by Paul Trachtman in The Smithsonian *(1984)*

— understand the meaning of process signs
— understand the arrangement of numbers on the page
— follow and remember the sequence of steps to be used in mathematical operations
— understand the principles of measurement
— read maps and graphs
— solve problems in arithmetic reasoning

More recently, several other explanations of the difficulty have been added. Reading difficulty may cause or compound math disorders (Lerner, 1976; Cawley, Fitzmaurice, Goldstein, Lepore, Sedlak, and Althaus, 1976; Bartel,

1975). Possible contributing causes range from ineffective instruction to disorders in abstract symbolic thinking.

Like reading disabilities, math disorders respond to specific instruction. In a large, long-term study of beginning teachers (Schneider, 1979), the level of interaction in learning was found to be the most important variable in mathematical achievement. Thornton and Reuille (1978) also suggested that students disabled in mathematics learn better when they practice to the point of "overlearning." This is not to suggest, however, that rote learning or meaningless practice should be emphasized. The pioneering work of Strauss and Lehtinen (1947) and the longitudinal work of Cawley et al. (1976) indicated that students disabled in mathematics require instruction that helps them to develop concepts and logical methods of problem solving. Another consistent recommendation is that concrete materials should be used to help students grasp abstract number concepts (Johnson and Myklebust, 1967; Horowitz, 1970; Schefflin and Seltzer, 1974).

Language. According to the definition, LD students have an overall deficit in one or more of the processes involved in language. An increasing number of researchers are suggesting that learning disabilities are related to overall language facility (Abrams, 1975; Vogel, 1975; Hessler and Kitchen, 1980; Wiig and Semel, 1980). A frequent observation is that disabled learners continue

Students using a microcomputer to develop language skills.

How are language deficits and learning disabilities related?

to use language incorrectly long after it has been mastered by children with comparable education and background. It has also been observed that academic achievement can be predicted from tests of oral language usage. Noel (1980) has shown that LD students have limited ability in oral communications involving labeling and verbal descriptions. Magee and Newcomer (1978) have investigated the relationship between oral language and academic achievement in LD children. They indicated that (1) correct grammar and understanding words and sentences are more closely related to academic achievement than are articulation and speech discrimination skills; (2) math proficiency is related to language ability; and (3) language skill seems to enhance children's ability to acquire general information about their environment.

Language problems also extend to written language. Wiig, Semel, and Abele (1981) found that the ability of 12-year-old LD students to interpret the meanings of ambiguous sentences differed from the ability of normal students of their age and was more nearly like the ability of normal 7- to 8-year-olds. Poplin, Gray, and Larsen (1980) found that third- through eighth-grade LD students scored significantly lower than did normals in their age group on the *Test of Written Language*.

These findings suggest that a general underlying problem with language sometimes extends to difficulty in learning, and they imply a need for emphasis on language development.

PSYCHOLOGICAL PROCESS DISORDERS

Much of the research on disabilities in reading, mathematics, and language suggests that LD students have some underlying disorders in the "basic psychological processes involved in understanding and in using language." Studies related to this hypothesis are summarized below. They have been divided into two groups. The first is the broad category of cognition, which includes perception, memory, and thought as related examples. The second is a narrower category called "attention"; this relates to the student's inability to focus and often occurs in conjunction with hyperactivity and the tendency to respond impulsively.

How can differences in cognitive processing influence labeling?

Cognitive disorders. This term includes disorders in the basic processes involved in learning: perception, memory, and thought. When pervasive cognitive disorders occur in students, they are labeled mentally retarded; when specific disorders are found in one or more of these processes, the student is more often labeled LD. This oversimplification is not intended to discount the difficulty of assessing learning processes; it acknowledges the confusion and overlap in the two labels. It is provided, rather, in an effort to clarify the description of the LD student as having one or more of these difficulties in some, but not all, school subjects.

Perception refers to the learner's ability to see and hear abstract stimuli, to label sights and sounds, and to distinguish between abstractions that look or sound familiar. Many LD students have difficulties with these tasks. Studies of disabled learners suggest that many of them are confused by words or numbers that look or sound alike. They may have trouble differentiating similar sounds (Wepman, 1960) and recognizing small visual differences (Strauss and Lehtinen, 1947; Cruickshank et al., 1961). Although some LD children have trouble receiving information that is presented auditorily or visually, a greater number experience difficulty in associating abstract auditory with visual stimuli (Abrams, 1975; Johnson and Myklebust, 1967; Guthrie, 1974). Recent research supports the assumption that auditory-visual integration is related to reading ability (Derevensky, 1977; Ward, 1977) but indicates that the variables are related in a complex manner, depending on the student's development, IQ, and economic background.

Does perceptual training improve learning performance?

Although the presence of perceptual problems in the LD population has been documented, there is little evidence to suggest that these problems are responsive to existing "treatment" programs. Hammill and Larsen (1978) have analyzed the research on perceptual treatment programs and concluded that the evidence does not justify their use. More recently, Luchou and Shepherd (1981) have indicated that multisensory (visual plus auditory and/or tactile) input does not improve the learning performance of LD students on a perceptual task not related to reading or math.

Memory is the process of retrieving and utilizing the sights and sounds that have been perceived. In cognition, memory involves letters, words, and numbers. It is difficult for many LD students, particularly when learning is not meaningful, to remember what they learn and to generalize their learning.

Morsink, Cross, and Strickler (1978) compared the abilities of disabled readers and normal learners to recall sequences of "meaningful" (bo, nup, . . .) and "meaningless" (fz, sdm, . . .) letters. They found that although the disabled readers were poorer than normal readers in both tasks, they were markedly inferior to normal readers on "meaningful" recall. This finding suggests that they didn't know how to simplify the task by grouping meaningful segments, that the segments were not meaningful to them, or both. Gibson's summary (1970) indicates that decoding instruction can improve the recall of abstract symbols, and Otto (1961) has shown that, though poor readers learn the "names" for symbols more slowly, they can remember verbal labels once they have learned them. Bryant (1965) and Abrams (1969) have suggested that disabled learners have extreme difficulty generalizing their knowledge of sound-symbol relationships to new situations. In an interesting study comparing the reading subskills of disabled readers and normal learners, Guthrie (1973) provided evidence that the reading subskills of normal learners are highly interconnected or are derived from an understanding of concepts common to all subskills. Among disabled readers, however, reading subskills may seem unrelated, and each subskill may have to be learned independently.

More recent research suggests that LD students can be taught to improve their performance on skills that require memory. Haines and Torgesen (1978) found that LD students with reading problems performed better on memory tasks when they became more active in the learning task through more efficient task strategies such as rehearsal. Similarly, Lewis and Kass (1982) found that learning material to criterion level and being taught that impulsive responses were incorrect were important factors in improving LD students' performance on memory tasks.

What is metacognition?

Baker (1982) has summarized the recent research on "metacognition," the use of congitive skills by LD students. Metacognition involves awareness of what is needed to perform a cognitive task plus the ability to be self-directing in completing the task. She indicates that LD students perform cognitive tasks like younger normal students, and that there has been some success in training children to improve their performance, but that a cause and effect relationship between this skill training and overall improvement of cognition has not yet been demonstrated.

Attention deficits. Many children with serious learning difficulties find it hard to focus their attention on a selected sound, word, number, or line of print (Cruickshank, Bentzen, Ratenburg, and Tannhauser, 1961; Strauss and Lehtinen, 1947). Ross (1976) suggests that the major difficulty is an ability to use attention selectively. He explains that children not using selective attention

This student is receiving individual attention from his teacher.

may look at the chalkboard or the fly on the eraser instead of the letter or word they should see. He also maintains that their attention may be overselective — for example, they may focus only on the circular part of the letter *b* and thus be unable to differentiate it from the *d*. Hallahan et al. (1978) compared disabled learners to "normal" teenagers on a task involving selective attention. They found that the LD group was deficient in giving selective attention to the central learning task, but not to the incidental details. A possible consequence, then, of an attention problem, is that students may focus on the irrelevant details while missing the central issue. Another possible problem is that children may guess at answers impulsively, without looking at the word, listening to the question, or thinking through their response.

What is an "attention deficit disorder"?

The presence of attention deficits in LD students is so pervasive that "attention deficit disorder" is one of the three current classifications of LD subgroups. Students with this disorder are described as overactive, restless, impulsive, inattentive, distractible, easily frustrated, aggressive, and unpredictable. Recent studies have provided further insight into this disorder. Brown (1981) has found that hyperactive children's ability to sustain attention to auditory stimuli improves with age but that improvement is not as great in regard to visual stimuli. In normal children, auditory and visual attention improve similarly as a function of age. Pihl and Niaura (1982) have suggested that the ability of LD children to sustain task attention deteriorates over time (most markedly after ten trials) rather than as a function of task complexity. It has not yet been shown that attention can be improved through training, although there has been promising research with relaxation training related to biofeedback (Dunn and Howell, 1982).

SOCIAL-EMOTIONAL DEFICITS

Social-emotional deficits have been suggested as characteristics of learning disabilities since the category was created, although social-emotional deficits are not included in the current federal definition. Two related issues, social perceptions and "learned helplessness," have received much attention recently.

How popular are children with learning disabilities?

Social perceptions. During the past decade, the peer popularity and self-image of LD students and their relationship to poor verbal and nonverbal communication skills have been studied extensively, most notably by Bryan. It has been noted that LD students are more likely than normal students to send and receive negative verbal messages and to interpret nonverbal behaviors inaccurately (Bryan and Bryan, 1978). Bryan, Sherman, and Fisher (1980) have indicated that LD boys are less likely to maintain eye contact or smile during an interview. Horowitz (1981) is among those who have shown that LD students are less popular than their peers and that they are aware of their unpopularity. Bryan, Donahue, and Pearl (1981) have indicated that LD children tend to take a submissive role in group problem-solving and that their suggestions are less likely to be included in the group's final choices.

There are some continuing questions in assessing social-emotional deficits as a characteristic of LD. Instruments have been developed to measure social perception; many are time-consuming and expensive, though it may be possible to assess these skills more quickly and easily (Axelrod, 1982). Maheady and Maitland (1982) caution that these assessment instruments may not measure the same things as would observation in the natural environment. Also, the same types of inappropriate social behaviors may be observed in groups other than LD children, notably the educable retarded and socially-emotionally disturbed (Maheady and Maitland, 1982). While not necessarily occurring in all students labeled LD, they probably occur more often in the LD subgroup with the hyperactivity syndrome.

Learned Helplessness. This is a second characteristic related to the LD student's social-emotional difficulties. It refers to the students' belief that success and failure are beyond their control. The term "attributions" is used frequently in this research, meaning an explanation the individuals give for their success and failure; most persons attribute success to ability or effort. There is also a second set of recurring terms, "internal locus of control," used to describe factors the individual can change, and "external locus of control," used to describe factors the individual cannot change.

Increasingly, the research suggests that LD students have poor self-esteem, poor motivation, and attributions suggesting an external locus of control. Pearl, Bryan, and Donahue (1980) found that LD students in their samples did not believe their achievement to be under their control; this learned helplessness seemed to extend beyond the areas in which students had abilities to other areas of academic learning. Tollefson, Tracy, Johnsen, Buenning, Farmer, and Barke (1982) have shown that, although their junior-high-age disabled learners verbalized a desire to do well, they failed to expend greater efforts and also predicted that they would score lower on subsequent tasks of equal difficulty.

What can teachers do about "learned helplessness"?

Most authors have suggested that teachers can and should assist students in overcoming learned helplessness by increasing their students' level of success and by providing direct instruction in coping with failure. Grimes (1981) cautions, however, against providing continuous success; it can have the opposite effect of leading students to believe that they lack ability when they ultimately experience failures. Grimes also emphasizes the importance of helping the LD student to cope with the unfairness of the situation in which an intelligent person must struggle so hard to learn. Mark (1983) believes that learned helplessness doesn't necessarily need to be changed; it may be an adaptive behavior that brings relief from excessive competition or peer and family pressure.

Several programs have been developed to help LD students improve their social-emotional skills. These include programs to help students understand the meanings of facial expression, gesture, and other forms of nonverbal communication (Minskoff, 1980) and work with others in cooperative learning groups (Bryan, Cosden, and Pearl, 1982). Some evidence is available on the effectiveness of training in social and problem-solving skills; it suggests that gains may be small for LD students compared to others (Hazel et al., 1981). In the area of learned helplessness, there is a need for a more uniform system to guide future research.

MOTOR SKILLS DISORDERS

What effect does motor training have on academic performance?

Like social-emotional deficits, motor skill disorders were listed as characteristics of LD from the beginning of the movement. Motor incoordination, which ranged from general awkwardness and difficulty with physical skills to poor handwriting, was often observed in students who had other characteristics of learning disabilities. Many pioneers in the LD movement developed educational programs that emphasized first the training of motor skills and then progressed through visual-motor integration to higher level cognitive skills (Kephart, 1971; Cratty, 1969; Getman, 1962; Frostig and Maslow, 1973). Although the well-designed studies of these programs indicated that training in motor skills had little effect on the student's academic performance (Arter and Jenkins, 1979), gross and fine motor incoordination are still observed in LD students with enough frequency to be considered a characteristic.

CONTINUUM OF CHARACTERISTICS

As indicated by the federal definition, any given child with a learning disability may exhibit academic skill deficits, psychological process disorders related to language comprehension and use, or both.

Mild to severe disabilities. Learning disabilities may range from mild to severe. When mild, they are usually treated by part-time special education focused on the area of disability (reading, math, etc.). When severe, they may require more intensive and long-term educational programming in an all-day special program plus service from related professionals such as speech therapists, counselors, and physicians.

Common learning problems. When reading the descriptions of LD characteristics, the reader may say, "I have that problem" or "That's just the way my nephew acts. . . . I wonder if he has a learning disability." Everyone experiences difficulties in learning certain things under particular conditions; these common learning problems are not characteristics of LD because they are mild and temporary. The following are some examples of common learning problems experienced by everyone.

How can problems in attention, perception, and thinking affect learning?

1. We all occasionally have problems focusing our attention. We may be distracted by other thoughts, or we may not know where to focus our attention. Can you read Figure 9-1? If you focused on the words hidden behind the lines, you read, "Are you paying attention?" The question, "Can you read Figure 9-1?" may have given you a clue to look for words. Materials that present distractions — as this one did — are particularly difficult for LD students. But difficulty in attending to the relevant stimuli in a distracting background is common to everyone.

2. You can understand part of the mystery of "perception" by reflecting on your experiences with visual illusions like the one in Figure 9-2. If you stare at the cube for about ten seconds, it seems to flip over. Your perception of its orientation changes. In a similar manner, some children with learning disabilities seem to be unstable in their perception of images. Johnson (1972, pp. 267-269) illustrates another aspect of differences in perception by presenting three pictures of a woman. One seems to be a pretty young woman with a feather in her hat; another, with one or two different lines, looks like a haggard old woman with a shawl. The third picture, which has both kinds of details, can be perceived as either a young or old woman, but viewers usually perceive it as the image of whichever picture they saw first. This experience illustrates a problem some LD children have. Many children have difficulty perceiving either details or whole configurations. They frequently have prob-

Figure 9-1

Figure 9-2

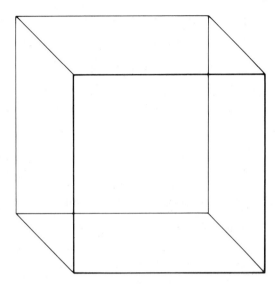

lems "shifting gears"; that is, they have trouble expanding their original perceptions and seeing things in a different way. Everyone has that difficulty sometimes, but it isn't a learning disability unless it's severe and persistent.

3. What kinds of things are hardest for you to remember? Try this experiment. Look at Figure 9-3 for 5 seconds. Write what you saw. Now try Figure 9-4. Look at it for 5 seconds. Write what you saw. Now check yourself.

Why was BRIOGANTRY easier? Probably because it looked more like a word, and the letters could be placed in larger groups to simplify learning them. Children with learning disabilities don't seem to know how to group things into meaningful parts to help them recall. Many children try to remem-

Figure 9-3

BRIOGANTRY

Figure 9-4

ber things one fragment at a time, just as you did with XTMSLFKBQH. They need help to understand how parts are meaningful and can be grouped. They also need lots of interesting practice and continued reinforcement to achieve mastery. But it is difficult for anyone to remember unrelated facts or abstract figures that don't make sense.

4. LD students have difficulty with cognitive skills. Try this example to see how you respond to problems that require careful thinking. Read this (Whimby, 1977, p. 255):

What follows the day before yesterday if two days from now will be Sunday?

Can you answer the question quickly? What did you try to do when you read this problem? If you're a systematic problem solver, you tried to take it apart and solve it one step at a time. But you were probably tempted to be a one-shot thinker, as many LD students are, and just guess at the answer. Of course, you'd find this problem harder to solve if it was read to you out loud and you had to hold the details in mind while solving each step. Certain circumstances can turn anyone into an impulsive learner, but unless the behavior occurs frequently and interferes with learning, it's not a characteristic of LD.

5. Language problems related to multiple meanings illustrate a common learning problem. Remember when you were little and thought shoe trees were trees that had shoes instead of leaves on them? Actor Fred Gwynne has written a delightful children's book called *A Chocolate Moose for Dinner* (Gwynne, 1976). It illustrates the child's simpler ideas of words that adults know have multiple meanings. It shows, for example, a picture of "shoe trees" and shows how "lions *pray* (prey) on other animals." (Picture that in your mind's eye!) Mort Walker, the creator of the Beetle Bailey comic strip, has also pictured this more concrete level of language in the verbal responses of his character named Zero. Zero is shown using a metal file to smooth down the general's papers after being told to "file these papers," and he goes to ask for the keys to the jeep when the general, in exasperation, moans, "You're

driving me to the psychiatrist's couch!" Such difficulties with language are understandable, because our language is filled with abstraction and multiple meanings. This behavior isn't a characteristic of LD unless it continues long after the child's language abilities have matured and the child has received good teaching.

All of our examples were, of course, vastly oversimplified for the purpose of illustration. They were intended to show that all of us have some of the problems often attributed to children with learning disabilities. It is important to remember that they may just be common problems and not symptoms of learning disabilities.

PROBE 9-3
Characteristics of Learning Disabilities

1. T F Disabled learners most often have deficits in the academic area of reading.

2. T F All disabled readers have difficulty in comprehension.

3. T F Language deficits may affect the LD student's ability to perform in math or in reading.

4. What is learned helplessness? What seems to be its relationship to LD?

5. T F Research has shown that academic performance can be improved by training visual-motor skills.

6. Describe a common problem you have had in learning. Explain how this problem differs from a learning disability.

TRENDS IN LEARNING DISABILITIES

You should be able to discuss the current trends in learning disabilities.

The major contemporary issue in learning disabilities is the same as it is in other areas of special education: How can we identify and meet the needs of a broad range of exceptional learners in the least restrictive environment? The question takes on added significance in the field of LD, because there has been so much disagreement over definition of the term and no resolution of the treatment controversy. In the future it will become increasingly important to separate — for treatment purposes — those few students with true disabilities from the much larger group of students with less complicated learning difficulties. Classification may become more important, but it won't be easier. The fact that learning difficulties range along a continuum from the mild to the severe and resist clear differentiation will continue to present problems. The following trends are emerging:

1. Service to LD children will be provided by a team of professionals rather than by a single specialist.
2. Research to identify the least restrictive educational environment will continue.
3. New theories about the causes, types, and treatments of learning disabilities will emerge.

THE SERVICE TEAM

The ecological, transdisciplinary team approach is designed to take advantage of aspects of the field that are still evolving. There are exciting developments in medical treatment and in educational approaches and new concepts in psychology and environmental research. All contribute to our understanding of learning disabilities, but the most effective approaches are derived from the entire range of sources. In addition, it was noted previously that a team decision is required for placement of an LD student and that teams have been found to make more appropriate decisions than do single individuals.

How has the role of the special education teacher changed?

As the diagnostic practices and treatment of the LD have evolved, the role of the special educator has changed as well. Special educators now act as team members rather than isolated specialists. In many cases the special educator serves as the teacher in a resource room, which provides part-time instruction for LD students. The special educator's role as a resource person will also be important for the severely disabled learner who requires initial placement in a special education setting. These children will need to be prepared for reentry into the educational mainstream. Reentry is a task that involves collaboration between the regular and special class teachers (Grosenick, 1971).

The new role of the special educator as a team member and resource person will require a new form of training, one that stresses professional interactions. Denemark, Morsink, and Thomas (1980) report that training for professional interactions should include practice in expressing ideas in simple, direct language and experiences in joint planning, team teaching, and collaborative evaluation of educational programs. The LD specialist of the future will have to know not only how to identify and teach the LD child but also how to work cooperatively as a member of a professional team as well.

LEAST RESTRICTIVE ENVIRONMENT

What is the least restrictive environment for an LD child?

For the severely disabled, special programs will be required. In many cases, however, the least restrictive environment for the LD student includes part-time placement in the regular classroom.

Heron and Skinner (1981) have attempted to establish criteria to define the regular classroom as the least restrictive environment for the learning disabled student. The variables chosen for their definition were selected from among those supported by recent research as contributing to the mainstreaming effort; these variables also addressed measurable factors in program design for learning disabled students. Their definition of the least restrictive environment is particularly interesting. It includes three components (Heron and Skinner, 1981, p. 116):

[This classroom]
1. "maximizes the LD student's opportunity to respond and achieve,"
2. "permits the regular teacher to interact proportionately with all students in the class," and
3. "fosters acceptable social relationships between nonhandicapped and LD students."

These criteria appear more specific and measurable than those previously used to define the least restrictive environment.

NEW THEORIES ABOUT CAUSES, TYPES, AND TREATMENTS

New information about the causes of learning disabilities is beginning to accumulate. This information appears to lead, on one hand, to greater differentiation among the various types of LD while at the same time supporting the existence of similarities among learning disabilities and other categories such as behavior disorders and mental retardation. It may be that this new evidence will lead to a new system of classification, and to an increased interest in treatment.

Current treatment emphasis. At the present time, most specialists believe that learning disabilities are caused primarily by educational rather than medical factors and that their treatment should have an educational focus. Coles (1980), for example, disputed the theory that many reading or learning disabilities are inherited. Although severe learning disabilities tend to run in families, Coles pointed out that the conclusion of hereditary causation is not supported, since there were often no control groups in these studies, and many failed to account for students' socioeconomic status, family relationships, or educational experiences. Coles argued that researchers who concluded that LD

How effective is skill-based instruction?

is hereditary did not search for alternate explanations of the problem and drew simplistic conclusions not supported by evidence.

The major educational treatments are skill-based; that is, they provide direct instruction on the specific skills in which the student is deficient. There is some research showing that the skill-based approach is effective with LD students but that its effectiveness depends on the way it is used by the teacher (Morsink and Otto, 1977). Face-to-face instruction is more effective than use of work sheets that students complete independently. Teachers who select instructional activities carefully, provide enough practice to ensure skill mastery, and show students how to apply the skills that they learn find their students retain information and generalize better.

Many educational interventions have included an emphasis on applied behavior analysis. Lovitt (1975) summarized this body of research as it applied to learning disabilities. He indicated that for reading instruction, reinforcement has been used effectively along with feedback and specific correction procedures. In handwriting, effective techniques include modeling, explicit instruction, teacher praise, and feedback. In arithmetic, techniques utilizing modeling, drill, praise, feedback, and tokens for correct responses have been successful. Lovitt urged that researchers also use applied behavior analysis to study more complex learning, such as reading comprehension and arithmetic problems, and that those who design programs for behavior management view self-management as the ultimate objective.

More recently there is additional evidence on the effectiveness of direct educational strategies in remedying learning disabilities. Deno and Chiang (1982) showed how to remedy reversals in letters. Wong (1979) increased LD students' reading comprehension through active listening strategies involving questioning and prompting. Cawley et al. (1976) developed an instructional program to increase LD students' performance on word problems in math. Accumulating evidence suggests that at least some learning disabilities can be remedied through careful instructional programming. LD reading and language specialists and classroom teachers are important partners in this effort.

Despite the effectiveness of educational treatments, however, there are some specialists who still believe the LD student's problems result from an internal physical deficit. This deficit could be a constitutional problem present at birth, such as a hereditary or congenital abnormality, or it could be a deficit occuring after birth: the result of infections, toxins, poor nutrition, injury, or illness (Baren, Liebel, and Smith, 1978).

Some intriguing questions along these lines continue to arise. It has been suggested that learning disabilities may be aggravated by allergies, induced by nutritional deficits, related to biochemical disorders, or even intensified by florescent lighting. (Hollander, 1977). Baren et al. (1978) add smog, flouride, aerosols, and auditory pollution to the list of possible causes of learning problems. There is some research on these controversial medical theories, but these findings should be regarded as inconclusive (Seiben, 1977).

De-emphasis of traditional categories. The difficulty of using current diagnostic procedures to place students in the LD category was discussed previously. Hallahan and Kauffman (1977) are among those who argue most strongly for the removal of the labels "learning disabilities," "behavior disorders," and "mental retardation" and the noncategorical treatment of these mildly handicapped students. The most serious mislabeling question relates to students who are culturally different. Although students' performance on tests of reading and language are thought to be the most accurate way to distinguish LD children from normal children, a few of these tests take dialect differences into account (Harber, 1980). Kavale (1980) has shown that the symptoms of learning difficulties in LD students are similar to the characteristics of those who are culturally different. Tucker (1980) has also documented the increase in the number and percentage of culturally different students placed in LD classes over the period 1970 to 1977. The question of labeling the culturally different student as learning handicapped is a very difficult one, since bias in testing can lead to misclassification; yet denying students needed services is equally inappropriate.

How are learning disabilities related to other exceptionalities?

Additionally, there are questions about the presence of learning disabilities, as defined by performance discrepancies, in other categories of exceptional students. It is possible that students labeled as behavior disordered and sensorily impaired may have the same types of discrepancies in learning strengths and weaknesses as do LD children. Pledgic (1982) shows that students with any handicapping conditon, including LD, can simultaneously have characteristics suggesting giftedness, and urges that teachers use systematic observation lists for identification of the gifted handicapped. On the other hand, Whitmore (1980) has documented the presence of learning disabilities in students identified as gifted underachievers. It would appear that all of this new information supports the development of new, more functional classification systems for students with learning difficulties.

In what ways can children with learning disabilities be classified?

New classification system. There is general agreement that the system of classifying students as learning disabled should be reconceptualized. A number of authors suggest ways in which this might be done.

Forness (1981) suggests that there are new questions about LD students' underlying perceptual and language problems. New evidence suggests that some LD students may have deficits in attention, in the use of memory strategies, or both. He states that it is also possible that there are at least two major types of language-related learning disorders: (1) those in which the student's skills mature more slowly and (2) those lasting deficits that cause later problems in language comprehension and use.

Komm (1982) indicates that what is now called LD should more accurately be subdivided into three more specific areas: conduct disorder, developmental disorder, and attention deficit disorder. The third, he suggests, is the most prominent and includes the related problems of inattention, impulsivity, and hyperactivity.

Wong (1979) describes three slightly different conceptual models of learning disabilities: (1) the interactional model, which focuses on educational factors and implies a need for accurate assessment and instruction, including applied behavior analysis and an emphasis on social perceptions; (2) the theory of a lag in selective attention; and (3) the conceptualization that the LD student is an inactive learner who does not process information effectively.

Two other promising developments may also yield new information on how LD students learn. Cole and Hall (1982) are currently conducting experiments in an interdisciplinary laboratory, to study learning environments and determine the relationship of classroom variables to student's learning. Finally, there is new research related to learning styles (see Davidman, 1981) and to right and left brain functioning (see Kaufman and Kaufman, 1983), which may have implications for reconceptualization of learning disabilities.

The growing knowledge base seems to suggest that the current term, "learning disabilities," is a generic description of a number of learning problems which range from mild to severe and may be found in students currently classified as LD or in other categories of exceptionality. Perhaps the classification of Adelman and Taylor (1983) is most logical. They divide learning disabilities into three groups according to other dimensions: (1) those caused by environmental variables, (2) those created by the interaction between the learner and the environment, and (3) (more severe) problems within the learner related to information processing or social-emotional dysfunctions.

It seems that future research, which emphasizes the cooperation of many related professionals, will be required to solve the mystery: "Does anybody know what a learning disability is?"

PROBE 9-4
Theories About Treatment of Learning Disabilities

Indicate whether each statement suggests an educational (ED) or medical (MD) explanation of learning disabilities:

__ 1. Since a special diet eliminating salicylates and certain artificial food colors and flavors seems to reduce hyperactivity in some children, the possibility that these substances contribute to learning disabilities should be explored further.

__ 2. One reason finger-tracing techniques are used in remedial reading is that this method is not associated with past failure.

__ 3. Abnormalities present at birth may cause or contribute to the development of learning disabilities.

___ 4. Careful planning, immediate correction of errors, and repeated practice were among the components suggested for the LD child's instructional program.

___ 5. Some learning disabled children benefit from certain types of drugs, whereas others don't.

___ 6. The characteristics of some children in LD programs suggest that they are neurologically impaired.

___ 7. According to the skill-referenced approach, LD students should receive instruction related directly to the skills they are having difficulty with.

SUMMARY

1. "Learning disabilities" is a relatively new term created to define and provide services for students with some abilities and some school-related difficulties.

2. Learning disabilities refers to a disorder in the psychological processes related to understanding and using language, is sometimes possibly neurological in origin, and manifests itself in poor academic achievement on specific tasks.

3. The learning disabilities definition is complex and controversial.

4. Definitions of learning disabilities vary from one state to another, and these differences result in varying prevalence figures for students who are so classified.

5. Referral of students suspected of having a learning disability should occur only after the student has been observed in the classroom and the teacher has implemented and measured the effectiveness of teaching alternatives.

6. Procedures for assessing learning disabilities are limited in scope and in accuracy.

7. Identification procedures should include assessment of the learning environment and interactions between student and teacher as well as the abilities listed in the definition of learning disabilities.

8. Placement in a learning disabilities program should be based on recommendations of a professional team and not just a single individual.

9. There is a trend to overidentify LD students, but new tests and procedures are being developed that may improve the process.

10. Everyone has learning difficulties, but these common problems should not be confused with LD characteristics, since they are of short duration and are mild rather than severe.

TASK SHEET 9
Field Study in Learning Disabilities

Select *one* of the following and complete the assigned tasks:

Program Visitation

Visit an educational program for children with learning disabilities. Talk with teachers, administrators, or other relevant staff. Describe the faculty you visited, the activities conducted, and any problems described by the staff. Summarize your reactions to this experience.

Program Comparison

Visit a program for children who have been diagnosed as having learning disabilities. Then visit either a regular elementary school program or a class for children who have been diagnosed as mentally retarded. Describe each visit and your general impressions of the students and the instructional programs. How were the groups and programs alike and how were they different?

Parent Interview

Interview the parent (or other family member) of a child who has been diagnosed as having a learning disability. Find out what the reactions were when the learning disability was first discovered. Describe the actions taken by the parents in obtaining educational services for the child. Determine the extent of satisfaction with the services that the child is receiving. Describe the problems that have been encountered by the parents.

Definitions

Ask two educators (teachers, principals, college professors, fellow teacher education students, etc.) to define what a learning disability is. Record their definitions. Analyze each of the definitions according to the four dimensions of learning disabilities described in this chapter.

Library Study

Read three articles related to the topic of learning disabilities and write a one-page abstract of each. You can find articles in the following journals:

Academic Therapy
Journal of Learning Disabilities
Learning Disabilities Quarterly

Agency Investigation

Write to these agencies and inquire about services they provide to children with learning disabilities. Write a three-page paper describing these services and how you might use them as a professional.

Association of Learning Disabled Adults
P. O. Box 9722, Friendship Station
Washington, DC 20016

Association for Children and Adults
with Learning Disabilities
4156 Library Road
Pittsburgh, PA 15234

Foundation for Children with Learning
Disabilities
99 Park Avenue, 6th Floor
New York, NY 11016

Design Your Own Field Experience

If none of the above learning activities fits your needs or circumstances, design one of
your own after discussing the idea with your instructor.

Peter

His voice is usually high-pitched, rapid, sing-song like: "What color is your house do you have a dog what's his name what's your dog's name does he have spots on his face where's your house do you have a dog what's his name what's your dog's name what's the color of your house do you have a dog my dog's name is Choo-Choo she has spots on her face what's your name your name is Laurie my name is Peter Lee Eaton Peter Lee Eaton that's my name you don't have a house you don't have a dog my dog's name is Choo-Choo my house is white what's your dog's name your name is Laurie . . ."

Sally

The children are coloring dittos. The teacher has her feet up on her desk, She is reading a novel, Sally is at her desk coloring. She begins to whistle a tune.

Teacher: "Please, please, if everyone did that we wouldn't get our work done."
Sally: Stops a few seconds then begins whistling again.
Teacher: "Sally, stop it. What did I just tell you?"
Sally: Continues whistling but at a lower volume.
Teacher: "Cut it out RIGHT NOW. . . . Do you want to go to the office?"
Sally: Begins laughing and loud singing.
Teacher: "STOP IT. . . . ALL RIGHT IF YOU WANT TO GO TO THE OFFICE THE REST OF THE DAY THAT'S WHAT YOU'LL DO. *RIGHT NOW.* . . . LET'S GO."
Sally: Gets up and runs across the room.
Teacher: Grabs Sally's arm and takes her back to her seat.
Sally: Sings loudly.
Teacher: Puts her hand over Sally's mouth and whispers in her ear.
Sally: Resumes coloring quietly while the teacher has her arm around her.

Source: "Peter" is from L. P. Van Veelan, Cheer Soap Opera, unpublished manuscript, University of Kentucky, 1975, p. 1. "Sally" is from B. Ray, Emotionally Disturbed, or "Sit Down, Shut Up and You'll Stay Out of Trouble," unpublished manuscript, University of Kentucky, 1978, p. 6. Reprinted by permission.

10

Behavior Disorders

C. Michael Nelson

C. Michael Nelson is a professor in the Department of Special Education at the University of Kentucky. Dr. Nelson has taught special education classes for adolescents, worked as a psychologist, and been involved in camping and residential treatment programs for behaviorally disordered children. He is past president of the Council for Children with Behavior Disorders.

The two children described on the facing page are behaving very differently from one another. Peter is talking almost nonstop, whereas Sally appears to be willfully misbehaving. Yet they have something in common: both have been identified and labeled by their school systems as behaviorally disordered or emotionally disturbed.[1]

Almost everybody would agree that something is wrong with the children in these situations — that they are different, strange, and don't fit in with other children or conform to our conception of "normal" behavior. But exactly what is wrong with them? Why are Peter and Sally different? How did they get that way? How do schools and parents cope with such children, and what happens to them when they grow up? We hope to provide answers to questions such as these in this chapter. You will find as you read that the answers are much more difficult to discern than the questions. The field of behavior disorders is fraught with controversy and conflicting opinions.

Whether you teach in a "regular" or a "special" classroom (for any disability group), you will frequently be involved with children labeled "behavior-

---

[1] The terms "behaviorally disordered" and "emotionally disturbed" are considered synonymous in this chapter.

ally disordered." According to Wood and Zabel (1978), as many as 30 percent of the children in any age group may be considered by teachers to have behavior problems. Although the proportion of children whose maladaptive behavior persists for a relatively long time is much smaller, it is likely that one or more pupils in any class of 30 will be difficult to manage in the classroom.

DEFINING BEHAVIOR DISORDERS

You should be able to define behavior disorders.

To organize diverse phenomena and group them according to common characteristics, modern society relies heavily on classifying and labeling. Peter and Sally have in common the label "behaviorally disordered." This label might lead one to expect that these two children are similar in more ways than they are different, but they aren't, of course. Like other children, they are different in many respects: age, sex, and other physical attributes, aptitude, achievement, personality, and importantly, the types of behaviors they display and the frequency with which they display them. The term "behavior disorders" encompasses an almost unlimited variety of behavior. What characteristics, then, do these children have in common?

FUNDAMENTAL CHARACTERISTICS OF BEHAVIOR DISORDERS

Several characteristics are considered in determining whether a child's behavior is disordered. These include (1) the perception that the child's behavior departs from acceptable standards, (2) the degree to which his or her behavior deviates from these standards, and (3) the length of time the behavior pattern has continued.

Who decides what a behavior disorder is?

Behavior That Departs from Acceptable Standards. In defining behavior disorders by referring to standards of behavior, we must ask what normal behavior is and who decides what is normal or abnormal. The answer to the first question is difficult to determine. Behaviors that are considered to be indications of psychological disorders (e.g., severe temper tantrums, tics, enuresis, behaviors suggestive of psychological tension) have been observed by parents and teachers of many "normal" children — those who have not been referred by their parents or teachers for help because of behavior problems (Ross, 1980). The behavior of children considered disordered or disturbed differs in degree, and not in kind, from that of those children considered normal (Ross, 1980). That is, disturbed children display higher rates of problem behaviors, rather than exhibiting entirely different behavior patterns than their non-disturbed peers. In answer to the second question, the judgment of whether a child's behavior is aberrant is made by an adult — a parent or teacher. Peers also make judgments and place labels on children, but these judgments rarely result in official action such as referral to a child guidance clinic or a special education program. Adults are responsible for the official deviant labels some of our children must wear to school every day.

Implicit in an adult's judgment that a child is behaviorally deviant is the assumption that the child's actions violate the standards of the culture or subculture. Social standards may be based on such factors as age, sex role, and setting. For example, thumb sucking is considered normal in two-year-olds, but in an eight-year-old the same behavior would be considered deviant. A ten-year-old boy who wears dresses and makeup would qualify for a deviant label in the American culture. Running and screaming are considered normal behaviors on a playground, but they are cause for alarm if they occur in church. Since it is adults who interpret these standards and apply them to children's behavior, whether or not a child is labeled deviant is largely a function of adult expectations (Kauffman, 1981).

The tolerance of adults for behavior, as well as their expectations, affects which children are identified as deviant. Thus, an extremely active child might not attract undue attention in teacher A's classroom; but teacher B, who values quiet and order, might find the same behavior intolerable. Because of the widespread use of labels, teachers have found that it is quite easy to get their judgments confirmed by mental health professionals. They are thus reinforced for identifying "problem" children by getting them moved from their classrooms into special education programs.

What distinguishes deviant from normal?

Degree of Deviation from Acceptable Standards. A second element of most definitions of behavior disorders is the judgment that the child's behavior is extreme. Sally is out of her seat too often. Too much of Peter's verbal behavior is repetitive and bizarre. Behavior can also vary to the opposite extreme, as in the case of children who are excessively isolated and withdrawn or grossly deficient in their ability to use language. Extremely high or low rates of behavior call attention to the child and are likely to result in his or her being labeled and assigned to a "deviant" category. Remember that it is the degree or amount of behavior and not a particular type of behavior that distinguishes deviant from normal children. In addition, extremely intense behavior, such as violent tantrums, can result in a child's being labeled deviant even if such behavior is infrequent.

Duration of the Behavior Pattern. Most definitions of behavior disorders also assume that the problem is chronic rather than transient (Hallahan and Kauffman, 1978). Peter has been strange since he was old enough to walk and talk. Sally's reputation as a behavior problem has extended through several years of school. Everyone is capable of behaving abnormally during periods of stress. The death of a loved one, failure in a marriage or career, or leaving home for the first time can all result in transient disturbances. It is only when such behavior patterns persist long after the stressful situation has passed that an individual is considered disturbed.

Should the child be labeled as disturbed?

Intense behavior problems of short duration occur rather frequently in children (Kauffman, 1981). While such transient behavior disorders may require professional help, it is better to label the *behavior* as disordered rather than the *child* as disturbed or disordered (Kauffman, 1981).

In summary, then, a child's behavior may be judged disordered (1) if it deviates from the range of behaviors for the child's age and sex that significant adults perceive as normal; (2) if it occurs very frequently or too intensely; or (3) if it occurs over an extended period of time.

WHO "OWNS" THE DISORDER

The question of "owning" a disorder may at first seem nonsensical. If a child is labeled "behaviorally disordered" or "emotionally disturbed," the problem is apparently that child's. Once again, however, the answer isn't that simple. If deviance is partially determined by environmental expectations, and if these expectations are influenced by adults' tolerance for behavior, it is possible that children could be labeled because the expectations made of them are inappropriate. Children so identified and labeled are just as stigmatized as those correctly labeled and become the targets of interventions designed to remedy or change their presumed behavior disorder. Most theories of psychopathology (e.g., the psychoeducational, behavioral, and biophysical theories) assume that the problem is the child's, and, therefore, that therapeutic change should occur in the person (Rhodes, 1970).

What is the ecological theory?

In recent years Rhodes (1967, 1970, 1975) has championed another view — that disturbance is the result of interactions between the child and the child's school, home, and peer group, also known as the child's "microcommunities." This theory is termed "ecological" because it is concerned with the interrelationships between behavior and environment. The ecological theory has influenced most contemporary definitions of behavior disorders (see, for example, Kauffman, 1981; Ross, 1980), and it has significant implications for treatment. Consider, for instance, how you would approach Sally differently if you viewed her disorder as a problematic interaction between her and her teacher rather than as a "characteristic" owned exclusively by Sally. One might accuse Sally's teacher of incompetence, or even of being behaviorally disordered herself, because her actions deviate from widely accepted standards for teachers' behavior. The ecological model, however, rejects the view that disturbance originates from individual psychopathology, either in children or in other significant people in the environment. Although we would like to bring Sally's teacher's behavior up to acceptable standards, our immediate concern would be to reduce the disturbing interactions occurring between the teacher and Sally.

The ecological model stresses that behavior is situation-specific. That is, a child may have a behavior problem in one situation but not in others. If, for example, Sally is disruptive in her third-grade class but isn't when she is on the playground, at home, or in her Sunday School class, is she behaviorally disordered? To label her as such may cause her to be stigmatized in settings in which her social interactions are not disturbing. The application of the label could establish expectations for disordered behavior that would become self-fulfilling prophecies. It would probably be better not to label her and to confine direct intervention to the setting in which the disturbance occurs. Peter, on the other hand, has disturbing encounters with people in all of his microcommunities. In his case, intervention (and a label, if it aids intervention) would be applied across all social settings. The extent to which intervention should be applied across settings or microcommunities is determined by the process of ecological assessment, which will be discussed later.

CONCEPTUAL MODELS OF BEHAVIOR DISORDERS

How do the psychodynamic, medical, and behavioral models differ?

How one conceptualizes a behavior disorder influences how one defines, identifies, and diagnoses it, and ultimately what kind of intervention one applies to it. The study of children's behavior disorders has been heavily influenced by Freudian psychology, which views mental disorders as disease processes that are essentially the same as physical diseases. According to this *psychodynamic* model, the disease produces symptoms, which are regarded as behavioral manifestations of the underlying disorder. To cure the disorder one must diagnose and treat the disease process that caused it. According to this view, the elimination of symptoms alone will result only in the appearance of new symptoms. And, in fact, it has been widely believed for many years that mental disorders should be treated medically. This "medical model" dominated the field from the turn of the twentieth century until the late 1950s and early 1960s, and medical treatment is still advocated by professionals who ascribe to a psychodynamic or a biophysical model of deviant behavior. The *biophysical* model seeks to explain disordered behavior in terms of biochemical, neurological, or genetic causes, whereas the psychodynamic model focuses more on past psychological experiences, especially those created by parental attitudes and behaviors. Both may be classified as medical models, in that both emphasize medically oriented treatments, such as psychoanalysis or psychoactive drugs.

In 1960 Thomas Szasz challenged the medical model, arguing that an analogy to physical disease is inappropriate when applied to social problems (i.e., those that involve living and getting along with other people). Problems in living cannot readily be traced back to neurological or other biochemical defects; and, moreover, labeling a behavior as a "symptom" of mental illness involves a subjective social judgment, not an objective physical diagnosis. Szasz also criticized the view that social relationships are naturally harmonious, since every person occasionally has problems in his or her social environment.

Ullmann and Krasner (1965) also criticized the medical model, offering as an alternative the *psychological* or *behavioral* model, which is derived from learning theory. Rather than concentrating on an underlying psychological pathology that is not directly observable, they emphasized the specification and direct treatment of overt behavior; that is, the treatment of symptoms themselves. This model explains behavior in terms of the environmental variables that influence it, particularly those that occur as a consequence of behavior. The behavioral model has had at least as much impact on the field of behavior disorders as Freudian theory. Techniques based on this model have been demonstrated to be very effective with both children and adults.

An important distinction between medical and behavioral models of deviant behavior concerns the different assumptions each model holds about the sources and nature of the child's problems. These assumptions influence the methods used in providing treatment. Persons advocating a psychodynamic or a biophysical model are more likely to apply treatment to underlying personality problems or to prescribe psychoactive drugs such as tranquilizers, stimulants, or antipsychotic or antidepressant medications (Miksic, 1983). The purpose of such treatment is to address the underlying problem (e.g., personality disturbance, neurological dysfunction) assumed to produce the behavioral symptoms, although psychoactive medications are frequently prescribed simply to control behaviors that interfere with the child's responsiveness to educational or psychological interventions. Professionals with a behavioral orientation, on the other hand, believe that replacing the child's inappropriate behavior with more adaptive behavior patterns constitutes effective treatment.

Like behaviorists, those who follow the *ecological* model tend not to attribute behavior to internal states. Rather, they view behavior disorders as the product of interactions between the child and others in the immediate environment. Whereas behaviorists traditionally focus on teaching the child appropriate behaviors while decreasing undesired behaviors, ecological practitioners also concentrate on changing the expectations, reactions, and behavior patterns of other persons in the child's microcommunities, as these factors are viewed as contributing significantly to the problem.

How do advocates of the sociological model and the counter theory approach treatment?

Two other models have influenced those who work with behavior disorders. The *sociological* model emphasizes conditions in the child's larger social environment (cultures and subcultures) that foster and maintain deviant behavior. Treatment is usually directed toward ameliorating these conditions or increasing the child's resistance to them. Finally, the *counter theory* model rejects theories that attempt to reduce disordered behavior to a limited set of theoretical assumptions. It focuses instead on advocacy for the deviant child and the delivery of effective services. The goal of intervention is often to change the broad social values and expectations that contribute to narrow views of behavior as deviant or normal. The ultimate goal of counter theorists is to change the educational system and society itself to encourage broader acceptance and understanding of individual differences.

Each of these models has contributed to the understanding and treatment of children's behavior disorders, and the trend today is to recognize the contribution of many different individual and environmental factors. Cullinan, Epstein, and Lloyd (1983) and Paul and Epanchin (1982) have offered more complete explanations of these models.

THE PROBLEM OF LABELING

Peter Lee has been tested several times and has been given a variety of labels: "severely retarded," "profoundly retarded," "moderately retarded," "hyperactive," "perceptually disordered," "emotionally disturbed." Usually the advice was "Do something about it now or else it will be a serious problem later." Peter knows the tricks of the I.Q. test. He can draw a man. The last time he went for testing, he wouldn't comply: Instead he hung himself upside-down in the closet, to the puzzlement of the psychiatrist. He yelled, "I'm a bat! I'm a bat!" (Van Veelan, 1975, pp. 10-11).

What are the steps in diagnosing behavior disorders?

The problems inherent in labeling handicapped children have been considered in some detail in Chapter 2. The issue is of particular concern to those who work with behaviorally disordered children, because such children can be labeled in so many different ways. The diagnostic fiasco involving Peter is an example. Children who have severe behavior disorders are especially likely to be given different labels by different diagnosticians and treatment agencies. There is also the problem of which label to aply to a child with multiple problems. For instance, is Peter emotionally disturbed, mentally retarded, or both? If both, which label will result in his getting the best services? The child and his parents are frequently deprived of special services while experts argue about which category the child belongs in.

How can labels harm children with behavior disorders?

In addition, labels tend to make us think in circles and come to be used as explanations for children's behavior (Ross, 1980). When we ask, "Why is Sally out of her seat so much?" the reply, "Because she's hyperactive," is almost automatic. If we then ask why the label "hyperactive" was assigned, a likely response is, "Because she's out of her seat so much." This may seem insignificant, but an unfortunate effect of such circular reasoning is that the child's label is used as an excuse to do nothing to help him or her. Sally's teacher may know how to keep her in her seat but have no idea how to reduce "hyperactivity." It is also very easy to fall into the trap of assuming that the label, originally used to describe the child's behavior, refers to a condition the child has (Ross, 1980). Thus, labeling Sally's behavior as hyperactive might be construed as meaning that she *has* hyperactivity. Semantic confusions like this tend to transfer ownership of the problem to the child and increase the likelihood that treatment will be applied only to the child, without consideration of inappropriate environmental expectations or practices.

Children exhibiting severe behavior disorders may be assigned a variety of labels. However, which diagnostic label best "fits" the child is less important than designing a special education program suited to her unique learning needs.

CONCEPTUAL AND EDUCATIONAL DEFINITIONS OF BEHAVIOR DISORDERS

Now that some of the problems involved in identifying, classifying, and treating children in school have been discussed, you should realize that labeling a child behaviorally disordered or emotionally disturbed may do more harm than good. An understanding of ecological theory, in particular, should lead professionals to reject attempts to define behaviorally disordered children in terms of their alleged characteristics.

Nevertheless, defining a population of behaviorally disordered children provides a central concept around which information about them can be organized and school practices can be guided. It is also necessary in most states for schools to identify and label students as behaviorally disordered in order to qualify for federal funds to support special education programs. PL 94-142 defines "seriously emotionally disturbed" as follows:

(i) A condition in which are exhibited one or more of the following characteristics over a long period of time and to a marked degree, which adversely affects educational performance:
  a. An inability to learn which cannot be explained by intellectual, sensory, or health factors;
  b. An inability to build or maintain satisfactory interpersonal relationships with peers or teachers;
  c. Inappropriate types of behavior or feelings under normal circumstances;
  d. A general pervasive mood of unhappiness or depression; or
  e. A tendency to develop physical symptoms or fears associated with personal or school problems.
(ii) The term includes children who are schizophrenic. The term does not include children who are socially maladjusted, unless it is determined that they are seriously disturbed (Federal Register, 1981, *46,* 3866).[2]

Why does the federal definition of "seriously emotionally disturbed" present problems?

Unfortunately, the federal definition does not provide clear guidelines for separating children with behavior disorders (serious emotional disturbance) from those who do not have behavior disorders. For instance, what constitutes a "marked degree"? What is "a long period of time"? How are practitioners to determine what constitutes "an inability to learn" or to build "satisfying relationships"? (Kerr and Nelson, 1983). The subjectivity of these statements makes it difficult to decide to whom the label should be applied and when treatment is necessary. Such ambiguity leaves a great deal to the discretion of

---

[2] A recent change in the federal regulations transferred autism from the category "seriously emotionally disturbed" to the category "other health impaired." Autistic children exhibit extreme behavior disorders, however, so autistic behaviors will be discussed in this chapter. The term "socially maladjusted" refers to children whose behavior is in accordance with deviant peer standards (e.g., a delinquent gang). Currently, the federal definition of "seriously emotionally disturbed" is being examined, and may be revised.

the person making the judgment. In view of the potential negative consequences of labeling a child in such circumstances, a different "working definition" is in order.

A noncategorical definition has been developed by Lilly (1970). He states
that his definition is one "in which it is not assumed that all school problems
are centered in the child and that removal of children from problem situations
will be beneficial for everyone involved" (p. 48). Lilly's position is compatible
with the ecological view, in that it focuses on factors in the environment as
well as within the child and emphasizes that intervention should be directed
at problems in the settings where they occur. Lilly replaced disability labels
with the term "exceptional school situations": "An exceptional school
situation is one in which interaction between a student and his teacher has
been limited to such an extent that external intervention (i.e., special
support services) is deemed necessary by the teacher to cope with the problem" (p. 48).

What is an "exceptional school situation"?

Obviously, Lilly's definition doesn't distinguish children with behavior
problems from the learning disabled, mentally retarded, or other alleged child
populations. This is in keeping with the growing opposition to labeling.
Special education is becoming less diagnostic — less oriented toward discovering "underlying" disorders — and more prescriptive or action-oriented.
Labeling the interaction between a teacher and child rather than the child alone
reflects our increasing awareness of the importance of ecological factors and a
more humanistic concern for children. It also reflects the special educator's
involvement in mainstreaming. Rather than removing the child to a special
setting and applying interventions to him or her alone, support services are
being taken to the child and the teacher.

These trends have made it necessary for special educators to move into new
roles. Instead of removing children from regular classrooms for the school
day, special education teachers are spending more time helping the regular
classroom teacher develop individualized approaches to working with all children, normal as well as exceptional (Lilly and Givens-Ogle, 1981; Reynolds
and Birch, 1982).

Although the federal definition employs the term "emotionally disturbed,"
the current trend is to use "behavioral disorders" instead. The latter term
offers the advantage of placing more emphasis on the behavior exhibited by
the child than on underlying emotional or pscyhological processes. Educators
and parents tend to be uncomfortable with the idea of dealing with underlying
dynamics and are usually not professionally trained to do so. Reactions to the
label "behaviorally disordered" are likely to be less negative, because this term
doesn't convey the implication that the child is emotionally unbalanced. Furthermore, research has shown that treating overt behavior is as effective as, if
not more than, treating presumed underlying difficulties (Kerr and Nelson,
1983).

PROBE 10-1
Defining Behavior Disorders

1. A teacher in your school is worried because he has learned that one of his new pupils has been identified as emotionally disturbed. Tell him why it is better to concern himself with specific behaviors and the settings in which they occur than to pay excessive attention to the label.

2. Explain why it is better to assume that behavior disorders are characteristics of the interactions between children and other people than it is to assume that they exist exclusively in the child.

3. T F Professionals typically consider peer evaluation rather than adult opinion in assessing behavior disorders.

4. What are the three characteristics common to most definitions of behavioral disorders?

TYPES, CLASSIFICATION, AND PREVALENCE OF BEHAVIOR DISORDERS

You should be able to identify different types of behavior disorders.

In view of the preceding discussion, you may be surprised by the suggestion that there are "types" of behavior disorders. You should keep in mind that the reason we discuss the concept in this manner is related more to the organization of the professional literature than to any practical considerations in working with children.

DIAGNOSIS OF BEHAVIOR DISORDERS

The determination of different categories of behavioral disorders begin with diagnosis. Diagnosis, in turn, consists of three steps: (1) initial screening, (2) identification, and (3) assignment to a diagnostic category. The purpose of screening is to identify children who may need special help. The identification process confirms which of the children identified during screening require therapeutic interventions. Diagnosis involves classification for the purpose of planning an intervention strategy.

During screening, children who may be having problems are identified by teachers, parents, peers, or in some cases, by self-report. It may involve simply asking which children have trouble getting along with classmates, following directions, or controlling themselves, or which have difficulty in other areas. It can also involve completing a standardized behavioral rating scale, such as the *Walker Problem Behavior Identification Checklist* (Walker, 1970), the *Behavior Evaluation Scale* (McCarney, Leigh, and Cornbleet, 1983), or the *Teacher Rating Scale* of the *Behavior Rating Profile* (Brown and Hammill, 1978). Teachers who use such devices can judge children's behavior fairly reliably.

What is target assessment?

Disordered children are identified by comparing these judgments or ratings to an external criterion. The most valid criterion for identifying children entails direct observation of behavior, or *target assessment*. The goal of target assessment is the identification of (1) behaviors that are causing problems to the child or others in the child's social environment, (2) environmental variables that might be influencing the target behaviors, and (3) variables that might be used to change these behaviors (Kerr and Nelson, 1983). A target behavior for Sally might be her disruptive classroom behavior or, more specifically, inappropriate noises and noncompliance. Influential environmental variables one might consider are how the teacher attends to Sally when she is disruptive, and whether the assigned work is appropriate for Sally. If the school had resources to help Sally and her teacher, the diagnostic process could end with target assessment, and the problem could be dealt with directly, without giving Sally a label. The tradition, however, is to continue diagnosis until something wrong with the child is found, and the process often continues to the next step.

The final step in diagnosis consists of assigning the child to a classification of behavior disorder and developing an intervention plan. The traditional approach at this level of diagnosis is to refer the child to a clinic for formal diagnostic testing. Generally, a battery of tests, which includes standardized intelligence and achievement instruments and, in some cases, projective techniques, is administered. Projective techniques are used to assess personality constructs that are not directly observable but may be "projected" through responses to ambiguous stimuli, such as ink blots or pictures. Depending on the theoretical persuasion and competence of the clinician, the child may emerge from the diagnostic testing session with any of a number of labels. Some of these include "attention deficit disorder with hyperactivity," "conduct disorder," "separation anxiety disorder," "oppositional disorder," and "schizoid disorder of childhood or adolescence" (American Psychiatric Association, 1980). Since these lables seldom translate into useful educational prescriptions, however, special educators infrequently use them to assign children to programs. The label "behaviorally disordered" or "emotionally disturbed" is sufficient to get the child into a special education program.

THE ECOLOGICAL APPROACH TO DIAGNOSIS

The ecological model provides a more practical approach to diagnostic assessment. The process begins when someone, usually a teacher or parent, reports a problem. The professional then assesses the problem in detail, focusing on the interaction of the child with those who are experiencing the problem, and not on the child in isolation. In addition to the problem situation, variables related to the school, the home, the child, the peer group, and the child's local community are studied. Intervention plans are developed for situations in which disturbing interactions occur. The ecological assessment process also specifies areas of strength and support that may be useful in planning treatment (Wahler and Cormier, 1970).

Why is ecological diagnosis so useful?

Because it carefully assesses environmental variables, the ecological model is especially useful in designing intervention strategies. Another advantage of this type of assessment is that it need not lead to a stigmatizing label; the emphasis is on the situation rather then the presumed underlying pathology of the child. For example, we would observe Sally's behavior in the playground, lunchroom, and gym as well as in her regular classroom. We might also interview other teachers and Sally's parents, to determine the extent of the behavior pattern displayed in her classroom and to identify other problems or potential problems. This would reveal how serious a problem Sally is and would also indicate whether intervention should be extended outside the major problem situation. In addition, ecological assessment could reveal whether an attempt should be made to change some of Sally's teacher's behavior. It could also uncover persons or activities from other microcommunities that could be incorporated into the intervention. For example, Sally's mother might be willing to give her daughter extra privileges at home when she brings home favorable reports from school. Or perhaps Sally is developing into a fine backgammon player and could get some of the attention she apparently desires by sharing her knowledge with the class.

CLASSIFICATION OF BEHAVIOR DISORDERS

Why do we attempt to classify behavior disorders? Scientists go through the process of classification to organize information, which permits them to make useful statements about the phenomena being classified. In the behavioral sciences these "useful statements" are used to provide treatment to individuals assigned to different categories. This means that one should be able to predict the behavior of individuals placed in a particular category when specific intervention techniques are applied. As was the case in assigning children to the broad category of "behavioral disorders," assigning them to subcategories may create more problems than it solves.

To make useful statements about the children assigned to a category of disordered behavior, it must (1) be demonstrated that the category actually exists; (2) be shown that children can be reliably assigned to that category; and (3) be proven that patterns of disordered behavior are related to their psychological antecedents and consequences. Few of the more than 24 proposed classification systems for children's behavior disorders have met these requirements (Quay, 1979).

What is DSM III?   Clinical diagnostic classification is usually accomplished by using the *Diagnostic and Statistical Manual,* third edition (DSM III) (American Psychiatric Association, 1980). This manual attempts to help the diagnostician arrive at a diagnostic classification by describing sets of symptoms, as well as etiological factors, which appear to be common to a given diagnostic category. DSM III groups behavior disorders of children and adolescents into five broad categories (American Psychiatric Association):

I.   Intellectual
    Mental Retardation
II. Behavioral (overt)
    Attention Deficit Disorder
III. Emotional
    Anxiety Disorders of Childhood or Adolescence
IV. Physical
    Eating Disorders
    Stereotyped Movement Disorders
    Other Disorders with Physical Manifestations
V.   Developmental
    Pervasive Developmental Disorders
    Specific Developmental Disorders

Within these categories, more specific diagnoses are achieved by comparing the child's presenting symptoms with descriptions under each specific diagnostic label. For example, the symptoms described on pages 418a and 418b of the DSM III are intended to help the clinician differentiate between "autism" and "childhood onset pervasive developmental disorder."

Although clinical diagnosis is usually done by a highly trained psychiatrist, psychologist, or social worker, the assignment of children into diagnostic categories tends to be unreliable; i.e., different diagnosticians may assign different labels to the same child (as in Peter's case, for example). This is partly because the diagnosis tends to be based on behaviors observed (or reported by the parents) in the clinician's office, and partly because there is a great deal of room for subjectivity (or "clinical judgment") by the diagnostician. For the most part, clinical diagnostic labels do not communicate information that is useful to educators, and therefore the clinical approach is not commonly used for the purpose of assigning pupils to educational programs.

Statistical Approach. In recent years, alternatives to the clinical approach have been developed. Several of these classification systems group clusters of observed behaviors statistically. This approach is better than the clinical methods because its categories are based on observable groups of behaviors. This permits teachers and parents to evaluate children's behavior more reliably (Quay, 1979). In numerous studies by Quay and his colleagues, four categories of behavior disorders have been identified (Quay, 1979):

1. Conduct disorders consist of aggressive verbal and physical behavior of an antisocial nature.
2. Anxiety-withdrawal is characterized by withdrawal rather than attack. Included are feelings of distress, fear, and anxiety, as well as physical compliants and expressed unhappiness.
3. Immaturity is characterized by age-inappropriate behaviors. It is much less prevalent than the two previous categories.
4. Socialized-aggressive disorders includes behaviors that may be encouraged by peer pressure or other environmental circumstances. For instance, stealing or fighting may be openly supported by a delinquent peer group.

What are behavioral excesses, deficits, and assets?

Functional-Analytic Approach. Kanfer and Saslow (1967) developed the functional-analytic approach to classify adult behavior disorders, but it has also worked well with children. It suggests three behavioral categories. *Behavioral excesses* are behaviors that are excessive in frequency, intensity, or duration, or that occur when socially inappropriate. *Behavioral deficits* are behaviors that fail to occur with sufficient frequency, with adequate intensity, in appropriate form, or under conditions in which they are socially expected. *Behavioral assets* are all nonproblematic behaviors. This category reflects the understanding that even highly deviant individuals have areas of strength. The functional-analytic approach can be used especially well with ecological assessment procedures. Derived from the behavioral model, its chief advantage is that it does not result in a label's being applied to a child. Instead, the child's maladaptive behaviors are specified, and strategies for change are suggested. Part of the intervention strategy is the identification of environmental variables that reinforce or maintain the problematic behavior. This approach is the same as target assessment, mentioned earlier.

Classification by Severity. Hallahan and Kauffman (1978) divided the behaviorally disordered into two groups on the basis of the severity of their disorders. Children with *mild and moderate* behavioral disorders can be managed by their teachers and parents with short-term consultation by a specialist. Children with *severe and profound* disorders, on the other hand, require intense and prolonged intervention, usually in a segregated setting. In calling attention to the problems involved in developing diagnostic classifications of children with extreme behavioral deviations, Kauffman (1981) observed that while there is not much controversy about whether children exhibiting severe behavior disorders can be identified as a group noticeably different from those less disordered, there is considerable debate concerning whether children categorized as severely and profoundly disordered can be meaningfully subdivided into categories such as "childhood schizophrenic" or "autistic." Using the information we have about Peter and Sally, we might consider Peter's disorders as severe and requiring intensive intervention; Sally's problems are probably relatively mild and could be addressed in the regular classroom.

What are the merits of classification by severity?

Classification by severity permits the efficient allocation of education services. But until criteria are established to differentiate children in need of intense and prolonged intervention from those who can profit from short-term help, there is a risk that children will be classified as severely or profoundly disordered merely to get them removed from regular classrooms.

The poor reliability and validity of projective techniques renders them useless for classifying children or for predicting their behavior (Salvia and Ysseldyke, 1981). In addition, while statistical approaches provide a useful conceptual scheme for organizing deviant child behavior, research has yet to demonstrate the effectiveness of these techniques for predicting child behavior and for planning treatment. The assessment of target behaviors and their ecological contexts, on the other hand, offers several advantages: (1) the child does not have to be labeled as a member of a deviant population; (2) problem behaviors and environmental variables are described in a fashion that leads directly to an intervention plan; (3) problems are assessed where they occur, not in a clinic; (4) the assets of the child and the situation are considered, not just the child's problems; and (5) the child's environment, and not just the child, is considered a potential cause of the problem (see Kerr and Nelson, 1983). The target assessment of functional-analytic approach is thus highly compatible with Lilly's (1970) definition of an exceptional school situation.

PREVALENCE FACTORS

How many children exhibit behavior disorders?

We stated earlier that teachers may perceive up to 30 percent of their pupils as having behavior problems. However, PL 94-142 indicates that the prevalence estimate for the seriously emotionally disturbed is 2 percent. As you have learned, many subjective factors (such as personal judgments regarding what constitutes normal behavior, or tolerance for deviant behavior) may go into identifying and labeling a child as behaviorally disordered. The 2 percent figure is used as a basis for allocating federal support of research, teacher training, and direct educational services. Estimates of the percentage of students needing special services for serious behavior problems vary considerably, but most prevalence figures are above 2 percent (Cullinan et al., 1983). Wood and Zabel (1978) have suggested that 3 percent of the school-age population is behaviorally disordered. Almost all of these pupils would be considered mildly or moderately disturbed, with severely and profoundly disturbed children accounting for only 0.1 percent (Hallahan and Kauffman, 1978).

Juvenile delinquency is a category of behavior disorder defined by the legal system. The population of children identified as delinquent overlaps the population of behaviorally disordered children. That is, children with behavior problems may or may not get into trouble with the law; adjudicated delinquents may or may not have been labeled behaviorally disordered. If this overlap is disregarded, the delinquency rate among children aged 10 to 17 is approximately 3 percent. In 1972, for example, 1 million cases were handled by the juvenile courts (U.S. Department of Health, Education, and Welfare, 1973).

Behavior disorders are not evenly distributed across ages, sexes, or socioeconomic levels. Although studies do not consistently find more boys than girls with behavior problems, boys tend to be overrepresented in programs for behaviorally disordered children by as much as ten to one (Rich, 1977). Schools have a particularly low tolerance for acting-out (aggressive) behavior, which is more often displayed by boys, members of minority groups (Rich, 1977), and children from lower socioeconomic levels (Kauffman, 1981). As girls grow older, their personality problems increase, whereas boys develop conduct problems or exhibit immaturity (Kauffman, 1981).

Two interesting questions about the later adjustment of behaviorally disordered children may be asked. Do behaviorally disordered children become maladjusted adults? What happens to children who receive treatment, compared to those who do not? Lewis (1965) reviewed the research on these questions and found that (you guessed it) the answers aren't simple. With regard to the first question, if the criterion for evaluating adult disturbance is admission to a psychiatric hospital, the answer is no. If however, the criterion is a diagnosed adult psychiatric disorder, the answer is yes. Considering both criteria together, Lewis (1965, p. 472) concluded, "The extent to which a childhood predisposition to mental illness influences appearance of problems in adult life is not entirely clear, but it is apparently not a determining factor." The child who acts out or has conduct problems is more likely to have serious adjustment problems as an adult than the withdrawn child (Kauffman, 1981; Lewis, 1965), and the prognosis for children with severe and profound behavior disorders is poor (Cullinan et al., 1983).

How effective is treatment for behavior disorders?

The second question concerning what happens to behaviorally disordered children as a result of treatment efforts is even more difficult to answer. Lewis (1965) reported that of those children who receive formal professional help in school or elsewhere, two-thirds to three-fourths improve, regardless of the treatment setting, the discipline of the therapist, or the age of the children. Evaluation of different treatment approaches is complicated by the difficulty of finding appropriate control groups, problems in equating treatments or treatment agents, the unavailability of a sufficient number of children with the same behavior problems, and the expense of tracking down terminated clients for follow-up assessments (Ross, 1980).

PROBE 10-2
Types and Classifications of Behavior Disorders

1. A teacher in your school complains about a "behaviorally disordered" child in her class. If you were using an ecological approach to the diagnosis of behavior disorders, would you agree with her use of this term? Why or why not?

2. List two behavior patterns a child diagnosed as having a conduct disorder might exhibit.

3. Why is a functional-analytic or target behavior approach to classification unlikely to result in a child's being labeled as behaviorally disordered?

4. T F Severely and profoundly behaviorally disordered school-age children account for approximately 0.1 percent of the total population of behaviorally disordered children.

5. Why do you think more boys than girls are identified as behavior problems?

6. A reasonable estimate of the number of school-age behaviorally disordered children is:
   a. 2 percent
   b. 1 percent
   c. 3 percent
   d. 10 percent

BIOPHYSICAL AND ENVIRONMENTAL CORRELATES

You should be able to describe the biophysical and environmental correlates of behavior disorders.

The hypothesis that behavior disorders have specific causes is derived from the medical model; the term "etiology" itself refers to the study of the causes of diseases. For the physician, finding the cause of a disease may be helpful in curing it, but that is not the case in the behavioral sciences. In the first place, the causes of disordered behavior may have occurred in the child's remote past, which makes them difficult to discover and impossible to treat. Second, it is usually not necessary to know the cause of a behavioral disorder to provide effective intervention (Kauffman, 1981). In addition, behavior is the result of the interaction of multiple "causes." As Ross (1980, p. 4) put it,

"Any specific behavior, taking place at any one time, represents the end point of the interaction of genetic-constitutional factors, the current physiological state of the person, current environmental conditions and past learning which in turn was a function of a similar interaction."

Nevertheless, behavioral scientists have been trying to understand causality for many years. There are many studies and much discussion of the subject, but they have yielded little valuable information. This is true largely because of limitations in the ways causal agents can be studied. Whereas medical researchers can isolate a suspected causal agent (a virus or bacterium, for example), inject it into a laboratory animal, and observe its effects while keeping all environmental variables constant, the behavioral scientist has to rely on less precise research strategies. Although Watson and Rayner (1920) developed a generalized conditioned fear response in the infant Albert, thereby establishing a direct cause-effect relationship, the ethics of this kind of research would be severely criticized today and the research halted. Another insurmountable problem is the control of environmental variables, which could be done only by raising experimental subjects in a laboratory.

What do statistical correlations show?

As a result of these factors, investigations of the causes of children's behavior disorders have usually involved retrospective examination of the case histories of children who have been given similar diagnostic labels. (The assumption that children having the same label are a homogeneous population is false, of course). These studies identify factors that are associated, or correlated, with behavioral disorders. Statistical correlation techniques demonstrate how factors vary together, but it is very important to understand that they do not establish that one factor causes another. Behavior disorders have been correlated with poor home environments, inadequate parental discipline, low socioeconomic status, learning problems in school, and other influences, but it would be a mistake to reason that these factors cause behavior disorders. Such factors are correlates, not necessarily causes, of behavioral disorders.

The relatively high correlation between a variable such as low socioeconomic status and behavior disorders does suggest that the former contributes to the disorder, but there is also a possiblity that a mutual relationship between these two conditions and a third unknown variable could account for the correlation. There are many variables associated with low socioeconomic status, such as the absence of a father in the home and the presence of deviant peer models (see Nelson and Polsgrove, 1981). Correlational studies that fail to take into account the simultaneous influence of such variables may inaccurately conclude that a single cause-effect relationship exists.

Inferences about causes must be made very carefully even when a behavior disorder is consistently related to a biophysical causal agent. For example, Lesch-Nyhan syndrome is a disorder of the nervous system that results in cerebral palsy, mental retardation, and apparently without exception, self-mutilating behavior, such as severe biting of the lips and fingers (Slater and Cowie, 1971). The consistent relationship of self-mutilation to this syndrome could lead one to conclude that Lesch-Nyhan syndrome causes self-mutilation (or more precisely, that the biochemical defect responsible for the syndrome produces all of its symptoms, one of which is self-mutilation). Anderson and Herrmann (1975) studied the effects of punishment, time-out from positive reinforcement, and positive reinforcement of behavior other than self-mutilation on five boys with Lesch-Nyhan. They found that these behavioral techniques quickly eliminated self-mutilation. The authors observed different rates of one subject's self-injurious behavior in the presence of his grandfather, grandmother, and mother. In a 15-minute session with another subject, following self-mutilation with social attention caused the behavior's rate of occurrence to triple. Furthermore, they observed that in all subjects the behavior occurred only in the presence of parents. These observations led Anderson and Herrmann to conclude that environmental factors play a role in the maintenance, if not the development, of the disorder.

One cannot assume, however, that because a particular behavior responds to a specific environmental event, the event caused the behavior in the first place. Specifically, that Anderson and Herrmann's subjects responded to adult attention does not mean that adult attention was the cause of the behavior's appearance. It does suggest, however, that a particular biochemical condition alone may not be able to produce a behavior disorder.

What are the implications of this for the behavioral scientist? All factors (biophysical and environmental) which may contribute to a behavior disorder must be investigated. "To assume that any one alone will provide a necessary and sufficient explanation is to ignore the complexity of the phenomenon that is human behavior" (Ross, 1980, p. 4). These factors cannot be indentified very accurately outside the laboratory. Accordingly, we discuss etiology in terms of *predisposing* causes, those that set the stage for a potential behavior disorder; *precipitating* causes, those which may trigger a behavior; and *contributing* factors, events that are consistently associated with behavior disorders and that may influence them (Hallahan and Kauffman, 1978). Thus, Lesch-Nyhan may predispose a child to develop self-injurious behavior, the presence of certain adults may precipitate it, and social attention may inadvertently contribute to its development and maintenance. These factors and conditions are not causes, but rather *etiological correlates*. These can be divided into two groups; biophysical and environmental.

BIOPHYSICAL CORRELATES

What types of behavior disorders appear to be most closely related to biological factors?

Biophysical factors include genetic, neurological, or biochemical conditions. Although the evidence is inconclusive, studies indicate that severe and profound behavior disorders are more frequently of biological origin than are milder disturbances (Kauffman, 1981). Biophysical agents have been linked to a variety of behavioral disorders, including infantile autism and hyperactivity. For example, Rimland (1964) suggested that autism is a defect in relating new stimuli to former experience, caused by lesions in the brain. Because autism tends to occur in children born prematurely, and such children were until recently exposed to pure oxygen, Rimland hypothesized that the cause of the neurological defect was hypersensitivity to oxygen.

A more direct approach to the question of etiology of behavior disorders was taken by Chess, Thomas, and Birch (1967), who monitored 136 children over a 10-year period. Thirty-nine children in their original sample developed behavioral disorders of various types and degrees of severity. From extensive interviews with the mothers of these children the authors developed patterns of reactivity that could be used to characterize three basic temperaments in the children in their sample. The "easy" child was biologically regular, approached new stimuli, adapted quickly and easily to change, and showed a predominantly positive mood. The "slow to warm up" child responded negatively to new stimuli and adapted slowly to new situations. The willingness of parents and teachers to let such children adapt at their own pace was important to their adjustment. The "persistent" child resisted interference and efforts to divert him or her from an activity. Arbitrary or forceful adult interference could cause adjustment problems for these children.

Chess et al. (1967) found that behavior problems were most likely to develop in children whose biological functions were irregular, who tended to withdraw when faced with new stimuli, who adapted slowly or not at all to new situations, whose moods were frequently negative, and who tended to react intensely. Whether children with these temperamental patterns acquired behavioral disorders depended on the way they were handled by their parents. The authors cautioned against concluding that the parents had a major role in the development of behavior problems, however. They found no evidence that the parents of difficult infants were different from the other parents studied. It can be concluded that the reciprocal influence of the infant's temperament on the parents and the parents' reaction to the child's temperament are more important in the etiology of disordered behavior than either innate behavioral tendencies or specific parental practices.

ENVIRONMENTAL CORRELATES

Because children spend most of their time in school and at home, the possible contributions of these environments to behavior disorders have been widely discussed.

Do parents cause behavior disorders?

Home Factors. Ever since the popularization of Freudian theory, parents of behaviorally disordered children have been accused of contributing to the problems of their children. Freud implicated parental discipline and toilet-training techniques, and others have blamed broken homes, maternal deprivation, parental reinforcement patterns, and faulty childrearing practices. Research, however, has not led to discovery of the origins of behavior disorders in family relationships. It is therefore inappropriate to hold parents responsible for the behavior disorders of their children.

Patterson, Reid, Jones, and Conger (1975) compared interactions in families with aggressive children to those in families of nonaggressive children. The interactions of the families of aggressive children tended to be hostile, whereas interaction in the families of nonaggressive children tended to be more positive. Studies such as this do *not* show whether the interaction pattern caused the behavior disorder or whether the behavior disorder was responsible for the disturbing interactions. It is likely that these factors affect each other reciprocally or that aggressive behavior is the result of other factors altogether.

How can schools contribute to behavior disorders?

School Factors. As Kauffman (1981) observed, the fact that many children develop behavior problems only after they enter school implies that schools may contribute to the appearance of behavior disorders. Studies of behaviorally disordered children in school indicate that, as a group, they do relatively poorly on tests of intelligence and achievement (Kauffman, 1981). This could lead one to assume that school failure may be a cause of disordered behavior, but it is also possible that behavior disorders cause school failure. Research on this topic has been inconclusive.

Some authorities have argued that schools themselves have become maladaptive social institutions, working in the service of the cultural values of conformity and mediocrity. Even if schools were above such criticism, it is clear that they tend to enforce conformity and punish children who violate standards of order and discipline, or who don't fit the pattern expected of the average child (Kauffman, 1981). Sally's teacher may not have caused her behavior problems, but she hasn't helped her overcome them either.

That schools sometimes contribute to behavior problems is also indicated by the fact that behavior disorders are more common among boys than girls in school, whereas parents report fewer problems with them at home. Ross (1980) cited evidence suggesting that this may be because boys have more learning difficulties than girls and may as a result find school more difficult. They may respond with behaviors that school personnel regard as hyperactive, aggressive, or antisocial.

Peer Factors. The peer group may also influence the development of behavioral disorders in school or other microcommunities. There has been little research on this subject, but children undoubtedly influence each other's behavior. This influence may exceed that of parents and other adult models, especially among older children.

Can we pinpoint the cause of behavior disorders?

A succinct summation of our understanding of the etiology of behavior disorders has been provided by Kauffman (1981, p. 146): "[T]he answer to the question 'Why did this child become emotionally disturbed?' is, in most cases, 'No one knows.'" This is true whether one is considering the case of a severely disordered child like Peter or a child such as Sally, who presents classroom management problems. Behavior disorders may be associated with predisposing, precipitating, or contributing factors. Research on the subject does little to increase our understanding because it must rely on correlational methods and because influential variables are almost impossible to control. As research into the causes of behavior disorders continues, additional correlates may be found. Recently, for example, the influence of viewing televised violence on children's aggressive behavior has been documented (Bandura, 1973; Lefkowitz, Eron, Walder, and Huesmann, 1977). Certain food additives also appear to be linked to hyperactivity (Rose, 1978). In the meantime, fortunately, effective intervention can be provided without identifying specific etiologies (Kauffman, 1981).

PROBE 10-3
Biophysical and Environmental Correlates

1. A noted psychiatrist, addressing a professional group of which you are a member, states that all severe mental illnesses are caused in part by genetic factors. You clear your throat, raise your hand, and rise to speak. All eyes turn toward you. What will you say?

2. Environmental correlates that may influence a child to exhibit behavior problems are (circle one):
   a. peers
   b. home
   c. school
   d. all of the above
   e. b and c only

3. What would you say to a parent who was worried that she had caused her child's behavior problem?

DISTURBING AND DISTURBED BEHAVIORS

> **You should be able to differentiate "disturbing" and "disturbed" behaviors and discuss intervention strategies for each.**

As mentioned earlier, there are many problems in defining a population of children. A "population" is nothing more than a convenient hypothetical construct around which information is organized. Describing children in terms of group averages leads us to think of them stereotypically. The "average" child from any population (whether "normal" or "behaviorally disordered") simply doesn't exist. There are children who meet the criteria of the PL 94-142 definition, but they should not be regarded as members of categories such as "hyperactive," "autistic," or "school phobic." They are individuals, and unless descriptions of their characteristics contribute to our understanding of them as individuals, they are of little worth to teachers and child advocates. Accordingly, a few of the exceptional teaching situations that a teacher might encounter in the classroom will be presented in this section.

Consistent with the ecological approach, behaviors will be grouped according to whether they are *disturbing* (i.e., they threaten classroom order and discipline, but tend to be specific to just one ecological setting) or *disturbed* (i.e., they occur with excessive intensity, frequency, or both, across several ecological settings).

DISTURBING BEHAVIORS

What is wrong with the term "hyperactivity"? Two general types of behavior are "disturbing" to classroom teachers: behaviors that cause management or discipline problems, and behaviors that affect the social climate of the classroom. The first group includes children who talk excessively, leave their seats, don't do their work, don't follow directions, or are generally disruptive. These children are frequently labeled "hyperactive." This label may be appropriate when children are consistently overactive in many different settings, but it is frequently applied to children who present problems only in a particular classroom. This label is so widely misused, and it has such undesirable ramifications, that in most cases target assessment is a preferable alternative.

Behaviors that threaten the teacher's authority and control also create management problems. Defiance and aggression toward authority figures are especially likely to alarm teachers and other school officials. Such behavior should be evaluated in the context of the demands and expectations of the adults in authority. Unless these behaviors extend to all authority figures or are extremely intense, as when a child strikes a teacher, it is best to provide

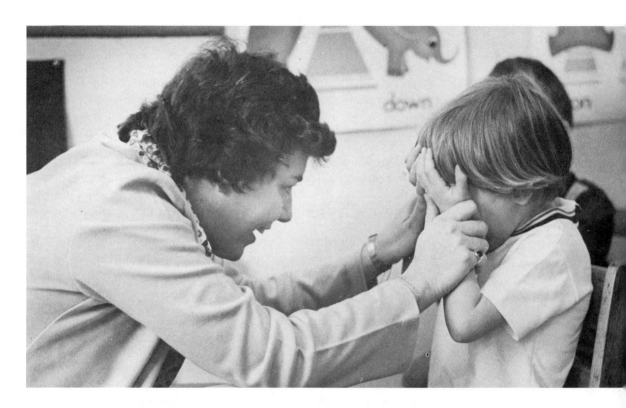

Children exhibiting "disturbed" behavior do so in many settings; "disturbing behavior" occurs with specific environments or persons. In either case, it is most productive to focus on the interaction between the child and those in his environment.

intervention where the problem occurs rather than moving the child to a segregated environment. This is in keeping with ecological strategy of dealing with problems where they happen rather than forcing the child to do all the changing.

Where is treatment for disturbing behaviors best applied?

Behaviors affecting the classroom social climate are disturbing because the teacher must take time from normal teaching functions to arbitrate disputes and encourage appropriate interaction with other children. This group of behaviors includes withdrawal and isolation as well as inappropriate social interactions. The child who fails to play with or talk to peers or who does not join group games or class discussions needs help to participate fully in the social life of the classroom. The child whose bullying or clowning causes classmates to react with rejection or ridicule also needs help. The teacher often has trouble dealing with such behavior because the variables controlling it (e.g., peer attention) are not under the teacher's control. Nevertheless, intervention is best applied where the problem occurs, because it is the "normal" classroom that the child must adjust to.

An important characteristic of disturbing behavior is that it tends to occur in some situations and not in others. A child who is a severe management problem in one teacher's classroom may be no problem at all in another's. Similarly, a child's behavior may be disturbing to some persons but not to others. During ecological assessment an effort is made to "map" the child's disturbance by determining in which situations the child is perceived as causing problems. Intervention is applied only in those settings where the disturbance occurs. Other settings may contribute resources for the intervention plan, but there is no need to intervene in situations where there are no problems. Disturbing behaviors are clearly the result of reciprocal interactions between the child and others in his environment. A child who is not regarded as a problem in all settings should not be considered the exclusive source of the problem.

The belief that disturbing children should receive intervention in the regular classroom is based on the assumption that the classroom teacher will be able to manage the child with special education consultation. These children, then, would be considered mildly and moderately disturbed according to Hallahan and Kauffman's (1978) definition. The attitude that a disturbance is the result of interactions between the child and persons in the environment is unpopular with many teachers and school administrators, who sometimes use special education programs as dumping grounds for problems that regular educators are unwilling to tackle. As a new special education teacher, you should realize that some teachers react defensively to the view that deviance is an interactive problem rather than a characteristic of a child. If you focus on the problem, however, and avoid labeling either the child or the teacher, you should quickly overcome this obstacle, provided of course that you are supported by a school policy that emphasizes teacher consultation and mainstreaming.

DISTURBED BEHAVIORS

It is tempting to characterize "disturbed" behaviors as symptomatic of an underlying pathology. We hope you need no further proof that such a conceptualization would be grossly inaccurate and, in practice, seriously abused. Even if it could be proven that underlying disorders exist, and they could be accurately diagnosed, there still would be the problem of designing effective interventions based on a child's diagnosis.

When can a behavior be considered to be "disturbed"?

Children in this category are likely to have severe and profound behavior disorders, according to the Hallahan and Kauffman (1978) definition. "Disturbed behavior" refers to behaviors that occur in diverse ecological settings, i.e., in the presence of different people and in various locations. The child exhibits undesired or maladaptive behaviors in most interactions, across all microcommunities. But it should never be assumed that a child who has been labeled "disturbed" meets this criterion. The conclusion that a child "owns"

TECHNOLOGY IN ACTION

Andrew was a hyperactive, disruptive pupil in his regular third-grade class. He had become such a management problem that he was referred for special education placement by his teacher. After an assessment and a conference with Andrew's parents, teacher, the principal, and the school special education consulting teacher, it was agreed that special services should be provided for Andrew in his regular classroom because: (1) he needed to learn appropriate student behaviors for "survival" in the regular classroom; (2) a special class environment would be too much unlike the regular classroom to facilitate his adjustment to the latter; and (3) his academic performance and general social maturity were on a par with his age-mates. His IEP goals were to reduce hyperactive and disruptive behaviors (calling out in class, getting out of his seat, interrupting the teacher and other students, making noises, and throwing things) and increase appropriate student behaviors (remaining in seat, completing assignments, obtaining permission to speak or leave seat).

The program the IEP team developed for Andrew involved the use of a kitchen timer and a behavior management strategy called the "hero procedure" (Kerr and Nelson, 1983). The consulting teacher divided the first 1-hour period of the day into brief, variable time intervals averaging 5 minutes in length. For several days she sat in the classroom to observe and record Andrew's behavior. He engaged in disruptive behavior an average of 67 percent of each 1-hour observation over five school days.

Following this "baseline" assessment, Andrew's teacher presented him with a set of special rules: (1) remain in your seat unless you have permission to leave; (2) do not talk out without first getting the teacher's permission; and (3) keep your eyes and hands on your own work. The teacher then explained that Andrew and his classmates would play a "timer game" (Wolf, Hanley, King, Lachowicz, and Giles, 1970). She would set the kitchen timer (according to a prearranged schedule) at her desk. If Andrew was following his rules when the timer rang, he would earn a point that could be exchanged at the end of the hour for an equivalent number of minutes of free time for the entire class. (This technique is called the hero procedure because Andrew's good behavior could earn a reinforcer desired by the whole group of students).

The timer game and hero procedure quickly reduced Andrew's disruptive behavior. One week later, the average amount of time Andrew spent engaging in disruptive behavior during the first hour was 12 percent, according to the consulting teacher's observations. The other children, who previously had avoided contact with Andrew, encouraged him to earn more points and praised him for his good behavior.

Over the next several weeks, the length of the timer intervals was gradually extended to an average of 20 minutes, and the game was expanded to encompass the entire school day. Earned free time was given at the end of the day instead of after each hour. Eventually the timer itself was phased out, and Andrew earned points for the group when the teacher periodically "caught him being good." Andrew's disruptive behavior remained at less than 10 percent per day (which was about the same as that of the other pupils in the class) for the remainder of the school year.

---

a behavior disorder can be made only after the child's behavior has been assessed in all ecological settings; and even then, the most useful view for intervention is that the disturbance is a reciprocal phenomenon between the child and the social environment. In fact, the term "disturbed" is used here only as a descriptive category. Its use as a label for children's behavior should be specifically avoided. A complete ecological assessment identifies environmental as well as personal variables that should be incorporated into a treatment plan. Interventions for disturbed behavior tend to involve intensive and prolonged treatment and removal of the child from the regular classroom.

A great variety of behaviors may be characterized as disturbed. The behaviors previously described as disturbing could be included if they occur across several ecological settings. The child who defies *all* authority figures, or the child who withdraws from *all* social contacts presents a different treatment problem than the child who acts in these ways only in some situations. Peter and Sally both may say inappropriate things, but Sally's performances tend to take place only in the classroom, whereas Peter babbles meaninglessly in all situations.

Behaviors that do not appear to be controlled by specific environmental stimuli may also be considered disturbed. For example, such self-stimulating behaviors as rocking, hand flapping, and head banging seem to occur without environmental reinforcement. [Recall, however, that Anderson and Herrmann (1975) showed that the severe self-mutilation associated with Lesch-Nyhan may be maintained by subtle environmental factors.] Failure to respond to verbal cues and directions is another example of lack of stimulus control, as anyone who has futilely yelled "stop" to a nonverbal child knows. In cases such as this the problem is one of communication. Verbal commands don't work with the child because the words don't have stimulus value for that child. To respond appropriately to the command "stop," the child must understand what the word means; i.e., the child must respond differently to the word "stop" than to another word, such as "go." Verbal deficits of this sort are severe and occur across different social settings. The syndrome labeled "autism" is often characterized as a verbal or language disorder, because children given this label often have no functional language, in addition to grossly inappropriate social behavior and low-level or nonexistent self-help skills. Once again, only a complete ecological assessment will reveal whether the failure to respond appropriately to verbal and nonverbal stimuli is generalized or occurs only in specific ecological settings.

Deficits in self-help or daily living skills also qualify as disturbed behavior. Children who do not feed or dress themselves or look after their own toilet needs require intensive educational efforts that extend beyond the school setting. Enuresis (bladder incontinence) and encopresis (lack of appropriate bowel control) are two behavior problems that can keep the child from entering the regular class. It is important to know whether the child is incontinent just before or during school or at other times as well. The child who wets his or her pants before reading group, for example, presents a very different problem than the child who has never acquired any bladder control.

Psychotic Behavior. The intense, chronic, and pervasive behavior displayed by Peter is an example of a "disturbed" behavior pattern that could be labeled psychotic. Such children "are frequently described as inaccessible, unreachable, or out of touch with reality, and they often function like children considered to be mentally retarded" (Kauffman, 1981, p. 68). As we pointed out earlier, while psychotic children can be differentiated rather easily from children whose behavior is less disordered (i.e., their behavior is both qualitatively and quantitatively different), it is much more difficult to separate them into meaningful subcategories. However, two major diagnostic categories have been described: autism and childhood schizophrenia (Kauffman, 1981).

Autism is a rare syndrome characterized by several specific factors, including the following:

What are the symptoms of autistic behavior?

1. Onset prior to 30 months of age.
2. Marked lack of responsiveness to other people.
3. Extreme language deficits, including total lack of functional language
4. If speech is present, unusual speech patterns, such as echolalia (meaningless repetition of words or phrases), reversal of pronouns (e.g., "he" for "I"), and metaphorical language (e.g., "I don't want any catsup" to indicate any negative response to a question).
5. Bizarre behavior, such as a marked resistance to any change in the environment or an unusual attachment to particular objects.
6. An absence of delusions or hallucinations, which characterize adult schizophrenia (American Psychiatric Association, 1980).

Parents of autistic children often report first suspecting that something is wrong with their child when the infant fails to make anticipatory responses to being picked up (i.e., holds its arms out to accept the parent's reach; Rimland, 1964). While some autistic children display normal intelligence, most function in the retarded range, although some display amazing skill in isolated areas (e.g., memorizing TV commercials or song lyrics). In addition, many display intense temper tantrums or aggressive behavior when thwarted, self-stimulatory behaviors such as rocking or twirling objects, or self-injurious behaviors such as head-banging or self-biting. They may have few self-help skills. It should be noted that while the syndrome of autism is quite rare, many children with severe developmental delays and even some with mild-to-moderate disabilities display some behaviors characteristic of autism. To avoid applying a label as potentially damaging as "autistic" to children, use of the term "autistic-like" is preferred (Strain, 1983).

The causes of autism are unknown. The failure to find close relatives of autistic children who also exhibit the syndrome suggests that genetic factors are not involved. Neurological dysfunction plays a role in most theories regarding etiology (see Cullinan et al., 1983).

What behaviors characterize schizophrenia?

Schizophrenia rarely occurs in children, emerging instead during adolescence or young adulthood. For diagnostic purposes, the classification "childhood onset pervasive developmental disorder" has replaced "childhood schizophrenia." In DSM III it is characterized by marked and chronic impairment of social relationships originating between the ages of 30 months and 12 years, and by the following behavior patterns:

1. Sudden excessive anxiety, catastrophic reactions to everyday events, inability to be consoled when upset, and unexplained attacks of panic.
2. Narrow or inappropriate affect and extreme lability of mood.
3. Resistance to change in the environment or insistence on sameness.
4. Odd movements, such as peculiar postures, hand movements, or walking movements.
5. Abnormal speech characteristics.
6. Oversensitivity or undersensitivity to stimuli.
7. Self-mutilation (American Psychiatric Association, 1980, p. 91).

As you can see, many of these characteristics also apply to autism. In fact, age of onset is the most common way to differentially diagnose these subgroups (Kauffman, 1981). Like autistic children, youngsters manifesting pervasive developmental disorders tend to function as retarded persons, although their retardation appears not to be as severe as that of most autistic children. Adding to the diagnostic confusion is the fact that many "psychotic" behaviors are observed in severely retarded children (Cullinan et al., 1983).

We indicated earlier that the prognosis for improvement in severely and profoundly disordered children tends to be very poor. However, some autistic children have been successfully mainstreamed into regular classrooms, provided they have the intellectual and academic ability and their autistic behaviors have been controlled (see Koegel, Rincover, and Egel, 1982).

PROBE 10-4
Disturbing and Disturbed Behaviors

1. You are a special education consultant, and a girl who displays aggressive behavior has been referred to you. Briefly describe the steps you would go through in assessing the problem. (Hint: think in terms of the settings in which you might want to study the behavior, the persons with whom you would talk about the child's behavior, and the kinds of information you would collect.)

2. How would you expect "disturbing" aggressive behavior to differ from "disturbed" aggressive behavior? How would the difference influence your intervention plan?

3. What are the differences between autism and childhood onset pervasive developmental disorder? Why is it often difficult to distinguish between these diagnostic groups?

EDUCATION AND TREATMENT OPTIONS

> **You should be able to describe the options for educating children with behavior disorders in the least restrictive environment.**

The educator of behaviorally disordered children is able to draw on a continually expanding array of service delivery options. The current emphasis on providing all school-related services in the least restrictive environment possible has added considerably to the educator's repertoire of intervention strategies. The cascade of services available to behaviorally disordered children and their families is vastly different today from what was available even a decade or two ago.

Special education for children with serious behavior problems scarcely existed before the middle of the twentieth century. Early school programs were heavily influenced by psychoanalytic theory. They were also affected by the work of Alfred Strauss and Laura Lehtinen, who pioneered a highly structured approach for children with learning and behavioral disorders (Strauss and Lehtinen, 1947). Strauss and Lehtinen's approach was based on the assumption that children exhibiting hyperactive, impulsive, or distractible behavior were brain injured. Brain damage was assumed to cause disorders in perception and attention as well, which was thought to account for significant learning problems in the same children. This constellation of symptoms or behaviors was termed the Strauss syndrome. The methods developed by Strauss and Lehtinen were later extended by Cruickshank (Cruickshank, Bentzen, Ratzeburg, and Tannhauser, 1961) and were applied by Haring and Phillips (1962) to children labeled emotionally disturbed.

What educational options are available for disturbed children?

During the 1960s and early 1970s, school programs for children exhibiting behavioral disorders expanded. Most of these programs exphasized the use of self-contained classrooms, the efficiency of which has been questioned in the light of follow-up studies of children returned to the regular classroom (e.g., Vacc, 1972). Critics of the widespread practice of assigning handicapped children to self-contained special classes welcomed the passage of PL 94-142 and its mandate for the least restrictive environment. The following continuum or cascade of services describes the educational environments presently available to children labeled "behaviorally disordered."

1. *Regular Classroom.* Most children with behavior problems are placed in this setting. Increasingly, however, special education consultants are available to help the regular classroom teacher develop and implement Individualized Educational Programs (IEPs).

2. *Resource rooms* are available for children requiring more intensive help with learning or behavior problems than the regular classroom teacher can

Many students with mild behavioral problems can be educated in a regular class.

provide. Some resource teachers also offer both consultation to the regular teacher and direct services to the child.

3. *Self-contained classrooms* accommodate children whose behaviors limit their access to the mainstream to such an extent that they need a highly structured, special environment for most of the school day. Because such classrooms are located within the school building, systematic efforts to mainstream pupils can be accomplished in gradual steps during the school year. The priority placed by PL 94-142 on serving the severely handicapped has prompted the development of public school programs for "autistic" and "psychotic" children. The lower intellectual functioning of these children, their lack of adequate language and self-care skills, and the relatively high frequency with which they exhibit bizarre and inappropriate behavior often dictate placement in a self-contained special class or a special school, the next step up the continuum of services. It should not, however, be assumed that a child labeled autistic, for example, cannot function at all in the mainstream. It is better to locate programs for such children in public schools than in segregated settings, where opportunities to model and learn more normalized behavior patterns are severely limited (see Koegel et al., 1982).

4. *Special day schools* are a relatively unusual option. These may be public or private, and may serve one or several categories of handicapped children. The child's access to the mainstream is severely restricted by physical removal from the public school building.

5. *Re-education schools* are a special type of residential school program found throughout the United States. Founded by Nicholas Hobbs (1966), "Re-ED" is based on the ecological model. The child is removed from the normal school environment only because he or she requires such extensive intervention. Contact is maintained with the child's natural ecology through intensive liaison work and through the child's home visits, which typically occur every weekend. Furthermore, the child's stay in the residential program is intentionally brief, averaging about 6 months. Re-ED support is provided from the time the child leaves the residential program until he or she and others in the child's microcommunities (e.g., parents, teachers) can function without it.

6. *Residential treatment programs* provide comprehensive intervention, which may include psychotherapy, chemotherapy, or other medical therapies in addition to education. The child's stay in such programs is generally relatively long — 1 or 2 years — and his or her contact with the natural ecology more severely limited. The trend today is away from custodial facilities.

In this continuum of services, fewer children and more severe behavior problems will be found as one moves up the continuum away from the least restrictive environment. In theory, children should be moved away from the least restrictive environment one step at a time, and they should be moved back down as soon as feasible (see Reynolds and Birch, 1982). In practice, however, the philosophy of "out of sight, out of mind" prevails; and except for programs like Re-ED, which provide support sytems for transitions from one level to another, there is little evidence that program placement is as flexible as it should be. Recent innovations in educational strategies are helping to overcome such problems, however. For example, special education programs that emphasize the development of skills needed to advance to less restrictive educational placements have paved the way for children exhibiting severely disordered behavior to progress from segregated environments to settings where they are integrated with their nondisabled peers (see Kerr and Nelson, 1983).

CURRENT TRENDS

What does the future hold for the education of behaviorally disordered children? There are several noteworthy trends. Of greatest importance is the provision of educational services to unserved children, including those with severe and profound behavioral disorders, preschool children exhibiting behavior problems, secondary-age youngsters, and delinquents. The provision of services to children on the basis of their labels is at odds with the philosophy of this chapter; but, nevertheless, programs for these children are badly needed. In the near future we hope services will be made available on the basis of children's needs instead of their labels. The practice of restricting special education services to children who meet rigid, formal definitions for categorical disabilities must be abolished before the special and regular educator can work as an effective team to help all children who have learning or adjustment problems (Reynolds and Birch, 1982).

A second promising trend is the increasing diversification of optional learning environments in the educational mainstream. This trend toward "alternative education" reflects greater sensitivity to the individuality of all children and gives the child who deviates from existing standards for "normal" behavior a chance to survive in the least restrictive appropriate environment (see Nelson, 1977).

What nontraditional roles are special education teachers being called upon to assume?

In addition, the current emphasis on mainstreaming has started a trend toward in-service teacher training and consultation by special educators — for example, mental health consultation provided by a crisis teacher or by a helping teacher to children or their teachers (Morse, 1980). Other special educators have expanded the role to include teacher training as well (Idol-Maestas, 1983). In the role of trainer, the special educator can provide a variety of instruction, including formal graduate courses, after-school workshops, demonstration teaching, and informal consultation. Two encouraging consequences of this trend are a reduction in labeling and an increase in the ability of regular classroom teachers to accept and foster individual differences in children. As regular classroom teachers assume greater responsibility, the in-service teacher trainer's role requires less direct intervention with children.

The special educator helps the teacher acquire the skills to deal with exceptional teaching situations rather than simply removing one participant in the disturbing interaction. Whether or not this trend becomes established will depend on the work of farsighted educators who realize that the best interests of handicapped children are not served by segregating them. You should realize, however, that this trend does not eliminate the need for more restrictive educational environments, such as self-contained classes. But in-service training and teacher consultation do reduce the population of such programs.

The treatment of children labeled psychotic is more likely to require intensive, systematic procedures that are applied throughout the day. Such youngsters also are more likely to require the services of professionals from other disciplines, such as neurology, psychiatry, and physical therapy. Therefore, more of these children tend to be placed in more restrictive educational environments, especially residential treatment programs. However, as indicated earlier, public school classes are being established for these pupils, and they are being educated with their nondisabled peers as much as possible. As educators have become more involved with parent training, it is possible to extend instruction throughout the child's day without the need for residential placement.

Finally, as the role of the educator as child advocate becomes more diversified, so do the demands placed on them. The in-service teacher trainer must sometimes work with teachers and administrations that resist change, the parent counselor or trainer must overcome guilt and denial, and classroom teachers must deal with children who progress very slowly or who reward them with verbal abuse at the end of a long day. As the efforts of special educators extend beyond traditional school boundaries, it is important to remember that the child is the client, and that one is dealing with microcommunities that have traditionally handled problems by rejecting problem children or making them scapegoats. Advocacy takes more than a strong personality, dedication, and tremendous patience, however; it takes great skill. Today's special educator must be familiar with a complex teaching technology, laws, and statutes affecting the handicapped, and counseling techniques and consultation strategies as well.

PROBE 10-5
Educational Environments

1. List the six levels of educational services generally available to the behaviorally disordered child. Identify each level's distinguishing characteristics.

2. You chair a school-based Admissions and Release Committee, which recommends educational placements for exceptional children. For each of the children described, indicate which of the six levels of the educational cascade you would recommend for placement and briefly explain your reasons.

a. Peter: A ten-year-old with "psychotic" behaviors. He has good speech and language but no academic skills. He has violent outbursts and behaves aggressively in many situations without apparent provocation.

b. Sally: An eight-year-old third grader who has been a discipline problem all year. She is about 1 year behind her grade level in arithmetic and functions at the readiness level in reading and language arts. Her teacher complains that she does not do assignments without constant supervision and disrupts the class with "silly" behavior.

c. Tim: A 14-year-old who spends most of his time in Spanish class sleeping or daydreaming. Although he has better than average intellectual potential, his teacher complains that he hasn't learned a thing.

d. James: A 12-year-old who has been expelled from school for aggressive attacks on a teacher and for vandalism. He already belongs to a street gang, and his parents are unable to control him.

e. Alice: A 17-year-old who is taking algebra (a required college-prep course) for the second time and still failing. Her work in other classes is average or slightly above average. Both Alice and her parents express a desire for her to attend college.

SUMMARY

1. Behavior disorders are best defined by considering characteristics common to the behaviors thought to be disordered.
2. There are a number of conceptual approaches to defining behavior disorders. The psychodynamic and behavioral orientations receive the most attention.
3. The ecological approach to the diagnosis and classification of behavior disorders has found wide acceptance by special educators.
4. Factors such as age, sex, and socioeconomic variables interact with prevalence estimates of behavior disorders.
5. Examination of the biophysical and environmental correlates of behavioral disorders is more productive for intervention than traditional investigations of etiological factors.
6. Rather than discuss the "characteristics" of behaviorally disordered pupils, teachers should differentiate "disturbing" behaviors, which tend to be specific to one setting, and "disturbed" behaviors, which occur with excessive intensity and/or frequency across several settings.
7. The provision of services to the behaviorally disordered in the least restrictive environment requires that a broad array of services to be available to the individual, the family, and the professionals involved.
8. Current trends in services for the behaviorally disordered person include provision for the previously unserved severely and profoundly disor-

dered, and in-service training of the regular educator to handle behavior problems in the mainstream of the school setting.

9. *Most important, do not label children as behaviorally disordered.*

TASK SHEET 10
Field Experience in Behavior Disorders

Complete *one* of the following:

Child Observation

Get permission from a building principal and the appropriate teachers to observe a child who has been identified by the school as behaviorally disordered. The child need not have been formally labeled. Observe the child for 30 minutes, if possible, in both a structured situation, such as a group lesson, and during free play.

1. What behaviors make the child "different" from his or her "normal" peers?
2. How are these behaviors different in terms of their frequency and intensity?
3. How do the teacher and the peer group react to the child's deviant behavior? Does their reaction seem to have anything to do with the behavior being a problem (i.e., do they call attention to it, give in to it, or seem to anticipate it)?

Parent or Teacher Interview

Interview a parent or regular classroom teacher regarding his perceptions of behavior disorders. Find out what he or she thinks the term means. You may use the term "emotionally disturbed" if you prefer.

1. Whom did you interview?
2. How did the person react to the term "behaviorally disordered" or "emotionally disturbed"? What did the person think it meant?
3. How would your interviewee's conception affect the way he or she reacted to or worked with a child having one of these labels?

Professional Interview

Interview a teacher, psychologist, or counselor who deals with children with behavior disorders. Describe the person you interviewed and his or her responsibilities. Identify rewards and problems encountered in working with these children.

Agency Investigation

Request information from the following agencies about the services they provide in the area of behavior disorders. Write a three-page paper summarizing these services and how you might use them if you were a professional working with children who exhibit behavior disorders:

American Psychiatric Association
1700 18th Street, N.W.
Washington, DC 20009

National Society for Autistic Children
169 Tampa Avenue
Albany, NY 12208

National Association for Mental Health
1800 North Kent Street
Arlington, VA 22209

Library Study

Locate three articles on behavior disorders. Write a one-page critique of each, concluding with a paragraph that summarizes your personal reaction to each. Here are the names of some journals in which you can find articles:

American Journal of Orthopsychiatry
Behavioral Disorders
Journal of Abnormal Child Psychology
Journal of Applied Behavior Analysis
Journal of Autism and Developmental Disorders

Design Your Own Field Experience

If none of the above activities fits your needs, design one of your own after discussing the idea with your instructor.

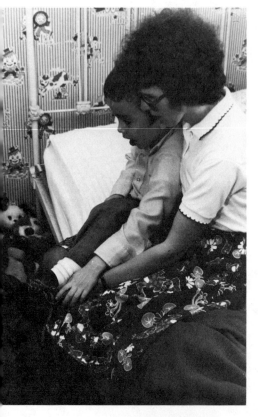

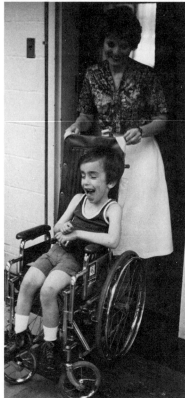

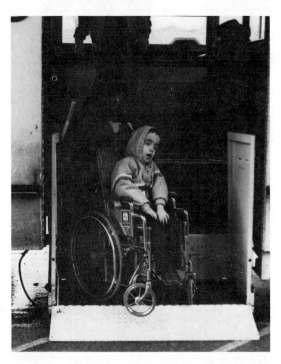

Brian, who has multiple disabilities, is helped to dress by his mother. A specially equipped bus picks him up for his trip to school, where he is met by his teacher. Part of his school day is spent with children who do not have disabilities. Following physical therapy, he has lunch. His afternoon is spent in a variety of individual lessons. Upon returning home, he plays with one of his neighborhood friends. After a full day it's time for a goodnight story and then to bed.

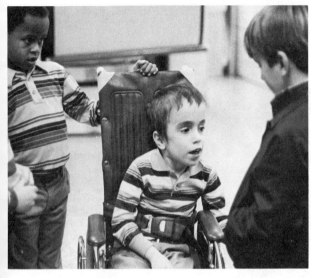

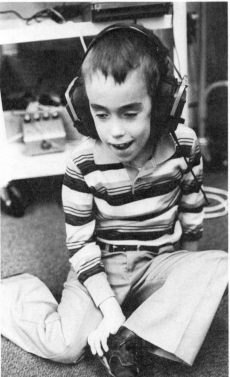

Jennifer:

The head nurse of a woman's locked ward introduces me to Jennifer. She is lying in a urine-soaked bed under a restraining sheet.

"How long has she been here?"

"Fifteen years. She gets up five to fifteen minutes every day."

"How about meals?"

"She is fed here in bed."

Later in the day I talked with one of the "brighter girls" (state school term), who has worked in the community and now serves the attendants assisting in feeding and cleaning.

"Ann, how long have you been here?"

"A long time."

"How long is that?"

"Seventeen years."

"How long has Jennifer been here?"

"About fifteen years."

"Does she ever get up?"

"Only on Mondays and Thursdays for a bath."

During the three hours I was present, Jennifer was not allowed out of her restraint. That evening another observer was able to see Jennifer's case history, including her medical record. According to that, Jennifer is receiving: Mellaril, 100 mg. three times a day; Valium, 5 mg. three times a day; phenobarbitol, 1½ gr. three times a day; and Dilantin sodium, 1½ gr. twice a day. . . .

Jennifer, of course, cannot put her own bib on, so it is done for her. Since she is not allowed out of the bed, she must eat lying flat. The urine-soaked bed was not cleaned before she ate lunch, nor was it cleaned before dinner. It has become her way of life.

Source: From Burton Blatt, *Souls in Extremis: An Anthology of Victims and Victimizers.* Boston: Allyn and Bacon, 1973, pp. 32-33. Reprinted by permission.

11

Severe Developmental Disabilities

David L. Gast and Mark Wolery

David Gast is Associate Professor in the Department of Special Education and Coordinator of personnel preparation programs in the area of the severely/profoundly handicapped at the University of Kentucky. Current areas of interest include designing data-based instructional programs and comparing errorless learning procedures used with severely handicapped learners. Mark Wolery is Associate Professor in the Department of Special Education at the University of Kentucky and coordinator of the early childhood education for the handicapped personnel program. Current interests include comparing errorless learning procedures and evaluating early intervention programs, teams, models, and physical therapy.

In the recent past, children like Jennifer who exhibited severe developmental delays and behavior problems and who lived in state residential institutions for the mentally retarded had very little chance for a quality life. Such children were typically denied access to educational programs that could maximize their ability to function independently. Their future was bleak indeed. However, with the passage of the Education for All Handicapped Children Act, PL 94-142, the right of these students to a free and appropriate education has been secured, regardless of their level of functioning or type of disability. Furthermore, their education must be designed to meet their individual needs.

The mandate securing children with severe and multiple handicaps a right to a community-based public education has presented a number of problems for local school districts. First, most districts were initially unable to hire special education teachers who had the skills to assess and teach children with severe developmental disabilities. Second, few school districts had money for the adaptive equipment and materials needed to provide an age-appropriate curriculum for multiply handicapped children. Third, some educational agencies objected to spending their limited resources on a population of students they believed would never be self-sufficient or productive citizens in the community. Fourth, many did not have the physical facilities accessible to students with such extensive disabilities. In short, most local education agencies were not prepared to address the needs of this most challenging population of students when PL 94–142 was passed.

During the period since the passage of PL 94–142, some school districts and community service agencies have met the challenge; others have not. In most communities considerable progress has been made in serving these students and their families. The gains are primarily because of the coordinated advocacy efforts of parents, professionals, and concerned citizens. Much has been accomplished in recent years to ensure that children like Jennifer have a brighter future. There is, however, much more that can be done.

In this chapter we discuss the instructional procedures, assessment strategies, curricula, and service delivery models for the education of students with severe developmental disabilities. As you read the chapter, you should realize that many of the concepts we present are new. Change will undoubtedly be made as new information becomes available about how best to meet these students' needs. Through continuing research and development, more effective instructional methodologies, curricula, and service delivery systems will be implemented. It is imperative that those who plan to work in this area of special education keep abreast of recent advances by attending professional conferences and reading the relevant professional literature.

CHARACTERISTICS OF CHILDREN WITH SEVERE DEVELOPMENTAL DISABILITIES

> **You should be able to describe the characteristics of children with severe developmental disabilities.**

This chapter focuses on children who have been identified as exhibiting severe learning and behavioral disabilities. These students have typically been assigned one of the following categorical labels: severely developmentally delayed, severely or profoundly mentally retarded, severely multiply handicapped, or severely/profoundly handicapped. Regardless of the specific label, these children are characterized by severe functional retardation, multiple disabilities, and a need for more services than children with mild and moderate disabilities require.

How diverse is the population of children with severe developmental disabilities?

Children with severe developmental disabilities are an extremely heterogeneous population in spite of their common categorical label. Their developmental delays may have been caused by a genetic irregularity, prenatal hazard, birth injury, or postnatal trauma as discussed in Chapter 8 (Mental Retardation). For many the cause of their developmental delay has gone unidentified.

They also differ in their sensory, motor, social, and cognitive abilities. Some are deaf, others are blind, some are deaf and blind. Some are ambulatory, others are nonambulatory. Some engage in bizarre self-stimulatory behaviors, others engage in "appropriate" social interactions. Most require highly structured educational programs to acquire new skills. A visitor to a classroom serving students with severe and profound handicaps would quickly conclude that this is a most diverse population.

Some people consider children with severe and multiple handicaps to be ineducable despite growing evidence to the contrary. Such an attitude is based on a very restricted definition of education and a lack of familiarity with or understanding of the educational research literature. One must keep in mind that this population has gained the attention of special educators only in the last decade. With few exceptions, severely handicapped children were denied

access to public education programs prior to 1975. Since the passage of PL 94–142 in that year, much money and effort have been spent to increase our understanding of how these children learn. Much remains to be learned, however. Efforts to maximize these children's learning capabilities are being furthered through the coordinated efforts of local educational agencies, state departments of education, university personnel preparation and research programs, and organizations such as The Association for Persons with Severe Handicaps (TASH), National Association for Retarded Citizens (NARC), Association for Behavior Analysis (ABA), and Council for Exceptional Children (CEC).

TOWARD A DEFINITION

Although there is general agreement among professionals about the behaviors that characterize persons with severe developmental disabilities, there is as yet no universally accepted definition of this population. Prior to 1977, the most common approach to defining severely and profoundly handicapped students was to list the medical and behavioral conditions professionals thought characterized the group (Sontag, Burke, and York, 1973). As you might imagine, using such an approach proved to be nearly impossible because of the heterogeneity of the population. In the years since severely handicapped persons gained the attention of special educators, several definitions have been forwarded, some based on general behavioral descriptors and service needs (Justen, 1976), and still others on service needs alone (Baker, 1979).

What are the common elements of definitions of the severely handicapped population?

At least two common threads are either directly stated or implied in all definitions of the severely handicapped population. First, students with severe developmental disabilities require instruction in basic adaptive behavior skills. Second, severely handicapped students require more services than moderately handicapped students to attain their maximum level of functioning. In keeping with these two fundamental components, the definition generated by a group of special educators from seven southeastern universities, the Southeastern Regional Coalition (1979, p. 39), is offered:

> The severely handicapped individual is defined for educational purposes as (1) having serious primary disabilities that are cognitive (e.g., –4 standard deviations below a normal IQ on a standardized test of intelligence such as the Revised Stanford-Binet Test of Intelligence) and/or behavioral (e.g., autistic or childhood schizophrenic), (2) having the high probability of additional physical and/or sensory handicaps, and (3) requiring significantly more resources than are provided for the mildly and moderately handicapped in special education programs.

According to this definition, an individual is described as severely/profoundly handicapped on the basis of his or her current level of functioning. The definition is educationally oriented in that it recognizes the need for additional services if effective instruction is to be provided. It also implies that instruction will focus on basic skills such as toileting, communication, personal hygiene, and vocational rather than academic skills.

Why is a definition so important?

Much effort has been devoted to defining the population, but why is the definition so important? Quite simply, an agreed-upon definition has a far-reaching influence on efforts to provide students appropriate services. Categorical labels are used by schools to establish classes for students with severe handicaps, determine placement criteria, and recruit and hire qualified teachers. State departments of education determine competencies needed by teachers of severely handicapped learners and set certification requirements. Universities develop teacher education programs and address teacher competencies based on a categorical system. All three must use the categorical definition adopted by the U.S. Office of Special Education to report prevalence data and to apply for supplemental funds (Sailor and Guess, 1983). Although many educators argue against adopting a new category of special education named severely handicapped, the fact remains that a categorical system is in place. If students with severe developmental disabilities are to receive their fair share of funds and receive appropriate educational services, educational agencies must agree upon a definition of what constitutes a severe developmental disability.

PREVALENCE

The number of severely and profoundly handicapped persons in the population is difficult to estimate. Based on a survey of handicapped children receiving special education and related services for the 1982-1983 school year, as reported by state agencies to the U.S. Department of Education, approximately 1.92 percent of the school-age population (ages 3 to 21) is mentally retarded. It is generally estimated that 0.1 percent of the total population can be categorized as severely/profoundly handicapped, although this is not specified in the USDE report. The 0.1 percent figure includes only those with severe and profound cognitive deficits; it does not include persons with severe speech, orthopedic, auditory, or visual impairment.

What percent of the school-age population is severely handicapped?

BEHAVIORAL CHARACTERISTICS

It is important to understand that the problems of the severely/profoundly handicapped differ in degree, not in kind, from the problems of other child populations. That is, it is the extent of the handicaps that results in the child's classification, not the type of handicap. Many children have visual, auditory, motor, or neurological impairments. Adaptive equipment such as glasses, hearing aids, or braces can correct some children's impairments. But children whose disabilities are so severe that they cannot be corrected with adaptive or prosthetic equipment may be rendered *functionally retarded*.

What is functional retardation?

The concept of functional retardation differs from the concept of mental retardation. Grossman (1983, p. 11) defined mental retardation as "significantly subaverage general intellectual functioning resulting in or associated with concurrent impairments in adaptive behavior and manifested during the developmental period." This definition, which is similar to the definition of "psychological retardation" discussed and criticized by Bijou (1981), implies defective mental functioning based on some biological abnormality that adversely affects adaptive behavior regardless of the environment in which the behavior occurs. In contrast, the concept of functional retardation emphasizes the importance of environmental events in shaping and maintaining adaptive behavior. Some environments in which people interact are deficient, providing insufficient support or structure for persons to attain their maximum potential. The result is retarded behavior. On the other hand, some environments provide maximum levels of support that minimize a disability's effects on an individual's ability to learn new skills and function more independently. Such an environment might provide students with adaptive devices (hearing aids, communication boards, wheelchairs) prosthetic equipment (artificial limbs), barrier-free access to activities (ramps, curb cut-outs, automatic doors), and consistent consequences for acquiring and using functional skills (differential reinforcement). With this distinction in mind, we can say that severely handicapped students are those for whom maximum environmental support has been provided and who in spite of this support continue to manifest functional retardation in adaptive behavior and require "a very high degree of dependence on caretakers and instructional personnel" (Sailor and Guess, 1983, p. 13).

As previously stated, severely handicapped children are a heterogeneous population. No two children have the same characteristics. Within this population, we find the following types of children (Sontag, Burke, and York, 1973, p. 21):

> Those who are not toilet trained; aggress toward others; do not attend to even the most pronounced social stimuli; self-mutilate; ruminate; self-stimulate; do not walk, speak, hear, or see; manifest durable and intense temper tantrums; are not under even the most rudimentary forms of verbal control; do not imitate; manifest minimally controlled seizures; and/or have extremely brittle medical existences.

An elaboration of some of the characteristics in this list will illustrate the wide variety of behaviors that a teacher of severely/profoundly handicapped children may encounter. The meaning of some of the characteristics is clear. The others can be explained as follows:

— *Aggression toward others* refers to behaviors that can inflict bodily harm on other persons, such as biting, kicking, hitting, hair pulling, and throwing things.
— *No attention to even the most pronounced social stimuli* means that the child does not make eye contact with adults and other children, does not look at instructional materials, and does not respond to simple verbal instructions.
— *Self-mutilation* refers to behaviors such as head banging, biting oneself, eye gouging, and hitting oneself on the head. This class of behaviors is commonly referred to as SIB, or self-injurious behavior.
— *Rumination* refers to self-induced vomiting after which a portion of the vomitus is chewed again and swallowed; this is a potentially life-threatening behavior disorder.
— *Self-stimulation* refers to purposeless, repetitive behaviors such as body rocking, hand flapping, and finger twirling; these may also be called stereotypic behavior.
— *Durable and intense temper tantrums* refers to a combination of physical aggression, self-mutilation, and/or self-stimulation occurring over an extended period.
— *Imitation* is the ability to mimic or repeat a behavior immediately after someone (referred to as the "model") demonstrates it; it is a primary mechanism for learning that is frequently absent in children with severe learning disabilities.
— *Extremely brittle medical existence* refers to the presence of life-threatening conditions, such as heart failure, respiratory difficulties, central nervous system disorders, digestive system malfunctions, and behaviors that threaten the life or safety of the individual.

What are stereotypic behaviors?

Children with severe developmental disabilities present a variety of handicapping conditions. Although these children have been assigned a common categorical label, they by no means represent a homogenous group. What they do share, however, is a need for systematic instruction and environmental adaption in order to acquire and maintain basic adaptive or life-sustaining skills. They are children who are dependent on others for their care and who manifest functional retardation. These students, as individuals, present a challenge to special educators. It should be remembered that the vast majority of these children had been placed in residential state institutions for their entire lives in the recent past. Not until the 1970s was it recognized that they can and do benefit from placement in public school educational programs.

PROBE 11-1
Characteristics of Persons with Severe Developmental Disabilities

1. What are the three primary components of the definition "severely/profoundly handicapped" presented in this chapter?

2. List five uses for population definitions and categorical labels of the severely and multiply handicapped population.

3. What is the prevalence of severely and profoundly handicapped persons in the general population?

4. What is meant by the statement, "severely/profoundly handicapped children differ in degree, not in kind"?

5. Describe how the concept of "functional retardation" differs from the concept of mental retardation.

6. Describe four characteristics commonly found in children enrolled in classrooms serving children with severe developmental delays.

EDUCABILITY OF CHILDREN WITH SEVERE DEVELOPMENTAL DISABILITIES

You should be able to discuss the arguments of opponents and proponents of the view that all students with severe and multiple handicaps are educable.

Can all children, regardless of the severity of their disability, benefit from an education? This question is being asked by lay persons and professionals alike regarding the educability of persons with severe and profound handicaps. That the question has been raised implies doubt on the part of some. It is important to note that our question is not whether all children have the *right* to an education — that right has been guaranteed by PL 94-142 — but whether all children can *benefit* from an education. The answer to this question is not as clear as one might think, particularly in light of the differences in the children who comprise the severely handicapped population. Undoubtedly there are students who have benefited considerably from their enrollment in public education programs. Children who had no means of communication prior to entry have learned to communicate through the use of nonspeech augmentative communication systems such as manual signs or communication boards. Other students who entered the public school system with a history of maladaptive or aberrant behaviors, such as hand flapping, eye gouging, or biting others, have learned to suppress these behaviors through systematic behavior management programs, which make them amenable to instruction in functional adaptive behavior skills. Still other children who were considered unlikely to learn to walk because of their physical disabilities, walk through participation in motor programs that inhibited abnormal reflexes and facilitated the use of normal motor patterns. Few would argue that these children and others like them have benefited from participation in educational programs. But what about those children whose development our educational system has not been able to enhance? It is these children who are often cited as being "ineducable," so the question of educability must revolve around them.

DEFINITION OF EDUCATION

The question of who is educable depends on how one defines education. Some think of education as learning to read, write, and do arithmetic, but by today's standards this definition would seem very restrictive. Webster's New World Dictionary (1976, p. 444) defines education as "the process of training and developing knowledge, mind, character, etc., esp. by formal schooling; teaching; training." The dictionary does not mention that a certain type of or level of skills are to be taught. Numerous court cases involving the right to education and the right to treatment, most of which addressed the rights of persons with severe developmental disabilities, have defined education without regard to the level of instruction. To quote Noonan, Brown, Mulligan, and Rettig (1982, p. 4):

What are the legal guarantees for educating severely handicapped children?

The judgment in *Maryland Association for Retarded Children* v. *Maryland* (1974) defined education as a plan "to help individuals achieve their full potential" (p. 186) with no distinction made between "training" and "education." *Mills* v. *D.C. Board of Education* (1972) stated that education must be suited to individual needs. *Pennsylvania Association for Retarded Children* v. *Commonwealth of Pennsylvania* (1971) similarly defined special education as appropriate to a student's learning capabilities; and *Armstrong* v. *Kline* (1979) ruled that education allows a child "within the limits of his or her handicap, to become self-sufficient" (p. 604) (p. 4).

These definitions of education suggest that it would be difficult to conclude that there is a class of children who could not benefit from education. Such a conclusion would have to be based on evidence that there are children who are incapable of learning *any* skill or behavior under optimal instructional conditions.

EDUCABILITY: BOTH SIDES OF THE ISSUE

A comprehensive discussion of the educability of persons with severe and multiple handicaps appears in a special issue of *Analysis and Intervention in Developmental Disabilities* (1981). In this issue, respected special educators and behavioral psychologists present numerous arguments on both sides of the issue. Three primary arguments have been forwarded by those who believe that not all children are educable. First, there is the argument that some children are not amenable to instruction because of their severe physical disabilities, damaged central nervous system, and profound mental retardation (Bailey, 1981). Second, some believe that if after extensive training by highly qualified professionals a child fails to acquire a "meaningful skill," that child can be presumed to be ineducable (Kauffman and Krouse, 1981). And third, for some children with certain disabilities, an adequate technology is lacking to improve significantly their functioning capabilities. Bailey's position (1981, p. 51) is typical of many who argue against the educability of all handicapped persons:

Why do some oppose education for severely handicapped children?

> The normalization movement has led us to believe that all clients can benefit from training, but the data do not support such a conclusion. I do not believe that the multiply physically handicapped, profoundly retarded, who have been unresponsive over an extended period to consistent efforts to train them ought to be subjected to further harassment. Our enthusiasm to train greatly exceeds our expertise, and that at this point we need to recognize the place of "stimulation programming" with the unresponsive profound individual. Lack of a functioning central nervous system is a limiting condition of habilitation, and our resources to provide such training are also severely limited. It is time to recognize these limiting conditions and to adjust our expectations accordingly. Stimulation programming, as opposed to teaching programming is, I believe, most appropriate with these clients, and this shift in emphasis represents an advance in our understanding of the right-to-treatment model. Such a shift in no way implies that our efforts to train the mildly, moderately, or severely retarded should be in any way reduced. Indeed, if the suggestion here is followed we should have more success with them, since trainers will be freed as the new adjustments are made.

Why are some in favor of education for severely handicapped children?

Proponents of the position that all children can benefit from an education base their argument on the belief that education, like development, is an ongoing process and that ineducability cannot be proven. As Baer (1981, pp. 96-97) has stated:

> A child cannot be declared unteachable in fact until teaching has been tried and has failed; teaching is too large a set of procedures (even in its own world) to have been tried and to have failed in its entirety, within the lifetimes of the child and the child's teachers. This point can also be stated in more mundane terms: The cost of truthfully affirming a child to be unteachable is no less than the cost of continuing to attempt teaching the child.
>
> Thus there is no way to affirm at the level of fact that some children cannot

be taught effectively; and there is no way to affirm at the level of fact that all children can be taught effectively. Any issue that hinges on either of these principles is automatically an eternally fruitless issue, if a factual answer is desired. . . . Extremely difficult-to-teach children constitute a challenge to their society and to the behavioral science of their society. I submit that it will enrich the society and the society's behavioral science to adopt, not as fact but as policy, the assumption that all children can be taught effectively.

For fear of not providing educational services to a child who has been arbitrarily declared ineducable and who might have benefited from education had services been provided, proponents of educability have adopted the position that all children can be taught effectively. In so doing they assure all children, regardless of the multiplicity and severity of their disabilities, a fair chance to achieve their full potential. Can a responsible profession deny children services that might improve their ability to function more independently in their community, home, or classroom? We think not. We must constantly keep in mind that educability is a relative term, and that one's ability to be educated depends on advances in educational technology. As more effective educational methods, adaptive equipment, and prosthetic devices are developed and used with students with severe developmental disabilities, who can predict what level of independent functioning these students might attain? Rather than relaxing our efforts to educate all children, it seems prudent that our efforts be intensified.

EARLY DETERMINANTS THAT AFFECT EDUCABILITY

What we do as special educators can make a difference. We can facilitate the growth and development of children who exhibit motor, sensory, social, and cognitive disabilities in a number of ways. First, we can serve as advocates for and participate in the early identification of children with developmental delays. Second, we can support the development of early education programs and the enrollment of high-risk children in those programs. Third, we can involve parents, brothers, and sisters in the habilitation process as early as possible. Educators must take each of these actions before children reach mandatory school age if multiply handicapped children are to reach their full potential.

Why is early identification important?

Early Identification. The longer the time between the child's being identified as having a disability and the start of intervention, the higher the probability that the disability will adversely affect the child's ability to acquire new and more functional skills. Special educators advocate that children with developmental disabilities be identified early because: (1) early experiences influence all areas of functioning — motor, sensory, cognitive, and social; (2) data support the notion that there are critical or optimal periods of central nervous system development during the first 3 years of life; (3) early intervention can inhibit or prevent the atrophy of muscles, thus avoiding the development of contractures; (4) failure to remedy one handicap can adversely affect other areas of development; (5) most handicapping conditons become worse as the child grows older without early intervention; and (6) there is growing evidence that early intervention helps (Hayden and McGinness, 1977).

High-risk children must be identified before they can receive services. Physicians, social workers, day care staff, and the general public must be educated about the behavioral indicators that may signal a possible disability. This can be accomplished through television and radio public service announcements, public forums, public speaking engagements at local organizations, and the dissemination of educational brochures. In conjunction with such an educational campaign, special educators, pediatricians, ophthalmologists, physical and occupational therapists, speech pathologists, audiologists, psychologists, and social workers must serve as advocates for and participate in the organization and maintenance of community-based infant identification or screening programs. Early identification does make a difference; the sooner children are identified as having a disability, the sooner they and their families can begin to receive services to minimize the long-term effect the disability may have on their ability to function. Early identification is the first step in making children with severe and multiple handicaps amenable to our educational efforts.

Early Intervention. As soon as a child with a disability has been identified, remediation of the disability should begin. Most communities offer some type of early intervention program through local chapters of the National Association for Retarded Citizens or United Cerebral Palsy, university medical centers and departments of special education, local public school systems, or child development state mental health and mental retardation agencies. If a community does not have an early education program for children with disabilities, as may be the case in some rural communities, such a program should be developed. Several communities can pool their financial and human resources to form an early education cooperative. Such cooperatives have been established in many states and have proven to be effective. Community-wide early education programs enhance the educability of the high risk children who attend (Bailey and Wolery, 1984).

Early intervention programs can take many forms. They can be home-based, center-based, or a combination of the two, as discussed in Chapter 3 (Early Childhood Education). The most important characteristic of an early intervention program, however, is that it be organized and operated along the lines of the transdisciplinary education and treatment model. Sailor and Guess (1983, p. 207) describe the transdisciplinary model as follows:

The transdisciplinary (TD) approach is an education/treatment model that effectively integrates program goals and objectives from various disciplines and professions. The integration begins in the assessment process and extends through direct programming effort. In this approach, each team member is responsible for sharing information and skills so that multiple interventions with the child can occur simultaneously.

Figure 11-1 schematically depicts a transdisciplinary team model for a home-based early intervention program. As indicated, the parents assume primary responsibility for implementing programs with their child. The facilitator, who may be any one of the team members, is responsible for assisting the parents and organizing the information from the various disciplines into a comprehensive intervention program plan for the child. Each discipline brings different yet equally important information to the team. By sharing this information, the transdisciplinary team can design and implement a coordinated and effective longitudinal program that will enhance a child's cognitive, motor, sensory, and social development. Table 11-1 presents a list of probable team members and the type of information and service each member can contribute to the development of an appropriate intervention program plan.

**Table 11-1
Transdisciplinary team members and their contributions**

Team Member	Contribution
Special Education Teacher	Assess cognitive and sensory motor skills; assist in the design of programs to facilitate cognitive development; maintain continuity in the children's programs as they move from infant to preschool to public school programs.
Physical Therapist	Assess gross motor skills; assist in the design of programs to facilitate normal motor development; teach care providers how physically to handle, position, and move a child; identify appropriate prosthetic and adaptive equipment.
Occupational Therapist	Assess fine and gross motor skills; assist in the design of appropriate feeding programs; recommend exercises to facilitate fine and gross motor skills.
Speech Pathologist	Assess communication and language skills; design programs to facilitate vocal and nonvocal communication skills; assess oral-muscular mechanism; assist in the design of feeding programs.
Psychologist	Assess cognitive skills; design programs to prevent or manage behavioral problems (self-stimulatory behaviors, self-injurious behaviors).

Table 11-1 (*cont.*)

Team Member	Contribution
Pediatric Nurse	Assist in monitoring and managing medical and health problems.
Nutritionist	Prescribe special feeding programs and diets.
Ophthalmologist	Assess for suspected visual problems and prescribe treatment.
Neurologist	Assess for seizures; prescribe medication for seizure control; monitor central nervous system activity.
Audiologist	Assess for suspected hearing problems.
Social Worker	Assist families in locating support services (e.g., family counseling, financial assistance).
Dentist	Monitor oral hygiene, including teeth and gum problems.
Orthopedist	Assess musculature and prescribe treatment to enhance physical development.

Source: Sailor and Guess, 1983. Used by permission.

What is the role of the family in treatment programs?

Early family involvement. Active parent and sibling participation is vitally important to the success of the multiply handicapped child's early education program. By consistently stimulating appropriate cognitive, sensory, motor, and social skill development, family members make the difference in whether disabled children learn to walk, talk, and interact effectively. Unlike non-handicapped children, severely handicapped children require an extraordinary level of consistency by their care providers. Although parents are the primary teachers of young children, brothers and sisters must also be taught how and how not to position, handle, feed, and communicate with their disabled brother or sister. This sharing of responsibility in a child's education program by siblings need not be so burdensome as it initially may sound. Teaching brothers and sisters how to play with their disabled sibling in the crib or on the floor in a way that promotes adaptive behaviors can be both fun and rewarding for all involved. Caring for a child with severe developmental disabilities can be a 24-hour-a-day job. Thus, it is important that *all* family members be familiar with the prescribed stimulation techniques and use those techniques in a consistent manner when interacting with the child throughout the day. Family participation and consistency in implementing an early intervention program designed by the transdisciplinary team can greatly influence a child's current and future developmental status.

Figure 11-1
Transdisciplinary model for providing direct services to severely handicapped infants in the home, using parents as the primary interventionists

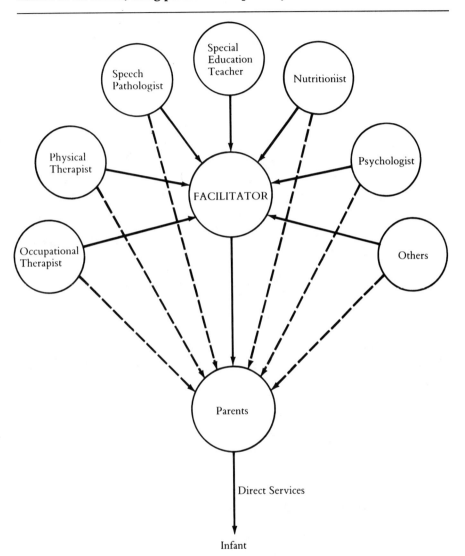

Note: It should be noted that a TD approach applied to a particular child does not have to have either the specific disciplines presented in this figure or as many.

Source: Sailor, W. & Guess, D. (1983) *Severely handicapped students: An instructional design.* Boston: Houghton Mifflin Co., p. 211. Used by permission.

PROBE 11-2
Educability

1. T F Children with severe developmental disabilities are ineducable according to current definitions of education.

2. What are three arguments forwarded by persons who believe children with severe and profound handicaps are *not* educable?

3. What is the primary argument forwarded by persons who believe that all children, regardless of the severity of their disability, can benefit from an education?

4. List four reasons why special educators urge that children with developmental disabilities be identified early.

5. T F Early intervention with a child with severe developmental disabilities should not begin before the child is 12 months old.

6. What are the two primary responsibilities of the transdisciplinary team facilitator working in a home-based early intervention program?

7. List two reasons why early family involvement in a severely handicapped child's program is important.

EDUCATIONAL ASSESSMENT PROCEDURES AND CONSIDERATIONS

You should be able to describe the general measurement strategies, models, and guidelines for assessing children for the purposes of identification and educational programming.

ASSESSMENT FOR IDENTIFICATION

Assessment for identification has at least three purposes. These are (1) identifying areas for further assessment, such as conducting a vision screening to decide whether an ophthalmological assessment is needed; (2) determining what resources are needed, such as the appropriate educational placement and related services and (3) determining the nature and severity of the disabilities (Dollar and Brooks, 1980). In part, the purpose dictates which tools and procedures are used, who conducts the assessment activities, what role teachers will play, and what behaviors are measured.

What are some of the tests used to assess severely handicapped children?

Measurement Strategies. A variety of measurement strategies, such as direct testing, direct observation, and interviews can be used to gather information for specific assessment purposes (Bailey and Wolery, 1984).

Direct testing may include *norm-referenced* measures, in which a student's performance is compared to the performance of a large population of other students on the same test. Examples of norm-referenced tests used with students with severe developmental disabilities are the *Bayley Scales of Infant Development* (Bayley, 1969) and the *TARC Assessment System* (Sailor and Mix, 1975). Norm-referenced tests may be used to determine the severity of a handicap and identify areas for further assessment; they are sometimes required for making placement decisions.

Criterion-referenced measures, in which performance is compared to levels of mastery on given skills, are also used. Examples of criterion-referenced tests are the *Learning Accomplishment Profile* (LeMay, Griffin, and Sanford, 1977), *Uniform Performance Assessment System* (White, et al., 1981), *Vulpé Assessment Battery* (Vulpé, 1977), and the *Behavioral Characteristics Progression* (Santa Cruz County Public School District, 1975). Criterion-referenced tests are used primarily to identify areas for further assessment and to plan instructional programs. They are also used to make decisions about placement and to determine what related services are needed.

Curriculum-referenced tools are usually criterion-referenced, but they include instructional activities that correspond to the assessment items. Examples include the *Pennsylvania Training Model Individual Assessment Guide* (Somerton and Turner, 1975), *Portage Guide to Early Education* (Bluma, Shearer, Froham, and Hilliard, 1976), *Carolina Curriculum for Handicapped Infants* (Johnson, Jens, and Attermeier, 1979), and the *Peabody Developmental Motor Scales* (Folio and Fewell, 1982). These tools are used primarily for instructional program planning.

How are direct observation and interviews used in assessment?

Besides using direct testing, teams assessing students with severe developmental disabilities rely heavily on direct observation. Important skills such as communication abilities and initiating and responding to social interactions are more effectively assessed by observation than by testing. Direct observation is useful in planning instructional programs, determining needed services, and identifying areas for further assessment. Billingsley and Liberty (1982), Cooper (1981), Repp (1983), Tawney and Gast (1984), and White and Haring (1980) describe procedures for using direct observation.

Another measurement strategy is the use of interviews. Parents, former teachers, and former therapists are frequently interviewed. Interviews are especially helpful in identifying areas for additional assessment and in planning instructional programs. Interviews are also useful in confirming or rejecting suspicions raised by other assessment activities (Powell, 1981). Some tests can be administered through interviews, such as *The Developmental Profile II* (Alpern, Boll, and Shearer, 1980) and the *AAMD Adaptive Behavior Scale* (Nahira, Foster, Shellhaas, and Leland, 1974). Other interview questions are individually generated to get information about students' responses to demands placed on them by their environments (Neel et al., 1982).

Guidelines. When the purpose of the assessment is identification, several guidelines should be followed (Dollar and Brooks, 1980). These guidelines currently represent the best professional practice, and some are required by PL 94-142 (Turnbull and Turnbull, 1978). Teams with members from disciplines such as special education, psychology, and physical, occupational, and speech and language therapy should conduct the assessment activities. Parents should also be members of the team and should be involved in planning and conducting the assessment and validating the results. Assessment activities should occur in settings that are relaxed, nonthreatening, free of interruptions and distractions, and familiar to the student. More than one setting should be used, and measurements should be taken more than once. Ideally, several sessions over several days in several settings should be used. Multiple measurement strategies should be used, and tests should be given only for the purposes for which they are valid. The team members should attempt to secure the child's best response to items.

ASSESSMENT FOR INSTRUCTIONAL PROGRAM PLANNING

What two steps are involved in assessment for program planning?

The primary purpose of assessment for instructional program planning is to determine *what* to teach students. Sailor and Guess (1983) propose a two-step process. First, one establishes yearly goals to increase students' independent functioning. Second, one determines the students' current abilities and generates a sequence of short-term objectives that will move students from their current level of ability to the achievement of the yearly objectives. Two types of current abilities are of interest: the student's best possible current performance and the student's usual performance in his or her natural environment. Large discrepancies between these two levels of performance may indicate a need to establish more reinforcing conditions in the students' usual environments. Another purpose of assessment for instructional program planning is to identify teaching methods that will be both effective and efficient.

What is the developmental milestones model?

Models. Three models can be used in conducting assessments for instructional program planning: the developmental milestones model, the developmental theory-based model, and the functional model (Bailey and Wolery, 1984).

The *developmental milestones* model is based on the view that as children grow, they develop certain skills and abilities (milestones) in an orderly, sequential fashion. Gesell and his colleagues (Gessell, 1928, 1938, 1940; Gesell and Amatruda, 1947) and others (Bayley, 1969; Cattell, 1940; Havinghurst, 1972) described this perspective and specified various milestones. They frequently developed norm-referenced tests to determine whether students had reached specific milestones. The purpose of the tests was to identify and diagnose children who showed developmental delays rather than to develop instructional program plans (Garwood, 1982).

When programs began serving young children with severe developmental disabilities, the programs frequently adapted or developed criterion- and curriculum-referenced tools and behavioral checklists from those tests (e.g., *Learning Accomplishment Profile; Portage Guide to Early Education*). Unfortunately, since the items were designed for discriminating between typical (normal) children of different ages rather than for instructional usefulness, the assessments frequently resulted in objectives that had little functional value for the children. Further, since the items were not designed for instruction, logical teaching sequences were nonexistent, incomplete, or were not obvious (Bailey and Wolery, 1984; Darby, 1979; Fewell, 1983a). Thus, although tools from the developmental milestones model are frequently used, their validity for identifying functional, worthwhile instructional objectives must be seriously questioned.

What is the developmental theory-based model?

The *developmental theory-based* model is based on the notion that theorists have adequately described a complete sequence of skills that leads to a specific ability. Piaget's (1963) description of the sensorimotor stage is an excellent example of such a sequence; others are the descriptions of attachment behavior (Ainsworth, 1973; Bowlby, 1969) and social play (Parten, 1932). From those descriptions, assessment tools and observational procedures can be developed. For example, the *Ordinal Scales of Psychological Development* (Uzrigis and Hunt, 1975; Dunst, 1980) measure the sensorimotor skills described by Piaget (Kahn, 1976, 1979). The *Parent Behavior Progression Scales* (Bromwich, 1981) measure the parent–child relationship, and Wintre and Webster (1974) describe the use of Parten's social play scale with "disturbed" children. Such assessment tools and procedures provide logical developmental objectives and instructional sequences. If these objectives were mastered, the students would have a broad range of skills to be used in a variety of possible environments.

However, the developmental theory-based model has some disadvantages. Given the severe developmental disabilities of some students, their slow rates of acquisition, and our present knowledge, it may be unrealistic to expect to provide sufficient training to establish broad developmental attainments. Further, assessment tools and procedures in the developmental theory-based approach are based on the assumption that the theory is an accurate representation of child development. Such assumptions may be false; for example, in the 1950s and 1960s it was assumed that there was a relationship between performance on perceptual-motor tests and academic performance, but remediation of perceptual-motor deficits did not result in consistent improvement in academic performance. Finally, in comparison to the developmental milestones model, the developmental theory-based model has generated relatively few practical assessment tools. Thus, while the developmental theory-based model has considerable appeal, transdisciplinary teams should use it cautiously.

The *functional model,* sometimes called the remedial model (Sailor and Guess, 1983) assumes that (1) the major goal of instruction (and thus assessment) is to promote independent functioning, and (2) sequences other than typical developmental sequences can be used to promote independence more quickly (Bailey and Wolery, 1984; Sailor and Guess, 1983). Initially the emphasis in this model was on determining which skills students with severe developmental disabilities would need to function independently as adults. This view was called the criterion of ultimate functioning (Brown, Nietupski, and Hamre-Nietupski, 1976). It is difficult to identify what skills young children with severe developmental disabilities will need as adults, however, so the focus was changed to the skills needed in immediate future environments. This view is called the criterion of the next educational environment (Sailor and Guess, 1983; Vincent et al., 1980).

In the functional model, students are assessed to determine how they perform important adaptive behaviors (called functional behaviors or critical functions) with tools such as the *Adaptive Performance Instrument* (API) (CAPE, 1980; for a detailed discussion of this tool see Sailor and Guess, 1983). Students' current and immediate future environments are also assessed to identify the skills required to function independently in those environments (Neel et al., 1982; Vincent et al., 1980). These environmental assessments, called ecological inventories, include interviews with persons in the environments and observations of the activities that take place in the environments. Behavioral expectations are also noted (Snell and Smith, 1983). Browder and Snell (1983) and Snell and Smith (1983) provide examples of ecological inventories and their function.

Use of the functional model should identify the skills (objectives) that students should acquire to function independently in their environments. Since environments differ from one another and the demands within similar environments may even vary, assessment activities must be individualized for each student (White, 1980). Any set of skills on a test or behavior checklist would not be appropriate for all students and might be inappropriate for most students. This fact makes conducting assessment in the functional model difficult and time-consuming. The issue of critical skills will be discussed further later in the chapter.

Selecting the Appropriate Model. Transdisciplinary teams must select the most appropriate assessment model before conducting assessments. At present, no research exists comparing the models' effectiveness or efficiency, but practice suggests the following guidelines. Because of the problems with the developmental milestones model discussed earlier, it should rarely be used.

When determining whether to use the developmental theory-based or functional model, the students' ages and the severity of their disabilities should be considered.

For older students, who are generally being taught to function independently, the functional model is usually more appropriate (Bailey and Wolery, 1984; Sailor and Guess, 1983). The functional model also appears to be more appropriate for children with quite severe disabilities. The developmental theory-based model would be most appropriate for infants and toddlers whose disabilities are mild or moderate.

Guidelines. The purpose of instructional program planning assessments is to specify the students' current levels of performance (both their best possible responses and their usual responses) and establish a sequence of objectives from that performance to their long-term (annual) objectives. To accomplish this task, as much information as possible must be gathered. Several guidelines should be followed.

1. A team approach must be used because no single professional is sufficiently competent to assess students with severe and multiple disabilities. Interdisciplinary (Allen, Holm, and Schiefelbusch, 1978) and transdisciplinary teams (Hart, 1977; Haynes, 1976) have been used. Under both models, team members communicate and interact a great deal and jointly plan the assessment activities (Fewell, 1983b). The major difference between the two types of teams is that in the transdisciplinary team, each member learns and assumes the role of other members; constant supervision and consultation, of course is needed (Lyon and Lyon, 1980; McCormick and Goldman, 1979). Some transdisciplinary teams use the *arena method,* in which one team member conducts the majority of the assessment activities, while other team members observe and score measures from their own areas of specialty (Dyk, 1983). Regardless of the team approach used, representatives from a number of disciplines who communicate effectively with each other must be involved.

What is the arena method of assessment?

2. Parents, family members, and significant others should be involved. Parents have a legal right to be involved in developing their child's individualized education plan (IEP). This involvement should begin with assessment. Parents and others can be valuable sources of information about what their children do, what items and activities serve as reinforcers, what skills they need to learn, what environments they are likely to encounter, and how they respond to various situations. Parents can also provide information on children's health, educational, and developmental backgrounds and collect information for the assessment team (Powell, 1981). They can help determine what demands are placed on the child in the home and

collect data on specific behaviors of interest. For example, they might count the number of times the child responds to social initiations or keep track of the amount and types of foods the child eats. Finally, parents and others can provide their judgment about the validity of assessment results. Frequently, parents can confirm or contradict findings from assessment activities.

3. All assessment activities should be conducted for a reason. Since assessments are time-consuming and require considerable effort, the assessment team must be careful to conduct only meaningful activities. Each activity should be designed to obtain specific information about the child to help plan the instructional program. Thus, it is probably inappropriate to administer a predetermined battery of tests. It would be better to use selected items from certain criterion- and curriculum-referenced tests, direct observation of important behaviors, and ecological inventories.

4. Multiple measurement strategies should be used and data should be collected reliably. As described earlier, assessment teams can use direct testing, direct observation, and interviews. Regardless of the strategy used, behaviors must be reliably recorded or the data will be useless for decisions about students' instructional program plans. The conditions under which the assessment occurred, such as the setting, time, people, and objects present should also be noted (Dollar and Brooks, 1980).

5. Students' responses during assessment activities should be reinforced. This guideline has two implications. First, for some students, no reinforcers will have been identified. In these cases, reinforcers should be identified before assessment is undertaken. Second, since we are attempting to measure students' best possible responses, it is important to use reinforcement correctly. Baer (1978), Alberto and Troutman (1982), and Wehman and McLoughlin (1981) have provided discussions on identifying and using reinforcers.

6. Students should be assessed by familiar persons in familiar settings and with materials they have previously used (Bailey and Wolery, 1984; Fewell, 1983a). Students are apt to perform best with people they know and in situations where they are familiar. Persons the students do not know should attempt to establish rapport with them before beginning assessment activities. Assessments should be conducted both in the child's classroom and in the various environments where the child interacts. Care should be taken to minimize auditory and visual distractions and interruptions. If students are unfamiliar with the materials being used, they should be allowed time to interact with the materials before the assessment.

7. Since student responses vary, they should be assessed in multiple sessions over several days and in a variety of settings. When planning for instructional programs, assessment activities should be conducted in each of the students' primary environments. Students should also be assessed in the same setting over several days, a practice which permits more accurate descriptions

and better predictions of their performance than does one day of measurement. When the assessment is completed, the conclusions must be regarded as tentative. The measures taken during the first few weeks of implementing the educational plan can be used to review the conclusions based on earlier testing sessions and observations.

8. Students' sensory and physical abilities should be assessed early (Fewell, 1983a). The team should determine how well a student hears and sees before assessment begins. If adaptive equipment such as hearing aids or glasses are needed, they should be used throughout the assessment. Test items should be adapted when necessary (Bailey and Wolery, 1984). Physical and occupational therapists can assess students' physical abilities. They can identify positions that will allow students to make their best movements and describe which movements are most appropriate for each student.

When assessment activities are completed, the conclusions are written. The report should describe the behaviors students can perform and the conditions under which they are performed. Assessment reports should also contain a list of objectives of functional responses.

What are functional responses?

Functional responses are those behaviors that produce an immediate effect on the environment, are natural to that environment, and result in more control of the environment (Sailor and Guess, 1983). They should also be responses frequently needed in the environment (Brown et al., 1979). When possible, the behaviors should be chronological age-appropriate; that is, similar to those performed by students who are the same chronological age as the severely disabled student (Brown et al., 1979). Examples of functional behaviors for many students with severe developmental disabilities are, among others, saying "yes" and "no," requesting food and drink, indicating the need to use the bathroom, reaching, grasping, and most self-care skills.

What are "critical functions"?

White (1980) suggested that when writing functional objectives, emphasis should be placed on the function (i.e., effect or result) of the skill rather than the form (specific behavior[s]) used to perform the skill. He called them critical functions and suggested that a variety of forms can be used. The form is less important than the fact that the function is accomplished. For example, asking for help is an important skill for students with severe developmental disabilities. The function (effect) is that the help is received. The form (topography of the behavior) used to ask for help may vary and is less important than the fact that help is requested. Examples of forms would be saying "help," manually signing "help," making a gesture and pointing to the situation for which one needs help, or activating a switch that would signal care givers that help is needed. Locomotion is another example of a critical function. The function (effect) is getting from one place to another. The possible forms (behaviors) used in locomotion may be walking, walking with crutches or a walker, crawling, using a wheelchair, or asking someone to transport the student to the desired location.

PROBE 11-3
Assessment Procedures

1. Give an example of a purpose for which each of the following measurement strategies should be used.
   a. Direct testing
   b. Direct observation
   c. Interviews

2. List an advantage and disadvantage of each of the following instructional programming models.
   a. Developmental milestones model
   b. Developmental theory-based model
   c. Functional model

3. Give one reason for each of the following guidelines for conducting instructional programming assessments.
   a. A team should conduct the assessments because _____ .
   b. Parents should be involved in the assessment because _____ .
   c. Students should be assessed by persons, in settings, and with materials that are familiar to them because _____ .

4. Give an example of a functional behavior.

CURRICULUM CONSIDERATIONS

You should be able to describe curriculum approaches, content areas, and evaluation issues related to curricula for students with severe developmental disabilities.

A curriculum is an organized description of what to teach; it should include basic strategies and activities for teaching, but the emphasis is on *what* to teach rather than *how* to teach (Wolery, 1983). Bailey, Jens, and Johnson (1983) suggest adding a third element to this definition: methods for measuring the effects of teaching. We describe the traditional developmental domains curriculum approach and the critical functions curriculum approach, means of evaluating curricula, and some specific curricula for various ages and school levels.

TRADITIONAL DEVELOPMENTAL DOMAINS CURRICULUM APPROACH

The traditional developmental domains curriculum approach grew out of the developmental milestones model of conducting assessments for instructional program planning. After the child has been assessed with a developmental milestones tool or set of tools, the curriculum for the child consists of the next items from the assessment sequences. As a result, curriculum domains are rather rigid. They include self-care, receptive and expressive language, fine and gross motor skills, social skills, cognitive skills, and sometimes recreation and leisure skills.

The *self-care* domain includes skills such as toileting, eating, self-feeding, dressing, undressing, and grooming activities such as brushing teeth and washing hands. Self-care skills are often taught through a task analysis approach rather than a developmental approach (Snell, 1978). Input is frequently obtained from occupational therapists (Copeland, Ford, and Solon, 1976).

The *language* domain includes receptive and expressive training, beginning with labeling and moving to the use of words in combination; vocal imitation is often viewed as a prerequisite skill. Nonvocal communication systems are sometimes used (Schiefelbusch, 1978). Emphasis is rarely placed on how students use language for communication, despite the fact that this area is now considered central to language training.

What is the difference between gross and fine motor skills?

The *gross motor* domain includes such skills as holding the head in mid-line, rolling, sitting, crawling, walking, and jumping. Input is frequently obtained from physical therapists, particularly those who use the neurodevelopmental treatment approach (Utley, Holvoet, and Barnes, 1977). The *fine motor* domain includes skills such as reaching, grasp patterns, and eye and hand coordination. These skills are often taught by using the manipulative materials commonly seen in preschool programs for nonhandicapped children.

Social skills are often poorly defined. Training usually involves reducing the occurrence of inappropriate or maladaptive behaviors such as self-stimulatory and self-injurious behaviors, tantrums, and noncompliance with adult requests, among others (Kauffman and Snell, 1977). Social interaction skills are also taught occasionally.

The *cognitive* domain frequently involves teaching students to make discriminations between materials of various sizes, shapes, colors, and number; reading traffic signs and other "functional" words such as "men" and "women"; and counting, money management, and other related math skills (Snell, 1978). It also includes basic interactions with objects in the environment such as looking at, grasping, and manipulating objects. These skills are sometimes associated with Piaget's description of the sensorimotor (Kahn, 1978, 1979; Robinson and Robinson, 1978).

What are the pros and cons of the traditional domains curriculum approach?

Advantage. The advantage of the traditional domain approach is the relative ease with which transdisciplinary teams can establish curriculum objectives. These are simply the skills just above students' current level of performance on the developmental sequences. Little attention is given to whether those skills are useful to the students when they are functioning in their natural

Exercises such as this help to stimulate gross motor development.

environments. Ease for the instructor is an important factor when evaluating educational practices, but it must assume less value than the effectiveness and efficiency of the practice.

Disadvantages. The problems with the traditional developmental domains curriculum approach are that (1) it is not particularly effective in establishing useful objectives for students; (2) if by chance useful skills are selected, the sequences that result are not necessarily the most efficient; and (3) it gives little attention to assessing the demands placed on students in their natural environments. A related disadvantage is the lack of individualization (White, 1980). Finally, the skills selected for instruction with this approach are sometimes impossible for students to perform because of specific sensory or physical disabilities.

FUNCTIONAL CURRICULUM APPROACH

What steps are involved in using the critical functions approach?

The functional curriculum approach emerged as a result of the problems with the traditional developmental domains approach. This newer approach attempts to individualize objectives for the unique needs of each student and the unique demands of their environments. Students are not matched to predetermined curricular sequences; rather, a curriculum is designed for each student. Brown et al. (1979) describe six steps for developing curricula that would teach *functional, chronological age-appropriate* skills in the natural environment.

1. Identify curriculum domains. Possible domains for students in middle childhood and older, for example, might be vocational skills recreation/ leisure skills, domestic living, community living, and communication.
2. Identify the environments in which students spend time, such as home, school, community, and vocational settings.
3. Identify and assess sub-environments within each environment, such as a vocational setting, break area, work station, cafeteria, and bathroom.
4. Identify and assess activities or routines that occur in each of the sub-environments, such as taking a break on the job, going to the bathroom, and performing the various task requirements of the job.
5. Identify skills needed to function independently in the activities, and also routines for each sub-environment, such as opening the bathroom door, removing appropriate clothing, sitting on the toilet, flushing the toilet, and washing hands.
6. Develop instructional programs to teach students to perform the skills identified in each routine.

What is a priority matrix?

Sailor and Guess (1983) suggest developing a *priority matrix*. One dimension of the matrix is the student's environments and perhaps sub-environments. The second dimension is various functional behaviors. A sample priority matrix for middle childhood and older students is shown in Figure 11-2.

When identifying critical functions, the child's age is a consideration. Sailor and Guess (1983) suggest using functional behaviors identified in the *Adaptive Performance Instrument (API)* (CAPE, 1980), for students who are nine years old or younger. The skill domains from the API include physical intactness, reflexes and reactions, gross motor skills, fine motor skills, self-care, sensorimotor skills, social skills, and communication. Each area includes target behaviors. Critical functions that occur across multiple environments in the priority matrix are taught first, and age-appropriate forms (behaviors) of the critical functions are used.

While the Brown et al. (1979) and the Sailor and Guess (1983) approaches differ slightly, both attempt to promote independent functioning in the natural environment with age-appropriate behaviors. However, students should not be excluded from some environments simply because they cannot perform

Figure 11-2
Priority Matrix
Environmental Domains

Critical Functions	School Classroom	School Lunchroom	Domestic Area	Communicative Center
Eating	Chew snack foods finger feed appropriate food	Chew meals	Chew meals finger feed appropriate foods	
Toileting	Answer "yes" or "no" to "Do you need to go to the bathroom?"	Answer "yes" or "no" to "Do you need to go to the bathroom?"	Answer "yes" or "no" to "Do you need to go to the bathroom?"	Answer "yes" or "no" to "Do you need to go to the bathroom?"
Expressive Communication	Request snack Greet teacher and fellow students	Request milk	Request toy Greet visitors	Greet people in appropriate situations
Receptive Communication	Follow 1 step commands Point to specified toy			
Hygiene/ appearance		Open mouth when teeth are brushed and hold toothbrush	Extend arms and legs during dressing	
Recreation/ leisure	Toy play 5 min.		Play 5 min social interaction with parents	Float in swimming pool
Social Interactions	Initiate social interaction with teacher		Initiate social interaction with parents	
Gross Motor	Extend arms to front, left, and right during protective extension exercises			

independently. Baumgart et al. (1982) suggest a system of *partial participation* in which various adaptions are devised through an eight-phase process that allows students to participate in a variety of environments. Although participation is not independent, the adaptions allow students to participate appropriately at some level.

Since curricula must be developed for individual students on the basis of their unique environments, relatively few comprehensive written curricula based on the functional approach have been developed. Some functional behaviors and some environmental demands are similar for many students, however, and it is possible to create an organized functional curriculum. The API is an example of an assessment tool that takes into account the need to identify and teach functional behaviors. Two curricula designed from the functional approach are the *Functional Speech and Language Program* (Guess, Sailor, and Baer, 1976, 1978) and the curriculum developed by the Innovative Model Program for Autistic Children and their Teachers (IMPACT) (Neel et al., 1982). The IMPACT materials describe critical communication functions and procedures used to teach those functions to autistic children. It is a useful model for persons attempting to implement or develop functionally based curricula.

What are the pros and cons of the functional curriculum approach?

Advantage. The obvious advantage of the functional curriculum approach is its emphasis on preparing students with severe developmental disabilities to function independently. Given our current knowledge and technology, this approach is the best way for educators to ensure that students live full, useful lives.

Disadvantages. The critical functions curriculum approach requires considerable competence, motivation, and ingenuity on the part of the team to develop individualized curricula for all students. Given the shortage of adequately trained personnel, successful implementation of this approach is the exception rather than the rule. Another disadvantage is that the functional approach moves many educational activities outside of traditional school settings, so implementation requires considerable flexibility on the part of school administrators. This disadvantage is more a fault of practices in our traditional educational system than of the approach itself, but it can present problems.

EVALUATING CURRICULA

Given the problem with the developmental domains curriculum approach (i.e., not attending to functional skills) and the difficulties of implementing the functional approach, the transdisciplinary team may choose to combine the two approaches. Thus, team members need to be able to evaluate curricula, both the written, commercial forms and those developed for individual students.

When dealing with a commercial curriculum, team members should evaluate the appropriateness of the curriculum for their students and settings, the extent to which it is to be used, and the curriculum's effectiveness. Procedures for conducting such evaluations have been described by Huberty and Swan (1977) and Wolery (1983). Teams rarely, if ever, choose to use only one commercial curriculum. The team more often selects specific sequences or activities from a variety of curricula.

What questions should be asked when evaluating curricula?

When evaluting curricula developed for students with disabilities, procedures for assessing their social validity or significance should be used (Kazdin, 1979; Wolf, 1978). Several questions should be asked. Are critical functions being taught? Will the functions be needed in future environments? Can the critical functions be used in more than one current environment? Do the critical functions require adaptions for physical or sensory disabilities? Do these adaptions look "natural" and blend into the real-world environment? Do the forms (behaviors) used to perform the critical functions look natural, like the behaviors nonhandicapped students use in those environments? Are the behaviors chronologically age-appropriate?

A more comprehensive list of questions to consider when evaluating curricula is presented in Table 11-2.

Table 11-2
Sample Questions for Evaluating Curricula

Sample Questions for Evaluating Applicability

1. Do the skill sequences in the curriculum include the skills needed by the students?
2. Are the steps between objectives in the skill sequences small enough?
3. Are teaching activities described adequately?
4. Are performance criteria for skill sequences specified?
5. Are functional skills and functional skill training routines included in the curriculum?
6. Are teaching activities for generalization of skills included and described in sufficient detail?

Sample Questions for Evaluating Implementation

1. Can children be placed in the skill sequences of the curriculum easily and efficiently?
2. Do all staff members, including those whose role is not educational, use the curriculum?
3. Can teaching activities suggested in the curriculum be used to teach corresponding objectives from the curriculum?

4. Are there enough teaching activities in the curriculum, or does staff need to develop additional activities?
5. Are staff members using the record-keeping system to make educational programming decisions?

Sample Questions for Evaluating Effectiveness

1. Do students acquire the behaviors targeted for instruction?
2. Do children perform behaviors learned in the curriculum in nontraining settings and situations?
3. Does the curriculum have a positive effect on interactions between team members?
4. Does the curriculum record-keeping system identify gains or lack of gains made by children?

Adapted from: Wolery, M. Evaluating curricula: Purposes and strategies. *Topics in Early Childhood Special Education,* 1983 *2*(4), 15-24.

When evaluating the use of individually developed curricula, the procedures for evaluating use described by Wolery (1983) are applicable. To evaluate effectiveness, special educators rely on direct observational measurement procedures coupled with single-subject research designs from behavioral psychology (applied behavior analysis) (Tawney and Gast, 1984).

AGE-APPROPRIATE CURRICULUM

As students grow older, their educational needs change. As a result, the focus of the curriculum must also change. In this section the focus of the curriculum is described at three points: early childhood, elementary school age, and secondary school age. Bailey, Jens, and Johnson (1983) provide a review of many of these curricula.

Early Childhood Curriculum. Many preschool projects have developed and published curricula for infants or young children with handicaps. Most of these projects are funded by the Handicapped Children's Early Education Program. The examples include the following:

— Carolina Curriculum for Handicapped Infants (Johnson, Jens, and Attermeier, 1979)
— Developmental Programming for Infants and Young Children (Schafer and Moersch, 1981)
— Guide to Early Developmental Training (Tilton, Liska, and Bourland, 1977 — Wabash Center)
— Hawaii Early Learning Profile (1979)

— HI-COMP Curriculum (Neisworth et al., 1980)
— Portage Guide to Early Education (Bluma, Shearer, Froham, and Hilliard, 1976)
— Programmed Environments Curriculum (Tawney, Knapp, O'Reilly, and Pratt, 1979)
— Teaching Research Curriculum for Moderately and Severely Handicapped (Fredericks et al., 1980)
— Teaching Your Down's Syndrome Infant (Hanson, 1977)

What features do different early childhood curricula share?

An interesting finding of the review by Bailey et al. (1983) was that although the curricula were from different theoretical orientations, the content areas were quite similar. Common domains were motor skills, cognitive skills, self-care, communication, and social skills. Functional skills or skills used to acquire functional skills should be taught in each area. It should be remembered that functionality is individually determined. The skills described here are included because they are likely to be functional for many young children with severe developmental disabilities.

The *motor* area includes gross motor skills, such as maintaining balance while stationary and during movement; inhibiting primitive postural reflexes; locomotion; and the development of automatic reactions, normalized muscle tone, and head control. Fine motor skills include functional grasp patterns and manipulation of objects with a variety of movements. For information on teaching motor skills see Baily and Wolery (1984), Bigge (1982), Bunker and Moon (1983), and Campbell (1983).

The *cognitive skills* in an early childhood curriculum include sensorimotor

Examples of communication boards.

skills, such as imitation, relating self and objects and other persons in space, means-ends or problem-solving, and manipulating objects in a variety of consistent ways. For infants, noting the relationships between any two events is thought to be a critical skill for later learning. Such relationships are called co-occurrences and are taught through frequent experiences with response-contingent events. Other cognitive skills may include sorting, matching, and problem solving. For information on teaching cognitive skills, see Bailey and Wolery (1984), Dunst (1981), Lockman (1983), and Robinson and Robinson (1983).

Self-care skills include eating, drinking, some form of self-feeding, toileting, dressing and undressing, and grooming (Bailey and Wolery, 1984; Snell, 1983b).

Communication skills involve learning the turn-taking needed in communicative exchanges; understanding what is communicated; responding by labeling objects, persons, and events; requesting; answering; greeting; and protesting. Other skills include following directions, functional use of objects, and imitation. Several sources describe communication skills training (Bailey and Wolery, 1984; Bricker, 1983; Carlson and Bricker, 1982; Coggins and Sandall, 1983; Guess, 1980; Musselwhite and St. Louis, 1982; Schiefelbusch, 1978). Students also need a means of communicating, such as speech, manual signs, communication boards, or some other nonvocal systems. Sailor ct al. (1980) described a method of determining the most appropriate mode of communication. One should devote less attention to manual signs, however, because of the small number of persons in the natural environment who understand sign language (Sailor and Guess, 1983).

Social skills involve toy and social play, and initiating, responding to, maintaining, and terminating interactions with peers and adults (Bailey and Wolery, 1984; Odom, 1983). Reducing the occurrence of inappropriate social behaviors is sometimes also a part of early childhood curricula (Gaylord-Ross, 1980).

During early childhood, students typically transfer from one program to another. For example, they may move from a home-based infant program to a center-based program serving preschoolers or from a preschool program to a public school program. Whenever such changes occur, the environment to which the child is moving should be assessed before the actual transition, and students should receive instruction on the functional skills that will be needed in the new environment (Fowler, 1982; Vincent et al., 1980).

What skills should be developed in the elementary school curriculum?

Elementary School Curriculum. The content areas of the elementary school curriculum reflect students' increasing age. The behaviors that students use to perform the critical functions should also be chronologically age-appropriate. At this level, some of the content areas in the early childhood curriculum are given less attention, while others are given more. For example, sensorimotor skills are less likely to be important during the elementary years.

Cognitive skills are given less emphasis with some children, but others may be taught functional reading and math. Snell (1983c) describes the content and procedures for teaching functional reading skills. At the most basic levels of instruction, reading would include words such as those used in pedestrian safety ("walk," "don't walk") and such words as "enter," "exit," "men," and "women." More complex reading skills would include directions for doing such things as reading recipes or bus schedules. Math skills might include ordering objects by size and counting in one-to-one correspondence, especially if such skills could be used in vocational placements. Handling money and telling time are examples of complex skills that might be appropriate for selected students.

In the *self-care* area, students who have mastered skills such as self-feeding and dressing may receive instruction on personal hygiene and grooming skills. If appropriate, skills such as housekeeping and cooking would also be taught (Browder and Snell, 1983). *Social skills* would receive continued emphasis for most students. These would include playing age-appropriate games with another peer or a small group of peers (Sailor and Guess, 1983). Considerable instruction is provided in communication skills. During the elementary school years, *prevocational* skills are introduced to the curriculum. In addition to skills involved in almost all vocational settings (task engagement, persistence), other vocational skills, such as task assembly, packaging, and sorting will be identified on the basis of possible future vocational placements of the students.

What is the primary focus of the secondary curriculum?

Secondary Level Education Curriculum. The secondary level education curriculum for students with severe developmental disabilities is quite different from the traditional curriculum. "All aspects of the curriculum at the secondary level are directed toward preparing the students to live in the particular community environments in which they are likely to reside upon completion of the public school curriculum" (Sailor and Guess, 1983, p. 283). Teachers in the secondary program must expand their role from interacting with students' families to interacting with a variety of additional community agencies and establishments. Ideally, much of the instruction in the secondary program would occur in the students' community rather than in the school classroom.

Sample curriculum content areas have been described by Sailor and Guess (1983) and Wilcox and Bellamy (1982a). One domain that remains from the elementary curriculum is *communication*. The major skill in the communication domain at the secondary level is to expand communication for use in various community settings. Students may also need to learn *domestic living* skills such as clothing selection, housekeeping, cooking, and clothing care (Browder and Snell, 1983; Vogelsberg, Williams, and Bellamy, 1982). Other important areas of instruction are *leisure time activities,* such as board games and listening to music; and *recreational skills,* including spectator events, such as movies and sporting events, and participation activities, such as swimming and bowling

(Voeltz, Wuerch, and Wilcox, 1982; Wehman, Schleien, and Kiernan, 1980). Another curriculum domain is *appropriate sexual behavior,* including dating and feminine hygiene care.

Several critical functions have been grouped under the broad heading of *community living.* These include "basic community interaction skills" (e.g., using public transportation and the telephone), "procurement of essential goods" (e.g., buying groceries and clothing), "procurement of essential services" (e.g., haircuts, banking, and medical care), and "participation in community activities" (e.g., eating in restaurants, going to church) (Sailor and Guess, 1983, p. 304).

A content area that receives considerable attention in the secondary level curriculum is *vocational* skills. These may include simulated work areas in the classroom and special training for sheltered and/or competitive employment (Bellamy, Bourbeau, and Sowers, 1983; Rusch, 1983; Sailor and Guess, 1983). Classroom employment training activities should be targeted for specific job placements in sheltered or competitive sites (Mithaug, Hagmeier, and Haring, 1977). When students move out of the classroom placement or from sheltered to competitive employment, a transitional program and various support services will be needed (Vogelsberg, Williams, and Friedl, 1980). Although the content areas of the secondary level curriculum may seem quite broad, Wilcox and Bellamy (1982b) point out that students do not need to know how to do every possible job or to engage in every possible recreational activity. Rather, they need to function independently on one or two jobs and engage in a small number of recreational activities available to them in their community.

PROBE 11-4
Curriculum Considerations

1. Define curriculum, and explain what type of information should be included in a curriculum.

2. What is the advantage of the critical functions curriculum approach compared to the developmental domains curriculum approach?

3. What three issues should be addressed when evaluating curricula?

4. List three early childhood curriculum areas and two types of behaviors in each area.

5. What are the differences between the early childhood curriculum and the elementary school-age curriculum?

6. What is the major thrust of the secondary curriculum?

INSTRUCTIONAL METHODS

You should be able to describe the four phases of learning, the prerequisites to learning, and the empirically verified procedures for teaching students with severe and multiple handicaps.

GOALS OF INSTRUCTION

The goal of all instruction, regardless of the student's age or level of functioning, is to teach skills that maximize independent functioning. To accomplish this goal, special educators individualize instruction by identifying and teaching skills that are both age-appropriate and functional for students. You will recall that age-appropriate skills are those performed by nonhandicapped persons of a similar chronological age; functional skills are skills that permit students more control over their own lives as soon as the skills are learned.

Skill Acquisition. The first step toward meeting this goal is called skill acquisition, during which students are taught skills not previously in their repertoires. Initially, a very specific set of instructional conditions may be necessary to teach a new skill. A teacher might begin by using one set of materials, controlling the pace at which materials are presented, adding cues or prompts to the task to reduce the number of errors a student makes, and delivering reinforcers contingent upon every correct response.

Skill Fluency. Once a skill has been acquired, instruction focuses on teaching students skill fluency, that is, performing the skill more proficiently and at more acceptable rates. For example, after a student has been taught the body mechanics of using a walker (acquisition phase) to facilitate independent mobility, the next instructional objective would be to teach proficient use of the walker to reduce the amount of time it takes the student to walk a specified distance. A second objective might be to teach the student to walk for longer periods of time and for longer distances.

How do teachers provide training in skill generalization?

Skill Generalization. The third phase is skill generalization. Unlike regular education teachers, special educators do not assume that a skill taught in the classroom will generalize to the community environment. They specifically program for skill generalization. Students must be able to perform skills in a variety of settings (classroom, lunch room, home) with several persons (teacher, teacher's aide, parent) and under natural environmental conditions.

To accomplish this, special education teachers systematically vary the conditions under which a skill is performed. They teach students to use natural cues and prompts by moving instruction to a student's home, neighborhood, and other sites where the student will find the skill useful. The cooperation of parents and the school district are essential for this part of the learning process. This phase is extremely important for teachers of severely and multiply handicapped students.

Skill Maintenance. The fourth and final phase of the learning process, skill maintenance, is to teach students to maintain a skill without the assistance of instructional supports such as artificial cues, prompts, and reinforcers. To facilitate skill maintenance, teachers attempt from the outset to make the instructional conditions similar to the conditions found in the student's natural environment. They use familiar and age-appropriate materials, teach functional skills, and utilize natural cues, prompts, and reinforcers to the maximum extent possible. Only when these natural cues and prompts prove to be inadequate for students to learn are less natural cues added and more intrusive prompts used.

Similarly, when natural consequences fail to result in skill acquisition, it may be necessary to supply artificial consequences contingent upon each correct response. Although added or exaggerated cues and prompts and unnatural positive reinforcers are often necessary for skill acquisition, they interfere with skill generalization and maintenance if they are not systematically removed. During the skill generalization phase of learning, instructional cues and prompts are faded out and control is transferred to more natural cues and prompts. In the skill maintenance phase, natural reinforcers replace artificial reinforcers, and the schedule of delivering these reinforcers is systematically thinned. During reinforcement schedule thinning, rather than reinforcing students every time they make a correct response (continuous reinforcement schedule), a reinforcer is delivered after every two correct responses (fixed ratio 2 reinforcement schedule), and then on the average of every third correct response (variable ratio 3 reinforcement schedule), and so on. Such reinforcement schedule thinning enhances the durability of a behavior over time and under natural environmental conditions (Koegel and Rincover, 1977).

A variety of instructional methods are available to teachers who must program for skill acquisition, fluency, generalization, and maintenance. The approach most commonly used by those who teach children with special needs, particularly students with moderate, severe, profound, and multiple disabilities, is applied behavior analysis (Alberto and Troutman, 1982). This methodology systematizes instruction and permits continuous evaluation of the student's performance toward his or her individualized instructional objectives.

What is reinforcement schedule thinning?

BEHAVIORAL MODEL OF TEACHING

The behavioral model of teaching is an instructional approach that places responsibility for a student's progress squarely on the shoulders of the teacher. If a student acquires a skill, then the teacher is credited with designing and implementing an effective instructional program. If a student fails to acquire, generalize, or maintain a skill, then the teacher takes responsibility for the student's lack of progress.

Basic assumptions. There are several basic assumptions associated with applied behavior analysis and the behavioral model of teaching. First, regardless of a student's etiology and whether deficiencies are cognitive, sensory, or motor, the child's problems are viewed as behavioral. Teachers who ascribe to the behavioral approach, then, believe all children can learn under appropriate instructional conditions. They believe their responsibility is to identify those optimal instructional conditions. In the educability debate presented earlier, the position espoused by Baer (1981) best reflects the behavioral model.

A second assumption of the behavioral model is that students learn best when teachers systematically order tasks in a sequence from easy to hard, beginning where the student is on a task and differentially reinforcing correct and incorrect responses. By systematically sequencing tasks, cues, and prompts and differentially reinforcing student responses, students can be taught complex functional skills with a minimum number of errors. It is differential reinforcement that causes the child to learn; the sequencing of tasks, cues, and prompts determines how efficiently a skill is learned (e.g., number of errors to criterion, number of trials to criterion, amount of direct instructional time to criterion).

What is "zero degree inference strategy"?

A third assumption of educators who adopt the behavioral approach to teaching is what Brown, Nietupski, and Hamre-Nietupski (1976) have referred to as a "zero degree inference strategy." According to the strategy, "no inferences are made that training to a criterion on any task in one situation will result in criterion performance in similar but different situations requiring similar or slightly different actions. Each time a situation changes for a severely handicapped student, it will be necessary to verify empirically that he or she can perform the skills required by that new situation" (p. 6). This strategy suggests that teachers need to design instructional programs that facilitate skill generalization and maintenance.

The fourth assumption subscribed to by behaviorally oriented educators is that instructional programs fail, not students. This assumption has led special educators to define teaching in functional terms. Teaching is defined as the arrangement of instructional conditions (pace, materials, cues, prompts, and consequences) such that a positive change in student behavior results. Such changes must be of practical value to students, permitting them greater independence and control over their environment. The responsibility and credit for positive behavior change rests with the student's teachers.

Given these four assumptions, it is not surprising that special educators who have adopted this model of teaching individualize instruction, systematically present cues, prompts, and reinforcers, and frequently evaluate the effectiveness of their instructional programs, modifying them based on the data.

How do pre-task, task, and post-task components differ?

Task Components. Simply described, the behavioral model of teaching breaks down any instructional task into three components: (1) pre-task, (2) task, and (3) post-task (Becker, Engelman and Thomas, 1975). The pre-task component requires that a teacher have the attention of students before presenting task materials and directions. Teachers can ensure student attention by requiring eye contact or having students make some other attentional response, such as saying "ready" or placing their hands in their laps or on the desk top.

Once the students are paying attention, the teacher can proceed to the task component. In the task component, the teacher presents the materials (fork and spoon), directions ("Pick up spoon"), cues (teacher holds up identical spoon), and response prompts (teacher assists student in grasping and scooping with the spoon). It is in this component that teachers tell students what to do and arrange cues and prompts to help them make the correct response with the least amount of assistance.

In the post-task component, teachers differentially reinforce correct and incorrect responses. This process may entail providing descriptive verbal praise ("Good, you picked up spoon") and a sticker for each correct response or initiating a correction procedure following an incorrect response (saying "Wrong. Pick up spoon" as the teacher physically guides the student through the correct response without delivering the sticker). It is important that each of these three components be addressed when designing instructional programs for severely and multiply handicapped students.

The behavioral model of teaching provides a framework within which to approach instruction. For teachers to teach, they must secure students' attention, consistently present directions, cues, and prompts which are appropriate for each student's level of functioning, and differently reinforce students' responses. As previously described, many severely handicapped students do not attend to even the most pronounced auditory and visual stimuli, do not imitate, and frequently engage in stereotypic behaviors. For these pupils, instructional programs must be designed that teach (1) attention to task, (2) motor imitation, and (3) suppression of inappropriate and interfering behaviors. Teachers of children with severe developmental delays give priority to such behaviors because they are viewed as prerequisites to learning.

DECREASING INAPPROPRIATE BEHAVIORS

Teachers of children with severe/profound mental retardation soon discover that many students engage in inappropriate behaviors that interfere with their learning functional skills. These children commonly engage in repetitive behaviors that have no apparent purpose, such as body rocking, hand flapping, or finger twirling. This class of behaviors is called stereotypic or self-stimulatory behavior. Although these behaviors frequently interfere with teaching, they seldom threaten the health or physical well-being of the student. Self-injurious behaviors, on the other hand, can be life-threatening, such as rumination, pica (craving unnatural foods or nonfoods), or head-banging, or at least physically harmful, such as eye-gouging, face-slapping, or self-biting. In a recent publication by the American Association on Mental Deficiency, Hollis and Meyers (1982) present a detailed analysis and comprehensive review of life-threatening behavior observed in persons with mental retardation. Because of the relatively high prevalence of self-injurious behavior (8 to 14 percent) among persons with severe mental retardation, special educators must be skilled at designing and implementing behavior management programs to suppress severe behavior problems (Maurice and Trudel, 1982). As Spradlin and Spradlin (1976) have pointed out, meaningful instruction can occur only after self-stimulatory, self-injurious, and other severe behavior problems are eliminated or reduced to acceptable levels.

How frequent is self-injurious behavior?

Not all behavior problems confronted by special educators working with severely handicapped students are as potentially devastating to a student's development and well-being as self-stimulatory and self-injurious behaviors. Some students may engage in behaviors that are simply embarrassing and annoying to teachers, parents, and school administrators (e.g., disrobing in public, smearing feces, or stealing food). Teachers should be able to control these behaviors through behavior modification techniques as well. They should be familiar with such procedures as differential reinforcement of appropriate behaviors incompatible with the inappropriate behavior, systematic ignoring, time out from positive reinforcement, and overcorrection. These and other behavior management procedures have been reviewed in detail by Snell and Smith (1983), Alberto and Troutman (1982) and Martin and Pear (1983).

TEACHING NEW SKILLS

What is "putting through"?

Several instructional procedures have been used successfully to teach new skills to students with severe learning and physical disabilities. The procedure used most frequently to teach complex skills is *physical prompting and fading,* sometimes referred to as physical guidance or "putting through." This procedure involves breaking down a skill into several component behaviors through a process known as *task analysis.*

Figure 11-3 is an example of how the self-care skill of putting on pants can be task analyzed into ten smaller steps or behaviors for instructional purposes. To teach this skill the teacher would begin by physically guiding the student through all ten steps. If the student does not resist teacher assistance during this first instructional session, the student is physically guided through Steps 2 through 10 during the next session. With each new session, if the student meets the criterion level on all steps to be performed independently, the teacher provides less assistance and requires the student to perform more steps independently.

It is important that students receive positive reinforcement each time they complete the sequence of steps. This increases the probability that they will continue to work on learning the skill. The procedure described here is an example of *backward chaining,* in which teacher assistance is systematically faded out beginning with the last step of the task analysis. With some skills it is preferable to fade out assistance on the first step of the task analysis as in assembly tasks; this is called *forward chaining.* Physical prompting and fading have been used to teach a variety of communication, self-care, motor, and vocational skills to students with severe and multiple handicaps (Snell, 1983). It is therefore imperative that special educators be thoroughly familiar with the design, implementation, and evaluation of this type of program.

How does a teacher use the "time delay procedure"?

Other instructional procedures that have proven successful with severely developmentally disabled students include the system of least prompts (Alberto and Schofield, 1979), stimulus shaping and stimulus fading (Westling and Koorland, 1979), and time delay (Snell and Gast, 1981). It is beyond the scope of this chapter to describe each of these instructional procedures, but the time delay transfer of stimulus control procedure deserves some discussion in light of its relatively recent introduction into special education classrooms. The time delay procedure has proven to be an effective, efficient way to teach a range of skills to severely handicapped learners, including eye contact, object recognition, manual sign reading, instruction following, and the initiation of verbal requests (Gast, 1983). Quite simply, the time delay procedure entails systematically increasing the amount of time between the time a teacher asks a student to make a response ("Show me the sign for *more*") and the time the teacher prompts the correct response (teacher models the manual sign for "more" for the student to imitate). Initially, the task direction and the prompt are paired. Over successive trials or blocks of trials, the teacher waits longer and longer (e.g., 1 second, 2 seconds, 3 seconds, and so on) before presenting the prompt. This allows the student more time over successive trials to perform the correct response independently. If the student is unsure of the correct response, he or she can wait, and the teacher will provide the prompt. Regardless of whether the student responds correctly before or after the prompt, the student will be reinforced. Only if he or she makes an incorrect response is the reinforcer withheld and a correction procedure employed. Severely handicapped students have typically anticipated the correct response 100 per-

Figure 11-3
Terminal Objective: Student unfolds pants and independently puts them on.

Step	Component Behaviors																				
1.	Pulls pants up from thighs to waist	10	10	10	10	10	10	10	10	10	10	10	10	10	10	10	10	10	10	10	10
2.	Pulls pants up from knees to thighs	9	9	9	9	9	9	9	9	9	9	9	9	9	9	9	9	9	9	9	9
3.	Pulls pants up from ankles to knees	8	8	8	8	8	8	8	8	8	8	8	8	8	8	8	8	8	8	8	8
4.	Stands up	7	7	7	7	7	7	7	7	7	7	7	7	7	7	7	7	7	7	7	7
5.	Puts on pants with one foot in and other started in the legs	6	6	6	6	6	6	6	6	6	6	6	6	6	6	6	6	6	6	6	6
6.	Puts on pants with one foot started in just past crotch	5	5	5	5	5	5	5	5	5	5	5	5	5	5	5	5	5	5	5	5
7.	Puts on pants when placed in front in correct position	4	4	4	4	4	4	4	4	4	4	4	4	4	4	4	4	4	4	4	4
8.	Positions pants in lap, front facing up	3	3	3	3	3	3	3	3	3	3	3	3	3	3	3	3	3	3	3	3
9.	Unfolds pants and puts them on	2	2	2	2	2	2	2	2	2	2	2	2	2	2	2	2	2	2	2	2
10.	Positions self correctly (sitting) and puts on pants	1	1	1	1	1	1	1	1	1	1	1	1	1	1	1	1	1	1	1	1
Sessions		1	2	3	4	5	6	7	8	9	10	11	12	13	14	15	16	17	18	19	20
Dates																					

Sessions/Dates

Adapted from *Teaching Research Infant and Child Center, the teaching research curriculum for moderately and severely handicapped: Self-help and cognitive.* Springfield, IL: Charles C. Thomas Publisher, 1980 p.86.

cent of the time before the 7-second delay period, i.e., they have achieved independent performance. Figure 11-4 is a diagnosis of the time delay procedure for a coin identification task. For more information on the time delay procedure, see Snell and Gast (1981).

A number of instructional procedures have proven effective in teaching functional skills to students once thought to be unteachable. Although optimal instructional methods have yet to be identified for some students, research continues, and for the vast majority of persons with severe learning disabilities an instructional technology is available. Teachers face the challenge of discovering new and more efficient procedures for teaching students with severe and multiple handicaps.

PROBE 11–5
Instructional Methods

1. Explain what is meant by a "functional age-appropriate skill" for an adolescent with a severe developmental disability.

2. List the four phases of learning and the instructional purpose of each.

3. List two basic assumptions about learning associated with the behavioral model of teaching (applied behavior analysis).

4. How do behaviors classified as self-injurious differ from those classified as self-stimulatory? Describe two behaviors in each category.

5. Describe the method of physical prompting and fading frequently used to teach severely handicapped students gross motor skills (e.g. dressing, bathing, throwing a ball, opening a can).

SERVICE DELIVERY

You should be able to describe the advantages of an integrative service delivery model and the types of services necessary to maintain persons with severe developmental disabilities in the community.

Philosophical, ethical, legal, and practical forces have shaped current service delivery systems for students with severe developmental disabilities. The roles of some of these forces are briefly described below.

Figure 11-4
Progressive Time Delay Teaching Model

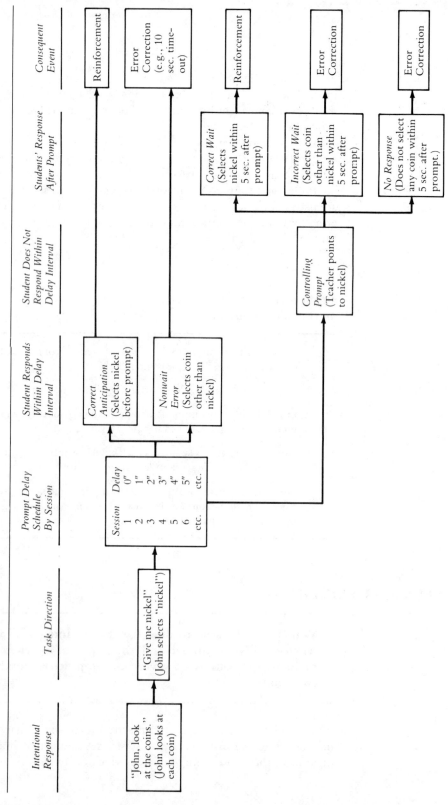

Anita is a nonverbal five-year-old child enrolled in a classroom that serves children with severe multiple handicaps. She seldom makes eye contact with adults when her name is called and does not imitate movements that are being presented by her teacher. A meeting with her parents and a communication specialist was called by Mr. Pitts, her teacher, to discuss this problem.

All parties at the meeting agreed that Anita must be taught to make eye contact with adults. The reason that this is so important is that eye contact is a prerequisite for learning other skills. For example, if eye contact can be established on command and maintained, then Anita can observe and learn things from others who share her environment. There was agreement at the meeting that Anita should be taught to make eye contact within 5 seconds of her name being called, and that eye contact should be maintained for a minimum of 10 seconds.

Before starting the eye contact training program, Mr. Pitts identified four items that Anita liked, which could be used as reinforcers for correct responses. He then developed two objectives, one for each phase of the eye contact program. His Phase 1 objective was "Anita will turn her head in the direction of the teacher within five seconds of her name being called 90 percent of the time over three consecutive days without teacher prompts." The Phase 2 objective was "Anita will turn her head in the direction of the teacher, make eye contact within five seconds of her name being called, and maintain eye contact for ten seconds 90 percent of the time over three consecutive days without teacher prompts."

Mr. Pitts taught the objective for Phase 1 (head orientation) through a progressive time delay procedure. For the first instructional session, he said, "Anita (pause), look at me" and immediately (zero-second delay) physically guided Anita's head so it was facing forward. He verbally praised Anita while holding her head in place and presenting her ·with a small spoonful of applesauce, which was one of the reinforcers that had been identified earlier. This zero-second delay procedure continued for all ten trials of the first training session.

In the second session, Mr. Pitts conducted trials exactly as in the first session, except that he waited 1 second before physically guiding Anita's head for-

ward. With each subsequent session, he waited an additional second before prompting Anita to turn her head. By the sixth session (5-second delay interval), Anita met the criterion for Phase 1; but she was not making eye contact with Mr. Pitts.

In the seventh training session, Mr. Pitts initiated Phase 2 training. To teach Anita to make and maintain eye contact, he said, "Anita (pause), look at me," which resulted in Anita's turning her head forward. Once the head was in this position, Mr. Pitts moved a strawberry (one of the other reinforcers) into her line of vision and slowly moved it to his eye level, making sure Anita was visually fixating on it the entire distance. When Anita was looking at the strawberry when positioned at Mr. Pitts's eye level, he covered it with his hand, said, "Good looking," and then immediately gave her the strawberry.

With each subsequent training session, Mr. Pitts made two subtle changes, provided that Anita met the preceding eye contact duration criterion. First, he required Anita to raise her head more each session (approximately 3 inches) in order for the reinforcer to be in her direct line of vision. Second, he covered the reinforcer with his hand for longer periods of time (session two for 1 second; session three for 2 seconds, etc.), while continuing to require Anita to maintain eye contact before delivering the reinforcer.

By systematically requiring Anita to perform more of the behavior independently and maintain eye contact for longer periods of time before receiving the reinforcer, Anita was taught an important basic skill in nearly errorless fashion. Mr. Pitts gradually eliminated the use of tangible reinforcers, and found that Anita would respond appropriately for a social reinforcer — praise.

Through this carefully designed instructional program, which used task analysis, a response prompting procedure (progressive time delay), behavioral shaping, and differential reinforcement, Anita was able to begin working on her next educational objective, which was motor imitation. Although some people may not see Anita's learning to establish and maintain eye contact on command as a significant achievement, it serves as a basic first step on the road to greater independence.

NORMALIZATION

As discussed in Chapter 2, the principle of normalization suggests that persons with disabilities should have the opportunity to live as much like nonhandicapped persons as possible and that this goal can be met by exposing them to the living conditions common to their culture (Wolfensberger, 1972). This philosophy provided the impetus for the deinstitutionalization of persons with severe developmental disabilities. It was hoped that the social interactions and demands of the community environment would result in adaptive behavior. This view is, of course, oversimplified. If students with severe developmental disabilities are to adapt to the community environment, then medical, educational, and other social services must be available. It is essential that these services be coordinated.

ACCESS TO EDUCATIONAL SERVICES

Litigation. As students moved out of residential institutions and as parents began to keep their children in the community rather than institutionalize them, parents began to seek educational services. However, students were frequently refused such services because of their disabilities. Parents sought help from the courts. One of the earliest and most important cases which addressed the educational rights of handicapped students was *Pennsylvania Association for Retarded Children* v. *the Commonwealth of Pennsylvania* (1971). This landmark case successfully secured the right to a free, appropriate, public education for all children with mental retardation (See Chapter 1 for a description of the provisions of this case). In another landmark case, *Mills* v. *Board of Education of the District of Columbia* (1972), the educational rights of students with mental retardation, secured in the *Pennsylvania* case, were extended to all children with a disability, regardless of type (mentally retarded, physically handicapped, or emotionally disturbed). These two cases, in conjunction with court cases addressing the right to treatment and rehabilitation of persons with mental illness residing in state institutions (*Wyatt* v. *Anderholt,* 1970; *Wyatt* v. *Stickney,* 1972), set in motion a movement on behalf of all disabled persons that changed the direction and model for service delivery.

Legislation. Advances were also made in Congress. Section 504 of the Rehabilitation Act of 1973 stated that persons with disabilities could not be discriminated against by any program receiving federal financial assistance. As a result of these successes and considerable cooperation between parent and professional groups, Public Law 94-142 (Education for All Handicapped Children Act) was written and passed. The provisions of this law were described in Chapter 1. It is mentioned here to emphasize that the provisions apply to students with severe developmental disabilities. One of the provisions of the law is that "to the maximum extent appropriate," students with handicaps are to be educated with nonhandicapped students.

What is the most appropriate educational placement for severely handicapped children?

Integration. While many persons understand the advantages of educating students with mild disabilities in schools with nonhandicapped children, two questions arise in relation to integrating students with severe developmental disabilities. First, is the public school the most *appropriate* educational setting, and second, is the public school mandated to provide such services? (Sailor and Guess, 1983, p. 46). The issue of appropriateness has many facets. Because sufficient research has not been conducted, it is not possible to specify the most appropriate educational environment for students with specific disabilities (Peck and Semmel, 1982). However, the rationale for integrating students with severe developmental disabilities into public schools deserves attention.

Brown et al. (1977) stated that integrated settings are more appropriate than segregated settings because they allow handicapped and nonhandicapped students the opportunity to interact with persons who are different from themselves. Such interactions are thought to be useful to both groups; students with severe developmental disabilities gain opportunities to learn through imitation of appropriate peer models, and nonhandicapped children learn more accurate views of persons with disabilities and thus become more tolerant and understanding of disabled persons. In fact, investigations of the effects of social contacts between the two groups suggest that typical students do acquire more positive attitudes, are willing to have more social contacts, and are less willing to agree with stereotyping statements (McHale and Simeonsson, 1980; Voeltz, 1980).

Integrated settings are also more apt to focus on the development of functional or adaptive behaviors than are segregated settings. This practice is especially true of institutions, where a medical treatment model may be used rather than a habilitative educational model. Further, integrated settings are more likely than segregated ones to provide longitudinal curricular activities to establish age-appropriate functional skills that will be useful in the natural environment (Brown et al., 1977).

Peck and Semmel (1982, p. 61) have indicated that special education's task now is not to compare integration and segregation, but to acquire the "knowledge of *how* integration may be accomplished that will allow educators to design programs that maximize the probability of successful instruction and social outcomes." Several papers have discussed this issue (Arknell, Thomason, and Haring, 1980; Hamre-Nietupski and Nietupski, 1981; Hamre-Nietupski, Nietupski, Bates, and Maurer, 1982; Taylor, 1982; Wehman and Hill, 1982).

Is the public school mandated to integrate students with severe developmental disabilities? The answer lies more with the legal system than with educational research. Sailor and Guess (1983) have concluded that such a mandate does exist; at issue is the form of that integration.

COMMUNITY-BASED SERVICES

The exodus of students from residential state institutions to the community and the provision of appropriate services for students in the community involve more than the educational system. Many families have shown that they can care for and provide stimulating environments for children with severe developmental disabilities. Not all families, however, have the desire or capability to do so. Further, as parents grow older and as they attempt to establish more independent behaviors in their young adult, alternative living arrangements are needed. Beyond foster or natural family living, Sailor and Guess (1983) have discussed a continuum of possibilities ranging from group homes to independent living. Options between the two extremes include cluster apartments and room-and-board facilities. One of the most common options is group homes, which are facilities in which a small group of students (usually six to ten) live under supervision. For information on the cost effectiveness of group homes, see Templeman, Gage, and Fredericks, (1982), and Gage, Fredericks, Johnson-Dorn, and Lindley-Southard (1982).

When is respite care needed?   Besides living arrangements, other family and student support services are needed. These include specialized medical care, dental care, recreation programs, arrangements for participation in religious services, transportation, and work centers (Kenowitz, Gallaher, and Edgar, 1977). Families will probably need *respite care*. Respite care involves someone other than a family member caring for the disabled person while the parents or family are away. The period of respite care may range from a few hours to several days.

Finally, it is unlikely that students with severe developmental disabilities will be maintained in the community without group and individual advocacy. Traditionally, groups of parents and professionals such as the National Association for Retarded Citizens, National Society for Autistic Children, United Cerebral Palsy, and others have served important functions. They have started new services, stimulated communities to start services, monitored services, initiated court cases, and helped develop and pass legislation. Professional groups such as The Association for Persons with Severe Handicaps and the Council for Exceptional Children have clarified issues, assisted in court cases, helped develop legislation, prompted research, and disseminated information. These activities are needed and must continue. However, a need also exists for persons in local communities to serve as advocates for individual students (Sailor and Guess, 1983). Such persons ensure that the students receive appropriate education and related services.

As Sailor and Guess (1983) indicate, the entry and maintenance of students with severe developmental disabilities into the educational system and community is an exciting yet demanding process. Although considerable gains have been made, there remains a need for innovative service delivery systems and applied research.

PROBE 11-6
Service Delivery

1. Describe the concept of normalization as it relates to providing services to developmentally disabled persons.

2. Name two court cases that helped establish the current level of services to students with severe developmental disabilities.

3. What are some advantages of integrating students with severe developmental disabilities into community schools?

4. List four types of services that must be available if students with severe developmental disabilities are to be successfully integrated into the community.

SUMMARY

1. Students with severe developmental disabilities are a heterogeneous population. They are characterized by low cognitive abilities and are likely to exhibit additional behavioral, physical, and sensory handicaps.

2. Research has shown that students with severe and multiple handicaps are educable and can benefit from instruction if it is systematic and data-based and focuses on the acquisition, fluency, generalization, and maintenance of functional skills.

3. Assessment of students with multiple handicaps requires input from professionals in a variety of disciplines. The transdisciplinary approach facilitates the design of educational program plans which address individual student needs across curriculum areas.

4. Teachers of severely handicapped students must be able to design, implement, evaluate, and modify instructional programs in accordance with applied behavior analysis principles and procedures. They must be able to handle severe behavior problems and to understand and manage a wide range of medical and physical problems.

5. Like other children with developmental disabilities, students with severe handicaps are entitled to be educated in the least restrictive environment appropriate.

TASK SHEET 11
Field Experiences with the Severely/Profoundly Handicapped

Select *one* of the alternatives and complete the required tasks. Write a report of no more than three pages about your activities.

Parent Interview

Interview the parents of a severely/profoundly handicapped child. Using great tact, try to determine some of the problems the parents have encountered in rearing their child and placing him or her in programs. Try to find out what other services the parents would find helpful.

Observation

Visit an educational program for severely/profoundly handicapped students, and talk with administrators, teachers, parents, aides, or other staff members. Describe the physical setting, the type of program, and the activities that you observed. Also, answer the following questions about the provision of the "least restrictive opportunity":

Facility

— Is the facility placed near the center of community activity?
— To what extent does the facility isolate children from other handicapped and non-handicapped children?
— How effectively are ancillary services, such as physical therapy, speech therapy, and medical services, delivered in each classroom?
— What architectural barriers did you observe?

Opportunities for Normal Integration

— What opportunities are the students given to practice skills learned in the classroom in the community?
— What opportunities are there for students to interact with less severely handicapped and nonhandicapped peers? How frequently are these opportunities offered?

Appropriate Educational Programming

Use your observations to comment on the training of the staff, the staff expectations for student performances, assessment procedures, the goals established for the children, adequacy of instruction, and evaluation procedures.

Participation

Volunteer your services at a facility serving severely handicapped individuals and record your activities, impressions, and questions. Describe the areas in which you think handicapped children would require intensive training before they could function in the community.

Agency Investigation

Write to three of the following agencies and inquire about the services that they provide for people with severe developmental disabilities. Write a three-page paper that synthesizes your findings, including how you might use their services if you were a professional working in this area:

Association for Behavior Analysis
Department of Psychology
Western Michigan University
Kalamazoo, MI 49008

American Association on Mental
Deficiency
5101 Wisconsin Avenue, N.W.
Washington, DC 20016

National Society for Autistic Children
169 Tampa Avenue
Albany, NY 12208

National Association for Retarded
Citizens
2709 Avenue E East
Arlington, TX 76011

The Association for Persons with Severe
Handicaps
7010 Roosevelt Way, NE
Seattle, WA 98115

Library Study

Use the library to identify at least three articles related to the education of children with severe developmental disabilities. Write a one-page abstract of each, concluding with a paragraph about your reactions to the article. Here are the names of some journals in which you can find articles:

Analysis and Intervention in Developmental Disabilities
American Journal of Mental Deficiency
Education and Training of the Mentally Retarded
Journal of the Association for Persons with Severe Handicaps
Journal of Applied Behavior Analysis
Journal of Autism and Developmental Disorders
Mental Retardation

Design Your Own Field Experience

If none of these alternatives appeals to you or you have an opportunity to perform some other task with the severely/profoundly handicapped, design your own field experience. Check with your instructor to determine its acceptability.

No ordinary handbook on child care could possibly have prepared Richard and Sally Hunter for their first baby. When he was just six months old, Kam Hunter began speaking in complete sentences. By the time he was 3, he had taught himself to read. As a first grader, he was allowed to enroll in Spanish courses at a high school near his elementary classroom in Ionia, Mich.; within a year, at the age of 7, he was a full-time high-school student. Today, Kam is a sophomore in the Honors College of Michigan State University. He is only 12 years old. "I just want to be treated like any other college student," says the handsome, blond youngster. "But I know that's probably not possible."

Kam Hunter is one of the gifted children — roughly 2.5 million young Americans who are endowed with academic, artistic or social talents far beyond those of their peers. They are not just the diagnosed geniuses, but comprise a widely varied group whose gifts range from prodigious prowess in chess or music to extraordinary facility in language, mathematics or the visual arts: a toddler in Seattle who amassed (and read) a library of more than 100 books before she was 2 years old; an 8-year-old chess champion from New York City who is well on his way to becoming a grand master; an inner-city 12-year-old from Baltimore whose paintings already hang in public galleries.

"They come from all levels of society, all races and both sexes," says Dr. Harold Lyon, former director of the Federal Office for the Gifted and Talented. "These are the future Beethovens, the Newtons, the Jeffersons, the Picassos, Baldwins and Martin Luther Kings. And like other minorities, they need help."

12

Gifted and Talented Children

Edwina D. Pendarvis

Edwina D. Pendarvis is Assistant Professor and Coordinator of the certification program for teachers of gifted children at Marshall University in Huntington, West Virginia. She has teaching experience in regular elementary and secondary classrooms and in a resource room serving gifted children in kindergarten through junior high school.

It may seem strange that Kam Hunter and children like him need special education. They have the ability to succeed at virtually any intellectual task they undertake. But ability is not the only factor in success; there are many factors that influence a child's development and performance. The purpose of this chapter is to help you gain a basic understanding of giftedness and the educational provisions that are best suited to gifted students.

DEFINITIONS AND NEED FOR PROGRAMS

> **You should be able to define giftedness and explain why gifted children should be provided with special education.**

MISCONCEPTIONS ABOUT THE GIFTED

Recognition of the importance of modifying instruction for gifted children is increasing (Mitchell, 1982); but exceptionally bright students still spend much

521

of their time in school practicing what they already know, reading books that are too easy for them, and answering questions that require little mental effort. Difficulty in bringing about necessary changes in the educational programs of gifted children stems, in large part, from common misconceptions about the gifted.

What common misconceptions lead people to have a negative view toward special education for the gifted?

Gifted Children Will Succeed Without Special Programs. Despite a large body of literature to the contrary, many educators think that gifted-student programs are unnecessary because gifted children will succeed without them. There are two flaws in this argument against special education for the gifted. One is that about half of the students who could qualify for gifted education are not recognized as gifted by their teachers (Pegnato and Birch, 1959). We cannot know that gifted children succeed if we do not know who they are. Another flaw in the argument that gifted children will excel without special programs is that research shows that many identified gifted children are unsuccessful both in their academic efforts and in their careers (Pringle, 1970; Terman and Oden, 1947; Whitmore, 1980).

It is true that history offers many examples of persons whose talents went unrecognized during their school years, but who later became eminent. Some famous examples are mentioned in a biography of Thomas Edison (Clark, 1977, p. 9):

> Here he [Thomas Edison] showed what has almost become a sign of genius: After only three months he returned home in tears, reporting that the teacher had described him as "addled." This was in fact no cause for alarm. Leonardo daVinci, Hans Anderson and Niels Bohr were all singled out in their youth as cases of retarded development; Newton was considered a dunce; the teacher of Sir Humphrey Davy commented, "While he was with me I could not discern the faculties by which he was so much distinguished"; and Einstein's headmaster was to warn that the boy "would never make a success of anything."

These gifted men did succeed without special education, at least as a part of their formal education; but many equally gifted persons may have failed. Research indicates that over half the gifted students in school are achieving far below their capabilities (Marland, 1972); many drop out of school early (French, 1975). Students such as these are far less likely to excel today than in Edison's era because success in most fields now requires many years of specialized, formal education.

Why are gifted programs sometimes considered elitist?

Gifted Programs Are Elitist. Belief that gifted programs are elitist presents another barrier to special provisions for talented children. Contributing to the elitist argument is the incontrovertible fact that minority groups are underrepresented in gifted programs (Perrone and Male, 1981). Until a larger proportion of gifted children from ethnic, racial, economic, and other minorities are included, the elitist label will not be eradicated. Although educators are becoming more sensitive to the need to employ equitable identification criteria in order to locate and serve gifted members of minority groups (Bernal, 1979), gifted-student education is still far from "culture-fair." Until programs have a more representational mix of majority and minority groups, advocates of gifted education can only document improvements and point out, as has Shirley Chisholm (Education of the Handicapped, 1979), that special programs benefit the large number of minority-group children who have already been identified as gifted.

A less serious charge that special education encourages snobbery in gifted students has been countered by the suggestion that undue feelings of superiority are promoted, not by gifted programs, but by the lack of them. In the regular classroom, gifted students can often, with little effort, outperform most other students. It is not elitist to give children appropriately difficult work and to allow them to discover that there are other children as talented as they.

Why do gifted children need special education?

Effective education depends on matching the level and pace of instruction with the students' level and rate of achievement (Bloom, 1976; Robinson, Roedell, and Jackson, 1979). Gifted students' advanced conceptual level and rapid learning rate make most regular classroom instruction inappropriate to their educational needs. Special education for the gifted provides instruction commensurate with their exceptional ability.

DEFINITIONS OF GIFTEDNESS

What purposes does a definition of giftedness serve?

Many people equate giftedness with a high IQ score, but giftedness can be defined in many ways. How giftedness is defined is critical because the definition (1) communicates to educators, as well as to the public, whom gifted education is intended to serve and (2) guides the development of identification procedures and the educational programs. If the definition is too narrow, children who need special education may go unserved because they are ineligible for the gifted program. If the definition is too broad, gifted children may be inadequately served because identification procedures and educational provisions are diluted in an effort to address the diversity of levels and types of ability that a broad definition may subsume. Both pragmatic and theoretical considerations enter into the task of developing a definition of giftedness.

How do pragmatic considerations affect definitions of giftedness?

Pragmatic Considerations in Defining Giftedness. Major pragmatic considerations for school systems or other agencies serving gifted children are (1) priorities regarding the type or types of ability the system is most concerned with developing and (2) budgetary constraints, or limits on funds that can be allocated to gifted education. These considerations determine both the content of the definition and the eligibility criteria that limit the scope of the definition.

The eligibility criteria establish the level of ability required for inclusion in the gifted program.

One school system may define giftedness as exceptional academic ability and give scope to its definition by requiring scores in the 95th percentile or above on standardized individually administered achievement or aptitude tests. Another system, with different educational priorities, may define giftedness as exceptional ability in any of several areas of giftedness: academics, performing arts, visual arts, etc. Given the same proportion of funds to spend on gifted education, the school district with the broader definition could limit its gifted population by establishing a high criterion level in each area. In general, the more limited the funds, the higher the level of giftedness required for eligibility for special programs. In recent years, because of budgetary cutbacks at the federal and state level, some gifted programs have had to raise their eligibility criteria and serve fewer children (Epstein, 1979).

If it seems strange that the condition of the economy can determine whether or not a child is gifted, you should recognize that budgetary allocations are, in effect, an expression of the public's educational priorities. In any society, the type of abilities that are cultivated and the level of effort directed to their development reflect the values of the culture (Laycock, 1979).

Theoretical Considerations. The concept of superior ability, particularly intellectual ability, is the critical attribute of most definitions of giftedness. Differences in definition that do not arise for pragmatic reasons may arise because the originators of the definitions subscribe to different theories about the nature of intelligence.

Who first applied statistical concepts to the study of intelligence?

Although interest in intelligence and its measurement has a long history, Francis Galton, whose *Hereditary Genius* was published in 1869, is often credited with laying the groundwork for quantitative investigation of ability by applying the concept of deviation from the mean to intellectual performance. Galton's conception of giftedness was broad, and he included in his studies several types of eminent persons: writers, statesmen, oarsmen, and wrestlers. Based on his investigation, Galton concluded that the necessary elements for outstanding achievement in any field are (1) capacity, (2) zeal, and (3) power to do laborious work.

In the early 1900s, influenced by Galton's work, Alfred Binet developed the prototype of intelligence tests in use today. Binet, who was interested in predicting children's scholastic performance, took a commonsense approach and assembled a variety of practical tasks, such as counting money (Gould, 1981). Based on the examinee's performance on the different tasks, Binet estimated the child's likelihood of success in school.

Binet's approach was relatively atheoretical (Gould, 1981), but Galton's work influenced theories of intelligence as well as its measurement. Among the most famous of those theories is that of Charles Spearman (1914). A contemporary of Binet, Spearman based his model of intelligence on factor analyses of children's performance on tests like Binet's (Gould, 1981). He hypothesized that performance on any intellectual task is determined by a general intellectual factor and by one or more specific factors relevant to the task at hand. Success in spelling, for example, is, according to this theory, determined by the speller's general intellectual ability level and by the level of those specific factors needed in spelling as opposed to some other task, such as solving arithmetic problems.

Who first defined giftedness in terms of IQ?

Spearman's theory provides the theoretical underpinning for the practice of representing cognitive ability by an IQ score, which indexes a general ability level (Gould, 1981). Thus, his theory forms the basis for definitions of giftedness such as that used by Lewis Terman (Terman and Oden, 1925), who revised a version of Binet's test to develop the Stanford-Binet Intelligence Scale and used it in the identification of approximately 1,500 gifted students (Terman and Oden, 1925). Because of the magnitude of Terman's longitudinal study of gifted students and its impact on education, defining giftedness in terms of superior general intellectual ability indicated by an IQ score in the 98th or 99th percentile has been common practice since the 1920s.

In contrast to definitions based on Spearman's two-factor model are definitions based on multi-factor models, such as J. P. Guilford's, which hypothesizes 120 independent cognitive factors (Guilford, 1967). He disagreed with the idea that there is a general factor that makes a significant contribution to performance on intellectual tasks. Rather, he proposed that performance on any task is a function of the interaction of three types of mental factors: (1) operations, (2) products or outcomes, and (3) content, or type of information the task requires (Guilford, 1967). The five types of operations are cognition, memory, divergent production, convergent production, and evaluation. The six products are units, classes, relations, systems, implications, and transformations. Four categories of content are semantic, symbolic, figural, and behavioral. Thus, there are 120 possible combinations of these three dimensions ($6 \times 6 \times 4$). According to Guilford's theory, a person could have a remarkable understanding of music, or mathematics, for example, and be average, or even below, in verbal understanding.

Research has not established the validity of Guilford's theory; nevertheless, his multi-factor model has influenced both educational policy and practice. A multi-factor perspective is reflected in the federal definition of giftedness in Section 902 of PL 95-561, The Gifted and Talented Children's Education Act of 1978:

> The term *gifted and talented children* means children and, whenever applicable, youth who are identified at the preschool, elementary, or secondary level as possessing demonstrated or potential abilities that give evidence of high performance capabilities in areas such as intellectual, creative, specific academic, or leadership ability, or in the performing and visual arts, and who by reason thereof, require services or activities not ordinarily provided by the school.

It has been estimated that, in applying a broad definition of giftedness, as in this federal definition, at least 3 to 5 percent of the total school-aged population would be considered gifted (Marland, 1972). This percentage includes talented children who might be excluded under a definition that is based only on general intellectual ability.

How has the changed concept of symbolization affected definitions of giftedness?

In defining giftedness, Gallagher (1975, p. 11) suggested that the ability to manipulate symbols may be the *sine qua non* of giftedness. In the first half of this century, symbolization was conceived primarily in terms of verbal symbolization and measured by intelligence tests comprised in large part of verbal content. In the late 1950s cognitive psychologists began to define "symbols" more broadly. Today, psychologists and educators advocate the development of literacy in several symbol systems: words, numbers, music, dance, and the visual arts (Eisner, 1983; Gardner, 1982). Definitions of giftedness increasingly reflect this changed perspective.

Current Definitions of Giftedness. Many states have adopted a definition of giftedness similar to the federal definition cited previously (Van Tassel-Baska, 1981). However, some states that mandate special education for the gifted have adopted definitions that focus on intellectual or academic ability. Although the general trend is toward broadening definitions, it is, because of funding difficulties, a gradual trend. Gradual expansion allows state or local school systems with limited funds an opportunity to conduct needs assessments, document the benefits of established gifted programs, and build support for larger funding allocations.

Do any definitions of giftedness include motivation as a criterion?

Another approach to defining giftedness is reminiscent of Galton's conclusions about outstanding achievement. Taking into consideration the large body of research that shows that achievement is not solely a function of high ability, Renzulli (1978) defined giftedness as a combination of (1) above average ability, (2) task commitment, and (3) creativity. This definition includes children who may not have extremely high IQ scores but who are talented in areas not measured by IQ tests. On the other hand, it excludes children who have high IQ scores but are not exceptionally creative or committed to a field of interest.

One of the major considerations in acceptance of this definition is whether the gifted program staff views task commitment as a given or as a quality that develops as students become expert in subjects in which they are interested and capable. Advocates of a definition that inclues task commitment, or motivation to achieve, point out that some gifted children never fulfill their potential and that talent alone does not determine success. Advocates of a definition that requires only evidence of superior ability are likely to subscribe to the view that if an appropriate education is provided, the task commitment will develop. There is research that supports this view as well, in that motivation improves as mastery over a discipline increases (Bloom, 1976).

The theoretical perspectives and pragmatic considerations important to the person or agency defining giftedness determine whether the federal definition, Renzulli's definition, Terman's definition, or another is adopted; but, as mentioned earlier, the issue is important because the definition determines who will receive special education. Each of the definitions discussed in this section describes overlapping but somewhat distinct populations of children; the characteristics of those populations suggest the types of indentification procedures, programs, and instruction that should be provided to gifted students.

PROBE 12-1
Definitions and Need for Programs

1. T   F   Gifted children seldom drop out of school.

2. T   F   Most gifted disadvantaged children are identified by using traditional assessment methods.

3. T   F   Gifted children consistently excel in school whether they receive special provisions or not.

4. List three common misconceptions about gifted children and programs for them.

5. Following the work of Lewis Terman in the 1920s, giftedness was often determined solely on the basis of _____ .

6. T   F   Some educators believe that high motivation is a necessary element in defining giftedness.

CHARACTERISTICS OF GIFTED CHILDREN

You should be able to describe the distinctive characteristics of gifted children.

No two children are alike, and there is great diversity among gifted children. Nevertheless, there are some traits that many gifted children share; knowledge of these traits enables educators to identify the gifted and place them in the most appropriate programs.

As you read this section, keep in mind that most of the studies designed to discover characteristics of gifted children have been based on samples composed largely of white, middle-, or upper-class children who are high achiev-

Kam Hunter as a twelve-year-old sophomore in the Honors College of Michigan State University. Obviously too young to play football, he participated as a student manager.

ers. The characteristics of these high-achieving gifted children are not necessarily descriptive of underachieving gifted children who are economically disadvantaged or members of another minority group.

INTELLECTUAL ABILITY

What are intellectually gifted children like?

Intellectually gifted children have many abilities that make them likely to succeed academically. They can memorize rapidly and retain what they have learned; they read with superior comprehension and often begin reading at an early age. They see relationships among ideas and have an advanced vocabulary (Ehrlich, 1982; Terman and Oden, 1947). These abilities enable them to master the basic school curriculum more quickly than other children. In fact, an early researcher in the field of gifted education (Hollingworth, 1942) estimated that children with IQ scores of 140 and above could master the 12 years of school in ½ to ¼ of the time. A large body of research documents that there is indeed a large discrepancy between the rate at which gifted children learn and the pace at which material is presented to them (Daurio, 1979). The lockstep nature of public instruction, in effect, tends to "normalize" gifted students by instructing them at a level two or more years below the level at which they could learn comfortably. The needs of children with such exceptional learning ability cannot be met without significant advancement of their education program.

Learning Preferences. Personality characteristics attributed to gifted students also suggest changes that should be made in their educational program. One of the most commonly cited qualities is an almost insatiable curiosity about a variety of subjects (Ehrlich, 1982; Terman and Oden, 1947). Because of this inquisitiveness, gifted children welcome instruction on topics such as geometry, astronomy, foreign languages, and others that may not be included in the regular school program at their grade level. The high levels of independence (Lucito, 1964) and motivation (Ehrlich, 1982) of many gifted students suggest that they are capable of planning and carrying out special interest projects without much supervision, and that they should be given opportunity for independent study. Their interest in abstract ideas (Hildreth, 1966) can cause gifted children to object to rote memory assignments and drill at least as strenuously as other children object to them, if not more so (Whitmore, 1980). The intellectually gifted excel in classes that offer opportunity for analysis, argument, and debate.

Are intellectually gifted children misfits?

Adaptive Behavior. The social and emotional development of intellectually gifted children generally equals or exceeds that of other children their age (Gallagher, 1975). Research on high-achieving gifted students shows that they are self-sufficient, resourceful, participate in many extracurricular activities, and tend to be well liked by other children, at least at the elementary school level (Gallagher, 1975; Terman and Oden, 1947).

These positive traits should not lead you to believe that gifted children are "superchildren," however. They have many problems in common with other children and some distinct problems resulting from feelings of being different. A teacher of gifted children reports, "They often get pressure because they're bright or different. They are not the elitists they're criticized for being. They're struggling for their own identities" (Maunder, 1977, p. 8). Pressure to conform and outright hostility may threaten the gifted child's social and emotional adjustment and result in the bitterness and frustration evident in this remark by a highly gifted student: "If I offend people just by existing that is not my fault" (Nevin, 1977, p. 81).

Gifted children sometimes contribute to their own alienation by being harshly critical of others. In contrast, many gifted children are too critical of themselves (Whitmore, 1980). These children need help in accepting failure as a valuable part of learning because it signals the need for renewed effort and suggests direction for the new effort to take. In short, gifted children need the same understanding and encouragement that all children need.

CREATIVITY

The nature and processes of creativity have been studied in a variety of ways by psychologists interested in defining and developing human capacities for original thought. In spite of extensive research on the subject, however, many issues are still unresolved. Researchers have found a positive correlation between intelligence as measured by IQ tests and creativity as measured by original work in science (Roe, 1953), creative writing (Gallagher, 1975), and performance on tests of divergent thinking (Torrance, 1974). Above average intelligence, although not necessarily in the very superior range, appears to be important in creative endeavors. However, special skills, certain personality traits, or a combination of both, appear to contribute an element of creative performance not explained by above average intelligence.

Are creativity and intelligence related?

Measuring Creativity. The requirements for creative accomplishment vary across disciplines (Gardner, 1982); different skills are needed for creativity in drama than are needed for creativity in physics or music, for example. However, the possibility that some cognitive or affective traits are common to creativity across all disciplines has formed a basic assumption in efforts to identify creative potential in young children. This assumption is, in part, a function of the desire to predict superior creativity rather than to judge creative accomplishment. Because children are not often highly skilled in a particular discipline, educators interested in early identification and development of creativity use instruments based on traits associated with creative products, processes, or persons (Callahan, 1978). The most commonly used cognitive tests of creativity measure *divergent thinking ability,* which is characterized by many original responses to questions or problems (Torrance, 1974).

What is divergent thinking?

Divergent thinking contrasts with convergent thinking, which seeks "correct" responses to questions or problems. High scorers on tests of divergent thinking, such as Torrance's (1966) *Test of Creative Thinking,* produce many unusual answers to questions that require imagination and knowledge. "List some ways to change textbooks to make them more interesting," or "List inventions that could be made by combining a video recorder and a typewriter," are examples of divergent thinking tasks similar to those used on both standardized and teacher-made tests of creativity.

How do children superior in divergent thinking differ from other children?

Learning Preferences. Studies show that children who earn high scores on divergent thinking tests share certain characteristics. They are intellectually playful, have a reputation for wild ideas, and respond to assignments in a novel way (Torrance, 1962). These children generally prefer loosely structured, open-ended learning activities that allow them to develop and express their own ideas (Torrance, 1974). Moreover, Strom and Torrance (1973) found that students who were good at divergent thinking not only expressed a strong dislike for programmed instruction, which is highly structured, they also learned less from that type of instruction than did other children. Not surprisingly, creative children sometimes become impatient with the routine in the regular classroom. As one highly creative child put it, "It's amazing how difficult a subject becomes if you study it slowly enough" (Aschner and Bish, 1965, p. 233).

SPECIAL TALENTS

What is "talent"?

Although the terms "giftedness" and "talent" are used interchangeably throughout this chapter, "talent" is often used to refer to specialized ability. Any discussion of talent, used in that sense, raises the issue of general intellectual ability versus special abilities. That musically gifted children, mathematically gifted children, and other children with exceptional aptitude in a particular field are likely to score above average on an IQ test has been determined by many research studies (Tannenbaum, 1983). It has also been found that children identified as gifted according to intelligence test scores tend to score above average on tests of special ability (Gallagher, 1975). However, there are many children who would qualify as gifted on the basis of their IQ score and not on the basis of a special aptitude test, and vice versa. Some children, of course, would qualify as gifted under either criterion (Hildreth, 1966; Stanley, 1977; Tannenbaum, 1983). Since most studies of children with special talents include many children with IQ scores in the highest percentiles, you should not be surprised to find that the characteristics of children identified as gifted in a specific field are similar to those discussed under intellectual ability. In addition, the characteristics attributed to one group of children with special abilities are also often attributed to children with other kinds of special ability.

Academic Talent. The children who are talented in academic areas are most likely to share skills common to those children who score high on IQ tests. Stanley (1976, p. 81) reported: "It would be rare, indeed, for a person to have excellent mathematical reasoning ability and yet be inferior to average thinkers in verbal reasoning ability. . . . Though its (Study of Mathematically Precocious Youth) participants are not chosen explicitly for high IQ, virtually none of them have average or below-average IQs."

Bloom (1982) found that mathematicians who enjoy an international reputation for their ability were, as children, characterized by (1) the abundance of questions they began asking at a very early age; (2) a great deal of time spent in solitary play; and (3) a proclivity for independent learning through books and observation of others. These characteristics, particularly preference for reading as a way to spend leisure time (see, e.g., Van Tassel-Baska, 1983), recur throughout the literature, not only in regard to mathematically talented children but to children with verbal ability and children who excel in science.

Although mathematically gifted boys and girls value theoretical pursuits and are less likely to seek as much social stimulation as more extroverted children seem to desire, they are as socially adroit and comfortable as most other children (Haier and Denham, 1976). Children who are identified on the basis of exceptional verbal ability also seem to value abstract ideas more than do other children their age (Fox, 1976). Although both groups are self-confident, girls who are identified as gifted on the basis of their mathematical ability tend to be much more unconventional than other girls of high ability (Haier and Denham, 1976).

Artistic Talent. Promising art students share with these children a preference for theoretical and aesthetic pursuits (Getzels, 1979). Ability to work alone and a preference for solitude may be important to outstanding achievement in both scholarly and artistic pursuits (Getzels, 1977).

The artistic disciplines that have received the most attention in the research literature on gifted children are music and the visual arts. Although artistically gifted children may be less likely to exhibit traits common to high-IQ children than are academically gifted children, there is still considerable overlap between the groups. This seems to be particularly true in music, which is a special interest of both mathematically and verbally gifted students (Van Tassel-Baska, 1983). One of the mathematically precocious students identified in the Johns Hopkins Study of Mathematically Precocious Youth project was recognized as the most outstanding high school composer of classical music in the United States (Getzels, 1977).

The characteristics that extremely talented musicians' parents report as distinguishing their children are a natural feeling for music and a great sensitivity and emotional responsiveness to it. At a young age, these gifted musicians were able to play by ear, and some displayed perfect pitch (Bloom, 1982). Specific attributes that may contribute to the general traits described by Bloom (1982) are (1) acute auditory sense, which allows discrimination of fine differences in tonal pitch, loudness, and timbre; and (2) tonal memory, which allows retention for comparative and reproductive purposes (Capurso, 1961).

The student who is gifted in the visual arts possesses traits analogous to those of the musically gifted student. Acute powers of observation, a vivid visual memory, a keen sense of color, and enjoyment of artwork are characteristics ascribed to promising artists (Tannenbaum, 1983).

Whatever the field, ability to learn new techniques, ideas, and processes

rapidly seems to be critical to the development of a high level of talent (Bloom, 1982). Researchers who have studied prodigious, specialized ability emphasize the role that early and increasingly advanced instruction seems to play in developing talent (Bloom, 1982; Feldman, 1979; Pressey, 1955). Bloom (1982) reported that among the world-class talented persons he studied, at least ten years of their life had been devoted to development of their talent. For at least that many years, the majority of their time and energy was devoted to that end.

Ability in the two other major arts, drama and dance, has received less attention in the literature on gifted education than has ability in music and the visual arts. We know less about the characteristics of children who are talented in these areas than about the academically gifted, the musically gifted, and children who are gifted in the visual arts. Some of the characteristics attributed to these groups are summarized in Table 12-1.

Table 12-1
Characteristics of Children with Special Talents

Talent Area	Abilities	Personality Attributes
Mathematics	Ability to manipulate symbolic material more effectively and more rapidly than classmates	Highly independent Enjoy theoretical and investigative pursuits Talented girls less conforming than general population
Science	Ability to see relationships among ideas, events, and objects Elegance in explanation; the ability to formulate the simplest hypothesis that can account for the observed facts	Highly independent "Loners" Prefer intellectually rather than socially challenging situations Reject group pressures Methodical, precise, exact Avid readers
Language Arts	Capability of manipulating abstract concepts, but sometimes inferior to the high general achiever in working with mathematical material Imagination and originality	Highly independent Social and aesthetic values (girls) Theoretical and political values (boys) Avid readers
Leadership	Ability to effect positive and productive change Good decision-making ability Proficiency in some area, such as athletics or academics Ability to communicate	Empathic Sensitive Charismatic — can transform the group through their enthusiasm and energy Superior communication skills

Table 12-1 (*cont.*)

Talent Area	Abilities	Personality Attributes
Psychomotor Ability	Gross motor strength, agility, flexibility, coordination, and speed Excellence in athletics, gymnastics, or dance Fine motor control, deftness, precision, flexibility, and speed Excellence in crafts — jewelry making, model building, mechanics, working with electronic equipment, etc. Ability to use complicated equipment with little or no training	Enjoy and seem to need considerable exercise Competitive Interested in mechanics, electronics, or crafts Have hobbies such as model building, origami, pottery
Visual or Performing Arts	Ability to disregard traditional methods in favor of their own original ones Resourcefulness in use of materials Ability to express their feelings through an art form Attention to detail in their own and others' artwork	Self-confident Competitive Prefer working alone Sensitive to their environment Gain satisfaction through expressing their feelings artistically Responsive to music, sculpture, etc.

Sources: Bloom, 1982; Ellison, Abe, Fox, Corey, and Taylor, 1976; Kough and DeHaan, 1958; Kranz, n.d.; Lindsay, 1977; Passow and Goldberg, 1962; Renzulli and Hartman, 1971; Roe, 1953; Stanley, George, and Solano, 1977.

Leadership. The federal definition of giftedness mentions another group that has received relatively little attention in schools' efforts to identify talented students: children with leadership ability. Some characteristics of this group, too, are included in Table 12-1; however, there has been less research on these children than on intellectually, academically, and artistically gifted children. This is, in part, because of the difficulty in distinguishing between sociability and leadership in young children. Identification of gifted leaders is problematic in that leadership, apart from a discipline in which to lead, seems to rely on traits associated with popularity. These traits may be irrelevant to skills needed to effect significant change in an important area. Identification for programs **What is leadership ability?** which seek to develop leadership ability usually entails peer nomination, teacher referral, and, less often, parent nomination (e.g., Epstein, 1979).

Psychomotor Ability. Although psychomotor ability is not mentioned in the definition of giftedness under PL 95-561, it was specified as an area of giftedness as defined in a United States Office of Education report to the Congress (Marland, 1972). Because psychomotor skill is important in many disciplines, traits associated with superior psychomotor ability are also provided in Table 12-1.

Since the definition of giftedness offered in the 1972 national survey on gifted education first referred to specific abilities, children with specialized talent have received increasing attention. Educators such as Stanley (1976), and Feldman (1979) suggest that schools should direct their attention to specific disciplines rather than global mental abilities in identifying and instructing gifted students.

PROBE 12-2
Characteristics of Gifted Children

1. T F Most intellectually gifted children are less emotionally and socially mature than other children their age.

2. The personality trait shared by children with high intellectual ability, specific academic ability, and creativity (See Table 12-1) is that they tend to be _____ .

3. Which of the following requires divergent thinking?
   a. As president of the United States, what would you do to solve the energy shortage problem?
   b. What were Mercutio's final lines in his famous death scene in *Romeo and Juliet?*
   c. What were the major causes of the Great Depression?

4. Describe the relationship between intelligence test scores and performance on measures of special ability.

5. Identify which kind of giftedness the following statements typify:
   a. Among her activities were membership in the debate society, the National Honor Society, and the band; still, her favorite pastime is reading.
   b. When asked what procedure should be followed, she had well-organized, goal-oriented suggestions to offer.
   c. Classmates are often critical of her original, sometimes bizarre, ideas and behavior.

6. T F Instruction plays only a minor role in development of outstanding talent.

7. The type of ability omitted from the federal definition of giftedness is. . . .
   a. creative ability
   b. leadership ability
   c. artistic ability
   d. psychomotor ability

IDENTIFYING GIFTED CHILDREN

> **You should be able to describe methods of identifying gifted children.**

IDENTIFICATION PROCEDURES

What are three stages in the identification process?

The definition of giftedness and characteristics of the student population subsumed by the definition guide the selection and development of identification methods. In general, the more kinds of ability included in the definition, the more complex the procedures needed to identify children who qualify for gifted education. No matter what definition is used, however, there are three overlapping but distinguishable stages in the identification process: (1) referral, (2) screening, and (3) evaluation.

Referral. The initial step in the identification process is the referral stage. At this stage, the names of children who may need special education are submitted to personnel responsible for screening and evaluation. Common referral strategies are (1) observation of performance in the classroom, (2) review of students' records of past performance, such as standardized achievement test scores, awards, grades, and anecdotal reports, and (3) completion of behavior checklists or rating scales by teachers, parents, peers, or the students under consideration for placement.

Is it easy to recognize which children should be referred for possible placement?

Unfortunately, many children who could qualify for gifted education are never referred because teachers have difficulty recognizing some students' exceptional ability (Jacobs, 1971; Pegnato and Birch, 1959; Whitmore, 1980). This difficulty is because, in part, the curriculum in the classroom is often at a level too low to elicit the advanced skills possessed by gifted children (Stanley, 1976). It also results from the influence of extraneous factors on teacher judgment of children's intellectual ability. For example, teachers tend to perceive children who participate readily in new learning activities as brighter than children who are more reluctant to participate (Roedell, Robinson, and Jackson, 1980); and attractive children tend to be given higher teacher ratings on intellectual ability than are unattractive children (Ysseldyke and Algozzine, 1982). Another difficulty stems from the fact that some gifted children achieve far below their ability level (Whitmore, 1980).

For reasons such as these, parents appear to be better at identifying superior ability in their children than are the children's teachers, at least in kindergarten and the early grades (Jacobs, 1971; Roedell, Robinson, and Jackson, 1980). Soliciting referrals from parents, as well as teachers and students, increases the possibility of locating talent at every grade level.

How can the effectiveness and efficiency of referrals be improved?

Questionnaires or behavior checklists are sometimes used to guide the observation of persons who are making the referral (Borland, 1978). Whether in the form of checklists, questionnaires, or rating scales, descriptions of characteristic behaviors or traits must be specific and must distinguish gifted children from other children (Roedell, Robinson, and Jackson, 1980). Specific items, such as "Does your child comment on words that have two or more meanings?" (Roedell, Robinson, and Jackson, 1980, p. 58), offer more guidance to the person rating the child than general descriptions such as "Has a good memory." Items that are too general are not reliable indicators of giftedness in that they can be interpreted in several ways.

Specificity alone is not sufficient to offer guidance to observers; the items must also correlate positively with superior performance on the measures used for screening and evaluation. To the extent that the behaviors on the checklist fail to correlate with those measures, they fail to identify gifted children and result in the referral of children who do not qualify for placement.

Since no referral procedures allow perfect correlation with performance on screening and evaluation instruments, testing all students at certain grade levels to identify children who may be gifted is an established practice in many school systems. Another practice used to increase the number of referrals that result in placement is the provision of programs or in-service training workshops to inform teachers and parents of the characteristics of gifted children and the procedures for referring children for screening or evaluation (Borland, 1978).

What are some strategies used to screen referrals?

Screening. Screening consists of the collection and review of easily obtainable information to determine the likelihood that the referred student will qualify according to evaluation criteria. This intermediate stage is sometimes combined with the referral process when, for example, teachers are asked to refer only children with test scores above a certain level. Common screening strategies are (1) administration of aptitude, intelligence, or achievement tests that do not require a psychologist to administer and interpret; (2) review, by a gifted education teacher or subject matter specialist, of work samples such as poems, essays, or musical compositions written by the referred student; and (3) review of checklists, rating scales, or questionnaires to determine eligibility for further evaluation.

Screening is required when evaluation measures are too time-consuming and costly to administer to all children referred to the program. This is often the case when specialized or noninstructional personnel such as psychologists, educational diagnosticians, or professional artists are needed for a comprehensive, in-depth evaluation.

As in referral, the screening process seeks maximum effectiveness and efficiency by including measures that identify as many children as possible who will qualify for placement while identifying as few children as possible who will not qualify. Selection or development of appropriate screening instruments and evaluation of the instruments' usefulness are essential elements of procedures to identify gifted children.

EVALUATION

The final stage in the identification process consists of collecting and analyzing information to determine referred children's eligibility for gifted education programs. Evaluation often consists of a comprehensive measure of ability and a committee review of relevant referral and screening information. Common evaluation strategies are (1) individual administration of a comprehensive intelligence test (Martinson, 1974); (2) auditions or review of student portfolios or projects (Mills and Ridlon, 1980); (3) administration of high-level achievement tests (George and Solano, 1976); and (4) analysis of case studies of children referred for placement (Renzulli and Smith, 1977). A summary of commonly used methods of evaluation is included in Table 12-2.

What are the results of using "multitalent" vs. "depth" approaches to determine placement eligibility?

Placement criteria usually represent either (1) a multitalent approach to determining eligibility or (2) an approach that seeks to locate the highest level of performance on a measure of talent. The former places greater emphasis on breadth or on high, but not necessarily outstanding, performance on a number of measures. The latter focuses on outstanding level of ability, or depth (Dirks and Quarforth, 1981). If a breadth model is used, students must qualify on more than one measure. They might, for example, qualify on the basis of superior scores on three out of five measures: grades, intelligence test, creativity test, achievement test, rating scale. This approach tends to identify students who are well-rounded achievers and to exclude children who are underachievers (Dirks and Quarforth, 1981). The depth approach may use a single-criterion model, which requires a high level of performance on a particular measure, such as an IQ test; or it may offer alternative placement criteria. In the latter instance, students must score in the highest range on any one of several measures, such as IQ tests, aptitude tests, or rating scales in order to qualify for special education. The depth model allows inclusion of children who score very high on one measure regardless of their performance on other measures. State or local educational priorities usually determine whether a breadth or depth model is used in evaluation of gifted children.

CONSIDERATIONS FOR SELECTING IDENTIFICATION INSTRUMENTS

Regardless of the evaluation model employed in determining eligibility for placement, the referral, screening, and evaluation instruments are the key factors in efforts to identify gifted students.

What are some limitations of the usefulness of IQ tests?

For many years, virtually the only way students could gain entrance into most gifted programs was by getting a high score on an IQ test. Although IQ scores are still considered important by most educators involved in the iden-

Table 12-2
Summary of Commonly Used Methods of Evaluation

Method	Strengths	Limitations	Comments
Teacher evaluation via behavior checklists or questionnaires	Familiar with student's work. Familiar with "normal" performance for grade level.	Teacher perceptions may be influenced by irrelevant factors such as appearance, willingness to conform, and attitudes toward classwork.	Teachers may fail to recognize as many as half the gifted students. Teacher nomination may be improved through in-service training on the characteristics of gifted children.
Peer evaluation via behavior checklists or questionnaires	Familiar with student's work. May be aware of interests or abilities of which the teacher is unaware.	Students' perceptions may be influenced by whether they like or dislike their classmate and whether or not the teacher appears to like their classmate.	Little research has been done on the effectiveness of peer evaluation.
Parent evaluation via behavior checklists or questionnaires	Familiar with child's development, interests, and abilities.	Parents may not know how their child's behavior compares with that of other children of the same age.	In kindergarten and at the primary level, parents may be better than teachers at identifying gifted children.
Grades	Information is readily available.	Review of grades fails to identify underachievers and children who are gifted in nonacademic areas.	Referral of children with an average of "B" or better results in the inclusion of most gifted children, but many nongifted children are referred as well.
Work samples	Can be collected in all talent areas, including the visual or performing arts.	Requires availability of experts such as music teachers and art teachers to judge the work sample.	Work samples reflect both the student's ability and commitment.

Table 12-2 (*cont.*)

Method	Strengths	Limitations	Comments
Interest inventories	Seem to be more "culture-fair" than IQ or achievement tests.	Ability level may not be as high as interest level.	One of the few measures that reflect commitment to an area of art or science.
Achievement tests	Indicate academic aptitude in particular subject areas. Test scores are usually on record in children's cumulative folders. They are a readily available source of information.	May fail to identify underachievers, especially children from culturally different environments and gifted handicapped children.	Success on most achievement tests requires superior verbal comprehension.
Group intelligence tests	Can indicate aptitude even when achievement is low. Test scores are often on record in children's cumulative folders.	If high cutoff points (e.g., 130 IQ or above) are used, as many as half the gifted children may be overlooked. Fails to differentiate the highly gifted from the moderately gifted.	For screening purposes, a relatively low cutoff point such as 115 IQ can reduce the number of gifted children missed.
Creativity tests	Usually considered more "culture-fair" than IQ or achievement tests.	Administration and interpretation often require special personnel. May be difficult to distinguish "original" but relevant responses from "bizarre" and irrelevant responses.	The relationship between ability to do well on a creativity test and consistent, outstanding creative performance hasn't been established.

(continued on following page)

Table 12-2 (*cont.*)

Method	Strengths	Limitations	Comments
Individual intelligence tests	Is most reliable single indicator of intellectual giftedness in middle- and upper-class socioeconomic levels. Many individual tests measure both verbal and nonverbal ability.	Require special personnel for administration and interpretation. Can be biased against minority groups and gifted handicapped children. Fail to assess important abilities such as specific artistic or academic aptitude.	Interpretation of the quality and character of responses by a competent tester can provide considerable insight into a child's ability.

tification of exceptionally able students, the use of the IQ score as the single, determining factor in identification has been harshly criticized. One of the most compelling criticisms is that the tests are biased against children who are not from white middle- or upper-class homes. Another is that IQ tests (particularly group IQ tests) often lack a sufficient number of questions difficult enough to distinguish the relatively few gifted children from other children who are above average in ability but not so significantly advanced as to require a highly differentiated program of instruction.

Are IQ tests diagnostic instruments?

Test Bias Against Minorities. IQ tests do not tap an innate dimension psychologically distinct from that reflected by achievement test scores (Mercer, 1981). Rather, they are distinguished primarily in that they draw from a broader domain of experience than do tests that are limited to particular subject areas. Intelligence tests are useful prognostic devices in that they predict scholastic performance with fair reliability; but they do not identify the cause of scholastic success or failure. Mercer (1981, p. 69) contends that IQ tests ". . . have been interpreted as if they yielded diagnostic information on the cause of the predicted outcome. Mental retardation, for example, is a diagnosis frequently made on the basis of performance on a single test that was designed as a prognostic measure."

Are non-verbal tests culture-fair?

The solution to the problem of test bias is not through development of culture-fair tests; in fact, it is clear that no test can be culture-fair (Mercer, 1981). Although some educators advocate the use of nonverbal tests on the grounds that they are less culturally biased, their use in identification of gifted children is not a satisfactory solution: In many instances, minority students tend to score lower on nonverbal tests, relative to majority norms, than on verbal IQ tests (Martinson, 1974; Sternberg, 1982).

Although some creativity tests offer the advantage that they do not penalize children from minority groups to as great a degree as IQ tests (Torrance, 1971), it is not clear that scores on creativity tests predict outstanding creative accomplishment. Therefore, their usefulness in planning educational programs for children who earn high scores is limited (Roedell, Jackson, and Robinson, 1980). Certainly, high creativity test scores should not be a determiner of eligibility for placement in a gifted program.

Establishment of separate norms for large minority groups or for economically disadvantaged schools is a promising solution to the problem of test bias. Using this approach, the highest-scoring 2 to 5 percent (for example), of the minority students might be identified as gifted even though their test scores are not in the highest percentiles according to the majority population on which the test was originally standardized. Limiting comparison to children with similar backgrounds is a strategy successfully used in projects designed to identify gifted disadvantaged children (e.g., Maker, Morris, and James, 1981).

Do all IQ tests adequately reflect children's intellectual strengths?

Low Test Ceilings. Most tests do not have enough difficult questions to distinguish the most brilliant children from other bright children. The result of this phenomenon is that two children with very different abilities may earn the same score on a test. A score of 124 IQ on a particular test, for example, may be reported for many children the same age, each having missed approximately the same number of questions on the test. However, the instrument tested the limits of some students' knowledge, while others might have been able to answer much more advanced questions. Since there were no higher-level questions on the test, both groups received the same score; yet, because of differences in their ability, the students would need quite different educational programs.

What is a solution to the problem of low test ceilings?

This problem applies to all standardized measures: achievement, aptitude, and IQ tests; but it can be avoided where higher-level tests are available, even though the tests may have been designed for older students. The Study of Mathematically Precocious Youth (Stanley and Benbow, 1982) relies on off-level testing to identify gifted children. Using the mathematical section of the College Entrance Examination Board's *Scholastic Aptitude Test* (SAT-M), the project identifies elementary and junior-high-school-aged students with extraordinary mathematical ability. According to Julian Stanley (1976), who initiated the project, "The harder tests spread out the top 2 percent over a wide range from good through excellent to superb. . . . Teachers may be able to identify the upper 1 percent or 2 percent by observation and with the aid of in-grade tests, but they can hardly be expected to find the top 1 in 200 or 500 or 10,000 without special assistance" (p. 313).

Identification of gifted children is one of the most important tasks facing educators who are interested in talent development. If exceptionally able children are not identified as gifted, it is unlikely that they will be provided an education that develops their abilities. Unfortunately, identification is as difficult as it is important. No single test can be relied on to identify giftedness. Educators responsible for identification determine which combination of assessment methods is most appropriate for the population defined as gifted in their schools and for the individual child who may qualify according to that definition. Factors such as the age, background, personality, and type of ability of the child must be weighed against the advantages and disadvantages of different instruments.

Important considerations in selecting and developing procedures and instruments that can be combined in the identification of gifted children are (1) the validity and reliability of the tests and checklists proposed for use in the referral, screening, and evaluation process, (2) alternative procedures, such as separate norms, for ethnic or racial minorities, economically disadvantaged, and handicapped students, and (3) tests that have high ceilings to assure adequate measurement of the extent of the referred students' mastery of advanced concepts.

What factors must be considered in selecting the best test or combination of tests for a particular child?

PROBE 12-3
Identifying Gifted Children

1. What are three steps in the identification process?

2. Give an example of an activity that might occur at each of the steps in the identification process.

3. For very young children, _____ is often more effective than teacher nomination in identifying the gifted.

4. T F Teacher referrals may miss many of the gifted students.

5. Give an example of a *poor* item that might appear on a gifted behavior checklist and tell why it is poor.

6. Write a better item for a gifted behavior checklist.

7. T F The multitalent approach to identification may miss highly gifted children who are not well-rounded in their interests.

8. T F In general, disadvantaged children perform better on nonverbal tests of intelligence.

9. Using tests designed for older students to identify young gifted students is an attempt to offset the problem of a _____ on tests designed for children the same age as the children to be identified.

10. T F Creativity tests are clearly superior to other measures in identifying children with potential to make original contributions in the arts and sciences.

EDUCATIONAL PROVISIONS FOR GIFTED CHILDREN

> **You should be able to describe the educational practices that are appropriate for gifted children.**

BARRIERS TO ACHIEVEMENT

What are some reasons for underachievement in gifted students?

Because instruction tends to be directed to the average achievement level for each grade in a school, meeting the educational needs of the most talented students requires modification of their program. For many of these students, underachievement is simply an effect of an instructional level that is too easy and an instructional pace that is too slow. For some students, however, there are additional barriers to achievement. Debilitating family circumstances, social stereotypes, or physical impairments render these students more vulnerable to the effects of inappropriate instruction. Special education includes strategies that recognize and address the major factors that place these students at risk for academic failure.

Inconsistent or Inappropriate Expectations at Home and in the Classroom. Damon is in the sixth grade. His unusual intellectual capacity is reflected by his high IQ score, 130 on the Stanford-Binet Intelligence Scale, and by his ready grasp of abstract ideas, reasoning ability, and insight into relationships between facts. However, Damon does C or D work in most of his subjects; since the second grade, his work has fallen far short of his intellectual capability.

Damon's written work is messy and almost always incomplete. He resents having to redo his papers and uses any excuse to get out of going to school. His parents and teachers have tried punishing, encouraging, coaxing, and lecturing to get him to try harder. When asked why he doesn't do well in class, Damon usually responds that classwork is boring, the teacher doesn't like him, and that he isn't all that smart anyway.

Damon is typical of a group of gifted underachievers who have been the subject of a great deal of research. Most of the research on the bright, middle-class underachievers was conducted during the period from the 1940s to the mid-1960s, when definitions of giftedness were based largely on intelligence test scores. Because the children studied had IQ scores in the 90th percentile and above, researchers looked for factors that affected the children's motivation and commitment to achieving in school. Among the factors investigated were personality traits, parent-child interactions, and attitudes toward school.

Although most of Terman's gifted children (Terman and Oden, 1947) grew up to be outstandingly productive adults, some of his subjects had a history of underachievement that began in the primary grades and continued throughout their lives. These students could be consistently differentiated from gifted achievers by four qualities: (1) inability or unwillingness to persist to achieve goals; (2) lack of integration of goals and a tendency toward purposelessness; (3) lack of self-confidence, and (4) feelings of inferiority (Terman and Oden, 1947).

Other studies have confirmed Terman's results. For example, in a study reported in *Able Misfits* (Pringle, 1970), lack of confidence was found to be the personality trait most frequently associated with underachieving gifted children. Some other personality traits associated with underachievement are immaturity, irresponsibility, and rigidity (Crow and Crow, 1959; Pringle, 1970). A study of highly intelligent dropouts, however, found the male dropouts more assertive and more independent, if more rebellious, than equally bright boys who stayed in school (French, 1975).

Although poor study habits and inconsistent work characterize gifted underachievers' school performance (Rimm, 1984), a plausible explanation for their negative attitude toward school is that, for various reasons, some gifted children have not learned that effort makes a difference in their academic performance (Rimm, 1984; Whitmore, 1980). According to Rimm (1984, p. 2), "Underachieving children don't believe that they could achieve even if they made appropriate efforts."

The reasons for the underachievers' negative attitude toward school have not been established, but poor parent-child relationships appear to be a contributing factor. Parents of gifted underachievers are often rejecting and inconsistent in their methods of discipline (Raph, Goldberg, and Passow, 1966).

What are some strategies for improving underachievers' performance?

Counseling gifted children and their parents, however, has not consistently resulted in improved performance (Gallagher, 1975). Educational modifications seem to have been more successful. Perhaps this is because the classroom as well as the home environment contributes to underachievement. Primary-grade-level underachievers identified by Whitmore (1980) report that several characteristics of the classroom have a debilitating effect on their performance; these factors include pressure to conform, a competitive climate, and the judgmental attitude of their teachers. Low teacher expectations and presentation of academic material below their conceptual level also contribute to gifted students' underachievement. Greater emphasis on academics can improve gifted students' underachievement so that they make nearly as much progress during the school year as do gifted achievers (Fearn, 1982).

The best way to remove the barriers to achievement may be to use a combination of methods. The Cupertino School District in California combined remediation behavior modification, techniques of self-control, and a stimulating curriculum in a supportive setting to create a program that has met with unusual success (Whitmore, 1980). The results of this program and others have implications for teachers (Gallagher, 1975; Whitmore, 1980):

—Don't give the students lectures or "pep talks" to get them to try harder. This has been shown to have detrimental effects on achievement.
—Show support and respect for the student's efforts.

— Establish appropriate standards and provide the instruction, guidance, and support to help students meet them.
— Encourage cooperation, rather than competition, in the classroom.
— Reward small gains in achievement and don't expect quick success.

What are some identified strengths of culturally different children?

Inadequate Exposure to the Cultural "Mainstream." Because of cultural biases in testing and instruction, many gifted children who are not from the white middle class are not identified and don't receive instruction that could develop their talents. Torrance (1977) suggests that these children should not be expected to exhibit the same strengths as white middle-class children; we should instead seek strengths that reflect their experiences. These strengths may include the ability to improvise with commonplace materials, responsiveness to concrete materials, and expressiveness in speech (Torrance, 1977). An example of the creative expressiveness of a young Appalachian student in a program for culturally different gifted children is provided in Hauck and Freehill's *The Gifted — Case Studies* (1972, p. 99):

The Worst Punishment for a Man
by
Junior ⎯⎯⎯⎯⎯

Sitting here at my desk, it seems that the day will never end. It's just now 3:30 P.M. and I have a conference with the Secretary of State at 4:00 P.M., at 5:00 P.M. a conference with Mike Mansfield and Senator Long. Oh God, I am tired. I'm not as young as I once was. The pages of history may contain but a paragraph about my life or my work, but at least I sure's hell have won the paragraph. "More critics than any U.S. President ever" — that's what the papers say. It seems nobody's satisfied with what I do. Viet Nam is really a hellava mess — and guess who gets all the blame for everything — me: Damn it! When will those demonstrators with the long hair and low morals and the intellectuals with no common sense learn that if we leave that little nation we are breaking our word, breaking our commitments, giving the communists another base of strength? Oh, damn it! Nobody listens to me . . . and this election coming up — McCarthy, Wallace and all the other S.O.B.'s who disapprove of the Great Society and how I try to run it. God help them though. Let one of 'em win — please. That's the worst punishment I can think of for a man — to be President of the United States.

The ability to see things from an unusual perspective, the concern for social issues, and the intellectual playfulness apparent in this composition illustrate the creativity sometimes found among children who come from environments not conducive to success in school. Special efforts must be made to counteract factors that can inhibit the performance of these children. These factors include (1) inexperience with the concepts and vocabulary of middle-class society; (2) the low expectations educators have for culturally different children; (3) the children's expectations of failure (Baldwin, Gear, and Lucito, 1978); and (4) the fact that achievement in school may conflict with peer loyalty (Hauck and Freehill, 1972).

What are some strategies for improving the academic performance of culturally different children?

The achievement of children from culturally different or economically disadvantaged environments can be improved by providing intensive, compensatory programs (Smilansky and Nevo, 1979) and by recognizing and developing the children's cognitive strengths (Maker, Morris, and James, 1981). Their achievement may also be improved by making teachers aware of the damaging effects that suppressed, but still prevalent, stereotypes and prejudice have on the performance of culturally different children (Thunberg, 1981).

Are some students both gifted and handicapped?

Handicaps and "Handicapism." Children can be both gifted and handicapped. Thomas Edison was deaf; Aldous Huxley was blind; Elizabeth Barrett Browning suffered from spinal injuries; and, according to some researchers, Einstein had learning disabilities. There is no handicapping condition that precludes giftedness. Talent has been found in every group, including the retarded. A recent discovery of giftedness among the handicapped was that of a Japanese boy with a reported IQ of 40, Yoshihiko Yamamoto (Figure 12-1), who won international acclaim for his artwork (Morishima, 1974). Using a broad definition of giftedness, June Maker, author of *Providing Programs for the Gifted Handicapped* (1977), suggests that the incidence of giftedness among the handicapped is 3 to 5 percent, about the same as in the nonhandicapped population.

Gifted handicapped children are often unusually difficult to identify, because a handicapping condition can mask unusual potential. For example, Krippner (1967) described the case of a deaf boy who was in a school for the mentally handicapped until he was 17 when he was discovered to be gifted — but only by accident. An employee of the institution happened to leave a transistor radio kit on a work table, and the handicapped youngster assembled it with ease.

The low expectations of many educators contribute to this failure to recognize giftedness in handicapped students. Low expectations not only prevent recognition of talent, they can destroy students' faith in their abilities. The low self-esteem that can result seems to be caused in part by the discrepancy between the extremely high goals gifted children set for themselves and the low expectations of others. Gifted handicapped adults suggest that educators who want to improve the performance of gifted handicapped children must expect more than mediocre performance (Maker, 1977).

How do boys and girls compare in school achievement?

Sex-Role Stereotypes. Research has yet to establish consistent differences in the intellectual ability of girls and boys, but there are significant differences in their achievement. Until puberty, when both boys and girls become more conscious of sex-role expectations, girls make better grades in all school subjects than do boys. Then, at the middle school or junior high school level,

Figure 12-1
Nagoya Castle, Produced by Yamamoto in the Ninth Grade

boys begin to outperform girls in mathematics and science, which are traditionally masculine pursuits (Horner, 1970). In math, the gap in achievement
continues to widen with age (Keating, 1976). As girls grow up they yield
progressively more to boys in achievement and competitiveness. Many
researchers feel that social stereotypes and expectations are responsible for
women's failure to pursue advanced study and careers commensurate with
their ability (Clark, 1983). Despite the feminist movement, girls are still
expected to be more conforming and less assertive than boys.

What are strategies for improving girls' achievement in traditionally masculine fields?

High general achievers and high arithmetic achievers are self-confident and
assertive (d'Heurle, Mellinger, and Haggard, 1959), but gifted girls tend to be
less self-confident than gifted boys. One study found that IQ was positively
correlated with expectations of success among boys, but the brighter a girl

was, the less well she expected to do (Morse, 1971). This lack of self-confidence may result from a conflict between characteristics of giftedness and society's perceptions of how a girl should behave. A recent research study on teacher and pupil stereotypes of gifted boys and girls (Solano, 1976) showed that although gifted boys are viewed favorably, gifted girls are viewed quite unfavorably. Disapproval by peers and teachers may undermine the confidence of bright girls.

Especially important to the achievement of gifted girls are (1) early entry into intellectually challenging programs, (2) provision of models that contradict sex-role stereotypes, and (3) provision of information about scholastic requirements for career alternatives in nonstereotypical disciplines (Callahan, 1979).

The following passage, written by Amelia Earhart earlier in this century, typifies the still-contemporary concern about the damaging effects of sex-role stereotypes:

> It has always seemed to me that boys and girls are educated very differently.
> . . . Too often little attention is paid to individual talent. Instead, education
> goes on dividing people according to their sex, and putting them in little feminine or masculine pigeonholes. Outside of school, similar differences are
> noticeable, too. In the home, boys and girls usually follow the pursuits which
> tradition has decreed for the one and the other. As different as what they do are
> ways of doing it. Girls are shielded and sometimes helped so much that they
> lose initiative and begin to believe the signs "Girls don't" and "girls can't"
> which mark their paths. Mrs. Bertrand Russell puts this fact very forcibly
> when she says women are bred to timidity. . . . Probably the most profound
> deterrent of all is tradition which keeps women from trying new things and
> from putting forth their whole effort.

PROGRAMS FOR GIFTED CHILDREN

Although there are many kinds of programs for gifted children, most of them have similar goals. Whether gifted children are placed in special schools, sent to resource rooms for part of the day, or given special assignments in the regular classroom, educational modifications are designed to

— Quicken the pace of learning by moving the students through activities faster than would be appropriate for children of average ability.
— Broaden the range of experiences and knowledge of gifted children by teaching subjects not offered in the regular curriculum at the children's grade level.
— Develop skills of analysis and expression in academic or artistic disciplines.
— Provide opportunity for concentrated, in-depth study of areas in which the students are especially interested or able.

How do horizontal and vertical programming differ?

As you will see from the descriptions of some of the most common types of programs in Chart 12-1, some programs emphasize one goal more than others. Programs that emphasize broadening the student's knowledge base can be described as *horizontal*. *Vertical* programs increase the pace of instruction or allow students to study more advanced subjects than in the regular program. Development of expressive and analytic skills is generally an important element of both types of program. It should be recognized that programs can be categorized according to their major emphasis. Few programs, however, consist entirely of horizontal or vertical experiences. Because no single program can meet the diverse needs of the talented children in a school system, every system needs a variety of program options (Feldhusen, 1982).

What are some methods for accomplishing the goals of gifted education?

Program Options. The goals of gifted education are accomplished through a combination of (1) grouping arrangements; (2) developmental placement based on consideration of individual students' achievement level and conceptual, physical, and social development (Christopherson, 1981); and (3) special activities in the regular classroom. Research offers stronger support for the first two approaches than for the third. Grouping bright children in homoge-

Chart 12-1
Programs for Gifted Children

Horizontal Programs	*Vertical Programs*
Exploration	*Acceleration*
Often used with students in kindergarten through third grade; allows the student to explore different subject areas according to his or her level of interest and ability. Emphasis is placed on encouraging enthusiasm for learning and stimulating curiosity. As in all gifted programs, higher levels of cognitive learning are encouraged.	Offers students the opportunity to move through their school career at the pace that is most suitable to their rate of learning. This may involve skipping several grades, early entrance to kindergarten, and early entrance to college. Advanced classes and honors programs are often considered forms of acceleration.
Enrichment	*Independent Study*
Expands students' experiential and informational base by exposing them to areas of study which they do not encounter in the regular curriculum. In this program, the stress is often on motivating the students to use their learning potential.	Allows students to delve into areas of particular interest. The teacher assists the students in locating resources and helps them define their goals and outline strategies for reaching them.
Seminars	*Tutorials*
Offer students an opportunity to learn through a series of discussions on topics not usually considered in depth in the regular curriculum.	Match tutors with students who are interested and talented in a subject that the teacher may lack time or expertise to offer. Tutors may be peers, older students, or adult volunteers.

neous classes has a significant, positive impact on their academic progress (Kulik and Kulik, 1982). The research in support of advancing students to placements more suited to their cognitive development is "both massive and impressive" (Tannenbaum, 1983, p. 201), with advantages reported by both parents and children (Alexander and Skinner, 1980). The practice of providing special instruction for gifted children in the classroom is not as well researched as are grouping and acceleration options. Since the size of most regular classrooms prohibits significant modifications in instruction to accommodate individual needs (Sizer, 1983), that option is probably best considered supplemental and not sufficiently differentiated to meet the educational needs of most gifted students.

Within each of these three classes of alternatives, there are a number of program options:

Grouping
— Cluster grouping (placing several gifted students in the same regular classroom)
— Resource center (on or off campus)
— Special class (seminars, honors, Advanced Placement)
— Self-contained classroom (all subjects taught by gifted education teacher)

Developmental Placement
— Early admission to kindergarten or first grade
— Grade skipping
— Cross-grade placement (acceleration in one or two subjects)
— Fast-paced classes (cover two years of material in one school year, for example)
— Credit by examination (students "test out" of units, courses, or grades)
— Early admission to college

Classroom Option
— Independent study with advanced level textbooks
— Independent and small-group projects/activities
— Autoinstructional materials
— School-wide enrichment programs or workshops
— Special interest clubs or classes

How can IEPs be used in educating gifted children?

IEPs for Gifted Children. Individualized education programs (IEPs) are an effective means of designing and implementing the combination of vertical and horizontal alternatives most suitable for each gifted student. Based on assessment that identifies the individual student's strengths and weaknesses, IEPs for gifted children ensure that they are not simply placed in an enrichment center for one day a week, or in an honors class, or some other option that constitutes the "gifted program." Instead, each child has an individualized program that combines a number of educational options in accordance with the child's assessed learning needs.

Depending on the children's level and type of ability, some may be best served in full-time programs, such as specialized arts school or a self-contained classroom for young gifted children. Some may need to enroll in college courses, and some may be adequately served through a combination of developmental placement and a resource room program. A range of options is needed at every grade level, but developmental factors influence the relative importance of different alternatives at the preschool and primary grade level, the intermediate and middle school level, and the high school and the post-secondary level of education.

How do preschool and primary grade programs accommodate the needs of young gifted children?

Preschool and Primary Grades. At the preschool level and in the primary grades, one of the major considerations in modifying instruction is the discrepancy between gifted children's conceptual development and their motor development. Although it is sometimes hard for teachers to accept that some five-year-olds who cannot write their name can read and understand books written for fifth- or sixth-graders (Epstein, 1979), they need to plan and provide academic tasks appropriate to the gifted child's conceptual level and motor tasks appropriate to their physical development.

The University of Washington Child Development Preschool program provides highly gifted preschoolers with individualized instruction using first- through seventh-grade workbooks and other instructional materials adapted to the young children's motor skill level (Roedell, Jackson, and Robinson, 1980).

Because of the large discrepancy between highly gifted children's academic skills and their physical development, self-contained classrooms with a small enough enrollment to allow individualization offer the most viable alternative for meeting their needs. Provisions for early admission to school, cross-grade placement, and grade skipping are also important at this age level.

Why is grouping important at the intermediate level?

Intermediate and Middle School. Grouping for special instruction is a primary means of meeting the educational needs of gifted children in the fourth through eighth grades. Resource rooms, resource centers, and advanced classes are common at this level. Emphasis on grouping is based partly on the belief that gifted children at this preadolescent and early adolescent stage need peers who share their interests and concerns (Clark, 1983). Otherwise, desire for acceptance by their classmates may have a negative effect on development; and the incidence of underachievement tends to increase (Clark, 1983).

A major consideration at this level of school is the need to counter effects of sex-role stereotyping on gifted students' cognitive development. Girls particularly are likely to begin underachieving during this period (Shaw and McCuen, 1960). As a consequence of their perception of science and mathematics as masculine subjects, they may lose interest in them and begin a pattern of opting out of taking high-level science and mathematics classes (Casserly, 1979).

Early admission to high school or early entry into a challenging program

Gifted children should be permitted to advance through school as quickly as their abilities allow.

may avoid problems encountered by educators who attempt to interest gifted girls in accelerated mathematics courses during the middle school or junior high school years when concerns about acceptance and interest in social interactions cause them to resist alternatives that separate them from long-time classmates or put them in highly competitive situations with boys (Callahan, 1979; Fox, 1976). Casserly (1979) suggests that high school girls who are interested in science and mathematics serve as role models for younger girls by giving science demonstrations and discussing the relevance of science or mathematics to various careers.

High School and Post-Secondary Level. The diversity of student interests and abilities within the gifted group is greater at the high school and the post-secondary school level than at any earlier point in the students' career. By high school, gifted students often surpass their teachers in some subjects (Renzulli, 1982). Because of this diversity and the high level of student ability, adequate provisions for gifted high school students require a variety of advanced materials as well as subject matter experts. Cooperative high school and college programs such as Advanced Placement courses, dual enrollment in high school and college, college correspondence courses, and early admission to college are important alternatives for students at this level.

Are there special schools for gifted students?

In some large cities, specialized schools provide gifted high school students needed access to full-time comprehensive programs in academic or artistic disciplines. The Bronx High School of Science and three other specialized schools are available to a small population of the most talented students in New York. A residential state school, the North Carolina School for the Performing Arts, is one of the most recently established specialized schools. It is innovative in that it provides both high school and college programs (Cox and Daniel, 1983). Because of the limited number of such schools, the majority of gifted high school and post-secondary school students are served through acceleration, special classes, and the cooperative high school and college programs mentioned earlier.

INSTRUCTION

Most educators of the gifted subscribe to a humanistic philosophy of education (Gowan, 1977). Inherent in this philosophy are a concern for the rights of the individual student and respect for individual differences. The qualities considered important for humanistic teaching include tolerance for diverse opinions, willingness to admit mistakes, and empathy with gifted children (Maker, 1975).

Must teachers of gifted children be gifted themselves?

Teacher Qualifications. Whether teachers of the gifted should be gifted themselves is a matter of some controversy. Some educators argue that it is sufficient for teachers of the gifted to be gifted at teaching. Others contend that the teachers should be gifted themselves if they are to empathize with the problems of gifted children, provide sufficiently challenging instruction, and even keep up with them as they learn. Some compromise positions are that teachers of the gifted should be above average in intelligence but not necessarily gifted; that teachers of elementary gifted children need not be gifted but that teachers of gifted high school students should be; and that teachers, whether gifted or not, should be familiar with many subjects and expert in at least one.

Lack of resolution of this issue is because, in large part, of teacher educators' reluctance to use procedures that could exclude persons capable of becoming excellent teachers of the gifted. A more pragmatic approach is to define the abilities and skills the teacher of the gifted should have and base teacher preparation on these. Listed among such skills needed by gifted education teachers are expertise in the subject or subjects they teach (Gallagher, 1975), knowledge and skills needed to assist in planning for individualization of gifted students' programs (Reynolds and Birch, 1977), and knowledge and skills needed to help students identify and expand their interests (Renzulli, 1977). Modifications of programs for gifted children focus on one or more of three dimensions of instruction: content, skills, and learning environment (Gallagher, 1975). Teachers of the gifted must be able to address each of these dimensions.

What constitutes enrichment for gifted children?

Enrichment in Gifted Programs. Because of the humanistic orientation of gifted programs and because the students are usually advanced in several subject areas and have mastered the basic skills taught at their grade level, the content of gifted programs is often based primarily on students' academic interests. Enrichment based on student interest alone, however, does not constitute a meaningful education for gifted students. Enrichment must be more than entertaining; it must be educationally relevant and challenging (Stanley, 1977). Popular gifted program activities such as field trips, creativity exercises, and educational games comprising a series of loosely related lessons are not defensible as differentiated instruction for the gifted (Renzulli, 1977).

The content and the learning environment of gifted programs should reflect the primary purpose of special instruction for talented students, that is, development of academic skills. A substantial and stimulating academic curriculum and a psychologically safe environment are crucial to high achievement (Whitmore, 1980). In this environment, the teacher acknowledges different levels of accomplishment but teaches students to persist in their efforts to master difficult concepts and skills.

What are some uses and limitations of the Enrichment Triad Model?

Much of the instruction designed for gifted children is intended to improve skills that are requisite for making original contributions to the arts, humanities, and sciences. The Enrichment Triad Model (Renzulli, 1977) suggests a possible approach to teaching these skills. One component of the model, exploration, assists students in identifying topics of interest to them. The second component, skill building, teaches research and communication skills related to various disciplines. The third component, investigation of real problems, encourages students to assume the role of a "professional" and develop an original product.

Although there is little research documenting its effectiveness, the Enrichment Triad Model is a widely used approach to differentiated instruction for the gifted (Maker, 1982). The model offers a coherent approach to independent study in students' areas of genuine interest; however, it must be used in combination with other educational alternatives. Alone, it addresses only the needs of students who are highly motivated to pursue independent work in an area of interest. It was not intended to address the needs of gifted underachievers, gifted students whose primary need is placement in a classroom setting in which the instructional level is commensurate with their achievement level, or gifted students whose talent is so highly developed that they need to attend a specialized school devoted to development of high-level talent in a particular discipline. Like most program models, the Enrichment Triad Model is but one of several alternatives to be considered in developing an IEP for a gifted child.

Evaluation of Instruction. Evaluation of the gifted education program is an important, but often neglected, activity. Evaluation not only documents the benefits of the program, it also identifies ways in which the program can be improved (Callahan, 1983). Input to planning, based on student progress measures; questionnaires completed by students, parents, and other involved persons; and program records, allows analysis of information to determine which elements of the program are effective and which need to be modified, strengthened, or eliminated.

What are some important principles in evaluating programs for gifted children?

Some principles of evaluation are particularly relevant to the evaluation of the effectiveness of gifted programs. First, progress tests must measure what was taught in the program. This basic principle is sometimes overlooked, and thus inappropriate tests are selected for evaluation. Because the tests fail to measure what the students learned, the program's benefits are not demonstrated (Howley, Howley, and Pendarvis, 1985). Second, tests used to evaluate student progress must have many difficult questions so that gains made by gifted students can be measured. Otherwise, if a pretest-posttest design is used to evaluate the program, and the students score very high on the pretest, they may score lower on the posttest simply because of carelessness or a statistical artifact, regression toward the mean. Thus, it could look as though students unlearned what they knew before instruction began! Finally, evaluation of student academic progress must include cognitive tests. Surveys of students' opinions about their progress are insufficient to document gains. Although the surveys provide valuable information and could comprise a part of the evaluation effort, they provide less compelling evidence than measures of skill or knowledge (Howley, Howley, and Pendarvis, 1985).

NEW TRENDS IN GIFTED PROGRAMS

Although the general trend in gifted education is toward more programs, the effectiveness of many existing programs has been questioned. Some enrichment programs have been criticized for being more entertaining than educational (Renzulli, 1977). Such criticisms have led educators to increase the use of acceleration and to develop IEPs for the gifted, in an effort to ensure high-quality education.

Is acceleration effective?

Another Look at Acceleration. In the past, acceleration has been viewed with distrust by many educators, but the work of Julian Stanley and his co-workers in their study of Mathematically Precocious Youth has compelled educators to take a new look at this method. Stanley has shown that unusually capable children who are eager to move ahead can meet the demands of college courses without suffering the social and emotional maladjustment predicted by opponents of acceleration (Stanley, 1977). Their findings confirm what many years of research have shown: The academic achievement of accelerated students is generally superior to that of nonaccelerated students of similar ability, and their social acceptance is equal to that of nonaccelerated peers (Daurio, 1979).

It is important to bear in mind, however, that acceleration should be contingent not on ability alone but on desire to move ahead in school as well. Seven of the children accelerated in Stanley's program, interviewed for an article in *Smithsonian* magazine, were all eager to get on with their studies, and they all placed a high value on intellectual pursuits. One of the youths, Michael Kotschenreuther, "burns to discover something 'that hasn't been known before' " (Nevin, 1977, p. 81).

Studies of early entrants to kindergarten indicate that this is another avenue that should be open to gifted children. Bright children who enter kindergarten 6 months to a year early compare favorably to their older classmates. Hobson (1963) found that early entrants graduated from high school with honors more frequently than similar children who entered school at the usual age. They also participated in more extracurricular activities, including social activities and athletics. The academic achievement and social acceptance of early entrants has been found to equal those of other children of similar intellectual ability (Birch, Tisdall, Barney, and Marks, 1965). Findings such as these imply a need for greater flexibility in admissions and promotions procedures through elementary and secondary school.

How is computer instruction in gifted programs different from that in regular education programs?

Computer Education. Computers in gifted education are used in much the same way as in other types of educational programs, but the emphases are different. Whereas the use of computers as purveyors of drill and practice programs is predominant in the regular education program (Tucker, 1983), in gifted education, computers are often used to teach computer programming and other computer skills. The early introduction of programming skills distinguishes computer education in gifted programs from computer education in regular classrooms. Instruction in computer programming begins at the first-grade level in many gifted programs (Doorly, 1981) and is not limited to simplified languages, such as LOGO, but teaches more difficult languages, such as BASIC (Nazarro, 1981). The argument about whether knowledge of programming skills is a component of computer literacy, still debated in regular education, seems to have been decided in the affirmative by educators of gifted children.

An introductory computer science course for high school students who plan to major in computer science or in another field that requires knowledge of computers and programming has been developed by the College Entrance Examination Board (1983) as part of its Advanced Placement program. The course curriculum requires the students to learn Pascal, a programming language that teaches widely applicable programming skills. Other goals of the course curriculum include learning how to design programs that solve different types of problems and learning the basic components and functions of computer hardware and software. Like other Advanced Placement courses, this course allows students to demonstrate mastery of the material by completing an examination. Many colleges and universities grant college credit for passing grades on Advanced Placement examinations. Thus, this option allows gifted students interested in computers an opportunity to earn both high school and college credit.

Individualized instruction, both accelerated and for enrichment, are provided in a limited fashion through computer programs that teach concepts not usually presented at the gifted students' chronological age grade level. Despite limits in the quality, quantity, and comprehensiveness of educational software, students can work through programs of basic skills in highly structured subjects such as mathematics, spelling, or grammar at a faster rate than through traditional instruction (Suppes, 1980). They can also be introduced to subjects that are not included in the curriculum at the elementary school level, such as chemistry, algebra, or physics. The enrichment provided by computer instruction in less-structured subjects, including literature and social studies, is not so well-documented as in convergent subjects (Kulik, Bangert, and Wiliams, 1983). However, enrichment through computer simulations, such as a simulation of weather conditions during an ocean crossing used to teach meteorological concepts (Barstow, 1981), are popular with gifted students and their teachers.

The use of the computer as a tool for solving problems is also emphasized in gifted education. Students at the North Carolina School of Science and Mathematics, for example, use computers to store and analyze data for their experiments (Davis and Frothingham, 1981). The word processing capabilities of computers lend themselves to students' efforts to compose original reports, essays, and stories (Papert, 1981). The capability to use computers and computer software to access information, process data, and improve verbal and graphic products are viewed by some educators as the most vital outcomes of computer education (Tucker, 1983).

Many young students have learned more about programming at home than at school. Children with access to home computers quite commonly develop skills that are far more advanced than those of adults who are responsible for computer instruction in the schools. Although these children almost always have a knowledgeable adult or older child they can go to for assistance, talented young programmers are primarily self-taught.

In a sense, computer programming is a "self-correcting" instructional ac-

TECHNOLOGY IN ACTION

The game is called "Snake Byte," and for lack of a better description, it could be called an arcade game, one of those electronic quarter-eaters you see from coast to coast these days. . . . The game isn't available in your local arcade just yet. But it's available for use on an Apple computer.

The inventor of the game is a 21-year-old Huntington native who stands to earn at least $25,000 from the invention in the next 12 months.

Chuck Sommerville is a first-generation child of the computer age. He didn't cut his teeth on an Apple home computer, but he has had one in his home for several years. It is from these "computer children" that the microcomputer will be developed into a powerful machine the limits of which cannot yet be imagined, the experts say (Peyton, 1982, p. 9).

Like many 13-year-olds, Chuck was fascinated by computers. When his teacher in the gifted program announced an upcoming class on computers, he was eager to participate. Unlike the other students, whose interest was satisfied with that one computer class, Chuck asked for and received permission to learn how to program on a computer in the science department of a nearby university. There he learned how to program in a now-obsolete language, FOCAL.

Because his programs used a great deal of memory and because he was taking science students' computer terminal time, Chuck was referred to the university's computer center and given a public account number for free computer time. Through a combination of trial and error and innumerable questions asked of the computer center staff, Chuck learned how to program in BASIC. However, he was spending so much time at the computer center that in an effort to keep him home more often, his father bought and assembled a computer terminal kit so that Chuck could use the university computer from his home. This arrangement worked well until the public account was closed. About that time, the first Apple microcomputers became available by mail order. By working at a local grocery store to help pay for it, Chuck was able to purchase his own microcomputer. Shutting himself in his room for all-night programming sessions, he quickly became a proficient programmer. By the time he was 15, he was earning money writing original programs.

Asked what appeal computers hold for him, Chuck responds that their primary appeal is their limitless potential and complexity. The computer, he says, is like an infinite puzzle with new features appearing all the time. Chuck compares the process of writing a difficult program to that of composing music. The programmer must have a conception of the whole program during the entire process. He must keep in mind all that has happened in the program, what he is trying to accomplish at the moment, and what will come later.

Currently designing computer hardware, Chuck relies most on the skills he acquired outside a formal school setting. Although some course work in his school program was certainly relevant, he feels that it did not go into sufficient depth in some critical areas, such as Boolean algebra.

tivity, and it lends itself to sequential skill development. Because mistakes in programming are usually immediately apparent when the program is run, the novice programmer is forced to ask questions and try different approaches until a solution is found. As the student's skills develop, more complex tasks are attempted. A computer and informational resources, such as other programmers, books, and magazines, seem to be sufficient for students who are highly motivated to learn how to program and who have unlimited access to the computer.

Feature articles, such as the one quoted in the vignette that follows, both reflect public interest in children who are talented programmers and typify the young programmer's history and attitudes.

EDUCATING GIFTED CHILDREN IN THE LEAST RESTRICTIVE ENVIRONMENT

Is the goal of normalization appropriate for gifted children's education?

The principle of education in the least restrictive environment is based on the belief that segregated settings impair the progress of handicapped children, in part because of the absence of nonhandicapped children to serve as models from whom they can learn appropriate behavior. In other words, educators hope to *normalize* the behavior of handicapped children. An awareness of this principle has caused some people to question whether gifted children should spend even part of the day away from the regular classroom. It is as important for the gifted to be educated in the least restrictive environment as it is for the handicapped, but what is the least restrictive environment for gifted children? Do we want the behavior of gifted children to be like that of other students? Full-time placement in the regular classroom may meet the goal of normalization, but in the case of gifted children that goal is not appropriate. Many gifted children in regular classrooms are already "normalizing" themselves by hiding their abilities so that they will be accepted by teachers and classmates.

Do some gifted children require totally differentiated programs?

Gifted children's potential for outstanding performance demands a different goal, one of *denormalization*. The learning characteristics of gifted children are different from those of other children, but they are positive differences and should be nurtured. For the realization of learning potential, the regular classroom can be the most restrictive environment for gifted children.

Coordination of Resources. Consider the problems of programming for David, a kindergarten-age child who "speaks a half-dozen languages, says his main interest is comparative philology, calculates mathematical equations, does chemistry experiments, studies the violin, reads the *New York Times* and college textbooks" (Bentsen, 1979). The regular elementary curriculum is as unsuitable for David as it would be for a profoundly handicapped child. The elementary teacher is unlikely to have the specialized knowledge necessary to help David pursue his interests independently, and it is unrealistic to suppose that experts can be brought into the classroom daily. David's education will probably require coordination of high school and college courses, independent study guided by teachers who are experts in his areas of interest, and in-school or out-of-school social experiences with children close to his own age.

Given the degree of "differentness" represented by extremely high IQ scores, it is unrealistic to expect that highly gifted children could profit from any but a radically different educational program. From early researchers such as Leta Hollingworth to contemporary experts in gifted education such as Julian Stanley, many educators have cautioned that the lockstep educational program is far too restrictive for many gifted children. For some of these children, extreme acceleration has been effected with positive results.

Although Kam Hunter, the gifted student described at the beginning of this chapter, had some initial difficulties adjusting to the notoriety of being the only 11-year-old on campus, he did not regret his choice to enter college early. As a 16-year-old graduate with a 3.6 grade point average in his double major of zoology and physiology, he summarized his feelings about college (*Michigan State University Today* 1982 p. 3): "My experiences and studies here have helped make me into both a better student and a better person, and I wouldn't trade them for anything."

Children like Kam and David are very rare; most gifted children will benefit from a more balanced combination of outside learning experiences and instruction in the regular classroom. The decisions about (1) how much instruction should be provided in the regular classroom and (2) in which grade level of the regular program to place the child, should be based on the ability of the teacher to provide individual instruction for the gifted, the support services and materials available, and the child's abilities and social and emotional development.

Cooperation Between Classroom and Special Education Teacher. Because most gifted children will be instructed in both the regular classroom and in a special class, the classroom teacher and the teacher of gifted classes share the responsibility for their education. The classroom teacher is in a position to observe the gifted child's work in all subjects. In some subjects the gifted child may be at the same level as the other children or may even need remedial work. In other subjects, the teacher may find that the child has already mastered the material at that grade level. The teacher of the gifted can assist in these subjects by planning activities and finding methods and materials for advancement. Together, the teachers can plan many alternative learning experiences involving independent study, cross-grade placement, directed readings, and learning centers.

Alternatives such as these can be used to provide individual instruction to all children, not just identified gifted children. The teacher may find that these learning experiences result in the discovery of previously unrecognized talent. As mentioned earlier (Stanley, 1976), giftedness may be overlooked if learning activities are not difficult enough to allow gifted children to display their exceptional ability. By providing advanced work, the teacher may find that some students are capable of accomplishing much more than was expected.

What is the least restrictive environment for gifted children?

The regular classroom teacher plays an important role in the social and emotional development of gifted children. It is a difficult role, and the responsibilities involved may be met more readily when the teacher has a strong conviction of the unique worth of every child in the classroom. The climate of support and recognition for individual differences that is based on such a conviction will forestall resentment of gifted children by their classmates and intellectual arrogance among the gifted.

In summary, the least restrictive environment for gifted children is that which provides instruction commensurate with ability and which includes provisions for social and emotional development. The variety of social, emotional, and instructional needs of gifted children requires a continuum of alternative settings, ranging from support in the regular classroom to full-time placement in a special school or college. The key to finding and providing the least restrictive environment for each gifted child is commitment to the idea of shared responsibility. Through the combined efforts of both general and gifted education personnel we can identify talented children and change their education from one of benign neglect to one which rewards their development.

PROBE 12-4
Educational Provisions for Gifted Children

1. Reread the case study of Damon at the beginning of this section. Identify four characteristics that are typical of classic underachievers or that contribute to underachievement.

2. Suggest some strategies that could be used to improve Damon's academic performance.

3. T F Educational modifications have been more successful than counseling in improving the performance of gifted underachievers.

4. T F A major difficulty in providing special programs for gifted children from minority groups is in finding procedures that offset bias in testing instruments.

5. Identify two factors that contribute to underachievement among the gifted handicapped.

6. T F Adolescent gifted girls usually respond favorably to accelerated mathematics classes.

7. Designate each of the following activities as horizontal (H) or vertical (V):
   ___ The students will complete a photographic essay depicting the ethnic composition of the class.
   ___ The students will visit a local art gallery.
   ___ The students will complete the third-grade mathematics book by the end of the first semester.

8. Check your knowledge of gifted programs by matching the following items:

___ A broad term for programs that expand students' experience or knowledge base.	a. Vertical
	b. Tutorial
___ A program usually offered children in kindergarten through third grade.	c. Horizontal
	d. Exploration
___ A program that matches gifted students with volunteers who are skilled in the student's ability or interest area.	e. Independent study
	f. Acceleration

___ Grade-skipping

___ A vertical learning program that permits a student to study in depth an area of special interest.

9. T   F   Research on acceleration has found no serious negative effect on social or emotional development of bright children.

10. T   F   Computer instruction for gifted children consists primarily of use of individualized software for drill and practice in basic academic skills.

11. Why may education in a regular classroom not be the least restrictive environment for gifted children?

12. T   F   Providing challenging instruction in the classroom may lead to identification of gifted students.

13. T   F   Most gifted students' needs may be adequately addressed in the regular classroom.

14. Describe at least three ways that the classroom teacher can improve education of gifted children in the regular classroom.

SUMMARY

1. Common arguments against special provision for the gifted are based on misconceptions about gifted children.

2. The concept of giftedness includes many kinds of ability.

3. Characteristics common to gifted children suggest the need for special educational programs.

4. The identification of gifted children is best accomplished through the combined use of a variety of evaluative methods.

5. Gifted programs typically seek to accelerate learning, broaden experience, develop academic skills, and provide opportunity for in-depth study.

6. A humanistic, student-centered approach is characteristic of gifted programs.

7. Acceleration is a desirable alternative for many gifted students.

8. IEPs for gifted children differ from IEPs for handicapped children in several respects.

9. Poor parent-child interaction patterns, social stereotypes, and learning, behavior, physical, or sensory handicaps inhibit the achievement of many gifted students.

10. Full-time placement in the regular classroom may be the most restrictive environment for many gifted children.

TASK SHEET 12
Field Study on Gifted Children

Select *one* of the following and complete the assigned tasks:

Definitions

Ask five people to define "giftedness." Record their answers and respond to the following questions:

1. What did the definitions have in common?
2. What was the narrowest definition?
3. What was the broadest definition?
4. How many definitions fell into each of the following categories?
   a. Very restrictive — few abilities would be included.
   b. Moderate — several or many abilities would be included.
   c. Broad — most or all abilities would be included.

Write your definition of giftedness.

Interview on Acceleration

Interview an educational administrator, a teacher, and a parent regarding their views on acceleration. Ask each to give at least two reasons supporting his or her views. Record the views and reasons given by each, and respond to the following:

1. Were the majority for or against acceleration?
2. Were some of the reasons given similar? If so, what were they?
3. On the basis of your reading and interviews, summarize and defend your position on acceleration.

Program Visitation

Visit a program for gifted children in a public or private school. Report on your visit, answering the following questions:

1. Where did you visit?
2. When were you there and for how long?
3. What activities did you observe?
4. What types of programming were used?
5. What did you observe that helped you categorize the program?
6. What did you learn, and what was your reaction to the visit?

Political Action

Write a letter to one of your legislators expressing your belief that gifted children need special education provisions. Submit a copy of the letter and the legislator's response. What was your reaction?

Agency Investigation

Request information from the following agencies about the services they provide in the area of gifted education. Write a three-page paper summarizing these services and how you might use them if you were a professional working with gifted children.

American Association for Gifted
Children
15 Gramercy Park
New York, NY 10003

Foundation for Gifted and Creative
Children
395 Diamond Hill Road
Warwick, RI 02866

National Association for Gifted Children   National Council for the Gifted
8080 Springvalley Drive   Box 222
Cincinnati, OH 45236   South Orange, NJ 07079

Library Study

Read three articles related to the gifted and write a one-page abstract of each *or* read a biography of a gifted person. Describe the characteristics of that person which are typical of the gifted. List any atypical characteristics. If you were the person's teacher, what modifications in educational programming would you have suggested? Why? You can find articles about gifted children in these journals:

Gifted Child Quarterly
G/C/T (Gifted/Creative/Talented)
The Journal for Gifted Education

Design Your Own Field Experience

If you know of a unique experience you can have with gifted people, or do not want to do any of the above alternatives, discuss your idea with your instructor and complete the tasks that you agree on.

Complementing Special Education Services

As the field of special education grew during the 1970s and early 1980s, the number and quality of complementary services increased as well. Many of these services were designed to draw parents into active involvement in educating their children, to help the handicapped adjust to life after graduation, or to assist the community in assimilating the handicapped. These services have often benefitted students without handicaps as well.

Space limitations do not permit a detailed discussion of all the complementary service areas involved in special education. We have selected two: career and vocational education, and working with families of exceptional children.

CAREER AND VOCATIONAL EDUCATION

An important aspect of today's special education is the preparation of the student for living and working in the community. In this chapter, we examine the circumstances that led to the development of career education. Models for providing career education are described, with particular emphasis on the one that is most appropriate for the handicapped — the competency-based model. We look at several instructional approaches, methods, and activities that are particularly useful in secondary-level career preparation. In addition, a description of vocational rehabilitation services is provided. We conclude with a discussion about the future directions of career education in special education.

THE FAMILIES OF CHILDREN WITH DISABILITIES

The role of the family in special education services has been a common theme throughout this text. The importance of parents and family members in the education of exceptional children has long been recognized, and since the passage of PL 94-142 in 1975, their involvement has been mandated. In this chapter, we examine the role not only of the parent but also the child in shaping parental involvement. Emphasis is placed on incorporating all family members into the process of educating the exceptional child. We also describe some family support organizations.

PART IV   COMPLEMENTING SPECIAL EDUCATION SERVICES

Merideth Moore is forcing down the unemployment rate — for the retarded. . . .

The mentally retarded men and women she places are trained at Metro Industrial Services of the Blue Grass Association for Mental Retardation, where Ms. Moore is a placement specialist.

"The employers really talk to one another," she said. "We have people who work out well in many jobs that previously have been high turnover positions."

"The six people from (Metro Industrial Services) are far better than employees I get off the street," said Doug Miller, manager of the Lafayette Club in Lexington. "There's a work-related attitude these people have — I am really amazed when I see someone nowadays who truly wants to work. . . ."

The supervisors say the people referred by the service get along well with other workers.

And the supervisors say they treat their retarded workers no differently than other employees — the service cautions employers not to do so.

"I'm satisfied," says James Burnell, the head steward. "I tell them what needs to be done and they do it."

Carlton Scully, the executive director of the Blue Grass Association for Mental Retardation, said the cost of training workers is about $13 a day, compared to about $100 a day for the care of a person placed in a residential institution. . . .

At the industrial service . . . workers are trained in different kinds of production. At the beginning, many work on projects where speed is not emphasized, so they can learn how to do the job. Others are placed in the Vocational Development Program, where high productivity is stressed — similar to the type of pressure they would face in a factory or other business. . . .

The trainees also learn about being punctual, paying attention to their work and getting along with supervisors and fellow employees. . . .

Source: From Eileon Levy, "Training of Mentally Retarded Employees Met with Praise, Job Offers." Lexington *Herald-Leader,* February 11, 1979. Reprinted by permission.

13

Career and Vocational Education

Patricia Thomas Cegelka

Patricia Thomas Cegelka, Professor and Chair of the Department of Special Education at San Diego State University, has been involved in the preparation of special education personnel for over a decade. Prior to that, she had been a teacher of secondary special education, a methods and materials consultant for learning disabled children, and a school psychologist. Her areas of professional interest, in addition to career and vocational education, include bilingual special education, secondary special education, personnel development, mental retardation, and learning disabilities.

The article on the facing page describes some of the practices involved in preparing one segment of the special education population for employment. Although work training practices may be a part of career preparation for anyone, including both nonhandicapped and handicapped students, career education is much more than simply preparing people to get jobs. Furthermore, it should begin when individuals enter the educational system as children and continue throughout their school careers. While a full range of career education experiences is important for all people, a well-conceptualized continuum is essential for special education students. Unfortunately, it frequently does not exist for the handicapped, or else it favors noncompetitive and sheltered work settings. A full range of career education experiences must be provided for exceptional learners if they are to become valued, full participants in the community.

In this chapter, the rationale for career education is presented, career education is defined, and the stages of career development are delineated. The relevance of career education to special education is explored, and models and instructional approaches for delivering career education to exceptional children are described. Special attention is given to career education at the secondary level, and the roles of both vocational education and vocational rehabilitation are discussed.

CAREER EDUCATION CONCEPTS

> **You should be able to define career education, explain its various stages, and describe its importance for special education.**

Career education has gained recognition over the past several years as an integral part of education programs. It reflects a change in the focus and the goals of education away from a narrow academic emphasis to a concern for the overall quality of life adjustment.

RATIONALE FOR CAREER EDUCATION

What problems prompted the career education movement?

Conceptualized in the early 1970s as an educational reform movement, career education was intended to offer a "comprehensive and long-range solution to many of America's social problems" (Gardner, 1973, p. 74). These problems, many of which were discussed by Hoyt (1975), included the following:

— School curricula were criticized as being narrowly focused on academics, not on meaningful real-life applications of academic information and knowledge.
— Students were frustrated by an educational curriculum that appeared to be irrelevant to their life needs; consequently, many students dropped out of secondary schools with neither the academic nor the vocational/occupational skills necessary for successful life adjustment.
— At the same time, the growing need for continuing education for adults was not being met.
— Workers' job dissatisfaction and alienation were attributed, at least in part, to educational practices that did not provide adequate preparation for adult work roles.
— Employers were frustrated with the poorly prepared, discontented, and unmotivated workers with whom they had to contend.
— The apparent demise of the work ethic in this country was of great concern to many.

These problems, identified several years ago, continue to be of concern to leaders in education and related fields. Data from the National Assessment of Educational Progress (1978a; 1978b) revealed that only about 2 percent of the 34,000 high school students surveyed considered school or academics as useful preparation for a job. Further, these same students had failed to acquire a variety of useful skills such as measuring, computing costs, writing job applications, and thinking critically. Finally, their occupational aspirations were judged by the investigators to be unrealistic. At the very time that society is

moving into a high technology, information-based age, our schools are grad-
uating students whose achievement levels are at an all-time low (Siccone,
1983). A report of the Carnegie Council of Policy Studies in Higher Education
(Kerr, 1979) revealed that nearly one-third of high school-age students were
ill-employed, ill-educated, and ill-equipped to make their way in society.
School dropout rates in some localities were shown to as high as 23 percent
for Caucasians, 35 percent for blacks, and 45 percent for Hispanics. This
alarming trend was attributed, in large part, to the perceived irrelevance of
the school curriculum.

How has career education made education more relevant to today's realities?
Career education has combined both academic and occupational orientations to education in an effort to respond to these problems. By emphasizing
the relationship of subject matter to various careers and occupations and by
developing needed work skills, career education has sought to make education
more relevant to the economic and employment realities of the day. Conceptualized as a major educational initiative of the Nixon administration, career
education has attempted to respond to problems arising from a changing
economy wherein an increasing proportion of the work force found itself in
jobs in which there was neither status nor personal satisfaction. By giving
respectability to all jobs, career education has sought to reduce the strong
societal bias (frequently reflected by teachers) in favor of white-collar jobs.
Recognizing the unsatisfying nature of many occupations, career education
has sought to increase the role of avocational work as a source of personal
satisfaction. In short, it has sought to increase the life satisfaction of workers,
restore the work ethic, and increase national productivity.

Although conceptualizations, delivery models, and definitions have been in
flux throughout this period, the basic thrust of career education has permeated
much of education. As discussed in more detail later, this has been particularly
true for special education, which has long had as its explicit goal the successful
adult adjustment of handicapped individuals. Special educators have embraced
career education as the missing link between academic and vocational preparation, and as the means for developing an integrated approach to the total
preparation of the handicapped student.

CAREER EDUCATION DEFINED

While occupational roles tend to be an important focus, career education is
not limited to concerns about employment. Career education has been defined
as the totality of experiences through which one learns about and prepares to
engage in work as part of one's way of living (Hoyt, 1975). Within this
context, work encompasses all productive activity, both paid and unpaid.
Work roles that might constitute the various life careers of the individual
include "(1) producer of goods and renderer of services; (2) member of a
family group; (3) participant in social and political life; (4) participant in avo-

**Chart 13-1
Council for Exceptional Children
Position Statement on Career Education**

Career education is the totality of experiences through which one learns to live a meaningful, satisfying work life. Within the career education framework, work is conceptualized as conscious effort aimed at producing benefits for oneself and/or others. Career education provides the opportunity for children to learn, in the least restrictive environment possible, the academic, daily living, personal-social and occupational knowledges and specific vocational work skills necessary for attaining their highest levels of economic, personal, and social fulfillment. The individual can obtain this fulfillment through work (both paid and unpaid) and in a variety of other societal roles and personal life styles including his/her pursuits as a student, citizen, volunteer, family member, and participant in meaningful leisure time activities.

Exceptional children, i.e., those whose characteristics range from profoundly and severely handicapped to those who are richly endowed with talents and/or intellectual giftedness, include individuals whose career potentials range from sheltered to competitive work and living arrangements. Exceptional children require career education experiences which will develop to the fullest extent possible their wide range of abilities, needs, and interests.

It is the position of CEC that individualized appropriate education for exceptional children must include the opportunity for every student to attain his/her highest level of career potential through career education experiences. Provisions for these educational experiences must be reflected in an individual educational program for each exceptional child which must include the following:

— Nondiscriminatory, ongoing assessment of career interests, needs, and potentials which assures the recognition of the strengths of the individual which can lead to meaningful, satisfying careers in a work-oriented society. Assessment materials and procedures must not be discriminatory on the basis of race, sex, national origin, or exceptionality.

— Career awareness, exploration, preparation, and placement experiences in the least restrictive school, living, and community environments which focus on the needs of the exceptional individual from early childhood through adulthood.

— Specification and utilization of community and other services related to the career development of exceptional individuals (e.g., rehabilitation, transportation, industrial and business, psychological, etc.).

— Involvement of parents or guardians and the exceptional student in career education planning.

Career education must not be viewed separately from the total curriculum. Rather, career education permeates the entire school program and even extends beyond it. It should be an infusion throughout the curriculum by knowledgeable teachers who modify the curriculum to integrate career development goals with current subject matter, goals, and content. It should prepare individuals for the several life roles which make up an individual's career. These life roles may include economic, community, home, avocational, religious or moral, and aesthetic roles. Thus, career education is concerned with the total person and his/her adjustment for community working and living.

Source: Council for Exceptional Children, (1978). *Position paper on career education.* Reston, VA: CEC.

How does the CEC view career education?

cational pursuits; and (5) participant in the regulatory functions involved in aesthetic, moral, and religious concerns" (Goldhammer, 1972, p. 129). This broad-based notion of career education is reflected in the official position statement of the Council for Exceptional Children, which describes career education as encompassing a range of functional levels and career potentials and as permeating the total school curriculum. The text of the position statement is included in Chart 13-1.

STAGES OF CAREER EDUCATION

How do career awareness, exploration, and preparation differ?

Career education is a developmental process that begins in childhood and continues throughout one's life. An aggregate of one's cognitive, affective, and psychomotor development, career education is typically conceptualized as involving three distinct phases or stages: (1) *career awareness;* (2) *career exploration;* and (3) *career preparation*. The career awareness stage during the elementary years focuses on the values of working and the different types of paid work. Beginning in about junior high school, the career exploration stage shifts to a focus on learning about specific occupations and the relationship of various occupational roles to the personal interests, aptitudes, and abilities of the individual. The career preparation stage, beginning in the senior high years, emphasizes the selection of specific occupational and vocational roles consistent with these attributes and with the life style that the individual desires. It includes either specific vocational preparation or preparation for the post-secondary education required to achieve one's career goals. Chart 13-2 on page 578 describes these stages in detail.

What is the fourth stage of career education?

It should be noted that while the three stages are depicted as discrete and sequential in nature, they are actually quite fluid and overlapping (Cegelka, 1981). Awareness, exploration, and preparation are not limited to set periods in one's life. Throughout life we continue to clarify and change personal values, to become aware of new abilities, to discover new opportunities, to explore new career options, and to seek advancement consistent with our personal development. In acknowledgement of the lifelong nature of the process through which we learn about, select, and alter career paths, Brolin (1982) has proposed a fourth stage of career education: the *career placement/follow-up/ continuing education* stage. This fourth stage reflects the fact that vocational roles shift, through personal choice or through economic circumstance, and that these shifts may require additional training, education, or other types of assistance if the individual is to adjust successfully.

CAREER EDUCATION AND SPECIAL EDUCATION

By and large, career education has been enthusiastically endorsed by special educators, who long have had a pragmatic appreciation for the relevance of career preparation to the successful adult adjustment of handicapped individ-

Chart 13-2
Career Education Stages

Career Awareness. The development of good work habits and realistic attitudes toward occupations and work roles, as well as the development of personal work values, characterize this stage. Children learn to differentiate among occupations by examining the work roles of members of their families, of the school staff, and of others with whom they come in contact. Field trips, such as to a dairy, a zoo, or a factory, expose them to the various occupations involved in the production of goods and/or the maintenance of a facility. Self-awareness, the development of self-confidence, and other attributes of a healthy work personality are stressed. A myriad of success experiences along with exposure to a wide variety of career options and work models are important features of this stage.

Career Exploration. This stage focuses on helping students discover their individual interests, abilities, values, and needs. Students examine a variety of specific occupations and learn to identify the similarities of occupational groupings or clusters as well as the characteristic worker traits for different occupations. They explore occupations through observations and experience with actual jobs, often in simulated work environments. Career guidance becomes increasingly important in organizing exploratory experiences around individual interests and abilities. The effects of various career choices on family life, leisure activities, and other life situations are stressed, as are the relationships between occupations and societal values and beliefs.

Career Preparation. The preparatory stage of career education is designed to ensure that every student either has acquired a salable skill before graduation or has selected an occupation for which advanced training is necessary. Opportunities for in-depth exploration of several jobs of particular interest to the student are provided. Some students participate in work experience programs, some enroll in specific vocational training programs, while others explore postsecondary preparation opportunities such as colleges, universities, technical schools, and other high level educational programs. Basic academic skills are still emphasized, as is the development of the personal social skills that enhance vocational opportunities. Additionally, attention is paid to the skills needed for family life, avocational pursuits, and citizenship.

---

uals. One authority noted in 1975 that "the form of career education, although not the name, had been the major curricular thrust for the handicapped since the early 1900s" (Kolstoe, 1975, p. 327). A major purpose of special education is to prepare handicapped individuals to lead productive, personally satisfying adult lives. A historical commitment to this goal was reflected in the unit approach (Ingram, 1935; Kirk and Johnson, 1951), which sought to make special education closely related to life needs, and the life-functions approach of Goldstein and Siegel's 1958 *Illinois Curriculum Guide*. During the 1950s and 1960s, the work-study model for secondary EMR students further reflected this orientation. Today's vocational education/career preparation emphasis for the mildly handicapped, and the community-based model to prepare severely handicapped persons for the "environments of ultimate functioning," are a modern extension of that same goal.

For many years, the work-study approach was universally endorsed as the major vehicle for work preparation in special education. Designed primarily for the educable mentally retarded, it was successfully applied to emotionally disturbed, blind, deaf, and orthopedically handicapped students. By the late 1960s, however, high interest in the relatively new category of learning disabilities resulted in shifts in special education priorities: from the mentally retarded to the learning disabled; from secondary to preschool; and from compensatory intervention to prevention and remediation. Growing out of PL 94-142, the mainstreaming movement signaled a further orientation toward remedial academics and away from life-adjustment preparation. As young handicapped children grew to adolescence, however, without having had their educational handicaps remedied, there was a renewed interest in special education on the secondary level. PL 94-142 requirements that appropriate education be provided handicapped students from ages 3 to 21 further underscored the need to develop meaningful offerings for older students. At this same time, employment sector data began to reveal serious problems of unemployment and underemployment for the disabled.

How do current career education concepts differ from earlier ones?

The career education movement, with its focus on the adult adjustment and employment needs of *all* students, helped rekindle interest in the career preparation of special education populations. More broadly conceptualized than earlier special education approaches, career education affords several advantages over the previous curriculum models. The broad, life preparation interpretation of career education reemphasizes the importance of both nonacademic and nonoccupational skills. Further, the comprehensive kindergarten-through-twelfth-grade-and-beyond nature of career education encourages special educators to develop instructional sequences for the full spectrum of competencies that relate to adult adjustment. Without attention to the developmental nature of these skills and experiences, special education curricula can lose precision and become fragmented. When this occurs, programs at the secondary level become little more than "latter-day head start" programs (D'Alonzo, 1977), with instruction focused on elementary-level prerequisite skills rather than important career preparation objectives.

Historically, special education programs have been concerned with the broad array of skills that seem to relate to adult adjustment. Many special educators have viewed career education as an opportunity to revitalize efforts in this area and to refocus on important goals and objectives temporarily shelved in the enthusiasm for mainstreaming. With its focus on maintaining handicapped learners in the regular classroom, mainstreaming has frequently resulted in the playing down of nonacademic curricular areas. Consequently, personal-social skills, daily living competencies, and work attitudes and behaviors have received less attention in special education programming, particularly for the mildly handicapped. The advent of career education has brought

How is career
education viewed
for different
exceptionalities?

a renewed awareness of the relevance of these additional skills to the adult adjustment of exceptional individuals.

While earlier work-study programs were designed to serve primarily educable mentally retarded students, career education has a more encompassing orientation, including the full range of handicapped, nonhandicapped, and gifted students. Consistent with the noncategorical orientation toward the mildly handicapped, most career education programs incorporate educable mentally retarded, learning disabled, and emotionally disturbed/behaviorally disordered children into a single program model. Authorities in each of these separate areas have endorsed the relevance of career education. Leading proponents in the area of learning disabilities view career education as adding a much-needed dimension to the learning disabilities curriculum, with the range of career preparation options sufficiently broad (from sheltered workshop to vocational education to college entrance) to meet the individual needs of all LD students (Williamson, 1975; Marsh, Gearheart, and Gearheart, 1978). Conceptualizing college preparation as one track within the career education program is particularly important given the increased number of learning disabled individuals who seek advanced academic preparation. Over the past ten years, a variety of model programs have developed in community colleges, comprehensive universities, and technical schools that provide academic assistance to identified learning disabled students.

Clark (1981) has made a strong case for the relevance of career education to the education of emotionally disturbed and behaviorally disordered students. He proposes that his school-based model (discussed later in this chapter) could prove instrumental in assisting these students to develop the attitudes, values, habits, knowledge, and skills needed to succeed in their life careers.

Career education has also been specifically endorsed for students with sensory impairments as well as for the moderately and severely mentally retarded. With the latter two groups, developing a curriculum frequently involves rewriting curricula designed for the mildly handicapped, extending the competencies and experiences downward to include more basic daily living, personal, social, and occupational skills (Boyan and House, 1979; Sirvis, 1979). The relevance of career education to these two groups was addressed in the CEC position statement, which points out that the career potentials of exceptional individuals range from sheltered to competitive arrangements and that all exceptional individuals, from the most gifted to the most severely and profoundly handicapped, should be assisted in obtaining fulfillment through their life careers.

At the other end of the ability spectrum, Hoyt and Hebeler (1974) have suggested that the unique abilities of gifted and talented students require special career education attention. These students may need special guidance in choosing professions that not only fully utilize their intellectual potential but lead to personal fulfillment as well.

PROBE 13-1
Career Education Concepts

1. List three societal concerns that contributed to the development of the career education movement.

2. T F Career education is basically the same as vocational education.

3. Define career education.

4. T F Career education should be viewed separately from the total curriculum.

5. Indicate the grade level at which each stage of career education would be emphasized and list one possible program feature of that stage.

Stage	Grades	Program Feature
Career Awareness	_____	_____
Career Orientation and Exploration	_____	_____
Career Preparation	_____	_____

6. The _____ approach to career education predominated in the special education programs of the 1950s.

7. T F Career education has relevance for all areas of special education.

LEGISLATIVE FOUNDATIONS OF CAREER EDUCATION

You should be able to describe the provisions of laws that provide the legislative foundation of career education.

Although career education is a recent movement, its roots run deep. Vocational goals have long been a part of the American education system: Two hundred years ago Ben Franklin's Academy combined liberal education with training in practical skills in an effort to facilitate the success and mobility of the middle classes. During the late nineteenth and early twentieth centuries, the combined influences of rising industrialism, increasing immigration, and expanding numbers of students attending secondary school brought about the development of vocational education programs.

The Smith-Hughes Act of 1917 endorsed vocational education in the secondary schools. A number of related laws were to follow that laid the legislative foundation for career education for exceptional children. Six of the most significant of these will be discussed in the following pages.

SECTIONS 503 AND 504 OF THE VOCATIONAL REHABILITATION ACT OF 1973

What is the difference between Sections 503 and 504 of the Rehabilitation Act?

Sections 503 and 504 of this act provide for equity in both training and employment of handicapped individuals. Section 503 requires all employers who have federal contracts of $2,500 or more to take affirmative action steps in the recruiting, hiring, training, transfer, and termination of handicapped individuals (*Federal Register,* April 16, 1976). Section 504 prohibits the exclusion of handicapped individuals, on the basis of their handicaps, from any preschool, elementary, secondary, or adult program that receives any form of federal financial assistance (direct grants, loans, and indirect support). Later amendments to this act have placed increased emphasis on servicing the severely handicapped, with assistance becoming available to support the community adjustment of those for whom employment is not a feasible objective.

THE EDUCATION AMENDMENTS OF 1974

What was the first law to allocate federal funds for career education?

This first career education legislation provided money to study and promote career education, including the development of state career education plans and the implementation of research and demonstration programs. It is important to note that the handicapped were specifically mentioned as beneficiaries of these services. Three basic career education policies were described in this act (Educational Amendments of 1974, PL 93-380):

1. Every child should, by the time he or she has completed secondary school, be prepared for employment and for full participation in society, according to his or her ability.
2. It is the obligation of each local educational agency to provide that preparation for all children in the school district, including those who are handicapped or otherwise disadvantaged.
3. Each state and local educational agency should provide a program of career education designed to prepare each child for maximum employment and participation in our society according to his or her ability.

THE EDUCATION OF ALL HANDICAPPED CHILDREN ACT OF 1975

What are the implications of PL 94-142 for career education?

This law, commonly referred to as PL 94-142, mandates that a free and appropriate education for all handicapped children be provided in the least restrictive environment possible. While neither the law nor its regulations mention career education specifically, career education is implied under the provision that appropriate education be provided. Insofar as career education has been deemed appropriate for all students, so is it appropriate for handicapped students; therefore, career education goals should be incorporated into the individual education plans of handicapped students. The regulations that implement PL 94-142 specifically refer to vocational education, defining it as

> organized educational programs which are directly related to the preparation of individuals for paid or unpaid employment or for additional preparation for a career requiring other than a baccalaureate or advanced degree (Section 121a. 14 (b) (3)).

VOCATIONAL EDUCATION AMENDMENTS OF 1976

What percent of federal vocational education funds must be spent on handicapped children?

When initially passed into law in 1963, the Vocational Education Act specified that handicapped children should have access to vocational education training programs. This intent was strengthened by the 1968 amendments, which specified that states must spend 10 percent of their basic state grant for educational programs and services for the handicapped. The 1976 amendments to this law further specified that these monies were to be used to the maximum extent possible to assist handicapped students in succeeding in regular vocational education programs. Further, the 10 percent set-aside monies were specifically earmarked for the excess costs for providing vocational education training to handicapped students, as opposed to the basic per-pupil costs incurred for any student.

CAREER EDUCATION INCENTIVE ACT OF 1977

What are the provisions of the Career Education Incentive Act?

This act, passed in 1977, was designed to "increase the emphasis placed on career awareness, exploration, decision-making and planning and to do so in a manner which will promote equal opportunity in making career choices through the elimination of bias and stereotyping in such activities, including bias and stereotyping on account of race, sex, economic status, and handicap" (U.S. Congress, *Career Education Incentive Act,* December 13, 1977). For the five years of its life, it provided money to support program planning and implementation; curriculum development; in-service training for teachers; cooperative efforts among schools, industry, business, and labor; guidance counseling; work experience programs for students; the purchase of materials; the development of resource centers; and the payment of salaries. These funds also supported the development by each state of state-wide career education plans. This act played an important role in the institutionalization of career education throughout the nation.

COMPREHENSIVE EMPLOYMENT AND TRAINING ACT OF 1978 (CETA)

How did CETA help the handicapped?

The purpose of this legislation was to provide employment and training opportunities for the economically disadvantaged, unemployed, and underemployed. Administered by the U.S. Department of Labor, CETA was designed to foster local solutions to local unemployment problems by providing funds to states, cities, counties, and combinations of local units with populations over 100,000 who design and submit acceptable plans. The 1978 Amendments to CETA demonstrated increased concern for youth employment and the unemployment of the handicapped. These amendments prohibited discrimination on the basis of handicap; required that the annual plan include affirmative action outreach, training, placement, and advancement of the handicapped; required that local agencies include descriptions of the employment and training services offered to handicapped individuals; required CETA advisory councils to include handicapped individuals; and required that efforts be made to remove architectural barriers to the employment of the handicapped. Programs for training personnel to work with handicapped persons were funded, and the maximum age limit of 22 years for the youth Jobs Corps program was waived for handicapped persons.

PROBE 13-2
Legislative Foundations

1. The _____ Act of 1917 endorsed vocational education in the secondary schools.

2. T   F   PL 94-142 was the first law to provide funds for career education programs.

3. Section _____ of the Rehabilitation Act of 1973 prohibits discrimination in hiring handicapped people to work on federally financed projects.

4. T   F   Career education is not mentioned in PL 94-142.

5. Is the Career Incentive Act of 1977 still in effect?

6. How did CETA help handicapped people?

CAREER EDUCATION MODELS IN SPECIAL EDUCATION

You should be able to identify and describe the salient features of the major models of career education that have evolved in special education.

Three models of career education are particularly relevant to exceptional populations. Two of these — Brolin and Kokaska's (1979) life-centered model and Clark's (1979) school-based model — were specifically developed to address the unique needs of handicapped learners. The third model, the Experience Based Career Education (EBCE) model, was developed for non-handicapped learners but is highly relevant to many exceptional learners. The first two models are quite similar in their emphasis on involving school, home, and community resources in the development of a variety of competencies. The life-centered, competency-based career education model was developed first and has had tremendous influence on the conceptualization of career education in special education. Clark's model differs primarily in the attention it gives to the development of attitudes, values, and personal relationships. The Clark model provides an excellent schematic representation of the developmental nature of career education and so will be presented first.

CLARK'S SCHOOL-BASED MODEL

What are the four domains of the school-based model of career education?

The school-based career education model developed by Clark depicts the kindergarten-through-adulthood developmental nature of career education. This conceptualization, shown in Figure 13-1, adds greater specificity to earlier generic school-based models by delineating four interrelated domains as fundamental to career education. These domains are: (1) values, attitudes, and habits; (2) human relationships; (3) occupational information; and (4) acquisition of actual jobs and daily living skills. It is a curriculum model that from initial school entry focuses on more than just occupational skill training. Although much of Clark's focus has been on development from kindergarten to ninth grade, these domains should remain important features of career education for exceptional students through the secondary school level.

The model depicts a variety of curriculum tracks as options for secondary school programming. Depending on the abilities and preferences of individual students, the most appropriate options for career education might be college preparatory, general education, vocational and technical education, fine arts education, cooperative education or work-study program, or the work evaluation and work adjustment option. Within each of these options or combination of options, the focus should be on preparing the student for either initial job entry or for further preparation at the post-secondary level. Again, the post-secondary career preparation options are varied, including undergraduate and graduate university preparation, community college or technical education, training within a rehabilitation facility, or other post-secondary preparation. The adult and continuing education component of the model stresses the necessity for additional training on a lifelong basis as individual interests and occupational requirements change.

Clark maintains that the four domains emphasized at the elementary level

Figure 13-1
A school-based career education model for the handicapped

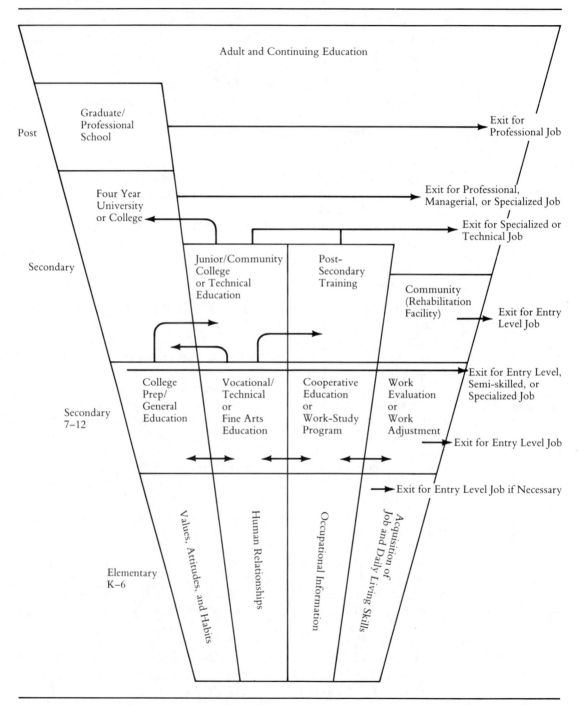

Source: From *Career education for the handicapped child in the elementary classroom* by G. M. Clark. Denver, CO: Love Publishing Co., 1979. Reprinted with permission.

are essential foundations for decision making and individual career achievement at the remaining stages of career education. More than any other career education model developed to address unique special education needs, it stresses the processes involved in establishing personal values, attitudes, and habits as well as human relationships. Clark (1981) points out that research literature on the adult adjustment of handicapped individuals as well as first-hand reports of handicapped adults indicate that the identification of these processes and attributes is an essential prerequisite to successful life adjustment.

LIFE-CENTERED COMPETENCY-BASED MODEL

Brolin's (1978) life-centered approach to career education has identified 22 competencies and 102 subcompetencies in three curriculum areas: (1) daily living skills, (2) personal-social skills, and (3) occupational guidance and preparation skills. (See Chart 13-3). According to this approach, the mildly handicapped student should have all these skills before leaving school. Because the competency statements encompass the skills everyone needs to succeed in community living, they are useful for other groups as well, from the nonhandicapped to the severely handicapped. Furthermore, they are broadly enough stated that they can be applied to all levels of instruction, from the primary grades through high school. They also can be taught using a variety of subject matter.

Chart 13-3
Career Education Competencies

A. *Daily Living Skills Curriculum Area*
1. Managing Family Finances
2. Caring for and Repairing Home Furnishing and Equipment
3. Caring for Personal Needs
4. Raising Children, Family Living
5. Buying and Preparing Food
6. Buying and Making Clothing
7. Engaging in Civic Activities
8. Utilizing Recreation and Leisure
9. Mobility in the Community

B. *Personal-Social Skills Curriculum Area*
10. Achieving Self-Awareness
11. Acquiring Self-Confidence
12. Achieving Socially Responsible Behavior
13. Maintaining Good Interpersonal Relationships
14. Achieving Independence
15. Making Good Decisions, Problem Solving
16. Communicating Adequately with Others

C. *Occupational Guidance and Preparation Curriculum Area*
17. Knowing and Exploring Occupational Possibilities
18. Making Appropriate Occupational Decisions
19. Exhibiting Appropriate Work Behaviors
20. Exhibiting Sufficient Physical and Manual Skills
21. Acquiring a Specific Salable Job. Skill is not included because the subcompetencies would be unique to the particular skill being acquired.
22. Seeking, Securing, and Maintaining Satisfactory Employment

Brolin provides suggestions for teachers in *Life Centered Career Education: A Competency-Based Approach* (1978). The curriculum plan details student objectives for each subcompetency, suggests instructional activities, and recommends ways that families and people in the community can assist in competency development. The following paragraphs illustrate methods of emphasizing competencies at all levels of instruction.

How are competencies incorporated into the curriculum?

The daily living skills curriculum area emphasizes the skills needed to care for oneself, to participate in family living, and to manage a home and personal finances. One of the subcompetencies for Competency 3, "Caring for Personal Needs," is "Dress Appropriately." At the elementary career awareness stage, the importance of appropriate dress could be emphasized — what clothes to wear in what weather, and to what activities, for example. During exploration, methods of buying and caring for clothes could be taught. At the career preparation stage, clothing construction and fashion could be studied, and more advanced methods of caring for clothes could be taught.

The personal-social curriculum area focuses on skills that foster self-understanding and independence. One of the subcompetencies involved in Competency 16, "Communicating Adequately with Others," is "Read at Level Needed for Future Goals." Students at the career awareness level might be taught to read and interpret important signs, such as traffic, safety, and restroom signs. At the next stage, students might begin studying the types of information provided in the newspaper and locating businesses and agencies by using the telephone book. At the career preparation stage, students could use help-wanted ads, newspaper advertisements, and the Yellow Pages to plan for real or simulated occupational or recreational pursuits.

Occupational guidance and preparation skills include competencies that can be developed at all instructional levels (Competencies 17, 18, and 19), and competencies that should be emphasized primarily at the high school level (Competencies 20, 21, and 22). The understanding of job classifications can be taught at all levels. During the career awareness stage the emphasis can be on the variety of jobs that are available in the school and community. At the career exploration level students can identify general job categories and discuss the ways jobs are classified: by salary, type of work, level of skill and training required, and location of work, for example. At the career preparation stage students can participate in actual job training.

The Competency-Based Model for Infusing Career Education into the Curriculum (see Figure 13-2) illustrates that all the stages of career education (awareness, exploration, preparation, placement, and follow-up) for each of the twenty-two competencies can be taught in conjunction with a variety of subject areas. The model further emphasizes the integral involvement of the school, home, and community in developing the twenty-two targeted competencies. In addition to participating in setting goals and objectives for their handicapped children, parents can provide home follow-through and reinforcement, provide required learning experiences, and model desired work

Figure 13-2
Competency-Based Model for Career Education

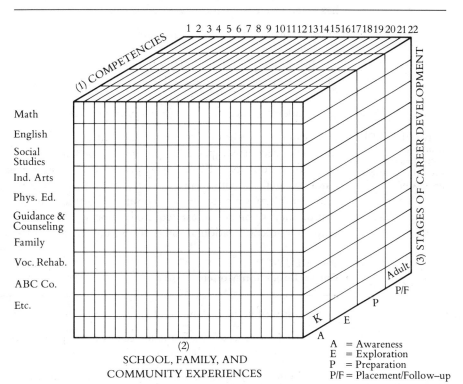

habits and values. The business and industry sectors, as the future employers of handicapped students, can be valuable resources in the design and implementation of career education programs.

EXPERIENCE-BASED CAREER EDUCATION MODEL

The Experience-Based Career Education (EBCE) model has been used successfully with nonhandicapped, mildly handicapped, and gifted youngsters at the secondary level. It is an individualized, highly structured, community-based alternative to traditional secondary education that attempts to make education relevant to the world of work. The experiential component of the program involves a series of community placements of 1 to 3 hours a day for 2 to 3 weeks each in such work settings as banks, publishing houses, hospitals, travel agencies, factories, and countless other job sites. A learning coordinator works with each student in selecting appropriate occupational placements and

What is the most distinguishing feature of the EBCE model?

related academic learning experiences. At the occupational site, students are given opportunities for observation and job-related experiences. Larson (1982) has listed five basic parameters of EBCE:

1. The program must be community based.
2. Scheduling is highly individualized.
3. Employer participation is voluntary.
4. The experiences are exploratory in nature, not oriented toward specific occupational skill development.
5. Academics are developed in conjunction with the learning site.

Why is the EBCE model so appropriate for special education programs?

Because the program is highly structured and at the same time highly individualized, it is especially appropriate for handicapped, nonhandicapped, and gifted students. EBCE can be provided in conjunction with college preparatory, general education, or vocational education curricula, or it can provide an alternative to high school for some students. High levels of community involvement are required, underscoring the basic career education emphasis on cooperation among school, family, and community.

PROBE 13-3
Career Education Models

1. List the four basic domains of Clark's model for career education.

2. T F   Competencies in the life-centered competency-based model can be used at all levels of instruction.

3. Community placement is the major distinguishing factor in the _____ model of career education.

4. Why would the EBCE program be appropriate for a handicapped secondary student?

INSTRUCTIONAL APPROACHES IN CAREER EDUCATION

You should be able to identify the instructional approaches used in career education programs.

THE INFUSION AND SEPARATE PROGRAMMING APPROACHES

There are two basic approaches to career education instruction: the *infusion approach* and the *separate programming approach*. The infusion approach integrates career education and the existing curriculum. Separate programming can involve (1) developing a separate curriculum devoted to career education, such as the EBCE program discussed earlier in this chapter; (2) developing separate career education classes; or (3) providing separate units devoted specifically to career education within courses on other subjects. The last approach is the one used most frequently.

The infusion approach relates curriculum content to adult careers, thereby increasing the relevance of education for the learner. In Brolin's Life-Centered Career Education program (Brolin, 1978), career education competencies are considered the primary goals, with academic skills playing a supportive role. Although basic academics are taught, instructional content is selected according to its value in facilitating the acquisition of competencies.

How can career education be infused into the curriculum?

Another method of infusing career education involves stressing the relevance of regular subjects to the problems of earning a living and other aspects of life after graduation. With this method, the focus of instruction is the academic subject matter. Here is a list of suggestions for ways that this type of instruction might be implemented:

Math: Emphasize the kinds of information communicated by numbers: age, weight, height, sizes of clothing, addresses, phone numbers, social security numbers, license numbers, and so on. Demonstrate practical applications of mathematical processes as in measuring, money management, construction plans, and computing wages and deductions. Have students interview adults to discover how they use math in their jobs and at home. Investigate how mathematics is used in the school cafeteria — altering recipes, determining the prices that should be charged, ordering food, and tallying receipts, for example. Use a token economy to demonstrate the relationship between work tasks and earnings.

Language Arts: The children can be acquainted with how people use language in different occupations through activities involving role playing. Application blanks, classified ads, résumés, and tax forms can be examined. Students can practice writing business and thank-you letters and using the telephone. The psychology of advertising can be studied.

Social Studies. Study the history and future of a particular job, business, or industry. Examine the variety of jobs and services available in a community. Teach map reading as an aid to student mobility, and explain how it can be useful in occupations such as delivering packages or driving a taxi. In the study of history or of different cultures, needs common to all people can be emphasized.

Health, Physical Education, and Fine Arts. Jobs and other pursuits that require strength, dexterity, and endurance can be discussed. The relationship between nutrition and exercise, and good health can be studied. Oral hygiene, cleanliness, and appropriate dress can be emphasized. The appreciation of the arts and of aesthetics can be taught as a leisure time activity.

Which approach to career education works best?

Clark (1979) suggests that students are served best through the use of a combination of the infusion and separate programming approaches. Infusion does not require that courses or units be added to an already crowded curriculum, and separate programming ensures that career education will be systematically approached. This combination approach permits a balance between academic skills and career education skills, providing a unique opportunity to tie together the two sets of competencies (Clark, 1979).

The ratio of separate programming to infusion found in any school program will be determined by such factors as the preparation and orientation of the teachers involved and the school's commitment to career education. The students' grade level, their degrees of handicap (if any), and the instructional setting are also considered. Clark (1979) has developed a schematic representation of career education delivery options based on these three considerations; it is shown in Table 13-1.

You will notice that separate programming is generally used for more severely handicapped children and for those in special class settings. In the regular classroom, career education is usually provided through infusion and unit teaching. Visually or hearing impaired children and the severely learning disabled may need separate career education courses in addition to that which has been infused into the regular class coursework.

INSTRUCTIONAL METHODS AND ACTIVITIES

A number of techniques and activities can be used in career education. Several of these will be discussed in the following pages.

Community Resources. One of the best is to invite family members and persons from business, industry, and social groups to visit the classroom and

Table 13-1
Delivery Systems for Career Education

	Mildly Handicapped		Moderately to Severely Handicapped	
	K-3	*4-6*	*K-3*	*4-6*
Regular Class or Resource Room	Infusion and unit teaching	Infusion and unit teaching	Infusion and separate subject	Infusion and separate subject
Special Class	Infusion and separate subject	Infusion and separate subject	Total curriculum	Total curriculum

Source: Clark, G. M. *Career Education for the Handicapped Child in the Elementary Classroom*, p. 165. Copyright 1979 by Love Publishing Company. Reprinted by permission.

discuss their work and social activities. A panel of several persons is an interesting forum for such discussions. Field trips to places of employment, community service agencies, and recreation facilities can also be effective. Field trips should be carefully planned around a set of objectives, and they should be integrated with activities in the classroom.

Why are simulations so useful in career education programs?

Simulation. Within the classroom, role playing, sociodramas, and simulation are excellent methods of developing specific career education concepts. Students can practice for situations such as riding a bus, making a date, or interviewing for a job, and they can develop sociodramas for acting out various social or occupational situations. Simulation can provide a realistic opportunity to learn about a particular occupation, business, or community agency. In special education settings, assembly lines, stores, banks, corporations, and restaurants have all been simulated successfully. Employment situations can be simulated through the use of time clocks, by designating work areas, and by assigning worker roles such as line leader, shade puller, and blackboard cleaner on a rotating basis. At the high school level Junior Achievement gives students the opportunity to develop their own companies, produce and sell products, and divide the profits. Class discussions, demonstrations, and inquiry or problem-solving techniques can be used effectively at both the elementary and secondary levels.

Unit Instruction. Unit instruction can be used to implement either the infusion or separate programming approach. Meyen (1976) has defined it as a "highly generic approach that allows skills and concepts to be couched in the context of themes meaningful to students." This means that a single instructional experience can be used to meet content, career development, and academic skill goals. A particular unit could emphasize the acquisition of information or the development of a specific skill, or it could be centered around a particular activity.

How can career education concepts best be infused into the curriculum?

The experience unit is probably the most appropriate for infusing career education concepts into the total instructional program. Kirk and Johnson (1951), in an early book on teaching the mentally retarded, suggested that a portion of the daily instruction be organized around a unit theme, with tool subjects (reading, writing, and arithmetic) and other activities (art, music, and recreation) connected with that theme. Meyen (1976) goes further and recommends that experiences in each of six core areas be incorporated into each unit, regardless of the unit's topic. The core areas he suggests are arithmetic, social competencies, communication skills, safety, health, and vocational information. A particular unit might emphasize one core area more than the others, depending on the topic, but experiences in all the core areas should be planned for each unit. For example, a unit on manufacturing could cover mathematics, science, health and safety, language arts, and other academic subjects. Mathematical skills could be related to wages, salaries, prices, and hours worked. Scientific principles could be explained in terms of machinery observed on a field trip. Health and safety could be approached through a discussion of special clothing worn by workers, company safety rules, and health services available at a factory. Interviewing, reading, films, sociodrama, and role playing could be related to language arts.

A unit devoted to career education could focus exclusively on that subject (such as Community Helpers), or it could be designed to help students meet other educational objectives as well. It could include such topics as community services, good work habits, and self-awareness. The unit approach is especially helpful to teachers of the handicapped, because it permits students to learn information and develop concepts by means other than reading, and it provides many opportunities for remediation. As mentioned earlier, the teacher may have to provide alternative methods of career education to handicapped students if they are not at the same developmental stage as the nonhandicapped.

In any group instruction, it is important for the teacher to remember that although the group may be focusing on a particular theme, there is room for individualization of objectives within that theme. Indeed, whether the student is mainstreamed or is in a self-contained setting, it is essential that objectives and activities be varied to meet the individual student's needs. A good way to ensure that both individual and group objectives are met is to include them in the daily lesson plan. This helps the teacher use time effectively and leaves a record of the teacher's approach to the unit, which can be used in subsequent years and shared with other teachers.

What is a learning center?

Learning Centers. A learning center is an instructional area where children teach themselves. These centers can be designed to teach or provide practice on a skill or concept that is being emphasized in an instructional unit. They can be developed for use by either individuals or groups.

Centers should focus on specific instructional objectives; they should provide direct sensory experiences through which concepts and learning skills can be developed (Beach, 1977). They should include a variety of activities — reading, listening, discussing, and watching, for example. Each center should offer activities appropriate for students at different levels.

The use of learning centers offers several advantages (Davidson et al., 1976):

> Learning centers can help you to personalize and individualize instruction. They can give children a choice. They can provide different modes of learning. They can buy time, time for you to say to a child, face to face: "My, I like that. Tell me about it." Centers can have specific activities for specific skills. They can be self-checking. They can provide activities that are open-ended and that encourage divergent thinking.

TECHNOLOGY IN ACTION

In the Fayette County School System of Lexington, Kentucky, vocational interest assessment begins, along with career exploration, in grade 7. During the 9th grade, every handicapped student in special or regular classes receives a complete vocational assessment for the purpose of identifying career and vocational education goals and objectives for their IEP. During the 1983–84 school year, more than 200 students were evaluated from 13 different schools within the school district.

This vocational assessment process has two levels: (1) screening and (2) comprehensive assessment. The screening assessment starts during the first few weeks of each school year when special education teachers and school-based teacher consultants administer a six-hour battery of tests that determine vocational interests and attitudes. Psychological and social histories and educational assessments are also obtained, as are medical records.

In each school, screening assessments including aptitudes, independent living skills, and basic work skills are done by a vocational assessment specialist and aides working with groups of three students. These assessments last approximately two hours. Personal interviews with the students also are conducted at this time.

The formal assessment is based upon need as determined by the screening phase. Each student needing intensive vocational evaluation spends approximately five hours at a vocational assessment center that is set up in one of the four high schools in the school district. This comprehensive assessment includes actual hands-on experience with job-related tasks in simulated work settings. Usually it is administered to groups of three students at a time.

After data have been collected from all of the assessment instruments, they are entered into a computer that has detailed analyses stored for over 1,500 primarily entry level jobs. The computer matches the abilities of the students with job requirements and identifies clusters of jobs that appear to be appropriate for each student.

Students are then provided with intensive job exploration activities in order to assist them in making decisions about the specific jobs in which they might be interested. Again, the computer is used to develop a more specific match between student and job. This time, the computer selects 7 or 8 specific jobs that might be appropriate for that student.

Any discrepancies between student characteristics and job requirements are identified at this time. These discrepancies then become the basis for goals and objectives for an Individualized Vocational Plan which is incorporated into the student's IEP. An internal steering committee evaluates student progress every 12 weeks. Updated matches between students and jobs can be done at any time through a telecommunication system between the secondary schools and the vocational assessment center.

The information generated by this system is also used to make decisions about the length of educational services needed for a particular student. Some students are encouraged to stay in school until age 21 in order to develop and refine their skills further. As students are about to graduate, school personnel work with vocational rehabilitation counselors and local agencies for placement of students into a continuum of community services. For those who need continued development, an inter-agency cooperative effort is underway to continue the implementation of the Individualized Vocational Plan formulated by the school system.

Another important aspect of learning centers it that they foster self-management, which is itself an important skill in career development. If the instructions for the center's use are clearly stated, students can enter the center and select an activity with little or no help from the teacher. The provision of more than one activity in the center will encourage children to exercise their ability to make choices.

An on-site learning center provides for the development of vocational skills.

EDUCATION FOR LEISURE

Career education has been conceptualized as including both paid and unpaid productive effort. The concept extends beyond economic factors to encompass one's total life style, including productive use of leisure time. People have more leisure time than ever before, a trend that futurists predict will increase. Improved technology has given us a shorter work week as well as massive worker displacement and unemployment. Highly specialized jobs, which are increasingly information-oriented rather than production- or people-oriented, are often uninvolving, uncreative, and unfulfilling. Clark (1979) notes that the emphasis in most mass media on leisure activities as the central focus of life in this country gives credence to the notion that paid work is becoming less important in terms of personal fulfillment. Increasingly, people seek satisfaction through their leisure time activities, with unpaid work becoming an important avenue to personal fulfillment and self-actualization.

Why is education for leisure important?

Educating the handicapped for leisure can help them overcome many of the social, economic, and attitudinal barriers that might otherwise keep them from enjoying the social and recreational life of the community. Some of the goals of leisure education of particular relevance to the handicapped are included in the following list (Leisure Information Service, 1976, pp. 42–43).

— Appreciation of the wide diversity of leisure choices and lifestyles.
— Recognition that understanding and appreciation of leisure experiences will be enhanced through direct exploration and participation.
— Development of specific skills necessary for participation in a variety of leisure time activities.
— Understanding of the contributions that leisure time provides for self-expression and physical and intellectual development.
— Development of interests and problem solving that will facilitate independent pursuits of leisure in the home, school, and community.

Some of the most popular leisure education activities take place out of doors. Instructional programs for the handicapped have been designed in backpacking, nature study, camping, and outdoor sports. Project EXPLORE (Expanding Programs and Learning in Outdoor Recreation and Education) provides a competency-based, skill-oriented curriculum designed to provide individualized, systematic, and direct instruction to handicapped children. Instructions have been developed in the areas of (1) camping and self-maintenance; (2) sports, games, and physical development; (3) arts and crafts; (4) safety and survival, and (5) nature study and development. The curriculum has been used successfully in special education classrooms, summer camps, and outdoor education programs with children whose handicaps ranged from mild to severe. Special instruction programs have also been developed for teaching swimming, bowling, skiing, horseback riding, wheelchair basketball, and other sports. The Special Olympics for the mentally retarded have increased public acceptance of the fact that everyone can benefit from participating and competing in sports.

What is the National Committee★Arts for the Handicapped?

Another recent focus of leisure education is the arts. Since the mid-1970s, the National Committee★Arts for the Handicapped (NCAH) has been promoting arts programming. The NCAH sponsors state and local Very Special Arts Festivals across the nation, funds exemplary Model Site programs, supports a variety of Special Project programs, and serves as a resource for information and technical assistance on arts and the handicapped. These activities

Learning to compete in leisure activities aids the personal adjustment of handicapped people. The competitive skills learned may then carry over into other parts of their lives.

are based on the recognition that children can learn by working in and observing the arts and that arts experiences promote social, emotional, and intellectual growth.

An example of a program that provides both art and leisure education is the Appalachian Folkcrafts Project for the Handicapped. In this project, curriculum materials were developed to teach handicapped children folk crafts as a leisure time activity. There was already a well-established crafts industry in Appalachia, so the development of these skills was a natural means of mainstreaming handicapped youngsters into the leisure activities of the region. Learning folk craft processes permitted the participants to develop a sense of regional pride, learn something about art, and attend social activities at craft fairs and associations. A set of guidelines for using this approach in other geographic areas was developed by the personnel of this project (Cegelka, 1979).

PROBE 13-4
Instructional Approaches in Career Education

1. What are the two approaches to career education?

2. T F An alternative to infusion is the unit approach to teaching.

3. T F Career education is best taught with a combination of infusion and separate programming.

4. T F Some subject matter content cannot be taught adequately through career education infusion.

5. The _____ approach is the best way to infuse career education concepts into the curriculum.

6. The use of _____ in career education helps to develop skills in self-management.

7. Explain why leisure education is important for handicapped people.

8. List four leisure activities in your community in which handicapped people could participate. Do not include activities that they could simply observe.

SELECTING THE LEAST RESTRICTIVE ENVIRONMENT

You should be able to describe the ways in which mainstreaming and career education interact.

Career education is applicable to persons of all ages across a variety of educational settings. As pointed out earlier, the goals of career education have long been advocated in slightly different form as the educational outcomes for the handicapped. Career education, in turn, has stressed the importance of these goals for all individuals.

What is the responsibility of the IEP committee with respect to career education?

Although the skills and objectives of a career education curriculum are appropriate for both handicapped and nonhandicapped youngsters, developmental lags of the former group could mean that somewhat different learning experiences are required within a given instructional program. The special education teacher can be a valuable resource to the regular class teacher in modifying career education programs to accommodate the handicapped student. In addition, at the secondary level particularly, the curricular focus of the regular academic classes may not be and often is not supportive of the career development needs of the mildly handicapped. There is frequently little about the lowest-track academic class to recommend it as attractive or even appropriate to the career development needs of slow students. Nonprescriptive mainstreaming can result in limiting the options of the special education student. Care must be taken by the students' IEP Committees to ensure that they are placed only in those settings that facilitate the development of specific competencies and that all career education competencies are developed.

Opportunities for handicapped students to participate in a variety of mainstream career preparation programs have expanded considerably in the past several years. PL 94-142, guaranteeing appropriate education for all handicapped children, specifically mentioned vocational education as appropriate for many handicapped individuals. The Vocational Education Act of 1963 and its amendments have provided that 10 percent of the research and demonstration money that each state received under this legislation be used for providing vocational education to the handicapped. In addition, the Vocational Rehabilitation Act of 1973 guarantees handicapped individuals access to all educational programs receiving federal money. These legislative efforts have greatly expanded the opportunities afforded the handicapped to obtain appropriate career preparation at both the secondary and post-secondary levels.

It is important that the full range of placements, from the completely segregated to the completely integrated, be considered for each child. Unfortunately, many educators interpret the "least restrictive environment" clause of PL 94-142 as meaning that students should be placed in the least restrictive environment *currently available,* without considering whether the environment meets the career education needs of the student. The lowest academic track in a school's secondary program may provide few benefits to the student with significant academic handicaps. Another half-grade level of achievement in reading or arithmetic may be less useful to the student than daily living, personal-social, and occupational skills.

What is the major criterion for making an educational placement for career education?

The best approach is to place students in classes on the basis of their need to acquire specific skills. Brolin (1973) suggests that student progress be carefully monitored, and that the student remain in a particular setting only until he or she attains specifically prescribed competencies. Segregated settings may be more frequently appropriate for students with severe or multiple handicaps, but even students with mild handicaps may need educational experiences available only through separate specialized programming efforts.

Whether the student is in a self-contained or a mainstream setting, the overall career education model has important implications for the level of achievement students attain. Carefully sequenced educational experiences at the elementary and junior high levels permit education at the secondary level to focus, when appropriate, on the development of specific occupational skills. The acquisition of desirable personal characteristics and attitudes is an important goal of all levels of career education. Education programs that combine training in academic, personal-social, daily living, and occupational skills hold great promise for developing the individual to his or her full potential.

SECONDARY PROGRAMMING

**How do career
education and
vocational
education differ?**

Despite the life-adjustment focus of many earlier special education programs,
until recently the more systematic career education efforts in special education
were focused at the secondary level. The work-study programs of the 1950s
and 1960s were the primary model for the occupational preparation of handicapped youth. Beginning in the early 1970s, increasing emphasis was given to
the specific vocational training available through vocational education programs. While people sometimes mistakenly equate career education and vocational education, they are not synonymous. Career education is a much
broader concept that encompasses vocational education, work attitudes, and
skills at the secondary and post-secondary levels. Vocational education is
geared toward providing specific vocational skill training and vocational adjustment; career education is concerned with the quality of the individual's
total life adjustment.

The broadly based conceptualization presented by Clark (1979) earlier in
this chapter has further expanded the arenas of career education to encompass
both college preparatory and general studies curricula. These options may be
particularly appropriate for children whose handicaps are other than mental
retardation, such as those with specific learning disabilities, behavior disorders, and visual or auditory handicaps. They would also be appropriate for
gifted and talented students, of course. For students who are less capable
intellectually, work evaluation or work adjustment program options may be
appropriate. These training programs can result in either competitive occupational placements or community rehabilitation or sheltered workshop placements. These options are not mutually exclusive, as students may participate
in two or more career preparation experiences. For example, students in the
college preparatory or general studies curricula might choose to participate,
perhaps during a summer session, in a work evaluation program in an effort
to understand better their occupational aptitudes and preferences.

**What are the main
features of a
work-study
program?**

Although traditional work-study programs are less prevalent than they
once were, they remain the curricular emphasis of many self-contained special
day programs at the secondary level. Ideally, these programs involve cooperative working relationships between special education and rehabilitation services, with the vocational rehabilitation counselor working closely with the
work-study teacher to provide work experiences and evaluation for the handicapped students. In the model programs as originally designed, students typically would rotate through a series of partial-day job exploration experiences
beginning in the sophomore year, with longer-term placements provided during the junior year. As seniors they would participate in paid, supervised
occupational placements as a prerequisite to graduation. These culminating
experiences usually were either half-day placements for the full academic year
or full-day placements for one semester. The integral involvement of the

This 22-year-old graduate of a special education program holds a clerical job in an office.

vocational rehabilitation counselor throughout the program meant that job placements appropriate to the skill levels of the individual students could be made. Further, the close supervision of the students by the counselor meant that during the school-based portion of the program, teachers could work to remedy work-related problems noted during the on-the-job observations.

The cooperative nature of these programs was the basis of their success. Rehabilitation counselors typically have information and skills relative to the world of work that special education teachers may lack. One former rehabilitation counselor who worked in a program that served primarily mildly retarded youngsters has written a text describing many of the problems and rewards in working with this population (Payne, Mercer, and Epstein, 1974):

Several years ago I was hired as a vocational rehabilitation counselor and I can readily recall my first day on the job. I was assigned a caseload of handicapped clients and my major responsibilities were too numerous and varied to list. . . . I was instructed to read the policy manual and find the clients.

"What do you mean, 'find the clients'?" I responded.

"The last counselor left unexpectedly and the first thing you need to do is find out who and where your clients are," I was matter-of-factly told. . . .

I picked the folder lying on top and arbitrarily chose this person to be my first client. After reading the folder, I decided to go to the restaurant where the client was listed as working. I pulled up to the restaurant in a state car and entered the place of business to find I had arrived at a busy time. Since the manager wasn't available to talk, I decided to have lunch. After eating, I was approached by the manager who informed me that the client had walked off the job four months ago. I hope counselors [will learn] to understand business routine, *schedule,* and business thinking.

It took me four days to find the client. He was at home, unshaven, watching television, and feeling sorry for himself. He was living in a place which smelled like urine and looked like a pigsty. I hope [that counselors will learn] about *people.*

Within a year under my counseling and guidance, this client was placed on, and walked off of, five different jobs. I hope [that counselors learn] something about *evaluation* and *training.*

One time I remember driving around the block three times to build up enough courage to talk with a hostile employer. He was mad and he had a right to be. My client lost his temper and broke the front window in the store. I hope [that counselors will learn] about *how to approach* an employer.

I once knew an eager counselor who placed six clients on jobs in one day. He thought he really had done something. During a follow-up session one month later, he couldn't find any of them — they all had been fired. I hope [that counselors will learn] about *follow-up.*

I heard of a client placed at the local humane society to care for animals. During the second week he felt sorry for the caged up animals and went around opening up all of the pens. There were dogs all over the county. It took over two weeks to round up the dogs. Yes, I hope [that counselors will understand] *people's feelings.*

I once worked with a client who had spent considerable time in jail for stealing bicycles. I took him to a grocery store to be interviewed for a job. Things were going fairly well until he spotted a bicycle shop across the street. I couldn't get his nose away from the window. He just kept muttering, "I want to work in a bicycle shop." I gave up at the grocery store, grabbed his arm, and quickly went across the street to inquire about a job in the bicycle shop. I don't know how, but the client somehow got a job that very day and worked there for several years before he was sent to prison for breaking into houses. You know, I hope [that counselors] really [do learn] about people, *all types of people.*

I have had clients hug me, laugh with me, cry with me, curse me, throw things at me, and spit on me. I have experienced joy and sorrow, success and failure. I have worked with clients I enjoyed seeing come into my office and I have worked with clients I enjoyed seeing walk *out* of my office. At times I really liked working for vocational rehabilitation and at other times I couldn't stand it.

What percent of the unemployed in the U.S. are handicapped?

For many years work-study programs were the major model for attempting to prepare special education students for adult employment. These programs emphasized the development of work attitudes and basic employee attributes and prepared students for entry-level jobs. The resulting entry levels of adult employment were interpreted as indicators of program efficacy. Subsequently, studies with both mildly handicapped and severely handicapped individuals have indicated that we frequently underestimated the employment potential of the handicapped. The disabled constitute 50 percent of the unemployed in this country, with 76 percent of all disabled women being unemployed. Of disabled individuals who are employed, 85 percent earn less than $7,000 per year and 52 percent earn less than $2,000 per year (Bowe, 1980). As many as two-thirds of all adults with handicaps are living below the poverty level (Bowe, 1979).

Data such as these, coupled with a greater recognition of the rights and abilities of handicapped individuals, resulted in various attempts to expand the range of vocational opportunities available to them. When the Vocational Education Act of 1963, which mandated that programs be extended to handicapped individuals, resulted in little identifiable change in practices, the 1968 Amendments specified that 10 percent of the funds allocated under Part B of this act be spent on providing services to handicapped students and another 15 percent on services for the disadvantaged. Despite these laws, considerable resistance to providing vocational education services to the handicapped persisted. Much of the set-aside funds were not expended on the handicapped, and funds that were spent frequently funded add-on segregated programs such as self-contained classes at the prevocational and vocational levels, instructional resource centers, and in-service training efforts for teachers. Funds were only infrequently spent on providing direct vocational education training of the handicapped, and few of these efforts involved mainstreaming into existing vocational education programs. A 1974 report of a federal program audit revealed that 70 percent of all handicapped students receiving vocational education were enrolled in segregated programs (Olympus Research Corporation, 1974).

In an effort to increase the efficiency and effectiveness of vocational education for special needs students, the 1976 Amendments designated that these students be integrated into regular vocational programs, with the facilities and programs being modified to meet their special needs. PL 94-142 specifically mentions vocational education as an appropriate educational provision for handicapped youth. Since 1973, rehabilitation legislation has emphasized service delivery to severely handicapped individuals; in addition, CETA services have now been expanded to include handicapped individuals, regardless of income, whose handicaps present substantial barriers to employment.

How many handicapped people are enrolled in vocational education programs?

Despite these strong and repeated mandates, appropriate vocational preparation opportunities for the handicapped have remained elusive. Although handicapped individuals constitute 10 to 12 percent of the general population, they account for only 2.56 percent of the total enrollment in vocational education programs, with ⅓ of these individuals receiving their training in segregated programs for the handicapped (Office of Civil Rights, 1979). Apprenticeship programs had the lowest percentage of handicapped student enrollments (0.37 percent), and work-study programs had the highest percentage (4.48 percent). These data led the Office of Civil Rights (1980) to conclude that handicapped enrollees appear to be clustered in those vocational education programs that prepare them for the lower-level occupations. Numerical underrepresentation of the handicapped is also apparent in other career preparation programs: 3 percent of the total CETA clients; 3 percent of community college enrollments; and 2 percent of enrollments in four-year colleges.

Why are handicapped people underrepresented in vocational programs?

A variety of factors contribute to this underrepresentation. Since the early 1970s, one of the most neglected areas of special education has been secondary-level programs, leading to student dropout rates that may be as much as five to six times higher than those for nonhandicapped students (President's Committee on Employment of the Handicapped, 1979). The focus of resource room programs at the secondary level is typically on maintaining students in the regular curriculum; when segregated career preparation programs exist, they tend to be taught by special education teachers who have little realistic understanding of the realities of the world of work and who have their strongest preparation in elementary level methodologies and curriculum. Finally, vocational education programs frequently have resisted including handicapped students. Historically, these programs have been geared toward providing specific training in skilled occupations to students of average and above average abilities. Taught by teachers without traditional college-based preparation but whose backgrounds are in the vocational skill areas they teach, these programs have not been geared toward notions of equality of opportunity and individualization of instruction. Many vocational education teachers have viewed the inclusion of handicapped students as denigrating to the status of their programs and have argued that because their programs are evaluated on the basis of job layoffs of former participants, inclusion of handicapped students jeopardizes their very existence. Additional concerns over integrating handicapped students into regular vocational education programs include the following (Minner, Knutson, and Aloia, 1979):

1. The perception that handicapped students are being "dumped" into vocational classes in the name of mainstreaming.
2. The belief that integration will jeopardize the quantity and quality of services and instruction provided to regular students.

3. The belief that the time factors involved in integrative programming are prohibitive.
4. The expectation that the skill level and abilities of handicapped students will be too low for success in vocational classes.
5. The fear that safety factors in certain classes will impose a liability on vocational teachers.
6. The belief that most handicapped students, even with training, are not capable of acquiring the necessary vocational competence allowing them to obtain a job in competitive employment.

What needs to be done to increase the availability of vocational education for handicapped students?

The previous discussion clearly demonstrates the impossibility of legislating emotions, attitudes, or a sense of commitment. Attention must be given to allaying many of the concerns and fears of vocational educators and of expanding their involvement from initial placement decisions to setting educational objectives and evaluating student success. Assurances must be provided that inclusion of handicapped students will not displace nonhandicapped students in these programs; the focus of vocational education must be broadened to provide greater emphasis on the development of general work skills and attitudes. In-service education must provide vocational education teachers with the needed instructional skills for working with students with disabilities, and program entrance requirements must be changed to reflect the competencies needed to perform the jobs targeted on the IEPs rather than the aptitudes required to complete an entire training program. Finally, program evaluation should be broadened to include the provision of services to special needs students and not limited to labor market layoffs.

VOCATIONAL REHABILITATION SERVICES

At the secondary and post-secondary level, vocational rehabilitation services can provide meaningful opportunities for career exploration, vocational evaluation, and occupational preparation. Founded in the early 1920s, the Vocational Rehabilitation Administration (now known as the Rehabilitation Services Administration) was established to provide training and related support for individuals, particularly war veterans, who became disabled as adults and needed rehabilitation to get jobs.

What services are provided by vocational rehabilitation agencies?

Both the range of services and the types of disabilities qualifying for services have expanded considerably since that time. Services funded by Rehabilitation money include medical, psychological, and vocational evaluations; the purchase of prosthetic devices; specific training costs (including prevocational, vocational, trade school, and college expenses) as well as living stipends; the purchase of tools, equipment, licenses, and supplies; and similar types of support. The type, duration, and goals of services provided are specified on an Individualized Written Rehabilitation Program (IWRP) developed for each client by the rehabilitation counselor.

Historically, one frequently found considerable resistance on the part of vocational rehabilitation counselors to providing services to those whose disabilities were developmental in nature, as contrasted to those whose disabilities were acquired after reaching adulthood. Traditional emphasis has been on rehabilitation, not *habilitation*. It was not until 1943 that the mentally retarded and mentally ill became eligible for services, and not until 1981 that the learning disabled became eligible. Emphasis on achieving case closures has lead rehabilitation counselors frequently to make conservative choices in selecting clients, with severity of handicap the most prevalent reason for denial of services (Laski, 1979). The language of the 1973 Rehabilitation Act, with its emphasis on providing services to the most severely handicapped, signaled a new direction. Some five years later, Rehabilitation Services funding was expanded to include those services required for the independent living of individuals for whom no vocational goal was deemed possible. Just as the CEC Position Statement on Career Education acknowledged that gainful employment was not a realistic career education expectation for everyone, this expansion similarly recognized that legitimate goals for some individuals do not include vocational outcomes.

While these developments have been positive ones for developmentally disabled individuals, many vocational rehabilitation programs are still reluctant to fund services for this segment of the population. The delivery of comprehensive, coordinated support services has been further plagued by a lack of clarity as to which type of program (special education, vocational education, or rehabilitation) was responsible for what type of service. As an example, partly as a function of PL 94-142's guarantee of appropriate educational services for handicapped individuals through age 21, many vocational rehabilitation agencies concluded that they were no longer responsible for providing services to handicapped individuals enrolled in special education programs. In a similar fashion, vocational educators questioned their continued responsibility for including handicapped students in their programs.

An important breakthrough came in 1977, when the Rehabilitation Services Administration and the U.S. Office of Education issued a *Memorandum of Understanding* that recognized the overlapping responsibilities of these agencies. The memorandum stated, "Education agencies are concerned with the overall life adjustment of handicapped young persons within their communities, including the ability to become employed. Vocational rehabilitation agencies are concerned with enabling handicapped individuals — particularly the severely disabled — to prepare for and engage in employment. These concerns are clearly compatible and every effort should be made to coordinate services" (*Federal Register,* October 3, 1977). Through this and two subsequent memoranda, chief state school officers and state directors of rehabilitation service agencies were encouraged to develop formal cooperative agreements among vocational rehabilitation, vocational education, and special education (Commissioners' Joint Memorandum, November 21, 1978) and to address the need to provide all handicapped persons with comprehensive vocational education services (*Federal Register,* September 25, 1978).

FUTURE DIRECTIONS

What impact will the "Information Age" have on career preparation for handicapped people?

Throughout this century the major purpose of special education has been to prepare handicapped individuals to lead productive, personally satisfying adult lives. Today's emphasis on vocational education and career preparation for the mildly handicapped and the community-based training approach to preparing the severely handicapped for "environments of ultimate functioning" are modern reflections of this goal. The career education movement has both expanded and validated these efforts. Today these efforts must all be reexamined in light of the technological advances that are having such a significant influence on our environment. The economic dislocations that we are currently experiencing in the form of energy shortages, factory closings, corporate bankruptcies, union breaking, and high levels of unemployment mirror futurist claims that our society is undergoing a dramatic and basic restructuring (Cegelka and Lewis, 1983). With the onset of the "Information Age," robots are replacing workers in countless jobs, work sites are becoming decentralized, and literacy is becoming more important.

These changes have profound implications for special educators. The focus of special education curricula will have to shift from teaching specific skills and responses to identifying and teaching those competencies that will generalize to many settings and will enhance individuals' ability to adapt to the new environments that emerge. Occupational and even life adjustment skills that are important today may become obsolete almost overnight. Technological advances can mean expanded employment opportunities for some handicapped individuals; those with severe orthopedic handicaps will be able to work at home, interacting with the workplace through telecommunications; bioengineering advances are already eradicating the debilitating effects of some sensory and physical disorders; and supportive environments are being engineered to provide technological compensation for other disabilities. However, these potentials must be viewed within the limitations that the new technologies will also impose. The current and predicted massive worker displacement could mean that highly capable individuals will be competing for low-level jobs, perhaps permanently displacing the least-skilled workers. Historically, in times of economic recession, the handicapped have been the most adversely affected. Tawney (1982, p. 391) has noted that information management skills (including logic, abstraction, synthesis, and generative thinking behavior) will become increasingly important, and "since these are the qualities in which mentally retarded individuals are most deficient, their integration into a future, high technology society appears to be more doubtful."

How will career education and vocational services need to be altered to meet the needs of our changing society?

This may mean that specific categories of public works programs will have to be reserved for those with conceptual handicaps (Cegelka and Lewis, 1983). Clearly, rehabilitative and social services will have to be restructured to provide for both continuous and periodic interventions to help disabled individuals make needed life adjustments. It may be that career education, by reemphasizing values and skills related to nonoccupational productivity and self-realization, can help fill this need. To date, however, its persisting emphasis on traditional forms of occupational adjustment suggests that career education may be ill prepared to respond to these changing needs.

What is the future of career education?

While the career education movement has survived for well over 10 years, its future is not clear. Ambiguity about its definitions and failure to engage in systematic program evaluation efforts have impeded its full development and acceptance. Educational critics complain about an already overburdened school curriculum that encompasses subjects such as consumerism, driver education, parenting, sex education, nutrition, and hygiene. Declining student achievement test scores, coupled with shrinking educational dollars, have fueled a "back to basics" movement that is narrowing the focus of educational efforts to specific academic skill areas. Changes in presidential administrations and in the federal educational leadership have resulted in new priorities and new program directions.

The combined effect of these limitations may mean that career education as a movement will go the way of previous educational enthusiasms and innovations. Should this occur, it is probable that many of its vestiges will remain. For decades to come, American education will continue to be enhanced by its emphasis on educational relevance, its involvement of the broader community in educational decision making and programming, and its developmental, lifelong learning orientation. Within special education, it is likely that career education will continue as an identifiable program feature. Benefits that have accrued to special education include the identification of the similarities that exist in the educational goals and objectives for all students, a refocusing on the scope and sequence of special education curricula, improved career preparation opportunities for adolescents, and increased involvement with community agencies and representatives. Continued concern with the life adjustment of exceptional individuals will characterize special education programs of the future.

PROBE 13-5
Least Restrictive Environment

1. The cooperative work-study programs of the 1960s had which of the following features?
   a. Vocational rehabilitation counselors worked with the schools in placing and evaluating the student during on-the-job training.
   b. The programs provided highly integrated, mainstream career education experiences.
   c. The programs provided a graduated sequence of occupational exploration experiences.
   d. As part of the program, problems observed during on-the-job training were remediated in the classroom.

e. They were supported jointly with funds from vocational rehabilitation and special education projects.

2. List four types of career preparation programming available today.

3. Name two factors that account for the reluctance of many vocational education teachers to work with special needs students.

4. What major historical factor contributes to a reluctance on the part of rehabilitation counselors to work with developmentally disabled individuals?

5. Describe two ways that career education facilitates the mainstreaming of mildly handicapped students.

6. Describe the detrimental effect that inappropriate mainstreaming can have on the career development of handicapped students.

7. Describe one way that technological advances may improve the employment possibilities for handicapped individuals and one way that they may be hindered by technology.

8. How has career education benefited special education?

SUMMARY

1. Career education is designed to improve the overall quality of life adjustment of all people, regardless of age, ability level, or handicap.
2. Career education developed out of a recognition that our education, social, and economic systems failed to prepare students for life as working adults.
3. The career education movement has received considerable support from state and federal legislation.
4. There are many definitions of career education, ranging from those that are narrowly occupational to those that encompass overall life adjustment.
5. The career development stages are career awareness, career orientation and exploration, and career preparation. These stages both are sequential and overlap.
6. Two common approaches to career education are the infusion approach and the separate programming approach. Most successful programs make use of both approaches.
7. A number of different techniques and exercises have been used successfully to teach career education, including unit teaching, learning centers, guest speakers, field trips, sociodramas, class discussions, demonstrations, and simulations.
8. In the past, the cooperative vocational rehabilitation/special education program was the model for career education in secondary special education.

9. Today the educational options for career preparation include the college preparatory or general studies curriculum, vocational education, experience-based career education, work-study programs, and work evaluation and adjustment programs.
10. Technological changes along with renewed emphasis on "back to basics" present strong challenges to the future directions of career education.

TASK SHEET 13
Field Experiences with Special Career Education

Select *one* of the following and complete the required tasks.

Workplace Visit

Visit one of the following and write a paper of no more than three pages about your experiences:
   a. a sheltered workshop
   b. a public school work-study program
   c. a rehabilitation agency

Interview on Employment

Interview one of the following people and write a three-page paper on the substance of your interview:
   a. A secondary work-study teacher
   b. A vocational rehabilitation counselor
   c. A sheltered workshop employee
   d. An employer who hires handicapped persons

Interview on Work Problems

Interview a handicapped person about the problems associated with employment. Write a three-page paper describing this person's responses.

Agency Investigation

Write to three of the following agencies and inquire about the services that they provide related to career education, vocational education, or vocational rehabilitation for handicapped people. Write a three-page paper which synthesizes your findings, including how you might use their services if you were a professional working in this area.

American Association for Health,
Physical Education, and Recreation
1201 Sixteenth Street, NW
Washington, DC 20036

National Committee★Arts for the
Handicapped
1701 K Street, NW
Washington, DC 20006

American Personnel and Guidance
Association
1607 New Hampshire Avenue, NW
Washington, DC 20009

National Rehabilitation Association
1522 K Street, NW, Suite 1120
Washington, DC 20005

National Rehabilitation Information
Center
8th & Varnum Streets, NE
The Catholic University of America
Washington, DC 20064

President's Committee on Employment
of the Handicapped
1111 Twentieth Street, NW, Suite 600
Washington, DC 20036

Social Security Administration
Washington, DC 20009

Your local or state office of Employment
Services or Rehabilitation Services

Library Study

Use the library to locate three articles on career education, vocational education, or vocational rehabilitation for handicapped people. Write a one-page abstract of each, concluding with a paragraph about your reactions to the article. Here are the names of some journals in which you can find articles:

Business Education Forum
Journal of Home Economics
Journal of Applied Rehabilitation Counseling
Journal of Rehabilitation
Rehabilitation Counseling Bulletin
Voc. Ed.

Design Your Own Field Experience

If you know of a unique experience you can have in the area of career education, or do not want to do any of the above alternatives, discuss your idea with your instructor and complete the tasks that you agree on.

Families of handicapped children should be actively involved in providing opportunities for education, home making, socialization, recreation, and other activities that are common among all families.

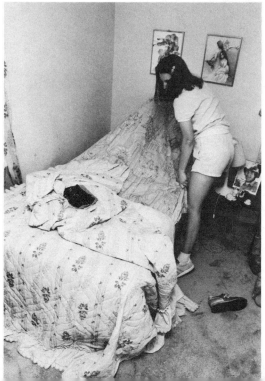

I always felt . . . that handicapped children only belonged to, oh, I don't know, "weird" people. They had one eye in their forehead, and they were either half-retarded themselves, or they were poor. It couldn't happen to a normal middle class person like myself.

I think there were definite stages, at least I went through definite stages of accepting Heather. The first one was disbelief. I just couldn't believe that she was not coming along normally. People would ask me in the store, you know, they could sense after she got so old that there was something wrong. I'd say, "Oh, she's just a little slow." But I would try to hide it from people, and I would just not believe it and not accept it.

And then, the second stage came where she was undeniably handicapped. I couldn't say any longer, "She's a little slow." It got to where it was unquestionable. And then I got to where I resented other healthy kids. This was a really bad stage for me. You'd see mothers wailing on their kids at the supermarket [and] I wanted to shake them, and say: "Look what you've got, you've got a beautiful, healthy, normal child. What are you doing? You know you don't appreciate her."

And I think a lot of people stay in that stage, and that's sad because they're very bitter, and all they can think of is feeling sorry for themselves — they're at this stagnant point in life. . . . If you get past that, and pull yourself up, and say: "O.K., it's nobody's fault, I'm not going to blame myself anymore." . . . I'm not being punished. Where can I go from here? What can I do for my child? What kind of a future can I plan for her? . . . I'm not helping her sitting here crying in my beer. What can I do now? I have to go on. Right now, there's no room in my heart for bitterness. I have to go on. You could destroy yourself if you sit around like that.

Source: Adapted from English, R. W., and Olson, K. K. *Parenting handicapped children: Earliest experiences. Center paper No. 106.* Eugene, Oregon: Rehabilitation Research & Training Center in Mental Retardation, 1976, 10-11.

14

The Families of Children with Disabilities

James A. McLoughlin

James A. McLoughlin is a Professor in the Department of Special Education at the University of Louisville. Dr. McLoughlin is a board member for a variety of parent organizations and is an author of many articles on the topic of families of children with disabilities.

At the beginning of the second decade since the passage of PL 94-142, an exciting period is beginning for the families of students with disabilities and for the educators of these students. As a result of federal recognition of their rights and responsibilities, parents are emerging as a group with a significant role in serving the needs of students with disabilities. They are increasingly involved in planning and carrying out their children's educational programs.

This requires considerable growth on the part of parents and other family members. In addition to making emotional adjustments to their children's disabilities, parents are learning skills to promote quality programs for their children and to participate in them more fully than ever before. At the same time, the educators of their children are developing both interpersonal and technical skills to facilitate greater family involvement. Educators are relating to parents more as the principal agents of treatment and change than as the principal causative agents (Paul and Porter, 1981). They are also learning to communicate better with parents and involve them more effectively in their children's programs. This progress is evident in the increasing number of parenting courses in teacher training programs (Edge, Fink, and Brause, 1978). Educators must apply themselves to involve families of the handicapped, but the rewards are many.

At the foundation of this effort is a close, trusting relationship between the families and educators. Unless both parents and teachers understand one another and appreciate each other's perspectives, little can be accomplished. The families of these children must wrestle with many emotional aspects of their children's disabilities. As we discuss in the following pages, educators must understand and relate to them in the context of these needs in order to encourage their participation.

RELATING TO FAMILIES

> **You should be able to describe how to relate effectively to the needs of families of students with disabilities.**

EMOTIONAL CHALLENGES

Current thinking about the emotional reactions of the family of students with disabilities stresses that they are both *natural* and *unique*. Once parents realize that their child is disabled, it is natural that they experience a series of profound emotional reactions as necessary precursors to accepting the situation. As with any traumatic event, the whole family is hurt, and it works together (consciously or unconsciously) to adapt to the situation (Seligman, 1979). The child with disabilities is not only the occasion for this process, but also an integral part of it.

The process is also unique. Families of children with disabilities have to learn to live with more emotional extremes and ultimately at deeper levels than most people (Paul and Porter, 1981). The disabilities of the children place more pervasive, intense, and enduring demands on the family's growth and development. That is why it is important to view emotional reactions to disabilities in a family context. Without understanding and assistance, these families may overprotect the children with disabilities, use them as scapegoats for other family problems, or break up as a family unit (Perosa and Perosa, 1981).

The changes in the modern family also have a strong effect on the family's ability to cope with a child's disability. Birth control, the movement for equal rights for women, alternative living styles (for example, unmarried couples living together), and the high rate of single-parent families are all influential (Lillie, 1981). Educators must appreciate how these social realities influence the emotional needs of the families of their students.

PARENTAL REACTIONS

Parents' reactions to the birth of a child with disabilities vary greatly. Such factors as religion, socioeconomic status, severity of handicap, obviousness of the disability, parental knowledge, and order of birth can all affect parental responses (Faerstein, 1981). A variety of descriptions of the emotional stages parents pass through before they accept their child's handicap have been offered, but they are highly speculative. Most parents, however, appear to experience periods of frustration, fear, guilt, disappointment, and uncertainty. Because of the intense feeling of loss felt by many parents, some experience a parallel to the adjustment process required by a loved one's death. Kübler-Ross (1969) describes these stages as denial, bargaining, anger, depression, and acceptance.

What is the initial reaction to learning that one's child is handicapped?

Shock. According to Kroth (1975), the initial reaction of parents is shock, even though they frequently suspect that their child has a problem before it is confirmed by professionals. Parents have described this stage by saying:

"My God, I couldn't believe this was happening to us."

"I felt like I was in a daze, and the doctor's voice was a thousand miles away."

"My head spun, I was sick to my stomach, and I fought the urge to faint."

"My wife turned white and started to shake and sob. I was so shaken, I couldn't do anything for her."

"I felt my world, my dreams, my plans were crushed. What an enormous disappointment!"

"I had a hunch about Tommy's problem, but I never anticipated how bad it was."

"I couldn't speak. I was deaf and dumb."

Educators and other professionals must appreciate the significance of this event for parents and other family members. They may be devastated, immobilized, and very vulnerable. Cold, impersonal and even cruel factual revelations can add to the blow and often delay the parental action necessary to obtain help.

Unfortunately, professionals who behave improperly are often themselves unhappy and upset about what they have to tell the parents and lack the skills, time, and other resources to do it well. Educators and other professionals have been known to say to parents:

"Mrs. Jones, I wish I had better news for you but Billy is permanently blind."

"I know this may sound like the end of the world, but your baby has a serious problem."

"There is not time now to get into all of it, but we have a problem."

Among themselves:

"God, I hate it when I have to tell parents that there is something wrong with their kid."

"I was so glad the principal was there. I knew that father was going to come after me."

"Could you believe how those parents reacted? They did not say a damn thing! That poor kid."

Educators must be ready to supply the correct mixture of information, frankness, comfort, and inspiration. They must recognize their own emotional investment in disclosing the disability and channel their feelings constructively.

Denial. Next, parents typically go through a period of denial. They may seek other professional opinions during this stage, hoping for a more promising diagnosis. Although parents' lives are often thrown into a state of confusion and turmoil, they may deny that the handicap has an emotional effect. Denial may also take the form of unrealistic planning for the child. This state is the result of a number of factors, including cultural pressure for the "ideal" child, the level of success expected by the parent, and parental identification with the exceptional child (that is, regarding the child's problem as a problem in oneself). One of the parents may be suffering in this way more than the other. Some typical denial reactions are:

"Are you sure? Can you do some more tests?"

"It's too soon to tell how well Johnny hears. Let's wait until he is five."

"That doctor is always telling people crazy things. Now Tammie doesn't look retarded, does she?"

"Even if there is any truth to what they said, she'll grow out of it. You'll see."

"These days they can do wonders. They'll operate and he'll walk."

"God's good. We'll find a way."

What is the danger in a denial reaction?

Educators must not get annoyed or frustrated with parents at this point. It is easy for the outsider to see the folly in something they say and do, but very hard to help them correct their course of action or thinking. The danger is that the child with the disability may not get any services or may receive inappropriate ones. Some examples of inappropriate feelings expressed by educators and others when confronted with parental denial are:

"Not that charlatan! You wasted your money and time having him test your child."

"Don't you think we are competent to help your child? I am insulted!"

"We are very busy here. If you can't recognize the facts about your child, then you had better go elsewhere."

"You're just shopping around, aren't you? That will not help anybody, especially your child."

The educator can help most by providing accurate assessment information that parents can understand. The implications for treatment and the future should be explained as clearly as possible. Parents can be given suggestions to guide their search for second opinions in order to minimize the possibility of their being victimized by incompetent people. The reactions of educators and other professionals must be governed by understanding when parents question their judgment and indicate their intention to confirm the diagnosis.

Guilt. After the denial stage, feelings of guilt often appear. Parents may blame themselves, circumstances, other people, or God. The effects of this fault-finding may be felt by physicians, teachers, family members, and other people in the community. Given the parents' emotional state and the pressure on them to act and make decisions (often in the absence of information and guidance), it is natural that they attempt to find some obvious or not-so-obvious reasons for the child's disability. Anger often accompanies these guilt feelings and gets mixed up in emotional outbursts, as the following statements illustrate:

"I can see your crazy brother in so many of Billy's actions. It scares me so!"

"I told you not to smoke grass when you were carrying the baby."

"That period of our life when I was carrying Susan was so traumatic. I never had a moment of peace."

"I will never set foot into that doctor's office again."

"Mrs. Harrison, you are his teacher and you don't teach. It's your fault."

"Why don't you people get your act together? One person tells us one thing, and another tells us something else."

There is some temptation for educators to assume some of the blame for the child's problem, and occasionally it's justified. Generally, though, educators must avoid the blaming game, and particularly avoid even indirectly reinforcing the impression that the disability is the fault of the parents. Some educators who have been caught up in this aspect of the situation have said:

"Look, Mr. Smith, if you weren't so tough on your son, maybe we could reason with him."

"We have the best of medical and educational care here, and your child has not responded. So don't blame us."

"Have you anything in your family background that would explain Mary's behavior?"

Whenever possible, it is helpful to clarify for parents any obvious reasons for their child's disability. Obtaining information for parents or directing them to other resources are also appreciated. When potentially volatile exchanges with parents are anticipated, it helps everyone involved to maintain composure and perspective if one's principal or another colleague is present.

Sorrow. A deep sense of sorrow and sadness is also evident in the families of children with disabilities. Sometimes parents and other family members have a difficult time keeping their spirits up in the face of the effort they must expend to meet the needs of the child with disabilities. Depressed parents may also withdraw into themselves and not seek aid for their child. They may find themselves overprotecting their child and, by so doing, overprotecting themselves. It is a small step for them to imagine that no one really understands or can work with their child as they do. Fear then takes over and adds to the battle parents must wage with themselves. Some have said of these feelings of depression:

> "I found myself just hanging around, withdrawing more and more into myself."

> "We were so miserable, so lost, that contact with anyone was painful. We even neglected one another."

> "I woke up every morning sick to my stomach. I was so sad I couldn't stop crying — for me, for my baby, for everything."

> "I just wanted everyone to go away and let my baby and me alone. I felt we could take care of ourselves."

As with guilty parents and angry parents, educators must avoid being drawn into counterproductive exchanges, such as:

> "I don't know how you do it, Mrs. Thompson. I never could."

> "What are you ever going to do when you move next month? I don't know how you will get along without the clinic."

> "My life is so much easier than those poor parents."

How can parents of handicapped children help each other?

Besides providing general encouragement and pointing out positive aspects of the situation, educators can best serve parents who have these feelings by putting them in touch with other parents of children with similar disabilities. These parents should be further along in the adjustment process and actively engaged in helping their children. Parents have a real knack of knowing what to say to one another. Parents also appreciate an educator who is accessible and who indicates a willingness to talk.

What can result from rejection?

Rejection. Another possible reaction is rejection of the child with disabilities. Regrettably, some parents abandon their children; others hand them over to someone else to care for. Child abuse is a frequent result of rejection. Unfortunately, other family members can contribute to devaluing the child with disabilities. The rejection is not overt, often being disguised with reasonable arguments and concern for other family members or for themselves. The following are some typical expressions of rejection:

"I am earning my place in heaven with this child."

"Johnny, don't bother me now. I have been one hour feeding that child. He'll be the death of me."

"Thank God that Mary is as bright as she is. If we had to help her as we do Lee, it would be impossible."

"Billy takes every ounce of patience we have. Sometimes I want to kill him or myself — anything to end the situation."

"I wonder if we should have put her away. The doctor may be right. What about us and the other kids?"

"Mom, I hate it when Susie and my other friends come for dinner and have to sit at the table with Tommy. He is sickening."

"Elizabeth, you are being a good mother, but you are too young to take the strain of raising a deaf child. I don't mean to meddle, but please see about that special school."

Parents and other family members are not likely to blatantly depreciate the child with disabilities in front of educators. However, educators may witness low expectations for the child and an unwillingness to challenge the child. They must avoid encouraging these attitudes and other forms of rejection by inappropriately saying:

"Yes, I bet she is a handful. How lucky you are to have a normal child as well as her."

"I wish I didn't always have bad reports to give you about Billy."

"I think Mary is going about as fast as she can. Maybe as far, too."

"Now, don't set your goals too high. These children are no Einsteins, you know."

Educators must be sensitive to signs of physical abuse and report cases as school system or agency policy dictates. Stressing the child's positive features and ignoring negative remarks by parents also help. Professionals must model an upbeat attitude. The child's self-concept is generally affected by these negative attitudes, and educators must counter them by arranging for successful and rewarding experiences. Parents have a hard time rejecting happy, successful children.

Acceptance. Finally, most parents reach the stage of acceptance. They admit that the child has a disability but feel no guilt and do not resent society. Some parents reach this stage quickly, some slowly, and some never fully face the realities of a disabling condition. The parents must face these realities over and over again. As any parent will tell you, they go to bed with them and they wake up with them. However, after the initial struggles and frustration, good information and supportive people help parents to understand. From their faith and inner strength they obtain the courage to face the situation. Most of all, their love for the child with the disabilities has its way and works wonders. They typically say at this stage:

> "I just realized that Judy was my *child*, not disabled child."

> "Once I got some information, calmed down, and got him into a good preschool, I felt better. Things started to flow."

> "The parent group has been a big help in understanding what is going on. I see things for what they are now."

> "Those first couple of months were hell. But then Sue and I got our heads together and started putting the pieces together."

Educators can seize upon these moments and reinforce parents' good feelings. Parents still need to be reassured and encouraged to have more confidence. Educators must be careful to let parents get their feet on the ground before propelling them into a high level of participation in programs. However, once parents have reached this point, they can benefit their child in a number of ways, both educationally and therapeutically. They can also start giving some advice to other parents struggling with their own children's disabilities.

What forms of interaction should teachers expect to have with parents?

In many ways, though, this point is the beginning of establishing a good working relationship with the family. Up to this point parents and educators have been forging the kind of bonds of trust and respect that come from sharing the hard times. Now the real work begins, as parents assume varying degrees of involvement. Educators of today can anticipate a full gamut of emotional exchanges with parents, among them the following:

1. Confidence: It is born of knowledge of and successful experience with their children. The educator's progress with the child adds to the parents' feeling of strength. The parents are more willing to take counsel, experiment, and challenge their children.
2. Assertiveness: The current legislative and political climate is very supportive of parents. Educators can expect parental demands, not requests. Also, parents and their advocates will often be very knowledgeable about provisions for service and suitable criteria for quality. Educators must relate to parents as responsible adults and not be threatened.
3. Happiness: Most parents of students with disabilities enjoy moments of success and contentment. They learn to appreciate the nature of their child's progress and are able to gauge "true" progress. Also, they begin

to structure their lives and carry on successfully in different areas. Educators can look forward to this state and remind parents of it when new challenges appear.

Educators must recognize the emotional impact of children's disabilities on their families. Educators also have their own feelings invested in the situation and must monitor them appropriately. If done effectively, parents and educators can establish the type of rapport needed to serve the child well.

THE CHILD'S ROLE

Children with disabilities obviously have a profound effect on their parents and other family members. There is evidence accumulating that children with disabilities influence how parents and others interact with them (Paul and Beckman-Bell, 1981).

How can handicapped children affect their parents?

Shaping Parent Behavior. The child's disability may directly shape parental behavior. For example, a severely handicapped child may require constant maternal care because he or she has a contagious disease or a certain feeding schedule. Mothers of blind infants may be slower to initiate self-feeding because of lack of child demand. In a comparative study of learning disabled and normal children, mothers of the learning disabled tended to exercise considerably more control but be less hostile (Humphries and Bauman, 1980), a finding which suggests that they perceived their children's need for structure.

Children also affect parents indirectly. Parental self-confidence and feelings of adequacy can be strained by lack of responsiveness from the child with disabilities. Nonverbal communication deficits, language disorders, and physical limitations can make it more difficult for parent-child interactions to develop well. For example, researchers note that the hyperactivity and language problems associated with most learning disabilities have a heavy impact on families. There is a special stress evident in these family histories (Delamater, Lahey, and Drake, 1981). Such families have a higher incidence of psychiatric disorders, criminal behavior, family hyperactivity (Singer, Stewart, and Pulaski, 1981), and family alcoholism (Idol-Maestas, 1981).

Self-concept. If there are some indications of how children with disabilities shape their family's behavior, there is a great deal of evidence indicating that the family forms the child's self-concept and feelings of self-worth. There is no doubt that parental attitudes influence their children with disabilities (Klein et al., 1981). When parents have a low regard for school authority, the children get the idea. Another debilitating result occurs when parents do not hold their children responsible for academic or other kinds of progress and deny the seriousness of the learning problems.

Of course, parents who regard their children as intellectually limited can convey that to the children, especially by their lack of interest. Children incorporate that attitude into their self-concepts. Parents of the learning disabled have been reported to attribute their children's successes less to ability and more to luck, while attributing failures more to a lack of ability and less to bad luck (Pearl and Bryan, 1982). These low estimations of their children's academic and social skills are often associated with pessimism about the future (Bryan, Pearl, Zimmerman, and Matthews, 1982).

Parents also transmit cultural values to children. Parents can overemphasize or de-emphasize academic progress and other forms of achievement, depending on their upbringing and experience. Either extreme can hurt the child. However understandable some of these feelings and attitudes might be, parents must monitor their behavior lest they add to the stress that a child is under by increasing the child's confusion, feelings of incompetence, and worry.

What child rearing practices are helpful with handicapped children?

Educators and others can be of assistance to children with disabilities and their families by encouraging parents to remember the following (Mesibov, 1978):

1. Help children understand matters related to their disability (e.g., hospitalization) with clear, direct, and concrete information.
2. Prepare children for situations (e.g., testing) by talking about what will happen, using pictures of the material involved, and visiting a facility ahead of time.
3. Give children a sense of control by letting them share in some decisions (e.g., what clothes to wear, what day of the week to go).
4. Guarantee as much emotional security as possible by maintaining regularity (e.g., regular bedtime, mealtimes, or time to see playmates) and familiarity (e.g., favorite games or clothes).
5. Offer incentives or treats for cooperating and working hard.
6. Structure in success and emphasize and reinforce it (e.g., charting progress or telling friends about it in front of the child).

THE FAMILY'S ROLE

Family members of children with disabilities are greatly influenced by the child and in turn influence the child. It is estimated that divorce rates in families with deaf-blind children are as high as 75 percent (Burley, 1977), and nine times higher than normal in families with spina bifida children (Tew, Lawrence, Payne, and Townsley, 1977). There is no telling if it is as high for other disabilities — it probably isn't for milder forms. Estimates of marital separations and divorces among parents of learning disabled children are 10 to 13 percent, while the child's learning disability seems a factor in a quarter to a third of the cases (Association for Children and Adults with Learning Disabilities, 1982; McLoughlin, Clark, and Petrosko, in press). However, there is mounting evidence that most disabilities of children contribute to a variety of family problems other than divorce and separation: stress; disruption of household routines, budget, parenting siblings, relationships with relatives and friends (McLoughlin et al., in press); and alcoholism and suicide (Block, 1978). To what degree these marital and family problems are part of a general trend in our society is also unclear.

Parents and Relatives. Considerable attention is being given to the needs of single parents of children with disabilities because of the greater incidence of academic and behavioral problems in these families (Werner, 1980). School difficulties are sometimes precipitated or at least exacerbated by the absence of one parent from the home, especially the father. The socioeconomic status of the family and the child's age at the time of the parents' separation make a difference (Roy and Fuqua, 1983). Certainly single parents need special consideration and understanding in meeting all their responsibilities. Educators can support them best by scheduling conferences at convenient times, avoiding criticizing them, and showing regard for the parent's knowledge and experience with the child (Werner, 1980).

The fathers of children with disabilities have also been receiving special attention lately, even though mothers tend to be the primary care givers and contact persons for educators. Some fathers may feel worse about the child's problem than mothers do. Fathers of language disordered children seem to find it more difficult to interact with their children (Kornblum, 1982). Societal mores and social pressure may deprive fathers of the opportunity to deal with their feelings appropriately. Educators should make a special effort to include them.

Grandparents play a significant role in how a family adjusts to a child's disability. Often they offer counsel at the difficult time of decision making and otherwise sustain their son or daughter and the family. The attitude they model and how they interact with the child can be a source of inspiration to everyone. As one grandmother remarked, she had to take the time and make the effort to get to know her cerebral-palsied grandson (McPhee, 1982). As you would expect, grandparents too must cope with their emotions.

Siblings. In large part, siblings adopt the attitudes of their parents toward the child with disabilities. Unless the family is well integrated, the child may become the scapegoat for the family's problems. Siblings may resent the amount of attention given to the disabled child if they are neglected in the process. Sibling responses are most favorable when the family is close and shares the same goals. Families with relatively independent children are generally better at accepting the exceptional child. Grossman (1972) found positive reactions among some of the normal siblings he interviewed.

By including their handicapped daughter in family activities, these parents are demonstrating their acceptance of her.

What concerns do children have about their handicapped siblings?

Sibling concerns may include (1) curiosity about the cause of the handicap and its effect on them, (2) inability to talk to their parents about the handicapped child in spite of their desire to do so, (3) worry about the reactions of their friends, and (4) worry about whether they will have to care for the handicapped child in the future (Cansler, Martin, and Valand, 1975). But, as an only sister of an autistic child indicated, the whole experience can be worthwhile, even being the "other mother" (Zatlow, 1982). She was prepared for probably caring for her brother in the future. Because of the skills he had and her past experience with him, that posed no threat.

A number of authors have addressed the subject of the exceptional child's interaction with the family. Moore and Morton (1976) suggest a number of books for children to read about disabilities. Landau, Epstein, and Stone (1978) have compiled an anthology of popular writings about exceptional people. Grossman (1972) has interviewed the normal siblings of retarded children and provides information useful in a cooperative family effort to integrate an exceptional child.

Cultural Values. Culturally different or minority families of children with disabilities may pose unique challenges (Marion, 1980). Minority parents seem less overwhelmed than nonminority parents. Feelings of protection and acceptance of children with disabilities are more typical than in other families, probably because of the support from strong extended family networks, the unique role of religion in their lives, or both.

The problems that do occur seem to arise when the child enters school. Parental concerns center on their negative image of educators, possibly discriminatory testing practices, and suspicion of educators' competence to evaluate their children's ability. These feelings of mistrust may result in angry confrontations with educators or in avoiding the student's program.

Educators must be prepared to meet the needs of minority parents (Rodriguez, 1981). Information should be shared in appropriate language, especially about their children's rights for services. Parents should be made to feel comfortable and welcome in schools for observations and invited to participate in programs informally. More casual formats for meetings should be developed.

What four crises do families with handicapped children face?

Transitional Periods. The families of children with disabilities, then, go through a variety of adjustments and modifications. Four major crises seem to be (1) when the parents first become aware of the problem, (2) when the child begins to receive educational services, (3) when the child leaves school, and (4) when aging parents can no longer care for the person with disabilities (MacKeith, 1973). Throughout all of these phases, educators and other professionals should be prepared to support families in their never-ending process of development as a social unit with a disabled member. For example, parents may need particular assistance when their children reach adolescence. As one mother described it, it was a time of excitement, uncertainty, pleasure, pride, and pain (Barnes, 1982).

It is to be hoped that parents of children with disabilities will work for the day when the children will attain more and more independence. Like all parents, they may find their children's movement into adulthood, bonding with peers, sexual awakening, and future planning particularly demanding (Daniels, 1982). Transitions are hard for everyone, but for these families they are especially challenging.

Parent/Educator Relationship. It should be clear by now that the parents of these students come to educators with a considerable emotional and cultural investment. Although both family and school have the child's best interest at heart, differences in values and experience between parents and educator may hinder the development of a working relationship.

What happens is that parents and educators may have preconceived conceptions of the other that hinder communication (Seligman, 1979). Parents may reject educators because they reject most authority figures, especially school-related ones. They may see teachers as mere academic instructors and resent any advice in other areas. Parents have expected some educators to serve as lawyers, priests, or in some other capacities.

On the other hand, educators may see parents as the cause of the child's problem. Some parents seem threatening, and teachers may feel vulnerable to their criticism. Repeated efforts to enroll parental help with the child's program may cause frustration and mistrust. There is also a possibility that teachers will have a different view of the student than the parents. To arrive at an effective working relationship, it is important to recognize the role of these cultural and value judgments. They must not be allowed to get in the way of an effective relationship with parents.

RESPONDING TO FAMILY NEEDS

For families to understand and adapt to their child's disability, educators and others must meet their many needs. They need information on a variety of topics and the skills to obtain quality services for their children.

Identifying Needs. A number of studies investigated the needs of parents and siblings. A group of parents of deaf-blind children listed their needs in this way: legal issues, curriculum and instruction, facts about the disability, behavior management; affective adjustment, family roles and interactions, and health, care, and maintenance (Kershman, 1982). While parents share common needs, regardless of their children's disabilities, there are unique emphases that will vary with the nature and extent of the child's problem. Families' needs may also vary depending on their stage of adjustment and on their level of participation. It is clearly advisable to establish parents' priorities for assistance regularly.

What is the first concern of parents?

Understanding the Disability. The first concern of most parents is to understand their child's problem. According to both professionals (Yoshida, Fenton, Kaufman, and Maxwell, 1978) and parents (Lusthaus, Lusthaus, and Gibbs, 1981), most conferences between parents and educators seem to be devoted to the parents' giving and receiving of information.

Families rely heavily on printed material and, more rarely, on nonprint media. While information from various agencies and school systems has improved over the last decade, parents still struggle with the reading level and vocabulary used in much printed matter (McLoughlin, Edge, Petrosko, and Strenecky, 1981). Parents are also put at a disadvantage because there is a real lag between the time research is completed and the time it reaches parents (Winton and Turnbull, 1982). Researchers seem to place a low priority on studying topics relevant to these families and reporting results in the lay press. In addition, even when clear, useful information is available through a variety of sources, parents have to know where to get it. Educators can be of great assistance by accumulating copies of information, developing accessible parent libraries, and encouraging agencies to develop appropriate material for parents (McLoughlin et al., 1983).

Parents must also become familiar with diagnostic procedures. Finding the appropriate specialists can present problems. Once they have been discovered, it is sometimes difficult to get unanimous opinions. A frequent complaint is that diagnostic information has been withheld or that information is presented in professional jargon that is difficult to understand. The three most common complaints made about physicians are their lack of knowledge about disabilities, their attitude toward and low expectations for children with disabilities, and their lack of skills in sharing information (Wolraich, 1982). Fortunately professionals in every field are improving in this area since they recognize the potential contributions parents can make if they are better informed.

Etiology. The etiology of the disorder is another area of interest, particularly in the case of genetic disorders such as Down's syndrome. Parents may also wonder whether exceptionalities such as learning disabilities and emotional disturbance will affect other children they may have planned to have. A knowledge of prenatal, perinatal, and postnatal causes of disabilities will be useful to parents genuinely interested in discovering whether they are responsible for their child's problem. Some exceptionalities, such as emotional disturbance, are influenced by environmental factors. When this is the case, parents may be relieved to discover that they can do something about the problem.

Potential for Development. An important area of parent concern is the child's potential for development. In a group of low-income mothers of retarded children, the future was reported to be the biggest concern (Eheart and Ciccone, 1982). They wanted parent groups and a program for the children to guarantee successful development. Of course, developmental potential is determined by such factors as the disability's severity and age of onset.

The parents of young children may be interested in such developmental areas as speech and language. Later concerns may be academic achievement and school behavior. The parents of exceptional adults may have questions about their child's employability and what approach to take regarding sexual relations. A recent study of the attitudes of parents with retarded children toward sterilization revealed 71 percent for involuntary and 67 percent for voluntary procedures (Wolf and Zarfan, 1982). Parents should be aware of the thinking of other parents.

As you can see, educators need accurate technical expertise in a variety of areas. Whenever possible, educators should also put parents in touch with older children with disabilities like their own child's so they can develop a realistic perspective on the possibilities for progress.

Available Services. Parents of exceptional children frequently do not know what services are available to them and where to get them. Here are some important questions that are asked about services:

What questions should teachers anticipate from parents of handicapped children?

1. How does one go about finding the specialists appropriate to the child's needs? Exceptional children may need assistance in several areas, such as language, academic skills, motor skills, vocational training, and social and emotional behavior. Each area has its own specialists.

2. What medical treatments and adaptive devices would benefit the child? Parents may have questions about drugs, vitamin therapy, diet control, sterilization, and other medical techniques. They may also be interested in finding out about the maintenance, use, and repair of braces, wheelchairs, hearing aids, glasses, and other devices.

When dealing with specialists, parents must be encouraged to state their child's problem clearly, demand respect, ask questions freely, refuse to be rushed, encourage their child's participation, and be objective about the child (Durio, 1980). Educators can also be a big help by being aware of the newest research on important issues.

3. How much will meeting the needs of the child cost? Specialists, medication, adaptive devices, and special schools are all expensive. Although PL 94–142 guarantees a free and appropriate education to all exceptional children, the cost of additional services can be substantial.

4. What school programs are available? Parents should be familiar with the various options available in the public and private schools and with their educational methods and materials. Some parents will be interested in home-based programs. In consultation with professionals, parents must decide which program is most suitable for their child.

5. Should the child be placed in a residential facility or kept at home? This is one of the most difficult decisions parents face. To determine the best course, parents must learn about the facility's procedures, accreditation, program objectives, administrator and teacher qualifications, philosophy and structure, and recreational and social facilities.

Parents should also be aware of what is involved in keeping their child at home, in respite care, or in a community residential facility (German and Maisto, 1982). Mothers who have not institutionalized their children tend to have a supportive extended family, have baby-sitters, not have another retarded child, and not have many behavior problems with their child. They are also more likely to be married. Educators should have similar facts available to guide parental decision making.

Support Groups. Families need support, information, and often inspiration to meet the challenges posed by disabilities. Parent organizations and training groups offer relevant and comfortable environments in which to learn how to adjust and grow. They offer information about transportation, baby-sitting, camps, and other topics meaningful to family life.

As one group of parents with Down's syndrome children reports, parent groups are particularly relevant when the children are very young, as an emotional support base (Spicker, 1982). They contribute to the accuracy of parental knowledge and to parental willingness to work with their child. It often takes other parents to snap a parent out of self-defeating activity. As one parent of a cerebral-palsied child says, parents must get over feeling guilty, use respite care and baby-sitters, and get out (Stanzler, 1982). Educators can encourage them in that direction.

Parent-Child Interactions. A universal area of concern for parents is how to relate to their exceptional children. The parent-child relationship is at the core of the child's successful development and happiness. A danger in programs' emphasizing how parents can train their children's skills is that parents get distracted from learning to love and relate to their child.

In one project, family consultants visit the homes of severely handicapped newborns and adapt suggestions in various areas to the parents' styles and goals (Affleck, McGrade, McQueeney, and Allen, 1982). This service is particularly helpful to mothers with less education, single mothers, and mothers of firstborn infants. Child management is an area of particular concern for many parents. They are interested in the child's behavior problems at school and want to learn strategies to be used in the home. Problems may arise in feeding, toileting, discipline, sexual activity, dating, and other areas. There are a variety of training programs and materials available that educators can provide to help parents handle such situations (Heward, Dardig, and Rossett, 1979).

Family Nurturing. The parents of children with disabilities must also tend to the needs of each other and their other children. Educators can do much by reminding parents of each other's needs and encouraging them to make opportunities to be together. While mothers generally get involved in programs more, many projects provide for father meetings and opportunities for father-care activities. At the University of Washington's Model Preschool Center for Handicapped Children, fathers and their infants attend Saturday morning classes together. Discussions and activities encourage awareness of child development and foster contact with the children. Mothers appreciate the respite and the sharing of responsiblity for the child. This type of experience fosters better relationships between parents.

Parents must also decide what to tell siblings about the exceptional child. Their other children may worry about a variety of things, such as frustration at being neglected or having to care for the child. Parents should also clarify how they feel about the normal siblings, since the child with disabilities may require so much attention. Siblings have to be reassured about their responsibility now and in the future for the exceptional child. Parent groups can offer advice on this topic. Educators can demonstrate awareness and sensitivity to sibling issues by considering their needs when making requests of parents. Also, children with disabilities can be taught to relate better to their siblings.

Advocacy. Parents often need to assert their right to quality programs. For example, parents of the learning disabled now struggle with a dearth of services for their children when they get into high school (McNutt and Heller, 1978) and as adults (Gray, 1981).

In addition, parents frequently complain that they are not included in decision making, that they are not informed about their child's progress, and that they have to maintain constant vigilance to ensure that the child is receiving the necessary services. Professionals should realize that parental anger is caused by society's frequent insensitivity and incompetence in meeting the needs of exceptional persons. It should be remembered that the enactment of PL 94-142 was largely the result of the activism of concerned parents. Parents today are going beyond asking for information; they want to be involved in deciding such things as what kinds of records are kept on their children, what medical services are needed, and what schools they transfer to (Lusthaus et al., 1981).

How can teachers help the advocacy efforts of parents?

Educators and others must be prepared to meet their needs and honor their legitimate requests. Some professionals train parents to perform advocate activities by teaching them to use professional terminology, to ask and understand the right questions, to be persistent but diplomatic when the answers they get are less than sufficient, and to recognize quality services and agencies (Muir, Milan, Branston-McLean, and Berger, 1982). Educators have an obligation to make parents aware of their rights and help them realize them.

Some problems are encountered only by the parents of children with a particular kind of disability. Reference works that describe the needs of these parents include the following: for the learning disabled, Wallace and McLoughlin (1979); for the autistic, Warren (1978); for the emotionally disturbed, Park and Shapiro (1976); for the multiply handicapped, Gordon (1977); for the retarded, Chinn, Drew, and Logan (1979); for the deaf and blind, Kershman (1982); for the physically handicapped, Joel (1975) and Finnie (1975); for the blind, Lowenfeld (1971); for the deaf, Bloom (1970); and for the speech and language impaired, Schreiber (1973). *Parents Speak Out* (Turnbull and Turnbull, 1978) is a collection of essays by parents of individuals with various exceptional conditions.

PROBE 14-1
Relating to Families

1. T F Parents should not discuss their exceptional child with their other children.

2. Name four of the emotional stages the parents of exceptional children typically pass through before they accept their child's condition.

3. What are three problems that the parents of exceptional children may encounter in searching for services?

4. Name six areas about which parents of exceptional children may need to find information.

INVOLVING PARENTS

You should be able to describe ways to involve parents in the education of their exceptional children.

The parents of exceptional children have played an important role in initiating and developing special education programs. They have supported every major effort to develop services. But it was not until after World War II that parents began to organize on behalf of their exceptional children. Groups such as the National Association for Retarded Citizens, the United Cerebral Palsy Association, and the Association for Children and Adults with Learning Disabilities have become very effective in determining policies and establishing programs for exceptional people. They have worked with the executive and legislative branches of government to develop a favorable public climate and to enact laws guaranteeing the rights of exceptional people. When necessary, parent organizations have turned to the courts to obtain the services and support they need (Turnbull, 1981).

In spite of the many contributions of parents, they have frequently been excluded from crucial aspects of their children's programs. For the most part, education has been left to the professionals. Some educators have been hesitant to involve parents in educational programs for a number of reasons (Seligman, 1979). One reason is that educators are sometimes reluctant to admit that they need help and that they do not have all the answers. Professionals have also claimed that parents are frequently uncaring or overprotective. Some professionals contend that the educational process is too complex for parents to understand, and that contact between the two groups should be limited to parent conferences several times a year. Finally, there have been claims that parents are incompetent in raising their children and that they would add little to educational programs if they became involved in them.

Fortunately, attitudes are changing and more positive approaches to working with parents are emerging, largely because of the enactment of PL 94-142, which mandates increased parent involvement. As a result, parents are assuming a broader role in the educational process. Educators realize that parents must participate in programs if they are to be as effective as possible. Parents are being blamed less for their children's disabilities (Paul and Porter, 1981). Parent and professional organizations are also working together more closely.

What are the legal rights of parents?

The parents of exceptional children have a number of rights specifically guaranteed by law:

1. The parents of the handicapped must receive written notice in their native language that the school is considering a change in their children's education program.
2. Parents must give permission for their children to be tested for the purpose of determining whether they should be placed in a special education program.
3. Parents have the right to an independent evaluation if they are dissatisfied with the evaluation performed by school personnel.
4. Parents have the right to be involved actively in the development of the children's individualized educational programs.
5. Parents must specifically approve the placement of their children.
6. Parents have the right to examine all school records related to their children and to remove inaccurate or misleading data from the children's file.
7. Parents may request an impartial due process hearing if they disagree with procedures or decisions relative to the placement of their children. The hearing officer may not be an employee of the school district. The parents have the right to legal counsel, and they may examine witnesses, present evidence, and obtain a written record of the hearing and findings. The hearing must be held no more than forty-five days after it is requested.
8. Parents may appeal the results of the due process hearing to the State Department of Education, which must review the appeal within 30 days. Parents can further appeal decisions to the federal courts if they are dissatisfied with the results of their appeal to the State Department of Education. Educators must ensure that proper procedures are established to notify parents about testing placement, nonbiased assessment, record keeping, and timetables. The information that is collected must be kept confidential.

The last decade has witnessed considerable experimentation in attempts to implement these rights. Parents have been incorporated into their children's programs in a variety of ways. Some are legislated by PL 94-142, others merely suggested by it and by common sense. In all cases considerable initiative and support are necessary from educators to make the involvement meaningful to parents and themselves.

The sections that follow describe ways to involve parents in the five more common aspects of their children's programs: identification and referral, assessment, planning, implementation, and evaluation (McLoughlin, Edge and Strenecky, 1978). Careful forethought and planning must go into these efforts. Some parents want and are able to get involved more than others (Kroth, 1980a). Individual family circumstances must be considered in planning, and families with less inclination to participate must be encouraged.

It is also important to remember that when children with disabilities start school, it represents a new phase for parents (Paul and Porter, 1981). They may have to acclimate to possibilities of active involvement. For other parents, more sophisticated opportunities may have to be provided (Cervone and O'Leary, 1982). Whatever the case, parent-teacher communication is the key (Swick, Flake-Hobson, and Raymond, 1980).

IDENTIFICATION AND REFERRAL

For reliable early identification of exceptional children, parents must be well informed. State departments of education and other educational agencies provide print material concerning traits of disabilities, available services, and the child's rights to a free and appropriate education (McLoughlin et al., 1981). Much improvement is necessary in this area; for example, such material must be made more accessible and readable. Greater cooperation is needed among educational agencies, parent organization, and governmental programs to improve the quality and flow of information (McLoughlin et al., 1983).

Other means of conveying information are the mass media, group instruction, and individual conferences. Mass media approaches seem limited tc arousing general awareness of disabilities, reinforcing and maintaining parental information and attitudes gained elsewhere, or both (Kurtz, Devaney, Strain, and Sandler, 1982). Group instruction is a better way to impart specific information about early identification, and it encourages follow-up. Efforts to incorporate parents more individually into screening for disabilities are also successful. Parental knowledge of such matters as general development and the child's knowledge of letters and numbers is a good predictor of the child's later successes and failures (Colligan, 1981).

The parents of children referred for special education services should be interviewed to obtain information useful in diagnosing the child's problem. Parents know a great deal about the child that would otherwise be unavailable to the diagnostician, including the child's personal traits, interests, health history, behavior when interacting with adults and other children, and attitudes. Information such as this is necessary for a complete, valid diagnosis.

How can teachers conduct effective parent interviews?

In seeking information from parents, it is important to be sensitive to parents' feelings. Only information relevant to the child's disability and the educational program should be solicited. Kroth and Simpson (1977) have suggested some guidelines for interviewing parents: (1) The interview should be conducted in a quiet, private setting. (2) The interview should be held in a positive atmosphere; at the same time, however, the interviewer should be prepared for hidden motivations and agendas. (3) Careful attention should be paid to the parents' nonverbal behavior as well as to their verbal responses; by the same token, interviewers should be aware of the messages they are sending. (4) In sharing the information obtained, the interviewer should respect the parents' right to privacy.

Through improved procedures and technology, educators can be trained to make initial contacts and interviews with parents more productive (Sawyer and Sawyer, 1981). It is critical to future interactions that such sessions go well. For the child's sake, the parents' knowledge and attitude must be carefully guided (Faerstein, 1981).

ASSESSMENT

The diagnostic phase of a child's program is strongly influenced by the degree of cooperation among parents and professionals. The ultimate results are shaped by the status of the referral agent, the degree of agreement between parents and professionals, and parental pressure, as well as the actual data (Bognar and Martin, 1982). It is imperative to involve parents constructively (McLoughlin and Lewis, 1981).

As discussed above, a verbal interview format and written case history forms are used to profile a child's development history and school background. The use of these approaches is particularly valuable because they acquaint you with the parents' perceptions of the child's problems and of the available educational opportunities.

More formally, parents are often asked to complete rating forms and other scales. On the *Behavior Rating Profile* (Brown and Hammill, 1978), parents rate their child's behavior at home; the scale is normed, and parental perceptions can be compared to those of teachers and the children. In the adaptive behavior area, the *Vineland Social Maturity Scale* (Doll, 1965) is frequently completed by parents. Because of the weight placed on data in such areas, educators must be aware of the possible bias in parental views. For example, one group of parents of the retarded tended to rate their children higher than teachers did in adaptive behavior, especially in self-help skills (Mealor and Richmond, 1980). While parents' experience and greater information in some areas may sometimes justify such results, there is an obvious need to have other independent and objective measures in order to complement parental information.

There are also ways to question parents about a child's basic skills (Mc-Loughlin, 1983). For example, when interested in the student's use of reading and math at home, educators can ask about the use of menus and newspapers or earning and using an allowance. Parents will be familiar with their child's use of these skills and will know what their child is interested in.

Another approach to involving parents in assessment is to have them observe their children at home, in school, or elsewhere. Parents often collect observational data in a systematic fashion as part of the preparation for a program to change some social or academic behavior (Cooper and Edge, 1981). There are a variety of materials available to train parents how to (1) select a specific behavior to observe, (2) design a system to keep track of how often or how much the behavior occurs, and (3) maintain a record of how the child performs over a period of time (Heward, Dardig, and Rossett, 1979).

What is the value of parental observation?

Parents may also gain a better understanding of their child's learning problems and of the instructional program if they observe in the classroom or in other settings. Educators can make such visits more effective and meaningful if they prepare parents in advance by explaining key aspects of the program, telling them where to sit and when to come and go, and suggesting how to behave when the children try to get their attention (Cansler et al, 1975). Parents also appreciate the opportunity to discuss what they witness.

Parents who prepare their children for testing or other assessment activities contribute greatly to the success of the effort. Children may feel uneasy about being tested and need to talk about their feelings. Brief explanations of procedures and materials help, as do advance visits to clinics and hospitals. Most of all, parents can avoid letting their own attitudes about the testing (e.g. fear, anger) transfer to the child. After the testing, parents can be encouraged to talk with their children about their feelings and answer their questions. These efforts may guarnatee the child's cooperation in similar activities later on.

Parental participation is particularly important in understanding the impact of their child's background and culture on his or her test performances. Multicultural assessments must have a strong parental component. For example, the completion of the *Adaptive Behavior Inventory for Children* by parents is an integral part of the total *System of Multicultural Pluralistic Assessment* designed by Mercer and Lewis (1977). They are asked to indicate their children's strengths and weaknesses in such areas as family, community, peer relations, and nonacademic school roles. Their experiences and insights are a safeguard against a biased assessment (Rodriguez, 1981).

CONFERENCES

What is the value of the IEP conference?

Parents of children with disabilities participate in conferences with educators and others for a variety of reasons: to find out the results of testing, to help

Frequent parent conferences lead to better educational programs for handicapped children.

design the Individualized Education Program (IEP), to decide how to deliver the needed services, and to help evaluate the child's progress in the program. The law requires that parents be involved in developing their exceptional child's IEP. The involvement of parents at this stage serves several purposes. First, it permits parents to understand their child's program better, which may create a more positive attitude at home toward the program. Second, parents are more likely to be interested in a program they are familiar with and helped to develop. Third, parental involvement eliminates the confusion and disagreement that may arise from misinformation and differing priorities. Fourth, parents are encouraged to serve as volunteers; they can provide valuable help and give teachers more time for individual instruction.

Parental Roles. In spite of a concerted effort over the past decade, parents tend to play a passive role in these conferences. At IEP conferences resource teachers tend to review the program while parents listen (Goldstein, Strickland, Turnbull, and Curry, 1980). Remarkably, some parents have been satsified with this situation in the past (Polifka, 1981). Their satisfaction seems to be related to whether they (1) are invited to the IEP review, (2) are asked to help prepare the IEP, (3) are informed of their right to appeal, and (4) feel that their child's special education placement is appropriate.

Considerable confusion about what should occur at conferences and who should do what seems to be at the root of the low level of participation. First, many professionals are not attending conferences; meetings usually consist of the child's mother and the special education teacher (Scanlon, Arick, and Phelps, 1981). The professionals who do attend such meetings, especially the educators, seem unsure of their goals and the functions they are to perform (Fenton, Yoshida, Maxwell, and Kaufman, 1979).

Parental Influence. Contrary to their legislated rights, parents are not influential at these conferences. Gilliam (1979) reported that meeting participants ranked parents as third in importance before attending meetings; after meetings, however, they ranked parents ninth in actual contribution. The initial estimation may be based on the assumption that parents know their children best, but in fact the main contributors to the conference tend to be members with hard data such as test scores, cumulative records, and diagnostic reports. Rather than gaining in influence and making greater contributions to different aspects of the IEP conference, parents seem to be losing ground (Gilliam and Coleman, 1981). Psychologists are perceived to be most influential in diagnosis; the special educator, in planning and implementation; the director, in placement; and the supervisor, in due process matters. According to PL 94-142, parents should be highly influential in final placement decisions, but in practice they defer to psychologists and special educators (Knoff, 1983).

Preparation. Both parents and educators are responding well to better preparation and training for such conferences, however. Such strategies as sending parents questions prior to the IEP conference with a follow-up telephone call and having the school counselor present as a parent advocate at the conference increase relevant contributions by parents (Goldstein and Turnbull, 1982). With the group of parents in the Goldstein and Turnbull study, the counselor's support was particularly helpful when he or she introduced the parents, directed questions to them, verbally reinforced their contributions, and summarized the discussion at the end of the conference. Classroom teachers who receive in-service training about their duties at these meetings speak much more than teachers who are not so prepared (Trailor, 1982). Seventy-five percent of the comments of these teachers were about student performance, behavior, and curriculum, and they were directed to parents.

Parents are also clarifying how they wish to participate in conferences. They seem satisfied with current practices in giving and receiving information about such topics as discipline, proper class placement, evaluation of the child's abilities, grouping for instruction, transportation, and provision of special resources (Lusthaus et al., 1981). They expect a greater part, however, in deciding about such topics as records kept about their children, medical services, and school transfers. A group of parents of retarded children has indicated the desire for greater power in deciding how and when their children's progress is evaluated (Soffer, 1982).

Educators must respond to these indications of interest and desire by encouraging relevant parent participation. Parents and professionals alike need to be educated to the possiblities of parental involvement. Current perceptions and practices may be more dysfunctional vestiges of the past than the result of considered deliberation.

Strategies. In addition to the conferences held to develop the IEP, meetings should be held at intervals to discuss such factors as the child's progress, school-home cooperative programs, and other issues of concern to parents and teachers. In all professional interactions it is important that professionals communicate candidly and clearly; parents complain that information is sometimes withheld from them and that educators use jargon they cannot understand.

Some rules of professional behavior dictate how educators should speak to parents (Losen and Diament, 1978). It is important to avoid an authoritarian or judgmental tone. Questioning should be designed to open up discussion rather than limit it. Educators must be considerate of parents' feelings and give parents the same rights and respect they might show parents who are professional colleagues. By following these guidelines, teachers and parents can improve the chances that conferences will be conducted in an atmosphere of cooperation and increase the likelihood of success.

When considering the educational placement of the handicapped child, the advantages and disadvantages of the various service arrangements should be carefully explained to parents. Parental objections to certain kinds of classes or teachers must be taken into account in making the placement decision. The consequences of diagnostic labels and the possible reactions of others to such labels should also be explained to parents.

School personnel must be as supportive of parents as possible, because parents must give their consent to the placement decision. Parents should be made to feel comfortable in the IEP conference. Their opinions should be solicited, and they should be encouraged to make suggestions about their child's needs. School personnel should express an interest in the child, and ample time should be provided to conduct the meeting. Finally, the staff should realize that the IEP conference can be very trying for parents, and they should be prepared to deal with parents' possible emotional reactions.

How can teachers make parent conferences more effective?

Educators can contribute to the success of conferences by anticipating the needs of parents. Some reasonable strategies to use at various phases of the conference process are:

1. Before the conference

   — inform parents of the time, place, and purpose
   — deliver oral and written messages in the parents' native language
   — send reminders
   — gather the necessary reports, material, etc.
   — choose a private and comfortable setting that allows for full participation by all
   — send parents some questions or ideas to consider
   — ask parents to bring certain information
   — designate someone to serve as advocate or sponsor for the parents at the meeting

2. Opening the meeting

   — introduce yourself and others
   — establish the purpose of the meeting and any time limitations
   — have people explain their roles
   — invite parental questions and input

3. Interpreting assessment results

   — avoid jargon
   — give examples of student test performances and show exhibits of work
   — relate the findings to parental experience
   — reconcile different findings for parents
   — ask parents for information
   — ask parents to confirm or evaluate the results from their experience

4. IEP development

   — ask about parental goals and priorities
   — incorporate goals suggested by parents
   — invite parents to help accomplish some school goals
   — describe ways parents can assist directly at school
   — explore the possiblities of home-based activities
   — demonstrate cooperation among the special and regular teachers responsible for the IEP
   — make sure all essential IEP features are included and meet with parents' satsifaction

5. Placement decision

   — explain pros and cons of different settings (e.g., special class, resource room, etc.)
   — clarify how often the child will be with his or her normal peers
   — avoid rushing parents to agree to the placement
   — invite parents to visit sample programs and placements

— provide the names and phone numbers of parents with children in the classes who have agreed to talk with such parents

— explain parents' right to appeal if they dislike the decision

— if applicable, describe how supportive services will be offered in conjunction with the main program

6. Closing the conference

— summarize the meeting by reviewing major decisions and explaining who will be responsible for follow-through

— offer copies of the IEP and other documents

— explain where the child's records are kept and the rules for confidentiality

— indicate how and when parents will get feedback about the child's progress

— ask about parental preferences for format and schedule in receiving progress reports

— set a date for at least an annual review of the IEP

— offer information about parent groups, materials, etc.

7. After the conference

— process all documents immediately

— send promised copies and other material

— perform the follow-up activities discussed in the session (Turnbull and Strickland, 1981; Katz et al., 1980)

INSTRUCTION

Parents of children with disabilities can be involved in teaching their children both at home and in the classroom. Many parents begin when their children are infants. Because of the proven efficiency of early intervention in the case of all disabilities and the paucity of services and professionals at this level, parents often serve as the primary instructors (Lillie and Trohanis, 1976). Of all possible forms of participation, parents most often assist in educational activities and therapy (Wiegerink and Hocutt, 1979).

Parent Roles. Parents of exceptional children become actively involved in instructional programs for a variety of reasons. Besides benefiting from the emotional support such programs provide, the parents who attend these programs seem to be having more trouble engaging their children as well as they would like (Spicker, 1982). This motivation for better parent-child interaction also guarantees greater follow-through with the program.

The lack of profitable communication between parents and children is a prime motivation for many parents to perform activities with their children.

While the frequency and length of verbal and nonverbal interactions does not seem to differ between parents of normal and language-disordered children, the quality does (Lasky and Klopp, 1982). The more linguistically mature child encourages parents to engage in richer verbal communication (i.e., questioning, providing information, acknowledging the child's statement) and nonverbal behaviors as well. Parents with exceptional children must be taught to communicate well, because their children may not naturally encourage them to do so.

Parents can be trained to teach language and other skills. One group of parents with language-disordered children was taught to increase their language stimulation skills by such activities as drawing the child's attention to an object, answering appropriately, and directing the child to do something (Lombardino and Mangan, 1983). Their children mastered a large percentage of the material taught.

Parents must also be taught to transfer their newfound skills to play and other more informal settings and to encourage the generalization of skills to the home. After a 10-week training period in sign language, one group of parents learned the sign system well, and their children advanced significantly (Williams, Lombardino, MacDonald, and Owens, 1982); but they did not use the system in unstructured settings. Parents of Down's syndrome toddlers learned how to prompt and reinforce speech better (Salzberg and Villani, 1983). After being given feedback through audiotapes and some ideas for adapting their strategies at home, they used the skills more effectively in informal settings.

Are parents natural teachers of their children?

Parent Training. Parents are not necessarily natural teachers, at least of material traditionally taught by educators. When mothers and teachers of the learning disabled were observed teaching the same tasks to the same child, the parents differed significantly in teaching style (Steinart, Campbell, and Kiely, 1981). The teachers gave information more useful to performing the task; structured the task more and asked more prompting questions; provided more noncontingent approval and positive feedback; and requested more independent activities from the children. There is obviously a need to train parents to teach their children effectively. For the child's sake, consistency in style as well as quality should be encouraged.

Even in the case of informal instruction and play, there is a need to shape parents' behavior as effective teachers. Compared to parents of nonretarded preschoolers, one group of parents with developmentally delayed children tended to dominate play sessions (Eheart, 1982). Their children responded less and initiated fewer interactions. Whether it was the parent or child controlling the situation is not important here. What is is the fact that parents can and must learn to be more effective even in playful and casual exchanges.

Efforts have been made to identify predictors of successful parental participation in educational activities. Their child rearing expectations seem to relate to their ability to benefit from language training programs (Strom, Rees, Slaughter, and Wurster, 1980). While socioeconomic status, education, and pretraining experience may affect parents' later retention of the behavior management material they learned, their actual performance during training may be the best predictor of whether they will successfully carry out programs with their children (Clark, Baker, and Heifetz, 1982).

Whether serving as tutors and teacher's aides at home or in the classroom, parents should be given goals that can be met in a short time (Shearer, 1976). If the activity is to be done at home, it should be designed in consideration of the home environment, family schedule, and other demands. Involving parents and siblings in planning the home activity is a wise strategy. Parents should be shown what to do and how to do it and should be given an opportunity to practice the skill under supervision. The criteria for completion should be explained. Parents should, of course, be reinforced for their participation. The activities parents are given to do at home or at school should be clear and contain all the necessary directions. When activities are sent home for completion, one must keep track of what is sent and plan for regular feedback from the families (Cansler et al., 1975).

Behavior Management. Of all the areas of instruction parents have participated in, behavior management has received the most emphasis. Parents are concerned about their exceptional children's socialization skills and emotional stability. Their interest extends to children's work habits at school, peer relations, and general obedience. Working alone or with educators, parents have learned and used the principles of applied behavioral analysis to modify their children's behavior. They have used the approach to encourage academic progress, speech and language skills, gains in physical therapy, and development in many other areas. Their success at learning and applying the principles is well documented (Cooper and Edge, 1981; O'Dell, 1974; Hall, Cristler, Cranston, and Tucker, 1970; Moore and Bailey, 1973). Many materials are available for parents who wish to use this approach (Becker, 1971; Patterson and Gullion, 1971; Smith and Smith, 1976).

Behavior-change programs such as these are often developed jointly by parents and educators. In one program, parents and teachers of learning disabled children cooperated in administering rewards to children who completed at least 80 percent of their independent seatwork (Hickey, Imber, and Ruggiero, 1979). Parents praised their children when they brought home a praise note for work completion, praised them in front of relatives and neighbors, displayed the praise note, and reminded the children each morning of the note system. Not only did the children's report card grades improve noticeably, but parents and teachers were able to maintain the system with a minimum of effort and communication. Parents also reported more enthusiasm and positive attitudes from the children.

What problems have arisen in some parent programs?

As in all areas of parent participation, however, certain legitimate concerns have arisen (Sapon-Shevin, 1982). Since some programs offer parents little guidance in choosing goals and many goals focus on eliminating undesirable behaviors, a potential conflict may arise between the parents' and the child's rights. Also, the selection and evaluation of reinforcers may be weak, and sanctioned use of punishment is a questionable practice. The parent training provided and professional follow-up and supervision given parent-directed programs may also be poor.

Such programs are often part of a broader effort by parents and educators to increase communication. A system of daily or weekly report cards or "smiley face" notes helps parents keep abreast of events in the classroom (Kroth, 1975; Dickerson, Spellman, Larsen, and Tyler, 1973). Generally the notes contain an indication of general academic or behavioral achievement for that day or week. Parents sign and return them, sometimes also providing rewards for high performance.

Innovative uses of the phone have enhanced not only parental involvement but also student achievement. When parents were called by educators to reinforce their tutoring of ten reading words each night and told of the child's progress, there was an increase in achievement and an improvement in parental attitudes toward the school (Heron and Axelrod, 1976). A telephone answering system has been used with similar efficacy to transmit instructions for parents, requests, and progress notes (Chapman and Heward, 1982).

Parents can serve in a variety of capacities in the school. They can assist in transportation, fund-raising projects, the construction of instructional materials, and classroom activities such as dressing and feeding. Volunteer programs must be well planned and coordinated; volunteers should be trained for specific responsibilities and carefully supervised.

Materials. A variety of materials are available for use by parents in the school or at home. Many of the nationally known preschool programs for the exceptional child, such as the Project MEMPHIS (Quick, Little, and Campbell, 1974) and the Portage Project (Shearer and Shearer, 1977), have special curricular material for parents. The *Learning Language at Home* program (Karnes, 1977) and *Peabody Early Experience Kit* (Dunn et al., 1976) are examples of materials designed with parents in mind. There are activities for the home in language arts and mathematics (Cooper and Heron, 1978). Wallace and Kauffman (1978) offer specific suggestions for remedying problems in the social-emotional and visual-motor areas, and in spoken language, written language, reading, and arithmetic. Ideas for informal assessment are arranged according to common problem areas, such as "Does the child have difficulty following directions?"

A Guide for Better Reading (Granowsky, Middleton, and Mumford, 1977) describes one school system's program to improve reading. In this program

TECHNOLOGY IN ACTION

Jill is a preschool child with cerebral palsy. She is having difficulty differentiating between the concepts of big and little. Mrs. Martin, her preschool teacher, believes that extra practice at home can help Jill overcome this problem. Jill's mother was willing to help at home, but she was at a loss about how to proceed.

Mrs. Martin developed a set of systematic procedures for Jill's mother to follow in providing direct instruction to Jill at home. These procedures involved presenting pictures of objects of different size, identifying the relative size of each, encouraging Jill's imitation of the label, reinforcing for correct imitations, and systematic record-keeping of the time involved in direct instruction.

Following is the parent activity sheet that Mrs. Martin developed for Jill's mother to use as a guide for home instruction (from Shearer, 1976). You can see from the activity chart that Jill's mother consistently met the goal of providing at least five minutes of daily instruction on the concepts. As it eventually turned out, Jill did learn to differentiate between big and little; and Mrs. Martin is convinced that the efforts of Jill's mother contributed greatly to this accomplishment.

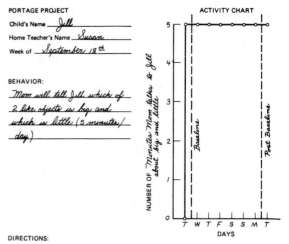

PORTAGE PROJECT

Child's Name _Jill_

Home Teacher's Name _Susan_

Week of _September 18th_

BEHAVIOR:

Mom will tell Jill which of 2 like objects is big and which is little (5 minutes/day)

DIRECTIONS:

1. Use paired objects or pictures that are the same - except for size.

2. Talk with Jill pointing to and naming the objects that are big and little, and encourage Jill to repeat the size word in imitation of you.

3. Praise her each time she imitates.

4. Use as many different examples of like pictures and objects as possible.

5. Record the number of minutes you spend naming big and little each day.

---

teachers assess reading skills and explain the findings to parents. The parents refer to the guide for activities to use in helping their child. Ideas for evaluation are also included.

Buist and Schulman (1969) have compiled a list of toys and games that can be used with exceptional children. They are described by age in four disability categories: perception, retention and recall, conceptualization, and expression. The play format permits parents to assist their exceptional children in a pleasant fashion. Finally, Moore and Morton (1976) offer a list of readings about working with their exceptional children. For each area of exceptionality they provide many examples of parents assisting their children, in some cases without professional support. Cansler et al. (1975) and Joseph P. Kennedy, Jr., Foundation's *Working with Your Child: For Families of the Developmentally Disabled* offer other suggestions to involve parents further in the instructional aspects of programs.

EVALUATION

How frequently must parents be involved in evaluating their handicapped child's progress?

Parents are required by law to be involved in at least one review of the child's individual education program a year. These evaluations are used to determine whether the program has been effective and whether changes in goals, objectives, placement, or procedures need to be made.

The effectiveness of parents' involvement in an annual evaluation is determined largely by the extent of communication between teachers and parents during the school year. Educators can communicate with parents in a number of ways. As discussed above, daily or weekly progress reports, graphs of child progress, and report cards that describe the child's skill levels rather than providing grades have all been used effectively (Kroth, 1975). "Smiley faces" can be used to reinforce children for meeting objectives. What is most important is that parents and teachers remain in regular contact, whether through phone calls, school conferences, written notes, home visits, casual meetings in the community, or parent groups. Every available opportunity should be used to share constructive comments about the child's behavior.

Efforts to include parents in the assessment and programming aspects of exceptional children's programs are teaching them what to look for in terms of their children's progress and program quality. Parents belonging to the National Association for Retarded Citizens place a high priority on this aspect of their children's program (Soffer, 1982). They demand a greater say in deciding when their children are evaluated and how they will get feedback. Professionals can help them and other parents by meeting more often, scheduling conferences better, and using language parents can understand. Parents can also be involved in the evaluation of their child's program by serving on advisory boards and steering committees. In these groups the opinions of parents can be solicited about a wide range of matters related to the education of exceptional children and ways to encourage productive interactions between professionals and parents.

PROBE 14-2
Involving Families

1. T F   Parents should not be involved in efforts to identify and refer exceptional children.
2. Describe three attitudes you might encounter among teachers opposed to parental involvement in the education of their exceptional children.
3. For each of the following stages of the educational process, describe a way that parents can be of assistance and how a professional could facilitate that particular parental effort.
   a. Identification
   b. Assessment

    c. Conferences
    d. Instruction
    e. Evaluation

4. Give three reasons that parents should be involved in the education of their exceptional children.

SUPPORTING FAMILIES

You should be able to describe ways to support parents and train them to perform their various roles and activities.

In addition to participating directly in their children's programs, parents find themselves performing many advocacy and program support roles. They are called upon to challenge inadequate and inappropriate services and to lobby for quality programs. They may need to interact with government officials, school administrators, and others. New programs are often developed and expanded as a result of an impetus created by parents. To them often falls the responsibility of arousing public awareness and creating sensitivity to the issues surrounding their children's needs by serving as speakers at meetings (Blackard and Barsh, 1982).

Parents must also continue to provide warm, supportive homes for their exceptional children and their siblings. Of all their possible activities, this one must be paramount (McLoughlin, 1979). Additionally, parents serve as vital resources to one another, as members of parent organizations or individually.

To perform these types of activities, families must be supported by professionals in various ways. These include safeguarding the rights of parents and serving as parent advocates.

FOSTERING PARENTAL RIGHTS

Are the rights of parents of handicapped children being fully observed?

Observance of the parental rights guaranteed by PL 94-142 has not been good. There seems to be an effort to meet the letter of the law, but efforts to meet the spirit of the law are lacking. For example, while prior notices concerning assessments are generally provided, they do not mention critical rights such as the parents' right to an independent evaluation that need not always be at their expense (Yoshida, 1982). Educators need to monitor such notices more closely for content and communication style.

As discussed earlier, the quality of parent participation at IEP conferences also leaves much to be desired. Parents cannot seem to remember what happens during these conferences (Hoff, Fenton, Yoshida, and Kaufman, 1978).

This situation is probably related to their lack of preparedness for the conferences, the technical jargon typically used, and parents' confusion about their role in the conference (Kotin and Eager, 1977).

There is reason to believe that some parents do not even attend the conferences; surveys of attendance (Pyecha et al., 1980) and audits of IEPs (Say, McCollum, and Brightman, 1980) indicate lower attendance than should be expected. When a group of parents of LD children were surveyed about their experience at the IEP conference, 25 percent could not recall the IEP process or confused it with other meetings (McKinney and Hocutt, 1982). While parents claimed that their job or home situation kept them away from such sessions, there was ample evidence that they lacked the knowledge to participate well and comfortably. Educators must serve as parent educators in regard to these conferences.

The profile of parental use of due process hearings is not very positive either (Strickland, 1982). While often vital to ensure the accountability of schools, due process seems to be a last, drastic recourse for parents who have tried everything. Parents who seek such hearings often have had numerous contacts, usually negative ones, with the schools about the problem and seem pushed to take a stand against the school's decision. Parents using this option are generally well educated and in the middle to upper socioeconomic levels.

In spite of the confidence these parents and schools have in the ability of the impartial hearing officer to make a fair decision, many decisions are not implemented. Parents report they would not ask for a due process hearing again, and many conflicts between parents and schools remain unresolved. In fact, relationships between the parties may get worse. Some positive, though indirect, outcomes of participating in hearings are that parents feel they are treated more as equals; the hearings are educational experiences; public awareness of the issues is highlighted; and federal and state policies regarding PL 94-142 are often clarified. All things considered, both parents and schools should consider a number of factors before requesting a due process hearing, including (1) the limited ability of the hearing and hearing officer to resolve the specific question at issue; (2) the investment of time, energy, and resources compared to the probable outcome; and (3) the potential harm to the child and stress on the family (Turnbull and Strickland, 1981). In this area, the saying "an ounce of prevention is worth a pound of cure" is particularly true.

To avoid formal due process hearings, some school districts and state departments use a process of mediation in which an intermediary helps the two conflicting parties reach a mutually acceptable solution to a problem. Mediation sometimes proves as adversarial, formal, and costly to participants as due process hearings, however (Yoshida and Byrne, 1979). Delays in using mediation after conflicts arise may create a level of tension and mistrust that make the technique less likely to be successful. Implementation of the approach requires improvement (Turnbull and Strickland, 1981), and many aspects of this technique need study (Yoshida, 1982). Educators in teaching and administrative roles must exercise understanding and restraint in the mediation process. It is likely that current usage of this procedure will probably improve as all parties learn how to function better in the mediation format.

PROFESSIONAL ADVOCACY

What advocacy roles should teachers assume?

Given the poor quality of current efforts to sustain parental rights, there are many avenues for providing support for parents. Much of what needs to be done can be considered a form of professional advocacy. There are two kinds of advocacy: external or internal to the system (McLoughlin, McLaughlin and Stewart, 1979). External advocacy, "an independent movement of consumers and their allies to monitor and change human service agencies" (Biklen, 1976), is untenable for educators since it requires that they be autonomous and engage in activities such as demonstrations, education boycotts, and so on. However, they can be internal advocates, engaged in a "continuous and cooperative process of interactions between parents and teachers as partners in guaranteeing the rights of the handicapped child to appropriate services" (McLoughlin, McLaughlin, and Stewart, 1979).

Parents have a crying need to know more about testing, conferences, due process, services for their children, and other aspects of special education. Their lack of knowledge seems to be at the heart of problems such as their difficulty participating at IEP meetings. Parents' lack of knowledge may influence professional perceptions of them and indirectly block fuller roles in decision making (Strickland, 1982).

While a recent study of all state departments of education indicated a commitment to provide information of this sort to families, the allocation of resources and strategies varied from state to state (McLoughlin, Edge, Strenecky, and Key, 1984). Better cooperative efforts among educational agencies and private parent and professional organizations will improve the quantity and quality of information. State education departments and other groups are stressing common criteria such as visual appeal, legibility, and content; they seem satisfied with their material. However, there are serious problems with readability, and gaps in content are evident (McLoughlin et al., 1981). Also while state education departments and other agencies involve parents in developing this material, participation is not broad enough to guarantee that the material will be appropriate for a parent audience.

Educators and other professionals also have an obligation to research issues relevant to parents (Winton and Turnbull, 1982). They need to become more flexible in deciding where and how they disseminate their research findings so that parents will hear about them and understand them. Creative use of the media can also influence parental awareness. For example, the Parent Education and Resource Center at the University of Louisville developed a set of 1-minute audiotapes with suggestions about child rearing practices in language, social-emotional, and physical development; they were broadcast over radio stations in Kentucky and elsewhere. Recorded telephone messages can increase parental knowledge as well as help children learn (Chapman and Heward, 1982).

Educators are also in an excellent position to provide information about two priority items for parents: the child's program and the teacher. Newsletters, and handbooks, and parent bulletin boards with information about the school program and the children's activities in it are very well received by parents. They often are willing to assist in such publication efforts (Cansler et al., 1975; Kroth, 1975).

Another way to develop a trusting relationship with parents is to make home visits (Cansler et al., 1975). Educators should have a clear purpose in mind for the visit and communicate it to the family when the appointment is made. Being positive about the child and indicating interest in the family's concerns are important for a successful visit. The family's privacy must be respected. These visits are also a great opportunity to model a good attitude toward the child for the parents and toward the parents for the child.

Educators who have a strong desire to serve as advocates are not deterred by difficult parents. The use of less structured and less traditional approaches often works (Cansler et al., 1975). Being accessible, sharing in their life situations, and approaching them as adults are good beginnings. More specific ideas include being visible in the neighborhood, associating with people the parents trust, sponsoring social events or programs involving their children, communicating clearly and seeking feedback, focusing on real needs, and encouraging parents in meaningful ways. With culturally different families and minorities, educators must be particularly sensitive to possible cultural discrepancies between themselves and the parents (Rodriguez, 1981).

Parental success in participating directly in different aspects of their children's program depends heavily upon professionals' conviction of their importance and efforts to make their role meaningful. When parents request mediation or a due process hearing, educators must remember that it is their duty to advocate the rights of the child in question.

PARENT PROGRAMS

Good relations with parents and the successful resolutions of problems depend on the educator's confidence in parents' knowledge and decision-making ability. That is why many educators see it as their role to provide enriching and training experiences for parents. The effort also benefits the children. In the long run, such efforts make the educator's job easier.

An important part of the program for the exceptional child should be the development of a parent program. In some cases parents will be involved with the school as part of the regular parent-teacher organization. Generally it is desirable to establish separate groups to deal with the needs of parents of exceptional children or to create formal programs to involve parents in the direct instruction of their children. Regardless of the type of program, the goal is to improve the educational process for everyone involved: parents, teachers, students, and administrators.

What good are parent programs?

Conceptual Basis. Parent programs serve many purposes. They are generally designed to give parents social and emotional support. By talking to parents who have similar problems and to professionals who can be of assistance, parents can learn to cope with feelings such as those described at the beginning of the chapter.

Parent programs can also provide a forum for the exchange of information. This can involve scheduling guest speakers, maintaining a lending library, or publishing a newsletter.

Parent programs frequently offer parents an opportunity to participate in their child's programs as teacher's aides, volunteers, tutors, data collectors, behavior managers, or field trip monitors. A major goal of all parent programs should be to improve the interactions between parents and their exceptional child. Parent groups can help parents develop appropriate expectations for their children and strategies for better communication (Lillie and Trohanis, 1976).

Several preschool programs have been developed that involve parents intensively in their children's education. In Portage Project, for example, a teacher visits the child's home for 1½ hours a week. During these visits, objectives for the child are developed and teaching strategies are demonstrated. The parents provide the child with the actual lessons and collect information on performance; this information is reviewed the next time the teacher visits (Shearer and Shearer, 1977). The PEECH project, on the other hand, trains parents to provide instructional assistance in the classroom. Some programs combine both techniques. Parents of older children generally do follow-up work at home.

Parent training must be approached carefully. It should be comprehensive, and not just develop isolated skills (Bricker and Casuso, 1979). Goals must be based on the family's needs, readiness, and learning style. Educators must recognize the importance of gaining the trust and confidence of parents (Simpson, 1982) or parent education will not yield major gains.

Content. Parent programs can involve a variety of topics and activities, depending on the parents' needs. Sometimes they are structured around organized, published material such as Smith and Smith's child management program (1976) or Becker's program (1971). In one program for fathers of deaf children, the topics included the physical causes of deafness and linguistic and cognitive development; the fathers also discussed common experiences in discovering and diagnosis of the problem and met deaf adults (Crowley, Keane, and Needham, 1982).

A program designed for siblings of exceptional children set out to familiarize them with the school's program and to provide some background on their disabilities (Cansler et al., 1975). Siblings had the opportunity to discuss their feelings, to learn games to play with the exceptional child, and to learn ways to relate better to them. Siblings benefit from sharing experiences among themselves, much as the parents do.

It is wise to cover material not related to school at parent meetings. Parents appreciate discussions about getting baby-sitters, going shopping or to a restaurant with the exceptional child, or going on vacation (Heward et al., 1979). Educators should not shy away from topics such as sex education, marriage, career possibilities, and living arrangements. Specialists should be sought when needed.

There are many print and nonprint materials available to facilitate the development of parent programs. *Strategies for Effective Parent-Teacher Interaction* (Kroth, 1980b) contains modules (lecture outlines, handouts, tapes and overlays, etc.) on topics such as conferencing and communication. *Parenting the Special Needs Child* (Felt, Coplon, and Sonnenschein, 1981) is a series of filmed vignettes of typical situations that parents of exceptional children find themselves in; it is an excellent means of stimulating a discussion. Parent Magazine Films, Inc., offers a set of filmstrips and cassettes on raising the exceptional child. Useful annotated bibliographies of training materials appropriate for parents and educators of exceptional children have been prepared by Strenecky, Strenecky, and Dare (1978) and Williams (1977).

Evaluation. Parent programs should be evaluated regularly. An initial needs assessment can establish appropriate topics, format, schedule and location, and desirable activities for the parents. When parents are trying to accomplish specific goals with their children, it is essential to provide for feedback lest they get discouraged or harm the child.

It is also helpful to attend to the characteristics and performance of parents in the group. Their socioeconomic status, education, and pretraining experience may dictate certain strategies; these traits were related to one parent group's later knowledge of behavior management techniques (Clark et al., 1982). However, if this group is indicative of what occurs generally, it is even more important to monitor parents' performance during the program; it seems to affect their follow-through activities.

The benefits to the children should also be examined, both in skill development and effect. Parental satisfaction and attitudes toward the child and school are other important indicators of success. Most of all, parent-child interactions should be examined for improvement.

Training Models. Current thinking about parent training stresses the need to make parents better consumers of educational services and more effective advocates for their children in such situations as evaluation sessions, IEP conferences, problem-solving sessions, and progress report conferences (Simpson, 1982). Training should be directed by a group of parents and educators. The format could consist ideally of attitude development activities, content sessions, opportunities for parents to express and share feelings, observations of acceptable role models, simulation activities (e.g. conferences), feedback activities, and follow-up arrangements.

In some cases, parents of exceptional children and educators can be trained together (McLoughlin, 1981). This tends to destroy misconceptions and build a working relationship more quickly. Suitable topics are communications and program areas about which parents and educators are frequently in communication, such as report cards and grades. Considerable planning is required to accommodate differences in learning style and background.

Parent Organizations and Resources. Various national organizations are prepared to provide parents and others with information about exceptional persons and services for them. Some of them, such as the National Association for Retarded Citizens, have state and local branches and offer conferences and informal meetings for parents. Such sessions are a vehicle for parents to keep current with the newest developments in the field, to participate in discussions designed for them, and to share useful strategies with other parents. Often parents are trained for advocacy activities. These organizations also provide parents regular newsletters, such as *Newsbriefs* from the Association for Children and Adults with Learning Disabilities. Siblings for Significant Change is a national group for people with exceptional brothers and sisters. *The Exceptional Parent* is a periodical specifically designed for parental interests and needs. See Task Sheet 14 for further details about these resources.

FUTURE TRENDS

The future in special education will be challenging for parents of exceptional persons of various ages. Since the passage of PL 94-142, parents have made significant progress toward participation in the development and implementation of services. However, too often the letter of the law has been observed, and not the spirit. The result has been an emphasis on involving the parents in procedural matters. Sometimes the goal of cooperation has been lost sight of in the midst of the paperwork and meetings.

For this reason, it is important for parents to avoid losing ground in this vital area. Their hard-won rights to participate may be overlooked if a backlash of political pressure objects to the necessary commitment of time and personnel to insure active parental involvement. Also, past experience suggests the need to clarify the best ways to have parents participate, since some parents have been unwilling and/or unable to do so effectively.

Parents can assist in directing their future involvement by making known how they want to be involved and how their concerns can be best met. There is growing awareness that some parents may have other concerns for their participation than professionals are aware of and may prefer alternative ways to be involved. Specifically, a broader family perspective to parent involvement seems more appropriate than a purely parental rights one. Such an approach would also ensure greater attention to parental concerns about their children's need during the preschool years and after they leave formal schooling.

What is the value of parent organizations?

Parent organizations must assume a major responsibility for guiding the initiative on behalf of parents of exceptional persons. It is necessary to counter the indifference of some parents whose children have received services and who are tempted to cease their advocacy activities. Professionals who are committed to the parent movement in special education must be suitably reinforced. The currency and quality of information provided to parents must also be monitored to prevent inappropriate and costly efforts by parents. The gains of the 1970s must be capitalized upon in the 1980s.

PROBE 14-3
Supporting Families

1. As a school official, describe three policies you would establish to ensure that the legal rights of parents are protected.

2. Describe four purposes served by parent programs.

3. T F Because professionals are familiar with the needs of parents, they should have the major responsibility in developing parent training programs.

4. T F Assessment of parental needs is the first step in developing a parent training program.

5. T F Parents and educators can never be trained together.

SUMMARY

1. Although reactions vary, the parents of disabled children may experience periods of shock, denial, guilt, fear, overprotectiveness, overt rejection, and disguised rejection before reaching the stage of acceptance.
2. The attitudes of parents can improve or adversely affect the behavior of their handicapped children.
3. The siblings of handicapped children generally adopt the attitudes of their parents toward the handicapped child.
4. The parents of handicapped children need a great deal of information about such subjects as diagnosis, treatment, management, and support services.
5. The relationship between parents and professionals concerned with handicapped children is gradually improving. Successful relationships depend on mutual trust and understanding.
6. Parents can assist in the identification, assessment, and programming of

their children and in the implementation and evaluation of their children's programs.

7. Parents have the legal right to be involved in all decisions regarding the education of their handicapped children. They also have the protection of due process if they are dissatisfied with the educational program that has been provided.

8. Parent programs should provide emotional support, a forum for the exchange of information, an opportunity to participate in the child's program, and parent-child interaction training.

9. Parent programs must be designed around their needs and directed toward making them better consumers and advocates.

10. A knowledge of parental needs, awareness of the ways they can get involved, and preparedness to support them are the main dimensions of a parent involvement program.

TASK SHEET 14
Field Experiences with Families of Exceptional Children

Select *one* of the following and complete the required tasks. Write a report of no more than three pages about your activities.

Family Interview

Interview the parents or other family members of a disabled or gifted child. Using great tact, ask about their reactions when they learned that their child was exceptional. Try to determine what problems the parents encountered in attempting to obtain services. Find out about their home life. If the parents have gone through the due process procedures mandated by PL 94-142, determine how they reacted to that experience.

Observation

Observe the meeting of a placement committee in your local school district. Describe how the professionals interacted with the parents at the meeting, and how the parents participated. Determine whether the parents' rights were correctly observed. What was your reaction to the procedure?

Professional Interview

Interview a professional person about his or her experience with parents of exceptional children. If the professional participates in parental involvement programs, ask him or her to describe them.

Participation

Offer your services to a parent training program or other program in which parents are involved.

Agency Investigation

Request information from three of the following agencies about the services they provide to parents of exceptional children. Write a three-page report summarizing these services and how you might use them if you were a parent of an exceptional child.

American Foundation for the Blind, Inc.
15 West 16th Street
New York, NY 10011

American Speech-Language-Hearing
Association
10801 Rockville Pike
Rockville, MD 20852

Association for Children and Adults
with Learning Disabilities
4156 Library Road
Pittsburgh, PA 15234

National Information Center for
Handicapped Children and Youth
Post Office Box 1492
Washington, DC 20013

International Parents' Organization of
the Alexander Graham Bell Association
for the Deaf
1537 35th Street, N.W.
Washington, DC 20007

National Assocation for Creative
Children and Adults
8080 Springvalley Drive
Cincinnati, OH 45236

National Association for the Deaf-Blind
2703 Forest Oak Circle
Norman, OK 73071

National Association for Retarded
Citizens
2709 Avenue E East
Post Office Box 6109
Arlington, TX 76011

National Easter Seal Society for Crippled
Children and Adults
2023 W. Ogden Avenue
Chicago, IL 60612

National Society for Autistic Children
169 Tampa Avenue
Albany, NY 12208

Siblings for Significant Change
823 United Nations Plaza
New York, NY 10017

Library Study

Use the library to locate three articles related to a topic associated with parents of exceptional children. Write a one-page abstract of each. In the last paragraph of your abstract indicate your personal reaction to the article. Here are the names of some journals in which you can find articles: *The Exceptional Parent* Periodical (605 Commonwealth Ave., Boston, MA 02215), newsletters and other publications available from the organizations mentioned above, and the special education journals mentioned elsewhere in this text.

Design Your Own Field Experience

If none of these alternatives is attractive to you, or if you have the opportunity to perform some other task with parents of exceptional children, design your own field experience. Check with your instructor to determine its acceptability.

PHOTOGRAPH CREDITS (Continued)

Photo essay: pp. 86–87, Judith Sedwick. *Chapter 3:* p. 91, Alan Carey/The Image Works, Inc.; p. 98, Paul Conklin; p. 123 © Susan Lapides; p. 135, Claudia Lewis. *Part II opening photo:* Reprinted by permission of Camp Kysoc, Kentucky Easter Seal Society. Photo by W.J. Wells. *Chapter 4:* p. 163, From W. C. Grabb, S. W. Rosenstein, and K. R. Bzoch (eds.), CLEFT LIP AND PALATE (Boston, Little, Brown and Co., 1971); p. 165, Courtesy of Dr. Thomas J. Vergo, Jr., Tufts University, School of Dental Medicine, Boston; p. 171, Courtesy of Western Electric; p. 178, Claudia Lewis. *Chapter 5:* p. 199, Claudia Lewis; p. 222, David Campione/Taurus Photos, Inc. *Photo essay:* pp. 232–233, Alan Carey/The Image Works, Inc. *Chapter 6:* p. 260, Courtesy of Wormald International; p. 262, Courtesy of Telesensory Systems, Inc.; p. 263, Courtesy of the Howe Press at Perkins School for the Blind, Watertown, Ma., U.S.A., 02172; p. 264, Courtesy of American Printing House for the Blind; p. 267, Claudia Lewis. *Chapter 7:* p.

294, Courtesy, Wright State University; p. 313, Bob Daemmrich/Texastock, Inc.; p. 320, Courtesy, Canadian Rehabilitation Council for the Disabled. *Photo essay:* pp. 334–5, Alan Carey/The Image Works, Inc. *Part III opening photo:* p. 336, Alan Carey/The Image Works, Inc. *Chapter 8:* all photos, Claudia Lewis. *Chapter 9:* p. 407, Paul Conklin; p. 410, Joan Liftin/Archive Pictures, Inc. *Chapter 10:* p 451, Alan Carey/The Image Works, Inc.; p. 458, Paul Conklin. *Photo essay:* pp. 466–7, Claudia Lewis. *Chapter 11:* p. 471, 494, Paul Conklin; p. 500 (left), Courtesy of Prentke Romich Co.; (right), Courtesy of Scitronics, Inc. *Chapter 12:* p. 528, Andrew Sacks; p. 533, Paul Conklin; p. 554, Claudia Lewis. *Unit IV opening photo:* Reprinted by permission of Camp Kysoc, Kentucky Easter Seal Society. Photo by W. J. Wells. *Chapter 13:* p. 596, Claudia Lewis; p. 598, 602, Paul Conklin. *Photo essay:* pp. 614–15, Paul Conklin. *Chapter 14:* p. 628, Paul Conklin; p. 640, Claudia Lewis.

TEXT CREDITS

Chapter 1: Excerpt, p. 9: From M. Satchell, "Ladies, Start Your Engines," *Parade,* May 6, 1979. Reprinted by permission. *Chapter 2:* Excerpt, pp. 54–55: From *Bluegrass Association for Retarded Citizens Newsletter,* July 1979. Reprinted by permission. Fig. 2-1: Based on figures from M. Reynolds, "A framework for considering some issues in special education," *Exceptional Children,* 28 (1962) and E. Deno, "Special education as developmental capital," *Exceptional Children,* 39 (1973). Reprinted by permission. *Chapter 3:* Fig. 3-1: Adapted from H. Knoblock and P. Pasamanick, eds., *Gesell and Amatruda's Developmental Diagnosis,* 3rd ed. Copyright © 1974 by Harper & Row, Publishers, Inc. Reprinted by permission. *Chapter 4:* Fig. 4-4 (left): From Harold Westlake and D. Rutherford, *Cleft Palate,* p. 57, © 1966. Reprinted by permission of Prentice-Hall, Inc., Englewood Cliffs, New Jersey. *Chapter 5:* Fig. 5-2: From Jerry L. Northern and Marion P. Downs, *Hearing in Children,* 3rd ed., p. 7. Copyright © 1984 by Williams & Wilkins. Reprinted by permission. Fig. 5-3: Diagram from *Your Health After 60,* edited by M. M. Blacker and D. R. Wekstein. Copyright © 1979 by Sanders-Brown Research Center on Aging and reproduced by permission of E. P. Dutton, Inc. Figs. 5-4 and 5-5 and Chart 5-1: William W. Green. Fig. 5-6: Courtesy of the National Association of the Deaf. *Chapter 6:* Excerpt on p. 243: From *Popular Computing,* April 1984, p. 34. Copyright © 1984 by McGraw-Hill, Inc. Reprinted by permission. Fig. 6-4: From the

National Society to Prevent Blindness, New York, N.Y. By permission. Fig. 6-5: Courtesy of Histacount Corporation. Fig. 6-11: Courtesy of American Printing House for the Blind. *Chapter 8:* Table 8-2: From C. J. Fogleman, ed., *American Association on Mental Deficiency Adaptive Behavior Scale Manual,* Rev. ed. (Washington, DC: American Association on Mental Deficiency, 1975). Reprinted by permission. Fig. 8-2: From *Journal of the American Medical Association,* September 9, 1983, Vol. 250, No. 10, p. 1249. Copyright 1983, American Medical Association. By permission. *Chapter 11:* Table 11-1 and Fig. 11-1: From Wayne Sailor and Doug Guess, *Handicapped Students: An Instructional Design.* Copyright © 1983 by Houghton Mifflin Company. Reprinted by permission. *Chapter 12:* Fig. 12-1: Courtesy of Akira Morishima. *Chapter 13:* Chart 13-1: From Council for Exceptional Children, *Position paper on career education.* Copyright 1978 by The Council for Exceptional Children. Reprinted with permission. Fig. 13-2: From Donn E. Brolin and Charles Kokaska, *Career Education for Handicapped Children and Youth,* p. 107. Copyright © 1979 by Bell & Howell Company. Reprinted by permission of Charles E. Merrill Publishing Company. Excerpt on pp. 603–604: Adapted by permission from J. S. Payne, C. D. Mercer, and M. H. Epstein, *Education and Rehabilitation Techniques* (New York: Behavioral Publications, 1974).

Glossary

Academic disciplines: The branches of knowledge and inquiry traditionally associated with scholarship in Western society, e.g., music, literature, history, physics.

Acceleration: Any of a number of educational provisions used to move students through the curriculum more rapidly than usual, e.g., early school admission, grade-skipping, accelerated classes.

Adaptive behavior: The effectiveness or degree with which an individual meets the standards of personal independence and social responsibility expected for age and cultural group.

Addition: Articulation disorder where a sound or sounds are added in normally nonoccurring positions in a word.

Advocacy (and consumerism): A trend in which parents and professionals are working in an assertive fashion to gain better services for handicapped persons.

Aesthetic and theoretical pursuits: As operationally defined on the Vernon-Allport-Lindzey *Study of Values,* these pursuits are artistic, such as sculpting, visiting art museums, or story-writing and scholarly, such as conducting experiments or discussing abstract ideas.

Agnosia: Inability to attach meaning to sounds, words, or visual experiences.

Air conduction test: A pure-tone hearing test using earphones.

Alchemy: A pseudoscience that alleges to create gold from other chemical compounds.

Amblyopia (lazy eye): A condition in which the brain will not tolerate double vision and suppresses what is being transmitted by the weaker eye.

Amniocentesis: A test that may be done during pregnancy to identify certain genetic disorders in the fetus. It consists of extracting a small amount of amniotic fluid, which surrounds the fetus in the womb, for examination.

Anoxia: Also referred to as asphyxia. The deprivation of oxygen in the blood to the extent that normal tissue functioning is not possible. Tissues of the brain or central nervous system are particularly susceptible to damage due to asphyxia.

Anterior: Refers to the front of the body.

Anvil (or incus): One of the bones of the middle ear that carries vibrations across the middle ear cavity.

Aphasia: Acquired language impairment caused by brain damage.

Applied behavior analysis: A structured approach to teaching and behavior management that employs observation and charting of student behavior, task analysis, systematic application of sequenced teaching procedures, reinforcement, and monitoring of student performance.

Apraxia: Difficulty with voluntary or purposeful muscular movement with no evidence of motor impairment.

Aqueous humor: Watery substance between the cornea and the lens of the eye.

Architectural barrier: A condition of the physical environment that can inhibit or prevent handicapped persons from using facilities or moving about.

Arthritis: Condition affecting the joints and muscles, causing pain, stiffness, and inflammation.

Arthrogryphosis: A congenital disease in which the muscles may be poorly developed with crooking or contraction of the joints.

Articulation: The movements of the vocal system that result in the production of speech sounds and words.

Articulation disorder: A communication disorder associated with substitutions, omissions, distortions, and/or additions of speech sounds.

Asthma: Chronic condition characterized by wheezing or labored breathing caused by a constriction of the air passages in the bronchial tubes and by an increased amount of thick secretions in the air tubes of the lungs.

Astigmatism: Blurred vision caused by uneven curvature of the cornea or lens.

Ataxia: A type of cerebral palsy in which lack of muscle coordination results in loss of coordinated movements, especially those relating to balance and position.

Athetosis: A form of cerebral palsy characterized by involuntary, jerky, purposeless, repetitive movements of the extremities, head, and tongue.

Atrophy: The degeneration or death of tissue.

Audiogram: A graphic portrayal of the results of hearing testing.

Audiologist: A specialist in evaluation and remediation of auditory disorders.

Audiology: A science concerned with hearing impairments, including their detection and remediation.

Auditory analysis: Ability to isolate components of an auditory message.

Auditory cortex: The portion of the brain covering that is associated with the hearing sense.

Auditory discrimination: Ability to detect the differences between sounds.

Auditory figure-ground perception: Ability to isolate a particular sound or a word from other sounds or words occurring simultaneously.

Auditory integration: Ability to associate a sound or sound combinations (word and sentences) with other experiences.

Auditory nerve: Cranial nerve VIII that carries auditory impulses from the cochlea to the brain.

Auditory perception: Use of the auditory channel to identify and attach meaning to specific recurring experiences (words) that are heard.

Auditory training: Training designed to teach a hearing impaired person to make best use of residual hearing.

Auditory-visual integration: Ability of the child to combine sound with symbol in understanding of, for example, phonetic symbols.

Aura: A condition that occurs in some individuals with epilepsy just before a seizure. The person may see unusual colors, hear ringing sounds, smell peculiar odors, or experience other phenomena during this time.

Auricle (pinna): The externally visible, flaplike, cartilaginous structure on the side of the head.

Autism: A severe behavioral disorder characterized by extreme withdrawal and self-stimulation, requiring intense and prolonged intervention, usually in a segregated setting.

Behavior checklists: A list of traits or behaviors that research has shown to be characteristic of a group of children. These checklists are often used to rate children to determine whether they should be referred for special services.

Behavior disorders: Disorders in which behavior deviates from a normal range, occurs over an extended period of time, and is extreme in terms of intensity and frequency.

Behavior modification: See introduction to Part III for list of concepts and their definitions.

Behavioral excesses: Behaviors that are excessive in terms of frequency, intensity, duration, or occurrence under conditions when their socially sanctioned frequency is close to zero.

Behavioral model: Assumptions that behavior disorders are primarily a result of inappropriate learning and that the most effective preventative actions and therapeutic interventions will involve controlling the child's environment in order to teach appropriate behaviors.

Biophysical model: Assumptions that behavior disorders are primarily a result of dysfunction of the central nervous system due to brain lesions, neurochemical irregularities, or genetic defects and that the most effective preventative actions and therapeutic interventions will involve prevention or correction of such biological defects.

Blind: Those whose visual acuity is 20/200 or less in the better eye with the best possible correction or a restriction in the field of vision to an angle subtending an arc of 20 degrees or less. These people must use braille, and tactile and auditory materials in their education.

Bone conduction test: A hearing test that measures the response of the sensorineural mechanism in the inner ear bypassing the outer and middle ear system.

Braille: A code developed for blind persons in which a system of raised dots allows the person to read with the fingertips.

Breadth and depth models of evaluation: These terms describe different criteria for determining giftedness. Breadth models require high performance on more than one measure. Depth models require high performance on only one measure.

Buckley Amendment: Guarantees parents control of the school records of their children.

Career: The totality of work one does in his or her lifetime.

Career awareness: Program emphasized during elementary years that examines the relationship of work to the total life process and emphasizes basic work values.

Career education: The totality of experiences through which one learns about and prepares to engage in work as part of his or her way of living.

Cascade of services: A hierarchy of educational service alternatives for handicapped persons, ranging from the least restrictive regular classroom to the highly restrictive hospital or institutional setting.

Casefinding: Activities designed to make initial contact with the target populations.

Cataract: Clouding of the lens of the eye that obstructs the passage of light.

Caudal: Reference to the tail-end or hind part of the body.

Central auditory disorder: Disorder of auditory comprehension, perception, and discrimination where there is no disorder or damage to the peripheral hearing mechanism.

Central nervous system (CNS): The part of the nervous system to which the sensory impulses are transmitted and from which motor impulses develop.

Cephalad: Reference to the head or anterior end of the body.

Cephalocaudal development: Development that proceeds from the head downward.

Cerebellum: An area of the brain which, if damaged, results in an inability to maintain balance and coordinated movement, or ataxia type cerebral palsy.

Cerebral palsy: An abnormal alternation of human movement or motor functioning arising from a defect, injury, or disease of the tissues of the central nervous system.

Cerumen: Bitter-tasting, waxlike material secreted by glands in the skin lining along the outer two-thirds of the auditory canal.

Chemotherapy: Administration of drugs to control or aid a problem.

Child find: A concerted effort by state and local educational agencies to identify all handicapped children in need of special education services.

Chorionic villi sampling: A prenatal diagnostic procedure accomplished by collecting a 30 mg sample from the chorion tissues surrounding the developing fetal placenta. The sample is collected by a catheter inserted through the uterus by way of the vagina and as such does not invade or break the wall of the patient's womb as is the case with amniocentesis. Can be safely used as early as the first eight to twelve weeks of pregnancy.

Choroid: Layer of the eye between the sclera and retina that contains blood vessels that provide nourishment to the retina.

Chromosomes: Human matter which contain genes and control heredity. Humans have 46 chromosomes acquired at conception, 23 from the mother and 23 from the father.

Cinefluoroscopy: X-ray motion pictures.

Circular pursuit: Visually following a moving object in a circular pattern.

Classroom performance: Academic behavior in the classroom. As indexed by grades, classroom performance is a common measure of achievement, but not always a valid one because of confounding influences on grades, e.g., teacher expectations.

Clubfoot: A congenital abnormality in which the foot is turned downward and inward at the ankle.

Cochlea: Snail-shell shaped auditory part of the inner ear. The sense organ of hearing.

Cognition: Awareness or understanding of information.

Computer skills: Ability to make informed use of major types of computer programs, such as word-processing, file storage, and data analysis programs. Computer skills also include, in many schools, programming in popular languages, such as BASIC or Pascal.

Concept: Thought, opinion, idea, or mental image.

Conduct disorder: A behavioral disorder characterized by a pattern including both verbal and physical aggressive behavior of an antisocial nature.

Conductive hearing loss: Hearing disorder caused by blockage or damage to the structures of the outer or middle ear.

Congenital condition: Condition present at birth.

Conjugate eye movement: Moving both eyes together in a coordinate manner.

Conjunctiva: Thin transparent layer that lines the eyelids and covers the front of the eye and prevents dust or other particles from entering.

Convergent thinking: Thinking that is intended to arrive at a "correct" answer such as a solution to a math problem or a definition of a vocabulary word.

CORE home: A cluster of community-based residential living options available to persons with mental retardation or other developmental disabilities. A client can move through the available options based on need, ability, and availability of those options.

Cornea: Transparent cover in front of the iris and pupil that refracts light rays.

Creativity: Production of original or imaginative work. Creativity is one of the five performance areas included in the federal definition of giftedness.

Cretinism: Congenital thyroid deficiency that can stunt physical growth and cause mental retardation.

Criterion-referenced test: A test of academic achievement in which a student's performance is compared to pre-established level of items correct.

Cultural bias: Partiality of educational practices in favor of the majority culture.

Cyanosis: A blue discoloration of the skin caused by a lack of oxygen in the blood.

Cystic fibrosis: A disease affecting mucous glands in the body causing respiratory and digestive problems.

Decibel: A dimensionless unit expressing the logarithmic ratio of two amounts of pressure, power, or intensity; measure of loudness of a particular sound. Abbreviated dB.

De-institutionalization: Term used to describe the movement away from placing handicapped people in large residential institutional facilities.

Developmental model: A model of development based on normal developmental milestones.

Developmental placement: Placing individual students into the grade level commensurate with their academic, social, and physical developmental level, rather than placing them only on the basis of chronological age.

Diabetes: A metabolic disorder in which the body is not able to properly utilize carbohydrates in the diet because of a failure of the pancreas to secrete an adequate supply of insulin.

Diabetic coma: A condition in which enough insulin is not available to help the body convert the intake of glucose.

Digital grasp: Grasping an object using the fingers (digits), rather than the whole hand.

Diphthong: Speech sound made with voicing that is a combination of two vowels coming together in the same syllable.

Direct instruction: A systematic teaching method that uses a model-lead-test format.

Disability: A condition due to the reduction of function or absence of a particular body part or organ (e.g., paraplegic, amputee); synonymous with disorder or dysfunction.

Discriminative stimulus: A stimulus which is consistently paired with reinforcement.

Disfluency: Speech marked by repetition, hesitation, prolongations, and in general, a lack of flow which calls attention to itself; referred to by some as stuttering.

Distal: Away from the body or trunk.

Distortion: Articulation disorders wherein an acceptable sound is replaced by a sound that doesn't exist in a given language.

Divergent thinking: Production of many different solutions to a problem or question which has no "right or wrong" answers.

Dominant gene: Genes that override the effect of recessive genes and determine the expression of certain traits. When one parent has a dominant gene for a particular trait there is a 50 percent chance that all offspring will exhibit that trait.

Down's Syndrome: A chromosomal aberration caused by improper cell division, which results in incorrect cell structure. Originally referred to as Mongolism, but this term is not accepted today. The syndrome is characterized by mild to moderate mental retardation, epicanthic folds of the eyelids (hence the approximation of an oriental or mongol appearance), large fissured tongue, broad and flat bridge of the nose, and typically poor muscle tone. It may account for the single largest number of persons manifesting mental retardation with a known cause. Can be detected prior to birth through either amniocentesis or chorionic villi sampling.

Dysarthria: Term referring to any speech disorder that has as its base an impairment of the central or peripheral nervous system.

Dyslexia: A severe disability in learning to read.

Eardrum (tympanic membrane): The semitransparent membrane which separates the outer and middle ear.

Echolalia: Imitation of the sounds of others.

Educable mentally retarded (EMR): A commonly used classification term in education for students with mild mental retardation. These students can typically profit from education and training in fundamental academic skills, including reading, arithmetic, science. Vocational training in both skilled and unskilled areas is typically feasible and as adults this group has proven to comprise highly dependable employees. Unsupervised living through adulthood is typically achieved by persons in the educational classification. The I.Q. parameters for this group are usually in the 50–55 to 70 range.

Educational lockstep: The practice of placing all students of the same chronological age into one grade level and ignoring other relevant criteria for grade placement.

Educational synthesizer: A teacher who incorporates available resources such as physical therapists into daily educational programs.

Electroencephalogram: Graphic record of the electrical output of brain waves.

Eligibility determination: The decision as to whether a student meets the criteria for placement in a program, such as a gifted education program.

Elitism: Partiality or favored treatment to a group on the basis of its supposed superiority.

Emmetropic eye: The normal eye; one that is perfectly focused for distance so that the image of an object focuses directly on the retina.

Encephalitis: A condition that causes inflammation of the brain which may result in brain damage.

Encopresis: Lack of bowel control.

Enrichment: Educational experiences not usually included in the curriculum, e.g., opportunities to study archeology, filmmaking, etc.

Enuresis: Lack of bladder control.

Epilepsy: A chronic condition of the central nervous system, characterized by periodic seizures accompanied by convulsions of the muscles, and, with more severe attacks, loss of consciousness.

Etiology: The causes or origins of a disease or condition.

Eustachian tube: Tubelike structure connecting the middle ear and the naso-pharynx.

Exceptional children: Those who have physical, mental, behavioral, or sensory characteristics that differ from the majority of children to such an extent that they require special education and related services in order to develop to their maximum capacity.

Expressive language: Ability to encode language and present it orally or in a written or gestural form.

Extensor muscle: Those muscles that are used to extend the arm, such as in reaching.

External auditory canal: An irregularly shaped, tubelike passage extending from the inside of the head to the middle ear. Approximately 1″ long in adults.

Fading: Gradual removal of additional stimuli such as prompts.

Fetal Alcohol Syndrome (FAS): FAS may be the third leading cause of mental retardation. Certainty regarding the amount of daily alcohol consumption and risk to the fetus has not been definitively determined. It is believed, however, that anything more than 89 ml (equivalent to 3 ounces) presents high risk for the fetus.

Fine motor skills: Use of small muscles for reaching, grasping, and manipulation of objects such as puzzles, formboards, cubes, and drawing materials.

Flexor muscles: Muscles used to pull your arm toward your body as if one were flexing the muscles.

Fragile-X Syndrome: A recently discovered chromosomal aberration that may rival Down's Syndrome for producing persons with mental retardation. A recessive gene trait, typically expressed only in males, as the chromosomal aberration occurs on the male chromosome, i.e., XY. Can be detected prior to birth through either amniocentesis or chorionic villi sampling.

Frequency: The number of vibrations which occur at the same rate over a period of time in a sound wave. Measured in Hertz (Hz).

Functional hearing loss: "Hearing loss" which has a psychological, as opposed to organic, cause.

Functional learning handicap: Handicap in learning that develops as a result of prolonged stress or environmental problems.

Generalization: Process of a skill being performed in different environments with different persons, different instructional materials, and different language cues.

Genes: The basic units of heredity. Genes direct and control the processes of human growth and development.

Gifted: A term used to refer to children with outstanding ability or potential. The term is usually applied to children who perform in the top three to five percent on measures of aptitude or achievement in such areas as general intellectual ability, specific academic aptitude, creativity, leadership or artistic ability.

Gifted handicapped children: Children who have both superior ability *and* a handicap, such as a learning disability, physical disability, or sensory disorder.

Glaucoma: Severe disorder that occurs when the aqueous fluid does not circulate properly and results in an elevation of pressure in the eye.

Global retardation: Profound, inclusive difficulty in learning, as opposed to specific difficulty in a single area such as reading or math.

Gower's sign: A symptom of Duchenne type of muscular dystrophy in which the child is seen "walking up" his lower limbs with his hands.

Grand mal seizure: A severe type of convulsive disorder involving loss of consciousness and extreme convulsions.

Gross motor skills: Use of large muscles for walking, running, and other whole body movements.

Grouping: Placing students of similar academic aptitude or achievement together for instruction; for example, high mathematics achievers grouped together for an advanced algebra class.

Habilitation: Refers to the training of skills and attitudes which are not part of an individual's past experiences.

Half-way house: A small residential facility established to bridge the gap from institution to community.

Handicap: Refers to problems that impaired or disabled people have as a result of interaction with their environment (e.g., inability of deaf person to hear a telephone or person in wheelchair to use a revolving door).

Hemiplegia: Paralysis of the extremities on one side of the body.

Horizontal programming: Instructional approach used with gifted children which broadens knowledge through the use of enrichment activities, exploration or internship experiences.

Hydrocephalus: A condition of excess cerebrospinal fluid in the brain that results in an enlargement of the head and mental retardation.

Hyperactivity: Excessive physical/muscular activity characterized by excessive restlessness and mobility; sometimes associated with learning disabilities.

Hyperopia (farsightedness): A condition that occurs when the eye is too short and the rays of light from near objects are not focused on the retina.

Hypertonicity: Refers to heightened state of excessive tension. Muscles are tight and tense.

Hypotonicity: Refers to flaccid muscle tone or inability to maintain tension or resistance to stretch.

Impairment: A condition resulting from diseased or defective tissue (e.g., cerebral palsy, birthmark, nearsightedness).

Individual educational program (IEP): A component of Public Law 94-142 that requires a written plan of instruction for each child receiving special services; the IEP must include a statement of the child's present levels of educational performance, annual goals, short-term objectives, specific services needed by the child, dates when these services will begin and be in effect, and when the child should be reevaluated.

Incidence: Refers to the estimates of the numbers of individuals in the population who may exhibit a particular characteristic at some time during their lifetime.

Incus (anvil): The second or middle bone in the chain of bones in the middle ear joining the malleus and stapes; anvil shaped.

Infusion approach: An approach to career education which stresses that career education should not be approached as a separate content area, but infused into the existing curriculum.

Instructional technology: A systematic way of designing, carrying out, and evaluating the total process of teaching. Media technology employs machines to accomplish this purpose while systems technology focuses upon methodology.

Insulin: A protein hormone produced by the pancreas and secreted into the blood where it regulates carbohydrate metabolism.

Intellectual ability: This term refers to a broad cluster of skills including memory, comprehension, and reasoning. Measures of intellectual ability typically index verbal or spatial skills.

Intelligence-quotient (IQ): Score on a test designed to measure intellectual abilities, such as memory, comprehension, and reasoning. The average score for the general population is usually 100.

Inter-individual differences: The differences between students.

Intermediate Care Facility/Mental Retardation/ Developmental Disabilities (ICF/MR/DD): A residential facility for persons with mental retardation or other developmental disabilities. Typically provides care and training throughout a client's life span.

Intra-individual differences: The differences within students.

Iris: Colored part of the eye that expands or contracts depending upon the amount of light passing through the eye.

Juvenile rheumatoid arthritis: A chronic condition common to school age children beginning with general fatigue, stiffness and aching of the joints.

Kinesthetic approach: An instructional technique that utilizes sensations derived from the student's muscles or movement sensations.

Kyphosis: A condition in which the back around the shoulder area is rounded.

Labeling: The process of assigning a child to a diagnostic category as a result of assessment. For example, a child may be labeled as "mentally retarded" after undergoing a psychological evaluation. Although useful for obtaining services, labeling may have negative psychological consequences.

Language: The systematic manner in which a people agree to symbolically represent their environment, thoughts, and emotions. This symbolic system depends on speech and consists of word and word combinations.

Laryngectomy: Removal of all or part of the larynx.

Least restrictive environment: A term used in education to refer to the learning setting that best permits a student to learn new skills regardless of existing handicapping conditions, disabilities, disorders or impairments.

Lens: Structure of the eye that refines and changes the light rays passing through the eye.

Linguistic functioning: Ability to use language.

Local norms: A distribution of test scores established for a particular school, community, or region. Local norms allow comparison of individual students with other students in a similar environment.

Lordosis: A condition in which the spine is curved inward, resulting in a swayback and/or protruding abdomen.

Mainstreaming: The educational placement of the child in the least restrictive educational setting.

Malleus (hammer): The first of a chain of three small bones in the middle ear extending from the eardrum to the incus; hammer shaped.

Manual communication: Communication which relies on hand signs or finger spelling.

Masking: The stimulation of one ear of a subject by controlled noise to prevent the hearing with that ear of the tone or speech being presented to the opposite ear.

Meningitis: Inflammation of the membranes that surround the brain and spinal cord.

Meningocele: A sac-like pouch that protrudes through an opening in the skull or spinal column.

Mental retardation: Significantly subaverage general intellectual functioning existing concurrently with deficits in adaptive behavior and manifested during the developmental period.

Microcephaly: A cranial disorder characterized by the development of a small head with a sloping forehead; retardation results from lack of space for brain development.

Minimal brain dysfunction: (controversial definition) Applies to children of average or above average intelligence who have learning disabilities associated with functional problems of the central nervous system.

Mixed hearing loss: Hearing disorder as the result of a combination of conductive and sensori-neural loss.

Monoplegia: Paralysis of one limb.

Multiple-factor theories of intelligence: Theories that propose that human intelligence is composed of a number of independent abilities which cannot be adequately indexed by a single score, such as an IQ score.

Multiple sclerosis: A disease or progressive deterioration in which the protective sheath surrounding the nerves degenerates and causes failure of the body's neurological system.

Muscular dystrophy: A hereditary disorder that causes a loss of vitality and progressive deterioration of the body as a result of death of muscle tissue.

Myopia (nearsightedness): Occurs when the eye is too long and the rays of light from distant objects are not focused on the retina.

Nasal sound: A sound produced by the blocking of the oral cavity, the opening of the velum and the emission of air via the nasal cavity (m, n, ŋ).

Neurologically impaired: Associated with problems in the functioning of the central nervous system.

Normalization: The concept that all handicapped persons should be provided with the opportunity to live according to the patterns and conditions of everyday life, which are as close as possible to the norms and patterns of the mainstream of society.

Norm-referenced test: Shows student's performance in comparison to the group of people on which the test was standardized.

Occipital lobe: A portion of the brain where visual stimuli are interpreted and "seeing" takes place.

Omission: Articulation disorder wherein a sound or sounds are omitted from words.

Operant conditioning: Changing behavior by altering its consequences; altering the future probability of the occurrence of a response by providing reinforcement or punishment as a consequence.

Ophthalmologist: A physician that specializes in treatment of the eye.

Optic nerve: The nerve that sends impulses to the occipital area of the brain where visual stimuli are interpreted.

Optician: A specialist trained to grind lenses to prescription.

Optometrist: A professional person who examines the eye for defects and/or refractive errors and prescribes corrective lenses.

Oral method: A method of teaching the hearing impaired that concentrates on teaching the child to speak and depend on lipreading or speech reading.

Organic learning handicap: Inherent, inborn, or constitutional handicap in learning.

Orthopedically handicapped: A disabling condition caused by physical impairments especially those related to the bones, joints, and muscles.

Ossicles: Three small bones of the ear that transfer sound waves from the eardrum.

Osteogenesis imperfecta: A congenital bone disease resulting in very fragile bones (often called brittle bone disease).

Otitis media: Middle ear infection.

Otosclerosis: Condition of the middle ear where a bony growth develops around the base of the stapes, impeding its movement.

Otolaryngologist: A physician who specializes in diseases of the ear and throat.

Otologist: A physician who specializes in diseases of the ear.

Otoscope: Small light used to examine the auditory canal and eardrum.

Paraplegia: Paralysis of the lower half of the body including both legs.

Partially seeing: Those whose visual acuity is between 20/200 and 20/70 in the better eye with the best possible correction or who in the opinion of an eye specialist need either temporary or permanent special education facilities. Partially seeing people can use ink print in their education.

Perceptual skills: Ability to select, organize, and interpret the stimuli that surround us.

Perinatal: The time during birth.

Petit mal seizure: A mild form of convulsive disorder characterized by dizziness and momentary lapse of consciousness.

Phenylketonuria (PKU): A genetic disorder which, if undetected, may cause mental retardation. May be detected at birth.

Phocomelia: A type of congenital deformity in which the hands and/or feet are directly attached to the torso and may resemble "seal flippers." Commonly found in children whose mothers took thalidomide to control morning sickness.

Pitch: The psychological attribute of auditory sensation by which man perceives the highness or lowness of a sound.

-plegia: Latin suffix referring to paralysis or inability to move.

Plosive sound: A sound that is produced by building pressure behind a complete articulatory closure and suddenly releasing it in an explosive manner (p, b, t, d, k, g).

Poliomyelitis (polio or infantile paralysis): An acute disease that inflames nerve cells of the spinal cord or brain stem and leaves a residual paralysis or muscular atrophy; is preventable through vaccination.

Postnatal: After birth.

Prehension: Grasping skills in fine motor development.

Prenatal: Occurring or existing before birth.

Prevalence: The number of individuals in the population who currently exhibit a particular characteristic.

Proximal: Refers to close to the body or trunk.

Proximodistal development: Development proceeds from the trunk outward.

Psychomotor: A term used to describe operations which combine cognitive and physical processes, e.g., playing a violin, playing tennis, handwriting, etc.

Psychomotor seizure: A seizure characterized by many automatic, stereotyped movements.

Pupil: The contractive opening in the middle of the iris.

Pure tone air conduction test: An audiometric test utilizing pure tones of varying frequencies which are presented through ear phones.

Pure tone bone conduction test: An audiometric test utilizing pure tones of varying frequencies which are presented through a vibrator.

Pyramidal tract: Area of the brain located between the motor and sensory areas of the cortex. Damage in this area results in spastic cerebral palsy.

Quadriplegia: Paralysis involving all four of the body extremities.

Receptive language: Ability to receive and understand transmitted language.

Recessive gene: Recessive genes are expressed only when both parents carry the gene. Children of parents who both carry a recessive trait gene have a 25 percent probability of exhibiting the trait, a 25 percent probability of not inheriting that gene trait nor exhibiting it, and a 50 percent probability of inheriting one gene from one parent and becoming a carrier of the recessive gene trait.

Refraction: The bending of light rays.

Rehabilitation: The retraining or reorganizing of skill patterns in individuals.

Relevant enrichment: This term, coined by J. C. Stanley, refers to special educational provisions matched to gifted students' individual area(s) of academic ability. Relevant enrichment is contrasted with enrichment provided gifted students without regard to individual aptitudes.

Reliability: The consistency with which a test measures a particular trait.

Retina: Back portion of the eye, containing nerve fibers connected to the optic nerve.

Retrolental fibroplasia: Eye disorder caused by too much oxygen in incubators of premature babies.

Rh incompatibility: A condition in which the fetus has Rh positive blood and the mother has Rh negative blood. The mother consequently builds up antibodies that attack the fetus, resulting in birth defects.

Rheumatic fever: Disease usually following a streptococcal infection that is characterized by acute inflammation of the joints, fever, chorea, skin rash, nosebleeds, and abdominal pains. It often damages the heart by scarring its tissues and valves.

Rigidity cerebral palsy: A type of cerebral palsy in which hypertension of the muscles creates stiffness.

Rubella (German measles): A communicable disease transmitted by a virus; infection of a woman during early stages of pregnancy produces a high probability of severe handicaps of the offspring.

Schizophrenia: A disorder characterized by split or dual personality, flights of ideas, distorted thought processes, and misconception of reality.

School phobia: Intense fear of a teacher, a classroom, peers, or any other aspect of the school. When it is time to go to school the child develops psychosomatic symptoms.

Sclera: Tough outer layer of eyeball which protects the contents as well as holding contents in place.

Scoliosis: Muscle weakness allowing a serious abnormal curvature of the spine which may be corrected with surgery or the use of a brace.

Screening: The process of testing a large number of people with a relatively fast, easy, and inexpensive procedure in order to identify those that may need further in-depth evaluation to determine whether they have a problem in need of treatment.

Seizure: An impairment of consciousness which may or may not be accompanied by active disruption of the motor state.

Semicircular canals: Three canals within the inner ear that function to maintain balance.

Sensorineural hearing loss: Hearing disorder caused by damage or dysfunction of the cochlea or VIII auditory nerve.

Severely handicapped individual: One who has serious primary disabilities that are cognitive, and/or behavioral, has the high probability of additional physical and/or sensory handicaps, and requires significantly more resources than are provided for the mildly and moderately handicapped in special education programs.

Severely/profoundly retarded (S/PR): A commonly used classification term in education for students with severe to profound mental retardation. These students can typically profit from training in basic self-help skills, ambulation, gross and fine motor skill development, object and symbol discrimination. Due to this group often having multiple handicapping conditions, intensive direct supervision is typically needed throughout their lives.

Sex-role stereotyping: Approval or disapproval of behavior based on preconceptions of what is masculine or feminine. Sex-role stereotyping inhibits students' endeavors in non-traditional roles, e.g., female mathematician.

Shaping: Reinforcement of successive approximations or better and better attempts of the target response.

Snellen chart: A white background with black letters or symbols of graded size used to test distant field visual acuity.

Spasticity: A type of cerebral palsy characterized by muscular incoordination resulting from muscle spasms, opposing contractions of muscles, and paralytic effects.

Special education: Instruction that is designed to meet the needs of children who cannot profit from the regular curriculum.

Specific learning disability: Disorder in one or more of the basic psychological processes involved in understanding or in using language, spoken or written, which may manifest itself in an imperfect ability to listen, think, speak, read, write, spell, or to do mathematical calculations.

Speech: The physical process involved in producing the sound and sound combinations of a language.

Speech reading: Interpreting the movements of the lips, face, head, and gestures as an aid to communication; also called lip reading or visual hearing.

Speech reception threshold (SRT): The lowest intensity at which a person can repeat two syllable words at least 50 percent of the time.

Spina bifida: Congenital defect, caused by a failure of the bony elements of a portion of the spine to close completely.

Spinal muscular atrophy: Disease that affects the spinal cord and results in progressive degeneration of motor nerve cells.

Stanford-Binet Intelligence Scale: An individually administered, comprehensive test of intellectual ability. The Stanford-Binet is often used to identify gifted students because it predicts scholastic success with fair reliability.

Stapes (stirrup): The last or innermost bone in the

chain of bones in the middle ear extending from the incus to the oval window; stirrup-shaped.

Standardized tests: Tests that are available from a test publisher that have been administered to a number of people under identical conditions.

Stereotypic or self-stimulatory behavior: Repetitive, bizarre behaviors that serve no observable function, e.g., body rocking, finger flipping.

Stoma: Opening at the base of the neck created to allow air to pass to the lungs of a laryngectomized person.

Strabismus: A condition in which the two eyes fail to move in a coordinated fashion, resulting in what appears to be crossed eyes.

Stroke, or CVA (cerebral vascular accident): Sudden interruption of blood flow to the brain.

Stuttering: *See* disfluency.

Substitution: Articulation disorder where one sound of a language is replaced by another sound of that language.

Symbolization: The representation of perceptions in memory, comprehension, and communication. Symbols used to represent perceptions may be iconic, linguistic, musical, etc.

Syndrome: A cluster or constellation of symptoms.

Syntax: The part of a grammar system that deals with the arrangement of word forms to show their mutual relations in the sentence.

Talented: A term often used synonymously with "gifted"; or to refer to superior ability in a specific area, e.g., talented musically, artistically, etc.

Task analysis: Breaking down of a skill into component behaviors, subskills, or subtasks.

Task commitment: One of three criteria suggested by J. S. Renzulli to define giftedness. Task commitment is evidenced by voluntary assumption of difficult and lengthy work in a particular field, such as mathematics.

Tay-Sachs Syndrome: A genetically transmitted (recessive gene) disease typically found only with persons from Northeastern European Jewish family backgrounds. Characterized by progressive paralysis, blindness, and usually death by early childhood, i.e., three years of age.

Test ceiling: The upper limits of a test's usefulness as an estimate of achievement or aptitude, e.g., a test designed for children 5 to 10 years of age often

does not adequately assess the knowledge and skills of bright children within that age who take the test.

Thalidomide: A drug taken as a relaxant that can cause congenital deformities when taken by pregnant women.

Threshold of hearing: The minimal value of sound wave pressure that will produce the sensation of sound; the point at which the person just begins to hear a sound.

Time delay procedure: Procedure used during acquisition of a response in which the presentation of the cue is systematically delayed.

Total communication: Philosophy of educators of the hearing impaired which recognizes the advantages of oral and manual systems and tries to blend them into a larger system.

Trainable mentally retarded (TMR): A commonly used classification term in education for students with moderate mental retardation. These students can typically profit from education and training in basic academic and self-help skills as well as unskilled vocational activities. Some form of supervision can typically be expected for this group through adulthood. The I.Q. parameters for this group are usually in the 20–25 to 50–55 range.

Triplegia: Paralysis of three of the body's limbs.

Tuberculosis: An infectious disease characterized by the formation of small nodules in the tissue of the lungs.

Underachiever: Any child whose scholastic performance is below that suggested by performance on IQ tests or other indicators of aptitude.

Validity: Refers to the extent to which a test measures what it purports to measure.

Vertical programming: Instructional approach used with gifted children which moves children up the curriculum ladder more rapidly than usual or deeper into subject matter than in the regular school program.

Visual acuity: Sharpness or clearness of vision.

Visual field (peripheral vision): Side vision which is measured in terms of degrees of visual arc.

Vitreous: A jelly-like clear substance in the center of the eyeball which helps hold the shape of the eye and has slight refractive power.

Vocation: Primary work role in which one is engaged at any particular time.

Voice disorder: Occurs when an individual's voice does not present an appropriate and consistent sound as a result of misuse of the voice structures or tissue change in the vocal tract.

Voiced sound: All sounds that use vocal fold vibration.

Work: Conscious effort aimed at producing benefits for oneself and/or others.

Probe Answers

Probe 1–1

p. 7
Terminology &
Prevalence

1. Components of the definition should include:
   - instruction that is part of the regular education program
   - instruction that is individually designed to meet the needs of exceptional children
   - designed for children whose needs cannot be met by the regular school curriculum
   - may call for supportive services

p. 7   2. False

p. 8   3. Disability refers to reduction of function or absence of a particular body part or organ; handicap refers to problems a disabled person may have as a result of interacting with the environment.

p. 12   4. 5.8; 9.5

p. 12   5. True

Probe 1–2

pp. 14–15   1. c; e; a; b; d; h; g

pp. 201–207
Total Mobilization

2. a. Education should be individualized.
   b. Tasks should be sequenced from easy to difficult.

p. 13   3. False
H/O

p. 15   4. False

p. 17   5. National Association for Retarded Citizens (NARC)

pp. 17–18
Advocacy & Litigation: 1950–1974

6. PARC verified that mentally retarded children were entitled to a publicly supported education. Mills extended this right to all exceptional children.

Probe 1–3

p. 21
Legislative
Implications

1. A law is made by elected representatives and generally represents broad policy. A regulation is written by appointed officials and specifies the procedures to be followed in the implementation of a law.

pp. 23–27   2. a. 504; b. 94–142; c. 94–142; d. 504; e. 504; f. 94–142; g. 504; h. 504; i. 94–142

p. 27   3. False

p. 26   4. b

Probe 1–4

p. 29
Impact of Technology

1. Although both use systematic approaches, media technology typically uses machines, while systems technology refers to procedures used by people.

p. 30 2. Direct instruction
p. 32 3. Competency-Based Teacher Education
pp. 33–34 4. False
pp. 34–35 5. Any three of the following:
Assistive & Adaptive Devices
   – Television systems that magnify
   – Captioned television
   – Communication boards
   – Speech synthesizers
   – Talking calculator
   – Optacon
   – Kurzweil Reader
   – Paperless braille
   – Micro Switches

pp. 35–37 6. Tutorial programs teach new concepts; drill and practice
The Special Potential of Microcomputers programs do not. The latter allow students opportunities to practice what they have learned.

pp. 35–36 7. False
p. 36 8. Branching moves students to different parts of the program based on their responses to questions.
Tutorial
p. 37 9. False
p. 39 10. SpecialNet
p. 40 11. ASET

Probe 2–1

p. 48 1. False
p. 47 2. False
p. 48 3. – Informal: teacher observation; anecdotal record; teacher made test
   – Formal: tests developed by publishers; IQ tests; standardized achievement tests; personality inventories

p. 48 4. Validity
p. 48 5. Reliability
Assessment

p. 48 6. Norm-referenced tests compare test results to those
Assessment achieved by the group of people upon whom the test was standardized, while criterion-referenced tests compare test results to a specific standard that has been set.

pp. 49–50 7. Identification; teaching
pp. 51–52 8. Any 3 of the following:
Labeling
   – labels are applied imprecisely
   – labeled children are stigmatized
   – labels yield too little information for planning
   – classification tends to be deviance oriented

– classification systems are insensitive to change
– classification can result in disregard of other factors, such as causes of conditions

p. 52
Labeling

9. Any of the following:
   – need to label to get funds to support programs
   – we use labels anyway and one set would just replace another
   – labels help to focus attention on a problem
   – for organizing and studying information about a particular category

Probe 2–2

p. 43	1. Deinstitutionalization; mainstreaming
p. 54	2. False
p. 54	3. True
p. 57	4. 7; 2; 10; 1; 8; 4; 6; 3; 9; 5
p. 57	5. Mainstreaming is the placement of handicapped children in the regular class for all or portion of the school day
pp. 58–59	6. False

Probe 2–3

p. 61 *Individualized* *Instruction*	1. True
p. 61	2. 8 IEP Requirements
p. 64	3. True
p. 65	4. False
p. 65	5. True

Probe 2–4

p. 67	1. True
p. 67	2. SOMPA
p. 68 *Attitudes of Students &* *Teachers*	3. – being handicapped – being a minority – being poor
p. 68 *Attitudes of Students &* *Teachers*	4. b. Cultural pluralism
pp. 68–69	5. True
p. 69	6. language

Probe 2–5

p. 71	1. False
p. 71	2. philosophy
p. 74 *Step Two*	3. – Level 1: Regular teachers with exceptional children in class – Level 2: Special education teachers at the building level

— Level 3: Special education specialists at the district level
— Level 4: Special educators at colleges and universities
— Level 5: Research and development specialists

p. 77	4. False
p. 78	5. objectives
p. 79	6. Exceptional Child Education Resources
p. 80	7. The Council for Exceptional Children (CEC)

Probe 3–1

p. 91 1st para.	1. a. birth to 8 or 9 years b. under age of 2 years c. between ages 2 and 5 years d. between 5 and 6 years e. 5 to 9 years
pp. 92–101	2. Any of the rationale provided on pages 92–101.
p. 96	3. True
pp. 93–94	4. 1. e; 2. f; 3. a; 4. c; 5. b
p. 99	5. Head Start Program of P.L. 93–644 (Does this question need to be . . . culturally disadvantaged?)
p. 100	6. 10 percent
p. 100	7. Develop experimental demonstration projects for pre-school handicapped children.
p. 100	8. True
p. 100	9. True

Probe 3–2

p. 103	1. False
p. 105	2. True; True; True; False; False; True
p. 109	3. True
p. 112	4. True
p. 120	5. True
p. 121	6. False
p. 123	7. True
p. 124	8. False

Probe 3–3

p. 127 para. 1	1. — brochures — radio/television announcements — newspaper articles — sending notes home with children in programs — personal contacts with agencies
p. 127 para. 3 & 4	2. before birth, amniocentesis for Tay-Sachs disease & Down's syndrome; at birth, urine test for glactosemia or PKU
pp. 128–129	3. False
p. 128	4. It must be accurate in order to provide information on a number of children needing services.
p. 128	5. PKU

p. 130 *para. 3*	6. They see the children more continuously and for longer periods of time than any other professional.
pp. 128–129	7. Any 3 of the following: – norm-referenced devices – criterion-referenced devices – piagetian measures – observation – logs – anecdotal records

Probe 3–4

pp. 131–132	1. Specialized equipment and personnel assembled at central location; Example: Model Preschool Center for Handicapped Children, University of Washington.
p. 132 *para. 3 & 4*	2. Example: PEECH Program. It serves handicapped children from the age of 3 along with normal children. Includes parental involvement and must meet state requirements of Illinois.
pp. 133–134	3. In rural and sparsely populated areas. Example: Portage Program in Wisconsin.

Probe 4–1

p. 145	1. Ten
pp. 146–147	2. False
p. 148	3. vocal fold vibrations
p. 148	4. exhaled
p. 151	5. lips; tongue
pp. 152–153	6. e; c; d; b; a
p. 148	7. False
p. 148	8. True
p. 148	9. False
p. 148	10. False
p. 148	11. True
p. 153	12. True
p. 153	13. False

Probe 4–2

p. 155	1. receptive language problems; expressive language problems; mixed receptive and expressive language problems.
p. 155	2. True
p. 155	3. transmission
p. 156	4. True
pp. 156–157	5. – auditory-perceptual abilities – memory skills – conceptual knowledge – retrieval skills
p. 158	6. semantics
p. 158	7. syntax

p. 158	8. pragmatics
p. 158–159	9. objectives
p. 159	10. cerebral vascular accident
p. 159–160	11. Any 2 of the following:
	– blocked blood vessel
	– burst blood vessel to the brain
	– injury to the brain

Probe 4–3

p. 161	1. – symptoms
	– physical explanation
	★– underlying neurological or physiological cause
p. 161	2. – substitutions
	– omissions
	– distortions
	– additions
p. 163	3. excess nasality
p. 164	4. a device that is inserted in the mouth to block off the air to the nasal cavity.
p. 165	5. lack of motor coordination may prohibit rapid enough movement of the articulators.
p. 168	6. If a normal voice mechanism is misused, it may break down and show the results of physical damage, which may be interpreted as an organic problem.
p. 169	7. denasal; nasal
p. 170	8. Ear, Nose, and Throat specialist or otorhinolaryngolosist
p. 170	9. He or she specializes in the treatment of problems of the ear, nose and throat.
p. 170	10. through a stoma (hole in the neck)
p. 168	11. False (unless they last longer than 6 months)
p. 169	12. excess or deficient nasality; breathiness; harshness; hoarseness
p. 171 (1–10)	13. Any five of one through ten
p. 172	14. It starts in childhood after a child begins to put words together.
p. 171	15. 2 1/2; 3 1/2
p. 174	16. – securing attention
	– expressing hostility
	– controlling the behavior of others
p. 176	17. False

Probe 5–1

p. 184	1. – transmitter – medium – receiver
p. 184 para. 4	2. Sound is created by the vibration of some object. This vibration is carried across some medium and can be heard by the ear.
p. 185	3. frequency; Hz; intensity; dB.

p. 185   4. 40–60 dB
pp. 185–187 5. – symbolic level – signal level – primitive or background level

Probe 5–2

pp. 188–190 1. 1. e.   5. d.
                   2. h.   6. a.
                   3. f.   7. i.
                   4. j.   8. b.

p. 188   2. False
p. 190   3. A transmission starts . . . nerve.
para. 3
p. 190   4. cortex
p. 190   5. fifth month

Probe 5–3

p. 192   1. deaf
p. 193   2. 100,000
pp. 194–197 3. – conductive – sensorineural – mixed-functional – central
p. 194   4. conductive; blocked auditory canal; otosclerosis
p. 196   5. functional
p. 195   6. sensorineural; viral; rubella
p. 197   7. central auditory disorder

Probe 5–4

p. 198   1. Any 4 of the following:
para. 3   – illness or disease of mother during pregnancy
                   – child does not react to loud sounds
                   – child does not engage in normal amount of vocal play
                   – child is delayed in speech and language development
                   – child does not pay attention in class
p. 202   2. audiogram
p. 200   3. False
pp. 200–202 4. – pure tone audiometric screening
                   – pure tone threshold audiometry
                   – speech audiometry
                   – sound field audiometry
                   – behavioral play audiometry
                   – impedance audiometer
                   – evoked response technique
p. 198   5. False
p. 202   6. 1. <   2.   3. ×   4. 0   5.]   6.
                   7. [8. >
p. 202   7. 500; 1,000; 2,000
p. 203   8. 1. 20–40 dB;   2. 80–100 dB;   3. 40–60 dB;
Chart   4. 0–20 dB;   5. 60–80 dB
p. 201   9. speech discrimination score from Speech Audiometry technique.

Probe 5–5

p. 207	1. – speech/language development
	– educational adjustment
	– vocational adjustment
	– social adjustment
	– personality and emotional adjustment
p. 209	2. 1 year
p. 209	3. False
p. 210	4. True
p. 210	5. True
pp. 207–208	6. 60; 2 years

Charts

p. 208	7. 80
Chart	

Probe 5–6

p. 212	1. Ventilate
p. 213	2. False
p. 213	3. body
p. 213	4. True
p. 215	5. Any 4 of the following:
	– earmold is not placed correctly in the ear
	– earmold is too loose
	– may need new earmold
	– earmold and receiver not firmly attached
	– plastic tube loose on ear-level aid
p. 217	6. auditory training
p. 217–218	7. lip reading or speech reading
p. 218	8. False

Probe 5–7

p. 219	1. Any 4 of the following:
para. 1	– history of hereditary hearing loss
(Identif.)	– infections or illness of mother during pregnancy
	– defects of child's ear, nose, or throat
	– low birth rate
	– prematurity
	– infections, diseases, or accidents sustained by the child
p. 220	2. Any 5 of the following:
para. 1	– frequent earaches or ear discharge
	– poor articulation of speech sounds or consonant sounds are omitted
	– incorrect answers to easy questions
	– child doesn't respond when spoken to in a normal manner
	– "hearing" appears to be better when child faces speaker.

– child often asks to have things repeated

– child turns up T.V. or radio too loud

p. 220 3. True

p. 220 4. False

p. 221 5. False

#6

p. 224 6. False

p. 224 7. oralists

p. 226 8. residential setting; day school, special class; resource room

Probe 6–1

p. 236 1. a; c; b; a; b; a; c; b; b; a

p. 238 2. The process of seeing begins when light is reflected from

1–8 an object and enters the eye. As the light rays pass through the cornea, aqueous, lens, and vitreous, they are refracted so that they will strike the retina in the macular area. From there, nerve impulses relay the impressions of visual stimuli to the brain, where "seeing" takes place.

Probe 6–2

p. 241 1. placing patch over unaffected eye; simple surgery to straighten the muscles involved

p. 239 2. False

p. 239 3. myopia

p. 242 4. retrolental fibroplasia (RLF); maternal rubella

p. 242 5. retrolental fibroplasia (RLF)

Probe 6–3

p. 244 1. Visually impaired children are those who differ from nor-

definitions mally seeing children to such an extent that it is necessary to provide them with specially trained teachers, specially designed or adapted curriculum materials, and specially designed educational aids, so that they can realize their full potential.

p. 244 2. blind; partially seeing

p. 244 3. 20/200; 20/70

p. 245 4. True

p. 245 5. The index of 20/150 means that an object which can be

para. 4 seen clearly from a distance of 150 feet by a normally seeing person must be 20 feet from the visually impaired person to be seen clearly.

pp. 245–247 6. visual arc

p. 248 7. A blind child is one whose visual loss indicates that he must use braille and other tactile and auditory materials to learn. A partially seeing child has some useful vision and uses print and other visual materials in his educational program.

Probe 6–4

p. 251	1. b; c; d; a
p. 250	2. Snellen Chart
p. 250	3. Any five of the following:
1–9	

- child appears clumsy and has trouble walking in new environments
- child holds head in awkward position or holds material very close to one's eyes
- child "turns out" when information is on blackboard or books he cannot read
- child constantly requests that someone tell him what is going on
- child is inordinately affected by glare and not being able to see things at certain times of day
- child has a pronounced squint
- child rubs eyes excessively
- child pushes eyeballs with fingers or knuckles
- child has obvious physical anomalies such as red, swollen lids, crust on eyes, or crossed eyes

| p. 252 | 4. True |

Probe 6–5

| p. 253 | 1. True |
| p. 255 (Concept Development) | 2. – restrictions in the range and variety of experiences they have had |

- restrictions in the ability to move about in the environment and observe people and objects around them
- restrictions in their integration into all aspects of environment

| p. 257–258 | 3. negative attitudes and reactions of those who can see; integration of blind and seeing and teacher training |

Probe 6–6

p. 257	1. True
p. 258	2. True
p. 266 para. 1	3. – eyeglass magnifiers – stand magnifiers – hand-held magnifiers – telescopic aids – television viewers
p. 258	4. orientation; mobility
p. 260	5. tactile; visual; auditory
pp. 260–267	6. Any three of the following:

- braille
- paperless braille
- microcomputer
- Optacon
- Kurzweil Reading Machine

p. 270	7. providing students access to computers
p. 270	8. electronic braille; Optacon; synthesized speech; enlarged print
p. 270	9. False

Probe 6–7

p. 271	1. residential
p. 272	2. True
p. 272	3. (residential schools — paragraph 2)
p. 273	4. 1–5
p. 274	5. False
p. 274	6. paragraphs 1 and 2
p. 274	7. True
p. 275	8. concept
pp. 275–276	9. 1–7
p. 276	10. 1–3
p. 276	11. False

Probe 7–1

p. 285	1. True
p. 285	2. plegia
p. 285	3. a. hemiplegia b. monoplegia c. quadraplegia d. paraplegia e. cephalad or superior f. anterior g. posterior h. caudal or inferior

Probe 7–2

p. 287	1. True
pp. 288–289	2. c; a; e; b; d
p. 289	3. prenatal; perinatal; postnatal
pp. 289–290	4. True
p. 290	5. False
p. 290	6. False
pp. 291–298	7. b; d; a; c; e; g; f
p. 299	8. thalidomide
p. 297	9. True
pp. 292–293	10. physical therapy
p. 292	11. False

Probe 7–3

p. 300	1. a congenital heart defect
p. 302	2. breathing
p. 301	3. diet and medication (insulin)
p. 301	4. True

Probe 7–4

p. 304	1. psychomotor
p. 304	2. grand mal
p. 304	3. petit mal seizure
p. 305	4. True
pp. 306–307	5. False
p. 307 *para. 2*	6. when seizure activity continues for more than five minutes, or when it appears that the person is going into repeated grand mal seizures

Probe 7–5

p. 309	1. Any 3 symptoms of child abuse.
p. 309	2. Any 3 symptoms of child neglect.
p. 284	3. Improved physical problems to the extent that he/she no
Definitions	longer requires special education.
p. 284	4. Physical impairment to the extent that child no longer has
	the ability to interact in regular classroom.
pp. 310–311	5. a. Does the child take medication?

        b. How will the child be transported to school?

        c. What methods are used to get the child on and off the school bus?

        d. Can the child write? Type? How?

        e. What equipment, such as a special feeding tray, does the child need?

        f. What positions for resting?

pp. 311–318	6. c; b; f; e; d; a
p. 312	7. An orthosis supports or assists a body function, and a prosthesis replaces a missing body part.
p. 314	8. when a careful evaluation of the potential effect of the
para. 2	device has not been conducted
p. 319	9. American National Standard Institute (ANSI)
p. 324	10. 32
p. 323	11. 4
p. 325	12. False
p. 323	13. False
pp. 324–325	14. False
p. 327	15. 40
p. 323	16. 1/2 inch
pp. 318–319	17. True

Probe 8–1

p. 346	1. "A retarded individual is one who has a limited repertory
para. 5	of behavior shaped by events that constitute his history." (Bijou, 1966, p.2)
p. 346	2. Its implications for teaching and identifying retarded children.
p. 347	3. Either of the following:
para. 1 & 2	– It does not take into account work of well-known developmental psychologists.
	– Does not quantify what is meant by limited behavioral repertoire.
p. 347	4. b
p. 347	5. "Mental retardation refers to significantly subaverage general intellectual functioning resulting in or associated with concurrent impairments in adaptive behavior and manifested during the developmental period." (Grossman, 1977, p. 5)
p 347	6. birth; her eighteenth birthday

Probe 8–2

p. 352	1. True
p. 350	2. intelligence quotient (IQ); mental age (MA)
p. 352	3. IQ; adaptive behavior
p. 351	4. a. 50–55 to 70
chart	b. 35–40 to 50–55
	c. 20–25 to 35–40
	d. Below 20 or 25
p. 353	5. False
p. 350	6. False
pp. 351–352	7. – size of normative sample
	– restricted sample of behaviors assessed
	– error of measurement
	– educational utility of IQ
p. 352	8. False
p. 352	9. ". . . refers to what people do to take care of themselves
para. 3	and to relate to others in daily living rather than the abstract potential implied by intelligence." (Grossman, 1983, p. 42)
p. 353	10. reliability and validity has been severely questioned and their appropriateness for classification purposes. Adaptive behavior is too subjective.
p. 353	11. – academic skills – interpersonal skill – social skill – independent functioning
p. 355	12. b

Probe 8–3

pp. 357–359	1. – etiology – clinical type – severity of symptoms
p. 359	2. c; b; a
p. 359	3. Any 2 of the following:
para. 4	– never able to gain total agreement on which factors should be classified
	– deciding on upper and lower boundaries within a subgrouping
	– in the assignment of individuals to a category
p. 359	4. – EMR – TMR – S/PR
p. 358	5. a cluster or constellation of symptoms
p. 360	6. True
p. 360	7. one

Probe 8–4

p. 361	1. False
p. 362	2. True
pp. 368–369	3. – intelligence; adaptive behaviors are at retarded levels of function
para. 1–4	– there is retarded intellectual functioning in the immediate family and usually the larger family circle
	– there is no clear evidence of brain damage in the child
	– the home environment is usually impoverished

p. 369	4. Traits result from the interaction of genetic and environmental factors.
pp. 362, 363, 366, 367 & 368	5. e; g; d; b; a; h; f; c
p. 369 *(Prevention)*	6. Any 5 of the following:

      – vaccination against rubella
      – surgery procedures to correct hydrocephalus
      – amniocentesis
      – drug therapy
      – blood transfusions
      – laws to protect against environmental danger
      – dietary treatment for PKU and galactosemia
      – improved maternal nutrition
      – genetic counseling

Probe 8–5

p. 372	1. True
p. 370	2. – ability to attend to task

      – memory
      – generalization
      – transfer
      – language development

p. 371 *para. 2*	3. – unable to differentiate the more significant aspects from those that are less useful

      – focus on specific clues; unable to shift attention to new clues
      – have a narrower breadth of attention

p. 372	4. They must demonstrate mastery of a skill

      – in the presence of at least 3 different persons;
      – in at least 3 different natural settings;
      – to at least 3 different sets of instructional material;
      – to at least 3 different appropriate language cues.

p. 372	5. False
p. 372	6. – difficulty of skills taught

      – actual skills or subjects covered

p. 370	7. True
p. 372	8. True

Probe 8–6

p. 376	1. They should be in upper range of classification in IQ and adaptive behavior
p. 378	2. True
p. 378	3. when child cannot attend public school because of a medical or physical problem
p. 378	4. False
pp. 381–382 *(1–10)*	5. Any four of one through ten.

pp. 379–386   6. Any 4 of the following:
Programs and facilities should not be physically segregated from the community; no more retardates should be congregated in one service facility than the surrounding community can readily integrate into its resources; daily routines taught to the retarded should be similar to those of all other persons in the community; grooming and dressing of the retarded should not be significantly different in style or type from that of others in the community; work should be provided that is culturally normal in type, quantity, and setting; services for adults and children should be separated; the retarded should be given maximum opportunity for contact with the nonretarded in their community; staff working with the retarded should meet the same standards as those providing services to comparable nonretarded persons

pp. 384–385   7. Any 3 of the following:
– group homes
– foster/family homes
– supervised apartment living
– natural home/family residence

p. 384   8. lack of training of foster parents

p. 385   9. group homes or Intermediate Care Facilities for the Mentally Retarded

p. 382   10. False

p. 379   11. mildly and moderately retarded; severely and profoundly retarded

pp. 379–380   12. – federal legislation
– developing programs and services for the severely/profoundly mentally retarded
– federal court decisions in institutional reform

p. 381   13. Efforts should be made to balance distribution of efforts more evenly.

Probe 9–1

p. 392   1. language; listen, speak, read, write, spell, or do mathematical calculations; visual, hearing or motor handicaps, or mental retardation, or of environmental, cultural, or economic disadvantage
(Definitions)

p. 393   2. discrepancy; deficit; focus; exclusions

p. 394   3. The percentage of special education students classified as L.D. rose to almost 44% between 1970 and 1977.

Probe 9–2

p. 396   1. False

pp. 396–397   2. – overall intelligence level and academic strengths and weaknesses; student's approach to the learning process; rules out other factors as primary causes of the problem
(Assessment Procedure)

p. 398	3. False
pp. 398–401	4. – need for ecological perspective – need for team decision
p. 402	5. Paragraphs 1 and 2 under sub-heading, "What should be included in an assessment?"

Probe 9–3

p. 404	1. True
p. 404	2. False
p. 408	3. True
p. 412	4. Learned helplessness refers to a student's belief that success and failure are beyond their control; L.D. students do not believe their achievements to be under their control.
p. 413	5. False
pp. 414–417	6. H/O

Probe 9–4

H/O	1. MD; 2. ED; 3. MD; 4. ED; 5. MD; 6. MD; 7. ED

Probe 10–1

pp. 433–434	1. – A label is a self-fulfilling prophecy. – It is circular and may not explain anything. – It may not be the "best" label in terms of getting the child the most appropriate special services. – It may not be child's problem. – Using a label will not solve the problem.
pp. 430–431	2. This assumption avoids harmful labeling; behavior might be situation-specific; and it does not scapegoat the child because the child does not "own" the problem.
p. 429	3. False
p. 428	4. three fundamental characteristics of behavior disorders

Probe 10–2

p. 439	1. You would not agree. The problem may not be "owned" by the child. A thorough assessment of the problem behavior(s), problem situation and child's ecological units needs to be completed before anyone can be blamed for the problem.
p. 441 *para. 1*	2. – aggressive verbal behavior – aggressive physical behavior of an antisocial nature
p. 441	3. It identifies a child's specific maladaptive behaviors and strategies for change are suggested.
pp. 442–443	4. True
p. 443	5. – Schools have a particularly low tolerance for acting-out (aggressive) behaviors often displayed by boys. – Boys develop conduct problems as they grow older or exhibit immaturity.
p. 442	6. c

Probe 10–3

    pp. 444–445   1. See biophysical and environmental correlates for reasons why evidence for this conclusion is weak.

    pp. 447–448   2. d

    3. Blaming either child or parent does little to relieve the situation since the influence on each other is reciprocal. Intervention should be stated and perhaps the parent can learn and deal with the child more effectively.

Probe 10–4

    pp. 453–454   1. – settings: classroom, playground, home or bus
- persons: teacher, parents, peers, siblings, or anyone in charge
- information: in which settings does the behavior occur, how persons in that setting react to the problem, different expectations by different adults, how management varies among adults and settings.

    pp. 450–456   2. Differences in behaviors and differences involving your intervention plan are discussed under disturbing and disturbed behaviors.

    pp. 455–456   3. Autism is characterized by several factors; 1–6, p. 455. Pervasive developmental disorders characterized by several behavior problems; 1–7, p. 456. The two sets of characteristics are similar. Age onset is the most common way to differentiate between these subgroups.

Probe 10–5

    1. – regular classroom; p. 457
- resource room; p. 457, 459
- self-contained; p. 459
- special day schools; p. 459
- re-education schools; p. 459
- residential treatment programs; p. 459

    pp. 457–458   2. a) residential treatment; see p. 459
    b) resource room plus consultation with regular classroom teacher; see pp. 457, 459
    c) regular classroom plus consultation for his teacher; p. 457
    d) Re-Ed; p. 459
    e) regular classroom or resource; see pp. 457, 459

Probe 11–1

    p. 472   1. – Primary disability is cognitive and/or behavioral.
- There is a high probability of additional physical and/or sensory handicaps.
- They require significantly more resources than the mildly or moderately handicapped.

    p. 473   2. Any 5 uses listed under "Why is a definition so important?"

p. 473   3. 1.92% of the school-age population; 0.1% of the total population.

p. 473   4. The extent of a severely handicapped child's disability differentiates him from other children, not the type of handicap.

p. 474   5. Mental retardation implies defective mental functioning based on some biological abnormality that adversely affects adaptive behavior regardless of the environment in which the behavior occurs. In contrast, the concept of functional retardation emphasizes the importance of environmental events in shaping and maintaining adaptive behaviors.

p. 474   6. Any 4 characteristics listed under Sontag, Burke, and York's (1973, p. 21) types of children.

Probe 11–2

p. 477   1. False

p. 478   2. – Some children are not amenable to instruction because of their severe physical disabilities, damaged central nervous system, and profound mental retardation.
   – After receiving extensive training child fails to acquire a "meaningful skill."
   – Adequate technology is lacking to significantly improve their functioning capabilities.

p. 478   3. They believe that education, like development, is an ongoing process and that ineducability cannot be proven.

pp. 479–480   4. Any 4 of the 6 reasons given under Early Identification.

pp. 479–480   5. False

p. 481   6. – assisting the parents
   – organizing the information from various disciplines into a comprehensive intervention program for the child

p. 482   7. – It is vitally important to the success of the multiply handicapped child's early education program.
   – It can influence a child's current and future developmental status.

Probe 11–3

p. 485   1. All three are useful for:
   – identifying areas for additional testing;
   – planning instructional programs;
   – making decisions about placements;
   – determining what related services are needed.

Model   2. a) discussed under: The development milestones model, pp. 486–487.
   b) discussed under: The development theory based model, pp. 487–488.
   c) discussed under: The functional model, p. 488.

Guidelines 3. a) #1, p. 489
         b) #2, pp. 489–490
         c) #6, p. 490

      4. Any of the following:
         – saying "yes" and "no"
         – requesting food or drink
         – indicating need to use bathroom
         – reaching
         – grasping
         – most self-care skills

Probe 11–4

p. 492 1. Curriculum is an organized description of what to teach; it should include basic strategies and activities for the teacher. Emphasis is on "what" to teach rather than "how" to teach.

p. 496 2. In the functional curriculum approach a curriculum is designed for each student; students are not matched to predetermined curricular sequences as with the developmental domains curriculum approach.

p. 498 3. – appropriateness of the curriculum for a particular student and his/her setting
         – the extent to which it is to be used
         – curriculum effectiveness

      4. Any 3 of the following:
         – motor; p. 500
         – cognitive; pp. 500–501
         – self-care; p. 501
         – communication; p. 501
         – social; p. 501

pp. 501–502 5. differences discussed under Elementary School Curriculum

      6. – preparing the student to live in the particular community environments in which they are likely to reside upon completion of the public school curriculum

Probe 11–5

p. 504 1. Age-appropriate skills are those performed by nonhandicapped persons of similar chronological age; functional skills are skills that permit students more control over their own lives as soon as the skills are learned.

pp. 504–505 2. – skill acquisition: students are taught skills not previously in their repertoires
         – skill fluency: performing the skill more proficiently and at more acceptable rates
         – skill generalization: students must be able to perform skills in a variety of settings, with several persons, and under natural environmental conditions

– skill maintenance: to teach students to maintain a skill without the assistance of instructional supports

pp. 506–507   3. Any 2 of the following:
- child's problems are viewed as behavioral
- students learn best when teachers systematically order task in sequence from easy to hard
- zero degree inference strategy, p. 506
- instructional programs fail, not students

p. 508   4. Self stimulatory behaviors seldom threaten the health or physical well-being of the student. Examples: body rocking, hand flapping, and finger twirling. Self-injurious behaviors can be life-threatening or physically harmful. Examples: rumination, pica, eye-gouging, and self-biting.

pp. 508, 510   5. Physical prompting and fading involves breaking down a skill into several component behaviors through task analysis and physically guiding a child through the steps with positive reinforcement for each step completed successfully. The teacher provides less assistance and requires the student to perform independently.

Probe 11–6

p. 514   1. A student with severe developmental disabilities can adapt to the community environment by being exposed to the living conditions common to his or her culture. Medical, educational, and other social services must be available and coordinated to help this normalization process.

p. 514   2. – *Pennsylvania Association for Retarded Children* v. *the Commonwealth of Pennsylvania* (1971)
- *Mills* v. *Board of Education of the District of Columbia* (1972)

p. 515   3. – allows handicapped and nonhandicapped students the opportunity to interact with persons who are different than themselves
- more apt to focus on development of functional or adaptive behaviors

4. Any 4 of the following:
- medical care
- dental care
- recreation programs
- participation in religious services
- transportation
- work centers

Probe 12–1

p. 522   1. False
p. 524   2. False
p. 522   3. False
pp. 522–524   4. – they are elitist
- they will succeed without special programs
- many people equate giftedness with a high IQ score

p. 525	5. an IQ score in the 98th or 99th percentile
p. 526	6. True

Probe 12–2

p. 529	1. False
p. 529	2. very independent
p. 531	3. a
p. 531	4. There are many children who would qualify as gifted on the basis of their IQ score (intelligence test) and not on the basis of a special aptitude test (special ability) and vice versa. Some would qualify as gifted under either criterion or both criteria.
p. 532	5. a) generally high IQ
p. 535	b) leadership
p. 531	c) divergent thinking
p. 534	6. False
p. 535	7. d

Probe 12–3

p. 537	1. – referral
	   – screening
	   – evaluation

pp. 537–539	2. – referral: observation, review of student's past performances, and completion of behavior checklist
	   – screening: administration of aptitude, intelligence, or achievement tests, review of work samples, and review of checklist or rating scales
	   – evaluation: individual administration of IQ tests, auditions or review of student projects, administration of high-level achievement tests, and analysis of case studies

p. 537	3. parent referral
p. 537	4. True
p. 538	5. Asking if the child has a "good memory" is too general and can be interpreted in several ways.
p. 538	6. "Does your child comment on words that have two or more meanings?"
p. 539	7. True
p. 542	8. False
p. 543	9. low test ceiling
p. 543	10. False

Probe 12–4

pp. 545–546	1. – unwillingness to persist to achieve goals
	   – tendency towards purposelessness
	   – lack of self-confidence
	   – feelings of inferiority

pp. 546–547	2. – Show support and respect for him. Ask his opinions and let him give input into his educational program.

        – Encourage cooperation, not competition in the classroom.

        – Praise him for even small improvements in academic performance.

p. 546   3. True

p. 547   4. True

p. 548   5. – society's lowered expectations for handicapped persons

        – society's failure to recognize and make provisions for superior ability in the handicapped population

pp. 548–549   6. False

p. 551   7. H; H; V

p. 551   8. c; d; b; f; e

p. 558   9. True

p. 558   10. False

p. 561   11. Education of the gifted in the regular classroom may meet the goal of normalization, but this goal is not appropriate for the gifted child. They have a tendency to "hide" their abilities from peers and teachers so that they will be accepted.

p. 562   12. True

p. 562   13. False

p. 562   14. Any 3 of the following:

        – planning activities and finding methods and materials for advancement

        – independent study

        – cross-grade placement

        – directed readings

        – learning centers

Probe 13–1

p. 574   1. Any 3 listed under Rationale for Career Education

p. 574   2. False

p. 575   3. Career education is the totality of experiences through which one learns about and prepares to engage in work as part of one's way of living.

p. 577   4. False

p. 577   5. – elementary years: values of working and different types of paid work

        – junior high years: learning about specific occupations and the relationship of various occupational roles to the personal interests, aptitudes, and abilities of the individual

        – senior high years: selection of specific occupational and vocational roles

p. 578   6. life skills, life-function, or Illinois

p. 579   7. True

Probe 13–2

p. 582   1. Smith-Hughes Act

p. 582	2. False
p. 582	3. 504
pp. 582–583	4. True, not mentioned specifically
p. 583	5. No
p. 584	6. See CETA of 1978

Probe 13–3

p. 585 1. – values, attitudes, and habits
   – human relationships
   – occupational information
   – acquisition of actual jobs and daily living skills

p. 587 2. True

p. 589 3. Experience-Based Career Education

p. 590 4. EBCE can be provided in conjunction with college preparatory, general education, or vocational education curricula, or it can provide an alternative to high school for some students.

Probe 13–4

p. 590 1. – infusion approach
   – separate programming approach

pp. 591–592 2. True

p. 591 3. True

p. 591 4. False

p. 590 5. infusion

p. 592 6. stimulation

p. 597 7. It can help them overcome many of the social, economic, and attitudinal barriers that might otherwise keep them from enjoying the social and recreational life of the community.

   8. Possibilities include backpacking, nature study, camping, arts and crafts, swimming, bowling, horseback riding, wheelchair basketball, and participation in Special Olympics.

Probe 13–5

pp. 601–602 1. a, b, c, and d

p. 601 2. – work-study
   – vocational education
   – college preparatory
   – work adjustment/work evaluation programs

p. 605 3. – Inclusion of handicapped students jeopardizes their programs.
   – They view it as denigrating to the status of their programs.

p. 607 4. Traditional emphasis has been on rehabilitation, not habilitation. There was a lack of clarity as to which type of program was responsible for what type of service.

   5. – experiential activities as normalizing experiences
   – Many vocational programs do not rely on academic

skills; consequently, handicapped students cannot compete in them.

6. Often a handicapped student is placed in the least restrictive environment currently available, which is not necessarily the most supportive of the student's career education needs.

p. 608 7. Any way listed under Future Directions.

p. 609 8. – identification of the similarities that exist in the educational goals and objectives for all students
   – a refocusing on the scope and sequence of special education curricula
   – improved career preparation opportunities for adolescents
   – increased involvement with community agencies and representatives

Probe 14–1

pp. 626–627 1. False

pp. 619–622 2. Any four of the following:
   – shock
   – guilt
   – denial
   – sorrow
   – rejection
   – acceptance

3. See pages 632–634

4. See pages 630–634

Probe 14–2

p. 637 1. False

p. 642 2. Authoritarian; inconsiderate of feelings; not respectful of legal rights

3. – Identification: see page 637
   – Assessment: see page 635
   – Conferences: see page 639
   – Instruction: see page 643 (strategies) to 644
   – Evaluation: see page 649

pp. 644–645 & 649 4. Instruction; Parent Training; Evaluation

Probe 14–3

p. 652 1. See Professional Advocacy

p. 655 2. See Conceptual Basis

p. 653 3. True

p. 654 4. True

p. 656 5. False

References

ABESON, A., & BALLARD, J. (1976). State and federal policy for exceptional children. In F. J. Weintraub, A. Abeson, J. Ballard, & M. L. LAVOR (EDS.), *Public policy and the education of exceptional children* (pp. 83–95). Reston, VA: The Council for Exceptional Children.

ABESON, A., BOLICK, N., & HAFF, J. (1976). *A primer on due process: Education decisions for handicapped children.* Reston, VA: The Council for Exceptional Children.

ABRAMS, J. (1969). Further considerations on the ego functioning of the dyslexic child: A psychiatric point of view. In G. Spache (Ed.), *Reading disability and perception* (pp. 16–21). Newark, DE: International Reading Association.

ABRAMS, J. (1975). Minimal brain dysfunction and dyslexia. *Reading World, 14,* 219–227.

ADAMSON, G. (1970). *Final report of the Educational Modulation Center.* Olathe, KS: Olathe Public Schools.

ADELMAN, H., & TAYLOR, L. (1983). *Learning disabilities in perspective.* Glenview, IL: Scott, Foresman.

ADELSON, E., & FRAIBERG, S. (1975). Gross motor development in infants blind from birth. In B. Z. Friedlander, G. M. Sterritt, & G. E. Kirk (Eds.), *Exceptional infant: Vol. 3. Assessment & Intervention.* New York: Brunner/Mazel.

ADES, H. W. (1959). Central auditory mechanisms. Ir J. Fields, H. W. Magoun, & V. E. Hall (Eds.), *Handbook of physiology: Vol. 1.* Washington, DC: American Psychological Society.

AFFLECK, G., McGRADE, B. J., McQUEENEY, M., & ALLEN, D. (1982). Relationship-focused early intervention in developmental disabilities. *Exceptional Children, 49,* 259–260.

AIELLO, B. (Ed.). (1976). *Places and spaces: Facilities planning for handicapped children.* Reston, VA: The Council for Exceptional Children.

AINSWORTH, M. D. S. (1973). The development of infant-motor attachment. In B. M. Caldwell & H. Ricciutti (Eds.), *Review of child development research.*

ALBER, M. B. (Ed.). (1978). *Listening: A curriculum guide for teachers of visually impaired students.* Springfield, IL: Specialized Educational Services Department, Materials Development and Dissemination Section, State Board of Education.

ALBERTO, P. A., & SCHOFIELD, P. (1979). An instructional interaction pattern for the severely handicapped. *Teaching Exceptional Children, 12*(1), 16–19.

ALBERTO, P. A., & TROUTMAN, A. C. (1982). *Applied behavior analysis for teachers.* Columbus, OH: Charles E. Merrill.

ALEXANDER, P., & SKINNER, M. (1980). The effects of early entrance on subsequent social and academic development: A follow-up study. *Journal for the Education of the Gifted, 3*(3), 147–150.

ALLEN, J. H. (1963). *May's diseases of the eye* (23rd ed.). Baltimore: Williams & Wilkens.

ALLEN, K. E., HOLM, V. A., & SCHIEFELBUSCH, R. L. (Eds.). (1978). *Early intervention–A team approach.* Baltimore: University Park Press.

ALLEN, R. M., & JEFFERSON, T. W. (1962). *Psychological evaluation of the cerebral palsied person: Intellectual, personal, and vocational applications.* Springfield, IL: Charles C. Thomas.

ALPERN, G., BOLL, T., & SHEARER, M. (1980). *The developmental profile II.* Aspen: Psychological Development Publications.

AMERICAN FOUNDATION FOR THE BLIND. (1961). *A teacher education for those who serve blind children and youth.* New York.

AMERICAN FOUNDATION FOR THE BLIND. (1978). *Sensory aids for the blind and visually handicapped.* New York.

AMERICAN PRINTING HOUSE FOR THE BLIND. (1981). *English braille American edition, 1959.* Louisville, KY: Author.

AMERICAN PRINTING HOUSE FOR THE BLIND. (1982). *Distribution of January 4, 1982 quota registrations by school, grades and reading media.* Louisville, KY: Author.

AMERICAN PSYCHIATRIC ASSOCIATION, COMMITTEE ON NOMENCLATURE AND STATISTICS. (1980). *Diagnostic and statistical manual of mental disorders* (3rd ed.). Washington, DC.

ANDERSON, L. T., & HERRMANN, L. (1975, December). *Lesch-Nyhan Disease: A specific learning disability?* Paper presented at the ninth annual convention of the Association for the Advancement of Behavior Therapy, San Francisco.

ANDERSON, W. R., HARTMAN, R. C., & REDDEN, M. R. (1981). *Federally funded programs for disabled students: Models for postsecondary campuses.* Washington, DC: American Council on Education. (ERIC Document No. 208 796)

APPELL, M. W. (1977). Infant stimulation programming for the deaf-blind. In E. L. Lowell & C. C. Rouin (Eds.), *State of the art.* Sacramento: California State Department of Education.

ARKELL, C., THOMASON, J., & HARING, N. G. (1980). Deinstitutionalization of a residential facility. *Journal of the Association for the Severely Handicapped, 5*(2), 107–120.

ARMSTRONG V. KLINE, 476 F. Supp. 590–92. 600 (1979).

ARONSON, A. (1980). *Clinical Voice Disorders.* New York: Thieme-Stratton.

ARTER, A., & JENKINS, J. R. (1979). Differential diagnosis-prescriptive teaching: A critical appraisal. *Review of Educational Research, 49,* 517–555.

Aschner, M. J., & Bish, C. E. (Eds.). (1965). *Productive thinking in education.* Washington, DC: National Education Association.

Ashcroft, S. (1984). Research on multimedia access to microcomputers for visually impaired youth. *Education of the Visually Handicapped, 15*(4), 109–118.

Ashcroft, S. C. (1963). Blind and partially seeing children. In L. M. Dunn (Ed.), *Exceptional children in the schools.* New York: Holt, Rinehart and Winston.

Ashcroft, S. C., & Bourgeois, M. S. (1980). Recent technological developments for the visually impaired: State of the art. *Journal of Special Education Technology, 3*(2), 5–10.

Associated Press. (1984, January 3). Old movie inspires man to invent new wheelchair. *Lexington Herald-Leader,* p. B2.

Association for Children and Adults with Learning Disabilities (ACLD). (1982). Vocational Committee Survey, *ACLD Newsbriefs, 145,* 21.

Axelrod, L. (1982). Social perception in LD adolescents. *Journal of Learning Disabilities, 15,* 610–613.

Baca, L., & Chinn, P. C. (1982). Coming to grips with cultural diversity. *Exceptional Education Quarterly, 2*(4), 33–45.

Baer, D. M. (1978). The behavioral analysis of trouble. In K. E. Allen, V. J. Holm, & R. L. Schiefelbusch (Eds.), *Early intervention — A team approach.* Baltimore: University Park Press.

Baer, D. M. (1981). A hung jury and a Scottish verdict: "Not proven." *Analysis and Intervention in Developmental Disabilities, 1*(1), 91–97.

Bagnato, S. J., & Neisworth, J. T. (1981). *Linking developmental assessment and curricula.* Rockville, MD: Aspen.

Bailey, D. B., Jens, K. G., & Johnson, N. (1983). Curricula for handicapped infants. In S. G. Garwood & R. R. Fewell (Eds.), *Educating handicapped infants.* Rockville, MD: Aspen.

Bailey, D. B., & Wolery, M. R. (1984). *Teaching infants and preschoolers with handicaps.* Columbus, OH: Charles E. Merrill.

Bailey, J. S. (1981). Wanted: A rational search for the limiting conditions of habilitation in the retarded. *Analysis and Intervention in Developmental Disabilities, 1*(1), 45–52.

Baker, D. B. (1979). Severely handicapped: Toward an inclusive definition. *American Association for the Education of the Severely/Profoundly Handicapped, 4*(1), 52–65.

Baker, L. (1982). An evaluation of the role of metacognitive deficits in learning disabilities. *Topics in Learning and Learning Disabilities, 2*(1), 27–35.

Baldwin, A. Y., Gear, G. H., & Lucito, L. J. (Eds.). (1978). *Educational planning for the gifted overcoming cultural, geographic, and socioeconomic barriers.* Reston, VA: Council for Exceptional Children.

Bandura, A. (1973). *Aggression: A social learning analysis.* Englewood Cliffs, NJ: Prentice-Hall.

Baren, M., Liebel, R., & Smith, L. (1978). *Overcoming learning disabilities: A team approach.* Reston, VA: Prentice-Hall.

Barnes, K. (1982). Life with our changing teenagers. *Exceptional Parent, 12,* 37–39.

Baroff, G. S. (1982). Predicting the prevalence of mental retardation in individual catchment areas. *Mental Retardation, 20,* 133–135.

Barraga, N. (1978, July). *Prevention of deficits: Preschool intervention.* Lecture presented at Project PAVE Special Study Institute, Louisville, KY.

Barraga, N. C. (1964). *Increased visual behavior in low vision children.* New York: American Foundation for the Blind.

Barraga, N. C. (1980). *Program to develop efficiency in visual functioning.* Louisville, KY: American Printing House for the Blind.

Barstow, D. (1981). The Talcott Mountain Science Center. In J. N. Nazzaro (Ed.), *Computer connections for gifted children and youth.* Reston, VA: Clearinghouse on Handicapped and Gifted Children.

Bartel, N. (1975). Problems in arithmetic achievement. In D. Hammill & N. Bartel (Eds.), *Teaching children with learning and behavior problems.* Boston: Allyn and Bacon.

Bateman, B. (1963). *Reading and psycholinguistic processes of partially seeing children* (CEC Research Monograph, Series A, No. 5). Arlington, VA: Council for Exceptional Children.

Bateman, B. (1964). The modifiability of sighted adults' perceptions of blind children's abilities. *New Outlooks for the Blind, 58,* 133–135.

Bauman, M. K. (1977). Group differences disclosed by inventory items. *International Journal for the Education of the Blind, 13,* 101–106.

Baumeister, A. A. (1979). *Processing of information in iconic memory: Differences between normal and retarded subjects.* Unpublished manuscript, George Peabody College of Vanderbilt University, Nashville, TN.

Baumgart, D., Brown, L., Pumpian, I., Nisbet, J., Ford, A., Sweet, M., Messina, R., & Schroeder, J. (1982). Principle of partial participation and individualized adaptions in educational programs for severely handicapped students. *Journal of the Association for the Severely Handicapped, 7*(2), 17–27.

Bayley, N. (1969). *Bayley scales of infant development.* New York: Psychological Corporation.

Beach, D. R. (1977). *Reaching teenagers: Learning centers for the secondary classroom.* Santa Monica, CA: Goodyear.

Beck, R. (1977). The need for adjunctive services in the management of severely and profoundly handicapped individuals: A view from primary care. In N. G. Haring & L. Brown (Eds.), *Teaching the Severely Handicapped* (Vol. 2). New York: Grune & Stratton.

Becker, W. C. (1971). *Parents are teachers.* Champaign, IL: Research Press.

Becker, W. C., & Carnine, D. W. (1980). Direct instruction: An effective approach to educational intervention with disadvantaged and low performers. In B. B. Lahey & A. E. Kazdin (Eds.), *Advances in clinical child psychology* (Vol. 3). New York: Plenum.

Becker, W. C., & Carnine, D. W. (1981). Direct instruction: A behavior theory model for comprehensive educational intervention with the disadvantaged. In S. W. Bijou & R. Ruiz (Eds.), *Behavior modification: Contributions to education*. Hillsdale, NJ: Lawrence Erlbaum Associates.

BECKER, W. C., ENGELMAN, S., & THOMAS, D. R. (1975). *Teaching 2: Cognitive learning and instruction*. Chicago, IL: Science Research Associates.

BEHR, S., & GALLAGHER, J. J. (1981). Alternative administrative strategies for young handicapped children: A policy analysis. *Journal of the Division for Early Childhood, 2,* 113–122.

BELL, S. (1970). The development of the concept of object as related to infant-mother attachment. *Child Development, 41,* 291–311.

BELLAMY, G. T., BOURBEAU, P. E., & SOWERS, J. (1983). Work and work-related services: Postschool options. In M. E. Snell (Ed.), *Systematic instruction of the moderately and severely handicapped* (2nd ed.). Columbus, OH: Charles E. Merrill.

BELMONT, J. M., & BUTTERFIELD, E. C. (1971). Learning strategies as determinants of memory deficiencies. *Cognitive Psychology, 2,* 411–420.

BENDER, E., SCHUMACHER, B., & ALLEN, H. A. (1976). *A resource manual for medical aspects of disabilities*. Carbondale, IL: Rehabilitation Counselor Training Program, Rehabilitation Institute, Southern Illinois University.

BENDER, Q., & ANDERMANN, K. (1965). Brain damage in blind children with retrolental filmoplasia. *Archives of Neurology, 12,* 644–649.

BENTSEN, C. (1979, June 18). The brightest kids. *New York, 12*(25), 36–40.

BERG, B. O. (1982). Convulsive disorders. In E. E. Bleck & D. A. Nagel (Eds.), *Physically handicapped children: A medical atlas for teachers* (pp. 171–181). New York: Grune & Stratton.

BERGER, K. W. (1972). *Speechreading: Principles and methods*. Baltimore: National Education Press.

BERLIN, C. M., JR. (1978). Biology and retardation. In J. T. Neisworth & R. M. Smith (Eds.), *Retardation: Issues, assessment and intervention* (pp. 117–137). New York: McGraw-Hill.

BERNAL, E. M. (1979). The education of the culturally gifted. In A. H. Passow (Ed.), *The gifted and the talented: Their education and development* (pp. 395–400). The seventy-eighth yearbook of the National Society for the Study of Education, Part 1. Chicago: University of Chicago Press.

BESSANT-BYRD, H. (1981). Competencies for educating culturally different exceptional children. In J. N. Nazzaro (Ed.), *Culturally different exceptional children in school*. Reston, VA: ERIC Clearinghouse on Handicapped and Gifted Children.

BETTELHEIM, B. (1950). *Love is not enough*. New York: Macmillan.

BETTELHEIM, B. (1967). *The empty fortress*. New York: Free Press.

BIGGE, J. (1982). *Teaching individuals with physical and multiple disabilities* (2nd ed.). Columbus, OH: Charles E. Merrill.

BIJOU, S. W. (1966). A functional analysis of retarded development. In N. R. Ellis (Ed.), *International review of research in mental retardation* (Vol. 1, pp. 1–19). New York: Academic Press.

BIJOU, S. W. (1981). The prevention of retarded development in disadvantaged children. In M. S. Begab, H. C. Haywood, & H. L. Garber (Eds.), *Psychosocial influences on retarded performance*. Baltimore: University Park Press.

BIKLEN, D. (1976). Advocacy comes of age. *Exceptional Children, 42,* 308–314.

BILLINGSLY, F. & LIBERTY, K. (1982). The use of time-based data in instructional programming for the severely handicapped. *Journal of the Association for the Severely Handicapped, 7*(1), 47–55.

BIRCH, H., & BELMONT, L. (1964). Auditory-visual integration in normal and retarded readers. *American Journal of Orthopsychiatry, 34,* 852–861.

BIRCH, H. R., RICHARDSON, S. A., BAIRD, D., HOROBIN, G., & ILLSLEY, R. (1970). *Mental abnormality in the community: A clinical and epidemiological study*. Baltimore: Williams & Wilkens.

BIRCH, J. W. (1974). *Mainstreaming: Educable mentally retarded children in regular classes*. Reston, VA: Council for Exceptional Children.

BIRCH, J. W. (1976). Mainstream education for hearing impaired pupils: Issues and interviews. *American Annals of the Deaf, 121,* 69–71.

BIRCH, J. W., & REYNOLDS, M. C. (1982). Special education as a profession. *Exceptional Education Quarterly, 2*(4), 1–13.

BIRCH, J. W., TISDALL, W., PEABODY, R., & STERRETT, R. (1966). *School achievement and effect of type size on reading in visually handicapped children* (Cooperative Research Project No. 1766, Contract No. OEC-4-10-028). Pittsburgh, PA: University of Pittsburgh.

BIRCH, J. W., TISDALL, W. J., BARNEY, W. D., & MARKS, C. H. (1965). *A field demonstration of the effectiveness or feasibility of early admission to school for mentally advanced children*. Pittsburgh, PA: University of Pittsburgh.

BISHOP, J. E. (1982, January 29). Gene defect linked to retarded males may solve mysteries — Does fragile-X chromosome account for many cases of hereditary condition? *Wall Street Journal*, pp. 1, 18, 19.

BLACKARD, M., & BARSH, E. (1982). Changing community attitudes. *Exceptional Parent, 12,* 43–46.

BLACKHURST, A. E. (1977). Competency-based special education personnel preparation. In R. D. Kneedler & S. G. Tarver (Eds.), *Changing perspectives in special education*. Columbus, OH: Charles E. Merrill.

BLACKHURST, A. E. (Ed.). (1985). *Using microcomputers in special education programs*. Boston: Little, Brown.

BLACKHURST, A. E., & BERDINE, W. H. (Eds.). (1981). *An introduction to special education*. Boston: Little, Brown.

BLACKHURST, A. E., & HOFMEISTER, A. M. (1980). Technology in special education. In L. Mann & D. Sabatino (Eds.), *Fourth review of special education*. New York: Grune & Stratton.

BLACKHURST, A. E., McLOUGHLIN, J. A., & PRICE, L. M.

(1977). Issues in the development of programs to prepare teachers of children with learning and behavior disorders. *Behavior Disorders, 2,* 157–168.

BLACKSHEAR, P. B., SULLIVAN, A. R., EWELL, Y., & ROGERS, K. (1980). *Black and gifted children.* Reston, VA: ERIC Clearinghouse on Handicapped and Gifted Children.

BLANKENSHIP, V., & LILLY, M. S. (1981). *Mainstreaming students with learning and behavior problems.* New York: Holt, Rinehart and Winston.

BLATT, B., & KAPLAN, F. (1966). *Christmas in purgatory.* Boston: Allyn and Bacon.

BLATT, B., OZOLINS, A., & McNALLY, J. (1979). *The family papers: A return to purgatory.* New York: Longman.

BLECK, E. E. (1982a). Anatomy — basic parts and terms of the nervous and musculo-skeletal systems. In E. E. Bleck & D. A. Nagel (Eds.), *Physically handicapped children: A medical atlas for teachers* (pp. 1–16). New York: Grune & Stratton.

BLECK, E. E. (1982b). Cerebral palsy. In E. E. Bleck & D. A. Nagel (Eds.), *Physically handicapped children: A medical atlas for teachers* (pp. 59–132). New York: Grune & Stratton.

BLECK, E. E. (1982c). Muscular dystrophy: Duchene type. In E. E. Bleck & D. A. Nagel (Eds.), *Physically handicapped children: A medical atlas for teachers* (pp. 385–394). New York: Grune & Stratton.

BLECK, E. E. (1982d). Myelomeningocele, meningocele, spina bifida. In E. E. Bleck & D. A. Nagel (Eds.), *Physically handicapped children: A medical atlas for teachers* (pp. 345–362). New York: Grune & Stratton.

BLECK, E. E. (1982e). Nonoral communication. In E. E. Bleck & D. A. Nagel (Eds.), *Physically handicapped children: A medical atlas for teachers* (pp. 145–169). New York: Grune & Stratton.

BLECK, E. E. (1982f). Osteogenesis imperfecta. In E. E. Bleck & D. A. Nagel (Eds.), *Physically handicapped children: A medical atlas for teachers* (pp. 405–412). New York: Grune & Stratton.

BLECK, E. E. (1982g). Traumatic paraplegia and quadriplegia. In E. E. Bleck & D. A. Nagel (Eds.), *Physically handicapped children: A medical atlas for teachers* (pp. 413–418). New York: Grune & Stratton.

BLECK, E. E. & Nagel, D. (Eds.). (1982) *Physically handicapped children: A medical atlas for teachers.* New York: Grune & Stratton.

BLOCK, J. (1978). Impaired children. *Children Today, 7,* 2–6.

BLOODSTEIN, O. (1981). *A handbook on stuttering.* Chicago: National Easter Seal Society for Crippled Children and Adults.

BLOOM, B. (1964). *Stability and change in human characteristics.* New York: John Wiley & Sons.

BLOOM, B. S. (1976). *Human characteristics and social learning.* New York: McGraw-Hill.

BLOOM, B. S. (1982). The role of gifts and markers in the development of talent. *Exceptional Children, 48*(6), 510–522.

BLOOM, F. (1970). *Our deaf children.* Washington, DC: Alexander Graham Bell Association.

BLOOM, L., & LAHEY, M. (1978). *Language development and language disorders.* New York: John Wiley & Sons.

BLUMA, S. M., SHEARER, M. S., FROHAM, A. H., & HILLARD, J. M. (1976). *Portage guide to early education.* Portage, WS: Cooperative Education Agency, No. 12.

BOGNAR, C. J., & MARTIN, B. W. (1982). A sociological perspective on diagnosing learning difficulties. *Journal of Learning Disabilities, 15,* 347–351.

BORLAND, J. (1978). Teacher identification of the gifted: A new look. *Journal for the Education of the Gifted, 2*(1), 22–32.

BOS, C. S. (1982). Getting past decoding: Assisted and repeated readings as remedial methods for learning disabled students. *Topics in Learning and Learning Disabilities, 1,* 51–57.

BOWE, F. (1979). *Handicapping America: Barriers to disabled people.* New York: Harper & Row.

BOWE, F. (1980). *Rehabilitating America.* New York: Harper & Row.

BOWER. T. G. R. (1977). *A primer of infant development.* San Francisco: W. H. Freeman.

BOWERMAN, M. (1976). Semantic factors in the acquisition of rules for word use and sentence construction. In D. Morehead & A. Morehead (Eds.), *Directions in normal and deficient child language.* Baltimore: University Park Press.

BOWLBY, J. (1969). *Attachment.* New York: Basic Books.

BOYAN, C., & HOUSE, C. (1979). Curriculum considerations in career education for the moderately handicapped. In G. M. Clark & W. J. White (Eds.), *Career education for the handicapped: Current perspectives for teachers.* Boothwyn, PA: Educational Resources Center.

BRICKER, D., & CASUSO, V. (1979). Family involvement: A critical component of early intervention. *Exceptional Children, 46,* 108–117.

BRICKER, D. D. (1983). Early communication: Development and training. In M. E. Snell (Ed.), *Systematic instruction of the moderately and severely handicapped* (2nd ed.). Columbus, OH: Charles E. Merrill.

BROLIN, D. E. (1973). Career education needs of secondary educable students. *Exceptional Children, 39,* 619–624.

BROLIN, D. E. (1982). *Vocational preparation of persons with handicaps.* Columbus, OH: Charles E. Merrill.

BROLIN, D. E., & KOKASKA, C. J. (1979). *Career education for handicapped children and youth.* Columbus, OH: Charles E. Merrill.

BROLIN, D. E., MALAVER, M., & MATYAS, G. (1976, June). *PRICE needs assessment study* (Project PRICE Working Paper 7). Columbia, MO: University of Missouri.

BROLIN, D. E., McKAY, D. J., & WEST, L. W. (1978). *Trainer's guide for life centered career education.* Reston, VA: Council for Exceptional Children.

BROLIN, D. E., & THOMAS, B. (Eds.). (1972). *Preparing teachers for secondary level educable mentally retarded: Proposal for a new model.* Minomonie, WS: University of Wisconsin — Stout.

BROLIN, E. (1978). *Life-centered approach to career education: A competency-based approach.* Reston, VA: Council for Exceptional Children.

BROMWICH, R. M. (1981). *Working with parents and infants: An interactional approach.* Baltimore: University Park Press.

BRONFENBRENNER, U. (1975). Is early intervention effective? In B. Z. Friedlander, G. M. Sterritt, & G. E. Kirk (Eds.), *Exceptional infant: Vol. 3: Assessment & intervention.* New York: Brunner/Mazel.

BROWDER, D. M., & SNELL, M. E. (1983). Daily living skills. In M. E. Snell (Ed.), *Systematic instruction of the moderately and severely handicapped* (2nd ed.). Columbus, OH: Charles E. Merrill.

BROWN, A. L., (1981). Metacognition: The development of selective attention strategies for learning from texts. In M. Kamil (Ed.), *30th Yearbook of the National Reading Conference.* Clemson, NC: National Reading Conference.

BROWN, L., BRANSTON, M. B., HAMRE-NIETUPSKI, S., PUMPIAN, I., CERTO, N., & GRUENEWALD, L. (1979). A strategy for developing chronological-age-appropriate and functional curricular content for severely handicapped adolescents and young adults. *Journal of Special Education, 13,* 81–90.

BROWN, L., NIETUPSKI, J., & HAMRE-NIETUPSKI, S. (1976). The criterion of ultimate functioning and public school services for severely handicapped children. In M. A. Thomas (Ed.), *Hey, don't forget about me!* Reston, VA: Council for Exceptional Children.

BROWN, L., WILCOX, B., SONTAG, E., VINCENT, B., DODD, N., & GRUENEWALD, L. (1977). Toward the realization of the least restrictive educational environments for severely handicapped students. *AAESPH Review, 2*(4), 195–201.

BROWN, L. L., & HAMMILL, D. D. (1978). *Behavior rating profile.* Austin, TX: PRO-ED.

BROWN, W. T., JENKINS, E. C., FRIEDMAN, E., BROOKS, J., WISNIEWSKI, K., SIMHACHALAM, R., & FRENCH, J. (1981, December). Fragile-X syndrome linked to autism: Giant steps. *The Journal of the New York State Office of Mental Retardation and Developmental Disabilities, 4,* 1–2.

BROWN, W. T., JENKINS, E. C., FRIEDMAN, E., BROOKS, J., WISNIEWSKI, K., SIMHACHALAM, R., & FRENCH, J. (1982). Autism is associated with the Fragile-X syndrome. *Journal of Autism and Developmental Disorders, 12*(3), 303–308.

BROWN V. TOPEKA BOARD OF EDUCATION, 347 U.S. 483 (1954).

BRUNER, J. S. (1960). *The process of education.* Cambridge, MA: Harvard University Press.

BRUNER, J. S. (1964). The course of cognitive growth. *American Psychologist, 19,* 1–15.

BRUNKEN, P. (1984). Independence for the visually impaired through technology. *Education of the Visually Handicapped, 15*(4), 127–133.

BRYAN, T., COSDEN, M., & PEARL, R. (1982). The effects of cooperative models on LD and MLD students. *Learning Disabilities Quarterly, 5,* 415–421.

BRYAN, T., DONAHUE, M., & PEARL, R. (1981). Learning disabled children's peer interactions during a small group problem-solving task. *Learning Disabilities Quarterly, 4,* 13–22.

BRYAN, T., PEARL, R., ZIMMERMAN, D., & MATTHEWS, F. (1982). Mothers' evaluations of their learning disabled children. *Journal of Special Education, 16,* 149–160.

BRYAN, T., SHERMAN, R. E., & FISHER, A. (1980). Learning disabled boys' nonverbal behaviors within a dyadic interview. *Learning Disabilities Quarterly, 3,* 65–72.

BRYAN, T. H., & BRYAN, J. H. (1978). Social interactions of learning disabled children. *Learning Disabilities Quarterly, 1,* 33–38.

BRYANT, N. D. (1965). Some principles of remedial instruction for dyslexia. *The Reading Teacher, 18,* 567–572.

BUEHLER, R. E., PATTERSON, G. R., & FURNISS, J. M. (1966). The reinforcement of behavior in institutional settings. *Behavior Research and Therapy, 4,* 157–167.

BUIST, C., & SCHULMAN, J. (1969). *Toys and games for educationally handicapped children.* Springfield, IL: Charles C. Thomas.

BUNKER, L. K., & MOON, S. (1983). In M. E. Snell (Ed.), *Systematic instruction of the moderately and severely handicapped* (2nd ed.). Columbus, OH: Charles E. Merrill.

BURGDORF, R. L. (1980). *The legal rights of handicapped persons: Cases, materials and text.* Baltimore: Paul H. Brooks.

BURGDORF, R. L., & SPICER, P. P. (1983). *The legal rights of handicapped persons: Cases, materials and text* (1983 Supplement). Baltimore: Paul H. Brooks.

BURLEY, M. (1977). A parent's perspective of the future. In G. Kranz & P. Varian (Eds.), *The needs of multiple handicapped individuals: Proceedings of the Annual Spring Conference.* Columbus, OH: Madison Co. Board of Education.

BUTTERFIELD, E. C., WAMBOLD, C., & BELMONT, J. M. (1973). On the theory and practice of improving short-term memory. *American Journal on Mental Deficiency, 77,* 654–669.

CALDWELL, B. M. (1971). Impact of interest in early cognitive stimulation. In H. Rie (Ed.), *Perspectives in psychopathology.* Chicago: Aldine-Atherton.

CALDWELL, B. M. (1976). Arbitration between the child and the family. In V. C. Vaughan III & T. B. Brazelton (Eds.), *The family — Can it be saved?* Chicago: Year Book Medical Publishers.

CALDWELL, B. M., & STEDMAN, D. J. (Eds.). (1977). *Infant education.* New York: Walker.

CALLAHAN, C. M. (1978). *Developing creativity in the gifted and talented.* Reston, VA: The Council for Exceptional Children.

CALLAHAN, C. M. (1979). The gifted and talented woman. In A. H. Passow (Ed.), *The gifted and the talented: Their education and development.* The Seventy-eighth Yearbook of the National Society for the Study of Education. Part 1 (pp. 401–423). Chicago: University of Chicago Press.

CALLAHAN, C. M. (1983). Issues in evaluating programs for the gifted. *Gifted Child Quarterly, 27*(1), 3–7.

CAMPBELL, P. (1983). Basic considerations in programming for students with movement difficulties. In M. E. Snell (Ed.), *Systematic instruction of the moderately and severely handicapped* (2nd ed.). Columbus, OH: Charles E. Merrill.

CANSLER, D. P., MARTIN, G. H., & VALAND, M. C. (1975). *Working with families.* Winston-Salem, NC: Kaplan.

CAPE PROJECT. (1980). *Adaptive Performance Instrument.* Moscow, ID: Department of Special Education, University of Idaho.

CAPURSO, A. (1961). Music. In L. A. Fliegler (Ed.), *Curriculum planning for the gifted.* Englewood Cliffs, NJ: Prentice-Hall.

CAPUTE, A., WACHTEL, R., SHAPIRO, B., PALMER, F., & ALLEN, M. (1983). Normal motor and reflex development. In J. Umbreit (Ed.), *Physical disabilities and health impairments: An introduction* (pp. 29–38). Columbus: Charles E. Merrill.

CAPUTE, A. J. (1975). Cerebral palsy and associated dysfunctions. In R. H. A. Haslam & P. J. Valletutti (Eds.), *Medical problems in the classroom: The teacher's role in diagnosis and management* (pp. 149–163). Baltimore: University Park Press.

CARHART, R. (1970). Development and conservation of speech. In H. Davis & S. R. Silverman (Eds.), *Hearing and Deafness.* New York: Holt, Rinehart and Winston.

CARLSON, L., & BRICKER, D. D. (1982). Dyadic and contingent aspects of early communicative intervention. In D. D. Bricker (Ed.), *Intervention with at-risk and handicapped infants.* Baltimore: University Park Press.

CARROLL, T. J. (1961). *Blindness: What it is, what it does, and how to live with it.* Boston: Little, Brown.

CARTWRIGHT, G. P. (1984). Computer applications in special education. In D. F. Walker & R. D. Hess (Eds.), *Instructional software: Principles and perspectives for design and use.* Belmont, CA: Wadsworth.

CASSERLY, P. L. (1979). Helping able young women take math and science seriously in school. In N. Colangelo & R. Zaffrann (Eds.), *New voices in counseling the gifted* (pp. 346–369). Dubuque, IA: Kendall/Hunt.

CATHEY, M. L., & JANSMA, P. (1979). Mainstreaming orthopedically disabled individuals in various activities, Part I. *The Directive Teacher, 2,* 9, 29.

CATON, H. (1979). A primary reading program for beginning braille readers. *Journal of Visual Impairment and Blindness, 73,* 309–313.

CATON, H., & BRADLEY, E. L. (1978–1979). A new approach to beginning braille readings. *Education of the Visually Handicapped, 10,* 66–71.

CATON, H., & RANKIN, E. (1980). Variability in age and experience among blind students using basal reading materials. *Journal of Visual Impairment and Blindness, 74,* 147–149.

CATON, H. R., PESTER, E., & BRADLEY, E. J. (1980–1983). *Patterns: The primary braille reading program.* Louisville, KY: American Printing House for the Blind.

CATTEL, R. B. (1971). *Abilities: Their structures, growth, and action.* Boston: Houghton Mifflin.

CATTELL, P. (1940). *The measurement of intelligence of infants and young children.* New York: Psychological Corporation.

CAWLEY, J., FITZMAURICE, A., GOLDSTEIN, H., LEPORE, A., SEDLAK, R., & ALTHAUS, V. (1976). *Project MATH.* Tulsa: Educ. Development Corp.

CEGELKA, P. T., (1979). Education for leisure. *Exceptional Teacher, 1,* 3–5.

CEGELKA, P. T. (1981). Career education. In J. Kauffman & D. Hallahan (Eds.), *Handbook of special education.* Englewood Cliffs, NJ: Prentice-Hall.

CEGELKA, P. T., & LEWIS, R. B. (1983). The once and future world: Portents for the handicapped. *The Journal for Special Educators, 19*(4), 61–72.

CENTER ON HUMAN POLICY. (1979). *The community imperative: A refutation of all arguments in support of institutionalizing anybody because of mental retardation.* Center on Human Policy, Syracuse University.

CERVONE, B. F., & O'LEARY, K. (1982). A conceptual framework for parent involvement. *Educational Leadership, 40,* 48–49.

CHAFFIN, J. D., MAXWELL, B., & THOMPSON, B. (1982). ARC-ED curriculum: The application of video game formats to educational software. *Exceptional Children, 42,* 173–178.

CHALKEY, T. (1982). *Your eyes: A book for paramedical personnel and the lay reader* (2nd ed.). Springfield, IL: Charles C. Thomas.

CHAPMAN, J. E., & HEWARD, W. L. (1982). Improving parent-teacher communication through recorded telephone messages. *Exceptional Children, 49,* 79–81.

CHASE, T. B. (1951). Developmental assessment of handicapped infants and young children: With special attention to the visually impaired. *AFB Practice Report.* New York: American Foundation for the Blind.

CHESS, S., THOMAS, A., & BIRCH, H. G. (1967). Behavior problems revisited: Findings of an anterospective study. *Journal of the American Academy of Child Psychiatry, 6,* 321–331.

CHINN, P. C., DREW, C. J., & LOGAN, D. R. (1979). *Mental retardation* (2nd ed.). St. Louis: C. V. Mosby.

CHRISTOPHERSON, S. L. (1981). Developmental placement in the regular school program. *G/C/T, 19,* 40–41.

CLARK, B. (1983). *Growing up gifted* (2nd ed.). Columbus, OH: Charles E. Merrill.

CLARK, D., BAKER, B., & HEIFETZ, L. (1982). Behavioral training for parents of mentally retarded children: Prediction of outcome. *American Journal of Mental Deficiency, 87,* 14–19.

CLARK, G. M. (1979). *Career education for the handicapped child in the elementary classroom.* Denver: Love.

CLARK, G. M. (1980). Career education: A concept. In G. M. Clark & W. J. White (Eds.), *Career education for the handicapped: Current perspectives for teachers.* Boothwyn, PA: Educational Resources Center.

CLARK, G. M. (1981). Career and vocational education. In G. Brown, R. L. McDowell, & J. Smith (Eds.), *Educating adolescents with behavior disorders.* Columbus, OH: Charles E. Merrill.

CLARK, M. (1983, February 7). A promising therapy for MS. *Newsweek,* p. 62.

CLARK, R. W. (1977). *The man who made the future.* New York: Putnam.

CODE OF ETHICS AND STANDARDS FOR PROFESSIONAL PRACTICE. (1983). *Exceptional Children, 50,* 205–209.

COGGINS, T. E., & SANDALL, S. (1983). The communicatively handicapped infant: Application of normal language and communication development. In S. G. Garwood & R. R. Fewell (Eds.), *Educating handicapped infants.* Rockville, MD: Aspen.

COHEN, H., CONROY, J. W., FRAZER, D. W., SNELBECKER, G. E., & SPREAD, S. (1977). Behavioral effects of interinstitutional relocation of mentally retarded residents. *American Journal of Mental Deficiency, 82*(1), 12–18.

COLE, M., & HALL, W. (Eds.). (1982). A model system for the study of learning difficulties. *The Quarterly Newsletter of the Laboratory of Comparative Human Cognition, 4,* 39–66. San Diego: University of California.

COLES, G. (1980). Evaluation of genetic explanations of reading and learning problems. *The Journal of Special Education, 14,* 365.

COLES, G. S. (1978). The learning disabilities test battery: Empirical and social issues. *Harvard Educational Review, 48,* 313–340.

COLLEGE ENTRANCE EXAMINATION BOARD. (1983). *Advanced placement course description: Computer science.* Princeton, NJ: College Entrance Examination Publication.

COLLIGAN, R. (1981). Prediction of reading difficulty from parental preschool report: A 3-year follow-up. *Learning Disability Quarterly, 4,* 31–37.

COMMISSION ON INSTRUCTIONAL TECHNOLOGY. (1970). *To improve learning: A report to the president and the congress of the United States.* Washington, DC: U. S. G.P.O.

Conference on Newborn Hearing Screening — Proceedings Summary and Recommendations. (1971). San Francisco: Maternal and Child Health Service, Health Services and Mental Health Administration, Public Health Service, Department of Health, Education, and Welfare.

CONLEY, R. W. (1979). Economics and mental retardation. In E. LaFramboise & G. Provencal (Eds.), *Where do we want to be in five years? A report of the American Association on Mental Deficiency's 1979 annual conference.*

CONNOR, F. P., WILLIAMSON, G. G., & SIEPP, J. M. (1978). *Program guide for infants and toddlers with neuromotor and other developmental disabilities.* New York: Teachers College Press.

COOPER, A., & HOLT, W. J. (1982). Development of social skills and the management of common problems. In K. E. Allen & E. M. Goetz (Eds.), *Early childhood education: Special problems, special solutions.* Rockville, MD: Aspen.

COOPER, J. (1981). *Measuring Behavior.* Columbus, OH: Charles E. Merrill.

COOPER, J. O., & HERON, T. (1978). Educational materials and strategies for home use. In D. Edge, B. Strenecky, & S. Mour (Eds.), *Parenting learning-problem children* (pp. 55–70). Columbus, OH: NCEMMH, Ohio State University.

COOPER, J. V., & EDGE, D. (1981). *Parenting: Strategies and educational methods.* Louisville, KY: Eston Corp.

COPELAND, M., FORD, L., & SOLON, N. (1976). *Occupational therapy for mentally retarded children.* Baltimore: University Park Press.

COREY, S. M. (1967). The nature of instruction. In P. C. Lange (Ed.), *Programmed instruction: The sixty-sixth yearbook of the National Society for the Study of Education (Part III).* Chicago: University of Chicago Press.

CORTER, C. M. (1977). Brief separation and communication between infant and mother. In T. Alloway, P. Pliner, & L. Krames (Eds.), *Attachment behavior: Advances in the study of communication and affect* (Vol. 3). N.Y.:Plenum.

COUNCIL FOR EXCEPTIONAL CHILDREN. (1978). *Position paper on career education.* Reston, VA: Author.

COWART, V. (1983, September 9). First-trimester prenatal diagnostic method becoming available in U.S. [Medical News]. *Journal of the American Medical Association, 250*(10), 1249–1250.

COWEN, E. L., UNDERBERG, R., VERILLO, R. T., & BENHAM, F. G. (1961). *Adjustment to visual disability in adolescence.* New York: American Foundation for the Blind.

COX, J., & DANIEL, N. (1983). Specialized schools for high ability students. *G/C/T, 28,* 2–9.

CRAIG, W. N., SALAM, J. M., & CRAIG, M. B. (1976). Mainstreaming and partial integration of deaf and hearing students. *American Annals of the Deaf, 121,* 63–68.

CRATTY, B. (1969). *Perceptual-motor behavior and educational processes.* Springfield, IL: Charles C. Thomas.

CROSS, D. P. (1983). Survey of classes for the physically disabled. Unpublished manuscript, University of Kentucky, Lexington.

CROSS, L. (1977). Casefinding. In L. Cross & K. W. Goin (Eds.), *Identifying handicapped children.* New York: Walker.

CROW, L. D., & CROW, A. (1959). *Educating the academically able: A book of readings.* New York: David McKay.

CROWLEY, M., KEANE, K., & NEEDHAM, C. (1982). Fathers: The forgotten parents. *American Annals of the Deaf, 127,* 38–40.

CRUICKSHANK, W. M., BENTZEN, F., RATENBURG, F., & TANNHAUSER, M. (1961). *A teaching method for brain-injured and hyperactive children.* Syracuse, NY: Syracuse University Press.

CRUICKSHANK, W. M., & JOHNSON, G. O. (Eds.). (1975). *Education of exceptional children and youth* (3rd ed.). Englewood Cliffs, NJ: Prentice-Hall.

CULATTA, R. (1976). Fluency: The other side of the coin. *American Speech and Hearing Association, 18,* 795–800.

CULATTA, R., & RUBIN, H. (1973). A program for the initial stages of fluency therapy. *Journal of Speech and Hearing Research, 16,* 556–559.

CULLINAN, D., EPSTEIN, M. H., & LLOYD, J. W. (1983). *Behavior disorders of children and adolescents.* Englewood Cliffs, NJ: Prentice-Hall.

CURTIS, J. (Ed.). (1978). *Processes and disorders of human communication.* New York: Harper & Row.

CUTSFORTH, T. D. (1932). The unreality of words to the blind. *Teachers Forum, 4,* 86–89.

CUTSFORTH, T. D. (1951). *The blind in school and society: A psychological study.* New York: American Foundation for the Blind.

D'ALONZO, B. J. (1977). Trends and issues in career education for the mentally retarded. *Education and Training of the Mentally Retarded, 12,* 156–158.

DANIELS, S. M. (1982). From parent-advocacy to self-advocacy: A problem of transition. *Exceptional Education Quarterly, 3,* 25–32.

DARBY, B. L. (1979). Infant cognition: Considerations for assessment tools. In B. L. Darby & M. J. May (Eds.), *Infant assessment: Issues and applications.* Seattle, WA: WESTAR.

DARELY, F., & SPRIESTERSBACH, D. (1978). *Diagnostic methods in speech pathology* (2nd ed.). New York: Harper & Row.

DAURIO, S. (1979). Educational enrichment versus acceleration: A review of the literature. In W. George, S. Cohn, & J. Stanley (Eds.), *Educating the gifted: Acceleration and enrichment.* Baltimore: Johns Hopkins University Press.

DAUTERMAN, W. L., SHAPIRO, B., & SWINN, R. M. (1967). Performance of intelligence for blind reviewed. *International Journal for the Education of the Blind, 17,* 8–16.

DAVIDMAN, L. (1981). Learning style: The myth, the panacea, the wisdom. *Phi Delta Kappan, 62,* 641–645.

DAVIDSON, T., FOUNTAIN, P., GROGAN, R., SHORT, B., & STEELY, J. (1976). *The Learning Center Book: An Integrated Approach.* Santa Monica: Goodyear, 3.

DAVIS v. SOUTHEASTERN COMMUNITY COLLEGE, 574 F.2D 1158 (4th Cir. 1978).

DAVIS, C. J. (1970). *New developments in intelligence testing of blind children.* Proceedings of the conference on new approaches to the evaluation of blind persons. New York: American Foundation of the Blind.

DAVIS, D. M. (1939). The relation of repetitions in the speech of young children to certain measures of language maturity and situational factors. *Journal of Speech Disorders, 4,* 303.

DAVIS, H., & SILVERMAN, S. R. (1970). *Hearing and deafness* (3rd ed.). New York: Holt, Rinehart and Winston.

DAVIS, S., & FROTHINGHAM, P. S. (1981). Computing at a new public high school for gifted students. In J. N. Nazzaro (Ed.), *Computer connections for gifted children and youth.* Reston, VA: Clearinghouse on Handicapped and Gifted Children.

DELAMATER, A., LAHEY, B., & DRAKE, L. (1981). Toward an empirical subclassification of "learning disabilities": A psychological comparison of "hyperactive" and "nonhyperactive" subgroups. *Journal of Abnormal Child Psychology, 9,* 65–77.

DeMOTT, R. (1974). Visually impaired. In N. G. Haring (Ed.), *Behavior of exceptional children: An introduction to special education* (pp. 529–563). Columbus, OH: Charles E. Merrill.

DENEMARK, G., MORSINK, C., & THOMAS, C. (1979). Accepting the challenge for change in teacher education. In M. Reynolds (Ed.), *A common body of practice for teachers: The Challenge of P. L. 94–142 to teacher education.* Minneapolis, MN: National Support System Projects.

DENHOFF, E. (1966). Cerebral palsy: Medical aspects. In W. M. Cruickshank (Ed.), *Cerebral palsy: Its individual and community problems* (2nd ed.) (pp. 24–100). Syracuse: Syracuse University Press.

DENO, E. (1970). Special education a developmental capital. *Exceptional Children, 37,* 229–237.

DENO, E. (1973). *Instructional alternatives for exceptional children.* Reston, VA: Council for Exceptional Children.

DENO, S., & CHIANG, B. (1979). An experimental analysis of the nature of reversal errors in children with severe learning disabilities. *Learning Disabilities Quarterly, 2,* 40–45.

DENO, S. L., MARSTON, D., SHINN, M., & FINDAL, G. (1983). Oral reading fluency: A simple datum for scaling reading disability. *Topics in Learning and Learning Disabilities, 2,* 53–59,

DEREVENSKY, J. L. (1977). Cross modal functioning and reading achievement. *Journal of Reading Behavior, IX(3),* 233–251.

DEUPREC, M. (1971). The muscles of voice and speech. In L. Travis (Ed.), *Handbook of speech pathology and audiology.* New York: Appleton-Century-Crofts.

DeVRIES, R., & KOHLBERG, L. (1977). Relations between Piagetian and psychometric assessments of intelligence. In L. G. Katz (Ed.), *Current topics in early childhood education.* Norwood, NJ: Ablex.

DeWEERD, J. (1981). Early education services for children with handicaps — Where have we been, where are we now, and where are we going? *Journal of the Division for Early Childhood, 2,* 15–24.

D'HEURLE, A., MELLINGER, J., & HAGGARD, E. (1959). Personality, intellectual and achievement patterns in gifted children. *Psychological Monographs, 73(13),* 1–28.

DIANA v. STATE BOARD OF EDUCATION. Civil Action No. C-70 37RFP (N.D. Cal. January 7, 1970).

DICKERSON, D., SPELLMAN, C. R., LARSEN, S., & TYLER, L. (1973). Let the cards do the talking: A teacher-parent communication program. *Teaching Exceptional Children, 5,* 170–176.

DIEDRICH, W., & YOUNGSTROM, K. (1966). *Alaryngeal speech.* Springfield, IL: Charles C. Thomas.

DIRKS, J., & QUARFOTH, J. (1981). Selecting children for gifted classes: Choosing for breadth vs. choosing for depth. *Psychology in the Schools, 18,* 437–449.

DOLL. E. (1962). A historical survey of research and management of mental retardation in the United States. In E. P. Trapp & P. Humelstein (Eds.), *Readings on the Exceptional Children.* New York: Appleton-Century-Crofts.

DOLL, E. (1965). *Vineland Social Maturity Scale.* Circle Pines, MN: American Guidance Service.

DOLLAR, S. J., & BROOKS, C. (1980). Assessment of severely and profoundly handicapped individuals, *Exceptional Education Quarterly, 1(3),* 87–101.

DONALDSON, J., & MARTINSON, M. C. (1977). Modifying attitudes toward physically disabled persons. *Exceptional Children, 43,* 337–341.

DOORLY, A. (1981). Microcomputers for gifted microtots. In J. N. Nazzaro (Ed.), *Computer connections for gifted children and youth.* Reston, VA: Clearinghouse on Handicapped and Gifted Children.

DuBose, R. F. (1978). Development of communication in nonverbal children. *Education and Training of the Mentally Retarded, 13,* 37–41.

Duffy, J. K. (1967). Hearing problems of school age children. In I. S. Fusfeld (Ed.), *A handbook of readings in education of the deaf and postschool implications.* Springfield, IL: Charles C. Thomas.

Dunn, F. M., & Howell, R. J. (1982). Relaxation training and its relationship to hyperactivity in boys. *Journal of Clinical Psychology, 38,* 92–100.

Dunn, L., Chun, L., Crowell, D., Dunn, L., Alevy, L., & Yackel, E. (1976). *Peabody Early Experience Kit.* Circle Pines, MN: American Guidance Service.

Dunst. C. J. (1980). *A clinical and educational manual for use with the Uzgiris and Hunt Scales of Infant Psychological Development.* Baltimore: University Park Press.

Dunst, C. J. (1981). *Infant learning: A cognitive-linguistic intervention strategy.* Hingham, MA: Teaching Resources Corporation.

Durio, H. F. (1980). Talking with your child's physician. *Pointer, 25,* 12–14.

Dyk, L. (1983, May 12). *Early intervention programs that work.* Paper presented at the HCEEP Rural Network — Appalachian Regional Workshop, Duffield, VA.

Eakin, W. M., Pratt, R. J., & McFarland, T. L. (1961). *Type size research for the partially seeing child.* Pittsburgh: Stanwix House.

Edge, D., Fink, A. H., & Brause, M. (1978). Developing parent training programs for professionals. In D. Edge, B. J. Strenecky, & S. I. Mour (Eds.), *Parenting learning-problem children: The professional educator's perspective.* Columbus, OH: NCEMMH, Ohio State University.

Education of the Handicapped: The Independent Biweekly News Service on Federal Legislation, Programs and Funding for Special Education. (1979). Washington, DC: Capitol Publications, Inc., 4(11), 4–5.

Edwards, J. S., & Edwards, D. (1970). Rate of behavior development: Direct and continuous measurement. *Perceptual & Motor Skills, 31,* 633–634.

Eheart, B. (1982a). Mother-child interaction with non-retarded and mentally retarded preschoolers. *American Journal of Mental Deficiency, 87,* 20–25.

Eheart, B. (1982b). Special needs of low-income mothers of developmentally delayed children. *American Journal of Mental Deficiency, 87,* 26–33.

Eheart, B., & Ciccone, J. (1982). Special needs of low-income mothers of developmentally delayed children. *American Journal of Mental Deficiency, 87,* 26–33.

Ehrlich, V. Z. (1982). *Gifted Children: A guide for parents and teachers.* Englewood Cliffs, NJ: Prentice-Hall.

Eisner, E. W. (1983). The art and craft of teaching. *Educational Leadership, 40*(4), 4–13.

Ellis, N. R. (1981). On training the mentally retarded. *Analysis and Intervention in Developmental Disabilities, 1*(1), 99–108.

Ellison, R., Abe, C., Fox, D., Corey, K., & Taylor, C. (1976, Winter). Using biographical information in identifying artistic talent. *The Gifted Child Quarterly, XX*(4), 402–413.

Enell, N. C., & Barrick, S. W. (1983). *An examination of the relative efficiency and usefulness of computer-assisted individualized education programs.* Grant Report Number 34–3651–67447–01–82, Office of Special Education, California State Department of Education.

Englemann, S., & Bruner, E. (1969). *DISTAR reading: An instructional system.* Chicago: Science Research Associates.

English, R. W., & Olson, K. K. (1976). *Parenting handicapped children: Earliest experiences. Center paper No. 106.* Eugene, OR: Rehabilitation Research and Training Center in Mental Retardation, 10–11.

Enzer, N. B., & Goin, K. W. (Eds.). (1978). *Social and emotional development: The preschooler.* New York: Walker.

Epilepsy Foundation of America. (1977). *Answers to most frequent questions people ask about epilepsy.* Washington, DC: Epilepsy Foundation.

Epps, S., Ysseldyke, J. E., & Algozzine, B. (1981, November). *Public Policy Implications of Different Definitions of Learning Disabilities* (Report 99). Institute for Research on Learning Disabilities.

Epstein, C. B. (1979). *The gifted and talented: Programs that work.* Arlington, VA: National School Public Relations Association.

Erb, L., & Mercer, C. D. (1979). Language disabilities. In C. D. Mercer (Ed.), *Children and adolescents with LD.* Columbus: Charles E. Merrill.

Erhardt, R. P. (1974). Sequential levels in development of prehension. *American Journal of Occupational Therapy, 28*(10), 592–596.

Evans. D., & Hampson, M. (1968). The language of mongols. *British Journal of Disorders of Communication, 3,* 171–181.

Faerstein, L. M. (1981). Stress and coping in families of learning disabled children: A literature review. *Journal of Learning Disabilities, 14,* 420–423.

Fallen, N. H., & McGovern, J. E. (1978). *Young children with special needs.* Columbus, OH: Charles E. Merrill.

Far West Laboratory for Educational Research and Development. (1980). *Educational programs that work.* San Francisco: Author.

Fearn, L. (1982). Underachievement and rate of acceleration. *Gifted Child Quarterly, 26,* 121–125.

Federal Register. (1977, December 29). p. 65083.

Federal Register. (1981). 46 (3866).

Feldhusen, J. (1982). Myth: Gifted education means having a program! Meeting the needs of gifted students through differentiated programming. *Gifted Child Quarterly, 26*(1), 37–41.

Feldman, D. (1979a). The mysterious case of extreme giftedness. In A. H. Passow (Ed.). *The gifted and the talented: Their education and development.* The seventy-eighth yearbook of The National Society for the Study of Education, Part 2 (pp. 335–351). Chicago: University of Chicago Press.

Feldman, D. (1979b). Toward a nonelitist conception of giftedness. *Phi Delta Kappan, 60*(9), 660–663.

Felt, M., Coplon, J., & Sonnenschein, P. (1981). *Par-*

enting the special needs child. Boston: Human Services Development.

FENICHEL, C. (1966). Psychoeducational approaches for seriously emotionally disturbed children in the classroom. In P. Knoblock (Ed.), *Intervention approaches in education for emotionally disturbed children.* Syracuse: Syracuse University Press.

FENTON, K. S., YOSHIDA, R. K., MAXWELL, J. P., & KAUFMAN, M. J. (1979). Recognition of team goals: An essential step toward rational decision making. *Exceptional Children, 45,* 638–644.

FEWELL, R. R. (1983a). Assessing handicapped infants. In S. G. Garwood & R. R. Fewell (Eds.), *Educating handicapped infants.* Rockville, MD: Aspen.

FEWELL, R. R. (1983b). The team approach to infant education. In S. G. Garwood & R. R. Fewell (Eds.), *Educating handicapped infants.* Rockville, MD: Aspen.

FIELD, T., ROSEMAN, S., DE STEFANO, L. J., & KOEWLER III, J. (1982, October). The play of handicapped preschool children with handicapped and nonhandicapped peers in integrated and nonintegrated situations. *Topics in Early Childhood Special Education, 2*(3), 28–38.

FINNIE, H. R. (1975). *Handling the young cerebral palsied child at home.* New York: E. P. Dutton.

FLAVELL, J. (1977). *Cognitive development.* Englewood Cliffs, NJ: Prentice-Hall.

FOGELMAN, C. J. (Ed.). (1975). *American Association on Mental Deficiency Adaptive behavior scale manual* (Rev. ed.). Washington, DC: American Association on Mental Deficiency.

FOLIO, R., & FEWELL, R. (1982). *Peabody development motor scales.* Hingham, MA: Teaching Resources Corporation.

FORD. F. R. (1966). *Diseases of the nervous system: In infancy, childhood and adolescence* (5th ed.). Springfield, IL: Charles C. Thomas.

FORNESS, S. (1981). Concepts of learning and behavior disorders: Implications for research and practice. *Exceptional Children, 48,* 56–65.

FOULDS, R. A., & LUND, B. L. (Eds.). (1976). *1976 conference on systems and devices for the disabled.* Boston: Tufts University Biomedical Engineering Center.

FOUNTAIN VALLEY SCHOOL DISTRICT. (1980). *Non oral communication.* Fountain Valley, CA.

FOWLER, S. (1982). Transition from preschool to kindergarten for children with special needs. In K. E. Allen & E. M. Goetz (Eds.), *Early childhood education: Special problems, special solutions.* Rockville, MD: Aspen.

FOX, L. (1976). Sex differences in mathematical precocity: Bridging the gap. In D. Keating (Ed.), *Intellectual talent research and development.* Baltimore: Johns Hopkins University Press.

FRAIBERG, S. (1975). Intervention in infancy: A program for blind infants. In B. Z. Friedlander, G. M. Sterritt, & G. E. Kirk (Eds.), *Exceptional infant, Vol. 3: Assessment & intervention.* New York: Brunner/Mazel.

FRANKENBURG, W. K., & CAMP, B. (1975). *Pediatric screening tests.* Springfield, IL: Charles C. Thomas.

FRANKENBURG, W. K., DODDS, J., & FANDAL, A. (1975).

Denver developmental screening test. Boulder, CO: University of Colorado Medical Center; Ladoca.

FREDERICKS, H. D., et al. (1980). *The teaching research curriculum for moderately and severely handicapped.* Springfield, IL: Charles C. Thomas.

FREEDMAN, R., WARNER, D. D., & COOK, P. (1973). *Exemplary programs for the handicapped. Volume III: Early childhood education.* Cambridge, MA: Abt.

FRENCH, J. L. (1975). The highly intelligent dropout. In W. B. Barbe & J. R. Renzulli (Eds.), *Psychology and education of the gifted* (2nd ed.). New York: Irvington.

FRENCH, J. N., & COZZI, P. (1981). Reading and the learning disabled student. *Education Unlimited, 3,* 6–8.

FRIEDMAN, J., & PASNAK, R. (1973). Attainment of classification and seriation concepts by blind and sighted subjects. *Education of the Visually Handicapped, 5,* 55–62.

FROSTIG, M., & MASLOW, P. (1973). *Learning problems in the classroom,* New York: Grune & Stratton.

FULLWOOD, N. N. (Ed.). (1977). *Technology and the handicapped: Telecommunications services in the rehabilitation of the blind.* Raleigh, NC: North Carolina State University School of Education.

FUREY, E. M. (1982). The effects of alcohol on the fetus. *Exceptional Children, 49*(1), 30–32.

FURTH, H. G. (1970). *Piaget for teachers.* Englewood Cliffs, NJ: Prentice-Hall.

FURTH, H. G. (1973). *Deafness and learning: A psychosocial approach.* Belmont, CA: Wadsworth.

GAGE, M. A., FREDERICKS, H. D., JOHNSON-DORN, N., & LINDLEY-SOUTHARD, B. (1982). Inservice training for staffs of group homes and work activity centers serving developmentally disabled adults. *Journal of the Association for the Severely Handicapped, 7*(4), 60–70.

GALLAGHER, J. (1979). Rights of the next generation of children. *Exceptional Children, 46*(2), 98–105.

GALLAGHER, J. J. (1975). *Teaching the gifted child* (2nd ed.). Boston: Allyn and Bacon.

GALTON, F. (1962). *Hereditary Genius.* London: Spottiswoode, Ballantyne & Company, Fontana Library.

GALTON, L. (1978). New devices to help the blind and near-blind. *Readings in Visually Handicapped Education.* Guilford, CT: Special Learning Corporation.

GANSCHOW, L., WHEELER, D., & KRETSCHMER, R. (1982). Contextual effects on reading of individual words by reading disabled adolescents with specific learning disabilities. *Learning Disabilities Quarterly, 5,* 145–151.

GARDNER, D. C. (1973). Career education in our town? *College Student Journal, 7*(3), 73–77.

GARDNER, H. (1982). *Art, mind, and brain.* New York: Basic Books.

GARFUNKEL, F. (1976). Early childhood special education for children with social and emotional disturbances. In H. H. Spicker, N. J. Anastasiow, & W. L. Hodges (Eds.), *Children with special needs: Early development and education.* Minneapolis, MN: Leadership Training Institute/Special Education.

GARRET, J. F. (Ed.). (1982). *Information systems on technical aids for the disabled: A transitional view.* New York: World Rehabilitation Fund, Inc.

GARRETSON, M. D. (1963). The need for multiple communication skills in the education process of the deaf. *Rocky Mountain Leader, 62,* 1–8.

GARWOOD, S. G. (1982a). (Mis)use of developmental scales in program evaluation. *Topics in Early Childhood Special Education,* 1(4), 61–69.

GARWOOD, S. G. (1982b). Piaget and play: Translating theory into practice. *Topics in Early Childhood Special Education,* 2(3), 1–13.

GARWOOD, S. G. ET AL. (1979). *Educating young handicapped children: A developmental approach.* Germantown, MD: Aspen.

GARWOOD, S. G., & FEWELL, R. R. (1983). *Educating handicapped infants: Issues in development and intervention.* Rockville, MD: Aspen.

GAST, D. L. (1983, May 29). *Time delay: Laboratory to classroom application.* Paper presented at the ninth conference of The Association for Behavior Analysis, Milwaukee, WS.

GASTAUT, H. (1970). Clinical and electroencephalographical classification of epileptic seizures. *Epilepsia, 11,* 102–113.

GAYLORD-ROSS, R. (1980). A decision model for the treatment of aberrant behavior in applied settings. In W. Sailor, B. Wilcox, & L. Brown (Eds.), *Methods of instruction for severely handicapped students.* Baltimore: Paul H. Brookes.

GEARHEART, B. R. (1974). *Organization and administration of educational programs for exceptional programs.* Springfield, IL: Charles C. Thomas.

GEARHEART, B. R. (1980). *Special education for the '80s.* St. Louis: C. V. Mosby.

GELOF, M. (1963). Comparisons of systems of classification relating degrees of retardation to measured intelligence. *American Journal of Mental Deficiency, 68,* 297–317.

GENSHAFT, J. L., DARE, N. L., & O'MALLEY, P. (1980). Assessing the visually impaired child: A school psychology view. *Journal of Visual Impairment and Blindness,* 74(9), 344–349.

GEORGE, W. C., & SOLANO, C. H. (1976). Identifying mathematical talent on a statewide basis. In D. P. Keating (Ed.), *Intellectual talent research and development* (pp. 55–89). Baltimore: Johns Hopkins University Press.

GERMAN, M., & MAISTO, A. (1982). The relationship of a perceived family support system to the institutional placement of mentally retarded children. *Education & Training of the Mentally Retarded, 17,* 17–23.

GESELL, A. (1928). *Infancy and human growth.* New York: Macmillan.

GESELL, A. (1938). *The psychology of early growth.* New York: Macmillan.

GESELL, A. (1940). *The first five years of life: A guide to the study of the preschool child.* New York: Harper.

GESELL, A., & AMATRUDA, C. S. (1947). *Developmental diagnosis.* New York: Harper & Row.

GESELL, A., & ILG, F. (1943). *Infant and child in the culture of today.* New York: Harper & Row.

GETMAN, G. (1962). *How to develop your child's intelligence.* Laverne, MN: G. N. Getman, O. D.

GETZELS, J. W. (Ed.). (1977). General discussion immediately after the Terman Memorial symposium. In J. C.

Stanley, W. C. George, & C. H. Solano (Eds.), *The gifted and the creative: A fifty-year perspective* (pp. 225–269). Baltimore: Johns Hopkins University Press.

GETZELS, J. W. (1979). From art student to fine artist: Potential, problem finding, and performance. In A. H. Passow (Ed.), *The gifted and the talented: Their education and development.* The seventy-eighth yearbook of the National Society for the Study of Education, Part 1 (pp. 372–387). Chicago: University of Chicago Press.

GIBSON, E. (1970). Learning to read. In H. Singer & R. RUDDELL (EDS.), *Theoretical models and processes of reading* (pp. 315–334). Newark, DE: IRA.

GILLIAM, J. (1979). Contributions and status rankings of educational planning committee participants. *Exceptional Children, 45,* 466–467.

GILLIAM, J. E., & COLEMAN, M. C. (1981). Who influences IEP committee decisions? *Exceptional Children, 47,* 642–644.

GILLUNG, T. B., & RUCKER, C. H. (1977). Labels and teacher expectations. *Exceptional Children, 43,* 464–465.

GIRAUD, F., AYMES, S., MATTEI, J. F., & MATTEI, M. G. (1976). Constitutional chromosomal breakage. *Human Genetics, 34,* 125–136.

GOLDBERG, M. J. (1983). Spinal muscular dystrophy. In J. Umbriet (Ed.), *Physical disabilities and health impairments: An introduction* (pp. 147–156). Columbus, OH: Charles E. Merrill.

GOLDHAMMER, K. A. (1972). A career curriculum. In K. Goldhammer & R. Taylor (Eds.), *Career education: Perspectives and promises.* Columbus, OH: Charles E. Merrill.

GOLDMAN, H. (1970). Psychological testing of blind children. *Research Bulletin,* American Foundation for the Blind, *21,* 77–90.

GOLDSTEIN, H., & SIEGLE, D. M. (1958). *The Illinois plan for special education of exceptional children: A curriculum guide for teachers of the educable mentally handicapped.* Danville, IL: Interstate Printers and Publishers.

GOLDSTEIN, S., STRICKLAND, B., TURNBULL, A. P., & CURRY, L. (1980). An observational analysis of IEP conference. *Exceptional Children, 46,* 278–286.

GOLDSTEIN, S., & TURNBULL, A. P. (1982). Strategies to increase parent participation in IEP conferences. *Exceptional Children, 48,* 360–361.

GOOD, C. V. (Ed.). (1959). *Dictionary of education* (2nd ed.). New York: McGraw-Hill.

GORDON, R. (1977). Special needs of multi-handicapped children under six and their families. One opinion. In E. Sontag (Ed.), *Educational programming for the severely and profoundly handicapped* (pp. 61–71). Reston, VA: Council for Exceptional Children, Division of Mental Retardation.

GOTTESMAN, I. I. (1963). Genetic aspects of intelligent behavior. In N. R. Ellis (Ed.), *Handbook of mental deficiency* (pp. 253–296). New York: McGraw-Hill.

GOTTESMAN, M. A. (1971). A comparative study of Piaget's developmental schema of sighted children with that of a group of blind children. *Child Development, 42,* 573–580.

GOTTESMAN, M. A. (1973). Conservation development in blind children. *Child Development, 44,* 824, 827.

GOTTESMAN, M. A. (1976). Stage development of blind children: A Piagetian view. *New Outlook for the Blind, 70,* 94–100.

GOULD, S. J. (1981). *The mismeasure of man.* New York: Norton.

GOWAN, J. C. (1977). Background and history of the gifted-child movement. In J. C. Stanley, W. C. George, & C. H. Solano (Eds.), *The gifted and the creative: A fifty-year perspective.* Baltimore, MD: Johns Hopkins University Press, 5–27.

GOWAN, A. G. (1957). *The war blind in American social structure.* New York: American Foundation for the Blind.

GRAHAM, M. D. (1965). Wanted: A readiness test for mobility training. *New Outlook for the Blind, 59,* 157–162.

GRANOWSKY, A., MIDDLETON, F., & MUMFORD, J. (1977). *A guide for better reading.* Asheville, NC: Tarmac.

GRAY, R. (1981). Services for the LD adult: A working paper. *Learning Disability Quarterly, 4,* 426–434.

GREENE, M. (1983). A tune beyond us, yet ourselves. *Design, 85*(2), 34–36.

GRIMES. L. (1981). Learned helplessness and attribution theory: Redefining children's learning problems. *Learning Disabilities Quarterly, 4,* 91–100.

GROSENICK, J. (1971, October). Integration of exceptional children into regular classes: Research and procedure. *Focus on Exceptional Children, 3*(5), 1–8.

GROSSMAN, F. K. (1972). *Brothers and sisters of retarded children.* Syracuse: Syracuse University Press.

GROSSMAN, H. (1973). *Manual on terminology and classification in mental retardation* (Rev. ed.). Washington, DC: American Association on Mental Deficiency.

GROSSMAN, H. (1977). *Manual on terminology and classification in mental retardation* (Rev. ed.). Washington, DC: American Association on Mental Deficiency.

GROSSMAN, H. (1983). *Manual on terminology and classification in mental retardation* (Rev. ed.). Washington, DC: American Association on Mental Deficiency.

GROSSMAN, H. J. (Ed.). (1977). *Manual on terminology and classification in mental retardation.* Washington, DC: American Association on Mental Deficiency.

GROSSMAN, R. P. (1978). LD and the problem of scientific definitions. *Journal of Learning Disabilities, 11*(3), 120–123.

GUESS, D. (1980). Methods in communication instruction for severely handicapped persons. In W. Sailor, B. Wilcox, & L. Brown (Eds.), *Methods of instruction for severely handicapped students.* Baltimore: Paul H. Brookes.

GUESS, D., SAILOR, W., & BAER, D. M. (1976). *Functional speech and language training for the severely handicapped. Part I: Persons and things.* Lawrence, KS: H & H Enterprises.

GUESS, D., SAILOR, W., & BAER, D. M. (1978). Children with limited language. In R. L. Schiefelbusch (Ed.), *Language intervention strategies.* Baltimore: University Park Press.

GUILFORD, J. P. (1956). The structure of the intellect. *Psychological Bulletin, 53,* 267–293.

GUILFORD, J. P. (1967). *The nature of human intelligence.* New York: McGraw-Hill.

GURALNICK, M. J. (Ed.). (1978). *Early intervention and the integration of handicapped and nonhandicapped children.* Baltimore: University Park Press.

GUSELLA, J. F., WEXLER, N. S., CONNELLY, P. M., NAYLOR, S. L., ANDERSON, M. A., TANZI, R. E., WATKINS, P. C., OTTINA, K., WALLACE, M. R., SAKAGUCHI, A. Y., YOUNG, A. B., SHOULSON, I., BONILLA, E., & MARTIN, J. B. (1983, November). A polymorphic DNA marker genetically linked to Huntington's disease. *Nature, 306*(17).

GUTHRIE, J. (1973). Models of reading and reading disability. *Journal of Educational Psychology, 65,* 9–18.

GUTHRIE, J. (1974, July). *Identification and instruction of children with reading disability.* Second Annual Report to the Spencer Foundation. (ERIC Document 098 516)

GWYNNE, F. (1976). *A chocolate moose for dinner.* New York: Windmill Books.

HAIER, R. J., & DENHAM, S. A. (1976). A summary profile of the nonintellectual correlates of mathematical precocity in boys and girls. In D. P. Keating (Ed.), *Intellectual talent research and development* (pp. 225–241). Baltimore: Johns Hopkins University Press.

HAINES. D. J., & TORGESEN, J. K. (1978). The effects of incentives on rehearsal and short-term memory in children with reading problems. *Learning Disabilities Quarterly, 2,* 48–55.

HALL, R. V., CRISTLER, C., CRANSTON, S. S., & TUCKER, B. (1970). Teachers and parents as researchers using multiple baseline designs. *Journal of Applied Behavior Analysis, 3,* 247–255.

HALLAHAN, D. P., GAJAR, A., COHEN, S., & TARVER, S. (1978). Selective attention and focus of control in learning disabled and normal children. *Journal of Learning Disabilities, 11*(4), 47–52.

HALLAHAN, D. P., & KAUFFMAN, J. M. (1977). Labels, categories, behaviors: ED, LD, EMR reconsidered. *The Journal of Special Education, 11,* 139–149.

HALLAHAN, D. P., & KAUFFMAN, J. M. (1978). *Exceptional Children: Introduction to special education,* Englewood Cliffs, NJ: Prentice-Hall.

HAMMILL, D. D., & LARSEN, S. C. (1978). The effectiveness of psycholinguistic training: A reaffirmation of position. *Exceptional Children, 44,* 402–414.

HAMMILL, D. D., LEIGH, J. E., McNUTT, G., & LARSEN, S. C. (1981). A new definition of learning disabilities. *Learning Disabilities Quarterly, 4,* 336–342.

HAMMILL, P., CRANDELL, J. M., & COLARUSSO, R. (1970). The Slossen intelligence test adapted for visually limited children. *Exceptional Children, 36,* 535–536.

HAMRE-NIETUPSKI, S., & NIETUPSKI, J. (1981). Integral involvement of severely handicapped students within regular public schools. *Journal of the Association for the Severely Handicapped, 6*(2), 30–39.

HAMRE-NIETUPSKI, S., NIETUPSKI, J., BATES, P., & MAURER, S. (1982). Implementing a community-based educational model for moderately/severely handicapped students: Common problems and suggested solutions. *Journal of the Association for the Severely Handicapped, 7*(4), 38–43.

HANSON, J. W., STREISGUTH, A. P., & SMITH, D. W.

(1978). The effects of moderate alcohol consumption during pregnancy on fetal growth and morphogenesis. *Journal of Pediatrics, 92,* 457–460.

HANSON, M. J. (1977). *Teaching your Down's syndrome infant.* Eugene, OR: University of Oregon.

HARBER, J. R. (1980). Auditory perception and reading: Another look. *Learning Disabilities Quarterly, 3,* 19–29.

HARING, N. G. (1970). The new curriculum design in special education. *Educational Technology, 10,* 24–31.

HARING, N. G., & PHILLIPS, E. L. (1962). *Educating emotionally disturbed children.* New York: McGraw-Hill.

HARING, N. G., & SCHIEFELBUSCH, R. L. (Eds.). (1976). *Teaching special children.* New York: McGraw-Hill.

HARLEY, R. K. (1973). Children with visual disabilities. In L. M. Dunn (Ed.), *Exceptional children in the schools* (2nd ed.). New York: Holt, Rinehart and Winston.

HARLEY, R. K., & LAWRENCE, G. A. (1977). *Visual impairment in the schools.* Springfield, IL: Charles C. Thomas.

HARLOW, H. F. (1974). Syndromes resulting from maternal deprivation. In J. H. Cullen (Ed.), *Experimental behavior: A basis for the study of mental disturbance.* New York: John Wiley & Sons.

HART, V. (1974). *Beginning with the handicapped.* Springfield, IL: Charles C. Thomas.

HART. V. (1977). The use of many disciplines with the severely and profoundly handicapped. In E. Sontag (Ed.), *Educational programming for the severely and profoundly handicapped.* Reston, VA: Council for Exceptional Children, Division on Mental Retardation.

HARVEY, B. (1982a). Asthma. In E. E. Bleck & D. A. Nagel (Eds.), *Physically handicapped children: A medical atlas for teachers* (pp. 31–42). New York: Grune & Stratton.

HARVEY, B. (1982b). Cystic fibrosis. In E. E. Bleck & D. A. Nagel (Eds.), *Physically handicapped children: A medical atlas for teachers* (pp. 255–264). New York: Grune & Stratton.

HARVEY, J., JUDGE, C., & WIENER, S. (1977). Familial X-linked mental retardation with an X chromosome abnormality. *Journal of Medical Genetics, 14,* 46–50.

HASSELBRING, T. S., & HAMLETT, C. L. (1984). Planning and managing instruction: Computer-based decision making. *Teaching Exceptional Children, 16,* 248–252.

HATLAN, P. H. (1980). *Important concerns in the education of visually impaired children: MAVIS sourcebook 5.* Boulder, CO: Social Science Education Consortium.

HAUCK, B. B., & FREEHILL, M. F. (1972). *The gifted: Case studies.* Dubuque, IA: William C. Brown.

HAVINGHURST, R. J. (1972). *Developmental tasks and education* (3rd ed.). New York: Longman.

Hawaii early learning profile. (1979). Palo Alto, CA: VORT Corporation.

HAYDEN, A. H. (1978). Early childhood education. In K. E. Allen et al. (Eds.), *Early intervention — A team approach.* Baltimore: University Park Press.

HAYDEN, A. H., & DMITRIEV, V. (1975). The multidisciplinary preschool programs for Down's syndrome children at the University of Washington model preschool center. In B. Z. Friedlander, G. M. Sterritt, & G. E. Kirk (Eds.), *Exceptional infant. Vol. 3: Assessment & Intervention.* New York: Brunner/Mazel.

HAYDEN, A. H., & EDGAR, E. B. (1977). Identification, screening, and assessment. In J. B. Jordan et al. (Eds.), *Early childhood education for exceptional children.* Reston, VA: Council for Exceptional Children.

HAYDEN, A. H., & HARING, N. D. (1976). Early intervention for high risk infants and young children. In T. D. Tjossem (Ed.), *Intervention strategies for high risk infants and young children.* Baltimore: University Park Press.

HAYDEN, A. H., & McGINNESS, G. D. (1977). *Educational programming for the severely and profoundly handicapped.* Reston, VA: Council for Exceptional Children.

HAYDEN, A. H., MORRIS, K., & BAILEY, D. (1977). The effectiveness of early education (Final report to the Bureau of Education for the Handicapped, U. S. O. E.). Seattle, WA: University of Washington, Model Preschool Center for Handicapped Children. Cited in K. E. Allen et al. (Eds.). (1978). *Early intervention — A team approach.* Baltimore: University Park Press.

HAYES, S. P. (1941). *Contributions to a psychology of blindness.* New York: American Foundation for the Blind.

HAYNES, U. B. (1976). The national collaborative infant project. In T. Tjossem (Ed.), *Intervention strategies for high risk infants and young children.* Baltimore: University Park Press.

HAYWOOD, H. C. (1979). What happened to mild and moderate mental retardation? *American Journal of Mental Deficiency, 83,* 427–431.

HAZEL, J. S., SCHUMAKER, J. B., SHERMAN. J. A., & SHELDON-WILDGEN, J. (1981). The development and evaluation of a group training program for teaching social and problem-solving skills to court-adjudicated youths. In D. Upper & S. M. Ross (Eds.), *Behavioral group therapy.* Champaign, IL: Research Press.

HEBB, D. O. (1942). The effect of early and late brain injury upon the test scores, and the nature of adult intelligence. *Proceedings of the American Philosophical Society, 85,* 275–292.

HEBER, R. F. (1959). *A manual on terminology and classification in mental retardation.* Washington, DC: American Association on Mental Deficiency.

HEBER, R. F. (1961). *A manual on terminology and classification in mental retardation.* Washington, DC: American Association on Mental Deficiency.

HEBER, R. F. (1970). *Epidemiology of mental retardation.* Springfield, IL: Charles C. Thomas.

HELTON, G. B., WORKMAN, E. A., & MATUSZEK, P. A. (1982). *Psychoeducational assessment — Integrating concepts and techniques.* New York: Grune & Stratton.

HERBST, D. S., & MILLER, J. R. (1980). Nonspecific X-linked mental retardation II: The frequency in British Columbia. *American Journal of Medical Genetics, 7,* 461–469.

HERON, T., & SKINNER, M. (1981). Criteria for defining the regular classroom as the least restrictive environment for LD students. *Learning Disabilities Quarterly, 4,* 115–119.

HERON, T. E., & AXELROD, S. (1976). Effectiveness of

feedback to mothers concerning their children's word recognition performance. *Reading Improvement, 13,* 74–81.

HERSHEY, M. (1977). Telephone instruction: An alternative educational delivery system for teacher in-service. *The Gifted Child Quarterly, 21,* 213–217.

HESSLER, G. L., & KITCHEN, D. W. (1980). Language characteristics of a pervasive sample of early elementary learning disabled students. *Learning Disabilities Quarterly, 3,* 36–41.

HEWARD, W. L., DARDIG, J. C., & ROSSETT, A. (1979). *Working with parents of handicapped children.* Columbus, OH: Charles E. Merrill.

HEWETT, F. M. (1968). *The emotionally disturbed child in the classroom.* Boston: Allyn and Bacon.

HICKEY, K. A., IMBER, S. C., & RUGGIERO, E. A. (1979). Modifying reading behavior of elementary special needs children: A cooperative resource-parent program. *Journal of Learning Disabilities, 12,* 444–449.

HICKS, D. E. (1975). Children with hearing impairments. In J. J. Gallagher (Ed.), *The application of child development research to exceptional children.* Reston, VA: Council for Exceptional Children.

HIGGINS, L. C. (1973). *Classification in congenitally blind children.* New York: American Foundation for the Blind.

HILDRETH, G. H. (1966). *Introduction to the gifted.* New York: McGraw-Hill.

HOBBS, N. (1966). Helping the disturbed child: Psychological and ecological strategies. *American Psychologist, 21,* 1105–1115.

HOBBS, N. (1974). Nicholas Hobbs. In J. M. Kauffman and C. D. Lewis (Eds.), *Teaching children with behavior disorders: Personal Perspectives.* Columbus, OH: Charles E. Merrill.

HOBBS, N. (1975). *The future of children.* San Francisco: Jossey-Bass.

HOBBS, N. (1978). Classification options: A conversation with N. Hobbs on exceptional child education. *Exceptional Children, 44,* 494–497.

HOBSON, J. R. (1963). High school performance of underage pupils initially admitted to kindergarten on the basis of physical and psychological examination. *Educational and Psychological Measurement, 23,* 159–170.

HOFF, M. K., FENTON, K. S., YOSHIDA, R. K., & KAUFMAN, M. J. (1978). Notice and consent: The school's responsibility to inform parents. *Journal of School Psychology, 16,* 265–273.

HOHMAN, I. R., & FREEDHEIM, D. K. (1958). Further studies on intelligence levels in cerebral palsied children. *American Journal of Physical Medicine, 37,* 9097.

HOLCOMB, R. K., & CORBETT, E. E. (1975). Mainstream: The Delaware Approach. Newark, DE: Newark School District (Sterk School).

HOLLANDER, S. K. (1977). A multidisciplinary approach to the etiology and management of learning disability. In P. D. Pearson & J. Hansen (Eds.), *Reading: Theory, research and practice,* 26th Yearbook of National Reading Conference. Clemson, SC: NRC 150–157.

HOLLINGWORTH, L. (1942). *Children above 180 IQ.* New York: Harcourt, Brace & World.

HOLLIS, J. H., & MEYERS, E. (Eds.). (1982). *Life-threatening behavior: Analysis and Intervention.* Washington, DC: American Association on Mental Deficiency.

HOLM, V. A., & KUNZE, L. H. (1969). Effect of chronic otitis media on language and speech development. *Pediatrics, 43,* 833.

HOPKINS, T. W., BICE, H. V., & COLTON, K. C. (1954). *Evaluation and education of the cerebral palsied child.* Arlington, VA: International Council for Exceptional Children.

HORNER, M. S. (1970). Femininity and successful achievement: Basic inconsistency. In J. M. Bardwick et al. (Eds.), *Feminine personality and conflict* (pp. 45–74). Monterey, CA: Brooks/Cole.

HORNER, M. S. (1972). Toward an understanding of achievement-related conflicts in women. *Journal of Social Issues, 18,* 157–175.

HOROWITZ, E. C. (1981). Popularity, decentering ability, and role-taking skills in learning disabled and normal children. *Learning Disabilities Quarterly, 4,* 23–38.

HOROWITZ, R. (1970, Fall). Teaching math to students with learning disabilities. *Academic Therapy, 6*(1), 17–35.

HORTON, K. B. (1976). Early intervention for hearing impaired infants and young children. In T. D. Tjossem (Ed.), *Intervention strategies for high risk infants and young children.* Baltimore: University Park Press.

HOWLEY, A., HOWLEY, C., & PENDARVIS, E. (1985). *Teaching gifted children.* Boston: Little, Brown.

HOYT, K. B. (1975). *An introduction to career education: A policy paper of the U.S. Office of Education.* Washington, DC: Office of Education.

HOYT, K. B. (1975, June). *Career education and the business-labor industry community.* Paper presented at the National Apprenticeship and Training Directors Conference, Washington, DC.

HOYT, K. B. (1980, June). Career education for persons with visual handicaps. Paper presented at the Helen Keller Centennial Conference, Boston.

HOYT, K. B., & HEBELER, J. R. (1974). *Career education for gifted and talented students.* Salt Lake City, UT: Olympus.

HUBERTY, C. J., & SWAN, W. W. (1977). Evaluation of programs. In J. Jordan, A. Hayden, M. Karnes, & M. Woods (Eds.), *Early childhood education for exceptional children.* Reston, VA: Council for Exceptional Children.

Human communication and its disorders: An overview (1969). Report of the National Advisory Neurological Diseases and Stroke Council, National Institute of Health, Public Health Services. Bethesda, MD: Department of Health, Education, and Welfare.

HUMPHREYS, R. P. (1979). The federal-state vocational rehabilitation program. *Amicus, 4,* 235–236.

HUMPHRIES, T. W., & BAUMAN, E. (1980). Maternal child rearing attitudes associated with learning disabilities. *Journal of Learning Disabilities, 13,* 459–462.

HUNT, J. McV. (1961). *Intelligence and experience.* New York: Ronald Press.

HUNT, J. McV., PARASKEVOPOULOS, J., SCHICKEDANZ, D., & UZGIRIS, I. C. (1975). Variations in the mean ages of achieving object permanence under diverse conditions of rearing. In B. Z. Friedlander, G. M. Sterritt, & G. E. Kirk (Eds.), *Exceptional infant, Vol. 3: Assessment & intervention.* New York: Brunner/Mazel.

IDOL-MAESTAS, L. (1981). Behavior patterns in families of boys with learning and behavior problems. *Journal of Learning Disabilities, 14,* 347–349.

IDOL-MAESTAS, L. (1983). *Special educator's consultation handbook.* Rockville, MD: Aspen.

ILLINGWORTH, R. S. (1972). *The development of the infant and young child.* Baltimore: Williams & Wilkins.

INGRAM, C. P. (1935). *Education of the slow-learning child.* Yonkers, NY: World Book.

INHELDER, B. (1968) *The diagnosis of reasoning in the mentally retarded.* New York: John Day.

ITARD, J. M. (1932). *The wild boy of Aveyron* (G. Humphrey & M. Humphrey, Trans.). New York: Appleton-Century-Crofts. (Originally published 1894)

JACOBS, J. C. (1971). Effectiveness of teacher and parent identification of gifted children as a function of school level. *Psychology in the Schools, 8,* 140–142.

JENKINS, J. R., & PANY, D. (1978). Standardized achievement tests: How useful for special education? *Exceptional Children, 44,* 448–453.

JENSEN, A. R., & FREDERICKSON, J. (1973). Free recall of categorized and uncategorized lists: A test of the Jensen hypothesis. *Journal of Educational Psychology, 3,* 304–314.

JOEL, G. (1975). *So your child has cerebral palsy.* Albuquerque, NM: University of New Mexico Press.

JOHNSON, D. (1972). *Reaching out* (pp. 267–269). Englewood Cliffs, NJ: Prentice-Hall.

JOHNSON, D., & MYKLEBUST, H. (1967). *Learning disabilities: Educational principles and practices.* New York: Grune & Stratton.

JOHNSON, D. J. (1975). Children with communication disorders. In J. J. Gallagher (Ed.), *The application of child development research to exceptional children.* Reston, VA: Council for Exceptional Children.

JOHNSON, N. M., JENS, K. G., & ATTERMEIER, S. A. (1979). *Carolina curriculum for handicapped infants.* Chapel Hill, NC: University of North Carolina, Frank Porter Graham Child Development Center.

JOHNSON, W. (1959). *The onset of stuttering.* Minneapolis: University of Minnesota Press.

JOHNSON, W., BROWN, S. F., CURTIS, J. F., EDNEY, C. W., & KEASTER, J. (1967). *Speech handicapped school children.* New York: Harper & Row.

JOHNSTON, R. B., & MAGRAB, P. R. (Eds.). (1976). *Developmental disorders: Assessment, treatment, education.* Baltimore: University Park Press.

JONES, J., & COLLINS, A. (1966). *Educational programs for visually handicapped children.* Washington, DC: U.S. Government Printing Office.

JONES. M. H. (1983). Cerebral Palsy. In J. Umbriet (Ed.), *Physical disabilities and health impairment: An introduction.* Columbus, OH: Charles E. Merrill.

JORDAN, J. B., HAYDEN. A. H., KARNES, M. B., & WOOD, M. M. (Eds.). (1977). *Early childhood education for exceptional children.* Reston, VA: Council for Exceptional Children.

JOSEPH P. KENNEDY JR. FOUNDATION. *Working with your child: For families of the developmentally disabled.* Washington, DC.

JUSTEN, J. E. (1976). Who are the severely handicapped?: A problem of definition. *American Association for the Education of the Severely/Profoundly Handicapped, 1*(5), 1–11.

KAHN, J. V. (1976). Utility of Uzgiris and Hunt Scales of Sensorimotor Development with severely and profoundly retarded children. *American Journal of Mental Deficiency, 80,* 663–665.

KAHN, J. V. (1978). Acceleration of object permanence with severely and profoundly retarded children. *AAESPH Review, 3,* 15–22.

KAHN, J. V. (1979). Applications of the Piagetian literature to severely and profoundly mentally retarded persons. *Mental Retardation, 17,* 273–280.

KAKALIK, J. S., BREWER, G. D., DOUGHERTY, L. A., FLEISCHAUER, P. D., & GENENSKY, S. M. (1973). *Services for handicapped youth.* (Report to the Department of Health, Education and Welfare, Washington, DC, Office of the Assistant Secretary for Planning and Evaluation). Santa Monica, CA: Rand Corporation.

KAMII, C. A. (1973). A sketch of the Piaget-derived preschool curriculum developed by the Ypsilanti Early Education Project. In B. Spodek (Ed.), *Early childhood education.* Englewood Cliffs, NJ: Prentice-Hall.

KAMINSKY, M., RUMEAU-ROUQUETTE, C., & SCHWARTZ, D. (1978). Correspondence. *New England Journal of Medicine, 298,* 55.

KANFER, F. H., & SASLOW, G. (1967). Behavioral analysis: An alternative to diagnostic classification. In T. Millon (Ed.), *Theories of Psychopathology.* Philadelphia: W. B. Saunders.

KANNER, L. (1964). *A history of the care and study of the mentally retarded.* Springfield, IL: Charles C. Thomas.

KARNES, M. (1977). *Learning language at home.* Reston, VA: Council for Exceptional Children.

KARNES, M. B., KOKOTOVIC, A. M., & SHWEDEL, A. M. (1982, December). Transporting a model program for young handicapped children: Issues, problems, and efficacy. *Journal of the Division for Early Childhood, 6,* 42–52.

KARNES, M. B., & ZEHRBACH, R. R. (1977a). Alternative models for delivering services to young handicapped children. In J. B. Jordan et al. (Eds.), *Early childhood education for exceptional children.* Reston, VA: Council for Exceptional Children.

KARNES, M. B., & ZEHRBACH, R. R. (1977b). Early education of the handicapped: Issues and alternatives. In B. Spodek & H. J. Walberg (Eds.), *Early childhood education: Issues and insights.* Berkeley, CA: McCutchan.

KATZ, S., BORTEN, J., BRASILE, D., MEISNER, M., & PARKER, C. (1980). The IEP process. *Pointer, 25,* 35–45.

KAUFFMAN. J. M. (1981). *Characteristics of children's behavior disorders* (2nd ed.). Columbus, OH: Charles E. Merrill.

KAUFFMAN, J. M., & KROUSE, J. (1981). The cult of educability: Searching for the substance of things hoped for; the evidence of things not seen. *Analysis and Intervention in Developmental Disabilities, 1*(1), 53–60.

KAUFFMAN, J. M., & PAYNE, J. S. (1975). *Mental retarda-*

tion: Introduction and personal perspectives. Columbus, OH: Charles E. Merrill.

KAUFFMAN, J. M., & SNELL, M. E. (1977). Managing the behavior of severely handicapped persons. In E. Sontag (Ed.), *Educational programming for the severely and profoundly handicapped.* Reston, VA: Council for Exceptional Children, Division on Mental Retardation.

KAUFMAN, A. S., & KAUFMAN, N. L. (1983). *The Kaufman assessment battery for children.* Circle Pines, MN: American Guidance Service.

KAVALE, K. A. (1980). Learning disability and cultural-economic disadvantage: The case for a relationship. *Learning Disabilities Quarterly, 3,* 97–112.

KAZDIN, A. E. (1979). Assessing the clinical or applied importance of behavior change through social validation. *Behavior Modification, 1,* 427–452.

KEATING, D. P. (1976). Creative potential of mathematically precocious boys. In D. P. Keating (Ed.), *Intellectual talent research and development* (pp. 262–272). Baltimore: Johns Hopkins University Press.

KEATS, S. (1965). *Cerebral palsy.* Springfield, IL: Charles C. Thomas.

KELLER, H. (1933) *Helen Keller in Scotland,* London: Methuen & Co., LTD.

KENOWITZ, L. A., GALLAHER, J., & EDGAR, E. B. (1977). Generic services for the severely handicapped and their families: What's available? In E. Sontag (Ed.), *Educational programming for the severely and profoundly handicapped.* Reston, VA: Council for Exceptional Children, Division on Mental Retardation.

KENT, L. A. (1961). A retraining program for the adult who stutters. *Journal of Speech and Hearing Disorders, 26,* 141–144.

THE KENTUCKY ASSOCIATION FOR RETARDED CHILDREN ET AL. V. KENTUCKY STATE BOARD OF EDUCATION ET AL., Civil Action No. 435 (E. D. KY, filed September 12, 1973).

KENTUCKY STANDARDS FOR PROGRAMS FOR VISUALLY IMPAIRED CHILDREN. (1980). Frankfort, KY: Kentucky State Department of Education, Bureau for Education of Exceptional Children.

KEOGH, B. (1970). Early identification of children with potential learning problems. *Journal of Special Education, 4*(3), 307–366.

KEPHART, N. (1971). *The slow learner in the classroom* (2nd ed.). Columbus, OH: Charles E. Merrill.

KERR, C. (1979). *Giving youth a better chance: Options for education, work.* Carnegie Council of Policy Studies in Higher Education. San Francisco: Jossey-Bass.

KERR, M. M., & NELSON, C. M. (1983). *Strategies for managing behavior problems in the classroom.* Columbus, OH: Charles E. Merrill.

KERSHMAN, S. (1982). The training needs of parents of deaf-blind-multihandicapped children. *Education of the Visually Handicapped, 13,* 98–108.

KESSALBRENNER V. ANONYMOUS, 33 N. Y. 2d 161, 305 N. E. 2d 903, 350 N. Y. S. 889 (1973).

KILLALEA ASSOCIATES. (1980). *State, regional, and national summaries of data from the 1978 civil rights survey of elementary and secondary schools.* Report prepared for the U.S. Office of Civil Rights. Alexandria, VA: Author.

KINDRED, M., COHEN, J., PENROD, D., & SHAFFER, T. (1975). *The mentally retarded citizen and the law.* New York: Free Press.

KIRK, E. C. (1981). *Vision pathology in education.* Springfield, IL: Charles C. Thomas.

KIRK, S. A. (1958). *Early education of the mentally retarded.* Urbana: University of Illinois Press.

KIRK, S. A., & ELKINS, J. (1975). Characteristics of children enrolled in the child service demonstration centers. *Journal of Learning Disabilities, 8,* 630–637.

KIRK, S. A., & GALLAGHER, J. J. (1979). *Educating exceptional children* (3rd ed.). Boston: Houghton Mifflin.

KIRK, S. A., & GALLAGHER, L. T. (1979). Children with visual impairments. In *Educating exceptional children* (3rd ed.). Boston: Houghton Mifflin.

KIRK, S. A., & JOHNSON, G. O. (1951). *Educating the retarded child.* Boston: Houghton Mifflin.

KLAUS, R. A., & GRAY, S. W. (1968). The early training project for disadvantaged children: A report after five years. *Monographs of the Society for Research in Child Development, 33* (4, Serial No. 120).

KLEIN, R. S., ALTMAN, S. D., DREIZEN, K., FRIEDMAN, R., & POWERS, L. (1981). Restructuring dysfunctional parental attitudes toward children's learning and behavior in school. *Journal of Learning Disabilities, 14,* 99–101.

KLIMENT, S. A. (1976). *Into the mainstream: A syllabus for a barrier-free environment.* Washington, DC: U.S. Government Printing Office. Superintendent of Documents, 3844.

KLINE, D. F. (1977). Child abuse and neglect: A primer for school personnel. Reston, VA: Council for Exceptional Children.

KNOBLOCK, P. (1973). Open education for emotionally disturbed children. *Exceptional Children, 39,* 358–365.

KNOBLOCK, H., & PASAMANICK, B. (Eds.). (1974). *Gesell and Amatruda's developmental diagnosis.* New York: Harper & Row.

KNOFF, H. M. (1983). Investigating disproportionate influence and status in multidisciplinary child study teams. *Exceptional Children, 49,* 367–369.

KOCH, F. P. (1958). A nursery school for children with cerebral palsy: Five year follow-up study of thirteen children. *Pediatrics, 22,* 329–335.

KOEGEL, R., & RINCOVER, A. (1977). Research on the difference between generalization and maintenance in extra-therapy responding. *Journal of Applied Behavior Analysis, 10,* 1–12.

KOEGEL, R. L, RINCOVER, A., & EGEL, A. L. (1982). *Educating and understanding autistic children.* San Diego, CA: College-Hill Press.

KOEHLER, J. (1982). Spinal muscular atrophy of childhood. In E. E. Bleck & D. A. Nagel (Eds.), *Physically handicapped children: A medical atlas for teachers* (pp. 477–481). New York: Grune & Stratton.

KOLSTOE, O. P. (1975). Secondary programs. In J. M. Kauffman & J. S. Payne (Eds.), *Mental retardation: Introduc-*

tion and personal perspectives. Columbus, OH: Charles E. Merrill.

KOMM, R. (1982). He's LD — I mean he's ADD! *Academic Therapy, 17,* 431–435.

KORNBLUM, H. (1982). A social worker's role with mothers of language disordered preschool children. *Journal of Learning Disabilities, 15,* 406–408.

KOTIN, L., & EAGER, N. (1977). *Due process in special education: A legal analysis.* Cambridge, MA: Research Institute for Educational Problems.

KOUGH, J., & DeHAAN, R. (1958). *Teachers' guidance handbook* (Vol. 1, Elementary Edition). Chicago, IL: Science Research Associates.

KRANZ, B. *Multidimensional screening device for the identification of gifted/talented children* (3rd ed.). Fairfax, VA: Fairfax County Public Schools.

KRIPPNER, S. (1967). *Characteristics of gifted and talented youth.* Paper presented at a workshop sponsored by Science Research Associates. Published by the U.S. Department of Health, Education, and Welfare, Office of Education. (ERIC Document, ED 015503)

KROTH, R. (1980). *Strategies for effective parent-teacher interaction.* Albuquerque, NM: University of New Mexico, Parent Involvement Center.

KROTH, R. L. (1975). *Communicating with parents of exceptional children.* Denver: Love.

KROTH, R. L. (1980). The mirror model of parental involvement. *Pointer, 25,* 18–22.

KROTH, R. L., & SIMPSON, R. L. (1977). *Parent conferences as a teaching strategy.* Denver: Love.

KÜBLER-ROSS, E. (1969). *On death and dying.* New York: Macmillan.

KULIK, C. C., & KULIK, J. A. (1982). Research synthesis on ability grouping. *Educational Leadership, 39*(8), 619–621.

KULIK, J. A., BANGERT, R. L., & WILLIAMS, G. W. (1983). Effects of computer-based teaching on secondary school students. *Journal of Educational Psychology, 75,* 19–26.

KURTZ, P. D., DEVANEY, B., STRAIN, P., & SANDLER, H. (1982). Effects of mass-media and group instruction on increasing parent awareness of early identification. *Journal of Special Education, 16,* 329–340.

KURZWEIL COMPUTER PRODUCTS. (1978, Summer). *The Kurzweil Report, 2,* 1–2.

KURZWEIL COMPUTER PRODUCTS. (1979, Spring). *The Kurzweil Report,* pp. 1–2.

LACKNER, J. (1968). A developmental study of language behavior in retarded children. *Neuropsychologia, 6,* 301–320.

LACROSSE, E. L. (1976). The contribution of the nursery school. In R. Koch & J. C. Dobson (Eds.), *The mentally retarded child and his family* (2nd ed.). New York: Brunner/ Mazel.

LAMBERT, N., WINDMILLER, M., COLE, L., & FIGUEROA, R. (1975). *Manual for American Association on Mental Deficiency Adaptive Behavior Scale Public School Version* (1974 revision). Washington, DC: American Association on Mental Deficiency.

LANCE, W. D. (1973). *Instructional media and the handi-*

capped. Stanford, CA: Stanford University. (ERIC Clearinghouse on Media and Technology).

LANCE, W. D. (1977). Technology and media for exceptional learners: Looking ahead. *Exceptional Children, 44,* 92–97.

LANDAU, E., EPSTEIN, S., & STONE, A. (1978). *The exceptional child through literature.* Englewood Cliffs, NJ: Prentice-Hall.

LANE, H. (1976). *The wild boy of Aveyron.* New York: Bantam Books.

LARRY P. v. RILES, Civil No. C-71-2270, 343 F. Supp. 1306 (N. D. Cal., 1972).

LARSON, C. (1982). Personal communication regarding the EBCE-MD/LD models, 1981. Cited in D. E. Brolin, *Vocational preparation of persons with handicaps.* Columbus, OH: Merrill.

LASKI, F. J. (1979). Vocational rehabilitation services for severely handicapped persons: Rights and reality. *Amicus, 4,* 237–245.

LASKY, E., & KLOPP, K. (1982). Parent-child interactions in normal and language disordered children. *Journal of Speech and Hearing Disorders, 47,* 7–18.

LAU v. NICHOLS, 94 S. Ct. 786 (1974), dicta on appropriateness of education.

LAWRENCE HALL OF SCIENCE. (1978). *SAUI Update: Science activities for the visually handicapped.* Berkeley, CA: Author.

LAYCOCK, F. (1979). *Gifted children.* Glenview, IL: Scott, Foresman.

LAZAR, I., & DARLINGTON, R. (1979, September). *Summary report, lasting effects after preschool.* DHEW Publication No. (OHDS) 79-30179. Washington, DC: U.S. Government Printing Office.

LEARY, P. A., & TSENG, M. S. (1974). The vocational rehabilitation process explained. *Journal of Rehabilitation, 40,* 9–34.

LEFKOWITZ, M. M., ERON, L. D., WALDER, L. O., & HUESMANN, L. R. (1977). *Growing up to be violent.* Elmsford, NY: Pergamon Press.

LEISURE INFORMATION SERVICE. (1976). *A system model for developing a leisure education program for handicapped children and youth (K-12).* Washington: Hawkins and Associates.

LeMAY, D. W., GRIFFIN, P. M., & SANFORD, A. R. (1977). *Learning accomplishment profile: Diagnostic edition* (Rev. ed.). Chapel Hill, NC: Chapel Hill Training and Outreach Project.

LENNEBERG, E. H. (1967). *Biological foundations of language.* New York: John Wiley & Sons.

LERNER, J., MARDELL-CZUDNOWKSI, C., & GOLDENBERG, D. (1981). *Special education for the early childhood years.* Englewood Cliffs, NJ: Prentice-Hall.

LERNER, J. W. (1981). *Learning disabilities: Theories, diagnosis, and teaching strategies* (3rd ed.). Boston: Houghton Mifflin.

LESSARD v. SCHMIDT. Civil No. 71-C-602 (E. D. Wisc. 1972).

LEWIS, M., & ROSENBLUM, L. A. (Eds.). (1978). *The development of affect.* New York: Plenum Press.

LEWIS, N. (1976). Otitis media and linguistic incompetence. *Archives of Otolaryngology, 102,* 387–390.

LEWIS, R.B. & DOORLAG, D. H. (1983). *Teaching special students in the mainstream.* Columbus, OH: Charles E. Merrill.

LEWIS, R. B., & KASS, C. E. (1982). Labelling and recall in LD students. *Journal of Learning Disabilities, 15,* 238–241.

LEWIS, W. W. (1965). Continuity and intervention in emotional disturbance: A review. *Exceptional Children, 31,* 465–474.

LILES-WHITEHURST, C. (1982, August). *Implementation of SBER 6A-6.3018 — special programs for students with specific learning disabilities.* Technical Assistance Paper #3. Tallahassee, FL: Department of Education.

LILLIE, D. (1981). Educational and psychological strategies for working with parents. In J. L. Paul (Ed.), *Understanding and working with parents of children with special needs* (pp. 89–118). New York: Holt, Rinehart and Winston.

LILLIE, D. C., & EDWARDS, J. D. (1983). *UNISTAR II: LD and EMH computer assisted IEP program.* Burlington, NC: Southern Micro Systems for Educators.

LILLIE, D. L., & TROHANIS, P. L. (Eds.). (1976). *Teaching parents to teach.* New York: Walker.

LILLY, M. S., & GIVENS-OGLE, L. B. (1981). Teacher consultation: Present, past, and future. *Behavioral Disorders, 6,* 73–77.

LILLY, S. M. (1970). Special education: A teapot in a tempest. *Exceptional Children, 37,* 43–49.

LINDER, T. W. (1983). *Early childhood special education.* Baltimore: Paul H. Brookes.

LINDSAY, B. (1977). Leadership giftedness: Developing a profile. *Journal for the Education of the Gifted, 11*(1), 63–69.

LIVINGSTON, J. S. (1958). Evaluation of enlarged test form used with partially seeing. *Sight Saving Review, 28,* 37–39.

LOCKMAN, J. J. (1983). Infant perception and cognition. In S. G. Garwood & R. R. Fewell (Eds.), *Educating handicapped infants.* Rockville, MD: Aspen.

LOMBARDINO, L., & MANGAN, N. (1983). Parents as language trainers: Language programming with developmentally delayed children. *Exceptional Children, 49,* 358–361.

LORENZ, K. (1971). *Studies in animal and human behavior* (Vol. 2). Cambridge, MA: Harvard University Press.

LOSEN, S. M., & DIAMENT, B. (1978). *Parent conferences in the schools.* Boston: Allyn and Bacon.

LOVAAS, O. I., SCHREIBMAN, L., KOEGEL, R., & REHM, R. (1971). Selective responding by autistic children to multiple sensory input. *Journal of Abnormal Psychology, 77,* 211–222.

LOVITT, T. (1975). Applied behavior analysis and learning disabilities. Part II: Research. *Journal of Learning Disabilities, 8,* 514–517.

LOVITT, T., & FANTASIA, K. (1980). Two approaches to reading program evaluation: A standardized test and direct assessment. *Learning Disabilities Quarterly, 3,* 77–87.

LOWENFELD, B. (1971). *Our blind children, growing and learning with them.* Springfield, IL: Charles C. Thomas.

LOWENFELD, B. (1973). History of the education of visually handicapped children. *The visually handicapped child in school.* New York: John Day.

LOWENFELD, B. (1975). *The changing status of the blind: From separation to integration.* Springfield, IL: Charles C. Thomas.

LOWENFELD, B., ABEL, G., & HATLEN, P. (1969). *Blind children learn to read.* Springfield, IL: Charles C. Thomas.

LOWREY, G. H. (1973). *Growth and development of children.* Chicago: Year Book Medical Publishers.

LUCHOU, J. P., & SHEPARD, M. (1981). Effects of multisensory training in perceptual learning. *Learning Disabilities Quarterly, 4,* 38–43.

LUCITO, L. (1964). Independence-conformity behavior as a function of intellect: Bright and dull children. *Exceptional Children, 31*(1), 5–13.

LUSTHAUS, C. S., LUSTHAUS, E. W., & GIBBS, H. (1981). Parents' role in the decision process. *Exceptional Children, 48,* 256–257.

LYNDON, W. T., & McGRAW, M. L. (1973). *Concept development for visually handicapped children.* New York: American Foundation for the Blind.

LYON, S., & LYON, G. (1980). Team functioning and staff development: A role release approach to providing integrated educational services to severely handicapped students. *Journal of the Association for the Severely Handicapped, 5,* 250–253.

MACE, R., & IASLETT, B. (1977). *An illustrated handbook of the handicapped section of the North Carolina state building code.* Raleigh, NC: The North Carolina State Building Code Council and the North Carolina Department of Insurance.

MacKEITH, R. (1973). The feelings and behavior of parents of handicapped children. *Developmental Medicine and Child Neurology, 15,* 524–527.

MacMILLAN, D. L. (1982). *Mental retardation in school and society* (2nd ed.). Boston: Little, Brown.

MacMILLAN, D.L., & FORNESS, S. R. (1973). Behavior modification: Savior or servant? In R. K. Eyman, P. E. Meyer, & G. Tarian (Eds.), *Sociobehavior studies in mental retardation.* Washington, DC: American Association on Mental Deficiency.

MAGEE, P. A., & NEWCOMER, P. L. (1978). The relationship between oral language skills and academic achievement of LD children. *Learning Disabilities Quarterly, 1,* 63–67.

MAGER, R. F. (1962). *Preparing instructional objectives.* Belmont, CA: Fearon.

MAHEADY, L., & MAITLAND, G. E. (1982). Assessing social perception abilities in learning disabled students. *Learning Disabilities Quarterly, 5,* 363–370.

MAKER, C. J. (1975). *Training teachers for the gifted and talented: A comparison of models.* Reston, VA: Council for Exceptional Children.

MAKER, C. J. (1977). *Providing programs for the gifted handicapped.* Reston, VA: Council for Exceptional Children.

MAKER, C. J. (1982). *Teaching models in education of the gifted.* Rockville, MD: Aspen.

MAKER, C. J., MORRIS, E., & JAMES, J. (1981). The Eugene Field project: A program for potentially gifted young children. In *Balancing the scale for the disadvantaged gifted*. Ventura, CA: Ventura County Superintendent of Schools Office.

MALONEY, M., & WARD, M. P. (1979). *Mental retardation and modern society*. New York: Oxford University Press.

March of Dimes Genetic Counseling. (1984). March of Dimes Birth Defects Foundation.

MARGALIT, M. (1982). LD children and their families: Strategies of extension and adaptation of family therapy. *Journal of Learning Disabilities, 15*, 594–595.

MARION, R. C. (1980). Communicating with parents of culturally diverse exceptional children. *Exceptional Children, 46*, 616–625.

MARK, S. (1983). To succeed or not to succeed: A critical review of learned helplessness. *Contemporary Educational Psychology, 8*, 1–19.

MARLAND, S. (1972). *Education of the gifted and talented*. Report to the Congress of the United States by the US Commissioner of Education. Washington, DC: United States Government Printing Office.

MARSH, G. E., GEARHEART, C. K., & GEARHEART, R. R. (1978). *The learning disabled adolescent: Program alternatives in the secondary school*. St. Louis: C. V. Mosby.

MARTIN, F. N. (1975). *Introduction to audiology*. Englewood Cliffs, NJ: Prentice-Hall.

MARTIN, G., & PEAR, J. (1983). *Behavior modification: What it is and how to do it*. Englewood Cliffs, NJ: Prentice-Hall.

MARTINSON, R. A. (1974). *The identification of the gifted and talented*. Ventura: CA: Office of the Ventura County Superintendent of Schools.

MARYLAND ASSOCIATION FOR RETARDED CHILDREN V. STATE OF MARYLAND, Equity No. 100-182-77676 (Cir. Ct., Baltimore County, May 31, 1974). (1980). In R. L. Burgdorf, Jr. (Ed.), *The legal rights of handicapped persons*. Baltimore: Paul H. Brookes, 182–187.

MARYLAND ASSOCIATION FOR RETARDED CHILDREN V. STATE OF MARYLAND, Equity No. 100-182-77676. (Cir. Ct., Baltimore, MD, 1974).

MAUNDER, J. (1977, August 28). Using one's gifts. *The Floridian*. St. Petersburg, FL: The Times Publishing Company, 6–11.

MAURICE, P., & TRUDEL, G. (1982). Self-injurious behavior prevalence and relationships to environmental events. In J. H. Hollis & E. Meyers (Eds.), *Life threatening behavior: Analysis and intervention*. Washington, DC: American Association on Mental Deficiency.

McAFEE, J. K., & VERGASON, G. (1979). Parent involvement in the process of special education. *Focus on Exceptional Children, 11*, 1–10.

McCARNEY, S. B., LEIGH, J. E., & CORNBLEET, J. A. (1983). *Behavior evaluation scale*. Columbia, MO: Educational Services.

McCARTHY, J. McR. (1975). Children with learning disabilities. In J. J. Gallagher (Ed.), *The application of child development research to exceptional children*. Reston, VA: Council for Exceptional Children.

McCay, V., GRIEVE, B., & SHAVER, K. (1980). Handicapping conditions associated with the congenital rubella syndrome. *American Annals of the Deaf, 125*(8), 993–997.

McCONNELL, F. (1973). Children with hearing disabilities. In L. M. Dunn (Ed.), *Exceptional children in the schools: Special education in transition* (2nd ed.). New York: Holt, Rinehart and Winston.

McCORMICK, D., BALLA, D. A., & ZIGLER, E. (1975). Resident care practices in institutions for retarded persons. *American Journal of Mental Deficiency, 80*, I, 14, 1–17.

McCORMICK, L., & GOLDMAN, R. (1979). The transdisciplinary model: Implications for service delivery and personnel preparation for the severely and profoundly handicapped. *AAESPH Review, 4*(2), 152–161.

McHALE, S. M., & SIMEONSSON, R. J. (1980). Effects of interaction on nonhandicapped children's attitudes toward autistic children. *American Journal of Mental Deficiency, 85*, 18–24.

McKINNEY, J. D., & HOCUTT, A. M. (1982). Public school involvement of parents of learning-disabled and average achievers. *Exceptional Education Quarterly, 3*, 64–73.

McKUSICK, V. A. (1978). *Mendelian inheritance in man* (5th ed.). Baltimore, MD: Johns Hopkins University Press.

McLOUGHLIN, J. A. (1979). Roles and practices of parents of children with learning and behavior problems. In D. Edge, B. Strenecky, & S. Mour (Eds.), *Training parents of children with learning problems: An educator's perspective*. Columbus, OH: Ohio State University Press.

McLOUGHLIN, J. A. (1981). Training together to work together: A parent/teacher education model. *Teacher Education and Special Education, 4*, 45–54.

McLOUGHLIN, J. A. (1983). Assessing secondary school students: Dilemmas and challenges. *Pointer, 27*, 42–46.

McLOUGHLIN, J. A., CLARK, F. L., & PETROSKO, J. (in press). LD adolescents and young adults and their families: A dynamic relationship. *Remedial and Special Education*.

McLOUGHLIN, J. A., EDGE, D., PETROSKO, J., & STRENECKY, B. (1981). PL 94-142 and information dissemination: A step forward. *Journal of Special Education Technology, 4*, 50–58.

McLOUGHLIN, J. A., EDGE, D., PETROSKO, J., STRENECKY, B., & DAVIS, C. (1983). Interagency cooperation to disseminate materials concerning exceptional people's needs. *Journal of Special Education Technology, 6*, 40–47.

McLOUGHLIN, J. A., EDGE, D., PETROSKO, J., STRENECKY, B., & KEY, P. (1984). Information about the handicapped: A nation's effort. *Parenting Studies, 1*, 33–37.

McLOUGHLIN, J. A., EDGE, D., & STRENECKY, B. (1978). Perspective of parent involvement in the diagnosis and treatment of learning disabled children. *Journal of Learning Disabilities, 11*, 291–296.

McLOUGHLIN, J. A., & LEWIS, R. (1981). *Assessing special students: Strategies and procedures*. Columbus, OH: Charles E. Merrill.

McLOUGHLIN, J. A., McLAUGHLIN, R., & STEWART, W. (1979). Advocacy for parents of the handicapped: A professional responsibility of challenge. *Learning Disability Quarterly, 2,* 51–57.

McNUTT, G., & HELLER, G. (1978). Services for learning disabled adolescents: A survey. *Learning Disability Quarterly 1,* 101–103.

McPHEE, N. (1982). A very special magic: A grandparent's delight. *Exceptional Parent, 12,* 13–16.

MEADOW, K. P. (1972). Sociolinguistics, sign language and the deaf sub-culture. In T. J. O'Rourke (Ed.), *Psycholinguistics and total communication: The state of the art.* Washington, DC: American Annals of the Deaf.

MEADOW, K. P. (1975). Development of deaf children. In E. M. Hetherington (Ed.), *Review of child development research* (Vol. 5). Chicago: University of Chicago Press.

MEALOR, D. J., & RICHMOND, B. O. (1980). Adaptive behavior: Teachers and parents disagree. *Exceptional Children, 46,* 386–393.

MEIER, J. H. (1976). *Developmental and learning disabilities: Evaluation, management, and prevention in children.* Baltimore: University Park Press.

MEISELS, S. J. (Ed.). (1979). *Special education and development.* Baltimore: University Park Press.

MELICHAR, J. F. (1977). *ISAARE* (vols. 1–7). San Mateo, CA: Adaptive Systems.

MELICHAR, J. F. (1978). ISAARE: A description. *AAESPH Review, 3,* 259–268.

MENOLASCINO, F. L. (1977). *Challenges in mental retardation: Progressive ideology and sources.* New York: Human Services Press.

MENYUK, P. (1972). *The development of speech.* Indianapolis, IN: Bobbs-Merrill.

MERCER, A. R., & MERCER, C. D. (1979). Reading disabilities. In C. D. Mercer (Ed.), *Children and adolescents with learning disabilities.* Columbus, OH: Charles E. Merrill.

MERCER, C., FORGNONE, C., & WOLKING, W. (1976). Definitions of LD used in the United States. *Journal of Learning Disabilities, 9,* 376–386.

MERCER, C. D., MERCER, A. R., & BOTT, D. A. (1984). *Self-correcting learning materials.* Columbus OH: Charles E. Merrill.

MERCER, J. R. (1973). The myth of the 3% prevalence. In R. K. Eyman, C. E. Meyers, & G. Tarian (Eds.), *Sociobehavioral studies in mental retardation: Papers in honor of Harry F. Dingman.* Monographs of the American Association on Mental Deficiency, *1,* 1–18.

MERCER, J. R. *System of multicultural and pluralistic assessment (SOMPA): Technical manual.* New York: Psychological Corporation.

MERCER, J. R. (1981). The system of multicultural pluralistic assessment: SOMPA. In National/State Leadership Training Institute on the Gifted, *Balancing the scale for the disadvantaged gifted.* Presentations from the Fourth Biennial National Conference on Disadvantaged Gifted/Talented. Ventura, CA: Ventura County Superintendent of Schools Office, 29–66.

MERCER, J. R., & LEWIS, J. F. (1977). *System of Multicultural Pluralistic Assessment.* New York: Psychological Corporation.

MESIBOV, G. B. (1978). Helping children cope with stress. In D. P. Cansler (Ed.), *Programs for parents of preschoolers.* Winston-Salem, NC: Kaplan Press, 63–73.

MEYEN, E. C. (1976). *Developing instructional units: Applications for the exceptional child.* Dubuque, IA: W. C. Brown.

MEYEN, E. L. (1978). *Exceptional children: An introduction.* Denver: Love.

MICHELSON, R. P., MERZENICH, M., & SHINDLER, R. (1975, October–November). The cochlear implant. *Audiology and Hearing Education, 1,* 2, 29.

Michigan State University Today. (1982). At 16, Kam's set for grad school. East Lansing, MI: Michigan State University Alumni Office, 3.

MIKSIK, S. (1983). Drug abuse and drug therapy. In M. M. Kerr & C. M. Nelson (Eds.), *Strategies for managing behavior problems in the classroom.* Columbus, OH: Charles E. Merrill.

MILISEN, R. (1971). The incidence of speech disorders. In L. Travis (Ed.), *Handbook of speech pathology and audiology.* New York: Appleton-Century-Crofts.

MILLER, C. K. (1969). Conversation in blind children. *Education of the Visually Handicapped, 12,* 101–105.

MILLER, J. J. (1982). Juvenile rheumatoid arthritis. In E. E. Bleck & D. A. Nagel (Eds.), *Physically handicapped children: A medical atlas for teachers.* New York: Grune & Stratton, 423–430.

MILLS, E. A., & RIDLON, J. A. (1980). A conversation about the NY state summer school of the visual arts. *School Arts, 79*(9), 62–68.

MILLS V. BOARD OF EDUCATION OF THE DISTRICT OF COLUMBIA, 348 F. Supp. 866 (D.D.C., 1972).

MINNER, S., KNUTSON, R., & ALOIA, G. (1979). *Concerns of vocational and special education teachers.* Unpublished manuscript, (Available from Project EMPLOY, Amphitheater School District, Tucson, AZ).

MINSKOFF, E. H. (1980). Teaching approach for developing nonverbal communication skills in students with social perception deficits. *Journal of Learning Disabilities, 13,* 118–124.

MITCHELL, B. M. (1982). An update on the state of gifted and talented education in the United States. *Phi Delta Kappan, 63,* 357–358.

MITCHELL, D. C., FIEWELL, E., & DAVY, P. (1983). Spina Bifida. In J. Umbriet (Ed.), *Physical Disabilities and Health Impairment: An Introduction.* Columbus, OH: Charles E. Merrill, 117–131.

MITHAUG, D. E., HAGMEIER, L. D., & HARING, N. G. (1977). The relationship between training activities and job placement in vocational education of the severely and profoundly handicapped. *AAESPH Review, 2,* 89–110.

MOORE, B. L., & BAILEY, H. (1973). Social punishment in the modification of a preschool child's "autistic-like" behavior with a mother as a therapist. *Journal of Applied Behavior Analysis, 6,* 497–507.

MOORE, C., & MORTON, K. (1976). *A reader's guide for parents of children with mental, physical and emotional disabilities.* Rockville, MD: U.S.O.E., Bureau of Community

Health Services, D.H.E.W. Publication No. (HSA) 77-5290.

MOORE, P. (1982). Voice disorders. In Shames & Wiig (Eds.), *Human communication disorders.* Columbus, OH: Charles E. Merrill.

MOORES, D. F. (1976). Early childhood special education for hearing handicapped children. In H. H. Spicker, N. J. Anastasiow, & W. L. Hodges (Eds.), *Children with special needs: Early development and education.* Minneapolis, MN: Leadership Training Institute/Special Education.

MONEY, J. (1962). *Reading disability: Progress and research needs in dyslexia.* Baltimore: Johns Hopkins University Press.

MORISHIMA, A. (1974). Another Van Gogh of Japan: The superior artwork of a retarded boy. *Exceptional Children, 41,* 92–96.

MORSE, J. A. (1971, April 18–24). *Gifted women: Barriers to development of potential.* Paper presented as the Annual International Convention of the Council for Exceptional Children. Miami Beach, FL.

MORSE, W. C. (1980). The crisis or helping teacher. In N. J. Long, W. C. Morse, & R. G. Newman (Eds.), *Conflict in the classroom* (4th ed.). Belmont, CA: Wadsworth.

MORSINK, C. (1977). *DELTA: A design for word attack.* Gainesville, FL: Author.

MORSINK, C., CROSS, D., & STRICKLER, J. (1978). How disabled readers try to remember words. *Reading Horizons, 18,* 174–180.

MORSINK, C., & OTTO, W. (1977). Special considerations in teaching LD children to read. In P. D. Pearson & J. Hansen (Eds.), *Reading: Theory, research, and practice,* twenty-sixth yearbook of the National Reading Conference. Clemson, SC: NRC, 163–167.

MORSINK, C. V. (1984). *Teaching special needs students in regular classrooms.* Boston: Little, Brown.

MOSS, J. W., & MAYER, D. L. (1975). Children with intellectual subnormality. In J. J. Gallagher (Ed.), *The application of child development research to exceptional children.* Reston, VA: Council for Exceptional Children.

MUIR, K., MILAN, M., BRANSTON-McLEAN, M., & BERGER, M. (1982). Advocacy training for parents of handicapped children: A staff responsibility. *Young Children, 37,* 41–46.

MUSSELWHITE, C. R., & ST. LOUIS, K. W. (1982). *Communication programming for the severely handicapped: Vocal and nonvocal strategies.* Houston, TX: College Hill Press.

MYERS, B. R. (1975). The child with a chronic illness. In R. H. A. Haslam & P. J. Valletutti (Eds.), *Medical Problems in the classroom: The teacher's role in diagnosis and management.* Baltimore: University Park Press, 97–127.

MYKLEBUST, H. R. (1960). *The psychology of deafness.* New York: Grune & Stratton.

MYKLEBUST, H. R. (1964). *The psychology of deafness* (2nd ed.). New York: Grune & Stratton.

NAHIRA, K., FOSTER, R., SHELLHAAS, M., & LELAND, H. (1974). *American Association on Mental Deficiency adaptive behavior scale.* Washington, DC: American Association on Mental Deficiency.

NASSARO, J. N. (1977). *Exceptional timetables: Historic events affecting the handicapped and gifted.* Reston, VA: Council for Exceptional Children.

NATIONAL ASSESSMENT OF EDUCATION PROGRESS (1978a). It's what you don't know that hurts. *NAEP Newsletter, 11*(5), 1(a).

NATIONAL ASSESSMENT OF EDUCATION PROGRESS (1978b). Wrap-up: Social studies/citizenship. *NAEP Newsletter, 11*(5), 1–2(b).

NATIONAL CENTER FOR HEALTH STATISTICS (1982). Unpublished Data from the 1980 National Health Survey.

NATIONAL SOCIETY FOR THE PREVENTION OF BLINDNESS. (1980). *Vision screening in schools.* New York: Author.

NAZZARO, J. N. (Ed.). (1981). *Computer connections for gifted children and youth.* Reston, VA: Clearinghouse on Handicapped and Gifted Children.

NEALIS, J. T. (1983a) Epilepsy. In J. Umbriet, *Physical disabilities and health impairment: An introduction.* Columbus, OH: Charles E. Merrill, 74–85.

NEALIS, J. T. (1983b). Human anatomy. In J. Umbriet, *Physical disabilities and health impairment: An introduction.* Columbus, OH: Charles E. Merrill, 3–15.

NEALIS, J. T. (1983c). Neuroanatomy. In J. Umbriet, *Physical disabilities and health impairment: An introduction.* Columbus, OH: Charles E. Merrill, 16–28.

NEEDLEMAN, H. (1977). Effects of hearing loss from recurrent otitis media on speech and language development. In B. F. Jaffe (Ed.), *Hearing Loss in Children.* Baltimore: University Park Press.

NEEL, R. S., BILLINGSLEY, F. F., McCARTY, F., SYMONDS, D., LAMBERT, C., LEWIS-SMITH, N., & HANASHIRO, R. (1982). *Teaching autistic children: A functional curriculum approach.* Seattle, WA: University of Washington.

NEILON, P. (1948). Shirley's babies after fifteen years: A personality study. *Journal of Genetic Psychology. 73,* 175–186.

NEISWORTH, J. T., & SMITH, R. M. (1978). (Eds.). *Retardation: Issues and assessments, and interventions.* New York: McGraw-Hill.

NEISWORTH, J. T., WILLOUGHBY-HERB, S. J., BAGNATO, S. J., CARTWRIGHT, C. A., & LAUB, K. W. (1980). *Individualized education for preschool exceptional children.* Rockville, MD: Aspen.

NELSON, C. M. (1977). Alternative education for the mildly and moderately handicapped. In R. D. Kneedler & S. G. Tamer (Eds.), *Changing perspectives in special education.* Columbus, OH: Charles E. Merrill, 185–207.

NELSON, C. M., & POLSGROVE, L. (1981). The etiology of adolescent behavior disorders. In G. B. Brown, R. L. McDowell, & J. Smith (Eds.), *Educating adolescents with behavior disorders.* Boston: Little, Brown.

NEVIN, D. (1977, October). Young prodigies take off under special program. *Smithsonian,* 76–82.

NEVIN, D. (1983). Everybody wants "computer literacy" so maybe we should know what it means. *The American School Board Journal, 170*(3), 25–29.

NEWBY, H. A. (1972). *Audiology.* New York: Appleton-Century-Crofts.

NIHIRA, K., FOSTER, R., SHELLHAAS, M., & LELAND, H. (1974). *American Association on Mental Deficiency: Adaptive behavior scale.* Washington, DC: American Association on Mental Deficiency.

NIRJE, B. (1969). The normalization principle and its human management implications. In R. B. Kugel & W. Wolfensberger (Eds.), *Changing patterns in residential services for the mentally retarded.* Washington, DC: U.S. Government Printing Office, 231–240.

NOEL, M. (1980). Referential communication abilities of learning disabled children. *Learning Disabilities Quarterly, 3,* 70–75.

NOLAN, C. Y. (1978). The visually impaired. In E. Meyer (Ed.), *Exceptional children and youth: An introduction.* Denver: Love.

NOLAN, C. Y. (1979). Thoughts on the future of braille. *Journal of Visual Impairment and Blindness, 73,* 333–335.

NOONAN, M. J., BROWN, F., MULLIGAN, M., & RETTIG, M.A. (1982). Educability of severely handicapped persons: Both sides of the issue. *Journal of the Association for the Severely Handicapped, 7*(1), 3–12.

NORTHCOTT, W. H. (1972). *Curriculum guide: Hearing impaired children — to three years — and their parents.* Washington, DC: The Alexander Graham Bell Association for the Deaf.

NORTHCOTT, W. H. (1973a). Implementing programs for young hearing impaired children. *Exceptional Children, 39*(6), 455–463.

NORTHCOTT, W. H. (Ed.). (1973b). *The hearing impaired child in a regular classroom: Preschool, elementary, and secondary years.* Washington, DC: The Alexander Graham Bell Association for the Deaf.

NORTHCOTT, W. H. (Ed.). (1973). *The hearing impaired child in a regular classroom: Preschool, elementary and secondary years.* Washington, DC: The Alexander Graham Bell Association for the Deaf.

NORTHERN, J. L., & DOWNS, M. P. (1974). *Hearing in children.* Baltimore: Williams and Wilkins.

O'BRIEN, R. (1976). *Alive . . . aware . . . a person: A development model for early childhood services with special definition for visually impaired children and their parents.* Rockville, MD: Montgomery County Public Schools.

O'DELL, S. (1974). Training parents in behavior modification: A review. *Psychological Bulletin, 81,* 418–432.

ODOM, S. L. (1983). The development of social interchanges in infancy. In S. G. Garwood & R. R. FEWELL (EDS.), *Educating handicapped infants.* Rockville, MD: Aspen.

OFFICE OF CIVIL RIGHTS REPORT. (1979). Washington, DC: U.S. Department of Health, Education and Welfare, Office of Education.

OFFICE OF CIVIL RIGHTS REPORT. (1980). Washington, DC: U.S. Department of Health, Education and Welfare, Office of Education.

O'LEARY, K. D., & O'LEARY, S. G. (1972). *Classroom management: The successful use of behavior modification.* New York: Pergamon.

OLYMPUS RESEARCH CORPORATION (1974). *An assessment of vocational education programs for the handicapped under Part B Amendements of the Vocational Education Act.* Salt Lake City: Olympus Research Corporation.

OMARK, D. R., & ERICKSON, J. G. (Eds.). (1983). *The bilingual exceptional child.* San Diego: College Hill Press.

ORTON, S. (1937). *Reading, writing, and speech problems in children.* New York: W. W. Norton.

OTTO, W. (1961). The acquisition and retention of paired associates by good, average, and poor readers. *Journal of Educational Psychology, 52,* 241–248.

OUELLETTE, E. M., & ERICKSON, H. L. (1976). A pilot prospective study of the fetal alcohol syndrome at the Boston City Hospital. Part II, The infants. *Annals of New York Academy of Sciences, 273,* 123–129.

OUELLETTE, E. M., ROSETTE, H. L., ROSMAN, N. P., & WEINER, L. (1977). Adverse effects on offspring of maternal alcohol abuse during pregnancy. *New England Journal of Medicine, 297,* 528–530.

PAPARELLA, M. (1979). Use and abuse of tympanostomy tubes. *Otitis Media.* Publication of the Second National Conference on otitis media. Columbus: Ross Laboratories, 86–89.

PAPARELLA, M., & JUHN, S. R. (1979). Otitis media: Definition and terminology. *Otitis Media.* Publication of the Second National Conference on otitis media. Columbus: Ross Laboratories, 2–8.

PAPERT, S. (1981). Computers and computer cultures. In J. N. Nazzaro (Ed.), *Computer connections in gifted children and youth.* Reston, VA; Clearinghouse on Handicapped and Gifted Children.

PARADISE, J. L. (1979). Medical Treatment of acute otitis media: A critical essay. *Otitis Media.* Publication of the Second National Conference on otitis media. Columbus, OH· Ross Laboratories, 79–84.

PARK, C., & SHAPIRO, L. (1976). *You are not alone.* Boston: Little, Brown.

PARKER, J. (1969). Adapting school psychological evaluation of the blind child. *New Outlook for the Blind, 63,* 305–311.

PARKER, L. A. (1977). Teleconferencing as an educational medium: A ten year perspective from the University of Wisconsin-Extension. In M. Monson, L. Parker & B. Riccomini (Eds.), *A design for interactive audio.* Madison, WI: University of Wisconsin-Extension.

PARKS, A. L., & Taylor, G. C. *Secondary special education programs: A procedures manual.*

PARTEN, M. B. (1932). Social participation among preschool children. *Journal of Abnormal and Social Psychology, 27,* 243–269.

Pace in Action on Special Education (PASE) v. Hannon, 506 F. Supp. 831 (N. D. Ill. 1980).

PASSOW, A. H., & GOLDBERG, M. L. (1962). *The Gifted: Digests of major studies.* Manuscript prepared for the Council on Exceptional Children, NEA. (ERIC document, ED 001303).

PATTERSON, G. R., & GULLION, M. E. (1971). *Living with children: New methods for parents and teachers.* Champaign, IL: Research Press.

PATTERSON, G. R., REID, J. B., JONES, R. R., & CONGER, R. E. (1975). *A social learning approach to family intervention: Vol. 1 Families with aggressive children.* Eugene, OR: Castalia.

PAUL, J. L., & BECKMAN-BELL, P. (1981). Parent perspectives. In J. L. Paul (Ed.), *Understanding and working with parents of children with special needs.* New York: Holt, Rinehart and Winston, 119–153.

PAUL, J. L., & EPANCHIN, B. C. (1982). *Emotional disturbance in children.* Columbus, OH: Charles E. Merrill.

PAUL, J. L., & PORTER, P. B. (1981). Parents of handicapped children. In J. L. Paul (Ed.), *Understanding and working with parents of children with special needs.* New York: Holt, Rinehart and Winston, 1–22.

PAYNE, J. S., KAUFFMAN, J. H., PATTON, J. R., BROWN, G. B., & DEMOTT, R. H. (1979). *Exceptional children in focus.* Columbus, OH: Charles E. Merrill.

PAYNE, J. S., MERCER, C. D., & EPSTEIN, M. H. (1974). *Education and rehabilitation techniques.* New York: Behavioral Publications.

PEABODY, R. L., & BIRCH, J. W. (1967). Educational implications of partial vision: New findings from a national study. *Sight Saving Review, 37,* 92–96.

PEARL, R., & BRYAN, T. (1982). Mothers' attributions for their learning disabled child's successes and failures. *Learning Disability Quarterly, 5,* 53–57.

PEARL, R., BRYAN, T., & DONAHUE, M. (1980). Learning disabled children's attributions for success and failure. *Learning Disabilities Quarterly, 3,* 3–9.

PECK, C. A., & SEMMEL, M. I. (1982). Identifying the Least Restrictive Environment (LRE) for children with severe handicaps: Towards an empirical analysis. *Journal of the Association for the Severely Handicapped, 7*(1), 56–63.

PEGNATO, C. W., & BIRCH, J. W. (1959). Locating gifted children in junior high schools: A comparison of methods. In W. B. Barbe & J. S. Renzulli (Eds.), *Psychology and education of the gifted* (2nd ed.). NY: Irvington, 431–432.

PEIRCE, R. L. (1979, March 6). Epileptics share a world of uncertainty and secrecy because of public's ignorance. *The Courier-Journal.*

PENNINGTON, F. M., & LUSZCZ, M. A. (1975). Some functional properties of iconic storage in retarded and nonretarded subjects. *Memory & Cognition, 3,* 295–301.

PENNSYLVANIA ASSOCIATION FOR RETARDED CHILDREN V. COMMONWEALTH OF PENNSYLVANIA, 334 F. Supp. 1257 (E.D. Pa. 1971).

PENNSYLVANIA ASSOCIATION FOR RETARDED CHILDREN V. COMMONWEALTH OF PENNSYLVANIA, 343 F. Supp. 279 (E.D. Pa. 1972), Consent Agreement.

PERA, T. B., & COBB, E. S. (1978). A microcomputer based learning analysis system for optimizing PSI instructional materials for the visually handicapped. *Behavior Research Methods and Instrumentation, 10,* 231–237.

PERKINS, W. (1977). *Speech pathology: An applied behavioral science* (2nd ed.). St. Louis: C. V. Mosby.

PEROSA, L., & PEROSA, S. (1981). The school counselor's use of structural family therapy with learning-disabled students. *The School Counselor, 29,* 152–155.

PERRONE, P. A., & MALE, R. A. (1981). *The developmental education and guidance of talented learners.* Rockville, MD: Aspen.

PETERSON, D. D. (1972). Children with physical disabilities and multiple handicaps. In B. R. Gearhart, (Ed.) *Education of the exceptional child: History, present practices, and trends.* San Francisco: Intext Educational Publishers, 243–273.

PETERSON, P. L. (1979). Direct instruction: Effective for what and for whom? *Educational Leadership, 37,* 46–48.

PEYTON, D. (1982, April 1). Video—Snake Byte OK for city native. *The Herald–Dispatch,* p. 9.

PFEIFFER, S. (1982). The superiority of team decision making. *Exceptional Children, 49,* 68–69.

PFEIFFER, S. I. (1981). The multidisciplinary team and nondiscriminatory assessment. *Arizona Personnel and Guidance Journal, 7*(1), 22–23.

PFLAUM, S., & BRYAN, T. (1980). Oral reading behaviors in the learning disabled. *Journal of Educational Research, 73,* 252–258.

PFLAUM, S., PASCARELLA, E. T., AUER, C., AUGUSTY, L., & BOSWICK, M. (1982). Differential effects of four comprehension-facilitating conditions on LD and normal elementary school readers. *Learning Disabilities Quarterly, 5,* 106–116.

PIAGET, J. (1950). *The psychology of intelligence.* New York: Harcourt Brace & World.

PIAGET, J. (1963). *The origins of intelligence in children.* New York: W. W. Norton.

PIHL, R. O., & NIAURA, R. (1982). Learning disability: An inability to sustain attention. *Journal of Clinical Psychology, 38,* 632–634.

PIKLER, E. (1971). Learning of motor skills on the basis of self-induced movements. In J. Hellmuth (Ed.), *Exceptional Infant Vol. 2: Studies in abnormality.* New York: Brunner/Mazel.

PINTNER, R. (1941). The deaf. In R. Pintner, J. Eisenson, & M. Stanton (Eds.), *The psychology of the physically handicapped.* New York: Appleton-Century-Crofts.

PINTNER, R., & REAMER, J. F. (1920). A mental and educational survey of schools for the deaf. *American Annals of the Deaf, 65,* 451.

PINTNER, R. J., EISENSON, J., & STANTON, M. (1941). *The psychology of the physically handicapped.* New York: Appleton-Century-Crofts.

PLEDGIC, T. K. (1982). Giftedness among handicapped children: Identification and programming development. *The Journal of Special Education, 16,* 221–224.

POLIFKA, J. C. (1981). Compliance with PL 94-142 and consumer satisfaction. *Exceptional Children, 48,* 250–253.

POLSGROVE, L., & REITH, H. (1985). Microcomputer applications to students with learning and behavior disorders. In A. E. Blackhurst (Ed.), *Using Microcomputers in Special Education Programs.* Boston: Little, Brown.

POOLEY, R. C. (1981). *Career development for dropout LD and ED adolescent boys: Two evaluation reports on activities between April 1, 1980–September 30, 1980 and October 1,*

1980–March 31, 1981. Norfolk, VA: James-Barry Robinson Institute. (ERIC Document No. 207 284)

POPLIN, M. S., GRAY, R., LARSEN, S., BANIKOWSKI, A., & MEHRING, L. (1980). A comparison of components of written expression abilities in learning disabled and non-learning disabled students at three grade levels. *Learning Disabilities Quarterly, 3,* 46–53.

PORTER, T. H., LYNN, M. S., & MADDOX, H. E. (1979, Fall–Winter). The cochlear implant. *Texas Journal of Audiology and Speech Pathology, 4, 3,* 24–27.

POWELL, M. L. (1981). *Assessment and management of developmental changes and problems in children* (2nd ed.). St. Louis: C. V. Mosby.

PRESIDENT'S COMMITTEE ON EMPLOYMENT OF THE HANDICAPPED (1979). *Affirmative action for disabled people: A pocket guide.* Washington, DC: U.S. Government Printing Office.

President's committee on mental retardation: Trends in state services. (1976). Washington, DC: U.S. Government Printing Office.

PRESSEY, S. L. (1955). Concerning the nature and nurture of genius. *Scientific Monthly, 81,* 123–129.

PRINGLE, M. L. (1970). *Able misfits.* London, England: Longman Groups.

PROCTOR, C. A., & PROCTOR, B. (1967). Understanding hereditary nerve deafness. *Archives of Otolaryngology, 85,* 23–40.

PRYZWANSKY, W. B. (1981). Mandated team participation: Implications for psychologists working in the schools. *Psychology in the Schools, 18,* 460–467.

PUBLIC LAW 90-538 (1968, September 30). Handicapped Children's Early Education Assistance Act.

PUBLIC LAW 93-380 (1974, August 21). Education Amendments of 1974.

PUBLIC LAW 93-644 (1975, January 4). The Head Start, Economic Opportunity, and Community Partnership Act of 1974.

PUBLIC LAW 95-602. The Rehabilitation, Comprehensive Services and Developmental Disabilities Amendments of 1978.

PUNCH, J. (1983). The Prevalence of Hearing Impairment. *ASHA, 25,* 27.

PYECHA, J., ET AL. (1980). *A national survey of individualized education programs (IEP's) for handicapped children. Final report.* Research Triangle Park, NC: Research Triangle Institution.

QUAY, H. C. (1972). Patterns of aggression, withdrawal and immaturity. In H. C. Quay & J. S. Werry (Eds.), *Psychopathological disorders of childhood.* New York: John Wiley & Sons, 1–29.

QUAY, H. C. (1979). Classification. In H. C. Quay & J. S. Werry (Eds.), *Psychopathological disorders of childhood* (2nd ed.). New York: John Wiley & Sons.

QUAY, H. C., & PETERSON, D. R. (1967). *Manual for the behavior problem checklist.* Unpublished manuscript, University of Illinois.

QUICK, A. D., LITTLE, T. C., & CAMPBELL, A. A. (1974). *Project MEMPHIS.* Belmont, CA: Lear Siegler/Fearon.

QUIGLEY, S. P. (1970). *Some effects of impairment upon school performance.* Manuscript prepared for the Division of Special Education Services, Office of the Superintendent of Public Instruction for the State of Illinois.

RABIN, A. T. (1982). Does vision screening tell the whole story? *Reading Teacher, 35*(5), 524–527.

RAMEY, C. T., & BRYANT, D. M. (1982). Evidence for prevention of developmental retardation during infancy. *Journal of the Division for Early Childhood, 5,* 73–78.

RAMSDELL, D. A. (1965). The psychology of the hard-of-hearing and the deafened adult. In H. Davis & S. R. Silverman (Eds.), *Hearing and deafness.* New York: Holt, Rinehart and Winston.

RAMSDELL, D. A. (1970). The psychology of the hard-of-hearing and the deafened adult. In H. Davis & S. Silverman (Eds.), *Hearing and deafness.* New York: Holt, Rinehart and Winston, 435–446.

RAPH, J., GOLDBERG, M., & PASSOW, A. (1966). *Bright underachievers.* New York: Teachers College Press, Columbia University.

REDL, F., & WINEMAN, D. (1954). *The aggressive child.* New York: Free Press.

REISBERG, L. (1982). Individual differences in LD students' use of contextual cuing. *Learning Disabilities Quarterly, 5,* 91–99.

RENZULLI, J. (1978). What makes giftedness? *Phi Delta Kappan, 60*(3), 180–184, 261.

RENZULLI, J. S. (1977). *The enrichment triad model: A guide for developing defensible programs for the gifted and talented.* Wethersfield, CT: Creative Learning Press.

RENZULLI, J. S. (1982). What makes a problem real: Stalking the illusive meaning of qualitative differences in gifted education. *Gifted Child Quarterly, 26*(4), 167–156.

RENZULLI, J. S., & HARTMAN, R. K. (1971). Scale for rating the behavioral characteristics of superior students. *Exceptional Children, 38,* 243–248.

RENZULLI, J. S., & SMITH, L. H. (1977). Two approaches to identification of gifted students. *Exceptional Children, 43*(8), 512–518.

RENZULLI, J. S., & SMITH, L. H. (1979). *A guide for developing individualized educational programs (IEP) for gifted and talented students.* Mansfield Center, CT: Creative Learning Press.

REPORT OF THE AD HOC COMMITTEE TO DEFINE DEAF AND HARD OF HEARING, (1975). *American Annals of the Deaf, 120,* 509–512.

REPP, A. (1983). *Teaching the mentally retarded.* Englewood Cliffs, NJ; Prentice-Hall.

REYNOLDS, M., & BIRCH, J. (1982). *Teaching exceptional children in all America's schools* (2nd ed.). Reston, VA: Council for Exceptional Children.

REYNOLDS, M. C., & BIRCH, J. W. (1977). *Teaching exceptional children in all American's schools.* Reston, VA: The Council for Exceptional Children.

RHODES, W. C. (1967). The disturbing child: A problem of ecological management. *Exceptional Children, 33,* 449–455.

RHODES, W. C. (1970). A community participation analysis of emotional disturbance. *Exceptional Children, 36,* 309–314.

RHODES, W. C. (1975). *A study of child variance, Vol. IV: The future.* Ann Arbor, MI: Institute for the Study of Mental Retardation and Related Disabilities.

RHODES, W. C., & TRACY, M. L. (Eds.) (1972). *A study of child variance: Vol. I Conceptual models.* Ann Arbor, MI: Institute for the Study of Mental Retardation and Related Disabilities.

RICH, H. L (1977). Behavior disorders and school: A case of sexism and racial bias. *Behavioral Disorders, 2,* 201–204.

RIMLAND, B. (1964). *Infantile autism.* New York: Meredith.

RIMM, S. (1984, January-February). Under achievement . . . or if God had meant gifted children to run our homes, she would have created them bigger. *G/C/T,* 27–29.

ROBINSON, C. C., & ROBINSON, J. H. (1978). Sensorimotor functions and cognitive development. In M. E. Snell (Ed.), *Systematic instruction of the moderately and severely handicapped.* Columbus, OH: Charles E. Merrill.

ROBINSON, C. C., & ROBINSON, J. H. (1983). Sensorimotor functions and cognitive development. In M. E. Snell (Ed.), *Systematic instruction of the moderately and severely handicapped* (2nd ed.). Columbus, OH: Charles E. Merrill.

ROBINSON, H. B., ROEDELL, W. C., & JACKSON, N. (1979). Early identification and intervention. In A. H. Passow (Ed.), *The gifted and the talented: Their education and development.* The Seventy-eighth yearbook of the National Society for the Student of Education, Part 1. Chicago: University of Chicago Press.

ROBINSON, N. M., & ROBINSON, H. B. (1976). *The mentally retarded child: A psychological approach* (2nd ed.). New York: McGraw-Hill.

RODRIGUEZ, R. F. (1981). The involvement of minority group parents in school. *Teacher Education and Special Education, 4,* 40–44.

ROE, A. (1953). *The making of a scientist.* New York: Dodd, Mead.

ROEDELL, W. C., JACKSON, N. E., & ROBINSON, H. B. (1980). *Gifted young children.* New York: Teachers College Press.

ROGERS, S. J., & PUCHALSKI, C. B. (1984, January). Social characteristics of visually impaired infants' play. *Topics in Early Childhood Special Education, 3*(4), 52–56.

ROSE, T. L. (1978). The functional relationship between artificial food colors and hyperactivity. *Journal of Applied Behavior Analysis, 11,* 439–446.

ROSS, A. (1976). *Psychological aspects of learning disabilities and reading disorders.* New York: McGraw-Hill.

ROSS, A. O. (1980). *Psychological disorders of children* (2nd ed.). New York: McGraw-Hill.

ROY, C., & FUQUA, D. (1983). Social support systems and academic performance of single-parent students. *The School Counselor, 30,* 183–192.

RUBIN, H., & CULATTA, R. (1971). A point of view about

fluency. *American Speech and Hearing Association, 13,* 380–384.

RUBIN, H., & CULATTA, R. (1974). Stuttering as an aftereffect of normal developmental disfluency. *Clinical Pediatrics 13*(2), 172–176.

RUBIN, M. (1976). *Hearing aids: Current developments and concepts.* Baltimore: University Park Press.

RUCONICH, S. (1984). Evaluating microcomputers access technology by use of visually impaired students. *Education of the Visually Handicapped, 15*(4), 119–125.

RUCONICH, S. K., ASHCROFT, S. C., & YOUNG, M. F. (1983). *Making microcomputers accessible to blind persons.* Unpublished manuscript. George Peabody College of Vanderbilt University.

RUSCH, F. R. (1983). Competitive vocational training. In M. E. Snell (Ed.), *Systematic instruction of the moderately and severely handicapped* (2nd ed.). Columbus, OH: Charles E. Merrill.

RYAN, J. (1975). Mental subnormality and language development. In E. Lenneberg & E. Lenneberg (Eds.), *Foundations of language development* (Vol. 2). New York: Academic Press.

RYAN, S. G., & BEDI, D. N. (1978). Toward computer literacy for visually impaired students. *Journal of Visual Impairment and Blindness, 72*(8), 302–306.

SAFFORD, P. L. (1978). *Teaching young children with special needs.* St. Louis: C. V. Mosby.

SAILOR, W., & GUESS, D. (1983). *Severely handicapped students: An instructional design.* Boston: Houghton Mifflin.

SAILOR, W., GUESS, D., GOETZ, L., SCHULER, A., UTLEY, B., & BALDWIN, M. (1980). Language and severely handicapped persons: Deciding what to teach to whom. In W. Sailor, B. Wilcox, & L. Brown (Eds.), *Methods of instruction for severely handicapped students.* Baltimore: Paul H. Brooks.

SAILOR, W., & MIX, B. (1975). *The TARC assessment system.* Lawrence, KS: H & H Enterprises.

SALVIA, J. (1978). Perspectives on the nature of retardation. In J. T. Neisworth & R. M. Smith (Eds.), *Retardation: Issues, assessment, and intervention.* New York: McGraw-Hill, 27–47.

SALVIA, J., & YSSELDYKE, J. E. (1981). *Assessment in special and remedial education* (2nd ed.). Boston: Houghton Mifflin.

SALZBERG, C., & VILLANI, T. (1983). Speech training by parents of Down Syndrome toddlers: Generalization across settings and instructional contexts. *American Journal of Mental Deficiency, 87,* 403–413.

SAMUELS, S. J. (1970). Reading disability? *The Reading Teacher, 24,* 267.

SANDERS, D. A. (1982). *Aural rehabilitation management model* (2nd ed.). Englewood Cliffs, NJ: Prentice-Hall.

SANDLER, A., COREN, A., & THURMAN, S. K. (1983). A training program for parents of handicapped preschool children: Effects upon mother, father, and child. *Exceptional Children, 49*(4), 355–358.

SANDMAIER, M. (1978). *Alcohol and your unborn baby.* Rockville, MD: National Institute on Alcohol Abuse and Alcoholism.

SANFORD, L. R. (1984). A formative evaluation of an instructional program designed to teach visually impaired students to use microcomputers. *Education of the Visually Handicapped, 15*(4), 135–144.

SANTA CRUZ COUNTY PUBLIC SCHOOL DISTRICT, (1975). *Behavior Characteristics Progression.* Santa Cruz, CA: Santa Cruz County Public School District.

SAPON-SHEVIN, M. (1982). Ethical issues in parent training programs. *Journal of Special Education, 16,* 341–358.

SAWYER, H., & SAWYER, S. (1981). A teacher-parent communication training approach. *Exceptional Children, 47,* 305–312.

SAY, E., McCOLLUM, J., & BRIGHTMAN M. (1980, April). *A study of the IEP: Parent and school perspectives.* Paper presented at the annual meeting of the American Educational Research Association, Boston.

SCANLON, C., ARICK, J., & PHELPS, N. (1981). Participation in the development of the IEP: Parents' perspective. *Exceptional Children, 47,* 373–376.

SCHAFER, D. S., & MOERSCH, M. S. (Eds.). (1981). *Developmental programming for infants and young children.* Ann Arbor: University of Michigan Press.

SCHAPIRO, J., & EIGERDORF, V. (1975). Options in living arrangements, workshop report F. In J. C. Hamilton & R. M. Segal (Eds.), *Proceeding — a consultation conference on the gerontological aspects of mental retardation.* Ann Arbor: University of Michigan, Institute of Gerontology.

SCHEERENBERGER, R. C. (1982). Public residential services, 1981: Status and trends. *Mental Retardation, 20,* 210–215.

SCHEFFLIN, M., & SELTZER, C. (1974, Spring). Math Manipulatives for Learning Disabilities. *Academic Therapy, 9,*(5), 357–362.

SCHERZER, A. L. (1974). Early diagnosis, management, and treatment of cerebral palsy, *Rehabilitation Literature, 35*(7), 194–199.

SCHIEFELBUSCH, R. L. (Ed.). (1978). *Language intervention strategies.* Baltimore: University Park Press.

SCHLESINGER, H. S., & MEADOW, K. P. (1972). *Sound and sign: Childhood deafness and mental health.* Berkeley: University of California Press.

SCHNEIDER, E. J. (1979, Fall). Researchers discover formula for success in student learning. *Educational R and D Report, 2,* 1–6.

SCHOFIELD, J. (1981). Computer based aids for the blind. *Inter-Regional Review, 69,* 4–9.

SCHOLL, G. (1973). Understanding and meeting developmental needs. In B. Lowenfeld (Ed.), *The visually handicapped child in school.* New York: John Day.

SCHOLL, G., & SCHNUR, R. (1976). *Measures of psychological, vocational, and educational functioning in the blind and visually handicapped.* New York: American Foundation for the Blind.

SCHREIBER, F. (1973). *Your child's speech.* Westminister, MD: Balantine Books,

SCHUBERT, M. A., & GLICK, H. M. (1981). Least restrictive environment programs: Why are some so successful? *Education Unlimited, 3*(2), 11–13.

SCHWEINHART, L. J., & WEIKART, D. P. (1981). Effects of the Perry Preschool Program on youths through age 15. *Journal of the Division for Early Childhood, 4,* 29–39.

SCOTT, E. P. (1982). *Your visually impaired student: A guide for teachers.* Baltimore, MD: University Park Press.

SEGUIN, E. (1866). *Idiocy and its treatment by the physiological method.* Albany, NY: Brandow.

SELIGMAN, M. (1979). *Strategies for helping parents of exceptional children.* New York: The Free Press.

SHAMES, G., & FLORENCE, C. (1982). Disorders of fluency. In Shames and Wiig (Eds.), *Human communication disorders.* Columbus, OH: Charles E. Merrill.

SHARRARD, W. J. W. (1968). Spina Bifida and its sequelae. South African Medical Journal, 1968, *42,* 915–918. In D. D. Peterson (Ed.), *The physically handicapped: A book of readings.* New York: MSS Educational, 207–210.

SHAW, M. C., & MCUEN, J. T. (1960). The onset of academic underachievement in bright children. *Journal of Educational Psychology, 51,* 103–106.

SHEARER, D., & SHEARER, M. (1977). The Portage Project: A model for early intervention. In T. Tjossem (Ed.), *Intervention strategies for high risk infants and young children.* Baltimore, MD: University Park Press.

SHEARER, M. S. (1976). A home-based parent-training model. In D. Lillie & P. Trohanis (Eds.), *Teaching parents to teach.* New York: Walker, 131–148.

SHEARER, M. S., & SHEARER, D. E. (1977). Parent involvement. In J. Jordan, A. Hayden, M. Karnes, & M. Wood (Eds.), *Early childhood education for exceptional children.* Reston, VA: Council for Exceptional Children, 208–235.

SICCONE, E. R. (1983). A strategic new vision for education. *Education Network News, 2,* pp. 2–3.

SIEBEN, R. (1977). Controversial medical treatments of learning disabilities. *Academic Therapy 13,* 133–147.

SIGEL, I. (1975). Concept formation. In J. J. Gallagher (Ed.), *The application of child development research to exceptional children.* Reston, VA: Council for Exceptional Children.

SILBERBERG, N. E., & SILBERBERG, M. C. (1977). A note on reading tests and their role in defining reading difficulties. *Journal of Learning Disabilities, 10,* 100–103.

SILVERMAN, S. R. (1971). The education of deaf children. In L. E. Travis (Ed.), *Handbook of speech pathology and audiology.* Englewood Cliffs, NJ: Prentice-Hall.

SILVERMAN, W. A. (1977). The lesson of retrolental fibroplasia. *Scientific American, 235*(6), 100–107.

SIMMONS-MARTIN, A. (1981). Efficacy report: Early Education Project. *Journal of the Division for Early Childhood, 4,* 5–10.

SIMNER, M. L. (1983, October). The warning signs of school failure: An updated profile of the at-risk kindergarten child. *Topics in Early Childhood Special Education, 3*(3), 17–27.

SIMPKINS, K., & STEPHENS, B. (1974). Cognitive development of blind subjects. *Proceedings of the 52nd Biennial Conference of the Association for the Education of the Visually Handicapped,* 26–28.

SIMPSON, R. L. (1982). Future training issues. *Exceptional Education Quarterly, 3,* 81–88.

SINGER, S., STEWART, M., & PULASKI, L. (1981). Minimal brain dysfunction: Differences in cognitive organization in two groups of index cases and their relatives. *Journal of Learning Disabilities, 14,* 470–473.

SINGLETON, R. (1981, December). *Applying the normalization principle in the United Kingdom: Barnardo's Skelmersdale Project.* Paper presented to the International Seminar on Planning for Integration of the Mentally Handicapped. Delft University, The Netherlands.

SIPERSTEIN, G. N., & BAK, J. T. (1980). Improving children's attitudes toward blind peers. *Journal of Visual Impairment and Blindness, 74*(4), 132–135.

SIRRIS, B. (1979). Career education for the severely handicapped. In G. M. Clark & W. J. White (Eds.), *Career education for the handicapped: Current perspectives for teachers.* Boothwyn, PA: Education Resources Center.

SIXTH ANNUAL REPORT TO CONGRESS ON THE IMPLEMENTATION OF PUBLIC LAW 94–142: THE EDUCATION FOR ALL HANDICAPPED CHILDREN ACT. (1984). Washington, DC: U.S. Department of Education.

SIZER, T. R. (1983). High school reform: The need for engineering. *Phi Delta Kappan, 64*(10), 679–683.

SKARNULIS, E. (1980). *Key concepts: Core and cluster.* Public information brochure. Division for Community Services for Mental Retardation. Bureau for Health Services. Department for Human Resources, Frankfort, KY.

SKEELS, H. M. (1966). Adult status of children with contrasting early life experiences: A follow-up study. *Monographs of the Society for Research in Child Development, 31* (39, Serial No. 105).

SKEELS, H. M., & DYE, H. B. (1939). A study of the effects of differential stimulation on mentally retarded children. *Proceedings and Addresses of the American Association on Mental Deficiency, 44*(1), 114–136.

SKINNER, F. (1977). *Telecommunications for vocational rehabilitation: Vol. 3 End instrument survey.* Washington, DC: Rehabilitation Services Administration Office of Human Development, Department of Health, Education and Welfare.

SLATER, E., & COWIE, V. (1971). *The genetics of mental disorders.* London: Oxford University Press.

SMILANSKY, M., & NEVO, D. (1979). *The gifted disadvantaged: A ten year longitudinal study of compensatory education in Israel.* New York: Gordon and Breach.

SMITH, E. W., KROUSE, S. W., & ATKINSON, M. M. (1961). *Educators encyclopedia.* Englewood Cliffs, NJ: Prentice-Hall.

SMITH, J., & SMITH, D. (1976). *Child management,* Champaign, IL: Research Press.

SMITH, R. M. (1971). *An introduction to mental retardation.* New York: McGraw-Hill.

SNELL, M. E. (Ed.). (1978). *Systematic instruction of the moderately and severely handicapped* (1st ed.). Columbus, OH: Charles E. Merrill.

SNELL, M. E. (1983a). Implementing and monitoring the IEP: Intervention strategies. In M. E. Snell (Ed.), *Systematic instruction of the moderately and severely handicapped* (2nd ed.). Columbus, OH: Charles E. Merrill.

SNELL, M. E. (1983b). Self-care skills. In M. E. Snell (Ed.), *Systematic instruction of the moderately and severely handicapped* (2nd ed.). Columbus, OH: Charles E. Merrill.

SNELL, M. E. (1983c). Functional reading. In M. E. Snell (Ed.), *Systematic instruction of the moderately and severely handicapped* (2nd ed.). Columbus, OH: Charles E. Merrill.

SNELL, M. E., & GAST, D. L. (1981). Applying time delay procedure to the instruction of the severely handicapped. *The Journal of the Association for the Severely Handicapped, 6*(3), 3–14.

SNELL, M. E., & SMITH, D. D. (1983). Developing the IEP: Selecting and assessing skills. In M. E. Snell (Ed.), *Systematic instruction of the moderately and severely handicapped* (2nd ed.). Columbus, OH: Charles E. Merrill.

SOCIAL SCIENCE EDUCATION CONSORTIUM. (1978). Project MAVIS materials adaptations for visually impaired students in the social studies. Boulder, CO.

SOFFER, R. (1982). IEP decisions in which parents desire greater participation. *Education and Training the Mentally Retarded, 17,* 67–70.

SOLANO, C. H. (1976, September 3–7). *Teacher and pupil stereotypes of gifted boys and girls.* Paper presented at the 84th annual conference of the American Psychological Association, Washington, DC.

SOMERTON, M.E., & TURNER, K. D. (1975). *Pennsylvania training model individual assessment guide.* Harrisburg, PA: Pennsylvania Department of Education.

SONTAG, E., BURKE, P., & YORK, R. (1973). Considerations for serving the severely handicapped. *Education and Training of the Mentally Retarded, 8,* 20–26.

SOUDER V. BRENNAN. Civil Action No. 482–73 (U.S. District Court for the District of Columbia, 1973).

SOUTHEASTERN REGIONAL COALITION. (1979). Issues in certification for teachers of the severely handicapped. In National Association of State Directors of Special Education, *Special Education Programs for Severely and Profoundly Handicapped Individuals: A Directory of State Education Agency Services.* Washington, DC; NASDSE, 32–50.

SPEARMAN, C. (1914). The heredity of abilities. *Eugenics Review, 6,* 219–237.

SPECIAL REPORT: PUBLIC POLICY, NAEYC–EPSDT. (1976). Early and Periodic Screening, Diagnosis, and Treatment. *Young Children, 31*(6), 486.

SPICKER, D. (1982). Parental involvement in early intervention activities with their children with Down's Syndrome. *Education and Training of the Mentally Retarded, 17,* 24–29.

SPITZ, H. H. (1973). Consolidating facts into the schematized learning and memory system of educable retardates. In N. R. Ellis (Ed.), *International review of research in mental retardation* (Vol. 6). New York: Academic Press.

SPIVACK, G., & SPOTTS, J. (1966). *Devereux Child Behavior (DCB) Rating Scale.* Devon, PA: Devereux Foundation.

SPIVEY, S. A. (1967). *The social position of selected children with a visual loss in regular classes in the public schools of At-*

lanta, Georgia. Specialist in education thesis. George Peabody College for Teachers, Nashville, TN.

SPODEK, B. (1977). Curriculum construction in early childhood education. In B. Spodek & H. J. WALBERG (EDS.), *Early childhood education: Issues and insights.* Berkeley, CA: McCutchan.

SPRADLIN, J. E., & SPRADLIN, R. R. (1976). Developing necessary entry skills for entry into classroom teaching arrangements. In N. G. Haring & R. L. Schiefelbusch (Eds.), *Teaching special children.* New York: McGraw-Hill.

SPREEN, O. (1965). Language functions in mental retardation: A review. *American Journal of Mental Deficiency, 69,* 482–494.

SPUNGIN, S. J., & SWALLOW, R. (1977). Psychoeducational assessment. Rate of psychologist to teacher of the visually handicapped. *AFB Practice Report.* New York: American Foundation for the Blind.

STANLEY, J. C. (1977). Rationale of the study of mathematically precocious youth (SMPY) during its first five years of promoting educational acceleration. In J. C. Stanley, W. C. George, & C. H. Solano (Eds.), *The gifted and the creative. A fifty-year perspective.* Baltimore: Johns Hopkins University Press, 75–112.

STANLEY, J. C., & BENBOW, C. P. (1981–82, Winter). Using the SAT to find intellectually talented seventh graders. *The College Board Review,* (122) 3–7, 26.

STANLEY, J. C., KEATING, D. P., & FOX, L. H. (Eds.). (1974). *Mathematical talent: Discovery, description, and development.* Baltimore, MD: Johns Hopkins University Press.

STANLEY, J. L., & LANMAN, J. T. (Eds.). (1976). History of oxygen therapy and retrolental fibroplasia. *Pediatrics, 54,*(4), 592–642.

STANLEY, J. S. (1976). The case for extreme educational acceleration in intellectually brilliant youths. *Gifted Child Quarterly 20*(1), 66–75.

STANZLER, M. (1982). Taking the guilt out of parenting. *Exceptional Parent, 12,* 51–53.

STEINART, Y. E., CAMPBELL, S. B., & KIELY, M. C. (1981). A comparison of maternal and remedial teacher teaching styles with good and poor readers. *Journal of Learning Disabilities, 14,* 38–42.

STEPHENS, B. (1978, July). *Piagetian approach to visually handicapped education: Research review.* Lecture presented at Project PAVE Special Study Institute, Louisville.

STEPHENS, T. M., BLACKHURST, A. E., & MAGLIOCCA, L. A. (1982). *Teaching mainstreamed students.* New York: John Wiley & Sons.

STERNBERG, R. J. (1982). Nonentrenchment in the assessment of intellectual giftedness. *Gifted Child Quarterly, 26*(2), Spring, 63–67.

STEVENS, G. (1962). *Taxonomy in special education for children with body disorders: The problem and a proposal.* Pittsburgh: University of Pittsburgh.

STIRVIS, B. (1980). Career education for the severely handicapped. In G. M. Clark & W. J. White (Eds.), *Career education for the handicapped: Current perspectives for teachers.* Boothwyn, PA: Education Resources Center.

STRAIN, P. S. (1983). Personal communication.

STRAUSS, A. A., & LEHTINEN, L. E. (1947). *Psychopathology and education of the brain injured child.* New York: Grune & Stratton.

STRENECKY, M., STRENECKY, B., & DARE, G. (1978). Parent involvement in the education of children with learning problems: An annotated bibliography. In D. Edge, B. Strenecky, & S. Mour (Eds.), *Parenting learning-problem children.* Columbus, OH: NCEMMH, Ohio State University, 127–134.

STRICKLAND, B. (1982). Parental participation, school accountability, and due process. *Exceptional Education Quarterly, 3,* 41–49.

STROM, R., REES, R., SLAUGHTER, H., & WURSTER, S. (1980). Role expectations of parents of intellectually handicapped children. *Exceptional Children, 47,* 144–148.

STROM, R. D., & TORRANCE, E. P. (1973). *Education for affective achievement.* Chicago, IL: Rand McNally.

STUMPHAUZER, J. S., AIKEN, T. W., & VELOZ, E. V. (1977). East side story: Behavioral analysis of a high juvenile crime community. *Behavioral Disorders, 2,* 76–84.

SUPPES, P. (1980). Impact of computers on curriculum in the schools and universities. In R. P. Taylor (Ed.), *The computer in the school: Tutor, tool, tutee.* New York: Teachers College Press, 236–247.

SWALLOW, R. (1977). Assessment for visually handicapped children and youth. *AFB Practice Report.* New York: American Foundation for the Blind.

SWALLOW, R., MANGOLD, S., & MANGOLD, P. (1978). Informal assessment of developmental skills for visually handicapped students. *AFB Practice Report.* New York: American Foundation for the Blind.

SWALLOW, R. M. (1981). Fifty assessment procedures commonly used with blind and partially seeing individuals. *Journal of Visual Impairment and Blindness, 75,* 2, 65–72.

SWICK, K. J., FLAKE-HOBSON, C., & RAYMOND, G. (1980). The first step establishing parent-teacher communication in the IEP conference. *Teaching Exceptional Children, 12,* 144–145.

SWITZSKY, H. N., HAYWOOD, H. C., & ROTATORI, A. F. (1982, December). Who are the severely and profoundly retarded? *Education and Training of the Mentally Retarded, 17*(14).

SYKES, K. S. (1971). A comparison of the effectiveness of standard print and large print in facilitating the reading skills of visually impaired students. *Education of the Visually Handicapped, 3,* 97–106.

SZASZ, T. S. (1960). The myth of mental illness. *American Psychologist, 15,* 113–118.

TANNENBAUM, A. J. (1983). *Gifted Children.* NY: Macmillan.

TAWNEY, J. W. (1977). Educating severely handicapped children and their parents through telecommunications. In N. G. Haring & L. J. Brown (Eds.), *Teaching the severely handicapped* (Vol. 2). New York: Grune & Stratton.

TAWNEY, J. W. (1982). The future. In P. T. Cegelka & H. J. Prehm (Eds.), *Mental Retardation.* Columbus, OH: Charles E. Merrill.

TAWNEY, J. W., & GAST, D. L. (1984). *Single subject research design in special education.* Columbus, OH: Charles E. Merrill.

TAWNEY, J. W., KNAPP, D. S., O'REILLY, O. D., & PRATT, S. S. (1979). *Programmed environments curriculum.* Columbus, OH: Charles E. Merrill.

TAYLOR, A. R. (1898). *The study of the child.* New York: D. Appleton.

TAYLOR, C. (Ed.). (1964). *Creativity: Progress and potential.* New York: McGraw-Hill.

TAYLOR, F. D., & SOLOWAY, M. M. (1973). The Madison School plan: A functional model for merging the regular classrooms. In E. N. Deno (Ed.), *Instructional alternatives for exceptional children.* Minneapolis: Leadership Training Institute/Special Education, University of Minnesota, 145–155.

TAYLOR, J. L. (1947). Selecting facilities to meet educational needs. In B. Lowenfeld (Ed.), *The blind preschool child.* New York: American Foundation for the Blind.

TAYLOR, O. (1973). Language, cultural contrasts, and the black American. In L. A. Bransford, L. Baca, & K. Lane (Eds.), *Cultural diversity and the exceptional child.* Reston, VA: Council for Exceptional Children, 34–41.

TAYLOR, S. J. (1982). From segregation to integration: Strategies for integrating severely handicapped students in normal school and community settings. *Journal of the Association for the Severely Handicapped, 7*(3), 42–49.

TELESENSORY SYSTEMS. (1973). *Optacon Training.* Palo Alto, CA: Author.

TELFORD, C. W., & SAWREY, J. M. (1977). *The exceptional individual* (3rd ed.). Englewood Cliffs, NJ: Prentice-Hall.

TEMPLEMAN, D., GAGE, M. A., & FREDERICKS, H. D. (1982). Cost effectiveness of the group home. *Journal of the Association for the Severely Handicapped, 6*(4), 11–16.

TERMAN, L. M., ET AL. (1925). *The mental and physical traits of a thousand gifted children. Vol. 1: Genetic studies of genius.* Stanford, CA: Stanford University Press.

TERMAN, L. M., & MERRILL, M. A. (1973). *The Stanford Binet Intelligence Scale* (3rd rev.). Boston: Houghton Mifflin.

TERMAN, L. M., & ODEN, M. H. (1947). *Genetic studies of genius. Vol. 4: The gifted child grows up.* Stanford, CA: Stanford University Press.

TEW, B. F., LAWRENCE, K. M., PAYNE, H., & TOWNSLEY, K. (1977). Marital stability following the birth of a child with spina bifida. *British Journal of Psychiatry, 131,* 77–82.

THIAGARAJAN, S., SEMMEL, D. S., & SEMMEL, M. I. (1974). *Instructional development for training teachers of exceptional chidlren: A sourcebook.* Reston, VA: Council for Exceptional Children.

THOMAS, C. C. (1983). *An examination of the efficacy of direct instruction techniques in special education classrooms.* Unpublished Doctoral Dissertation, University of Kentucky, Lexington, KY.

THOMPSON, G. A., IWATA, B. A., & POYNTER, H. (1979). Operant control of pathological tongue thrust in spastic cerebral palsy. *Journal of Applied Behavior Analysis, 12,* 325–334.

THORKILDSEN, R., BICKEL, W. K., & WILLIAMS, J. G. (1979). Microcomputer/videodisc CAI package to teach the retarded. *Education and Industrial Television. II,* (5), 40–42.

THORNTON, C. A., & REUILLE, R. (1978). The Classroom Teacher, the LD Child, and Math. *Academic Therapy, 14,* pp. 15–21.

THUNBERG, U. (1981). The gifted in minority groups. In B. S. Miller & M. Price (Eds.), *The gifted child, the family, and the community.* NY: Walker

THURLOW, M. L., & YSSELDYKE, J. E. (1979). Current assessment and decision-making practices in model programs for the learning disabled. *Learning Disabilities Quarterly, 2,* 15–24.

TILLMAN, M. H., & OSBORNE, R. T. (1969). The performance of blind and sighted children on the Wechsler Intelligence Scale for children: Interaction effects. *Education of the Visually Handicapped, 1,* 1–4.

TILTON, J., LISKA, D., & BOURLAND, J. (Eds.). (1977). *Guide to early developmental training.* Boston: Allyn and Bacon.

TJOSSEM, T. D. (Ed.). (1976). *Intervention strategies for high risk infants and young children.* Baltimore: University Park Press.

TOBIN, J. J. (1972). Conversation of substance in the blind and sighted. *British Journal of Educational Psychology, 42*(2), 192–197.

TOLLEFSON, N., TRACY, D. B., JOHNSEN, E. P., BUENNING, M., FARMER, A., & BARKE, C. R. (1982). Attribution patterns of learning disabled adolescents. *Learning Disabilities Quarterly, 5,* 14–20.

TOMBLIN, J. B. (1978). *Processes and disorders of human communication.* (Curtis, Ed.). New York: Harper & Row.

TORRANCE, E. P. (1962). *Guiding creative talent.* Englewood Cliffs, NJ: Prentice-Hall.

TORRANCE, E. P. (1966). *Tests of creative thinking.* Princeton: Personnel Press.

TORRANCE, E. P. (1971). Are the Torrance Tests of Creative Thinking biased against or in favor of disadvantaged groups? *Gifted Child Quarterly, 15,* 75–80.

TORRANCE, E. P. (1974a). Broadening concepts of giftedness in the 70's. In S. A. Kirk & F. E. Lord (Eds.), *Exceptional children: Educational resources and perspectives.* Boston: Houghton Mifflin.

TORRANCE, E. P. (1974b). *Norms-technical manual: Torrance tests of creative thinking.* Lexington, MA: Ginn & Company.

TORRANCE, E. P. (1977). *What research says to the teacher: Creativity in the classroom.* Washington, DC: National Education Association.

TRAILOR, C. B. (1982). Role clarification and participation in child study teams. *Exceptional Children, 48,* 529–530.

TREMBLEY, P. W. (1982). Vertical word processing: A new approach for teaching written language to the learning disabled adolescent. *Journal of Learning Disabilities, 15,* 587–593.

TUCKER, J. (1980). Ethnic proportions in classes for the learning disabled: Issues in nonbiased assessment. *Journal of Special Education, 14,* 93–105.

TUCKER, J., STEVENS, L. J. & YSSELDYKE, J. E. (1982). *Learning disabilities: The experts speak out.* Research Report No. 77. Minneapolis: University of Minnesota, Institute for Research on Learning Disabilities.

TUCKER, M. (1983). Computers alone can't save education or protect us in the world economy. *The American School Board Journal, 170*(3), 31–32.

TURNBULL, A. P., & STRICKLAND, B. (1981). Parents and the educational system. In J. L. Paul (Ed.), *Understanding and working with parents of children with special needs.* New York: Holt, Rinehart and Winston, 231–263.

TURNBULL, A. P., & TURNBULL III, H. R. (1978). *Parents speak out.* Columbus, OH: Charles E. Merrill.

TURNBULL, H. R., & TURNBULL, A. P. (1978). *Free appropriate public education: Law and implementation.* Denver Love.

TURNBULL III, H. R. (1981). Parents and the law. In J. L. Paul (Ed.), *Understanding and working with parents of children with special needs.* New York: Holt, Rinehart and Winston, 205–230.

TURNER, G., & OPITZ, J. M. (1980). Editorial comment: X-linked mental retardation (Special issue on (fra[X]). *American Jouranl of Medical Genetics, 7,* 407–415.

TYMITZ, B. L. (1980, September). Instructional aspects of the IEP: An analysis of teachers' skills and needs. *Educational Technology,* 13–20.

TYMITZ, B. L. (1983). Do teachers need a philosophy of education: An exploratory study. *Journal for Special Educators, 19,* 1–10.

TYMITZ-WOLF, B. (1982, March). Guidelines for assessing IEP goals and objectives. *Teaching Exceptional Children,* 198–201.

ULLMANN, L. P., & KRASNER, L. (Eds.). (1965). *Case studies in behavior modification.* New York: Holt, Rinehart and Winston.

UMBREIT, J., & OSTROW, L. S. (1980). The fetal alcohol syndrome. *Mental Retardation, 18,* 109–111.

UMSTED, R. G. (1975). Children with visual handicaps: In J. J. Gallagher (Ed.), *The application of child development research to exceptional children.* Reston, VA: Council for Exceptional Children.

U.S. DEPARTMENT OF EDUCATION. (1980). *To assure the free appropriate public education of all handicapped children: 2nd annual report to Congress on the implementation of Public Law 94-142, The Education for all Handicapped Children Act.* Washington, DC: Departmnt of Education.

U.S. DEPARTMENT OF HEALTH, EDUCATION AND WELFARE, OFFICE OF INCIDENCE YOUTH DEVELOPMENT. (1973). *Juvenile court statistics: 1972.* Washington, DC: Government Printing Office.

U.S. DEPARTMENT OF HEALTH, EDUCATION AND WELFARE, PUBLIC HEALTH SERVICES, NATIONAL INSTITUTE OF HEALTH. (1976). *Interim Report of the National Advisory Eye Council 1976.* (DHEW Publication No. 76-1098).

U.S. GOVERNMENT PRINTING OFFICE. (1983). *Physical disabilities and health impairments: An introduction.* Columbus, OH: Charles E. Merrill.

U.S. OFFICE OF EDUCATION. (1975). *Estimated number of handicapped children in the United States, 1974–75.* Washington, DC: Bureau of Education for the Handicapped.

UTLEY, B., HOLVOET, J., & BARNES, K. (1977). Handling, positioning, and feeding the physically handicapped. In E. Sontag (Ed.), *Educational programming for the severely and profoundly handicapped.* Reston, VA: Division on Mental Retardation, Council for Exceptional Children.

VAGIRIS, I. C., & HUNT, J. Mc V. (1975). *Assessment in infancy: Ordinal scales of psychological development.* Urbana: University of Illinois Press.

VACC, N. C. (1972). Long term effects of special class intervention for emotionally disturbed children. *Exceptional Children, 39,* 15–22.

VANDERHEIDEN, G. (1982). *Comparison of Apple, Epson, IBM, . . . Microcomputers for applications in rehabilitation systems for persons with physical handicaps.* Madison, WI: Trace Research and Development Center for the Severely Communicatively Handicapped.

VANDERHEIDEN, G. C. (1978). *Non-vocal communication resource book.* Baltimore: University Park Press.

VANDU KOLK, C. J. (1976). Intelligence testing for visually impaired persons. *Journal of Visual Impairment and Blindness, 71,*(4), 158–163.

VANDU KOLK, C. J. (1977). Demographic etiological, and functional variables related to intelligence in the visually impaired. *Clinical Psychology, 33*(3), 782–786.

VAN ETTEN, J., & ADAMSON, G. (1973). The fail save program: A special education service continuum. In E. Deno (Ed.), *Instructional alternatives for exceptional children.* Reston, VA: Council for Exceptional Children.

VAN RIPER, C. (1978). *Speech correction: Principles and methods* (6th ed.). Englewood Cliffs, NJ: Prentice-Hall.

VAN TASSEL-BASKA, J. (1981). *An administrator's guide to the education of gifted and talented children.* Washington, DC: National Association of State Boards of Education.

VAN TASSEL-BASKA, J. (1983). Profiles of precocity: The 1982 midwest talent search finalists. *Gifted Child Quarterly, 27*(3), 139–144.

VAN VEELAN, L. P. (1975). *Cheer soap opera.* Unpublished manuscript. University of Kentucky.

VAUGHAN, D., & ASBURY, T. (1974). *General opthalmology* (7th ed.). Los Altos, CA: Lange Medical.

VAUGHAN, D., & ASBURY, T. (1980). *General ophthalmology* (9th ed.). Los Altos, CA: Lange Medical.

VAUGHAN, R. W. & HODGES, L. (1973). A statistical survey into a definition of learning disabilities: A search for acceptance. *Journal of Learning Disabilities, 6,* 658–664.

VAUTOUR, J. A. (1976). A study of placement decisions for exceptional children determined by child study teams and individuals (Doctoral dissertation, University of Connecticut, 1975). *Dissertation Abstracts International, 36,* 6007-A.

VERNON, M., & BROWN, D. A. (1964). A guide to psychological tests and testing procedures in the evaluation of deaf and hard of hearing children. *Journal of Speech and Hearing Disorders, 29,* 414–423.

VERNON, M., & PICKETT, H. (1976). Mainstreaming: Issues and a model plan. *Audiology and Hearing Education, 2,* 5–11.

VINCENT, L. J., SALISBURY, C., WALTER, G., BROWN, P., GRUENWALD, L. J., & POWERS, M. (1980). Program evaluation and curriculum development in early childhood/special education: Criterion of the next environment. In W. Sailor, B. Wilcox, & L. Brown (Eds.), *Methods of instruction for severely handicapped students.* Baltimore: Paul H. Brookes.

VOELTZ, L. (1980). Children's attitudes toward handicapped peers. *American Journal of Mental Deficiency, 84,* 455–464.

VOELTZ, L. M., WUERCH, B. B., & WILCOX, B. (1982). Leisure and recreation preparation for independence, integration, and self-fulfillment. In B. Wilcox & G. T. Bellamy (Eds.), *Design of high school programs for severely handicapped students.* Baltimore: Paul H. Brookes.

VOGEL, S. (1974). Syntactic abilities in normal and dyslexic children. *Journal of Learning Disabilities, 1,* 103–109.

VOGELSBERG, R. T., WILLIAMS, W., & BELLAMY, G. T. (1982). Preparation for independent living. In B. Wilcox & G. T. Bellamy (Eds.), *Design of high school programs for severely handicapped students.* Baltimore: Paul H. Brookes.

VOGELSBERG, R. T., WILLIAMS, W., & FRIEDL, M. (1980). Facilitating systems change for the severely handicapped: Secondary and adult services. *Journal of the Association for the Severely Handicapped, 5*(1), 73–85.

VULPE, S. G. (1977). *Vulpe assessment battery.* Toronto: National Institute on Mental Retardation.

WADSWORTH, B. J. (1978). *Piaget for the classroom teacher.* New York: Longman.

WAHLER, R. G., & CORMIER, W. H. (1970). The ecological interview: A first step in out-patient child behavior therapy. *Journal of Behavior Therapy and Experimental Psychiatry, 1,* 279–289.

WALKER, H. M. (1970). *Walker problem behavior identification checklist.* Los Angeles: Western Psychological Services.

WALLACE, G., & KAUFFMAN, J. (1978). *Teaching children with learning problems* (2nd ed.). Columbus, OH: Charles E. Merrill.

WALLACE, G., & LARSEN, S. C. (1978). *Educational assessment of learning problems: Testing for teaching.* Boston: Allyn and Bacon.

WALLACE, G., & McLOUGHLIN, J. A. (1975). *Learning disabilities: Concepts and characteristics.* Columbus, OH: Charles E. Merrill.

WALLACE, G., & McLOUGHLIN, J. A. (1979). *Learning disabilities: Concepts and characteristics.* Columbus, OH: Charles E. Merrill.

WALLACH, M. A. (1970). Creativity. In P. H. Mussen (Ed.), *Carmichael's manual of child psychology.* NY: John Wiley & Sons.

WALSHE, F. (1963). *Disease of the nervous system.* Baltimore: Williams & Wilkin.

WARD, L. O. (1977). Variables influencing auditory-visual integration in normal and retarded readers. *Journal of Reading Behaviors, 9*(3), 290–295.

WARREN, D. H. (1977). *Blindness and early childhood development.* New York: American Foundation for the Blind.

WARREN, F. A. (1978). A society that is going to kill your children. In A. P. Turnbull & H. R. Turnbull, III (Eds.), *Parents speak out.* Columbus, OH: Charles E. Merrill, 176–197.

WATSON, J. B., & RAYNER, R. (1920). Conditioned emotional reactions. *Journal of Experimental Psychology, 3,* 1–14.

Webster's New World Dictionary. (1976). p. 444.

WECHSLER, D. (1974). *Wechsler Intelligence Scale for Children: A manual.* New York: Psychological Corporation.

WEHMAN, P., & HILL, J. W. (1982). Preparing severely handicapped youth for less restrictive environments. *Journal of the Association for the Severely Handicapped, 7*(1), 33–39.

WEHMAN, P., & McLOUGHLIN, P. J. (1981). *Program development in special education.* New York: McGraw-Hill.

WEHMAN, P., SCHLEIEN, S., & KIERNAN, J. (1980). Age appropriate recreation programs for severely handicapped youth and adults. *Journal of the Association for the Severely Handicapped, 5*(4), 395–407.

WEINTRAUB, F. J. & ABESON, A. (1976). New education policies for the handicapped: The quiet revolution. In F. J. Weintraub, A. Abeson, J. Ballard, & M. L. LaVor (Eds.), *Public policy and the education of exceptional children.* Reston, VA: Council for Exceptional Children, 7–13.

WEINTRAUB, F. J., ABESON, A., BALLARD, J., & LAVOR, M. L. (Eds.). (1976). *Public policy and the education of exceptional children.* Reston, VA: Council for Exceptional Children.

WEINTRAUB, F. J., ABESON, A. R., & BRADDOCK, D. L. (1971). *State law and education of handicapped children: Issues and recommendations.* Arlington, VA: Council for Exceptional Children.

WEIZENBAUM, J. (1976). *Computer power and human reason.* San Francisco: W. H. Freeman.

WELSH, R. L., & BLASCH, B. B. (1980). *Foundations of orientation and mobility.* New York: American Foundation for the Blind.

WEPMAN, J. (1960). Auditory discrimination, speech, and reading. *Elementary School Journal, 60,* 325–333.

WERNER, M. S. (1980). Single parents and adolescent school crisis: Alienation or alliance. *The Pointer, 25,* 46–51.

WESTLING, D. L., & KOORLAND, M. A. (1979). Some considerations and tactics for improving discrimination learning. *Teaching Exceptional Children, 11*(3), 97–100.

WHIMBY, A. (1977). Teaching sequential thought: A cognitive-skills approach. *Phi Delta Kappan, 59,* 255.

WHITE, O. R. (1980). Adaptive performance objectives: Form versus function. In W. Sailor, B. Wilcox, & L. Brown (Eds.), *Methods of instruction for severely handicapped students.* Baltimore, MD: Paul H. Brookes.

WHITE, O. R., EDGAR, E. B., HARING, N. G., AFFLECT, J., HAYDEN, A., & BENDERSKY, M. (1981). *Uniform performance assessment system.* Columbus, OH: Charles E. Merrill.

WHITE, O. R., & HARING, N. G. (1980). *Exceptional teaching.* Columbus, OH: Charles E. Merrill.

WHITMORE, J. (1980). *Giftedness, conflict, and underachievement.* Boston: Allyn and Bacon.

WIECK, P. R. (1979, March 1). Van meets handicapped regulations for now. *Albuquerque Journal.*

WIEGERINK, R., & HOCUTT, A. M. (1979). Parent involvement in preschool programs for handicapped children: A national perspective. In H. Leler et al., (Eds.), *Proceeding of the Ira J. Gordon Memorial Conference on Parent Education and Involvement.* Chapel Hill, NC: University of North Carolina, School of Education.

WIIG, E. H., & SEMEL, E. M. (1980). *Language assessment and intervention for the learning disabled.* Columbus, OH: Charles E. Merrill.

WIIG, E. H., SEMEL, E., & ABELE, E. (1981). Perception and interpretation of ambiguous sentences by learning disabled twelve year olds. *Learning Disabilities Quarterly, 4,* 3–12.

WILCOX, B., & BELLAMY, G. T. (1982). Curriculum content. In B. Wilcox & G. T. Bellamy (Eds.), *Design of high school programs for severely handicapped students.* Baltimore, MD: Paul H. Brookes.

WILLIAMS, B. R., & VERNON, M. (1970). Vocational guidance for the deaf. In H. Davis & S. R. Silverman (Eds.), *Hearing and deafness* (3rd ed.). New York; Holt, Rinehart and Winston.

WILLIAMS, D. (1957). A point of view about "stuttering." *Journal of Speech and Hearing Disorders, 22,* 390–397.

WILLIAMS, D. (1977). *Parenting in 1977: A listing of parenting materials,* Austin, TX: Parenting Materials Information Center, SEDL.

WILLIAMS, D. (1978). Stuttering. In J. Curtis (Ed.), *Processes and disorders of communication.* New York: Harper & Row.

WILLIAMS, L., LOMBARDINO, J., MacDONALD, J., & OWENS, R. (1982). Total communication: Clinical report on a parent-based language training program. *Education and Training of the Mentally Retarded, 17,* 293–298.

WILLIAMSON, A. P. (1975). Career education: Implications for secondary learning disabled students. *Academic Therapy, 10,* 193–200.

WILSON, K. (1979). *Voice problems of children.* Baltimore: Williams & Wilkins.

WINDSOR, C. E., & HURTT, J. (1974). *Eye muscle problems in childhood: A manual for parents.* St. Louis: C. V. Mosby.

WINTON, P., & TURNBULL, A. (1982). Dissemination of research to parents. *Exceptional Parent, 12,* 32–36.

WINTRE, M. G., & WEBSTER, C. D. (1974). A brief report on using a traditional social behavior scale with disturbed children. *Journal of Applied Behavior Analysis, 7,* 345–348.

WOLERY, M. (1983). Evaluating curricula: Purposes and strategies. *Topics in Early Childhood Special Education, 2*(4), 15–24.

WOLF, J. M. (1969). Historical perspective of cerebral palsy. In J. M. Wolf (Ed.), *The results of treatment in cerebral palsy,* Springfield, IL: Charles C. Thomas, 5–44.

WOLF, L., & ZARFAN, D. (1982). Parents' attitudes toward sterilization of their mentally retarded children. *American Journal of Mental Deficiency, 87,* 122–129.

WOLF, M. M. (1978). Social validity: The case for subjective evaluation or how applied behavior analysis is finding its heart. *Journal of Applied Behavior Analysis, 11,* 203–214.

WOLF, M. M., HANLEY, F. L., KING, L. A., LACHOWICH, J., & GILES, D. K. (1970). The times gone: A variable interval contingency for the management of out-of-seat behavior. *Exceptional Children, 37,* 113–117.

WOLF V. LEGISLATURE OF UTAH, CIV. No. 182464 (3rd Dist., Salt Lake City, Jan. 8. 1969).

WOLFENSBERGER, W. (1971). Will there always be an institution? II: The impact of new service models, *Mental Retardation, 9*(6), 31–38.

WOLFENSBERGER, W. (1972). *The principle of normalization in human services.* Toronto: National Institute on Mental Retardation.

WOLFENSBERGER, W. (1976). The origin and nature of our institutional models. In R. B. Kugel & A. Shearer (Eds.), *Changing patterns in residential services for the mentally retarded* (rev. ed.). Washington, DC: President committee on mental retardation.

WOLRAICH, M. L. (1982). Communication between physicians and parents of handicapped children. *Exceptional Children, 48,* 324–331.

WONG, B. (1979). Research and educational implications of some recent conceptualizations in learning disabilities. *Learning Disabilities Quarterly, 2,* 63–68.

WONG, B. Y. L. (1979). Increasing retention of main ideas through questioning strategies. *Learning Disabilities Quarterly, 2,* 42–47.

WONG, B. Y. L. (1982). Understanding learning disabled students' reading problems. *Topics in Learning and Learning Disabilities, 1,* 43–50.

WONG, B. Y. L., WONG, R., & LAMARE, L. (1982). The effects of knowledge of criterion task on comprehension and recall in normally achieving and learning disabled children. *The Journal of Educational Research, 16,* 119–126.

WOOD, F. H., & ZABEL, R. (1978). Making sense of reports on the incidence of behavior disorders/emotional disturbances in school-aged children. *Psychology in the Schools, 15,* 45–51.

WOODWARD, M. (1959). The behavior of idiots interpreted by Piaget's theory of sensorimotor development. *British Journal of Educational Psychology, 29,* 60–71.

WORMALD INTERNATIONAL SENSORY AIDS. (1979). *Electronic Travel Aids.* Bensenville, IL.

WRIGHTSTONE, J. W., ARANOW, M. S., & MOSKOWITZ, S. (1963). Developing reading test norms for deaf children. *American Annals of the Deaf, 108,* 311–316.

WYATT V. ANDERHOLT Vol. 503. 2d, 1305, (1970).

WYATT V. STICKNEY, 325 F. Supp. 781, 784 (M. D. Ala. 1972).

WYATT V. STICKNEY, Civil Action No. 3195–N. (U.S. District Court, Middle District of Alabama, North Division, 1972).

YOSHIDA, R. K. (1982). Research agenda: Finding ways

to create more options for parent involvement. *Exceptional Education Quarterly, 3,* 74–80.

YOSHIDA, R. K., & BYRNE, C. (1979). Mediation in special education: The right idea in the wrong form? *School Administrator, 36,* 18–19.

YOSHIDA, R. K., FENTON, K. S., KAUFMAN, M. J., & MAXWELL, J. P. (1978). Parental involvement in the special education pupil planning process: The school's perspective. *Exceptional Children, 44,* 531–534.

YOUNG, M., & ASHCROFT, S. C. (1980–81). *Survey of microcomputer access in programs serving the visually impaired.* Unpublished manuscript, Available from M. Young & S. C. Ashcroft, Peabody College of Vanderbilt University, Nashville, TN.

YSSELDYKE, J. E., & ALGOZZINE, B. (1979). Perspectives on assessment of learning disabled students. *Learning Disabilities Quarterly, 2,* 3–13.

YSSELDYKE, J. E., & ALGOZZINE, B. (1982). *Critical issues in special and remedial education.* Boston: Houghton Mifflin.

YSSELDYKE, J. E., ALGOZZINE, B., SHINN, M., McGUE, M. (1982). Similarities and differences between low achievers and students classified learning disabled. *The Journal of Special Education, 16,* 73–85.

ZATLOW, G. (1982). A sister's lament. *Exceptional Parent, 12,* 50–51.

ZEAMAN, D., & HOUSE, B. J. (1963a). An attention theory of retardate discrimination learning. In N. R. Ellis (Ed.), *Handbook of mental deficiency.* New York: McGraw-Hill.

ZEAMAN, D., & HOUSE, B. J. (1963b). The role of attention in retardate discriminative learning. In N. R. Ellis (Ed.), *Handbook of mental deficiency.* New York: McGraw-Hill, 159–223.

ZEAMAN, D., & HOUSE, B. J. (1979). In N. R. Ellis (Ed.), *Handbook of mental deficiency, psychological theory and research* (2nd ed.). Hillsdale, NJ: Lawrence Erlbaum.

ZEHRBACH, R. R. (1975). Determining a pre-school handicapped population. *Exceptional Children, 42*(2), 76–83.

Name Index

Subject Index

Club foot, 295–296, 298–299
Cochlear implants, 116
Code of Ethics and Standards for Professional Practice, 82
Cognitive development, 113, 156, 408–410, 493, 500–501, 502
Commission on Instructional Technology, 29
Communication aids, 34, 39
Communication disorders, 10, 118, 145–181, 314, 315
  language disorders, 154–160
  role of teacher and speech pathologist in, 170, 177–179
  speech and language concepts, 146–154
  speech disorders, 161–176, 289
Communication skills, 106, 115, 120–121, 501, 502
Communications satellites, 34
Community living skills, 503
Community residential services, 381–382
Competency-Based Model for Infusing Career Education into the curriculum, 588
Competency-Based Teacher Education (CBTE), 32–33
Comprehensive Employment and Training Act of 1978 (CETA), 584, 604–605
Comprehensive Rehabilitation Services Amendments of 1978 (PL 95-1780), 345–346
Computer assisted instruction (CAI), 36
Computers, 35, 65. *See also* Microcomputers; Technology
Conceptual development, 105, 117–118, 255
Conceptual knowledge, 157
Conduct disorders, 441. *See also* Behavior disorders
Conductive hearing loss, 194–195, 196, 200
Confidentiality of records, 26
Congenital heart defects, 300
Consonants, 151
Continuum of special education services, 56–57
Convulsive disorders, 290, 303–308
Core Home, 382–383, 384
Correlation, defined, 444–445
Cortisone, 298
Council for Exceptional Children (CEC), 34, 40, 70, 80–82, 318, 321, 472, 516, 576
Counter theory model, 432
Creativity, 526, 530–531, 543, 547
Cretinism, 358, 363
Criterion-referenced tests, 48, 397, 485, 487
Cultural factors, 12
  and acceptance of disabilities, 629
  and assessment of gifted children, 522–523, 542–543, 547, 548
  and behavior disorders, 445
  in mental retardation, 368–369
  in special education practices, 66–70

Curriculum. *See also* names of disabilities
  age-appropriate, 496, 499–503, 504
  in early childhood, 499–502
  and norms, 105
Curriculum-referenced assessment, 485, 487
CVA. *See* Cerebral vascular accident
Cystic fibrosis, 301

Daily living skills, 259
Davis case, 19
Day schools, 7, 72–73, 378, 459
Deafness, 192. *See also* Hearing disorders
Deinstitutionalization, 54–55
Denormalization, 561
Desensitization, 341
Development, child, 102–126, *See also* Language development
  major areas of, 105–125
  normal, 103–105, 106
  visually impaired, 253–254
Developmental Disabilities Act (PL 95-602), 100–101
Developmental milestones model, 486
Developmental theory-based model, 487–488
Developmentally disabled children, 10, 469–519
  causes of developmental delays, 470–471
  characteristic behavior of, 470–476
  curriculum approaches, content, 492–503
  definitions, 472–473
  early identification and intervention, 479–482, 484
  educability of, 98–99, 471, 476–483
  educational assessment procedures, 484–491
  instructional program planning, 486–491
  intervention programs, 480–483
  service delivery, community, 513–517
Diabetes, 289, 301–302, 365
Diana v. State Board of Education in California, 19
Differentiation, 103
Dilantin, 305
Disability, defined, 8
Disfluency, 171–175
Disorder. *See* Disability
DISTAR reading materials, 31
Disturbed behaviors, 450, 452–456
Disturbing behaviors, 450–452
Divergent thinking, 531
Domestic living skills, 502
Down's syndrome, 97, 127, 132, 195, 358, 363
Dressing. *See* Self-help skills
Drive control units, 318
DSM III (Diagnostic and Statistical Manual), 440
Duchenne muscular dystrophy, 291

Due process, 25
Dysfunction. *See* Disability

Ear, 188–191
Ear, Nose, and Throat (ENT) specialist, 170
Early and Periodic Screening, Diagnosis, and Treatment Program (EPSDT), 129
Early childhood education, 89–136. *See also* Development, child
  defining, 90–92
  education and treatment options, 131–138
  for the gifted, 553
  history and importance of, 92–95
Early Education Project, 133
Eastern Nebraska Community Office of Retardation (ENCOR), 384, 385
Eating. *See* Self-help skills
Ecological approach, 339, 399, 430–431, 432, 436, 439
Educability
  of developmentally disabled, 471, 476–483
  of mentally retarded, 359, 360, 361, 376, 377, 378
Educable mentally retarded (EMR), 359, 360, 361, 376, 377, 378
Education, defined, 477
Education Amendments of 1974 (PL 93-380), 23, 582
Education for All Handicapped Children Act (PL 94-142), 20, 23, 24–29, 30, 47, 58, 60, 61, 64, 100, 271, 274–275, 309, 345, 378, 379, 392, 393, 394, 435, 442, 450, 457, 469–470, 471, 486, 514–515, 579, 582–583, 600, 604, 607, 617, 636, 650–651
Educational media, 33
Educational Resources Information Center (ERIC), 79
Electrolarynx, 172
Elementary and Secondary Education Act (PL 90-247), 22
Emotionally disturbed. *See* Behavior disorders
Encopresis, 454
ENCOR, 384, 385
Enrichment Triad Model, 556
Enuresis, 454
Epilepsy, 303–307
Esophageal speech, 170
Eugenic scare, 16
Exceptional Child Education Resources (ECER), 79
Exceptional children, defined, 7
Expanding Programs and Learning in Outdoor Recreation and Education (EXPLORE), 597
Experience Based Career Education (EBCE), 585, 589–590
Extinction, 340
Eye, 236–239, 240
Eye-contact, 512